T0210905

Lecture Notes in Computer Science　　9837

Commenced Publication in 1973
Founding and Former Series Editors:
Gerhard Goos, Juris Hartmanis, and Jan van Leeuwen

Editorial Board

Advanced Research in Computing and Software Science
Subline of Lecture Notes in Computer Science

Subline Series Editors

Subline Advisory Board

More information about this series at http://www.springer.com/series/7408

Xavier Rival (Ed.)

Static Analysis

23rd International Symposium, SAS 2016
Edinburgh, UK, September 8–10, 2016
Proceedings

 Springer

Editor
Xavier Rival
Ecole Normale Supérieure
Paris
France

ISSN 0302-9743 ISSN 1611-3349 (electronic)
Lecture Notes in Computer Science
ISBN 978-3-662-53412-0 ISBN 978-3-662-53413-7 (eBook)
DOI 10.1007/978-3-662-53413-7

Library of Congress Control Number: 2016950412

LNCS Sublibrary: SL2 – Programming and Software Engineering

Printed on acid-free paper

This Springer imprint is published by Springer Nature
The registered company is Springer-Verlag GmbH Berlin Heidelberg

Preface

Static Analysis is increasingly recognized as a fundamental tool for program verification, bug detection, compiler optimization, program understanding, and software maintenance. The series of Static Analysis Symposia has served as the primary venue for the presentation of theoretical, practical, and applicational advances in the area. Previous symposia were held in Saint-Malo, Munich, Seattle, Deauville, Venice, Perpignan, Los Angeles, Valencia, Kongens Lyngby, Seoul, London, Verona, San Diego, Madrid, Paris, Santa Barbara, Pisa, Aachen, Glasgow, and Namur. This volume contains the papers presented at SAS 2016, the 23rd International Static Analysis Symposium. The conference was held on September 8–10, 2016 in Edinburgh, UK.

The conference received 55 submissions, each of which was reviewed by at least three Program Committee members. The Program Committee decided to accept 21 papers, which appear in this volume. As in previous years, authors of SAS submissions were able to submit a virtual machine image with artifacts or evaluations presented in the paper. In accordance with this, 19 submissions came with an artifact. Artifacts were used as an additional source of information during the evaluation of the submissions.

The Program Committee also invited four leading researchers to present invited talks: Jade Alglave (Microsoft Research UK), Thomas A. Henzinger (IST Austria, Klosterneuburg, Austria), Fausto Spoto (University of Verona, Italy), and Martin Vechev (ETH Zurich, Switzerland). We deeply thank them for accepting the invitations.

SAS 2016 was collocated with the Symposium on Logic-Based Program Synthesis and Transformation (LOPSTR 2016) and the Symposium on Principles and Practice of Declarative Programming (PPDP 2016) and it featured five associated workshops: the Workshop on Static Analysis and Systems Biology (SASB 2016) and the Workshop on Tools for Automatic Program Analysis (TAPAS 2016) were held before SAS, on the 7th of September; the Numerical and Symbolic Abstract Domains Workshop (NSAD 2016), the Workshop on Static Analysis of Concurrent Software, and REPS AT SIXTY were held after SAS, on the 11th of September.

The work of the Program Committee and the editorial process were greatly facilitated by the EasyChair conference management system. We are grateful to Springer for publishing these proceedings, as they have done for all SAS meetings since 1993.

Many people contributed to the success of SAS 2015. We would first like to thank the members of the Program Committee, who worked hard at carefully reviewing papers, holding extensive discussions during the on-line Program Committee meeting, and making final selections of accepted papers and invited speakers. We would also like to thank the additional referees enlisted by Program Committee members. We thank the Steering Committee members for their advice. A special acknowledgment goes to James Cheney for leading the local organization of the conference and to the University of Edinburgh for hosting the Conference. Finally, we would like to thank our sponsors: Facebook, Fondation de l'ENS, and Springer.

July 2016   Xavier Rival

Organization

Program Committee

Bor-Yuh Evan Chang	University of Colorado Boulder, USA
Patrick Cousot	New York University, USA
Vijay D'Silva	Google Inc., USA
Javier Esparza	Technical University of Munich, Germany
Jérôme Feret	Inria/CNRS/Ecole Normale Supérieure, France
Pierre Ganty	IMDEA Software Institute, Spain
Roberto Giacobazzi	University of Verona, Italy
Atsushi Igarashi	Kyoto University, Japan
Andy King	University of Kent, UK
Francesco Logozzo	Facebook, USA
Roman Manevich	Ben-Gurion University of the Negev, Israel
Matthieu Martel	Université de Perpignan Via Domitia, France
Jan Midtgaard	Technical University of Denmark, Denmark
Ana Milanova	Rensselaer Polytechnic Institute, USA
Mayur Naik	Georgia Institute of Technology, USA
Francesco Ranzato	University of Padua, Italy
Xavier Rival	Inria/CNRS/Ecole Normale Supérieure, France
Sukyoung Ryu	KAIST, South Korea
Francesca Scozzari	Università di Chieti-Pescara, Italy
Caterina Urban	ETH Zürich, Switzerland
Bow-Yaw Wang	Academia Sinica, Taiwan
Kwangkeun Yi	Seoul National University, South Korea

Additional Reviewers

Adje, Assale	Hur, Chung-Kil	Seidl, Helmut
Amato, Gianluca	Jourdan, Jacques-Henri	Seladji, Yassamine
Brutschy, Lucas	Kang, Jeehoon	Si, Xujie
Chapoutot, Alexandre	Kong, Soonho	Singh, Gagandeep
Chawdhary, Aziem	Lee, Woosuk	Stein, Benno
Chen, Yu-Fang	Meier, Shawn	Suwimonteerabuth,
Cho, Sungkeun	Meyer, Roland	Dejvuth
Dogadov, Boris	Miné, Antoine	Tsai, Ming-Hsien
Garoche, Pierre-Loic	Mover, Sergio	Walukiewicz, Igor
Haller, Leopold	Oh, Hakjoo	Werey, Alexis
Heo, Kihong	Seed, Tom	Zhang, Xin

Contents

Invited Papers

Simulation and Invariance for Weak Consistency 3
   Jade Alglave

Quantitative Monitor Automata 23
   Krishnendu Chatterjee, Thomas A. Henzinger, and Jan Otop

The Julia Static Analyzer for Java 39
   Fausto Spoto

Full Papers

Automated Verification of Linearization Policies 61
   Parosh Aziz Abdulla, Bengt Jonsson, and Cong Quy Trinh

Structure-Sensitive Points-To Analysis for C and C++ 84
   George Balatsouras and Yannis Smaragdakis

Bounded Abstract Interpretation 105
   Maria Christakis and Valentin Wüstholz

Completeness in Approximate Transduction 126
   Mila Dalla Preda, Roberto Giacobazzi, and Isabella Mastroeni

Relational Verification Through Horn Clause Transformation 147
   Emanuele De Angelis, Fabio Fioravanti, Alberto Pettorossi,
   and Maurizio Proietti

Securing a Compiler Transformation 170
   Chaoqiang Deng and Kedar S. Namjoshi

Exploiting Sparsity in Difference-Bound Matrices 189
   Graeme Gange, Jorge A. Navas, Peter Schachte, Harald Søndergaard,
   and Peter J. Stuckey

Flow- and Context-Sensitive Points-To Analysis Using Generalized
Points-To Graphs 212
   Pritam M. Gharat, Uday P. Khedker, and Alan Mycroft

Learning a Variable-Clustering Strategy for Octagon from Labeled
Data Generated by a Static Analysis 237
   Kihong Heo, Hakjoo Oh, and Hongseok Yang

Static Analysis by Abstract Interpretation of the Functional Correctness
of Matrix Manipulating Programs   257
    Matthieu Journault and Antoine Miné

Generalized Homogeneous Polynomials for Efficient Template-Based
Nonlinear Invariant Synthesis   278
    Kensuke Kojima, Minoru Kinoshita, and Kohei Suenaga

On the Linear Ranking Problem for Simple Floating-Point Loops   300
    Fonenantsoa Maurica, Frédéric Mesnard, and Étienne Payet

Alive-FP: Automated Verification of Floating Point Based Peephole
Optimizations in LLVM.   317
    David Menendez, Santosh Nagarakatte, and Aarti Gupta

A Parametric Abstract Domain for Lattice-Valued Regular Expressions   338
    Jan Midtgaard, Flemming Nielson, and Hanne Riis Nielson

Cell Morphing: From Array Programs to Array-Free Horn Clauses   361
    David Monniaux and Laure Gonnord

Loopy: Programmable and Formally Verified Loop Transformations   383
    Kedar S. Namjoshi and Nimit Singhania

Abstract Interpretation of Supermodular Games.   403
    Francesco Ranzato

Validating Numerical Semidefinite Programming Solvers
for Polynomial Invariants.   424
    Pierre Roux, Yuen-Lam Voronin, and Sriram Sankaranarayanan

Enforcing Termination of Interprocedural Analysis   447
    Stefan Schulze Frielinghaus, Helmut Seidl, and Ralf Vogler

From Array Domains to Abstract Interpretation Under Store-Buffer-Based
Memory Models   469
    Thibault Suzanne and Antoine Miné

Making k-Object-Sensitive Pointer Analysis More Precise
with Still k-Limiting   489
    Tian Tan, Yue Li, and Jingling Xue

Author Index   511

Invited Papers

Simulation and Invariance for Weak Consistency

Jade Alglave[1,2]($\boxtimes$)

[1] Microsoft Research Cambridge, Cambridge, UK
j.alglave@ucl.ac.uk
[2] University College London, London, UK

Abstract. We aim at developing correct algorithms for a wide variety of weak consistency models $M_0, \ldots, M_n$. Given an algorithm A and a consistency model $M \in \{M_0, \ldots, M_n\}$, at quite a high-level examining the correctness of the algorithm A under M amounts to asking, for example, "can these executions happen?", or "are these the only possible executions?". Since a few years, Luc Maranget and myself have been designing and developing the herd7 simulation tool: given a *litmus test*, *i.e.* a small piece of code and a *consistency model*, *i.e.* a set of constraints defining the valid executions of a program, the herd7 tool outputs all the possible executions of the litmus test under the consistency model. In recent works with Patrick Cousot, we have developed an invariance method for proving the correctness of algorithms under weak consistency models. In this paper I would like to give a general overview of these works.

1 Introduction

Weak consistency models (WCMs) are now a fixture of computing systems: for example Intel x86 or ARM processors, Nvidia graphics cards, programming languages such as C++ or OpenCL, or distributed systems such as Amazon AWS or Microsoft's Azure. In this context, the execution of a concurrent program no longer is an interleaving of the instructions involved on the different processes that constitute the program, unlike what is prescribed by Lamport's Sequential Consistency (SC) [Lam79a].

On the contrary, semantics of programs need to take into account possible *reordering of instructions* on one process, or *propagation delays* between processes, for example due to hardware features such as *store buffers* and *caches*.

Different *consistency semantics* styles can be used to describe WCMs. *Operational models* define *abstract machines* in which executions of programs are sequences of transitions made to or from formal objects modelling *e.g.* hardware features such as store buffers and caches. *Axiomatic models* abstract away from such concrete features and describe executions as relations over *events* modelling *e.g.* read or write memory accesses, and synchronisation.

Different *program semantics* styles can be used to describe program executions (operational, denotational, axiomatic, *etc.*). The approach taken by the herd7 tool, formalised later with Patrick Cousot, is as follows. Computations are described as individual traces of processes on the one hand, and anarchic

© Springer-Verlag GmbH Germany 2016
X. Rival (Ed.): SAS 2016, LNCS 9837, pp. 3–22, 2016.
DOI: 10.1007/978-3-662-53413-7_1

(unrestrained) communications between processes. Specific WCMs are taken into account by placing restrictions on communications only.

We aim at developing correct algorithms for a wide variety of weak consistency models $M_0, \ldots, M_n$. Given an algorithm A and a consistency model $M \in \{M_0, \ldots, M_n\}$, at quite a high-level examining the correctness of the algorithm A under M amounts to asking, for example, "can these executions happen?", or "are these the only possible executions?".

1.1   Simulation, or Building All the Possible Executions

A first way to try to address this question is by simply building all the possible executions of A under M and examining to what extent the subset of executions under scrutiny (the ones which possibility we question above) is included in the set of all possible executions.

Since a few years, Luc Maranget and myself have been designing and developing the herd7 simulation tool: given a *litmus test, i.e.* a small piece of code and a *consistency model, i.e.* a set of constraints defining the valid executions of a program, the herd7 tool outputs all the possible executions of the litmus test under the consistency model.

1.2   Invariance, or Building Invariant Specifications of Executions

Another way to try to address this question is to build *invariant specifications* of the algorithm; in other words to state properties that all executions satisfy, at all execution points. Then one needs to check that these specifications indeed are invariant. Once this is done one can assess whether the executions under scrutiny satisfy the specification, in which case they can well happen.

In recent works with Patrick Cousot, we have developed such a method for proving the correctness of algorithms under weak consistency models.

1.3   Overview

In this paper I would like to give a general overview of these works. In both cases

- we get given
    1. an algorithm A, and
    2. a consistency model M.
- we need to build
    1. a description of the semantics of each thread, and
    2. a description of the communications between threads.
- we need to invent a specification of how the program should behave.

As an illustration, we will use the classical mutual exclusion algorithm of Peterson [Pet81]. Our algorithms will be written in our Litmus Instruction Set Architecture (LISA) language. Our consistency models will be written in our cat language.

2 Semantics

In this section we examine, on a *store buffering* litmus test, the following points:

1. write the litmus test in the *Litmus Instruction Set Architecture* (LISA) language of the herd7 tool; this includes:
   - writing a small piece of concurrent code;
   - writing a question about which executions can happen;
2. build all the possible executions of the litmus test;
3. write several consistency models in the cat language;
4. examine to what extent the executions we have asked about can happen under a certain model.

2.1 Writing a Litmus Test in LISA

We give the code of a store buffering litmus test in LISA in Fig. 1. The test uses two shared variables F1 and F2. This snippet is at the heart of Peterson's algorithm, which we will examine later; essentially F1 and F2 are flags which each thread uses to indicate that they would like to enter their critical sections.

```
LISA SB
{F1=0; F2=0}
 P0          | P1          ;
 w[] F1 1    | w[] F2 1    ;
 r[] r1 F2   | r[] r3 F1   ;
 exists (0:r1=0 /\ 1:r3=0)
```

Fig. 1. A *store buffering* litmus test (sb)

Let's read the LISA code; our litmus test is composed of:

- a prelude at line 0:, between curly brackets, which initialises the variables F1 and F2 to 0;
- two processes P0 and P1, each depicted as a column; let's detail the first process, on the left-hand side: at line 1:, we write 1 to the variable F1—the LISA syntax for writes is "w[] x e" where x is a variable and e an expression over registers, whose value is written to x. At line 5: we read the value of shared variable F2 and place it into register R1, which is private to the first thread.
- a question about the final state of registers R1 and R2; here we ask: "is it possible that R1 and R2 both contain the value 0?".

This outcome is possible on machines that feature *store buffers* for example. Indeed the two writes—the write of F1 on P0 and the write of F2 on P1—can be made to the respective private store buffers of P0 and P1. Then the two reads can be made from memory, *i.e.* the read of F2 on P0 reads the initial value 0, and *idem* for the read of F1 on P1. Finally, the two writes are flushed to memory.

2.2   Build All the Possible Executions of a Litmus Test

We now show all the possible executions of the sb litmus test, in Fig. 2.

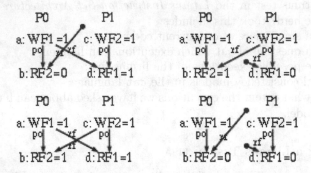

Fig. 2. All possible executions of the store buffering litmus test of Fig. 1

At the top left-hand corner, we see an execution where the read of F1 on P1 takes its value from the write of F1 by P0, hence reads the value 1. We depict by with a *read-from* arrow (rf), between the write and the read of F1.

In the same execution, we see that the read of F2 on P0 takes its value from the inital state. We depict this by a read-from. Here we have omitted the initialisation events to F1 and F2, hence the rf arrow has a little stub at its source, instead of a write event.

At the top right-hand corner, we see an execution where the read of F1 takes its value from the initial state, whilst the read of F2 takes its value from the write of F2 by P1.

At the bottom left-hand corner, we see an execution where both reads take their values from the updates: the read of F1 reads 1 as written by P0, idem for the read of F2.

Finally at the bottom right-hand corner, we see an execution where both reads take their values from the inital state. This is the execution that leads to both registers holding the value 0 in the end, as asked by the question at the bottom of the sb litmus test in Fig. 1.

Now, let's take a closer look at that last execution. We reproduce it in Fig. 3, with some additional information.

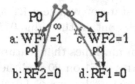

Fig. 3. The execution of sb leading to the final state in question

In Fig. 3, we have added *coherence* arrows. Coherence relates writes to the same variable. By convention, the initialisation write of a given variable is ordered in coherence before any update of that variable. Thus the write of F1 by P0 appears in coherence after the initialisation write of F1, idem for F2.

Now, observe that the execution in Fig. 3 exhibits a *cycle*: 1: w[] F1 true — po ⟶ 5: r[] R1 F2 — rf^-1 ⟶ 0: w[] F2 false — co ⟶ 21: w[] F2 true — po ⟶ 25: r[] R3 F1 — rf^-1 ⟶ 0: w[] F1 false — co ⟶ 1: w[] F1 true. This is the sequence that the consistency model needs to forbid to ensure that this final state is never reached.

2.3 Write Consistency Models in cat

Now we can examine these questions through the prism of various consistency models. Before detailing how we write models, we give a glimpse of the cat language. In this paper we will focus on:

- Sequential Consistency [Lam79a] (SC), where executions of a program are interleavings of the instructions appearing on the threads of the program, and
- Total Store Order [SPA94, OSS09] (TSO), which allows store buffering scenarios as seen in Fig. 1, and is the model of Sparc TSO and x86 machines.

However we note that the cat language has been used to define a variety of models, such as IBM Power [AMT4b], ARM [AMT4b], Nvidia [ABD+15], HSA [ACM15b], C++ [BDW16], OpenCL [BDW16].

The cat language (see [ACM15b]) is a domain specific language to describe consistency models succinctly by constraining an abstraction of program executions into a candidate execution ⟨e, po, rf, IW⟩ providing

- *events e*, giving a semantics to instructions; for example a LISA write w[] x v yields a write event of variable x with value v. Events can be (for brevity this is not an exhaustive list):
  - *writes*, gathered in the set W, unless they come from the prelude of the program in which case they are gathered in the set of *initial writes* IW;
  - *reads*, gathered in the set R;
  - *fences*, gathered in the set F.
- the program order po, relating accesses written in program order in the original LISA program;
- the read-from rf describing a communication between a write and a read.

The language provides additional basic built-in semantics bricks:

- the relation loc relating events accessing the same variable;
- the relation ext relating events from different processes;
- operators over relations, such as intersection &, union |, inverse of a relation ^-1, closure +, cartesian product *, set difference \.

The cat user can define new relations using let, and declare constraints over relations, such as irreflexivity or acyclicity constraints, using the eponymous keywords irreflexive r and acyclic r (*i.e.* irreflexive r+).

Preliminary definitions. In all the models shown below we use the following two definitions:

- we define the relation co as relating initial writes (*viz.*, the writes from the prelude) to the writes in the program that access the same variable. In cat speak, the set of initial writes is written IW, the set of writes in the program is W, the relation between accesses to the same variable is loc (for location) and the intersection is &;
- we define a shorthand fr (for *from-read*) for the sequence of relations rf^-1 and co that appears twice in the cycle in Fig. 3. We refine this relation further, to the relation fre, which is fr restricted to accesses that belong to different processes—in cat speak this is denoted by the relation ext (for external).

When M is SC. In cat speak, SC is modelled as in Fig. 4 (see *e.g.* [Alg10] for an equivalence proof). The first two lines define co and fr as above. The last line states that there cannot be a cycle in the union (depicted by |) of the program order po, the read-from rf, the coherence co and the from-read fr.

```
let co = (IW*W) & loc
let fr = (rf^-1;co)
acyclic po | rf | co | fr as sc
```

Fig. 4. SC in cat

When M is TSO. In cat speak, TSO is modelled as given in Fig. 5 (see *e.g.* [Alg10] for an equivalence proof). The first two lines define co and fr as above.

Then we define a new relation po-loc, as the restriction of the program order po to accesses relative the same variable (see the intersection with the relation loc). Next up we require the acyclicity of the union of po-loc with all the communication relations: read-from rf, coherence co and from-read fr. We call this acyclicity check scpv, which stands for "SC per variable". This check is required to ensure that all the values read and written by accesses to a same variable are reachable on SC. Less formally, this enforces *coherence* properties, *e.g.* that a read of a variable cannot read from a write of the same variable appearing later on the same thread.

We then define the relation ppo (for *preserved program order*) as the program order po relieved from (see the setminus operator \) the write-read pairs (W*R). Then we define the relation rfe (for external read-from) as the restriction of the read-from rf to accesses that belong to different threads (denoted by the relation ext). Finally we require the acyclicity of the union of the preserved program order, the external read-from, the coherence and the from-read relations. We call this acyclicity check tso, as it is the main distinguishing feature of the TSO model (the SC per variable check appearing in most other models that we have studied, *e.g.* IBM Power).

```
let co = (IW*W) & loc
let fr = (rf^-1;co)
let po-loc = po & loc
acyclic po-loc | rf | co | fr as scpv

let ppo = po \ (W*R)
let rfe = rf & ext
acyclic ppo | rfe | co | fr as tso
```

Fig. 5. TSO in `cat`

2.4 Answer Our Question About the Final State

Recall the question that we have asked about the final state: "is it possible that
R1 and R2 both contain the value `false`?". Recall that the consistency model
needs to forbid the cycle given in Fig. 3 to ensure that this final state is never
reached. In other words, a consistency model will forbid this execution if it
ensures that the sequence `po; fre; po; fre` is irreflexive, *i.e.* communications
between the two processes of `sb` should not be such that taking a step in program
order `po`, then a step of `fre`, landing on the other process, then a step of `po`,
then a step of `fre` again, goes back to the starting point. Overall this leads to
the `cat` specification given in Fig. 15 (Fig. 6):

```
let co = (IW*W) & loc
let fre = (rf^-1;co) & ext
irreflexive po; fre; po; fre as sb-forbid
```

Fig. 6. A possible specification of `sb`

When M is SC. Now, note that the sequence s forbidden by sb's specification
is also a cycle in the union of relations which the SC model of Fig. 4 requires
to be acyclic, hence a contradiction: an execution containing s is also forbidden
when M is SC.

When M is TSO. An execution forbidden by our specification of `sb` (see
Fig. 15) will not be forbidden by the TSO model given in Fig. 5. This is because
any execution forbidden by our specification of `sb` involves a pair write-read in
program order (see the two `po` edges in the sequence s for example). Moreover,
the write-read pairs are explicitly removed from the `tso` acyclicity check given
on the last line of the TSO model of Fig. 5, thus will not contribute to executions
forbidden by the model.

Adding fences. LISA fences can be added to have a correct implementation of
`sb`. The fence semantics must be defined by a `cat` specification (F is the set of
fence events) and the specification of `sb` must be strengthened as given in Fig. 7.

```
let fhw = (po & (_ * F)); po
let fre = (rf^-1;co) & ext
irreflexive fhw ; fre ; fhw ; fre as sb-forbid
```

Fig. 7. A stronger specification of sb

3   Specifications

In this section we will examine, on Peterson's algorithm, the following points:

1. write the algorithm in the *Litmus Instruction Set Architecture* (LISA) language of the herd7 tool [AM15]. Along the way, we use LISA's special fence instructions, which allow to indicate between which program points (perhaps sets of program points) synchronisation is needed for correctness.
2. state an invariant specification S_{inv} of the algorithm;
3. state an invariant communication specification S_{com} of the algorithm.

3.1   Writing the Algorithm in LISA

We give the code of Peterson's algorithm in LISA in Fig. 8. The algorithm uses three shared variables F1, F2 and T:

- two shared flags, F1 for the first process P0 (resp. F2 for the second process P1), indicating that the process P0 (resp. P1) wants to enter its critical section, and
- a turn T to grant priority to the other process: when T is set to 1 (resp. 2), the priority is given to P0 (resp. P1).

Let's look at the process P0: P0 busy-waits before entering its critical section (see the do instruction at line 3:) until (see the while clause at line 6:) the process P1 does not want to enter its critical section (*viz.*, when F2=false, which in turn means ¬R1=true thanks to the read at line 4:) or if P1 has given priority to P0 by setting turn T to 1, which in turn means that R2=1 thanks to the read at line 5:.

LISA code. Let's read it together; our algorithm is composed of:

- a prelude at line 0:, between curly brackets, which initialises the variables F1 and F2 to **false** and the variable T to 0;
- two processes, each depicted as a column; let's detail the first process, on the left-hand side: at line 1: we write **true** to the variable F1—the LISA syntax for writes is "w[] x e" where x is a variable and e an expression over registers, whose value is written to x. At line 2 we write 2 to T. At line 3: we see a do instruction which ensures that we iterate the instructions at lines 4 and 5 until the condition expressed at line 6 (*viz.*, R1 ∧ R2 ≠ 1) is false. At line 4: we read the variable F2 and write its value into register R1, and at line 5: we read the variable T and write its value into register R2. At line 7: we have a skip instruction, simply to signify the critical section, and at line 8: we write **false** to F1.

```
0:{ w F1 false; w F2 false; w T 0; }
P0:                                || P1:
1:w[] F1 true                      || 10:w[] F2 true;
2:w[] T 2                          || 11:w[] T 1;
3:do {i}                          || 12:do {j}
4:    r[] R1 F2 {⤳ F2₄ⁱ}           || 13:    r[] R3 F1; {⤳ F1₁₃ʲ}
5:    r[] R2 T  {⤳ T₅ⁱ}            || 14:    r[] R4 T;  {⤳ T₁₄ʲ}
6:while R1 ∧ R2 ≠ 1 {i_end}        || 15:while R3 ∧ R4 ≠ 2; {j_end}
7:skip (* CS1 *)                   || 16:skip (* CS2 *)
8:w[] F1 false                     || 17:w[] F2 false;
9:                                 || 18:
```

Fig. 8. Peterson algorithm in LISA

Annotations. We have placed a few annotations in our LISA code, to be used later in invariants and proofs:

– *iteration counters*: each do loop, at line 3: and at line 12:, is decorated with an iteration counter, *e.g.* i for the first process and j for the second process. We also decorate the line of each until clause (*i.e.* lines 6: and 15:) with a symbolic name (i_{end} and j_{end}) to represent the iteration counter when exiting the loop.
– *pythia variables*: each read, at lines 4 and 5 for the first process, and lines 13 and 14 for the second process, is decorated with a pythia variable. More precisely a read ℓ: r[] R x at line ℓ:, reading the variable x and placing its result into register R, is decorated with the pythia variable $\{⤳ x_\ell^n\}$, where ℓ is the line of the read in the program, x is the variable that the read is reading, and n is an instance of the iteration counter.

Our invariants use pythia variables as opposed to simply the shared variables because WCMs are such that there is no notion of instantaneous value of the shared variables that the invariants could refer to. Instead, we use pythia variables, which give us a unique way to denote the values read during computation.

3.2 Stating an Invariant Specification S_{inv}

Figure 9 gives an invariant specification of our implementation of Peterson: the specification states that both processes cannot be simultaneously in their critical sections.

3.3 Stating a Communication Specification S_{com}

The next step in our specification process consists in stating an invariant communication specification S_{com}, expressing which inter-process communications are allowed for the algorithm A. We take the reader through this process using again Peterson's algorithm as an illustration.

$$1: \{true\} \quad 10: \{true\}$$
$$\cdots \qquad \cdots$$
$$7: \{\neg at\{16\}\} \; 16: \{\neg at\{7\}\}$$
$$\cdots \qquad \cdots$$
$$9: \{true\} \qquad 18: \{true\}$$

Fig. 9. Invariant specification S_{inv} for Peterson's algorithm

Peterson can go wrong under WCMs. Under certain WCMs, such as x86-TSO or any weaker model, Peterson's algorithm is incorrect (*i.e.* does not satisfy the specification S_{inv} given above in Fig. 9, that both processes cannot be simultaneously in their critical section).

To see this, consider Fig. 10. The red arrows are an informal representation of a communication scenario where:

- on the first process (see the left-hand side), the read at line 4: reads the value that F2 was initialised with at line 0:, so that R1 contains `false`. The read at line 5: reads from the update of T by the right-hand side process, so that R2 contains the value 1.
- on the second process, the read at line 13: reads from the initial value of F1, so that R3 contains `false`; the read at line 14: reads from the left-hand side process, so that R4 contains 2.

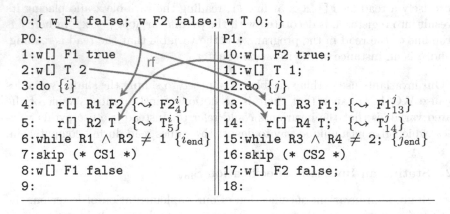

Fig. 10. Incorrect execution of Peterson algorithm with WCM

In this situation (which is impossible under SC), both loop exit conditions can be true so that both processes can be simultaneously in their critical section, thus invalidating the specification S_{inv}.

Communication specification S_{com}. Let us express the communication scenario depicted in red in Fig. 10 as an invariant. We write the pythia triple pythia$\langle \ell, \mathsf{x}_\theta, v \rangle$ to mean that the read ℓ' : r[] R x $\{ \rightsquigarrow \mathsf{x}_\theta \}$, or more precisely its pythia variable x_θ, takes its value v from evaluating the expression e of the write ℓ: w[] x e, and the local invariant at ℓ implies that e $= v$.

We give a communication specification for Peterson's algorithm in Fig. 11.

$$S_{com} \triangleq \neg [\exists i, j \,.\, \text{pythia}\langle 0, \text{F2}_4^i, \textsf{false} \rangle \wedge \text{pythia}\langle 11, \text{T}_5^i, 1 \rangle \wedge$$
$$\text{pythia}\langle 0, \text{F1}_{13}^j, \textsf{false} \rangle \wedge \text{pythia}\langle 2, \text{T}_{14}^j, 2 \rangle]$$

Fig. 11. A communication specification for Peterson's algorithm

In words, our communication specification S_{com} states that the scenario in Fig. 10 is impossible, which in turn ensures that both processes cannot be simultaneously in their critical section. Therefore, there cannot be two iteration counters i and j such that:

- the read at line 4: and i^{th} iteration (corresponding to the pythia variable F2$_4^i$) takes its value, **false**, from the initialisation of the variable F2 (which has been made in the prelude at line 0:);
- the read at line 5: and i^{th} iteration (corresponding to the pythia variable T$_5^i$) takes its value, 1, from the write at line 11;
- the read at line 13 and j^{th} iteration (corresponding to the pythia variable F1$_{13}^j$) takes its value, **false**, from the initialisation of the variable F1 (which has been made in the prelude at line 0:);
- the read at line 14 and j^{th} iteration (corresponding to the pythia variable T$_{14}^j$) takes its value, 2, from the write at line 2.

3.4   And Now to the Proofs!

Our method is articulated as follows—we detail each of these points in turn below, and show a graphical representation in Fig. 12:

1. Design and specifications:
   - write the algorithm A, including *synchronisation markers* if needed
   - state an invariant specification S_{inv} (see Sect. 3.2)
   - state a communication specification S_{com} (see Sect. 3.3);
2. Proofs:
   - prove the correctness of the algorithm A w.r.t. the invariant specification S_{inv}, under the communication specification S_{com} (see Sect. 4);
   - prove that the consistency model M guarantees the communication specification S_{com} that we postulated for the correctness of A (see Sect. 5).

Recall Fig. 12; given an algorithm A (*e.g.* Peterson's algorithm as given in Fig. 8) and a WCM M, we first need to invent:

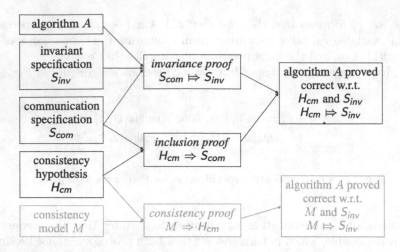

Fig. 12. Our method

1. an invariant specification S_{inv}, *e.g.* the one in Fig. 9 for Peterson's algorithm;
2. a communication specification S_{com}, *e.g.* Fig. 11 for Peterson's algorithm.

With these two specifications at hand, we can now start proving away; our method is articulated as follows:

1. *Conditional invariance proof* $S_{com} \Mapsto S_{inv}$: we need to prove that if the communications occur like prescribed by S_{com}, then the processes satisfy the invariant S_{inv};
2. *Inclusion proof* $M \implies S_{com}$: we need to validate the hypotheses made in the communication specification S_{com}, *viz.*, we need to ensure that the WCM M guarantees them.

We now detail each proof in turn.

4   Conditional Invariance Proof $S_{com} \Mapsto S_{inv}$

Given an algorithm A, and the specifications S_{inv} and S_{com}, we need to prove that each process of the algorithm satisfies a given invariant S_{inv} under the hypothesis S_{com}; to do so we:

1. invent a stronger invariant S_{ind}, which is inductive;
2. prove that S_{ind} is indeed inductive, i.e. satisfies verification conditions implying that if it is true, it stays true after one step of computation or one step of communication that satisfies S_{com}; effectively we prove $S_{com} \Mapsto S_{ind}$.
3. prove that S_{ind} is indeed stronger than S_{inv} (i.e. $S_{ind} \implies S_{inv}$);

Thus we have:

- $S_{com} \Mapsto S_{ind}$, saying that S_{ind} is invariant for the algorithm under communication hypothesis S_{com};
- $S_{ind} \implies S_{inv}$, saying that the inductive invariant S_{ind} is stronger than the invariant S_{inv}.

This allows us to conclude that $S_{com} \Mapsto S_{inv}$, which was our goal. We now illustrate the correctness proof process on Peterson.

4.1   Invent a Stronger Invariant S_{ind}, which is inductive

An inductive invariant S_{ind}, stronger than S_{inv} is given in Fig. 13. More precisely, Fig. 13 gives local invariants (depicted in blue in curly brackets) for each program point of each process, as in the Owicki-Gries and Lamport proof methods [OG76, Lam77]. Our invariants can depend on registers (both the ones local to the process under scrutiny, and from other processes), pythia variables and, as in Lamport's method [Lam77], on the program counter of the other processes (thus avoiding auxiliary variables [OG76]). The invariants cannot depend on shared variables.

```
0: { w F1 false; w F2 false; w T 0; }
{F1=false ∧ F2=false ∧ T=0} }
1:{R1=0 ∧ R2=0}                        10:{R3=0 ∧ R4=0}
   w[] F1 true                            w[] F2 true;
2:{R1=0 ∧ R2=0}                        11:{R3=0 ∧ R4=0}
   w[] T 2                                w[] T 1;
3:{R1=0 ∧ R2=0}                        12:{R3=0 ∧ R4=0}
   do {i}                                 do {j}
4:{ (i=0 ∧ R1=0 ∧ R2=0) ∨           13:{(j=0 ∧ R3=0 ∧ R4=0) ∨
    (i>0 ∧ R1=F2₄^{i-1} ∧ R2=T₅^{i-1})}  (j>0 ∧ R3=F1₁₃^{j-1} ∧ R4=T₁₄^{j-1})}
   r[] R1 F2 {⤳ F2₄^i}                   r[] R3 F1 {⤳ F1₁₃^j};
5:{R1=F2₄^i ∧ (i=0 ∧ R2=0) ∨        14:{R3=F1₁₃^j ∧ (j=0 ∧ R4=0) ∨
           (i>0 ∧ R2=T₅^i)}                     (j>0 ∧ R4=T₁₄^j)}
   r[] R2 T {⤳ T₅^i}                     r[] R4 T; {⤳ T₁₄^j}
6:{R1=F2₄^i ∧ R2=T₅^i}              15:{R3=F1₁₃^j ∧ R4=T₁₄^j}
   while R1 ∧ R2≠1 {i_end}                while R3 ∧ R4≠2 {j_end} ;
7:{¬F2₄^{i_end} ∧ T₅^{i_end}=1}     16:{¬F1₁₃^{j_end} ∧ T₁₄^{j_end}=2}
   skip (* CS1 *)                         skip (* CS2 *)
8:{¬F2₄^{i_end} ∧ T₅^{i_end}=1}     17:{¬F1₁₃^{j_end} ∧ T₁₄^{j_end}=2}
   w[] F1 false                           w[] F2 false;
9:{¬F2₄^{i_end} ∧ T₅^{i_end}=1}     18:{¬F1₁₃^{j_end} ∧ T₁₄^{j_end}=2}
```

Fig. 13. Invariants of Peterson algorithm

Let us read the local invariants for the first process of Peterson:

- line 0: simply reflects the initialisations made in the prelude, thus we have F1=false ∧ F2=false ∧ T=0;

- at line 1: LISA assumes that all registers local to P1 (*viz.*, R1 and R2) are initialised to 0, thus we have R1=0 ∧ R2=0—we separate the initialisation of shared variables (*e.g.* F1, F2 and T), factored out in the prelude, and the initialisation of local registers, which is made at the top of each concerned process;
- at line 2:, we have just passed a write of F1, which leaves the invariant unchanged, thus we still have R1=0 ∧ R2=0;
- similarly at line 3:, we just passed a write of T, which leaves the invariant unchanged, thus we still have R1=0 ∧ R2=0;
- at line 4:, we are about to enter, or have entered, a loop, whose iterations are indexed by i as indicated by the annotation after the do instruction; the loop invariant states that:
  - either we have not entered the loop yet (i=0), in which case the registers are unchanged, *viz.*, R1=0 ∧ R2=0, or
  - we have entered the loop (i>0), in which case the registers contain updated values, more precisely updated pythia variables: for example $R1=F2_4^{i-1}$ indicates that in the $i-1$ iteration of the loop, there has been, at line 4:, a read of the variable F2, resulting in the pythia variable $F2_4^{i-1}$ being placed into register R1;
- at line 5: we have just passed a read of the variable F2, yielding the pythia variable $F2_4^i$: this leads to the updated local invariant $R1=F2_4^i$ ∧ ((i=0 ∧ R2=0) ∨ (i>0 ∧ $R2=T_5^{i-1}$));
- at line 6: we have just passed a read of the variable T, yielding the pythia variable T_5^i: this leads to the updated local invariant $R1=F2_4^i$ ∧ $R2=T_5^i$;
- at line 7:, we have just exited the loop—as symbolised by the annotation i_end—thus we have met the exit condition, *viz.*, ¬R1 ∨ R2=1; this is reflected in the invariant ¬ $F2_4^{i_{end}}$ ∧ $T_5^{i_{end}}$=1, as we know from the invariant at line 6: that $R1=F2_4^i$ and $R2=T_5^i$;
- at line 8:, we just passed a skip, which leaves the invariant unchanged;
- at line 9:, we just passed a write, which leaves the invariant unchanged.

4.2 Prove that S_ind Is Indeed Inductive

S_{ind} is inductive under the hypothesis S_{com}; we prove this in several steps:

- *Initialisation proof:* we must prove that the invariant at the entry of each process (*e.g.* R1=0 ∧ R2=0 for P0) is true when all processes are at their entry, all registers hold the value 0, and there is no pythia variable;
- *Sequential proof:* we must prove that the invariants are true when executing a process sequentially. This is simple since:
  - a read r [] R x ⤳ x_ℓ^i updates the value of register R to the adequate pythia variable x_ℓ^i,
  - a write is handled like a skip, *i.e.* has no effect on the invariant, and
  - loops are handled classically:
    * the loop invariant at line 4: must be true upon the first loop entry (*i.e.* R1=0 ∧ R2=0 when i=0), and

* on the ith iteration, if the invariant at line 6: is true after the previous iteration (*i.e.* R1=F2$_4^{i-1}$ ∧ R2=T$_5^{i-1}$), and the exit condition is false (*i.e.* we do not have ¬F2$_4^{i-1}$ ∧ T$_5^{i-1}$=1), then the loop invariant at line 4: must be true for i (*i.e.* R1=F2$_4^{i-1}$ ∧ R2=T$_5^{i-1}$ since the registers hold the values read at the previous iteration), and

* if the invariant at line 6: is true at the end of the loop *i.e.* when i_{end}= i and the while test is false, then the invariant at line 7: must be true, *i.e.* ¬ F2$_4^{i_{end}}$ ∧ T$_5^{i_{end}}$=1.

– *Absence of interference proof:* we must prove that if an invariant is true at a given program point of a process, and another process takes one step of computation, the invariant stays true. In our example, the invariants of each process depend only on its own registers and pythia variables which are not modified by the other process (the upcoming communication proof takes into account the fact that the pythia variables can be modified by the communications).

– *Communication proof:* we must prove that if an invariant is true at some process point ℓ of a process p and a read for x_θ is performed then the value received into x_θ is that of a matching write. Of course only the communications allowed by the communication invariant S_{com} have to be taken into account.

In our case, the invariants do not say anything on the value assigned to the pythia variables so that the invariants are true for any value carried by the pythia variables. More precisely, the read at line 4: can read from the writes at line 0:, 10: or 17:. The invariant at line 4: does not make any distinction on these cases and just states that some value F2$_4^i$ has been read—this value can be **true** or **false**—and assigned to R1. Similarly the read of T at line 5: can read from the writes at line 0:, 2:, or 11:. Again the invariant does not make any distinction between these cases just stating that some value T$_5^i$ is read and assigned to R2. So the communications can be anarchic and the invariance proof does not make, on that example, any use of the communication hypothesis S_{com}. It is however used in the next proof, that S_{ind} is stronger than S_{inv}.

4.3   Prove that S_{ind} Is Indeed Stronger than S_{inv}

S_{ind} is stronger than S_{inv} under the hypothesis S_{com}; we establish our *mutual exclusion proof* by reductio ad absurdum. More precisely, we want to prove that $(S_{com} \wedge S_{ind}) \Longrightarrow S_{inv}$. We choose to prove the equivalent $(S_{ind} \wedge \neg S_{inv}) \Longrightarrow \neg S_{com}$. Thus we assume that at$\{7\}$ and at$\{16\}$ do hold and get a contradiction:

at 7 ∧ at 16

$\Longrightarrow \neg F2_4^{i_{end}} \wedge T_5^{i_{end}} = 1 \wedge \neg F1_{13}^{j_{end}} \wedge T_{14}^{j_{end}} = 2$

$\wr$i.e. the invariants at lines 7: and 16: hold$\wr$

$\Longrightarrow \neg S_{com}$ $\wr$since by taking $i = i_{end}$ and $j = j_{end}$, we

have $F2_4^i = $ false $\wedge$ $T_5^i = 1 \wedge F1_{13}^j = $ false $\wedge$

$T_{14}^j = 2$ $\wr$

5 Inclusion Proof $M \Longrightarrow S_{com}$

Recall that we have proved that the algorithm A satisfies the invariant S_{inv} under a certain communication hypothesis specified by S_{com}. To ensure that S_{inv} holds in the context of the consistency model M, we need to ensure that M guarantees that the communication specification S_{com} holds.

This is essentially an inclusion proof, that all the behaviours allowed by M are allowed by S_{com}, which we write $M \Longrightarrow S_{com}$. Proving that $M \Longrightarrow S_{com}$ is the only bit of proof that must be adapted when considering a different model M'.

To make this inclusion proof easier, we translate our specification S_{com} into the same language as the model M. Recall that we use the `cat` language to describe our model M; hence we need to find a `cat` specification H_{cm} that encompasses our specification S_{com}.

We now take the reader through this process using again Peterson's algorithm (see Fig. 8) with S_{com} being Fig. 11 in Sect. 3.3 as an illustration. More precisely, we proceed as follows:

1. we build the communication scenario corresponding to the pythia triples;
2. we write the corresponding `cat` specification H_{cm};
3. we prove that all the behaviours allowed by H_{cm} are allowed by S_{com};
4. we prove that all the behaviours allowed by M are allowed by H_{cm}.

5.1 Building the Communication Scenario Corresponding to the Pythia Triples

This requires us building several relations between accesses:

- the *read-from* relation rf links a write w of a variable to a read r of the same variable, such that r takes its value from w;
- the *coherence* relation co links an initial write of a variable in the prelude to all the writes of that variable in the program;
- the *program order* relation po links accesses (*i.e.* read/write events) that appear in program order on a process.

More precisely, given the code of the algorithm A (*e.g.* Peterson's in Fig. 8) and an anarchic invariant (*i.e.* without any restriction on possible communications, *e.g.* Peterson's in Fig. 13), we build the following relations (see Fig. 14 with plain or dotted arrows):

- *read-from* rf: for each pythia triple, we depict the read-from relation in red; for example for pythia$\langle 0, F2_4^i, \text{false} \rangle$, we create a read-from relation between a write and a read of the variable F2 with value `false`. The write comes from line 0:, and the read from line 4, at the ith iteration.
- *coherence* co: we depict the coherence edges relative to the variables mentioned by the pythia triples, in our case F1, F2 and T: see in Fig. 14 the edge in blue between the write of F1 (resp. F2, T) in the prelude at line 0: and the write of F1 (resp. F2, T) at line 1: (resp. 10: for F2 and 2:, 11: for T).

– *program order* po: we also depict the program order edges between the accesses which are either the source or the target of a communication edge (*viz.*, read-from and coherence): see in Fig. 14 the po edges in purple between the lines 1:, 2:, 4:, and 5: on the first process, and similarly on the second process. po is irreflexive and transitive (not represented on Fig. 14).

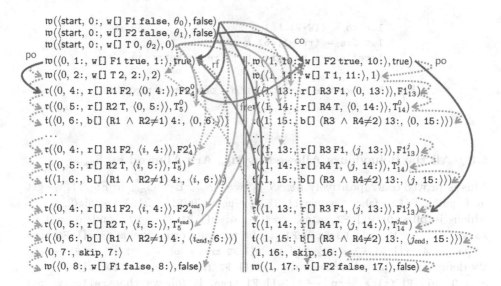

Fig. 14. Communications corresponding to the pythia triples for Peterson

Now in Fig. 14 (where dotted lines can be ignored), note the reflexive sequence 1: w[] F1 true — po ⟶ 4: r[] R1 F2 — rf^-1 ⟶ 0: w[] F2 false — co ⟶ 10: w[] F2 true — po ⟶ 13: r[] R3 F1 — rf^-1 ⟶ 0: w[] F1 false — co ⟶ 1: w[] F1 true. This is the sequence that our cat specification H_{cm} will forbid.

5.2   Writing the Corresponding cat Specification H_{cm}

Writing the corresponding cat specification H_{cm} goes as follows (see Fig. 15 for the definition of H_{cm} in cat):

– we define the relation co as relating initial writes (*viz.*, the writes from the prelude) to the writes in the program that access the same variable. In cat speak, the set of initial writes is written IW, the set of writes in the program is W, the relation between accesses to the same variable is loc (for location) and the intersection is &;
– we define a shorthand fr (for *from-read*) for the sequence of relations rf^-1 and co that appears twice in the cycle in Fig. 14. We refine this relation further, to the relation fre, *viz.* fr restricted to accesses that belong to different processes—in cat this is denoted by the relation ext (for external);

– we require the sequence po; fre; po; fre to be irreflexive, *i.e.* communications between the two processes of Peterson should not be such that taking a
step in program order po, then a step of fre, landing on the other process,
then a step of po, then a step of fre again, goes back to the starting point.

Overall this leads to the cat specification given in Fig. 15:

```
let co = (IW*W) & loc
let fre = (rf^-1;co) & ext
irreflexive po; fre; po; fre as Peterson
```

Fig. 15. A possible specification H_{cm} of Peterson algorithm

5.3   All the Behaviours Allowed by H_{cm} Are Allowed by S_{com}

This is proved contrapositively *i.e.* $\neg S_{com} \implies \neg H_{cm}$. By $\neg S_{com}$ in Fig. 11, we get
$\exists i, j$. pɳtɧia$\langle 0,$ F2$_4^i$, false$\rangle \wedge$ pɳtɧia$\langle 11,$ T$_5^i$, 1$\rangle \wedge$ pɳtɧia$\langle 0,$ F1$_{13}^j$, false$\rangle \wedge$ pɳtɧia$\langle 2,$ T$_{14}^j$, 2$\rangle$
which implies 0: w[] F2 false — rf ⟶ 4: r[] R1 F2 ⤳ F2$_4^i$ and 0: w[] F1
false— rf ⟶ 13: r[] R3 F1 ⤳ F1$_{13}^j$. The program order yields 1: w[] F1 true
— po ⟶ 4: r[] R1 F2 ⤳ F2$_4^i$ and 10: w[] F2 true — po ⟶ 13: r[] R3 F1 ⤳ F1$_{13}^j$.
By definition of the coherence order 0: w[] F2 false — co ⟶ 10: w[] F2 true
and 0: w[] F1 false — co ⟶ 1: w[] F1 true. It follows that reflexive po;
fre; po; fre is true proving $\neg H_{cm}$.

Now, note that the sequence s forbidden by Peterson's specification is exactly
the same as the one we examined for the sb litmus test in Section 2.4. Thus all
conclusions are identical, and one needs to add fences as in sb to make Peterson
correct under TSO or weaker models.

5.4   All the Behaviours Allowed by M Are Allowed by H_{cm}

This is proved by reductio ad absurdum. Suppose an execution of Peterson that is forbidden by H_{cm} yet allowed by M. Such an execution
involves a sequence s of accesses a, b, c, d such that $s =$ a — po ⟶b
— fre ⟶ c —po ⟶ d — fre ⟶ a. This may be forbidden by the WCM
M (*e.g.* SC) or prevented by adding fences (*e.g.* TSO).

The consistency model M (*e.g.* SC with fhw = no fence; TSO with fhw =
mfence) must then be shown to implement H_{cm} by the proof method of [ACM15a]
(Fig. 16).

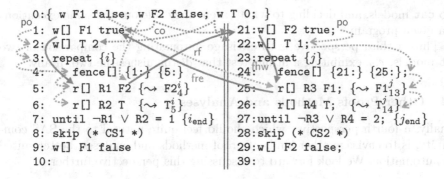

Fig. 16. Peterson algorithm for WCM with fences

6 Perspectives

To conclude we list here a few perspectives for future work.

6.1 From Algorithms to Programs, or the Other Way Around

A first perspective is to envisage verifying *programs* rather than algorithms written in LISA. However our theoretical developments, and to a lesser extent our tool developments, are based on LISA and its semantics. Ideally one could design and prove their algorithms in LISA, then translate the algorithms into the language of their choice, or conversely translate a program of interest into a LISA algorithm. In both cases this requires:

1. a formal comparison of the semantics of both languages, to ensure that the translation does not introduce any unsoundness;
2. some automation to help with fiddly translations.

6.2 From Consistency Hypothesis to Communication Specification, or the Other Way Around

Recall from Sect. 5.3 that we need to link our consistency hypothesis H_{cm}, which expresses in cat a constraint over the communications of our algorithms, with our communication specification, which morally should express the same constraint using pythia variables.

Thus a second perspective is to envisage automating the link between the two, for example producing the communication specification used in the invariance proof from the consistency hypothesis in cat.

6.3 Checking to What Extent a Given Consistency Model Satisfies a Consistency Hypothesis

Recall from Sect. 5.4 that we need to show that our consistency hypothesis H_{cm} is satisfied under a given consistency model M. This essentially requires comparing two `cat` models, and deciding to what extent they rule out the same executions of a given program.

Thus a third perspective is to envisage automating the comparison of two `cat` models, *e.g.* exhibiting a litmus test that distinguishes the two, if any.

6.4   Other Proofs Methods and Analyses

Finally, a fourth perspective, which should feel quite natural to the SAS community, is to envisage other kinds of proof methods and analyses, better suited for automation. We look forward to discussing this perspective further.

Acknowledgements. We thank Luc Maranget and Patrick Cousot for the thrilling years spent working together, hoping for many more to come. We thank Vincent Jacques for comments on a draft.

References

[ABD+15] Alglave, J., Batty, M., Donaldson, A.F., Gopalakrishnan, G., Ketema, J., Poetzl, D., Sorensen, T., Wickerson, J.: GPU concurrency: weak behaviours and programming assumptions. In: ASPLOS (2015)

[ACM15a] Alglave, J., Cousot, P., Maranget, L.: La langue au chat: cat, a language to describe consistency properties, 31 January 2015. Unpublished manuscript

[ACM15b] Alglave, J., Cousot, P., Maranget, L.: Syntax and semantics of the cat language. HSA Foundation, Version 1.1:38 p., 16 October 2015

[Alg10] Alglave, J.: A Shared Memory Poetics. Ph.D. thesis, Université Paris 7 (2010)

[AM15] Alglave, J., Maranget, L.: herd7, 31 August 2015. virginia.cs.ucl.ac.uk/herd

[AMT4b] Alglave, J., Maranget, L., Tautschnig, M.: Herding cats: modelling, simulation, testing, and data-mining for weak memory. TOPLAS **36**(2), 1–74 (2014)

[BDW16] Batty, M., Donaldson, A.F., Wickerson, J.: Overhauling SC atomics in C11 and OpenCL. In: POPL (2016)

[Lam77] Lamport, L.: Proving the correctness of multiprocess programs. IEEE Trans. Software Eng. **3**(2), 125–143 (1977)

[Lam79a] Lamport, L.: How to make a multiprocessor computer that correctly executes multiprocess programs. IEEE Trans. Comput. **28**(9), 690–691 (1979)

[OG76] Owicki, S.S., Gries, D.: An axiomatic proof technique for parallel programs I. Acta Inf. **6**, 319–340 (1976)

[OSS09] Owens, S., Sarkar, S., Sewell, P.: A better x86 memory model: x86-TSO. In: Berghofer, S., Nipkow, T., Urban, C., Wenzel, M. (eds.) TPHOLs 2009. LNCS, vol. 5674, pp. 391–407. Springer, Heidelberg (2009)

[Pet81] Peterson, G.L.: Myths about the mutual exclusion problem. Inf. Process. Lett. **12**(3), 115–116 (1981)

[SPA94] SPARC International Inc. The SPARC Architecture Manual Version 9 (1994)

Quantitative Monitor Automata

Krishnendu Chatterjee[1]([✉]), Thomas A. Henzinger[1], and Jan Otop[2]

[1] IST Austria, Klosterneuburg, Austria
krish.chat@gmail.com
[2] University of Wroclaw, Wroclaw, Poland

Abstract. In this paper we review various automata-theoretic formalisms for expressing quantitative properties. We start with finite-state Boolean automata that express the traditional regular properties. We then consider weighted ω-automata that can measure the average density of events, which finite-state Boolean automata cannot. However, even weighted ω-automata cannot express basic performance properties like average response time. We finally consider two formalisms of weighted ω-automata with monitors, where the monitors are either (a) counters or (b) weighted automata themselves. We present a translation result to establish that these two formalisms are equivalent. Weighted ω-automata with monitors generalize weighted ω-automata, and can express average response time property. They present a natural, robust, and expressive framework for quantitative specifications, with important decidable properties.

1 Introduction

In this work we review various automata-theoretic formalisms for expressing quantitative properties. We start with the motivation for quantitative properties.[1]

Traditional to quantitative verification. The traditional formal verification problem considers Boolean or functional properties of systems, such as "every request is eventually granted". For analysis of resource-constrained systems, such as embedded systems, or for performance analysis, quantitative properties are necessary. Hence recently significant research activities have been devoted to quantitative aspects such as expressing properties like "the long-run average success

---

This research was supported in part by the Austrian Science Fund (FWF) under grants S11402-N23 (RiSE/SHiNE) and Z211-N23 (Wittgenstein Award), ERC Start grant (279307: Graph Games), Vienna Science and Technology Fund (WWTF) through project ICT15-003 and by the National Science Centre (NCN), Poland under grant 2014/15/D/ST6/04543.

[1] We use the term "quantitative" in a non-probabilistic sense, which assigns a quantitative value to each infinite run of a system, representing long-run average or maximal response time, or power consumption, or the like, rather than taking a probabilistic average over different runs.

© Springer-Verlag GmbH Germany 2016
X. Rival (Ed.): SAS 2016, LNCS 9837, pp. 23–38, 2016.
DOI: 10.1007/978-3-662-53413-7_2

rate of an operation is at least one half" or "the long-run average (or the maximal, or the accumulated) resource consumption is below a threshold".

Automata-based properties. Automata have been one of the standard ways to express specifications of system properties. For example, for Boolean properties, automata provide a robust way to express all ω-regular properties [28], and all formulas expressed in Linear-time Temporal Logic (LTL) can be translated to finite-state ω-automata [26]. We review in this paper various automata-based frameworks to express quantitative properties.

Natural ways for extension. The first natural way to express quantitative properties is to consider automata with counters. However, computational analysis of such models quickly leads to undecidability (such as two-counter machines), and a classical way to limit expressiveness for decidability is to consider *monitor counters*, i.e., the counter values do not influence the control. The second approach is to consider automata with weights (or weighted automata). We describe below various approaches that explore the two above possibilities.

Weighted automata over finite words. The first extension of automata with weights was considered as weighted automata over finite words, where the weights come from a semiring [22]. The weighted automata framework for example can express the worst-case execution time, where every transition is labeled with a weight that represents the instruction execution time, and the automaton can choose the supremum over all traces. The weighted automata framework has been significantly enhanced as cost register automata [2]. However, both the weighted automata and the cost register automata framework are restricted to finite words only. In this work we focus on automata over infinite words.

Weighted ω-automata. The counterpart of weighted automata for infinite words is called *weighted ω-automata* (also referred to as *quantitative automata* in [14]). In weighted ω-automata, which extend finite automata, every transition is assigned a rational number called a weight. Hence every run gives rise to an infinite sequence of weights, which is aggregated into a single value by a value function. For non-deterministic weighted ω-automata, the value of a word w is the infimum value of all runs over w. Weighted ω-automata provide a natural and flexible framework for expressing quantitative properties [14]. For example, the property of long-run average of the ratio of requests to grants can be expressed with weighted ω-automata, but not weighted automata over finite words. However, even weighted ω-automata cannot express the following basic property [18].

Example 1. Consider infinite words over $\{req, gra, \#\}$, where req represents requests, gra represents grants, and $\#$ represents idle. A basic and interesting property is the average number of #'s between a request and the corresponding grant, which represents the long-run average response time of the system. We consider two variants: first, when at any point at most one request can be pending, and in general, arbitrarily many requests can be pending.

Weighted automata with monitors. To express quantitative properties such as average response time, weighted ω-automata can be extended with monitors.

The monitors can be of two types: (a) counters; and (b) weighted automata over finite words. We explain the two approaches below.

Automata with monitor counters. Automata with monitor counters are similar in spirit to cost register automata, but for infinite words. They are automata equipped with counters. At each transition, a counter can be started, terminated, or the value of the counter can be increased or decreased. However, the transitions do not depend on the counter values, and hence they are referred to as monitor counters. The values of the counters when they are terminated give rise to the sequence of weights. A value function aggregates the infinite sequence into a single value. Automata with one monitor counter can express the average response time property with at most one request pending (in general at most k requests pending with k counters), which weighted ω-automata cannot.

Nested weighted automata. The second way to enrich expressiveness of weighted ω-automata is to consider weighted automata over finite words as monitors. This gives rise to the framework of *nested weighted automata (NWA)* [18]. An NWA consists of a master automaton and a set of slave automata. The master automaton runs over input infinite words. At every transition the master can invoke a slave automaton that runs over a finite subword of the infinite word, starting at the position where the slave automaton is invoked. Each slave automaton terminates after a finite number of steps and returns a value to the master automaton. Each slave automaton is equipped with a value function for finite words, and the master automaton aggregates the returned values from slave automata using a value function for infinite words. In other words, the slave automata are weighted automata over finite words, whereas the master automaton is an weighted ω-automaton. For Boolean finite automata, nested automata are equivalent to the non-nested counterpart, whereas NWA are strictly more expressive than non-nested weighted ω-automata [18], for example, NWA can express the long-run average response time property (see [18, Example 5]). The NWA framework provides a specification framework where many basic quantitative properties, that cannot be expressed by weighted ω-automata, can be expressed easily, and it provides a natural framework to study quantitative run-time verification (see [18, Sect. 5]). NWA can express the average response time property with any number of requests pending.

The relationship. We establish a close relationship between NWA and automata with monitor counters. More precisely, we show that automata with monitor counters form a special class of NWA. An NWA has width k if at any point at most k slave automata can be active. An NWA with bounded width is an automaton that has width at most k, for some k. We show that the class of automata with monitor counters exactly coincides with the class of NWA with bounded width. Thus the two different ways of adding monitors to weighted ω-automata coincide and give a robust formalism for quantitative specifications. Note that NWA in general allow to have unbounded number of monitor counters, and are more interesting as a theoretical framework, and also more challenging to establish decidability results.

Decidability results. Finally, several interesting computational problems for NWA are decidable [18]. For example, for a subclass of NWA that can express the average response time property, the fundamental automata theoretic questions of emptiness and universality are decidable [18, Theorem 15].

Summary. In summary, NWA provide a natural, expressive, and robust specification framework for quantitative properties: it is a natural extension of weighted ω-automata with nesting, which can express basic performance properties such as average response time, and robust since two different formalisms of monitors lead to the same expressive power. Moreover, it enjoys nice computational aspects, such as decidability of the basic questions. A pictorial description of the landscape of the various automata theoretic formalisms to express quantitative properties is shown in Fig. 1.

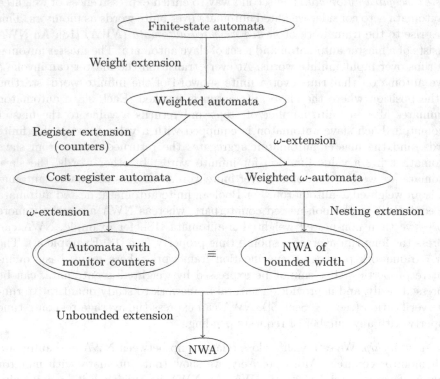

Fig. 1. An overview of the automata models discussed in this paper. The arrows are labeled with a new feature introduced by a more general model, i.e., assigning values to words (weight extension), allowing infinite words (ω-extension), allowing counter monitors (register extension), allowing nesting (nesting extension), and allowing unbounded number of monitors (unbounded extension).

Related works. While in this work we focus on weighted automata for infinite words, we briefly mention the other related works. Weighted automata over finite words (see the book [22] for an excellent collection of results) as well as infinite words without monitors [13, 14, 23] have been extensively studied. The extension to weighted automata with monitor counters over finite words has been considered as cost register automata in [2]. A version of NWA over finite words has been studied in [6]. NWA over infinite words were introduced in [18]. NWA with bounded width have been studied in [16]. Several quantitative logics have also been studied, such as [1, 5, 7]. While we will consider the basic decision problems of emptiness and universality for weighted ω-automata, the study of quantitative properties on other models (such as probabilistic models) or other semantics (like probabilistic semantics) have also been studied extensively [3, 4, 8–11, 15, 17, 19, 20, 24, 25, 27].

2   Finite State Automata

In this section we consider Boolean finite-state automata to express qualitative (i.e., functional or regular) properties.

Words. We consider a finite *alphabet* of letters Σ. A *word* over Σ is a (finite or infinite) sequence of letters from Σ. We denote the i-th letter of a word w by $w[i]$. The length of a finite word w is denoted by $|w|$; and the length of an infinite word w is $|w| = \infty$.

Automata. An *automaton* $\mathcal{A}$ is a tuple $\langle \Sigma, Q, Q_0, \delta, F \rangle$, where (1) Σ is the alphabet, (2) Q is a finite set of states, (3) $Q_0 \subseteq Q$ is the set of initial states, (4) $\delta \subseteq Q \times \Sigma \times Q$ is a transition relation, and (5) F is a set of accepting states, An automaton $\langle \Sigma, Q, q_0, \delta, F \rangle$ is *deterministic* if and only if δ is a function from $Q \times \Sigma$ into Q and Q_0 is a singleton. In definitions of deterministic automata we omit curly brackets in the description of Q_0 and write $\langle \Sigma, Q, q_0, \delta, F \rangle$.

Semantics of automata. A *run* π of an automaton $\mathcal{A}$ on a word w is a sequence of states of $\mathcal{A}$ of length $|w| + 1$ such that $\pi[0]$ belong to the initial states of $\mathcal{A}$ and for every $0 \leq i \leq |w| - 1$ we have $(\pi[i], w[i], \pi[i+1])$ is a transition of $\mathcal{A}$. A run π on a finite word w is *accepting* iff the last state $\pi[|w|]$ of the run is an accepting state of $\mathcal{A}$. A run π on an infinite word w is *accepting* iff some accepting state of $\mathcal{A}$ occurs infinitely often in π. For an automaton $\mathcal{A}$ and a word w, we define $\mathsf{Acc}(w)$ as the set of accepting runs on w. Finally, we define a language *recognized* by an automaton $\mathcal{A}$ as the set of words w such that $\mathsf{Acc}(w) \neq \emptyset$.

Example 2 (Responsiveness). We consider a system with three types of events: requests ($\boldsymbol{r}eq$), grants ($\boldsymbol{g}ra$) and null instructions ($\#$). We consider the following specifications express that the system is responsive:

SB1 $\mathbf{G}(\boldsymbol{r}eq \rightarrow \neg\boldsymbol{r}eq\mathbf{U}\boldsymbol{g}ra)$: *requests and grants are organized in non-overlapping pairs*

SB2 $\mathbf{G}(\boldsymbol{r}eq \rightarrow \mathbf{F}\boldsymbol{g}ra)$: *every request is followed by a grant,*

SB3 $\mathbf{GF}\boldsymbol{r}eq \rightarrow \mathbf{GF}\boldsymbol{g}ra$: *if infinite number of request is issued, the system issues infinitely many grants*

The above properties are ordered from the strongest to the weakest, i.e., the first property implies the second and the second implies the third. The converse implications do not hold.

Every LTL formula φ can be translated to a Büchi automaton, which recognize words satisfying φ. In particular, properties SB1, SB2 and SB3 can be expressed by automata presented in Fig. 2.

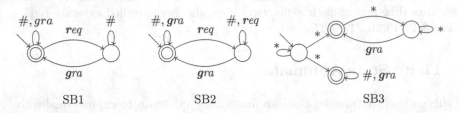

Fig. 2. Finite-state automata expressing properties SB1, SB2 and SB3. Double circles denote accepting states, the state the most to the left is an initial state and $*$ denotes all letters $req, gra, \#$.

Results. A basic question for automata is the language emptiness (resp., universality) problem that asks whether there exists a word that is accepted (resp., all words are accepted). The emptiness problem is NLOGSPACE-complete whereas the universality problem is PSPACE-complete [28].

3   Weighted Automata

In this section we present weighted automata over finite words and infinite words. We call weighted automata over infinite words as weighted ω-automata (which was originally called *quantitative automata* [14]). For brevity, if it is clear from the context that we consider infinite words, then we simply use weighted automata instead of weighted ω-automata. These automata assign numbers to words, and hence can express quantitative properties such as *workload* of a system. The following definitions are common for finite- and infinite-word automata.

Labeled automata. For a set X, an X-*labeled automaton* is an automaton extended by a function C assigning elements of X to transitions of $\mathcal{A}$. Formally, X-labeled automaton $\mathcal{A}$ is a tuple $\langle \Sigma, Q, Q_0, \delta, F, C \rangle$, where $\langle \Sigma, Q, Q_0, \delta, F \rangle$ is an automaton and $C : \delta \mapsto X$ is a labeling function.

Weighted automata. A *weighted automaton* is a $\mathbb{Z}$-labeled automaton, where $\mathbb{Z}$ is the set of integers. The labels are called *weights*.

Semantics of weighted automata. We define the semantics of weighted automata in two steps. First, we define the value of a run. Second, we define the value of a word based on the values of its runs. To define values of runs, we will consider *value functions* f that assign real numbers to sequences of integers.

Given a non-empty word w, every run π of $\mathcal{A}$ on w defines a sequence of weights of successive transitions of $\mathcal{A}$, i.e., $C(\pi) = (C(\pi[i-1], w[i], \pi[i]))_{1 \leq i \leq |w|}$; and the value $f(\pi)$ of the run π is defined as $f(C(\pi))$. We denote by $(C(\pi))[i]$ the weight of the i-th transition, i.e., $C(\pi[i-1], w[i], \pi[i])$. The value of a non-empty word w assigned by the automaton $\mathcal{A}$, denoted by $\mathcal{L}_{\mathcal{A}}(w)$, is the infimum of the set of values of all *accepting* runs; i.e., $\inf_{\pi \in \mathrm{Acc}(w)} f(\pi)$, and we have the usual semantics that the infimum of an empty set is infinite, i.e., the value of a word that has no accepting run is infinite. Every run π on an empty word has length 1 and the sequence $C(\pi)$ is empty, hence we define the value $f(\pi)$ as an external (not a real number) value $\bot$. Thus, the value of the empty word is either $\bot$, if the empty word is accepted by $\mathcal{A}$, or ∞ otherwise. To indicate a particular value function f that defines the semantics, we will call a weighted automaton $\mathcal{A}$ an f-automaton.

Value functions. We will consider the classical functions and their natural variants for value functions. For finite runs we consider the following value functions: for runs of length $n + 1$ we have

1. *Max and min:* $\mathrm{MAX}(\pi) = \max_{i=1}^{n}(C(\pi))[i]$ and $\mathrm{MIN}(\pi) = \min_{i=1}^{n}(C(\pi))[i]$.
2. *Sum and absolute sum:* the sum function $\mathrm{SUM}(\pi) = \sum_{i=1}^{n}(C(\pi))[i]$ and the absolute sum $\mathrm{SUM}^{+}(\pi) = \sum_{i=1}^{n} \mathsf{Abs}((C(\pi))[i])$, where $\mathsf{Abs}(x)$ is the absolute value of x.

We denote the above class of value functions for finite words as $\mathsf{FinVal} = \{\mathrm{MAX}, \mathrm{MIN}, \mathrm{SUM}, \mathrm{SUM}^{+}\}$. For infinite runs we consider:

1. *Supremum and Infimum, and Limit supremum and Limit infimum:* $\mathrm{SUP}(\pi) = \sup\{(C(\pi))[i] : i > 0\}$, $\mathrm{INF}(\pi) = \inf\{(C(\pi))[i] : i > 0\}$, $\mathrm{LIMSUP}(\pi) = \limsup\{(C(\pi))[i] : i > 0\}$, and $\mathrm{LIMINF}(\pi) = \liminf\{(C(\pi))[i] : i > 0\}$.
2. *Limit average:* $\mathrm{LIMAVG}(\pi) = \limsup_{k \to \infty} \frac{1}{k} \cdot \sum_{i=1}^{k}(C(\pi))[i]$.

We denote the above class of value functions for infinite words as $\mathsf{InfVal} = \{\mathrm{SUP}, \mathrm{INF}, \mathrm{LIMSUP}, \mathrm{LIMINF}, \mathrm{LIMAVG}\}$.

Example 3 (Workload). Recall the setting of requests and grants from Example 2 and properties regarding responsiveness of the system. However, property 1 is satisfied by a trace $r \, eqg \, rar \, eq^2 \, gra \ldots r \, eq^i \, gra \ldots$ in which the average number of requests per grant tends to infinity. Property 1 implies the long-time average of requests per grant is 1, but it is much stronger as it requires a pending request to be matched with a grant before a new request can be issued. With LIMAVG-automata we can specify the *workload* of the system, which is defined as the long-term average of difference between requests and grants.

Results. The classical decision questions for automata, emptiness and universality have their counterparts in the quantitative framework. The emptiness (resp., universality) problem that asks, given a weighted automaton and a threshold, whether there exists a word whose value does not exceed the threshold (resp., values of all words do not exceed the threshold). The complexity of these problems depends on the value function. For the finite words, a comprehensive account of the results is available in [22]. Below we discuss the results for infinite words. For the considered values functions, the emptiness problem is in PTIME [14, Theorem 3], whereas complexity of the universality problem ranges between PSPACE-complete [14, Theorem 7] and undecidable ([12, Theorem 5] which follows from [21, Theorem 4]).

4   Automata with Monitor Counters

In this section we consider automata with monitor counters, which extend weighted ω-automata.

Automata with monitor counters. An *automaton with n monitor counters* $\mathcal{A}^{\text{m-c}}$ is a tuple $\langle \Sigma, Q, Q_0, \delta, F \rangle$ where (1) Σ is the alphabet, (2) Q is a finite set of states, (3) $Q_0 \subseteq Q_0$ is the set of initial states, (4) δ is a finite subset of $Q \times \Sigma \times Q \times (\mathbb{Z} \cup \{s, t\})^n$ called a transition relation, (each component refers to one monitor counter, where letters s, t refer to starting and terminating the counter, respectively, and the value from $\mathbb{Z}$ is the value that is added to the counter), and (5) F is the set of accepting states. Moreover, we assume that for every $(q, a, q', \boldsymbol{u}) \in \delta$, at most one component in $\boldsymbol{u}$ contains s, i.e., at most one counter is activated at each position. Intuitively, the automaton $\mathcal{A}^{\text{m-c}}$ is equipped with n counters. The transitions of $\mathcal{A}^{\text{m-c}}$ do not depend on the values of counters (hence, we call them monitor counters); and every transition is of the form $(q, a, q', \boldsymbol{v})$, which means that if $\mathcal{A}^{\text{m-c}}$ is in the state q and the current letter is a, then it can move to the state q' and update counters according to v. Each counter is initially inactive. It is activated by the instruction s, and it changes its value at every step by adding the value between $-N$ and N until termination t. The value of the counter at the time it is terminated is then assigned to the position where it has been activated. An automaton with monitor counters $\mathcal{A}^{\text{m-c}}$ is *deterministic* if and only if Q_0 is a singleton and δ is a function from $Q \times \Sigma$ into $Q \times (\mathbb{Z} \cup \{s, t\})^n$.

Semantics of automata with monitor counters. A sequence π of elements from $Q \times (\mathbb{Z} \times \{\bot\})^n$ is a *run* of $\mathcal{A}^{\text{m-c}}$ on a word w if (1) $\pi[0] = \langle q_0, \bot \rangle$ and $q_0 \in Q_0$ and (2) for every $i > 0$, if $\pi[i-1] = \langle q, \boldsymbol{u} \rangle$ and $\pi[i] = \langle q', \boldsymbol{u}' \rangle$ then $\mathcal{A}^{\text{m-c}}$ has a transition $(q, w[i], q', \boldsymbol{v})$ and for every $j \in [1, n]$ we have (a) if $v[j] = s$, then $u[j] = \bot$ and $u'[j] = 0$, (b) if $v[j] = t$, then $u[j] \in \mathbb{Z}$ and $u'[j] = \bot$, and (c) if $v[j] \in \mathbb{Z}$, then $u'[j] = u[j] + v[j]$. A run π is *accepting* if some state from F occurs infinitely often on the first component of π, infinitely often some counter is activated and every activated counter is finally terminated. An accepting run π defines a sequence π^W of integers and $\bot$ as follows: let the counter started at position i be j, and let the value of the counter j terminated at the earliest position after i be x_j, then $\pi^W[i]$ is x_j. The semantics of automata with monitor counters is given, similarly to weighted ω-automata, by applying the value function to π^W.

More general counter operations. In our framework, the counter operations we allow are: activation, adding an integer, and termination. More generally, we can allow other operations such as terminating a counter and discarding its value, or adding the value of one counter to another and terminating it. These operations are similar in spirit to the operations on registers with the copyless restriction in the cost register automata [2]. In [2] it has been shown that the copyless sum of registers can be eliminated using a variant of the subset construction. We can apply this construction to our framework, and this more general operations do not add expressive power as compared to the basic operations that we consider. Hence for simplicity, and ease of establishing equivalence with other models, we consider the basic and fundamental set of counter operations for automata with monitor counters.

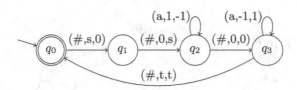

Fig. 3. The automaton $\mathcal{A}_{\text{diff}}$ computing the maximal difference between the lengths of blocks of a's at odd and the following even positions.

Example 4 (Blocks difference [16]). Consider an alphabet $\Sigma = \{a, \#\}$ and a language $\mathcal{L}$ of words $(\#^2 a^* \# a^* \#)^{\omega}$. On the words from $\mathcal{L}$ we consider a quantitative property "the maximal block-length difference between odd and even positions", i.e., the value of word $\#^2 a^{m[1]} \# a^{m[2]} \#^3 \ldots$ is $\sup_{0 \leq i} |m[2*i+1] - m[2*i+2]|$. This property can be expressed by a SUP-automaton $\mathcal{A}_{\text{diff}}$ with two monitor counters depicted in Fig. 3.

The automaton $\mathcal{A}_{\text{diff}}$ has a single initial state q_0, which is also the only accepting state. It processes the word w in subwords $\#^2 a^k \# a^m \#$ in the following way. First, it reads $\#^2$ upon which it takes transitions from q_0 to q_1 and from q_1 to q_2, where it starts counters 1 and 2. Next, it moves to the state q_2 where it counts letters a incrementing counter 1 and decrementing counter 2. Then, upon reading $\#$, it moves to q_3, where it counts letters a, but it decrements counter 1 and increments counter 2. After reading $\#^2 a^k \# a^m$ the value of counter 1 is $k - m$ and counter 2 is $m - k$. In the following transition from q_3 to q_0, the automaton terminates both counters. The aggregating function of $\mathcal{A}_{\text{diff}}$ is SUP, thus the automaton discards the lower value, i.e., the value of $\#^2 a^k \# a^m \#$ is $|k - m|$ and the automaton computes the supremum over values of all blocks. It follows that the value of $\#^2 a^{m[1]} \# a^{m[2]} \#^3 \ldots$ is $\sup_{0 \leq i} |m[2*i+1] - m[2*i+2]|$.

Example 5 ((Well-matched) average response time). Consider a system from Examples 2 and 3 and assume that it satisfies property SB1, i.e., at every position there is at most one pending request. Then, an automaton with a single monitor counter can compute the average response time (ART) property, which asks for the long-run average over requests of the number of steps between a request and the following grant. E.g. ART of the trace $(req\#\#g\,ra\,req\#gra)^{\omega}$ is 1.5.

Note that ART of a word can be unbounded, whereas weighted ω-automata with the limit average value function return values which are bounded by the value of the maximal weight in the automaton. Therefore, the ART property cannot be expressed by weighted ω-automata with the limit average value function or any other value function considered in the literature. Below, we define an automaton with monitor counters, which expresses a more general property.

We consider an extension on the ART property, called the 2-ART property, which is essentially the ART property in systems with two types of requests req_1, req_2 and grants gra_1, gra_2. In these systems, requests are satisfied only by grants of an appropriate type. The automaton with two monitor counters depicted in Fig. 4 computes the 2-ART property.

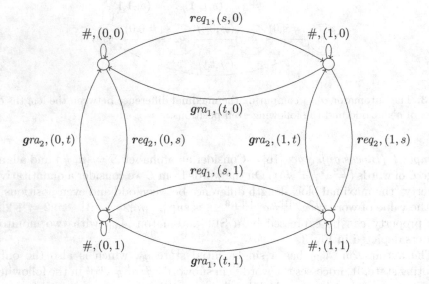

Fig. 4. The automaton computing the 2-ART property

Results. In the following section, we show equivalence of automata with monitor counters and nested weighted automata of bounded width. Due to this equivalence, we refrain from complexity discussion here.

5 Nested Weighted Automata

In this section we describe nested weighted automata introduced in [18], and closely follow the description of [18]. For more details and illustration of such automata we refer the reader to [18]. We start with an informal description.

Informal description. A *nested weighted automaton* consists of a labeled automaton over infinite words, called the *master automaton*, a value function f for infinite words, and a set of weighted automata over finite words, called *slave automata*. A nested weighted automaton can be viewed as follows: given a word, we consider the run of the master automaton on the word, but the weight of each transition is determined by dynamically running slave automata; and then the value of a run is obtained using the value function f. That is, the master automaton proceeds on an input word as an usual automaton, except that before it takes a transition, it starts a slave automaton corresponding to the label of the current transition. The slave automaton starts at the current position of the word of the master automaton and works on some finite part of the input word. Once a slave automaton finishes, it returns its value to the master automaton, which treats the returned value as the weight of the current transition that is being executed. The slave automaton might immediately accept and return value $\perp$, which corresponds to *silent* transitions. If one of slave automata rejects, the nested weighted automaton rejects. In the sequel, a master automaton is always a weighted ω-automaton, and the slave automata are weighted automata. For brevity and uniformity, we simply use weighted automata. We define this formally as follows.

Nested weighted automata. A *nested weighted automaton* (NWA) $\mathbb{A}$ is a tuple $\langle \mathcal{A}_{\mathrm{mas}}; f; \mathfrak{B}_1, \ldots, \mathfrak{B}_k \rangle$, where (1) $\mathcal{A}_{\mathrm{mas}}$, called the *master automaton*, is a $\{1, \ldots, k\}$-labeled automaton over infinite words (the labels are the indexes of automata $\mathfrak{B}_1, \ldots, \mathfrak{B}_k$), (2) f is a value function on infinite words, called the *master value function*, and (3) $\mathfrak{B}_1, \ldots, \mathfrak{B}_k$ are weighted automata over finite words called *slave automata*. Intuitively, an NWA can be regarded as an f-automaton whose weights are dynamically computed at every step by a corresponding slave automaton. We define an $(f; g)$-*automaton* as an NWA where the master value function is f and all slave automata are g-automata.

Semantics: runs and values. A *run* of an NWA $\mathbb{A}$ on an infinite word w is an infinite sequence $(\Pi, \pi_1, \pi_2, \ldots)$ such that (1) Π is a run of $\mathcal{A}_{\mathrm{mas}}$ on w; (2) for every $i > 0$ we have π_i is a run of the automaton $\mathfrak{B}_{C(\Pi[i-1], w[i], \Pi[i])}$, referenced by the label $C(\Pi[i-1], w[i], \Pi[i])$ of the master automaton, on some finite word of $w[i, j]$. The run $(\Pi, \pi_1, \pi_2, \ldots)$ is *accepting* if all runs $\Pi, \pi_1, \pi_2, \ldots$ are accepting (i.e., Π satisfies its acceptance condition and each $\pi_1, \pi_2, \ldots$ ends in an accepting state) and infinitely many runs of slave automata have length greater than 1 (the master automaton takes infinitely many non-silent transitions). The value of the run $(\Pi, \pi_1, \pi_2, \ldots)$ is defined as the value of f applied to the sequence of values of runs of slave automata $\pi_1, \pi_2, \ldots$ with $\perp$ values removed. The value of a word w assigned by the automaton $\mathbb{A}$, denoted by $\mathcal{L}_{\mathbb{A}}(w)$, is the infimum of the set of values of all *accepting* runs. We require accepting runs to contain infinitely many non-silent transitions because f is a value function over infinite sequences, so we need the sequence $v(\pi_1)v(\pi_2) \ldots$ with $\perp$ symbols removed to be infinite.

Deterministic nested weighted automata. An NWA $\mathbb{A}$ is *deterministic* if (1) the master automaton and all slave automata are deterministic, and (2) slave automata recognize prefix-free languages, i.e., languages $\mathcal{L}$ such that if $w \in \mathcal{L}$, then no proper extension of w belongs to $\mathcal{L}$. Condition (2) implies that no accepting run of a slave automaton visits an accepting state twice. Intuitively, slave automata have to accept the first time they encounter an accepting state as they will not see an accepting state again.

Example 6 (Average response time). Consider an alphabet Σ consisting of requests req, grants gra, and null instructions $\#$. The average response time (ART) property asks for the average number of instructions between any request and the following grant. An NWA computing the average response time is depicted in Fig. 5. At every position with letter req the master automaton $\mathcal{A}_{mas}$ of $\mathbb{A}$ invokes the slave automaton $\mathfrak{B}_1$, which computes the number of letters from its initial position to the first following grant. The automaton $\mathfrak{B}_1$ is a SUM^+-automaton. On letters $\#$ and gra the automaton $\mathcal{A}_{mas}$ invokes the slave automaton $\mathfrak{B}_2$, which is a dummy automaton, i.e., it immediately accepts and returns no weight. Invoking such a dummy automaton corresponds to taking a silent transition. Thus, the sequence of values returned by slave automata ($54311\ldots$ in Fig. 5), is the sequence of response times for each request. Therefore, the averages of these values is precisely the average response time; in the NWA $\mathbb{A}$, the value function f is LIMAVG. Also this property cannot be expressed by a non-nested automaton: a quantitative property is a function from words to reals, and as a function the range of non-nested LIMAVG-automata is bounded, whereas the ART can have unbounded values (for details see [18]).

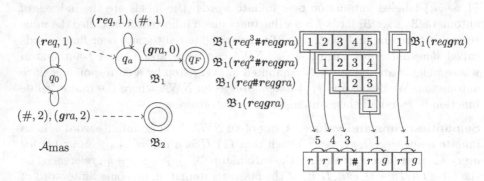

Fig. 5. An NWA $\mathbb{A}$ computing ART. The master automaton $\mathcal{A}_{mas}$ and slave automata $\mathfrak{B}_1, \mathfrak{B}_2$ are on the left. A part of a run of $\mathbb{A}$ on word $req\,req\,req\#req\,gra\,req\,gra\ldots$ is presented on the right.

5.1   NWA of Bounded Width

In this section we define a subclass of NWA, called NWA of bounded width, and we discuss properties of this subclass.

Bounded width. An NWA has *bounded width* if and only if there exists a bound C such that in every run at every position at most C slave automata are active.

Example 7 (Non-overlapping ART). Consider the NWA $\mathbb{A}$ from Example 6 depicted in Fig. 5, which does not have bounded width. The run in Fig. 5 has width at least 4, but on word $req\,gra\,ra\,req^2\,gra\,ra\,req^3\,gra\ldots$ the number of active slave automata at position of letter gra in subword $req^i\,gra$ is i. We consider a variant of the ART property, called the 1-ART property, where after a request till it is granted additional requests are not considered. Formally, we consider the ART property over the language $\mathcal{L}_1$ defined by $(req\#^* gra\#^*)^\omega$ (equivalently, given a request, the automata can check if the slave automaton is not active, and only then invoke it). An NWA $\mathbb{A}_1$ computing the ART property over $\mathcal{L}_1$ is obtained from the NWA from Fig. 5 by taking the product of the master automaton $\mathcal{A}_{mas}$ (from Fig. 5) with an automaton recognizing the language $\mathcal{L}_1$, which is given by the automaton for the property SB1 presented in Fig. 2. The automaton $\mathbb{A}_1$, as well as, $\mathbb{A}$ from Example 6 are $(\text{LIMAVG}; \text{SUM}^+)$-automata and they are deterministic. Indeed, the master automaton and the slave automata of $\mathbb{A}_1$ (resp., $\mathbb{A}$) are deterministic and the slave automata recognize prefix-free languages. Moreover, in any (infinite) run of $\mathbb{A}_1$ at most one slave automaton is active, i.e., $\mathbb{A}_1$ has width 1. The dummy slave automata do not increase the width as they immediately accept, and hence they are not considered as active even at the position they are invoked. Finally, observe that the 1-ART property can return unbounded values, which implies that there exists no (non-nested) LIMAVG-automaton expressing it.

Lemma 1 (Translation Lemma [17]). *For every value function $f \in \text{InfVal}$ on infinite words we have the following: (1) Every deterministic f-automaton with monitor counters $\mathcal{A}^{m\text{-}c}$ can be transformed in polynomial time into an equivalent deterministic $(f; \text{SUM})$-automaton of bounded width. (2) Every non-deterministic (resp., deterministic) $(f; \text{SUM})$-automaton of bounded width can be transformed in exponential time into an equivalent non-deterministic (resp., deterministic) f-automaton with monitor counters.*

Proof **(Translation of automata with monitor counters to NWA):** Consider a deterministic f-automaton $\mathcal{A}^{m\text{-}c}$ with k monitor counters and the set of states Q^{m-c}. We define an $(f; \text{SUM})$-automaton $\mathbb{A}$, which consists of a master automaton $\mathcal{A}_{mas}$ and slave automata $\{\mathfrak{B}_{i,q} : i \in \{1, \ldots, k\}, q \in Q^{m-c}\} \cup \{\mathfrak{B}_\perp\}$. The slave automaton $\mathfrak{B}_\perp$ is a dummy automaton, i.e., it has only a single state which is both the initial and the accepting state. Invoking such an automaton is equivalent to taking a silent transition (with no weight). Next, the master automaton $\mathcal{A}_{mas}$ and slave automata $\{\mathfrak{B}_{i,q} : i \in \{1, \ldots, k\}, q \in Q^{m-c}\}$ are variants of $\mathcal{A}^{m\text{-}c}$, i.e., they share the underlying transition structure. The automaton $\mathcal{A}_{mas}$ simulates $\mathcal{A}^{m\text{-}c}$, i.e., it has the same states and the transitions among these states as $\mathcal{A}^{m\text{-}c}$. However, whenever $\mathcal{A}^{m\text{-}c}$ activates counter i, the master automaton invokes the slave automaton $\mathfrak{B}_{i,q}$, where q is their current state (both $\mathcal{A}_{mas}$ and the simulated $\mathcal{A}^{m\text{-}c}$). The accepting condition of $\mathcal{A}_{mas}$ is the same as of $\mathcal{A}^{m\text{-}c}$. For every $i \in \{1, \ldots, k\}$, the slave automaton $\mathfrak{B}_{i,q}$ keeps track of counter i, i.e., it simulates $\mathcal{A}^{m\text{-}c}$ and applies instructions of $\mathcal{A}^{m\text{-}c}$ for counter i to its value. That is, whenever $\mathcal{A}^{m\text{-}c}$ changes the value of counter i by m, the automaton $\mathfrak{B}_{i,q}$ takes a transition of the weight m. Finally, $\mathfrak{B}_{i,q}$ terminates precisely when $\mathcal{A}^{m\text{-}c}$ terminates counter i. The semantics of automata with monitor counters implies that $\mathbb{A}$ accepts if and only if $\mathcal{A}^{m\text{-}c}$ accepts and, for every word, the sequences of weights produced by the runs of $\mathbb{A}$ and $\mathcal{A}^{m\text{-}c}$ on that word coincide. Therefore, the values of $\mathbb{A}$ and $\mathcal{A}^{m\text{-}c}$ coincide on every word.

(Translation of NWA of bounded width to automata with monitor counters): We show that non-deterministic (resp., deterministic) f-automata with monitor counters subsume non-deterministic (resp., deterministic) $(f; \text{SUM})$-automata of bounded width. Consider a non-deterministic $(f; \text{SUM})$-automaton $\mathbb{A}$ with width bounded by k. We define an f-automaton $\mathcal{A}^{\text{m-c}}$ with k monitor counters that works as follows. Let Q_{mas} be the set of states of the master automaton of $\mathbb{A}$ and Q_s be the union of the sets of states of the slave automata of $\mathbb{A}$. The set of states of $\mathcal{A}^{\text{m-c}}$ is $Q_{mas} \times Q_s \times \ldots \times Q_s = Q_{mas} \times (Q_s)^k$. The automaton $\mathcal{A}^{\text{m-c}}$ simulates runs of the master automaton and slave automata by keeping track of the state of the master automaton and states of up to k active slave automata. Moreover, it uses counters to simulate the values of slave automata, i.e., whenever a slave automaton is activated, $\mathcal{A}^{\text{m-c}}$ simulates the execution of this automaton and assigns some counter i to that automaton. Next, when the simulated slave automaton takes a transition of the weight m the automaton $\mathcal{A}^{\text{m-c}}$ changes the value of counter i by m. Finally, $\mathcal{A}^{\text{m-c}}$ terminates counter i when the corresponding slave automaton terminates.

Since $\mathbb{A}$ has width bounded by k, the simulating automaton $\mathcal{A}^{\text{m-c}}$ never runs out of counters to simulate slave automata. Moreover, as it simulates runs of the master automaton and slave automata of $\mathbb{A}$, there is a one-to-one correspondence between runs of $\mathcal{A}^{\text{m-c}}$ and runs of $\mathbb{A}$ and accepting runs of $\mathbb{A}$ correspond to accepting runs of $\mathcal{A}^{\text{m-c}}$. Finally, the sequence of weights for the master automaton determined by a given run of $\mathbb{A}$ coincides with the sequence of weights of $\mathcal{A}^{\text{m-c}}$ on the corresponding run. Therefore, the values of $\mathbb{A}$ and $\mathcal{A}^{\text{m-c}}$ coincide on every word. Thus, non-deterministic f-automata with monitor counters subsume non-deterministic $(f; \text{SUM})$-automata of bounded width. Moreover, the one-to-one correspondence between runs of $\mathbb{A}$ and $\mathcal{A}^{\text{m-c}}$ implies that if $\mathbb{A}$ is deterministic, then $\mathcal{A}^{\text{m-c}}$ is deterministic. Therefore, deterministic f-automata with monitor counters subsume deterministic $(f; \text{SUM})$-automata of bounded width. This completes the proof.

Results. Complexity of the emptiness and the universality problems depends on the value functions for the master automaton and slave automata. Both problems can be undecidable. However, in decidable cases the problems are in PTIME for fixed width and PSPACE-complete if the width is given in input. The detailed complexity results are summarized in Tables 1–4 in [18] and Table 1 in [16].

5.2   NWA of Unbounded Width

NWA of unbounded width express the unrestricted average response time property, where there is no restriction on the number of pending requests. This property has been showed in Example 6.

Significance of results. The above example shows that NWA with unbounded width can express properties such as average response time. As compared to NWA with bounded width, analysis of NWA with unbounded width is more challenging as there is no bound on the number of active slave automata.

This model also corresponds to automata with monitor counters, where fresh counters can be activated, and there is no bound on the number of counters. Thus establishing positive results (such as decidability and complexity bounds) is much more challenging and non-trivial for NWA with unbounded width. Below we discuss the results about NWA with unbounded width.

Results. Complexity of the emptiness and the universality problems depends on the value functions for the master automaton and slave automata. Both problems can be undecidable. In decidable cases the complexity ranges between PSPACE-complete and EXPSPACE. The detailed complexity results are summarized in Tables 1–4 in [18].

6   Conclusion

In this work we considered various automata-theoretic formalisms to express quantitative properties. The two different extensions of weighted ω-automata with monitors, namely, with counters, or with weighted automata, have the same expressive power and provide a robust framework for quantitative specifications. There are several interesting directions of future works. First, we consider specific value functions, such as limit-average. A framework of quantitative specifications with general value functions and their characterization is an interesting direction of future work. Second, to explore the effectiveness of weighted automata with monitors in verification, such as in runtime verification, is another interesting direction of future work.

References

1. Almagor, S., Boker, U., Kupferman, O.: Discounting in LTL. In: Ábrahám, E., Havelund, K. (eds.) TACAS 2014 (ETAPS). LNCS, vol. 8413, pp. 424–439. Springer, Heidelberg (2014)
2. Alur, R., D'Antoni, L., Deshmukh, J.V., Raghothaman, M., Yuan, Y.: Regular functions and cost register automata. In: LICS 2013, pp. 13–22 (2013)
3. Baier, C., Dubslaff, C., Klüppelholz, S.: Trade-off analysis meets probabilistic model checking. In: CSL-LICS 2014, pp. 1:1–1:10 (2014)
4. Baier, C., Klein, J., Klüppelholz, S., Wunderlich, S.: Weight monitoring with linear temporal logic: complexity and decidability. In: CSL-LICS 2014, pp. 11:1–11:10 (2014)
5. Boker, U., Chatterjee, K., Henzinger, T.A., Kupferman, O.: Temporal specifications with accumulative values. ACM TOCL 15(4), 1–25 (2014)
6. Bollig, B., Gastin, P., Monmege, B., Zeitoun, M.: Pebble weighted automata and transitive closure logics. In: Gavoille, C., Kirchner, C., Meyer auf der Heide, F., Spirakis, P.G., Abramsky, S. (eds.) ICALP 2010. LNCS, vol. 6199, pp. 587–598. Springer, Heidelberg (2010)
7. Bouyer, P., Markey, N., Matteplackel, R.M.: Averaging in LTL. In: Baldan, P., Gorla, D. (eds.) CONCUR 2014. LNCS, vol. 8704, pp. 266–280. Springer, Heidelberg (2014)

8. Brázdil, T., Brozek, V., Chatterjee, K., Forejt, V., Kucera, A.: Two views on multiple mean-payoff objectives in Markov decision processes. In: LICS 2011, pp. 33–42 (2011)
9. Brázdil, T., Chatterjee, K., Forejt, V., Kucera, A.: Multigain: a controller synthesis tool for MDPs with multiple mean-payoff objectives. In: TACAS 2015, pp. 181–187 (2015)
10. Chatterjee, K.: Markov decision processes with multiple long-run average objectives. In: Arvind, V., Prasad, S. (eds.) FSTTCS 2007. LNCS, vol. 4855, pp. 473–484. Springer, Heidelberg (2007)
11. Chatterjee, K., Doyen, L.: Energy and mean-payoff parity Markov decision processes. In: Murlak, F., Sankowski, P. (eds.) MFCS 2011. LNCS, vol. 6907, pp. 206–218. Springer, Heidelberg (2011)
12. Chatterjee, K., Doyen, L., Edelsbrunner, H., Henzinger, T.A., Rannou, P.: Mean-payoff automaton expressions. In: Gastin, P., Laroussinie, F. (eds.) CONCUR 2010. LNCS, vol. 6269, pp. 269–283. Springer, Heidelberg (2010)
13. Chatterjee, K., Doyen, L., Henzinger, T.A.: Expressiveness and closure properties for quantitative languages. LMCS, 6(3) (2010)
14. Chatterjee, K., Doyen, L., Henzinger, T.A.: Quantitative languages. ACM TOCL 11(4), 23 (2010)
15. Chatterjee, K., Forejt, V., Wojtczak, D.: Multi-objective discounted reward verification in graphs and MDPs. In: McMillan, K., Middeldorp, A., Voronkov, A. (eds.) LPAR-19 2013. LNCS, vol. 8312, pp. 228–242. Springer, Heidelberg (2013)
16. Chatterjee, K., Henzinger, T.A., Otop, J.: Nested weighted limit-average automata of bounded width. To appear at MFCS 2016 (2016)
17. Chatterjee, K., Henzinger, T.A., Otop, J.: Quantitative automata under probabilistic semantics. To appear at LICS 2016 (2016)
18. Chatterjee, K., Henzinger, T.A., Otop, J.: Nested weighted automata. In: LICS 2015, pp. 725–737 (2015)
19. Chatterjee, K., Komárková, Z., Kretínský, J.: Unifying two views on multiple mean-payoff objectives in Markov Decision Processes. In: LICS 2015, pp. 244–256 (2015)
20. Chatterjee, K., Majumdar, R., Henzinger, T.A.: Markov decision processes with multiple objectives. In: Durand, B., Thomas, W. (eds.) STACS 2006. LNCS, vol. 3884, pp. 325–336. Springer, Heidelberg (2006)
21. Degorre, A., Doyen, L., Gentilini, R., Raskin, J.-F., Toruńczyk, S.: Energy and mean-payoff games with imperfect information. In: Dawar, A., Veith, H. (eds.) CSL 2010. LNCS, vol. 6247, pp. 260–274. Springer, Heidelberg (2010)
22. Droste, M., Kuich, W., Vogler, H.: Handbook of Weighted Automata, 1st edn. Springer, Heidelberg (2009)
23. Droste, M., Rahonis, G.: Weighted automata and weighted logics on infinite words. In: Ibarra, O.H., Dang, Z. (eds.) DLT 2006. LNCS, vol. 4036, pp. 49–58. Springer, Heidelberg (2006)
24. Filar, J., Vrieze, K.: Competitive Markov Decision Processes. Springer, New York (1996)
25. Forejt, V., Kwiatkowska, M., Norman, G., Parker, D., Qu, H.: Quantitative multi-objective verification for probabilistic systems. In: Abdulla, P.A., Leino, K.R.M. (eds.) TACAS 2011. LNCS, vol. 6605, pp. 112–127. Springer, Heidelberg (2011)
26. Pnueli, A., The temporal logic of programs. In: 18th Annual Symposium on Foundations of Computer Science, pp. 46–57. IEEE (1977)
27. Puterman, M.L., Processes, M.D.: Discrete Stochastic Dynamic Programming, 1st edn. Wiley, New York (1994)
28. Thomas, W.: Automata on infinite objects. In: Handbook of Theoretical Computer Science, vol. b, pp. 133–191. MIT Press, Cambridge (1990)

The Julia Static Analyzer for Java

Fausto Spoto[(✉)]

Dipartimento di Informatica, Università di Verona, and Julia Srl, Verona, Italy
fausto.spoto@univr.it

Abstract. The Julia static analyzer applies abstract interpretation to the analysis and verification of Java bytecode. It is the result of 13 years of engineering effort based on theoretical research on denotational and constraint-based static analysis through abstract interpretation. Julia is a library for static analysis, over which many checkers have been built, that verify the absence of a large set of typical errors of software: among them are null-pointer accesses, non-termination, wrong synchronization and injection threats to security. This article recaps the history of Julia, describes the technology under the hood of the tool, reports lessons learned from the market, current limitations and future work.

1 Introduction

The Julia analyzer applies static analysis to Java bytecode, based on abstract interpretation [7]. Its internal technology has been published already [9,10,21, 22,24,25,28–33] and the rest is a major, at times painful engineering effort, aimed at making theory match the complex reality of modern software, as such of virtually no direct interest to the scientific community. Hence, the goal of this invited article is twofold: give a brief overview of the technology, meant as a reference to other, more detailed articles; and report experience gathered from the transformation of the tool into a company that survives on the market, something that research scientists typically overlook but, at the end, is the sole justification for the existence of a research community that does not want to remain confined inside pure theoretical speculation.

Julia was born in 2003 to perform experiments that could complement and support the formalizations presented in scientific articles. Figure 1 shows the timeline and main milestones of the development of the tool. The main guideline was the development of a *sound* static analyzer. That is, Julia was meant to find all errors, without any false negatives. For this reason, abstract interpretation was the preferred theoretical basis. In practice, this means that the main issue has been the fight against false positives, whose reduction proved essential once the tool was incorporated into a company and customers started using it. Currently, the Julia analyzer is unique on the market in applying sound non-trivial static analyses to large Java programs, such as nullness, termination, synchronization and injection attacks (see Sects. 3, 4, 5 and 6). In particular, it is the only sound analyzer able to find SQL-injections and cross-site scripting attacks [20] in Java.

The Julia company was incorporated in 2010, after 7 years of software development, as a university startup, together with Roberto Giacobazzi from Verona

© Springer-Verlag GmbH Germany 2016
X. Rival (Ed.): SAS 2016, LNCS 9837, pp. 39–57, 2016.
DOI: 10.1007/978-3-662-53413-7_3

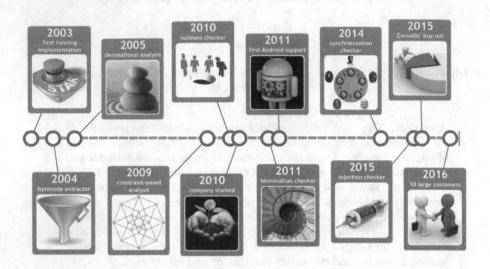

Items:

2003
Julia was born as a Java project for research experiments with static analysis of Java bytecode, based on abstract interpretation

2004
Julia parses Java bytecode through the BCEL library. The reachable portion of code and libraries is extracted by using class analysis. Only that portion of code is analyzed

2005
The bottom-up nature of denotational analysis is ideal for abstract interpretation of compositional properties, typically implemented through a functional approximation based on BDDs

2009
Constraints allow a simple and fast definition of abstract software properties. In this context, a constraint is a graph whose nodes are program points and whose edges are control links

2010
Null-pointer exceptions are the typical software error in Java. Julia includes many abstractions that contribute to the definition of a very precise static analysis for nullness

2010
Julia is incorporated as a startup company of the University of Verona, Italy. Fausto Spoto is the majority shareholder, together with other professors from Verona and Réunion

2011
Software termination guarantees that programs will not hang forever. Julia proves termination by using polyhedral constraints or bounded differences

2011
Julia can analyze Android code by generating Java bytecode from the IDE. Support of the Android library and object lifecycle is essential for precision

2014
Julia checks consistency of synchronization in multithreaded Java programs, extensively used in web and mobile applications and nowadays supported by multicore hardware

2015
Injections allow external agents to inject special data into web applications, access classified information and potentially compromize the system

2015
Corvallis SpA buys the control share of the Julia company and starts selling the tool to its customers, in partnership with other Italian and foreign companies

2016
Julia is used by banks, insurance companies and large industrial groups, in Italy and abroad. Experience with customers is key for further improvements of the tool

Fig. 1. Timeline of the development of the Julia static analyzer and company (courtesy of ReadWriteThink: www.readwritethink.org).

and Fred Mesnard and Étienne Payet from Réunion. Nevertheless, the tool needed further technological evolution to become strong enough for the market. From 2015, Julia Srl is part of the larger Italian group Corvallis and enjoys the support of its commercial network. The tool is currently used by banks and insurance companies as well as by large industrial groups, in Italy and abroad.

This article is organized as follows. Section 2 shows the technology implemented by the Julia library. Sections 3, 4, 5 and 6 show the most significant examples of analyses built over that library. Section 7 describes problems and solutions for the analysis of real software, which is never pure Java. Section 8 reports our experience with the engineering of a static analyzer. Section 9 reports problems faced when a university startup hits the market and a sound static analyzer must become a tool used on an everyday basis by non-specialized personnel. Section 10 concludes.

Throughout this article, examples are made over two simple Java classes. Figure 2 shows a synchronized vector, implemented through an array, that collects comparable, nullable objects and sort them through the `bubblesort()` method. Method `toString()` returns an HTML itemized list of the strings. Figure 3 is a Java servlet, *i.e.*, an entry point for a web service. It expects four parameters and collects their values inside a `Collector` of strings. It sorts those values and writes their HTML list as output (typically shown on a browser's window).

2   A Library for Static Analysis

Julia is a parallel library for static analysis of Java bytecode based on abstract interpretation, over which specific analyses can be built, called *checkers*. As of today, Julia has been used to build 57 checkers, that generate a total of 193 distinct classes of warnings, and a code obfuscator. The construction of the representation of a program in terms of basic blocks (Sect. 2.1) is done in parallel, as well as type inference. Checkers run in parallel. However, each single analysis is sequential, since its parallel version proved to be actually slower. The computation of a static analysis is asynchronous and yields a *future* (a token that allows blocking access to the result of a running computation [14]), hence it is still possible to launch many static analyses in parallel with a performance gain, as long as they do not interact.

We describe below the support provided by the Julia library and then the four scientifically more appealing checkers that have been built over that library.

2.1   Representation of Java Bytecode

The library provides a representation of Java bytecode which is:

ready for abstract interpretation: all bytecodes[1] are state transformers, including those modelling exceptional paths; the code is a graph of basic blocks;

---

[1] In this article, *bytecode* refers both to the low-level language resulting from the compilation of Java and to each single instruction of that language. This is standard terminology, although possibly confusing.

```
1  import com.juliasoft.julia.checkers.guardedBy.GuardedBy;
2
3  public class Collector<T extends Comparable<T>> {
4      private final @GuardedBy("itself") T[] arr;
5
6⊖     public Collector(T[] arr) {
7          this.arr = arr;
8      }
9
10⊖    public T get(int index) {
11         synchronized (arr) {
12             return arr[index];
13         }
14     }
15
16⊖    public void set(int index, T value) {
17         synchronized (arr) {
18             arr[index] = value;
19         }
20     }
21
22⊖    public void bubblesort() {
23         T[] x;
24
25         synchronized (arr) {
26             x = arr;
27         }
28
29         for (int count = 0; count < x.length; count++)
30             swap(x);
31     }
32
33⊖    private void swap(T[] x) {
34         int pos = 0;
35         while (pos < x.length - 1)
36             if ((x[pos] == null && x[pos + 1] != null) ||
37                     (x[pos] != null & x[pos + 1] != null
38                         && x[pos].compareTo(x[pos + 1]) > 0)) {
39                 T temp = x[pos];
40                 x[pos] = x[pos + 1];
41                 x[pos + 1] = temp;
42                 pos++;
43             }
44     }
45
46⊖    @Override
47     public String toString() {
48         StringBuilder sb = new StringBuilder();
49
50         sb.append("<ul>");
51
52         synchronized (arr) {
53             for (T x: arr) {
54                 sb.append("<li>");
55                 sb.append(x);
56                 sb.append("</li>");
57             }
58         }
59
60         sb.append("</ul>");
61
62         return sb.toString();
63     }
64 }
```

Fig. 2. A collector of comparable values.

```
 1 import java.io.IOException;
 2 import java.io.Writer;
 3 import javax.servlet.http.HttpServlet;
 4 import javax.servlet.http.HttpServletRequest;
 5 import javax.servlet.http.HttpServletResponse;
 6
 7 @SuppressWarnings("serial")
 8 public class Parameters extends HttpServlet {
 9
10     @Override
11     protected void doGet(HttpServletRequest request, HttpServletResponse response)
12             throws IOException {
13         response.setContentType("text/html;charset=UTF-8");
14
15         Writer writer = response.getWriter();
16
17         Collector<String> collector = new Collector<>(new String[4]);
18         collector.set(0, request.getParameter("id0"));
19         collector.set(1, request.getParameter("id1"));
20         collector.set(2, request.getParameter("id2"));
21         collector.set(3, request.getParameter("id3"));
22         collector.bubblesort();
23
24         writer.write(collector.toString());
25     }
26 }
```

Fig. 3. A servlet that reads four parameters, sorts them and writes them as a list.

fully typed and resolved: bytecodes have explicit type information available about their operands, the stack elements and locals. Instructions that reference fields or methods are resolved, *i.e.*, the exact implementation(s) of the field or methods that are accessed/called are explicitly provided;

analysis-agnostic: it makes no assumption about the checker that will be applied, hence it does as few instrumentation as possible; in particular, it does not transform stack elements into locals not translate the code into three-address form.

For instance, Fig. 4 shows the representation of the bytecode of bubblesort() from Fig. 2. It shows exceptional paths, that are implicit in the source code and correspond to situations where a runtime exception is raised and thrown back to the caller. More complex exceptional paths are generated for explicit exception handlers. Figure 4 shows that field accesses and method calls are decorated with their resolved target(s), under square brackets. For instance, the access to the field signature arr is resolved into an access to field Collector.arr of type Comparable[]. The call to the method signature swap() is resolved into a call to Collector.swap(Comparable[]). In more complex situations, resolution is less trivial. For instance, Fig. 5 shows that the call to signature compareTo() at line 38 in Fig. 2 is resolved into a call to String.compareTo(Object), since the program stores only strings inside a Collector. Field resolution is static in Java bytecode, while method resolution is dynamic and Julia applies a specific algorithm [23], known as *class analysis*. For simplicity, Fig. 4 does not show static types for each stack element and local variable at each bytecode. However, Julia infers them and makes them available in this representation.

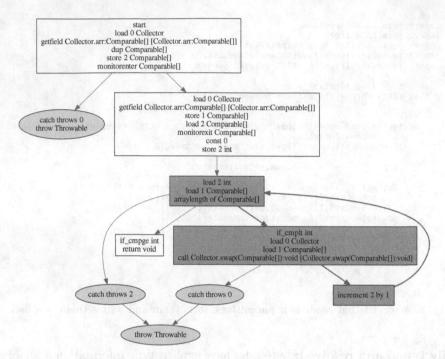

Fig. 4. The representation that Julia builds for method `bubblesort()` in Fig. 2. Ellipses are blocks implementing exceptional paths. Filled rectangles are the compilation of the `for` loop.

The Julia library builds over BCEL [13], for parsing the bytecode, whose later version makes Julia able to parse the latest instructions used for the compilation of lambda expressions and default methods in Java 8. An important issue is the portion of code that should be parsed, represented in memory and analyzed. Parsing the full program and libraries might be possible but programs use only a small portion of the libraries (including the huge standard library), whose full analysis would be prohibitive in time and space. Since Java bytecode is an object-oriented language where method calls are dynamic, determining the boundaries of the code to analyze is non-trivial. Julia solves this problem with class analysis [23], whose implementation has been the subject of extreme optimization, to let it scale to very large codebases, that possibly instantiate many classes and arrays. This implementation is called *bytecode extractor* and is a delicate component of Julia that takes into account many situations where objects are created by reflection (for instance, injected fields in Spring [18]). It is important to know the entry points of the application from where the extraction starts. Julia assumes by default that the `main()` method and callback redefinitions (such as `equals()` and `hashCode()`) are entry points. But it can be instructed to consider all public methods as entry points, or methods explicitly annotated as `@EntryPoint`.

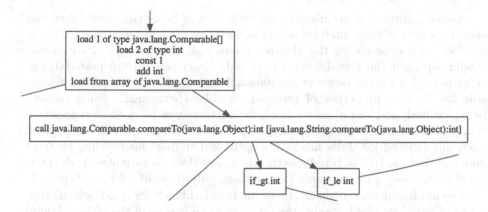

Fig. 5. A portion of the representation that Julia builds for method `swap()` in Fig. 2.

2.2 Denotational Analyses

Support for denotational analyses has been the first provided by Julia, by applying to imperative object-oriented programs previous results for logic programs. Denotational semantics is a way of formalizing the semantics of programs [34], based on the inductive, bottom-up definition of the functional behavior of blocks of code. The definition is direct for the smaller components of the code and is inductive for larger components, made up of smaller ones. For loops and recursion, a fixpoint computation saturates all possible execution paths. By *semantics of programs*, in the context of Julia one must always understand *abstract semantics*, defined in a standard way, through abstract interpretation [7], so that it can be computed in finite time.

Julia is completely agnostic about this abstraction. In general, for Julia an abstract domain is a set of elements $A = \{a_1, \ldots, a_n\}$, that can be used to soundly approximate the behavior of each bytecode instruction, together with operations for least upper bound ($\sqcup$) and sequential composition ($\circ$) of abstract domain elements. Consider for instance Fig. 4. A denotational analyzer starts by replacing each non-`call` bytecode with the best abstraction of its input/output behavior (from pre-state to post-state) provided by A (Fig. 6). Then the analyzer merges abstractions sequentially, through the $\circ$ operator of A (Fig. 7). This process is known as *abstract compilation* [17]. The fixpoint computation starts at this point: Julia keeps a map ι from each block in the program to the current approximation computed so far for the block (an *interpretation*). Each `call` bytecode gets replaced with the $\sqcup$ of the current approximations $\iota(b_1) \ldots \iota(b_k)$ of its k dynamic targets (modulo variable renaming) and sequentially merged ($\circ$) with the approximation inside its block (as $a31$ in Fig. 7). Then $\iota(b)$ is updated with the approximation inside b sequentially composed ($\circ$) with the least upper bound ($\sqcup$) of the current approximations of its f followers: $\iota(b_1) \sqcup \ldots \sqcup \iota(b_f)$. This process is iterated until fixpoint. At the end, $\iota(b)$ is the abstraction of all execution traces starting at each given block b.

A nice feature of denotational analysis is that of being completely flow and context sensitive, fully interprocedural and able to model exceptional paths. In practice, this depends on the abstract domain A. In particular, its elements should represent functional behaviors of code (from pre-state to post-state) in order to exploit the full power of denotational analysis. In practice, this is achievable for Boolean properties of program variables (being null, being tainted, being cyclical, and so on), since Boolean functions can be used as representation for functional behaviors and efficiently implemented through binary decision diagrams (BDDs) [5]. Julia has highly optimized support for building abstract domains that use BDDs, It reduces the number of Boolean variables by abstracting the variables of interest only (for nullness, only those of reference type).

The implementation of denotational analysis is difficult for non-Boolean properties of variables (for instance, the set of runtime classes of the objects bound to a variable or the set of their creation points). Moreover, it provides only functional approximations of the code, rather than approximations of the state just before a given instruction. The latter problem is solved at the price of a preliminary transformation [24], that Julia implements.

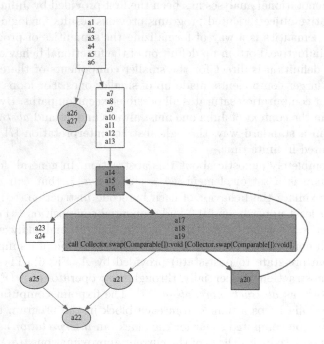

Fig. 6. The abstraction of the non-call bytecodes of method bubblesort() in Fig. 2.

2.3   Constraint-Based Analyses

A constraint-based analysis translates a Java bytecode program into a set-constraint, whose nodes are (for instance) blocks of code and whose edges

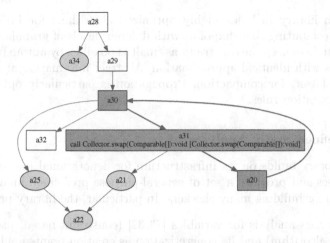

Fig. 7. The sequential merge of the abstraction of method `bubblesort()` in Fig. 2.

propagate abstract information between nodes. The approximation at a node is the least upper bound of the abstract information entering the node from each in-edge. Abstract information is propagated along the edges until fixpoint. The constraint for Fig. 4 might be as in Fig. 8, where each node contains the fixpoint abstract information at that node and arrows represent propagation of abstract information. Method calls have been flattened by linking each call place to the first node of the target(s) of the call. Each `return` instruction inside a callee is linked back to the non-exceptional followers of the `calls` in the callers. Each `throw` bytecode inside a callee is linked back to the exceptional followers of the `calls` in the callers. There might exist a direct link from a `call` instruction to its subsequent instructions, such as between the node approximated with $a6$ and that approximated with $a9$ in Fig. 8. This edge can model side-effects induced by the execution of the method, if they can occur.

The nice feature of constraint-based analysis is that it can be easily applied to every kind of abstract domain, also for non-Boolean properties. For instance, abstract information might be the set of already initialized classes; or undirected pairs of variables that share; or directed pairs of reachable variables. Moreover, there is large freedom about the granularity of the constraint: nodes might stand for approximations at blocks of code; but also for approximations at each single instruction (by splitting the blocks into their component instructions); or even for approximations of each single local variable or stack element at each program point. The latter case allows one for instance to compute the set of creation points for each variable; or the set of runtime classes for each variable; or the set of uninitialized fields for each variable. Finally, edges can propagate abstract information by applying any propagation rule, also one that might transform that information during the flow. The limitation of constraint-based analysis is that it is inherently context-insensitive, since method calls have been flattened: there is a merge-over-all-paths leading to each given method.

The Julia library includes highly optimized algorithms for building constraints and computing their fixpoint, with different levels of granularity. These algorithms strive to keep the constraint as small as possible, by automatically collapsing nodes with identical approximation. Abstract information at each node is kept in a bitset, for compaction. Propagation is particularly optimized for additive propagation rules.

2.4 Predefined Static Analyses

The Julia library builds on its infrastructure for denotational and constraint-based analyses and provides a set of general-purpose predefined analyses, that can be useful for building many checkers. In particular, the library provides:

- a possible class analysis for variables [23,32] (constraint-based, used for the extraction algorithm) and its concretization as creation-points analysis;
- a definite aliasing analysis between variables and expressions [21] (constraint-based);
- a possible sharing analysis between pairs of variables [29] (constraint-based);
- a possible reachability analysis between pairs of variables [22] (constraint-based);
- a numerical analysis for variables, known as *path-length* [33] (denotational);
- a possible cyclicity analysis for variables [28] (denotational);
- a possible nullness analysis for variables [30] (denotational);
- a definite non-`null` analysis for expressions [30] (constraint-based);
- a definite initialization analysis for fields [31] (constraint-based);
- a definite locked expressions analysis [10] (constraint-based);
- a possible information flow analysis for variables [9] (denotational).

3 Nullness Checker

A typical error consists in accessing a field or calling a method over the `null` value (a *dereference* of `null`). This error stops the execution of the program with a `NullPointerException`. Julia can prove that a program will never raise such exception, but for a restricted set of program points where it issues a warning. The Nullness checker of Julia uses a combination of more static analyses. A first analysis approximates the Boolean property of being `null` for program (local) variables, by using BDDs that express constraints on all possible nullness behaviors of a piece of code [30]. However, object-oriented programs store values in fields and not just local variables. This makes things much more difficult, since a field holds `null` by default: hence Julia proves also that a field is always initialized before being read [31]. Moreover, expressions might be locally non-`null` because of some previous non-nullness check. Julia can prove it, provided the expression does not change its value between check and dereference [30].

Consider for instance the code in Figs. 2 and 3. The Nullness checker of Julia issues *only* the following warning:

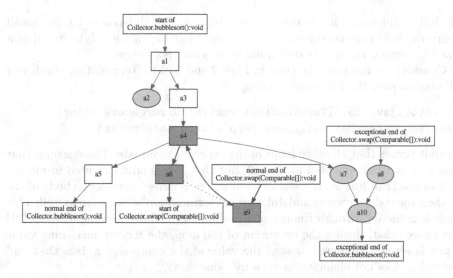

Fig. 8. A constraint generated for method `bubblesort()` in Fig. 2.

`Collector.java:38: [Nullness: FormalInnerNullWarning]`
`  are the elements inside formal parameter "x" of "swap" non-null?`

First of all, this proves that the program will *never* raise a NullPointer
Exception elsewhere. Let us check that warning then. At line 38 of Fig. 2 the
value of x[pos] can actually be null, since the array x is allowed to hold null
elements (parameters of a servlet are null when missing) and the test x[pos]
!= null at line 37 is not enough to protect the subsequent dereference at line
38. The reason is that the programmer at line 37 has incorrectly used the eager &
operator, instead of the lazy &&. Hence the dereference at line 38 will be eagerly
executed also when x[pos] holds null.

In order to appreciate the power of this checker, consider that, after fixing the bug, by replacing & with && at line 37, the Nullness checker does not
issue any warning anymore, which proves that the program will *never* raise
a NullPointerException. This is achieved through the expression non-null
analysis [30], that now proves expression x[pos] to be non-null at line 38.

4   Termination Checker

Most programs are expected to terminate. A non-terminating program will never
provide an answer to a query or will hang a device. The Termination checker
of Julia proves that loops terminate, by translating Java bytecode into logic
programs over linear constraints [2,33], whose termination is subsequently proved
by using traditional techniques for logic programs [4,6,19,26]. Since imperative
programs allow shared data structures and destructive updates, the inference
of linear constraints needs the support of sharing and cyclicity analysis [28,

29]. Julia implements linear constraints with bounded differences [8]. For small programs, Julia can use the more precise and more expensive polyhedra [3] or a mixed implementation of bounded differences and polyhedra.

Consider for instance the code in Figs. 2 and 3. The Termination checker of Julia issues *only* the following warning:

```
Collector.java:35: [Termination: PossibleDivergenceWarning]
  are you sure that Collector.swap always terminates?
```

Hence it proves that all other loops in the program terminate. The reason is that variable `pos` is incremented at line 42, but that line is only executed inside the body of the `if` at line 36. If the statement `pos++` is moved outside the body of the `if`, then the code is correct and Julia proves termination of this loop as well. This result is achieved through the use of a preliminary definite aliasing analysis [21] that proves that, during the execution of the loop, the strictly increasing value of `pos` is always compared against the value of the expression `x.length-1` and that value does not change, not even by side-effect.

5   Synchronization Checker

Concurrency is more and more used in modern software. It supports performance, by running algorithms in parallel on multicore hardware, but also responsivity, by running long tasks on threads distinct from the user interface thread (typical scenario in Android programming [15]). But concurrency is difficult and programmers tend to write incorrect concurrent code. Code annotations have been proposed [14] as a way of specifying synchronization policies about how concurrent threads can access shared data to avoid *data races* (concurrent access to the same data). The semantics of such annotations has been recently formalized [11] and tools exist nowadays that check and infer them [10]. Julia has a GuarbedBy checker that is able to prove the correctness of annotations already provided by the programmer, but can also infer sound annotations for fields and method parameters [10], that were not explicitly written in code.

Consider for instance Fig. 2 and 3. Field `arr` at line 4 of Fig. 2 is annotated as `@GuardedBy("itself")`. This means that a thread can dereference the *value* of field `arr` only at program points where that thread locks the value itself [11]. For instance, this is what happens at lines 12, 18 and 53. Nevertheless, the GuardedBy checker of Julia issues the following warning:

```
Collector.java: [GuardedBy: UnguardedFieldWarning]
  is "itself" locked when accessing field "arr"?
```

Indeed, the value of `arr` is copied into variable x at line 26 and later dereferenced at line 29 and inside method `swap()`, without holding the lock on that value. The programmer might have expected to optimize the code by reducing the span of the critical section to line 26 only. But this is incorrect since it protects, inside the critical section, only the *name* arr (which is irrelevant) rather than the *value* of `arr` (which is semantically important). If the synchronization starting at line

25 is extended until the end of line 30, Julia does not issue any warning anymore and infers the @GuardedBy("itself") annotation for field arr.

6 Injection Checker

Injection attacks are possibly the most dangerous security bugs of computer programs [20], since they allow users of a web service to provide special input arguments to the system, that let one access sensitive data or compromize the system. The most famous attacks are SQL-injection and cross-site scripting (XSS). Julia has an Injection checker that applies taintedness analysis through an abstract domain for information flow, made of Boolean formulas and implemented as BDDs [9].

Consider for instance the code in Figs. 2 and 3. The Injection checker of Julia issues only the following warning:

```
Parameters.java:24: [Injection: XSSInjectionWarning]
  possible XSS-injection through the 0th actual parameter of write
```

Lines 18–21 in Fig. 3 actually store some parameters of the request inside the collector and such parameters can be freely provided by an attacker. They are then sorted at line 22 and written to the output of the servlet as an HTML list, at line 24. Hence, if the attacker provides parameters that contain special HTML of Javascript tags, they will be rendered by the browser and hence open the door to any possible attack.

The power of Julia's analysis is related to a new notion of taintedness for data structures, that does not classify fields as tainted or untainted on the basis of their name, bur considers instead an object as tainted if tainted data can be *reached* from it [9]. For instance, if another Collector would be created in the code in Fig. 3, populated with strings not coming from the parameters of the request, and written to the output of the servlet, then Julia would not issue a warning for that second write(). Both collectors would be implemented through field arr (Fig. 2) but only one would actually reach tainted data. This object-sensitivity justifies the precision of the Injection checker of Julia, compared to other tools [9].

7 Frameworks: Java Does Not Exist

Julia is a static analyzer for Java bytecode. But real programs nowadays are very rarely pure Java code. Instead, they are multilanguage software based on a large variety of *frameworks*. For instance, Java often integrates with Java Server Pages (JSPs), another programming language that is used to program the views of web applications. If a static analyzer does not understand JSPs, then it will miss part of the code, non-nullness information, information flows and injection attacks. A framework is, instead, a library that simplifies the implementation of frequently used operations and very often modifies the semantics of the language by introducing new behaviors through reflection. The typical example, in the banking sector, is Spring [18], that provides declarative configuration of software applications through XML or annotation-based specification of *beans*; as well as simplified implementations of web services and of the model-view-controller design pattern for web applications; it also provides aspect-oriented programming. Spring applications are often built on top of a persistence framework, typically Hibernate [16].

If a static analyzer does not understand the multilanguage nature of software or does not understand the semantical modifications that frameworks induce in Java, then it will issue many false alarms and also miss actual bugs. That is, it will become imprecise and unsound. Julia manages JSPs by compiling them into Java code through the Jasper compiler [12]. Julia embeds partial support for Spring, in particular for bean instantiation and their injection as dependencies. Nevertheless, this is work in progress and the evolution of the frameworks tends to be faster than our ability to deal with their new features.

A notable framework is Android. Knowledge about the Android standard library is essential to avoid many false alarms. For instance, Julia has been instructed to reason about the way views are constructed in an Android activity from their XML specification, in order to reduce the number of false alarms about wrong classcasts and null-pointer dereferences [25]. A big problem is that Julia analyzes Java bytecode, but Android applications are packaged in Dalvik bytecode format. Currently, it is possible to export the Java bytecode from the integrated development environment or convert Dalvik into Java bytecode, with the Dex2Jar tool [1].

8   Engineering Problems

A static analyzer for a real programming language is very complex software. It implements involved semantical definitions; it is highly optimized in order to scale to the analysis of large programs; it uses parallel algorithms, whose implementation requires experience with multithreading; it must be clear, maintainable and expandable, which requires object-orientation and design pattern skills. The natural question is then who can ever write such software. Julia has been developed in 13 years, largely by a single person, who is a university researcher and a passionate programmer. It is possibly the case that a very professional development team could have be used instead, but a deep involvement of researchers in the development effort seems unavoidable. In particular, the complexity and duration of the effort seems to us incompatible with spotty development by students or PhD's, which would result in fragmentation, suboptimal implementation and final failure. However, researchers are usually reluctant to spending so much time with activities that do not translate into published papers. This is understandable, since their production is typically measured in terms of publications only. It seems to us necessary to find alternative ways of measuring the production of researchers, by including their direct involvement in technology transfer, at the right weight.

After a static analyzer has been developed by researchers, it must eventually be entrusted to professional programmers, who will continue with the less critical development of the tool. This is a delicate moment and requires time. Knowledge can pass from researchers to programmers but this is a long term investment with no immediate monetary benefit. As with any complex software, the alternative is to lose experience and finally memory about the code, which would mean utter disaster. The best solution is to open-source the code of the analyzer, if this is compatible with the business model of the company.

Maintenance of a static analyzer is another difficult engineering task. In our experience, a small *improvement* of the analyzer might change its precision or computational cost very much, or introduce bugs. Hence it becomes important to find ways for reducing the risk of regression. Since Julia is written in Java, we have of course applied Julia to Julia itself from time to time, found errors and debugged the analyzer. But this is not possible for functional bugs. Testcases are more helpful here, but there is little experience with testing of static analyzers. We have developed hundreds of higher level tests, that run the static analysis of a given program and compare the result with what was obtained in the past. Such tests must be updated from time to time, since Julia performs more and more checks and becomes more and more precise. Of course, this process cannot be done by hand. Instead, Julia has the ability to translate, automatically, the result of a static analysis into a JUnit test class, that can later be used to check for non-regression. Hence testcases can be updated automatically. For instance, the following JUnit testcase is automatically generated from the analysis of the code in Fig. 2 and 3 with the checkers Nullness, Termination, GuardedBy and Injection. It re-runs the analyses, asserts the existence of the expected warnings and the non-existence of other warnings:

```
@Test
public void test() throws WrongApplicationException, ClassNotFoundException {
  Program program = analyse();
  ClassMembersBuilder classMembersBuilder = new ClassMembersBuilder(program);

  assertWarning(new UnguardedFieldWarning("Collector.java", "arr", "itself"));
  assertWarning(new PossibleDivergenceWarning
    (classMembersBuilder.getMethod("Collector", "swap", "void", "Comparable[]")));
  assertWarning(new FormalInnerNullWarning("Collector.java", 38, "Collector", "swap", 0));
  assertWarning(new XSSInjectionWarning("Parameters.java", 24,
    classMembersBuilder.getMethodReference("java.io.Writer", "write", "void", "String"), 0));
  assertNoMoreWarnings();
}
```

9   From Research to Market

Pushing new technology from laboratory to market is definitely exciting, but it is also source of deception. In the case of Julia, the key point of *soundness* has been the hardest to communicate to the market. Customers often already use a static analysis tool, which is typically highly unsound, and do not see soundness as a reason to change. Instead, they tend to highlight non-scientific aspects, such as the ability to integrate the tool into their organization, its ease of use, the quality of the graphics of the reports, the classification of the warnings inside well-known grids, the ability to work on specific software technology, which is typically multilanguage and based on frameworks. Very few customers seem impressed by soundness. Instead, customers tend to support other tools that do *everything*, without questioning how good such tools actually are at doing this *everything*. This situation might change in the future, but decades of misinformation will not be easily forgotten. From this point of view, the dichotomy between scientific publication and industrial communication must be eventually resolved, but this requires good will on both sides.

Hitting the market is also an opportunity to discover how *real* software looks like and hence what a static analyzer should be able to analyze. For instance, very often programmers do not initialize objects inside their constructors, but leave them uninitialized and later call *setter methods*. This is sometime the consequence of the use of frameworks, such as Java Beans or Hibernate, or it s just a programming pattern. In any case, it hinders static analysis, since uninitialized fields hold their default value in Java (`null` or 0), which induces the analyzer to issue hundreds of warnings, since objects can be used before being fully initialized. Similarly, programmers never check for nullness of the parameters of public methods, which leads to warnings if such parameters are dereferenced. We stress the fact that all these warnings are real bugs, in principle. But programmers will never see it that way, since they assume that methods are called in a specific order and with specific non-`null` arguments. Of course, this is not documented, not even in comments. Julia reacts to this situation with analyses of different strictness: for instance, together with the Nullness checker, Julia has a BasicNullness checker that is optimistic *w.r.t.* the initialization of fields and the nullness of the parameters passed to public methods.

Another problem faced with *real* software is that this is written against all programming recommendations. We found methods of tens of thousands of lines, with hundreds of variables. This means that abstract domains based on BDDs or linear inequalities typically explode during the analysis. We applied worst-case assumptions, triggered when computations become too complex, although this results in more false alarms. But naive triggers are sensitive to the order of computation of the abstract analysis, *i.e.*, they might fire non-deterministically, which is unacceptable in an industrial context. Hence we had to find more robust triggers for the worst-case assumption, that do not depend on the order of computation of the analysis.

10 Conclusion

The Julia static analyzer is the result of 13 years of research and engineering. It is the proof that research from academia can move to the market and provide a solution to an actual market need. It is exciting to see theoretical results about static analysis, BDDs, polyhedra and fixpoint computation applied to solve real problems of large banks, insurance companies, automobile industries and simple freelance programmers around the world.

This article presents a synthetic view of the history of Julia and of its underlying technology and strengths. It acknowledges the problems faced once the tool is used to analyze actual software, written in peculiar ways and using reflection, also through several frameworks, and the expectations that customers have about such technology. These aspects are the real issues that still jeopardize the success of sound static analysis outside the academic world.

The development of Julia continues. There are many open problems that need an answer. First of all, concurrency is an opportunity not yet completely exploited, that can improve the efficiency of the tool by using more parallel algorithms. It is also a problem, since the analysis of concurrent programs is difficult and current techniques are often unsound in that context. Also the presentation of the warnings needs improving. Instead of a flat list, possibly organized into static priority classes, it might be possible to rank warnings *w.r.t.* their *features*, by using machine learning [27]. Finally, the applicability of Julia will be expanded. The translation from CIL bytecode into Java bytecode is already implemented and should allow, in the near future, to analyze safe CIL code with Julia, such as that derived from the compilation of C#. The application to other programming languages is possible in principle, but seems more difficult. Large parts of the Julia library might be recycled for other languages, in particular the fixpoint algorithms, but the specific analyses need to be built again from scratch.

References

1. Dex2Jar. https://sourceforge.net/projects/dex2jar
2. Albert, E., Arenas, P., Genaim, S., Puebla, G., Zanardini, D.: COSTA: design and implementation of a cost and termination analyzer for java bytecode. In: de Boer, F.S., Bonsangue, M.M., Graf, S., de Roever, W.-P. (eds.) FMCO 2007. LNCS, vol. 5382, pp. 113–132. Springer, Heidelberg (2008)
3. Bagnara, R., Hill, P.M., Zaffanella, E.: The parma polyhedra library: toward a complete set of numerical abstractions for the analysis and verification of hardware and software systems. Sci. Comput. Program. **72**(1–2), 3–21 (2008)
4. Bagnara, R., Mesnard, F., Pescetti, A., Zaffanella, E.: A new look at the automatic synthesis of linear ranking functions. Inf. Comput. **215**, 47–67 (2012)
5. Bryant, R.: Symbolic boolean manipulation with ordered binary-decision diagrams. ACM Comput. Surv. **24**(3), 293–318 (1992)
6. Codish, M., Lagoon, V., Stuckey, P.J.: Testing for termination with monotonicity constraints. In: Gabbrielli, M., Gupta, G. (eds.) ICLP 2005. LNCS, vol. 3668, pp. 326–340. Springer, Heidelberg (2005)
7. Cousot, P., Cousot, R.: Abstract interpretation: a unified lattice model for static analysis of programs by construction or approximation of fixpoints. In: Proceedings of Principles of Programming Languages (POPL 1977), pp. 238–252 (1977)
8. Dill, D.L.: Timing assumptions and verification of finite-state concurrent systems. In: Sifakis, J. (ed.) Automatic Verification Methods for Finite State Systems. LNCS, vol. 407, pp. 197–212. Springer, Heidelberg (1990)

9. Ernst, M.D., Lovato, A., Macedonio, D., Spiridon, C., Spoto, F.: Boolean formulas for the static identification of injection attacks in Java. In: Davis, M., et al. (eds.) LPAR-20 2015. LNCS, vol. 9450, pp. 130–145. Springer, Heidelberg (2015). doi:10. 1007/978-3-662-48899-7_10

10. Ernst, M.D., Lovato, A., Macedonio, D., Spoto, F., Thaine, J.: Locking discipline inference and checking. In: Proceedings of Software Engineering (ICSE 2016), Austin, TX, USA, pp. 1133–1144. ACM (2016)

11. Ernst, M.D., Macedonio, D., Merro, M., Spoto, F.: Semantics for locking specifications. In: Rayadurgam, S., Tkachuk, O. (eds.) NFM 2016. LNCS, vol. 9690, pp. 355–372. Springer, Heidelberg (2016). doi:10.1007/978-3-319-40648-0_27

12. The Apache Software Foundation. Jasper 2 JSP Engine How To. https://tomcat. apache.org/tomcat-8.0-doc/jasper-howto.html

13. The Apache Software Foundation. Apache Commons BCEL. https://commons. apache.org/proper/commons-bcel. 24 June 2016

14. Goetz, B., Peierls, T., Bloch, J., Bowbeer, J., Holmes, D., Lea, D.: Java Concurrency in Practice. Addison Wesley, Reading (2006)

15. Göransson, A.: Efficient Android Threading. O'Reilly Media, Sebastopol (2014)

16. Red Hat. Hibernate. Everything Data. http://hibernate.org

17. Hermenegildo, M., Warren, D.S., Debray, S.K.: Global flow analysis as a practical compilation tool. J. Logic Program. **13**(4), 349–366 (1992)

18. Pivotal Software Inc. Spring Framework. https://projects.spring.io/ spring-framework

19. Lee, C.S., Jones, N.D., Ben-Amram, A.M.: The size-change principle for program termination. In: Proceedings of Principles of Programming Languages (POPL 2001), pp. 81–92. ACM (2001)

20. MITRE/SANS. Top 25 Most Dangerous Software Errors. http://cwe.mitre.org/ top25. September 2011

21. Nikolić, Đ., Spoto, F.: Definite expression aliasing analysis for Java bytecode. In: Roychoudhury, A., D'Souza, M. (eds.) ICTAC 2012. LNCS, vol. 7521, pp. 74–89. Springer, Heidelberg (2012)

22. Nikolić, Đ., Spoto, F.: Reachability analysis of program variables. ACM Trans. Program. Lang. Syst. (TOPLAS) **35**(4), 14 (2013)

23. Palsberg, J., Schwartzbach, M.I.: Object-oriented type inference. In: Proceedings of Object-Oriented Programming, Systems, Languages & Applications (OOPSLA 1991). ACM SIGPLAN Notices, vol. 26(11), pp. 146–161. ACM, November 1991

24. Payet, É., Spoto, F.: Magic-sets transformation for the analysis of Java bytecode. In: Riis Nielson, H., Filé, G. (eds.) SAS 2007. LNCS, vol. 4634, pp. 452–467. Springer, Heidelberg (2007)

25. Payet, É., Spoto, F.: Static analysis of android programs. Inf. Softw. Technol. **54**(11), 1192–1201 (2012)

26. Podelski, A., Rybalchenko, A.: A complete method for the synthesis of linear ranking functions. In: Steffen, B., Levi, G. (eds.) VMCAI 2004. LNCS, vol. 2937, pp. 239–251. Springer, Heidelberg (2004)

27. Raychev, V., Bielik, P., Vechev, M.T., Krause, A.: Learning programs from noisy data. In: Proceedings of Principles of Programming Languages (POPL 2016), St. Petersburg, FL, USA, pp. 761–774. ACM (2016)

28. Rossignoli, S., Spoto, F.: Detecting non-cyclicity by abstract compilation into boolean functions. In: Emerson, E.A., Namjoshi, K.S. (eds.) VMCAI 2006. LNCS, vol. 3855, pp. 95–110. Springer, Heidelberg (2006)

29. Secci, S., Spoto, F.: Pair-sharing analysis of object-oriented programs. In: Hankin, C., Siveroni, I. (eds.) SAS 2005. LNCS, vol. 3672, pp. 320–335. Springer, Heidelberg (2005)
30. Spoto, F.: Precise null-pointer analysis. Softw. Syst. Model. **10**(2), 219–252 (2011)
31. Spoto, F., Ernst, M.D.: Inference of field initialization. In: Proceedings of Software Engineering (ICSE 2011), Waikiki, Honolulu, USA, pp. 231–240. ACM (2011)
32. Spoto, F., Jensen, T.P.: Class analyses as abstract interpretations of trace semantics. ACM Trans. Program. Lang. Syst. (TOPLAS) **25**(5), 578–630 (2003)
33. Spoto, F., Mesnard, F., Payet, É.: A termination analyzer for Java bytecode based on path-length. ACM Trans. Program. Lang. Syst. (TOPLAS) **32**(3), 1–70 (2010)
34. Winskel, G.: The Formal Semantics of Programming Languages: An Introduction. MIT Press, Cambridge (1993)

Full Papers

Full Papers

Automated Verification of Linearization Policies

Parosh Aziz Abdulla, Bengt Jonsson, and Cong Quy Trinh[✉]

Uppsala University, Uppsala, Sweden
cong-quy.trinh@it.uu.se

Abstract. We present a novel framework for automated verification of linearizability for concurrent data structures that implement sets, stacks, and queues. The framework requires the user to provide a *linearization policy*, which describes how linearization point placement in different concurrent threads affect each other; such linearization policies are often provided informally together with descriptions of new algorithms. We present a specification formalism for linearization policies which allows the user to specify, in a simple and concise manner, complex patterns including non-fixed linearization points. To automate verification, we extend thread-modular reasoning to bound the number of considered threads, and use a novel symbolic representation for unbounded heap structures that store data from an unbounded domain. We have implemented our framework in a tool and successfully used it to prove linearizability for a wide range of algorithms, including all implementations of concurrent sets, stacks, and queues based on singly-linked lists that are known to us from the literature.

1 Introduction

Data structures that can be accessed concurrently by many parallel threads are a central component of many software applications, and are implemented in several widely used libraries (e.g., `java.util.concurrent`). Linearizability [17] is the standard correctness criterion for such concurrent data structure implementations. It states that each operation on the data structure can be considered as being performed atomically at some point, called the *linearization point (LP)*, between its invocation and return. This allows client threads to understand the data structure in terms of atomic actions, without considering the complications of concurrency.

Linearizable concurrent data structures typically employ fine-grained synchronization, replacing locks by atomic operations such as compare-and-swap, and are therefore notoriously difficult to get correct, witnessed, e.g., by a number of bugs in published algorithms [8,20]. It is therefore important to develop efficient techniques for automatically verifying their correctness. This requires overcoming several challenges.

One challenge is that the criterion of linearizability is harder to establish than standard correctness criteria, such as control state reachability; in fact, proving linearizability with respect to a given data structure specification is undecidable, even in frameworks where verification of temporal safety properties is

© Springer-Verlag GmbH Germany 2016
X. Rival (Ed.): SAS 2016, LNCS 9837, pp. 61–83, 2016.
DOI: 10.1007/978-3-662-53413-7_4

decidable [5]. This has lead to verification techniques that establish some form of simulation between concurrent and sequential executions, and whose mechanization requires an interactive theorem prover (e.g., [6,7,25,26]). Automation has been successful only under simplifying assumptions. A natural one is that LPs are *fixed*, i.e., can be affixed to particular statements in method implementations [1,3,30]. However, for a large class of linearizable implementations, the LPs are not fixed in the code of their methods, but depend on actions of other threads in each particular execution. This happens, e.g., for algorithms that employ various forms of *helping mechanisms*, in which the execution of a particular statement in one thread defines the LP for one or several other threads [13,14,34,35].

Another challenge is that verification techniques must be able to reason about fine-grained concurrent programs that are infinite-state in many dimensions: they consist of an unbounded number of concurrent threads, which operate on an unbounded domain of data values, and use unbounded dynamically allocated memory. This challenge has been addressed by bounding the number of accessing threads [2,32,33], restricting the class of algorithms that can be verified [15,31], or requiring auxiliary lemmas [24,36].

Contributions. In this paper, we present a novel uniform framework for automatically verifying linearizability of concurrent data structure implementations, which handles the above challenges. In our framework, the user provides (i) a C-like description of the data structure implementation, (ii) a specification of sequential data structure semantics, using the simple technique of *observers* [1], and (iii) a *linearization policy*, which describes how LP placement in different concurrent threads affect each other; such linearization policies are often provided informally together with descriptions of new data structure implementations. Our framework then automatically checks that the requirement of linearizability (wrp. to the data structure specification) is satisfied when LPs are placed according to the given linearization policy. Ours is the first framework that can automatically verify all linearizable singly-linked list-based implementations of sets, stacks, and queues that have appeared in the verification literature, requiring only a small amount of user annotation (of linearization policies). Our framework relies on a number of advancements over the state-of-the-art.

1. We handle non-fixed LPs by a novel formalism for specifying linearization policies, by means of so-called *controllers*. Linearization policies capture inter-thread constraints on LP placement. They are often described informally by the algorithm designers together with each new data structure implementation when explaining why it is linearizable. Our controllers offer a way to express such policies in a simple and uniform manner. They can express complex patterns for linearization that are much more general than fixed LPs, including all the ones that are known to us from the literature, such as helping and flat-combining [12–14,23,24,34,35]. Each method is equipped with a controller, whose task is to announce the occurrence of potential linearization points for that method. The controller is defined by a few simple rules that are triggered by its thread, and may also interact with controllers of other

threads, in order to properly announce LPs. We specify the data structure semantics by adapting the technique of *observers* [1], that check correctness of the sequence of LP announcements. We extend previous usage of observers by allowing a controller to announce an LP several times. This extension allow us to handle implementations where the occurrence of a (non-fixed) LP is conditional on some predicted future condition; a false prediction can then (under some restrictions) be corrected by a renewed LP announcement. In previous approaches, such situations were handled by prophecy variables or backward simulation (e.g., [25]), that make automated verification significantly more difficult. The use of observers and controllers reduces verification to establishing that each method invocation generates a sequence of LP announcements, the last of which may change the state of the observer and conforms to the method's call and return parameters, such that that the total sequence of LP announcements is not rejected by the observer. The establishment of these conditions can be reduced to control state reachability using standard techniques; our framework accomplishes this by automatically generated *monitors*.

2. We handle the challenge of an unbounded number of threads by extending the successful thread-modular approach which verifies a concurrent program by generating an invariant that correlates the global state with the local state of an arbitrary thread [3]. We must extend it to handle global transitions where several threads synchronize, due to interaction between controllers. We show that the number of synchronizing threads that need to be considered in the abstract postcondition computation is bounded by $3 \cdot (\#\mathcal{O}) + 2$ where $\#\mathcal{O}$ is the diameter of the observer. Furthermore, we define a condition, which we call *stuttering*, that allows to reduce the number of synchronizing threads to only two. The stuttering condition can be verified through a simple syntactic check and is indeed satisfied by all the examples that we have considered.

3. In order to reason about concurrent programs that operate on an unbounded data domain via dynamically allocated memory, we present a novel symbolic representation of singly-linked heap structures.

For stacks and queues Chakraborty et al. [15], and later Boujjani et al. [4], showed that linearizability can be checked by observing only the sequence of method calls and returns, without considering potential LP placement. This technique cannot check linearizabilitiy of sets. We can adapt their technique to our framework. By using observers as defined in [4,15] and adapting controllers accordingly, we can use our symbolic verification technique to automatically verify stacks and queues without considering potential LP placement.

We have implemented our technique in a tool, and applied it to specify and automatically verify linearizability of all the implementations of concurrent set, queue, and stack algorithms known to us in the literature, as well as some algorithms for implementing atomic memory read/write operations. To use the tool, the user needs to provide the code of the algorithm together with the controllers that specify linearization policies. To our knowledge, this is the first time all these examples are verified fully automatically in the same framework.

Related Work. Much previous work has been devoted to the *manual* verification of linearizability for concurrent programs. Examples include [18, 28]. In [24], O'Hearn *et al.* define a *hindsight lemma* that provides a non-constructive evidence for linearizability. The lemma is used to prove linearizability of an optimistic variant of the lazy set algorithm. Vafeiadis [29] uses forward and backward simulation relations together with history or prophecy variables to prove linearizability. These approaches are manual, and without tool implementations. *Mechanical* proofs of linearizability, using interactive theorem provers, have been reported in [6, 7, 25, 26]. For instance, Colvin *et al.* [6] verify the lazy set algorithm in PVS, using a combination of forward and backward simulations.

There are several works on *automatic* verification of linearizability. In [31], Vafeiadis develops an automatic tool for proving linearizability that employs instrumentation to verify logically pure executions. However, this work can handle non-fixed LPs only for read-only methods, i.e., methods that do not modify the heap. This means that the method cannot handle algorithms like the *Elimination* queue [23], *HSY* stack [14], *CCAS* [12], *RDCSS* [12] and *HM* set [16] that we consider in this paper. In addition, their shape abstraction is not powerful enough to handle algorithms like *Harris* set [11] and *Michael* set [22] that are also handled by our method. Chakraborty *et al.* [15] describe an "aspect-oriented" method for modular verification of concurrent queues that they use to prove linearizability of the Herlihy/Wing queue. Bouajjani et al. [4] extended this work to show that verifying linearizability for certain fixed abstract data types, including queues and stacks, is reducible to control-state reachability. We can incorporate this technique into our framework by a suitable construction of observers. The method can not be applied to sets. The most recent work of Zhu *et al.* [36] describe a tool that is applied for specific set, queue, and stack algorithms. For queue algorithms, their technique can handle queues with helping mechanism except for *HW* queue [17] which is handled by our paper. For set algorithms, the authors can only handle those that perform an optimistic contains (or lookup) operation by applying the *hindsight lemma* from [24]. Hindsight-based proofs provide only *non-constructive* evidence of linearizability. Furthermore, some algorithms (e.g., the unordered list algorithm considered in Sect. 8 of this paper) do not contain the code patterns required by the hindsight method. Algorithms with non-optimistic contains (or lookup) operation like *HM* [16], *Harris* [11] and *Michael* [22] sets cannot be verified by their technique. Vechev *et al.* [33] check linearizability with user-specified non-fixed LPs, using a tool for finite-state verification. Their method assumes a bounded number of threads, and they report state space explosion when having more than two threads. Dragoi *et al.* [10] describe a method for proving linearizability that is applicable to algorithms with non-fixed LPs. However, their method needs to rewrite the implementation so that all operations have linearization points within the rewritten code. Černý *et al.* [32] show decidability of a class of programs with a bounded number of threads operating on concurrent data structures. Finally, the works [1, 3, 30] all require fixed linearization points.

We have not found any report in the literature of a verification method that is sufficiently powerful to automatically verify the class of concurrent set implementations based on sorted and non-sorted singly-linked lists having non-optimistic contains (or lookup) operations we consider. For instance the lock-free sets of *HM* [16], *Harris* [11], or *Michael* [22], or unordered set of [35].

2   Data Structures, Observers, and Linearizability

Data Structure Semantics. A *data structure* DS is a pair $\langle \mathbb{D}, \mathbb{M} \rangle$ where $\mathbb{D}$ is the *data domain* and $\mathbb{M}$ is the alphabet of method names. An *operation op* is of the form $\mathtt{m}(d^{in}, d^{out})$ where $\mathtt{m} \in \mathbb{M}$ is a method name and $d^{in}, d^{out} \in \mathbb{D}$ are the *input* resp. *output* data values. A *trace* of DS is a sequence of operations. The behavior $[\![DS]\!]$ of DS is the set of traces. We often identify DS with its behavior $[\![DS]\!]$. For example, in the Set data structure, the set of method names is given by $\{\mathtt{add}, \mathtt{rmv}, \mathtt{ctn}\}$, and the data domain is the union $\mathbb{Z} \cup \mathbb{B}$ of the sets of integers and Booleans. Input and output data values are in $\mathbb{Z}$ and $\mathbb{B}$ respectively. For instance, the operation $\mathtt{add}(3, \mathtt{tt})$ successfully adds the value 3, while $\mathtt{ctn}(2, \mathtt{ff})$ is a failed search for 2 in the set.

Observers. We specify traces of data structures by *observers*, as introduced in [1]. Observers are finite automata extended with a finite set of *registers* that assume values in $\mathbb{Z}$. At initialization, the registers are nondeterministically assigned arbitrary values, which never change during a run of the observer. Formally, an observer $\mathcal{O}$ is a tuple $\langle S^{\mathcal{O}}, s^{\mathcal{O}}_{\mathrm{init}}, \mathbb{X}^{\mathcal{O}}, \Delta^{\mathcal{O}}, s^{\mathcal{O}}_{\mathrm{acc}} \rangle$ where $S^{\mathcal{O}}$ is a finite set of *observer states* including the *initial state* $s^{\mathcal{O}}_{\mathrm{init}}$ and the *accepting state* $s^{\mathcal{O}}_{\mathrm{acc}}$, a finite set $\mathbb{X}^{\mathcal{O}}$ of

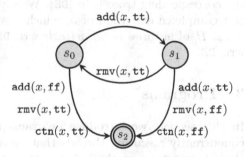

Fig. 1. Set observer.

registers, and $\Delta^{\mathcal{O}}$ is a finite set of *transitions*. Transitions are of the form $\langle s_1, \mathtt{m}(x^{in}, x^{out}), s_2 \rangle$ where x^{in} and x^{out} are either registers or constants, i.e., transitions are labeled by operations whose input or output data may be parameterized on registers. The observer accepts a trace if it can be processed in such a way that an accepting state is reached. Observers can be used to give *exact* specifications of the behaviors of data structures such as sets, queues, and stacks. The observer is defined in such a way that it accepts precisely those traces that do *not* belong to the behavior of the data structure. This is best illustrated by an example. Figure 1 depicts an observer that accepts the sequences of operations that are *not* in $[\![\mathrm{Set}]\!]$.

Linearizability. An operation $\mathtt{m}(d^{in}, d^{out})$ gives rise to two *actions*, namely a *call action* $(\mathtt{eid}, \mathtt{m}, d^{in}) \downarrow$ and a *return action* $(\mathtt{eid}, \mathtt{m}, d^{out}) \uparrow$, where $\mathtt{eid} \in \mathbb{N}$ is an *action identifier.* A *history* h is a sequence of actions such that for each return action a_2 in h there is a unique *matching* call action a_1 where the action identifiers in a_1 and a_2 are identical and different from the action identifiers of all other actions in h and such that a_1 occurs before a_2 in h. A call action carries always the same method name as its matching return action. A call action which does not match any return action in h is said to be *pending*. A history without pending call actions is said to be *complete*. A *completed extension* of h is a complete history h' obtained from h by appending (at the end) zero or more return actions that are matched by pending call actions in h, and thereafter removing pending call actions. For action identifiers eid_1, eid_2, we write $eid_1 \preceq_h eid_2$ to denote that the return action with identifier eid_1 occurs before the call action with identifier eid_2 in h. We say that a history is *sequential* if it is of the form $a_1 a_1' a_2 a_2' \cdots a_n a_n'$ where a_i' is the matching action of a_i for all $i : 1 \le i \le n$, i.e., each call action is immediately followed by the matching return action. We identify a sequential history of the above form with the corresponding trace $op_1 op_2 \cdots op_n$ where $op_i = \mathtt{m}(d_i^{in}, d_i^{out})$, $a_i = (eid_i, \mathtt{m}, d_i^{in}) \downarrow$, and $a_i = (eid_i, \mathtt{m}, d_i^{out}) \uparrow$, i.e., we merge each call action together with the matching return action into one operation. A complete history h' is a *linearization* of h if (i) h' is a permutation of h, (ii) h' is sequential, and (iii) $eid_1 \preceq_{h'} eid_2$ if $eid_1 \preceq_h eid_2$ for each pair of action identifiers eid_1 and eid_2. We say that a sequential history h' is *valid* wrt. DS if the corresponding trace is in $[\![DS]\!]$. We say that h is *linearizable* wrt. DS if there is a completed extension of h, which has a linearization that is valid wrt. DS. A set H of histories is *linearizable* wrt. DS if all members of H are *linearizable* wrt. DS.

3   Programs

In this section, we introduce programs that consist of arbitrary numbers of concurrently executing threads that access a concurrent data structure. Each thread executes a method that performs an operation on the data structure. Each method declares local variables and a method body. Variables are either pointer variables (to heap cells), or data variables, assuming values from an infinite (ordered) domain, or from some finite set $\mathbb{F}$ that includes the Boolean values $\mathbb{B}$. We assume w.l.o.g. that the infinite set is given by the set $\mathbb{Z}$ of integers. The body is built in the standard way from atomic commands, using standard control flow constructs (sequential composition, selection, and loop constructs). Each statement is equipped with a unique label. We assume that the set of local variables include the parameter of the method in addition to the program counter pc whose value is the label of the next statement to be executed. Method execution is terminated by executing a **return** command, which may return a value. The global variables can be accessed by all threads, whereas local variables can be accessed only by the thread which is invoking the corresponding method. We assume that all global variables are pointer variables, and that they are initialized, together with the heap, by an initialization method, which is executed once at the beginning of program execution.

Heap cells have a fixed set $\mathcal{F}$ of fields, namely data fields that assume values in $\mathbb{Z}$ or $\mathbb{F}$, and lock fields. Furthermore, each cell has one pointer field, denoted next, and hence heap cells are organized into singly-linked lists. We use the term $\mathbb{Z}$-field for a data field that assumes values in $\mathbb{Z}$, and the terms $\mathbb{F}$-field and lock field with analogous meaning. Atomic commands include assignments between data variables, pointer variables, or fields of cells pointed to by a pointer variable. The command new Node() allocates a new structure of type Node on the heap, and returns a reference to it. The compare-and-swap command CAS(&a,b,c) atomically compares the values of a and b. If equal, it assigns the value of c to a and returns true, otherwise, it leaves a unchanged and returns false. We assume a memory management mechanism, which automatically collects garbage, and also ensures that a new cell is fresh, i.e., has not been used before by the program; this avoids the so-called ABA problem (e.g., [21]).

Figure 2 depicts a program Lazy Set [13] that implements a concurrent set containing elements from $\mathbb{Z}$. The set is implemented as an ordered singly linked list. The program contains three methods, add, rmv, and ctn, corresponding to operations that add, remove, and check the existence of an element in the set, respectively. Each method takes an element as argument, and returns a value which indicates whether or not the operation has been successful. For instance, the operation add(e) returns the value true if e was not already a member of the set. In such a case a new cell with data value e is added to its appropriate position in the list. If e is already present, then the list is not changed and the value false is returned. The program also contains the subroutine locate that is called by add and rmv methods. A cell in the list has two data fields: mark:$\mathbb{F}$, where $\mathbb{F} = \{0,1\}$, and val:$\mathbb{Z}$, one lock field lock, and one pointer field next. The rmv method first logically removes the node from the list by setting the mark field, before physically removing the node. The ctn method is wait-free and traverses the list ignoring the locks inside the cells.

4   Linearization Policies

In this section, we introduce our formalism of *controllers* for expressing linearization policies. A linearization policy is expressed by defining for each method an associated controller, which is responsible for generating operations announcing the occurrence of LPs during each method invocation. The controller is occasionally activated, either by its thread or by another controller, and mediates the interaction of the thread with the observer as well as with other threads.

To add controllers, we first declare some statements in each method to be *triggering*: these are marked by the symbol •, as in Fig. 2. We specify the behavior of the controller, belonging to a method m, by a set R^m of *reaction rules*. To define these rules, we first define different types of events that are used to specify their behaviors. Recall that an *operation* is of the form $m(d^{in}, d^{out})$ where m is a method name and $d^{in}, d^{out} \in \mathbb{D}$ are data values. Operations are emitted by the controller to the observer to notify that the thread executing the method performs a linearization of the corresponding method with the given input and

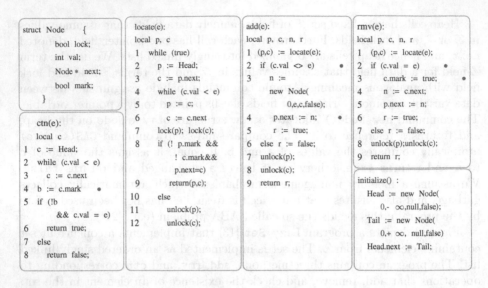

Fig. 2. Lazy Set.

---

add
ρ_1 **when** • **provided** pc=4 **emit** add(e,true) **broadcast** add(e)
ρ_2 **when** • **provided** pc=2 && (c.val = e) **emit** add(e,false)
rmv
ρ_3 **when** • **provided** pc=3 **emit** rmv(e,true)
ρ_4 **when** • **provided** pc=2 && c.val <> e **emit** rmv(e,false)
ctn
ρ_5 **when** • **provided** pc=4 && !b && c.val = e **emit** ctn(e,true)
ρ_6 **from** q_0 **when** • **provided** pc=4 && !(!b&&c.val=e) **emit** ctn(e,false) **goto** q_0
ρ_7 **from** q_0 **when** (add(e),before) **provided** 1<=pc<=4 **emit** ctn(e,false) **goto** q_1

Fig. 3. Reaction Rules for Controllers of Lazy Set.

output values. Next, we fix a set Σ of *broadcast messages*, each with a fixed arity, which are used for synchronization between controllers. A message is formed by supplying data values as parameters. In reaction rules, these data values are denoted by expressions over the variables of the method, which are evaluated in the current state when the rule is invoked. In an operation, the first parameter, denoting input, must be either a constant or the parameter of the method call.

– A *triggered* rule, of form **when** • **provided** *cnd* **emit** *op* **broadcast** *se*, specifies that whenever the method executes a triggering statement and the condition *cnd* evaluates to **true**, then the controller performs a *reaction* in which it emits the operation obtained by evaluating *op* to the observer, and broadcasts the message obtained by evaluating *se* to the controllers of other threads. The broadcast message *se* is optional.

– A *receiving* rule, of form **when** $\langle re, \text{ord} \rangle$ **provided** *cnd* **emit** *op*, specifies that whenever the observer of some other thread broadcasts the message obtained by evaluating *re*, and *cnd* evaluates to `true`, then the controller performs a reaction where it emits the operation obtained by evaluating *op* to the observer. Note that no further broadcasting is performed. The interaction of the thread with the observer may occur either *before* or *after* the sender thread, according to the flag `ord`.

A controller may also use a finite set of states, which restrict the possible sequences of reactions by a controller in the standard way. Whenever such states are used, the rule includes source and target states using kewords **from** and **goto**. In Fig. 3, the rule ρ_7 changes the state from q_0 to q_1, meaning that no further applications of rules ρ_6 or ρ_7 are possible, since they both start from state q_0. Rules that do not mention states can be applied regardless of the controller state and leave it unchanged.

Let us illustrate how the reaction rules for controllers in Fig. 3 specify LPs for the algorithm in Fig. 2. Here, a successful `rmv` method has its LP at line 3, and an unsuccessful `rmv` has its LP at line 2 when the test `c.val = e` evaluates to `false`. Therefore, both these statements are marked as triggering. The controller has a reaction rule for each of these cases: in Fig. 3: rule ρ_3 corresponds to a successful `rmv`, whereas rule ρ_4 corresponds to an unsuccessful `rmv`. Rule ρ_4 states that whenever the `rmv` method executes a triggering statement, from a state where `pc=2` and `c.val <> e`, then the operation `rmv(e,false)` will be emitted to the observer.

A successful `add` method has its LP at line 4. Therefore, the controller for `add` has the triggered rule ρ_1 which emits the operation `add(e,true)` to the observer. In addition, the controller also broadcasts the message `add(e)`, which is received by any controller for a `ctn` method which has not yet passed line 4, thereby linearizing an unsuccessful `ctn(e)` method by emitting `ctn(e,false)` to the observer. The keyword **before** denotes that the operation `ctn(e,false)` will be presented before `add(e,true)` to the observer. Since the reception of `add(e)` is performed in the same atomic step as the triggering statement at line 4 of the `add` method, this describes a linearization pattern, where a `ctn` method, which has not yet reached line 4, linearizes an unsuccessful `ctn`-invocation just before some other thread linearizes a successful `add` of the same element.

To see why unsuccessful `ctn` method invocations may not have fixed LPs, note that the naive attempt of defining the LP at line 4 provided that the test at line 5 fails will not work. Namely, the `ctn` method may traverse the list and arrive at line 4 in a situation where the element e is not in the list (either e is not in any cell, or the cell containing e is marked). However, before executing the command at line 4, another thread performs an `add` operation, inserting a new cell containing the element e into the list. The problem is now that the `ctn` method cannot "see" the new cell, since it is unreachable from the cell currently pointed to by the variable b of the `ctn` method. If the `ctn` method would now try to linearize an unsuccessful `ctn(e)`, this would violate the semantics of a set, since the `add` method just linearized a successful insertion of e.

A solution to this problem, following [13], is to let an unsuccessful ctn(e) method linearize at line 4 *only if* no successful add(e) method linearized since its invocation. If some other thread linearizes a successful add(e) before the ctn(e) method executes line 4, then the ctn(e) method should linearize immediately before the add(e) method. This solution is expressed by the rules in Fig. 3. Note, however, that it is now possible for an invocation of a successful ctn(e) to emit several operations: It can first emit ctn(e,false) together with the linearization of a successful add(e), and thereafter emit ctn(e,true) when it executes the statement at line 4, if it then finds the element e in the list (by rule ρ_5). In such a case, both operations are fine with the observer, and the last one is the event that causes the method to return true, i.e., conforms with the parameters and returns values.

Verifying Linearization Policies. By using an observer to specify the sequential semantics of the data structure, and defining controllers that specify the linearization policy, the verification of linearizability is reduced to establishing four conditions: (i) each method invocation generates a non-empty sequence of operations, (ii) the last operation of a method conforms to its parameters and return value, (iii) only the last operation of a method may change the state of the observer, and (iv) the sequence of all operations cannot drive the observer to an accepting state. Our verification framework automatically reduces the establishment of these conditions to a problem of checking control state reachability. This is done by augmenting the observer by a *monitor*. The monitor is automatically generated. It keeps track of the state of the observer, and records the sequence of operations and call and return actions generated by the threads. For each thread, it keeps track of whether it has linearized, whether it has caused a state change in the observer, and the parameters used in its last linearization. Using this information, it goes to an error state whenever any of the above four conditions is violated. The correctness of this approach is established in the next section, as Theorem 1.

5   Semantics

In this section, we formalize the semantics of programs, controllers, observers, and monitors, as introduced in the preceding sections. We do this in several steps. First, we define the state of the heap and the transition relation induced by a single thread. From this we derive the semantics of the program and use it to define its history set. We then define the semantics of observers, and its augmentation by the monitor; the observer is embedded in the monitor. Finally, we define the product of the augmented program and the monitor. On this basis, we can formally state and prove the correctness of our approach, as Theorem 1.

For a function $f : A \mapsto B$ from a set A to a set B, we use $f[a_1 \leftarrow b_1, \ldots, a_n \leftarrow b_n]$ to denote the function f' such that $f'(a_i) = b_i$ and $f'(a) = f(a)$ if $a \notin \{a_1, \ldots, a_n\}$.

Below, we assume a program $\mathcal{P}$ with a set $\mathtt{X}^{\mathsf{gl}}$ of global variables, a data structure $\mathtt{DS}$ specified as an observer $\mathcal{O}$. We assume that each thread $\mathtt{th}$ executes one method denoted $\mathtt{Method(th)}$.

Heaps. A *heap (state)* is a tuple $\mathcal{H} = \langle \mathbb{C}, \mathtt{succ}, \mathtt{Val}^{\mathsf{gl}}, \mathtt{Val}^{\mathbb{C}} \rangle$, where (i) $\mathbb{C}$ is a finite set of cells, including the two special cells $\mathtt{null}$ and $\bot$ (dangling); we define $\mathbb{C}^- = \mathbb{C} - \{\mathtt{null}, \bot\}$, (ii) $\mathtt{succ} : \mathbb{C}^- \to \mathbb{C}$ is a total function that defines the next-pointer relation, i.e., $\mathtt{succ}(\mathtt{c}) = \mathtt{c}'$ means that cell $\mathtt{c}$ points to $\mathtt{c}'$, (iii) $\mathtt{Val}^{\mathsf{gl}} : \mathtt{X}^{\mathsf{gl}} \to \mathbb{C}$ maps the global (pointer) variables to their values, and (iv) $\mathtt{Val}^{\mathbb{C}} : \mathbb{C} \times \mathcal{F} \to \mathbb{F} \cup \mathbb{Z}$ maps data and lock fields of each cell to their values. We assume that the heap is initialized by an initialization thread, and let $\mathcal{H}_{\mathtt{init}}$ denote the initial heap.

Threads. A *local state* $\mathtt{loc}$ of a thread $\mathtt{th}$ wrt. a heap $\mathcal{H}$ defines the values of its local variables, including the program counter $\mathtt{pc}$ and the input parameter for the method executed by $\mathtt{th}$. In addition, there is the special initial state $\mathtt{idle}$, and terminated state $\mathtt{term}$. A *view* $\mathtt{view}$ is a pair $\langle \mathtt{loc}, \mathcal{H} \rangle$, where $\mathtt{loc}$ is a local state wrt. the heap $\mathcal{H}$. A thread $\mathtt{th}$ induces a transition relation $\to_{\mathtt{th}}$ on views. Initially, $\mathtt{th}$ is in the state $\mathtt{idle}$. It becomes active by executing a transition $\langle \mathtt{idle}, \mathcal{H} \rangle \xrightarrow{(\mathtt{th},\mathtt{m},d^{in})\downarrow}_{\mathtt{th}} \langle \mathtt{loc}^{\mathtt{th}}_{\mathtt{init}}, \mathcal{H} \rangle$, labeled by a call action with $\mathtt{th}$ as the event identifier and $\mathtt{m} = \mathtt{Method(th)}$. It moves to an initial local state $\mathtt{loc}^{\mathtt{th}}_{\mathtt{init}}$ where d^{in} is the value of its input parameter, the value of $\mathtt{pc}$ is the label of the first statement of the method, and the other local variables are undefined. Thereafter, $\mathtt{th}$ executes statements one after one. We write $\mathtt{view} \xrightarrow{\lambda}_{\mathtt{th}} \mathtt{view}'$ to denote that the statement labeled by λ can be executed from $\mathtt{view}$, yielding $\mathtt{view}'$. Note that the next move of $\mathtt{th}$ is uniquely determined by $\mathtt{view}$, since $\mathtt{th}$ cannot access the local states of other threads. Finally, $\mathtt{th}$ terminates when executing its $\mathtt{return}$ command giving rise to a transition $\langle \mathtt{loc}, \mathcal{H} \rangle \xrightarrow{(\mathtt{th},\mathtt{m},d^{out})\uparrow}_{\mathtt{th}} \langle \mathtt{term}, \mathcal{H} \rangle$, labeled by a return action with $\mathtt{th}$ as event identifier, $\mathtt{m} = \mathtt{Method(th)}$, and d^{out} as the returned value.

Programs. A *configuration* of a program $\mathcal{P}$ is a tuple $\langle \mathtt{T}, \mathtt{LOC}, \mathcal{H} \rangle$ where $\mathtt{T}$ is a set of threads, $\mathcal{H}$ is a heap, and $\mathtt{LOC}$ is a *local state mapping* over $\mathtt{T}$ wrt. $\mathcal{H}$ that maps each thread $\mathtt{th} \in \mathtt{T}$ to its local state $\mathtt{LOC(th)}$ wrt. $\mathcal{H}$. The initial configuration $c^{\mathcal{P}}_{\mathtt{init}}$ is the pair $\langle \mathtt{LOC}_{\mathtt{init}}, \mathcal{H}_{\mathtt{init}} \rangle$, where $\mathtt{LOC}_{\mathtt{init}}(\mathtt{th}) = \mathtt{idle}$ for each $\mathtt{th} \in \mathtt{T}$, i.e., $\mathcal{P}$ starts its execution from a configuration with an initial heap, and with each thread in its initial local state. A program $\mathcal{P}$ induces a transition relation $\to_{\mathcal{P}}$ where each step corresponds to one move of a single thread. This is captured by the rules P1, P2, and P3 of Fig. 4 (here ε denotes the empty word.) Note that the only visible transitions are those corresponding to call and return actions. A *history* of $\mathcal{P}$ is a sequence of form $a_1 a_2 \cdots a_n$, such that there is a sequence $c_0 \xrightarrow{a_1}_{\mathcal{P}} c_1 \xrightarrow{a_2}_{\mathcal{P}} \cdots c_{n-1} \xrightarrow{a_n}_{\mathcal{P}} c_n$ of transitions from the initial configuration $c_0 = c^{\mathcal{P}}_{\mathtt{init}}$. We define $\mathcal{H}(\mathcal{P})$ to be the set of histories of $\mathcal{P}$. We say that $\mathcal{P}$ is linearizable wrt. $\mathtt{DS}$ if the set $\mathcal{H}(\mathcal{P})$ is linearizable wrt. $\mathtt{DS}$.

Controllers. The controller of a thread th induces a transition relation $\rightarrow_{\mathtt{cntrl(th)}}$, which depends on the current view view of th. For an expression *expr* denoting an operation, broadcast message, or condition, let view(*expr*) denote the result of evaluating *expr* in the state view. For a predicate *cnd*, we let view $\models$ *cnd* denote that view(*cnd*) is true. Transitions are defined by the set $R^{\mathtt{Method(th)}}$ of rules ($R^{\mathtt{th}}$ for short) associated with the method of th. Rule C1 describes transitions induced by a triggered rule, and states that if *cnd* is true under view, then the controller emits the operation obtained by instantiating *op* and broadcasts the message obtained by instantiating *se*, according to view. Rule C2 describes transitions induced by receiving a message e', and states that if *re* equals the value of e' in view, and *cnd* evaluates to true in view, then the operation view(*op*) is emitted. In both cases, the controller also emits to the observer the identity th of the thread. This identity will be used for bookkeeping by the monitor (see below.)

Augmented Threads. An *augmented view* $\langle q, \mathtt{loc}, \mathcal{H} \rangle$ extends a view $\langle \mathtt{loc}, \mathcal{H} \rangle$ with a state q of the controller. We define a transition relation $\rightarrow_{\mathtt{aug(th)}}$ over augmented views that describes the behavior of a thread th when augmented with its controller. For a label λ of a statement we write $\lambda^\bullet$ to denote that the corresponding statement is triggered. Rule TC1 states that a non-triggered statement by the thread does not affect the state of the controller, and does not emit or broadcast anything. Rule TC2 states a return action by the thread. Rule TC3 states that when the thread th performs a triggered statement, then the controller will emit an operation to the observer and broadcast messages to the other threads. The reception of broadcast messages will be described in Rule R.

Augmented Programs. An *augmented program* $\mathcal{Q}$ is obtained from a program $\mathcal{P}$ by augmenting each thread with its controller. A *configuration* c of $\mathcal{Q}$ is a tuple $\langle \mathtt{T}, \mathtt{Q}, \mathtt{LOC}, \mathcal{H} \rangle$, which extends a configuration of $\mathcal{P}$ by a *controller state mapping*, $\mathtt{Q}$, which maps each thread th $\in$ T to the state of its controller. We define the size $|c| = |\mathtt{T}|$ and define ThreadsOf $(c) = \mathtt{T}$. We use $\mathcal{C}^{\mathcal{Q}}$ to denote the set of configurations of $\mathcal{Q}$. Transitions of $\mathcal{Q}$ are performed by the threads in T. The rule Q1 describes return action or a non-triggered statement in which only its local state and the heap may change. Rule Q2 describes the case where a thread $\mathtt{th}_s$ executes a triggered statement and hence also broadcasts a message to the other threads. Before describing this rule, we describe the effect of message reception. Consider a set T of threads, a heap $\mathcal{H}$, a controller state mapping Q over T, and a local state mapping LOC over T wrt. $\mathcal{H}$. We will define a relation that extracts the set of threads in T that can receive e from $\mathtt{th}_s$. For ord $\in \{\mathtt{before}, \mathtt{after}\}$, define enabled $(\mathtt{T}, \mathtt{Q}, \mathtt{LOC}, \mathcal{H}, e, \mathtt{ord}, \mathtt{th}_s)$ to be the set of threads th $\in$ T such that (i) th $\neq \mathtt{th}_s$, i.e., a receiver thread should be different from the sender thread, and (ii) $\langle \mathtt{LOC(th)}, \mathcal{H} \rangle : \mathtt{Q(th)} \xrightarrow{\langle \mathtt{th}, op \rangle | \langle e, \mathtt{ord} \rangle ?}_{\mathtt{cntrl(th)}} q'$ for some q' and op, i.e., the controller of th has an enabled receiving rule that can receive e, with the ordering flag given by ord. The rule R describes the effect of receiving a message that has been broadcast by a sender thread $\mathtt{th}_s$. Each thread that can receive the message will do so, and the thread potentially will all change their controller state and

$$\frac{\langle \mathtt{idle}, \mathcal{H}\rangle \xrightarrow{(\mathtt{th},\mathtt{m},d^{in})\downarrow}_{\mathtt{th}} \langle \mathtt{loc}^{\mathtt{th}}_{\mathtt{init}}, \mathcal{H}\rangle}{\langle \mathtt{T}, \mathtt{LOC}, \mathcal{H}\rangle \xrightarrow{(\mathtt{th},\mathtt{m},d^{in})\downarrow}_{\mathcal{P}} \langle \mathtt{T}, \mathtt{LOC}[\mathtt{th} \leftarrow \mathtt{loc}^{\mathtt{th}}_{\mathtt{init}}], \mathcal{H}\rangle} \; P1 \qquad \frac{\langle \mathtt{loc}, \mathcal{H}\rangle \xrightarrow{(\mathtt{th},\mathtt{m},d^{out})\uparrow}_{\mathtt{th}} \langle \mathtt{term}, \mathcal{H}\rangle}{\langle \mathtt{T}, \mathtt{LOC}, \mathcal{H}\rangle \xrightarrow{(\mathtt{th},\mathtt{m},d^{out})\uparrow}_{\mathcal{P}} \langle \mathtt{T}, \mathtt{LOC}[\mathtt{th} \leftarrow \mathtt{term}], \mathcal{H}\rangle} \; P2$$

$$\frac{\langle \mathtt{loc}, \mathcal{H}\rangle \xrightarrow{\lambda}_{\mathtt{th}} \langle \mathtt{loc}', \mathcal{H}'\rangle}{\langle \mathtt{T}, \mathtt{LOC}, \mathcal{H}\rangle \xrightarrow{\varepsilon}_{\mathcal{P}} \langle \mathtt{T}, \mathtt{LOC}[\mathtt{th} \leftarrow \mathtt{loc}'], \mathcal{H}'\rangle} \; P3$$

$$\frac{\begin{array}{c}\mathtt{view} \models cnd\,,\, \mathtt{m}(d^{in}, d^{out}) = \mathtt{view}(op)\,,\, e = \mathtt{view}(se)\,,\\ (\mathbf{from}\; q\; \mathbf{when}\; \bullet\; \mathbf{provided}\; cnd\; \mathbf{emit}\; op\; \mathbf{broadcast}\; se\; \mathbf{goto}\; q') \in R^{\mathtt{th}}\end{array}}{\mathtt{view} : q \xrightarrow{(\mathtt{th},\mathtt{m}(d^{in},d^{out}))|e!}_{\mathtt{cntrl(th)}} q'} \; C1$$

$$\frac{\mathtt{view} \models cnd\,,\, \mathtt{m}(d^{in}, d^{out}) = \mathtt{view}(op)\,,\, e' = \mathtt{view}(re)\,,\, (\mathbf{from}\; q\; \mathbf{when}\; re\; \mathbf{provided}\; cnd\; \mathbf{emit}\; op\; \mathbf{goto}\; q') \in R^{\mathtt{th}}}{\mathtt{view} : q \xrightarrow{(\mathtt{th},\mathtt{m}(d^{in},d^{out}))|\langle e',\mathtt{ord}\rangle?}_{\mathtt{cntrl(th)}} q'} \; C2$$

$$\frac{\langle \mathtt{loc}, \mathcal{H}\rangle \xrightarrow{\lambda}_{\mathtt{th}} \langle \mathtt{loc}', \mathcal{H}'\rangle\,,\, \neg\lambda^{\bullet}}{\langle q, \mathtt{loc}, \mathcal{H}\rangle \xrightarrow{\varepsilon}_{\mathtt{aug(th)}} \langle q, \mathtt{loc}', \mathcal{H}'\rangle} \; TC1 \qquad \frac{\langle \mathtt{loc}, \mathcal{H}\rangle \xrightarrow{(\mathtt{th},\mathtt{m},d^{out})\uparrow}_{\mathtt{th}} \langle \mathtt{loc}', \mathcal{H}'\rangle}{\langle q, \mathtt{loc}, \mathcal{H}\rangle \xrightarrow{(\mathtt{th},\mathtt{m},d^{out})\uparrow}_{\mathtt{aug(th)}} \langle q, \mathtt{loc}', \mathcal{H}'\rangle} \; TC2$$

$$\frac{\langle \mathtt{loc}, \mathcal{H}\rangle \xrightarrow{\lambda}_{\mathtt{th}} \langle \mathtt{loc}', \mathcal{H}'\rangle\,,\, \lambda^{\bullet}\,,\, \langle \mathtt{loc}, \mathcal{H}\rangle : q \xrightarrow{(\mathtt{th},op)|e'!}_{\mathtt{cntrl(th)}} q'}{\langle q, \mathtt{loc}, \mathcal{H}\rangle \xrightarrow{(\mathtt{th},op)|e'!}_{\mathtt{aug(th)}} \langle q', \mathtt{loc}', \mathcal{H}'\rangle} \; TC3$$

$$\frac{\mathtt{enabled}\,(\mathtt{T},\mathtt{Q},\mathtt{LOC},\mathcal{H},e,\mathtt{ord},\mathtt{th}_s) = \{\mathtt{th}_1,\ldots,\mathtt{th}_n\}\,,\, \forall i : 1 \leq i \leq n : \langle \mathtt{LOC}(\mathtt{th}_i), \mathcal{H}\rangle : \mathtt{Q}(\mathtt{th}_i) \xrightarrow{(\mathtt{th}_i,op_i)|\langle e,\mathtt{ord}\rangle?}_{\mathtt{th}_i} q_i}{\langle \mathtt{T}/\mathtt{th}_s, \mathtt{LOC}, \mathcal{H}\rangle : \mathtt{Q} \xrightarrow{op_1 \cdots op_n|\langle e,\mathtt{ord}\rangle?} \mathtt{Q}[\mathtt{th}_1 \leftarrow q_1,\ldots,\mathtt{th}_n \leftarrow q_n]} \; R$$

$$\frac{\mathtt{LOC}(\mathtt{th}) = \mathtt{loc}\,,\, \langle q, \mathtt{loc}, \mathcal{H}\rangle \xrightarrow{\tau}_{\mathtt{aug(th)}} \langle q, \mathtt{loc}', \mathcal{H}'\rangle\,,\, \tau \in \{\varepsilon, (\mathtt{th},\mathtt{m},d^{out})\uparrow\}}{\langle \mathtt{T}, \mathtt{Q}, \mathtt{LOC}, \mathcal{H}\rangle \xrightarrow{\tau}_{\mathcal{Q}} \langle \mathtt{T}, \mathtt{Q}, \mathtt{LOC}[\mathtt{th} \leftarrow \mathtt{loc}'], \mathcal{H}'\rangle} \; Q1$$

$$\frac{\begin{array}{c}\langle q, \mathtt{loc}, \mathcal{H}\rangle \xrightarrow{(\mathtt{th}_s,op)|e!}_{\mathtt{aug(th}_s)} \langle q', \mathtt{loc}', \mathcal{H}'\rangle\,,\\ \langle \mathtt{T}/\mathtt{th}_s, \mathtt{LOC}, \mathcal{H}\rangle : \mathtt{Q} \xrightarrow{w_1|\langle e,\mathtt{before}\rangle?} \mathtt{Q}'\,,\, \langle \mathtt{T}/\mathtt{th}_s, \mathtt{LOC}, \mathcal{H}\rangle : \mathtt{Q}' \xrightarrow{w_2|\langle e,\mathtt{after}\rangle?} \mathtt{Q}''\end{array}}{\langle \mathtt{T}, \mathtt{Q}, \mathtt{LOC}, \mathcal{H}\rangle \xrightarrow{w_1 \bullet \langle \mathtt{th}_s,op\rangle \bullet w_2}_{\mathcal{Q}} \langle \mathtt{T}, \mathtt{Q}''[\mathtt{th}_s \leftarrow q'], \mathtt{LOC}[\mathtt{th}_s \leftarrow \mathtt{loc}'], \mathcal{H}'\rangle} \; Q2$$

$$\frac{\langle s, \mathtt{m}(x^{in}, x^{out}), s'\rangle \in \Delta^{\mathcal{O}}\,,\, \mathtt{Val}\,(x^{in}) = d^{in}\,,\, \mathtt{Val}\,(x^{out}) = d^{out}}{\langle s, \mathtt{Val}\rangle \xrightarrow{\langle \mathtt{th},\mathtt{m}(d^{in},d^{out})\rangle}_{\mathcal{O}} \langle s', \mathtt{Val}\rangle} \; O1$$

$$\frac{\forall x^{in}.x^{out}.s'.\, \neg\left(\langle s, \mathtt{m}(x^{in}, x^{out}), s'\rangle \in \Delta^{\mathcal{O}} \wedge \mathtt{Val}\,(x^{in}) = d^{in} \wedge \mathtt{Val}\,(x^{out}) = d^{out}\right)}{\langle s, \mathtt{Val}\rangle \xrightarrow{\langle \mathtt{th},\mathtt{m}(d^{in},d^{out})\rangle}_{\mathcal{O}} \langle s, \mathtt{Val}\rangle} \; O2$$

$$\frac{\langle s, \mathtt{Val}\rangle \xrightarrow{\mathtt{m}(d^{in},d^{out})}_{\mathcal{O}} \langle s, \mathtt{Val}\rangle\,,\, \mathtt{Lin}\,(\mathtt{th}) \in \{0,1\}\,,\, \mathtt{Method}\,(\mathtt{th}) = \mathtt{m}}{\langle \mathtt{T}, \langle s, \mathtt{Val}\rangle, \mathtt{Lin}, \mathtt{RV}\rangle \xrightarrow{\langle \mathtt{th},\mathtt{m}(d^{in},d^{out})\rangle}_{\mathcal{M}} \langle \mathtt{T}, \langle s, \mathtt{Val}\rangle, \mathtt{Lin}[\mathtt{th} \leftarrow 1], \mathtt{RV}[\mathtt{th} \leftarrow d^{out}]\rangle} \; M1$$

$$\frac{\langle s, \mathtt{Val}\rangle \xrightarrow{\langle \mathtt{th},\mathtt{m}(d^{in},d^{out})\rangle}_{\mathcal{O}} \langle s', \mathtt{Val}\rangle\,,\, s' \neq s\,,\, \mathtt{Lin}\,(\mathtt{th}) \in \{0,1\}\,,\, \mathtt{Method}\,(\mathtt{th}) = \mathtt{m}}{\langle \mathtt{T}, \langle s, \mathtt{Val}\rangle, \mathtt{Lin}, \mathtt{RV}\rangle \xrightarrow{\langle \mathtt{th},\mathtt{m}(d^{in},d^{out})\rangle}_{\mathcal{M}} \langle \mathtt{T}, \langle s', \mathtt{Val}\rangle, \mathtt{Lin}[\mathtt{th} \leftarrow 2], \mathtt{RV}[\mathtt{th} \leftarrow d^{out}]\rangle} \; M2$$

$$\frac{c \xrightarrow{\langle \mathtt{th},\mathtt{m}(d^{in},d^{out})\rangle}_{\mathcal{O}} \langle s^{\mathcal{O}}_{\mathtt{acc}}, \mathtt{Val}\rangle}{\langle \mathtt{T}, c, \mathtt{Lin}, \mathtt{RV}\rangle \xrightarrow{\langle \mathtt{th},\mathtt{m}(d^{in},d^{out})\rangle}_{\mathcal{M}} \mathbf{error}} \; M3 \qquad \frac{\mathtt{Lin}\,(\mathtt{th}) = 0}{\langle \mathtt{T}, c, \mathtt{Lin}, \mathtt{RV}\rangle \xrightarrow{(\mathtt{th},\mathtt{m},d^{out})\uparrow}_{\mathcal{M}} \mathbf{error}} \; M4$$

$$\frac{\mathtt{Lin}\,(\mathtt{th}) = 2}{\langle \mathtt{T}, c, \mathtt{Lin}, \mathtt{RV}\rangle \xrightarrow{\langle \mathtt{th},\mathtt{m}(d^{in},d^{out})\rangle}_{\mathcal{M}} \mathbf{error}} \; M5 \qquad \frac{\mathtt{RV}\,(\mathtt{th}) \neq d^{out}}{\langle \mathtt{T}, c, \mathtt{Lin}, \mathtt{RV}\rangle \xrightarrow{(\mathtt{th},\mathtt{m},d^{out})\uparrow}_{\mathcal{M}} \mathbf{error}} \; M6 \qquad \frac{}{\mathbf{error} \xrightarrow{e}_{\mathcal{M}} \mathbf{error}} \; M7$$

$$\frac{\forall i : 0 \leq i < n : c_i \xrightarrow{e_{i+1}}_{\mathcal{M}} c_{i+1}}{c_0 \xrightarrow{e_1 \cdots e_n}_{\mathcal{M}} c_n} \; M8 \qquad \frac{c_1 \xrightarrow{w}_{\mathcal{Q}} c_1'\,,\, c_2 \xrightarrow{w}_{\mathcal{M}} c_2'}{\langle c_1, c_2\rangle \to_{\mathcal{S}} \langle c_1', c_2'\rangle} \; QM$$

Fig. 4. Inference rules of the semantics.

emit an operation. Notice that the receiver threads are collected in a set and therefore the rule allows any ordering of the receiving threads. We are now ready to explain the rule Q2. The sender thread th_s broadcast a message e_2 that will be received by other threads according to rule R. The sender thread and the receiver threads, all emit operations (e_1 and w respectively). Depending on the order specified in the specification of the controller, a receiving thread may linearize *before* or *after* th_s. Notice that the receiver threads only change the local states of their controllers and the state of the observer. An *initial configuration* of $Q \in \mathcal{C}^Q$ is of the form $\langle \text{T}, \text{Q}_{\text{init}}, \text{LOC}_{\text{init}}, \mathcal{H}_{\text{init}} \rangle$ where, for each $\text{th} \in \text{T}$, $\text{LOC}_{\text{init}}(\text{th})$ is the initial state of the controller of th, and $\text{LOC}_{\text{init}}(\text{th}) = \text{idle}$.

Observers. Let $\mathcal{O} = \langle S^{\mathcal{O}}, s^{\mathcal{O}}_{\text{init}}, \text{X}^{\mathcal{O}}, \Delta^{\mathcal{O}}, s^{\mathcal{O}}_{\text{acc}} \rangle$. A configuration c of $\mathcal{O}$ is a pair $\langle s, \text{Val} \rangle$ where $s \in S^{\mathcal{O}}$ is an observer state and Val assigns a value to each register in $\mathcal{O}$. We use $\mathcal{C}^{\mathcal{O}}$ to denote the set of configurations of $\mathcal{O}$. The transition relation $\rightarrow_{\mathcal{O}}$ of the observer is described by the rules O1 and O2 of Fig. 4. Rule O1 states that if there is an enabled transition that is labeled by a given action then such a transition may be performed. Rule O2 states that if there is no such a transition, the observer remains in its current state. Notice that the rules imply that the register values never change during a run of the observer. An initial configuration of $\mathcal{O} \in \mathcal{C}^{\mathcal{O}}$ is of the form $\langle s^{\mathcal{O}}_{\text{init}}, \text{Val} \rangle$.

Monitors. The monitor $\mathcal{M}$ augments the observer. It keeps track of the observer state, and the sequence of operations and call and return actions generated by the threads of the augmented program. It reports an error if one of the following happens: (i) a thread terminates without having linearized, (ii) the parameters of call and return actions are different from those of the corresponding emitted operation, (iii) a thread linearizes although it has previously changed the state of the observer, or (iv) Q generates a trace which violates the specification of the data structure DS. The monitor keeps track of these conditions as follows. A *configuration* of $\mathcal{M}$ is either (i) a tuple $\langle \text{T}, c, \text{Lin}, \text{RV} \rangle$ where T is a set of threads, c is an observer configuration, $\text{Lin} : \text{T} \mapsto \{0, 1, 2\}$, and $\text{RV} : \text{T} \mapsto \mathbb{Z} \cup \mathbb{F}$; or (ii) the special state **error**. For a thread $\text{th} \in \text{T}$, the values $0, 1, 2$ of $\text{Lin}(\text{th})$ have the following interpretations: 0 means that th has not linearized yet, 1 means that th has linearized but not changed the state of the observer, and 2 means that th has both linearized and changed the state of the observer. Furthermore, $\text{RV}(\text{th})$ stores the value returned by th the latest time it performed a linearization. In case c is of the first form, we define $\text{ThreadsOf}(c) = \text{T}$. We use $\mathcal{C}^{\mathcal{M}}$ to denote the set of configurations of $\mathcal{M}$. The rules M1 through M8 describe the transition relation $\rightarrow_{\mathcal{M}}$ induced by $\mathcal{M}$. Rule M1 describes the scenario when the monitor detects an operation $\text{m}(d^{in}, d^{out})$ performed by a thread th such that $\mathcal{O}$ does not change its state. In such a case, the flag Lin for th is updated to 1 (the thread has linearized but not changed the state of the observer), and the latest value d^{out} returned by th is stored RV. Rule M2 is similar except that the observer changes state and hence the flag Lin is updated to 2 for th. Notice that in both rules, a premise is that th has not changed the observer state previously (the flag Lin for th is different from 2.) Rules M3, M4, M5, and M6 describe the conditions (i), (ii), (iii), and (iv) respectively described above that lead to the error state. The rule M7 describes the fact that the error state is a sink, i.e., once $\mathcal{M}$ enters that state then it will never leave it. Finally, rule M8 describes the reflexive transitive closure of the relation $\rightarrow_{\mathcal{M}}$. An initial configuration of $\mathcal{M} \in \mathcal{C}^{\mathcal{M}}$ is of the form $\langle \text{T}, c_{\text{init}}, \text{Lin}_{\text{init}}, \text{RV}_{\text{init}} \rangle$ where $c_{\text{init}} \in c_{\text{init}}^{\mathcal{O}}$ is an initial configuration of $\mathcal{O}$, $\text{Lin}_{\text{init}}(\text{th}) = 0$ and $\text{RV}_{\text{init}}(\text{th})$ is undefined for every thread $\text{th} \in \text{T}$.

Product. We use $\mathcal{S} = \mathcal{Q} \otimes \mathcal{M}$ to denote the system obtained by running $\mathcal{Q}$ and $\mathcal{M}$ together. A (initial) configuration of $\mathcal{S}$ is of the form $\langle c_1, c_2 \rangle$ where c_1 and c_2 are (initial) configurations of $\mathcal{Q}$ and $\mathcal{M}$ respectively such that $\text{ThreadsOf}(c_1) = \text{ThreadsOf}(c_2)$. We use $\mathcal{C}^{\mathcal{S}}$ to denote the set of configurations of $\mathcal{S}$. The induced transition relation $\rightarrow_{\mathcal{S}}$ is described by rule QM of Fig. 4. Intuitively, in the composed systems, the augmented program and the monitor synchronize through the actions they produce. For a configuration $c \in \mathcal{C}^{\mathcal{S}}$, we define $\text{Post}(c) = \{c' \mid c \rightarrow_{\mathcal{S}} c'\}$. For a set C of system configurations, we define $\text{Post}(C) = \bigcup_{c \in C} \text{Post}(c)$. We say that that **error** is reachable in $\mathcal{S}$ if $c \rightarrow_{\mathcal{S}}^{*} \langle c', \textbf{error} \rangle$ for an initial configuration c of $\mathcal{S}$ and configuration c' of $\mathcal{Q}$.

Verifying Linearizability. The correctness of this approach is established in the following theorem.

Theorem 1. *If* **error** *is not reachable in* $\mathcal{S}$ *then* $\mathcal{P}$ *is linearizable wrt.* DS.

Proof. To prove $\mathcal{P}$ is linearizable wrt. DS. We must establish that for any history h of $\mathcal{P}$, there exists a history h' such that h' is linearization of h and h' is valid wrt. DS. So, consider a history h of $\mathcal{P}$. From Condition (i) in the paragraph about monitors in Sect. 5, h is a complete history. Then from Conditions (ii) and (iii), each action in h has a LP and whose call and return parameters are consistent with the corresponding emitted operation by the controller. Therefore, there exists a complete sequential history h' which is a permutation of h whose actions are ordered according to the order of their LPs in h. Therefore h' is linearization of h. From Condition (iv), h' is *valid* wrt. DS. Therefore, h is *linearizable* wrt. DS.   □

6   Thread Abstraction

By Theorem 1, linearizability can be verified by establishing a reachability property for the product $\mathcal{S} = \mathcal{Q} \otimes \mathcal{M}$. This verification must handle the challenges of an unbounded number of threads, an unbounded heap, and unbounded data domain. In this section, we describe how we handle an unbounded number of threads by adapting the thread-modular approach [3], and extending it to handle global transitions where several threads synchronize, due to interaction between controllers.

Let a heap cell c be *accessible* from a thread th if it is reachable (directly or via sequence of next-pointers) from a global variable or local variable of th_1.

A *thread abstracted* configuration of $\mathcal{S}$ is a pair $\langle c^{ta}, \texttt{private}\rangle$, where $c^{ta} \in \mathcal{C}^{\mathcal{S}}$ with $\texttt{ThreadsOf}\,(c^{ta}) = \{\texttt{th}_1\}$, such that each cell in the heap of c^{ta} is accessible from $\texttt{th}_1$ (i.e., the heap has no garbage), and where $\texttt{private}$ is a predicate over the cells in the heap of c^{ta}. For a system configuration $c^{\mathcal{S}}$, let $\alpha_{\texttt{thread}}\,(c^{\mathcal{S}})$ be the set of thread abstracted configurations $\langle c^{ta}, \texttt{private}\rangle$, such that (i) c^{ta} can be obtained by removing all threads from $c^{\mathcal{S}}$ except one, renaming that thread to $\texttt{th}_1$, and thereafter removing all heap cells that are not accessible from $\texttt{th}_1$, (ii) $\texttt{private}(c)$ is true iff in $c^{\mathcal{S}}$, the heap cell c is accessible only from the thread that is not removed. For a set C of system configurations, define $\alpha_{\texttt{thread}}\,(C) = \bigcup_{c^{\mathcal{S}} \in C} \alpha_{\texttt{thread}}\,(c^{\mathcal{S}})$. Conversely, for a set C of thread abstracted configurations, define $\gamma_{\texttt{thread}}\,(C) = \{c^{\mathcal{S}} \mid \alpha_{\texttt{thread}}(\{C\}) \subseteq C\}$. Define the postcondition operation $\texttt{Post}^{ta}$ on sets of thread abstracted configurations in the standard way by $\texttt{Post}^{ta}\,(C) = \alpha_{\texttt{thread}}(\texttt{Post}\,(\gamma_{\texttt{thread}}(C)))$. By standard arguments, $\texttt{Post}^{ta}$ then soundly overapproximates $\texttt{Post}$.

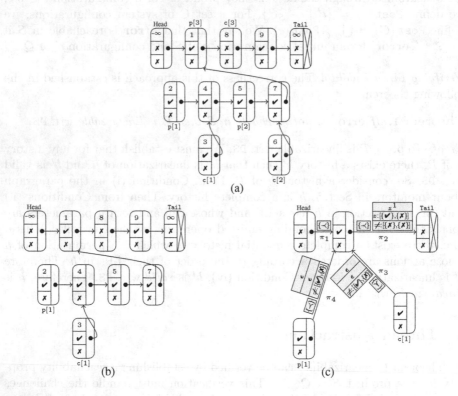

Fig. 5. Example of (a) heap state of Lazy Set algorithm, (b) its thread-abstracted version, and (c) symbolic version. The observer register x has value 9.

In Fig. 5 (a) is a possible heap state of the Lazy Set algorithm of Fig. 2. Each cell contains the values of $\texttt{val}$, $\texttt{mark}$, and $\texttt{lock}$ from top to bottom, where ✔ denotes $\texttt{true}$, and ✗ denotes $\texttt{false}$ (or *free* for lock). There are three threads,

1, 2, and 3 with pointer variable p[i] of thread i labeling the cell that it points to. The observer register x has value 9. Figure 5 (b) shows its thread abstraction onto thread 1.

We observe that the concretization of a set of abstract configurations is a set of configurations with arbitrary sizes. However, as we argue below, it is sufficient to only consider such sizes up to $3 \cdot (\#\mathcal{O}) + 2$. The reason is that the thread abstraction encodes, for an arbitrary thread th, its view, i.e., its local state, the state of the heap, and the observer. In order to preserve soundness, we need not only to consider the transitions of th, but also how the transitions of other threads may change the states of the heap and the observer. Suppose that a different thread th′ performs a transition. We consider two cases depending on whether th′ sends a broadcast message or not. If not, it is sufficient for th to see how th′ alone changes the heap and the observer. If th′ sends a message an arbitrary number of threads may receive it. Now note that only th′ may change the heap, while the receivers only change the state of the observer (Sect. 5). Also note that the values of the observer registers never change. The total effect is that th′ may change the state of the heap, while the other threads only change the state of the observer. Any such effect can be accomplished by only considering at most $3 \cdot (\#\mathcal{O}) + 2$ threads. The diameter $\#\mathcal{O}$ of $\mathcal{O}$ is the length of the longest simple path in $\mathcal{O}$. Formally, define $\gamma_{\text{thread}}^{k}(C) = \{c \mid (c \in \gamma_{\text{thread}}(C)) \cap |c| \leq k\}$, i.e., it is the set of configurations of in the concretization of C with at most k threads.

Lemma 1. *For a set of abstract configurations C, we have* $\text{Post}^{ta}(C) = \alpha_{\text{thread}}\left(\text{Post}\left(\gamma_{\text{thread}}^{k}(C)\right)\right)$ *where* $k = 3 \cdot (\#\mathcal{O}) + 2$.

As we mentioned above, when we perform helping transitions, the only effect of receiver threads is to change the state of the observer. When the receivers do not change the observer to a non-accepting state, we say that the transition is *stuttering* wrt. the observer. The system S is *stuttering* if all helping transitions of S are *stuttering*. This can be verified by a simple syntactic check of the observer and controller. In all the examples we have considered, the system turns out to be stuttering. For instance, the receiver threads in the Lazy Set algorithm are all performing stuttering ctn operations. Hence, the concretization needs only consider the sender thread, together with the thread whose view we are considering, reducing the number of threads to two.

Lemma 2. *For a set abstract configurations C of S, if S is stuttering, then* $\text{Post}^{ta}(C) = \alpha_{\text{thread}}\left(\text{Post}\left(\gamma_{\text{thread}}^{2}(C)\right)\right)$.

7 Symbolic Shape and Data Abstraction

This section describes how we handle an unbounded heap and data domain in thread-abstracted configurations. We assume that each heap cell contains exactly one $\mathbb{Z}$-field.

The abstraction of thread-abstracted configurations we use is a variation of a well-known abstraction of singly-linked lists [19]. We explicitly represent only a finite subset of the heap cells, called the *relevant* cells. The remaining cells are summarized into linked-list segments of arbitrary length. Thus, we intuitively abstract the heap into a graph-like structure, whose nodes are relevant cells, and whose edges are the connecting segments. More precisely, a cell c (in a thread-abstracted configuration) is *relevant* if it is either (i) pointed to by a (global or local) pointer variable, or (ii) the value of c_1.next and c_2.next for two different cells $c_1, c_2 \in \mathbb{C}$, one of which is reachable from some global variable, or (iii) the value of c'.next for some cell $c' \in \mathbb{C}$ such that private(c') but ¬private(c). Each relevant cell is connected, by a linked-list segment, to a uniquely defined next relevant cell. For instance, the thread abstracted heap in Fig. 5(b) has 5 relevant cells: 4 cells that are pointed to by variables (Head, Tail, p[1], and c[1]) and the cell where the lower list segment meets the upper one (the second cell in the top row). The corresponding symbolic representation, shown in Fig. 5(c), contains only the relevant cells, and connects each relevant cell to its successor relevant cell. Note that the cell containing 4 is not relevant, since it is not globally reachable. Consequently, we do not represent the precise branching structure among cells that are not globally reachable. This is an optimization to limit the size of our symbolic representation.

Our symbolic representation must now represent (A) data variables and data fields of relevant cells, and (B) data fields of list segments. For (A) we do as follows.

1. Each data and lock variable, and each data and lock field of each relevant cell, is mapped to a domain which depends on the set of values it can assume: (i) variables and fields that assume values in $\mathbb{F}$ are mapped to $\mathbb{F}$, (ii) lock variables and fields are mapped to $\{th_1, other, free\}$, representing whether the lock was last acquired by th_1, by another thread, or is free, (iii) variables and fields that assume values in $\mathbb{Z}$ are mapped to $[X^{\mathcal{O}} \mapsto \{=, \neq\}]$, representing for each observer register $x \in X^{\mathcal{O}}$, whether or not the value of the variable or field equals the value of x.
2. Each pair of variables or fields that assume values in $\mathbb{Z}$ is mapped to a subset of $\{<, =, >\}$, representing the set of possible relations between them.=

For (B), we define a domain of *path expressions*, which capture the following information about a segment.

- The possible relations between adjacent $\mathbb{Z}$-fields in the heap segment, represented as a subset of $\{<, =, >\}$, e.g., to represent that the segment is sorted.
- The set of observer registers whose value appears in some $\mathbb{Z}$-field of the segment. For these registers, the path expression provides (i) the order in which the first occurrence of their values appear in the segment; this allows, e.g., to check ordering properties between data values for stacks and queues, and (ii) whether there is exactly one, or more than one occurrence of their value.
- For each data and lock field, the set of possible values of that field in the heap segment, represented as a subset of the domain defined in case 1 above. This subset is provided both for the cells whose $\mathbb{Z}$-field is not equal to any observer register, and for the cells whose $\mathbb{Z}$-field is equal to each observer register.

To illustrate, in Fig. 5(c), each heap segment is labeled by a representation of its path expression. The first component of each path expression is $\{<\}$, i.e., the segment is sorted. The path expression at the top right has as its second component the sequence x^1, expressing that there is exactly one cell whose $\mathbb{Z}$-field has the same value as the observer register x. The row $x : [\{✔\}, \{✗\}]$ expresses that the cells whose $\mathbb{Z}$-value is equal to that of x, have their mark field true, and their lock field free. The row $\neq: [\{✗\}, \{✗\}]$ expresses that the other cells have their mark field false, and their lock field free. The two lower path expressions express that no cell has a value equal to that of x, and summarize the possible values of fields.

The symbolic representation combines the above described shape and data representations, representing thread-abstracted configurations by *symbolic configurations*. These are tuples of form $\Phi = \langle \mathrm{I}, \mathrm{Val}^v, \mathtt{nextrel}, \pi, \mathrm{Val}^d, \mathrm{Val}^r, \mathtt{private} \rangle$, where

- I is a finite set of *indices*, denoting the relevant cells of the heap,
- Val^v maps each (global or local) pointer variable to an index in I,
- nextrel maps each index i to $\mathrm{I} \cup \{\mathtt{null}, \bot\}$,
- π maps each index i to a path expression; intuitively, if the index i represents the relevant cell c, then $\mathtt{nextrel}(i)$ represents the next relevant cell, and $\pi(i)$ summarizes the heap segment between c and the cell represented by $\mathtt{nextrel}(i)$,
- Val^d maps data variables and fields of relevant cells to appropriate domains, and Val^r maps pair of those that assume values in $\mathbb{Z}$ to a subset of $\{<, =, >\}$.
- private is a predicate on indices.

We define a satisfaction relation between thread-abstracted and symbolic configurations. A *symbolic representation* Ψ is a set of symbolic configurations. A set of thread-abstracted configurations then satisfies a symbolic representation Ψ if each of its thread-abstracted configuration satisfies some symbolic configuration in Ψ.

Symbolic Postcondition Computation. It remains to define a symbolic post operation $\mathtt{Post}^{symb}$ on symbolic representations that reflects $\mathtt{Post}^{ta}$ on sets of thread-abstracted configurations. Given a set Ψ of symbolic configurations representing possible views of single threads, it first generates all ways of merging them to symbolic representations of combined views of k threads; thereafter computing their postconditions wrp. to the next statement in each thread; and finally projecting the results onto each of the k participating threads. As follows from Lemmas 1 and 2, it is sufficient to consider only bounded values of k, and indeed $k = 2$ is sufficient for all examples that we considered.

8   Experimental Results

Based on our framework, we have implemented a tool in OCaml, and used it for verifying 19 concurrent algorithms (both lock-based and lock-free) including two

Algorithms	Time (s)	Algorithms	Time (s)
MS two-lock queue [21]	0.32	Treiber stack [27]	0.18
MS lock-free queue [21]	21.07	HSY stack [14] ✓	83.89
Elimination queue [23] ✓	105.56	DGLM queue [9]	16.99
Vechev-CAS set [34] ✓	24.01	Optimistic set [16]	60.43
Vechev-DCAS set [34]	16.02	Lazy set [13] ✓	289
Harris lock-free set [11]	1512	O'Hearn set [24] ✓	12.01
Michael lock-free set [22]	110	HM lock-free set [16] ✓	462.01
Pessimistic set [16]	1.51	CCAS [12] ✓	0.04
Unordered set [35] ✓	2301	RDCSS [12] ✓	0.26

(a)

Algorithms	Time (s)	Algorithms	Time (s)
MS two-lock queue [21]	1.80	Treiber stack [27]	140.03
MS lock-free queue [21]	287	DGLM queue [9]	500
		HW queue [17]	6.99

(b)

Fig. 6. Experimental Results for verifying concurrent programs

stacks, five queues, nine ordered sets, one unordered set and two CAS algorithms. The user needs to provide the program code and the set of controllers. The experiments were performed on a desktop 2.8 GHz processor with 8 GB memory. The results are presented in Fig. 6, where running times are given in seconds. Figure 6(a) provides the verification results for all algorithms except for HW queue with provided linearization policies, using the technique of controllers introduced in the paper. Figure 6(b) provides the verification results for queues and stack without LP placement, using the technique adapted from [4,15]. All experiments start from the initial heap, and end either when the analysis reaches the fixed point or when a violation of linearizability is detected.

Helping. The algorithms marked by ✓ use helping. We run some of the algorithms with two different helping patterns (such as the ones described in Sect. 3), and report the execution time for each.

Arrays. Our tool does not currently support arrays, and hence we have transformed arrays to singly-linked lists in the algorithms that use the former.

Safety Properties. Our tool is also capable of verifying memory related safety properties such as the absence of null pointer dereferencing, dangling pointers, double-freeing, cycles, and dereferencing of freed nodes, as well as sortedness. In fact, for each algorithm, the time reported in Fig. 6 is the sum of the times taken to show linearizability and all the properties mentioned above.

Running Times. As can be seen from the table, the running times vary in the different examples. This is due to the types of shapes that are produced during the analysis. For instance, the CCAS, RDCSS, stack and queue algorithms without an elimination produce simple shape patterns and hence they have shorter running times. Several features may make shapes more complex, such as insertion/removal of elements in the middle of a list in the ordered set algorithms, and having two linked lists (instead of one) in the elimination queue and stack algorithms. Also, the unordered set algorithm generates complex shapes since it allows physically removed elements to re-appear in the set.

Error Detection. In addition to establishing correctness of the original versions of the benchmark algorithms, we tested our tool with intentionally inserted bugs. For example, we emitted broadcast messages in the controllers or inserted bugs into the codes of algorithms. In all cases, the tool, as expected, successfully detected and reported the bug. In the Lazy Set algorithm, when we emitted rule ρ_7 in Fig. 3, the tool reported an error. As another example, when we removed the statement in line 4 of the add method in the Lazy Set algorithm, the tool also reported an error.

9 Conclusions

We have presented a uniform framework for automatically verifying linearizability of singly-linked list-based concurrent implementations of sets, stacks, and queues, annotated with linearization policies. Our contributions include a novel formalism for specifying linearization policies with non-fixed LPs, an extension of thread-modular reasoning, and an extension of existing symbolic representations of unbounded singly-linked-list structures containing data from an unbounded domain. We have verified all linearizable singly-linked list-based implementations known to us in the literature. In the future, we intend to extend the framework to more complex data structures.

Acknowledgments. We thank the reviewers for helpful comments. This work was supported in part by the Swedish Foundation for Strategic Research within the ProFuN project, and by the Swedish Research Council within the UPMARC centre of excellence.

References

1. Abdulla, P.A., Haziza, F., Holík, L., Jonsson, B., Rezine, A.: An integrated specification and verification technique for highly concurrent data structures. In: Piterman, N., Smolka, S.A. (eds.) TACAS 2013 (ETAPS 2013). LNCS, vol. 7795, pp. 324–338. Springer, Heidelberg (2013)
2. Amit, D., Rinetzky, N., Reps, T., Sagiv, M., Yahav, E.: Comparison under abstraction for verifying linearizability. In: Damm, W., Hermanns, H. (eds.) CAV 2007. LNCS, vol. 4590, pp. 477–490. Springer, Heidelberg (2007)
3. Berdine, J., Lev-Ami, T., Manevich, R., Ramalingam, G., Sagiv, M.: Thread quantification for concurrent shape analysis. In: Gupta, A., Malik, S. (eds.) CAV 2008. LNCS, vol. 5123, pp. 399–413. Springer, Heidelberg (2008)

4. Guha, S., Indyk, P., Muthukrishnan, S.M., Strauss, M.J.: On reducing linearizability to state reachability. In: Widmayer, P., Triguero, F., Morales, R., Hennessy, M., Eidenbenz, S., Conejo, R. (eds.) ICALP 2002. LNCS, vol. 2380, pp. 95–107. Springer, Heidelberg (2002)
5. Bouajjani, A., Emmi, M., Enea, C., Hamza, J.: Verifying concurrent programs against sequential specifications. In: Felleisen, M., Gardner, P. (eds.) ESOP 2013. LNCS, vol. 7792, pp. 290–309. Springer, Heidelberg (2013)
6. Colvin, R., Groves, L., Luchangco, V., Moir, M.: Formal verification of a lazy concurrent list-based set algorithm. In: Ball, T., Jones, R.B. (eds.) CAV 2006. LNCS, vol. 4144, pp. 475–488. Springer, Heidelberg (2006)
7. Derrick, J., Dongol, B., Schellhorn, G., Tofan, B., Travkin, O., Wehrheim, H.: Quiescent consistency: defining and verifying relaxed linearizability. In: Jones, C., Pihlajasaari, P., Sun, J. (eds.) FM 2014. LNCS, vol. 8442, pp. 200–214. Springer, Heidelberg (2014)
8. Doherty, S., Detlefs, D., Groves, L., Flood, C., Luchangco, V., Martin, P., Moir, M., Shavit, N., Steele Jr., G.: DCAS is not a silver bullet for nonblocking algorithm design. In: SPAA 2004, pp. 216–224. ACM (2004)
9. Doherty, S., Groves, L., Luchangco, V., Moir, M.: Formal verification of a practical lock-free queue algorithm. In: de Frutos-Escrig, D., Núñez, M. (eds.) FORTE 2004. LNCS, vol. 3235, pp. 97–114. Springer, Heidelberg (2004)
10. Drăgoi, C., Gupta, A., Henzinger, T.A.: Automatic linearizability proofs of concurrent objects with cooperating updates. In: Sharygina, N., Veith, H. (eds.) CAV 2013. LNCS, vol. 8044, pp. 174–190. Springer, Heidelberg (2013)
11. Harris, T.L.: A pragmatic implementation of non-blocking linked-lists. In: Welch, J.L. (ed.) DISC 2001. LNCS, vol. 2180, pp. 300–314. Springer, Heidelberg (2001)
12. Harris, T.L., Fraser, K., Pratt, I.A.: A practical multi-word compare-and-swap operation. In: Malkhi, D. (ed.) DISC 2002. LNCS, vol. 2508, pp. 265–279. Springer, Heidelberg (2002)
13. Heller, S., Herlihy, M.P., Luchangco, V., Moir, M., Scherer III, W.N., Shavit, N.N.: A lazy concurrent list-based set algorithm. In: Anderson, J.H., Prencipe, G., Wattenhofer, R. (eds.) OPODIS 2005. LNCS, vol. 3974, pp. 3–16. Springer, Heidelberg (2006)
14. Hendler, D., Shavit, N., Yerushalmi, L.: A scalable lock-free stack algorithm. J. Parallel Distrib. Comput. **70**(1), 1–12 (2010)
15. Henzinger, T.A., Sezgin, A., Vafeiadis, V.: Aspect-oriented linearizability proofs. In: D'Argenio, P.R., Melgratti, H. (eds.) CONCUR 2013 – Concurrency Theory. LNCS, vol. 8052, pp. 242–256. Springer, Heidelberg (2013)
16. Herlihy, M., Shavit, N.: The Art of Multiprocessor Programming. Morgan Kaufmann, San Francisco (2008)
17. Herlihy, M., Wing, J.M.: Linearizability: a correctness condition for concurrent objects. ACM Trans. Program. Lang. Syst. **12**(3), 463–492 (1990)
18. Liang, H., Feng, X.: Modular verification of linearizability with non-fixed linearization points. In: PLDI, pp. 459–470. ACM (2013)
19. Manevich, R., Yahav, E., Ramalingam, G., Sagiv, M.: Predicate abstraction and canonical abstraction for singly-linked lists. In: Cousot, R. (ed.) VMCAI 2005. LNCS, vol. 3385, pp. 181–198. Springer, Heidelberg (2005)
20. Michael, M., Scott, M.: Correction of a memory management method for lock-free data structures. Technical Report TR599, University of Rochester, Rochester, NY, USA (1995)
21. Michael, M., Scott, M.: Simple, fast, and practical non-blocking and blocking concurrent queue algorithms. In: PODC, pp. 267–275 (1996)

22. Michael, M.M.: High performance dynamic lock-free hash tables and list-based sets. In: SPAA, pp. 73–82 (2002)
23. Moir, M., Nussbaum, D., Shalev, O., Shavit, N.: Using elimination to implement scalable and lock-free FIFO queues. In: SPAA, pp. 253–262 (2005)
24. O'Hearn, P.W., Rinetzky, N., Vechev, M.T., Yahav, E., Yorsh, G.: Verifying linearizability with hindsight. In: PODC, pp. 85–94 (2010)
25. Schellhorn, G., Derrick, J., Wehrheim, H.: A sound, complete proof technique for linearizability of concurrent data structures. ACM Trans. Comput. Log. 15(4), 31:1–31:37 (2014)
26. Schellhorn, G., Wehrheim, H., Derrick, J.: How to prove algorithms linearisable. In: Madhusudan, P., Seshia, S.A. (eds.) CAV 2012. LNCS, vol. 7358, pp. 243–259. Springer, Heidelberg (2012)
27. Treiber, R.: Systems programming: Coping with parallelism. Technical Report RJ5118, IBM Almaden Res. Ctr. (1986)
28. Turon, A.J., Thamsborg, J., Ahmed, A., Birkedal, L., Dreyer, D.: Logical relations for fine-grained concurrency. In: POPL 2013, pp. 343–356 (2013)
29. Vafeiadis, V.: Modular fine-grained concurrency verification. PhD thesis, University of Cambridge (2008)
30. Vafeiadis, V.: Shape-value abstraction for verifying linearizability. In: Jones, N.D., Müller-Olm, M. (eds.) VMCAI 2009. LNCS, vol. 5403, pp. 335–348. Springer, Heidelberg (2009)
31. Vafeiadis, V.: Automatically proving linearizability. In: Touili, T., Cook, B., Jackson, P. (eds.) CAV 2010. LNCS, vol. 6174, pp. 450–464. Springer, Heidelberg (2010)
32. Černý, P., Radhakrishna, A., Zufferey, D., Chaudhuri, S., Alur, R.: Model checking of linearizability of concurrent list implementations. In: Touili, T., Cook, B., Jackson, P. (eds.) CAV 2010. LNCS, vol. 6174, pp. 465–479. Springer, Heidelberg (2010)
33. Vechev, M., Yahav, E., Yorsh, G.: Experience with model checking linearizability. In: Păsăreanu, C.S. (ed.) Model Checking Software. LNCS, vol. 5578, pp. 261–278. Springer, Heidelberg (2009)
34. Vechev, M.T., Yahav, E.: Deriving linearizable fine-grained concurrent objects. In: PLDI, pp. 125–135 (2008)
35. Zhang, K., Zhao, Y., Yang, Y., Liu, Y., Spear, M.: Practical non-blocking unordered lists. In: Afek, Y. (ed.) DISC 2013. LNCS, vol. 8205, pp. 239–253. Springer, Heidelberg (2013)
36. Zhu, H., Petri, G., Jagannathan, S.: Poling: SMT aided linearizability proofs. In: Kroening, D., Păsăreanu, C.S. (eds.) CAV 2015. LNCS, vol. 9207, pp. 3–19. Springer, Heidelberg (2015)

Structure-Sensitive Points-To Analysis
for C and C++

George Balatsouras[✉] and Yannis Smaragdakis

Department of Informatics, University of Athens, 15784 Athens, Greece
{gbalats,smaragd}@di.uoa.gr

Abstract. We present a points-to analysis for C/C++ that recovers much of the available high-level structure information of types and objects, by applying two key techniques: (1) It records the type of each abstract object and, in cases when the type is not readily available, the analysis uses an *allocation-site plus type* abstraction to create multiple abstract objects per allocation site, so that each one is associated with a single type. (2) It creates separate abstract objects that represent (a) the fields of objects of either struct or class type, and (b) the (statically present) constant indices of arrays, resulting in a limited form of array-sensitivity.

We apply our approach to the full LLVM bitcode intermediate language and show that it yields much higher precision than past analyses, allowing accurate distinctions between subobjects, v-table entries, array components, and more. Especially for C++ programs, this precision is invaluable for a realistic analysis. Compared to the state-of-the-art past approach, our techniques exhibit substantially better precision along multiple metrics and realistic benchmarks (e.g., 40+% more variables with a single points-to target).

1 Introduction

Points-to analysis computes an abstract model of the memory that is used to answer the following query: *What can a pointer variable point-to, i.e., what can its value be when dereferenced during program execution?* This query serves as the cornerstone of many other static analyses aiming to enhance program understanding or assist in bug discovery (e.g., deadlock detection), by computing higher-level relations that derive from the computed points-to sets. In the literature, one can find a multitude of points-to analyses with varying degrees of precision and speed.

One of the most popular families of pointer analysis algorithms, *inclusion-based* analyses (or Andersen-style analyses [1]), originally targeted the C language, but has been extended over time and successfully applied to higher-level object-oriented languages, such as Java [3,4,17,22,24]. Surprisingly, precision-enhancing features that are common practice in the analysis of Java programs, such as field-sensitivity or online call-graph construction are absent in many analyses of C/C++ [5,7,8,11,12,25].

© Springer-Verlag GmbH Germany 2016
X. Rival (Ed.): SAS 2016, LNCS 9837, pp. 84–104, 2016.
DOI: 10.1007/978-3-662-53413-7_5

In the case of field-sensitivity, the reason behind its frequent omission when analyzing C is that it is much harder to implement correctly than in Java. As noted by Pearce et al. [21], the crucial difference is that, in C/C++, it is possible to have the address of a field taken, stored to some pointer, and then dereferenced later, at an arbitrarily distant program point. In contrast, Java does not permit taking the address of a field; one can only load or store to some field directly. Hence, `load/store` instructions in Java bytecode (or any equivalent IR) need an extra field specifier, whereas in C/C++ intermediate representations (e.g., LLVM bitcode) `load/store` requires only a single address operand. The precise field affected is not explicit, but only possibly computed by the analysis itself.

The effect of such difference in the underlying IRs, as far as pointer analysis is concerned, is far from trivial. In C, the computed points-to sets have an expanded domain, since now the analysis must be able to express that a variable p *at some offset* i may point-to another variable q *at some offset* j, with these offsets corresponding to either field components or array elements.

The best-documented approach on how to incorporate field-sensitivity in a C/C++ points-to analysis is that of Pearce et al. [20,21]. The authors extend the constraint-graph of the analysis by adding (positive) weights to edges; the weights correspond to the respective field indices. For instance, the instruction "`q = &(p->f`$_i$`)`" would be encoded as a constraint $q \supseteq p + i$. However, this approach does not take types into account. In fact, types are not even statically available at all allocation sites, since most standard C allocation routines are type-agnostic and return byte arrays that are cast to the correct type at a later point (e.g., `malloc()`, `realloc()`, `calloc()`). Thus, field i is represented with no regard to the type of its base object, even when this base object abstracts a number of concrete objects of different types. As we shall see, the lack of type information for abstract objects is a great source of imprecision, since it results in a prohibitive number of spurious points-to inferences.

We argue that type information is an essential part in increasing analysis precision, even when it is not readily available. The abstract object types should be rigorously recorded in all cases, especially when indexing fields, and used to filter the points-to sets. In this spirit, we present a *structure-sensitive* analysis for C/C++ that employs a number of techniques in this direction, aiming to retrieve high-level structure information for abstract objects in order to increase analysis precision:

1. First, the analysis records the type of an abstract object when this type is available at the allocation site. This is the case with stack allocations, global variables, and calls to C++'s `new()` heap allocation routine.
2. In cases where the type is not available (as in a call to `malloc()`), the analysis deviates from the allocation-site abstraction and creates multiple abstract objects per allocation site: one for every type that the object could have. Thus, each abstract object of type T now represents the set of all concrete objects of type T allocated at this site. To determine the possible types for a given allocation site, the analysis creates a special type-less object and records the cast instructions it flows to (i.e., the types it is cast to), using the existing

points-to analysis. This is similar to the use-based *back-propagation* technique used in past work [15,16,23], in a completely different context—handling Java reflection.

3. The field components of abstract objects are represented as abstract objects themselves, as long as their type can be determined. That is, an abstract object S0 of struct type S will trigger the creation of abstract object S0.f_i, for each field f_i in S. (The aforementioned special objects trigger no such field component creation, since they are typeless.) Thus, the recursive creation of subobjects is bounded by the type system, which does not allow the declaration of types of infinite size.

4. Finally, the analysis treats array elements similarly to field components (i.e., by representing them as distinct abstract objects, if we can determine their type), as long as their respective indices statically appear in the source code. That is, an abstract object A0 of array type [T×N] will trigger the creation of abstract object A0[c], if the constant c is used to index into type [T×N]. The object A0[*] is also created, to account for indexing at unknown (variable) indices.

As we shall see, the last point offers some form of array-sensitivity as well and is crucial for analyzing C++ code, lowered to an intermediate representation such as LLVM bitcode, in which all the object-oriented features have been translated away. To be able to resolve virtual calls, an analysis must precisely reason about the exact v-table index that a variable may point to, and the method that such an index may itself point-to. That is, a precise analysis should not merge the points-to sets of distinct indices of v-tables.

In summary, our work makes the following contributions:

– It presents a structure-sensitive pointer analysis that employs key techniques, essential in retrieving high-level structure information of heap objects, thus significantly increasing the precision of the analysis.
– The analysis is implemented and evaluated in cclyzer[1], a new pointer analysis framework that operates on LLVM Bitcode. The pointer analysis is expressed in a fully declarative manner, using Datalog.
– We evaluate the precision of our structure-sensitive analysis by comparing to a re-implementation of the Pearce et al. [20,21] analysis, also operating over the full LLVM bitcode language. We show that our techniques provide a major precision enhancement for realistic programs.

2   Background and Motivation

We next discuss essential aspects of precise pointer analysis for C and C++, as well as the key features of the LLVM bitcode intermediate language.

---

[1] cclyzer is publicly available at https://github.com/plast-lab/cclyzer.

2.1 C/C++ Intricacies and Issues

Research on pointer analysis in the last decade has shifted much of its focus from the low-level C language to higher-level object-oriented (OO) languages, such as Java [3,4,17,22,24]. To a large extent, the industry's paradigm shift to object oriented programming and Java's rising popularity naturally ignited a similar interest shift in the research community.

In points-to analysis, however, one could argue that object-oriented languages in general, and Java, in particular, are better targets than C, for a number of reasons. First, the points-to abstraction [6] is more suited to OO programming, where dynamic object allocations are more common. Furthermore, Java offers a clear distinction: only variable *references* are allocated on the stack, whereas the allocated objects themselves are stored on the heap. Also, class fields can only contain references to other objects, not entire subobjects. Thus, variables point to (heap) objects and objects can only point to each other through their fields. This leads to a clear memory abstraction as well, where objects are commonly represented by their allocation site. A points-to analysis in Java has to compute two sets of edges: (i) a set of unlabeled edges from variables to abstract heap objects, and (ii) a set of field-labeled edges between abstract objects.

This is not the case for C/C++, where:

1. Objects can be allocated both on the stack and on the heap.
2. An object can contain another *subobject* as a field component. In fact, a field may even contain a fixed-size array of subobjects.
3. Any such subobject can have its address taken and stored to some variable, which can be dereferenced later (as can any normal pointer variable) to return the subobject's exact address (i.e., the address of the base object plus the relative byte offset of the given subobject).

Figure 1 illustrates the above points. The `Outer` struct type contains a 3-element array of `Inner` subobjects via its field `in`. Unlike in Java, all these subobjects are stored inside the `Outer` instance's allocation; no dereference is needed to access them. On Fig. 1b, variable `ptr` will hold the address of some subobject of variable (or stack-allocated object) `obj` of the `Outer` type. Variable `ptr` is then used later to store to this field of `obj`. (Note that the two instructions, the store instruction at line 4 and the instruction that returns the field address at line 3, can even reside in different functions.) In a precise analysis, this should establish that the `in[1].x` field of abstract object $\widehat{o_1}$ (representing the stack allocation for `obj` at line 1), may point to abstract object $\widehat{o_2}$ (representing the heap allocation of line 2).

In contrast, a *field-insensitive* approach (which is common among C/C++ analyses [5,7,8,11,12,25]) is to not record offsets at all. This affords simplicity, at the expense of significant loss of precision. A field-insensitive analysis would disregard any offsets of any field or array accesses it encounters and simply compute that $\widehat{o_1}$ points-to (somewhere inside) $\widehat{o_2}$. Any subsequent instruction that accesses *any* field of $\widehat{o_1}$ would have to consider $\widehat{o_2}$ as a possible target. In the case of line 5, the field-insensitive analysis would (over-)conservatively infer that variable `q` may point to $\widehat{o_2}$.

```
1   typedef struct Inner {
2       int **x;
3       int *y;
4   } Inner;
5
6   typedef struct Outer {
7       void *x;
8       Inner in[3];
9   } Outer;
```

(a) Nested struct declaration

```
1   Outer obj;              // alloc: ô₁
2   int *g = malloc(...); // alloc: ô₂
3   int ***ptr = &(obj.in[1].x); ...
4   *ptr = &g;
5   void *q = obj.x;
```

(b) Complex Field Access

```
1   Inner i;
2   Inner *ip = &i;
3   ip = (Inner *) &ip->y;
```

(c) Positive Weight Cycles

Fig. 1. C example with nested struct types

The line of work by Pearce et al. [20,21] introduces a form of *field-sensitivity*, such that the analysis differentiates between different fields of an object by representing them with distinct symbolic offsets. For instance, the i-th field of p is encoded as $p + i$. Thus, the effect of an *address-of-field* instruction such as "q = &(p->f$_i$)" — f$_i$ being the name of the i-th field of p — would add the edge (p, q) labeled with i to a constraint graph, to encode that $q \supseteq p + i$: the points-to set of variable q is a superset of that of the i-th field of any object pointed-to by p.

There are several issues with this approach:

1. First, it is not clear how the approach generalizes to nested structures, as in Fig. 1a. Had a heap allocation $\hat{o}$ (of unknown type) flowed to the points-to set of variable p, how could an expression like $p + i$ differentiate between the i-th field of $\hat{o}$ and the i-th field of $\hat{o}$'s first subobject? (Note that the two fields could be of entirely incompatible types.)
2. As Pearce et al. note, imprecision in the analysis may introduce positive weight cycles that lead to infinite derivations, if no other action is taken. For instance, in Fig. 1c:
   i. Due to the instruction "ip = &i;", the points-to set of ip should include at least i: $ip \supseteq \{i\}$.
   ii. Due to instruction "ip = (Inner *) &ip->y;", the corresponding constraint, $ip \supseteq ip + 1$, would induce: $ip \supseteq \{i, i.y, i.y.y, i.y.y.y, \ldots\}$. Of course, an object like $i.y.y$ would make no sense given that no such field exists.

As a way to overcome this, Pearce et al. assign unique indices to all (local) program variables and their fields, and also record their symbolic ranges (that is, the index where the enclosing lexical scope of each variable ends). Then, they ensure that field accesses only reference memory locations within the same enclosing scope. However, this does not prohibit all redundant derivations: $ip + 1$ may still add to the points-to set irrelevant variables or fields that happen to be in the same enclosing scope.

Also, this does not work well for heap allocations, since their type, and hence the number of their fields, is unknown. Instead, they are assumed to define as many fields as the largest struct in the program, which will also lead to many redundant derivations.

3. This approach greatly decreases the analysis precision in the presence of factory methods or wrapper functions for allocation routines. Consider the xmalloc() function of *GNU Coreutils* in Fig. 2, which is consistently used instead of malloc() to check if the allocation succeeded and abort the program otherwise. The allocation site it contains will represent the union of all struct types, dynamically allocated via xmalloc(), by the same abstract object. The *i*-th field of this abstract object will then represent the *i*-th field of this union type, losing essential type information by merging unrelated fields (whose types we statically know to be completely different).

```
1  /* Allocate N bytes of memory dynamically, with error checking. */
2  void * xmalloc (size_t n) {
3      void *p = malloc (n);
4      if (!p && n != 0) xalloc_die ();
5      return p;
6  }
```

Fig. 2. Generic malloc() wrapper with error checking that aborts the program when allocation fails

The common denominator of all these limitations is that they lose any association between abstract objects and their types, due to cases in which type information is not readily available (as in heap allocations). What we propose instead is that the analysis strictly record types for all abstract objects (any abstract object must have a *single* type) and use this type information to filter redundant derivations that arise from analysis imprecision. For heap allocations specifically, where a single allocation site could be used to allocate objects of many different types, we propose a deviation from the standard allocation-site abstraction that creates multiple abstract objects per allocation site (one for each different type allocated there).

2.2   The LLVM IR

Our analysis targets C/C++ programs translated to LLVM bitcode. LLVM bitcode is a low-level intermediate representation, similar to an abstract assembly language, and forms the core of the LLVM umbrella project. It defines an extensive *strongly-typed* RISC instruction set, and has the following distinguishing features:

– Instead of a fixed set of registers, it uses an infinite set of temporaries, called *virtual registers*. At the register allocation phase, some of the virtual registers

will be replaced by physical registers while the rest will be spilled to memory. All virtual registers are kept in SSA form.
– Program variables are divided into two categories:
i. variables whose address is taken and can be referenced by pointers
ii. variables that can never be referenced by pointers.
The latter are converted to SSA, whereas the former are kept in memory by using: (i) `alloca` instructions to allocate the required space on stack, and (ii) load/store instructions to access or update, respectively, the variable contents, at any point (hence escaping SSA form). This technique has been termed "partial SSA" [10].
– Like address-taken variables, global variables are also kept in memory and are always represented by a pointer to their "content" type. However, their space is allocated using a global initializer instead of an `alloca` instruction.

The example of Fig. 3 illustrates these points regarding the LLVM translation. Figure 3a shows the original source code, while Fig. 3b shows the corresponding LLVM bitcode. Local variable p is stored in memory (since its address is taken) and virtual register %p holds its address. %p's value can be updated multiple times, using `store` instructions. Likewise, global variable gv (of type `int*`) is also kept in memory and pointer @gv (of type `int**`) is used to access it. As will be clear later, our analysis follows the variable representation conventions of LLVM and decouples memory allocations from virtual registers (or global variable references). Figure 3c depicts the relevant points-to relationships, which capture that gv points to p. Dashed edges are used to represent *variable points-to edges* (whose source is a virtual register), while solid edges are *dereference edges* between abstract objects.

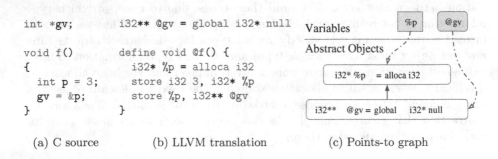

(a) C source   (b) LLVM translation   (c) Points-to graph

Fig. 3. Partial SSA example

3 Approach

Our analysis approach adds more detail to object abstractions, which serve both as sources and as targets of points-to edges, allowing a more detailed representation of the heap. Although our approach is applicable to C/C++ analysis in general, it is best to see it in conjunction with the LLVM bitcode intermediate language. Just as LLVM bitcode is a strongly-typed intermediate language, we assign types and offsets to every abstract object value and its points-to relationships. The challenge is that, unlike in the LLVM bitcode type system, such information is not readily available by local inspection of the code—it needs to be propagated by the analysis reasoning itself.

We next discuss the various abstractions of our analysis, in representing its input and output relations. Then, we express the main aspects of our analysis as a set of inference rules.

3.1 Abstractions

Figure 4 presents the input and output domains of our analysis. We represent functions as a subset of global entities. Thus, G contains all symbols referencing global entities—everything starting with symbol "@" in LLVM bitcode. Set V holds temporaries only (i.e., virtual registers), and not global variables. We represent the union of these two sets with P, which stands for *pointer variables* (i.e., any entity whose value may hold some memory address). Our analysis only introduces the set of abstract objects O, that correspond to memory locations.

T	set of program types
L	set of instruction labels
C	program (integer) constants
V	set of virtual registers
G	set of global variables
$F \subseteq G$	program functions
$P = V \cup G$	pointer variables
O	set of abstract objects

Fig. 4. Analysis domains

The LLVM IR defines an extensive instruction set. However, only a small subset is relevant for the purposes of pointer analysis. Figure 5 presents a simplified version of these relevant instructions. The first two instructions are used to allocate memory on the stack and on the heap, respectively. As previously discussed, `alloca` instructions are used for address-taken variables. They accept an extra type argument (absent in `malloc` instructions), which specifies the exact type of the allocation (virtual registers are strongly typed), and the allocation size is a constant. Next, we have `cast` instructions, used solely to satisfy LLVM's type checker since they do not change any memory contents, and `phi` instructions that choose a value depending on the instruction's predecessor. Apart from the standard `load`/`store` instructions, we have two more instructions that, given a memory address operand, return a new address by adding a relative offset that corresponds to either a field or an array element. (Only `load` instructions

LLVM Instruction	Operand Types	Description
$p = \texttt{alloca T}, nbytes$	$V \times T \times C$	Stack Allocations
$p = \texttt{malloc } nbytes$	$V \times (V \cup C)$	Heap Allocations
$p = (\texttt{T}) \, q$	$V \times T \times (P \cup C)$	(No-op) Casts
$p = \texttt{phi}(l_1 : a_1, l_2 : a_2)$	$V \times (L \mapsto (P \cup C))^2$	SSA Phi Node
$p = *q$	$V \times P$	Load from Address
$*p = q$	$P \times (P \cup C)$	Store to Address
$p = \texttt{\&q->}f$	$V \times P \times C$	Address-of-field
$p = \texttt{\&q}\,[idx]$	$V \times P \times (V \cup C)$	Address-of-array-index
$p = a_0(a_1, a_2, \ldots, a_n)$	$V \times (F \cup V) \times (P \cup C)^n$	Function Call
$\texttt{return p}$	$P \cup C$	Function Return

Fig. 5. LLVM IR instruction set. We also prepend a label $l \in L$ to each instruction (that we omit in this figure). Each such label can be used to uniquely identify its instruction.

dereference memory, however.) Finally, we have call and return instructions. Call instructions may also accept a variable (function pointer), as their first argument.

Abstract Objects. Our analysis defines several different kinds of abstract objects that express the exact nature of the allocation. Any abstract object must fall into one of the following categories:

- $\widehat{o_i}$ A stack or heap allocation for instruction (allocation site) $i \in L$.
- $\widehat{o_{i,\texttt{T}}}$ A (heap) allocation for instruction $i \in L$, specialized for type $\texttt{T} \in T$.
- $\widehat{o_g}$ A global allocation for global variable or function $g \in G$.
- $\widehat{o.fld}$ A field subobject that corresponds to field "fld" of base object $\widehat{o} \in O$.
- $\widehat{o[c]}$ An array subobject that corresponds to the element at constant index $c \in C$ of base object $\widehat{o} \in O$.
- $\widehat{o[*]}$ An array subobject that corresponds to any elements at unknown indices of base object $\widehat{o} \in O$.

When not using any special notation, we shall refer to a generic abstract object that could be of any of the above forms.

By representing field and array subobjects as separate abstract objects themselves, the handling of instructions that return addresses anywhere but at the beginning of some allocation becomes straightforward. As we shall see at Sect. 3.2, all our analysis has to do is return the relevant abstract object that represents the given subobject of its base allocation. This abstract subobject will have its own distinct points-to set, which will be tracked separately from that of its base allocation or any of the rest of its fields. Thus, it will allow the analysis to retain a certain degree of precision that would be otherwise impossible.

Our analysis computes four main relations:

Variable points-to edges. Edge $p \mapsto \widehat{o} \in P \times O$ records that pointer variable (either virtual register or global variable) p may point to abstract object $\widehat{o}$. Note that virtual registers that correspond to source variables will always point to a single object: the corresponding stack allocation. Temporaries introduced by LLVM bitcode, though, may point to many abstract objects.

Dereference edges. Edge $\widehat{po} \rightsquigarrow \widehat{o} \in O \times O$ records that abstract object $\widehat{po}$ may point to abstract object $\widehat{o}$. Any object that has a non-empty points-to set (i.e., the object has outgoing dereference edges) may represent a pointer. Dereference edges can only be established by `store` instructions.

Abstract object types. The partial function $type : O \rightharpoonup T$ records the type of an abstract object. An abstract object can be associated with one type at most, or none at all. Since our analysis uses types to filter redundant derivations, the more types it establishes for abstract objects, the more points-to edges it will compute.

Call-graph edges. Edge $i \xrightarrow{calls} f \in L \times F$ records that invocation site i may call function f. This also accounts for indirect calls that use function pointers.

3.2 Techniques - Rules

Figure 6 presents the main aspects of the analysis as a set of inference rules. The first two rules handle stack and heap allocation instructions. All they do is create a new abstract object representing the given allocation site, and assign it to the target variable. In the case of stack allocation, we also record the type of the object, since it is available at the allocation site. The next pair of rules handle global allocations for global variables and functions, respectively, in a similar way. In contrast to the previous rules, we create abstract objects for all global entities, regardless of any instructions (since their allocation in LLVM bitcode is implicit), and record their types.

For cast instructions, we copy any object that flows in the points-to set of the source variable to the points-to set of the target variable. Phi instructions are treated similarly, but we have to consider both of the instruction's operands, regardless of their corresponding labels, since our result must be an over-approximation.

Store instructions are the only way in which the analysis establishes dereference edges. For a store instruction, $*p = q$, we have to perform the following:

1. First, find the corresponding abstract objects that the two instruction operands point to, by following their outgoing variable points-to edges. Namely: (i) the memory allocation of the value to be stored (abstract object $\widehat{o}$), and (ii) the memory allocation that $\widehat{o}$ is going to be stored into (abstract object $\widehat{po}$).
2. Then, establish a dereference edge between any two such abstract objects returned, expressing that object $\widehat{po}$ may point to object $\widehat{o}$.

$$\text{STACK} \quad \frac{i: \; \mathtt{p} = \mathtt{alloca} \; \mathtt{T}, \, nbytes}{\mathtt{p} \mapsto \widehat{o_i} \qquad type(\widehat{o_i}) = \mathtt{T}} \qquad \text{HEAP} \quad \frac{i: \; \mathtt{p} = \mathtt{malloc} \; nbytes}{\mathtt{p} \mapsto \widehat{o_i}}$$

$$\text{GLOBAL} \quad \frac{f \in F}{f \mapsto \widehat{o_f} \qquad type(\widehat{o_f}) = type(f)} \qquad \frac{\mathtt{g} \in (G \setminus F)}{\mathtt{g} \mapsto \widehat{o_g} \qquad type(\widehat{o_g}) = type(\mathtt{g})}$$

$$\text{CAST} \quad \frac{i: \; \mathtt{p} = (\mathtt{T}) \, \mathtt{q} \qquad \mathtt{q} \mapsto \widehat{o}}{\mathtt{p} \mapsto \widehat{o}} \qquad \text{PHI} \quad \frac{i: \; \mathtt{p} = \mathtt{phi}(l_1 : a_1, \, l_2 : a_2)}{\forall j: \; a_j \mapsto \widehat{o} \Rightarrow \mathtt{p} \mapsto \widehat{o}}$$

$$\text{LOAD} \quad \frac{i: \; \mathtt{p} = {*}\mathtt{q} \qquad \mathtt{q} \mapsto \widehat{po} \qquad \widehat{po} \rightsquigarrow \widehat{o}}{\mathtt{p} \mapsto \widehat{o}} \qquad \text{STORE} \quad \frac{i: \; {*}\mathtt{p} = \mathtt{q} \qquad \mathtt{p} \mapsto \widehat{po} \qquad \mathtt{q} \mapsto \widehat{o}}{\widehat{po} \rightsquigarrow \widehat{o}}$$

$$\text{FIELD} \quad \frac{i: \; \mathtt{p} = \&\mathtt{q}\text{->}f \qquad \mathtt{q} \mapsto \widehat{o} \qquad type(\widehat{o}) = S \qquad type(q) = S}{\mathtt{p} \mapsto \widehat{o.f} \qquad type(\widehat{o.f}) = type(S.f)}$$

$$\text{ARRAY} - \text{CONST} \quad \frac{i: \; \mathtt{p} = \&\mathtt{q} \, [c] \qquad \mathtt{q} \mapsto \widehat{o} \qquad type(\widehat{o}) = [\mathtt{T}] \qquad type(q) = [\mathtt{T}]}{\mathtt{p} \mapsto \widehat{o[c]} \qquad type(\widehat{o[c]}) = \mathtt{T}}$$

$$\text{ARRAY} - \text{VAR} \quad \frac{i: \; \mathtt{p} = \&\mathtt{q} \, [j] \qquad \mathtt{q} \mapsto \widehat{o} \qquad type(\widehat{o}) = [\mathtt{T}] \qquad type(q) = [\mathtt{T}]}{\mathtt{p} \mapsto \widehat{o[*]} \qquad type(\widehat{o[*]}) = \mathtt{T}}$$

$$\text{CALL} \quad \frac{i: \; \mathtt{p} = a_0(a_1, \, a_2, \, \ldots, \, a_n) \qquad a_0 \mapsto \widehat{o_f}}{i \xrightarrow{calls} f(p_1, \, p_2, \, \ldots, \, p_n) \qquad \forall j: \; a_j \mapsto \widehat{o} \Rightarrow p_j \mapsto \widehat{o}}$$

$$\text{RET} \quad \frac{i: \; \mathtt{p} = a_0(\ldots) \qquad i \xrightarrow{calls} f(\ldots) \qquad j: \; \mathtt{return} \; \mathtt{q} \qquad j \in body(f) \qquad \mathtt{q} \mapsto \widehat{o}}{\mathtt{p} \mapsto \widehat{o}}$$

$$\text{HEAP-BP} \quad \frac{i: \; \mathtt{p} = \mathtt{malloc} \; nbytes \qquad j: \; \mathtt{w} = (\mathtt{T}) \, \mathtt{q} \qquad \mathtt{q} \mapsto \widehat{o_i}}{\mathtt{p} \mapsto \widehat{o_{i,\mathtt{T}}} \qquad type(\widehat{o_{i,\mathtt{T}}}) = \mathtt{T}}$$

Fig. 6. Inference rules

The first step simply bypasses the indirection introduced by LLVM bitcode, where operands are represented as virtual registers that point to memory locations. Load instructions perform the opposite operation, and thus are treated symmetrically. For instruction $\mathtt{p} = {*}\mathtt{q}$, we first (i) find the corresponding abstract object that the address operand may point to (abstract object $\widehat{po}$), (ii) then follow any outgoing dereference edge of object $\widehat{po}$ to get any memory location $\widehat{po}$ may point to (object $\widehat{o}$), and finally (iii) establish a new variable points-to edge for target variable $\mathtt{p}$, recording that $\mathtt{p}$ may now also point to object $\widehat{o}$.

The next three rules (FIELD, ARRAY–CONST, ARRAY–VAR) model field-sensitivity. The rule handling field accesses, such as $\mathtt{p} = \&\mathtt{q}\text{->}f$, finds any object $\widehat{o}$ that base variable $\mathtt{q}$ may point to, and returns $\widehat{o}$'s relevant field subobject $\widehat{o.f}$. However, a key element is that $\widehat{o}$ is only considered as a base object if its type matches the declared (struct) type of $\mathtt{g}$ (recall that LLVM bitcode is strongly typed). This precludes any untyped heap allocations as possible base objects. Otherwise, the analysis would end up creating untyped field subobjects too, further fueling imprecision. Thus, we are able to maintain an important invariant of our structure-sensitive analysis: *only create field (or array) subobjects whose types we are able to determine*. Effectively, LLVM bitcode imposes *strong typing on variables*, while our analysis extends the treatment to *abstract objects*.

Array element accesses are treated similarly and they, too, maintain this invariant. However, we distinguish array accesses using a constant index from those using a variable (i.e., unknown) index. In the former case, we return the array subobject $\widehat{o[c]}$, which represents the subobject at index c. In the latter case, we return $\widehat{o[*]}$, which represents the *unknown* index. Essentially, this treatment allows our analysis to track independently the points-to sets of array indices that are statically known to be different, yielding a form of *array-sensitivity*.

Call and return instructions as modeled as assignments: (i) from any actual argument a_j to its respective formal parameter f_j, and (ii) from any returned value q to the target variable of the call instruction p. Like cast instructions, they simply copy the points-to sets from the assignment's source to its target. However, the rule that handles call instructions also records call-graph edges. When the function operand a_0 may point to abstract object o_f, representing function f, we record an edge from the given call site to function f. This handles both direct and indirect calls (i.e., via function pointers).

How to produce type information for unknown objects. Our analysis only allows taking the address of fields of objects whose type is known. This prevents loading and storing from/to fields of objects without types. Such objects can only be used as identity markers. Yet C and C++ allow the creation of untyped objects. Their handling is a key element of the analysis.

The HEAP-BP rule implements the *use-based back-propagation* technique [15, 16, 23], which creates multiple abstract objects per (untyped) allocation site. The rule states that when an (untyped) heap object $\widehat{o}_i$ (allocated at instruction i) flows to some cast instruction j, where it is cast to type T, we augment the points-to set of i's target variable p with a new abstract object $\widehat{o_{i,T}}$, specialized for the given type. The insight behind this rule is that, even when the program performs an allocation via a type-agnostic routine like `malloc()`, the allocation will be later cast to its intended type before being used. By using this technique, the original untyped allocation will be prevented from creating any untyped subobjects, but as soon as the possible type of the allocation is discovered, the new abstract typed object will succeed where the untyped one has failed. Note that instructions i and j could occur in distant parts of the program, as long as the analysis can establish that the object allocated at instruction i flows to j.

This treatment successfully deals with generic allocation wrappers or factory methods. In this case, the wrapped allocation will flow to multiple cast instructions, and thus create multiple typed variations of the original object. However, in each case, only the object with the correct matching type will be used as a base for any subsequent address-of-field instructions. The rest of the objects will be filtered, since they are indeed irrelevant.

3.3 Partial Order of Abstract Objects

As the observant reader may have noticed, the rules of Fig. 6 about accesses or array elements are not sound. Consider the example of Fig. 7. Variable p points to a heap allocation. Three different store instructions take place: (i) one that stores &i to index 1, (ii) one that stores &j to index 3, and (iii) one that stores &k to some variable index. When loading from index 1, the analysis has to return both &i and &k (since the value of variable idx may be equal to 1), but not &j, which is stored to a different index. Conversely, when loading from a variable index, the analysis has to return all three addresses, since the index could be equal to any constant.

```
int i, j, k, idx;
...
int **p = malloc(...);
p[1] = &i;
p[3] = &j;
p[idx] = &k;
int *x = p[1];   // yields { i, k }
int *y = p[2];   // yields { k }
int *z = p[j];   // yields { i, j, k }
```

Fig. 7. Accessing array elements.

Using our array-sensitive approach, we ensure that indices 1, 3, and "*" (unknown) are associated with separate points-to sets that are not merged. To handle loads correctly, though, we have to be able to reason about implicit associations of abstract objects, due to possible index aliases. Thus, we say that object $\widehat{o[*]}$ "generalizes" object $\widehat{o[c]}$ (for the same base object $\widehat{o}$), since loading from $\widehat{o[*]}$ must always return a superset of the objects returned by loading from $\widehat{o[c]}$, for any constant c. This concept extends even to deeply nested subobjects. For instance, an object $o.\widehat{f_1[*][2]}.f_2[*]$ generalizes object $o.\widehat{f_1[4][2]}.f_2[*]$.

We can think of this binary relation between abstract objects as a partial order over domain O and define it appropriately.

Definition 1 *Abstract Object Generalization Order.* An abstract object $\widehat{y} \in O$ *generalizes* an abstract object $\widehat{x}$, denoted $\widehat{x} \sqsubseteq \widehat{y}$, if and only if:

$$\widehat{x} = \widehat{y}$$

$$\vee$$

$$(\widehat{x} = \widehat{p[*]} \vee \widehat{x} = \widehat{p[c]}) \wedge \widehat{y} = \widehat{q[*]} \wedge \widehat{p} \sqsubseteq \widehat{q}$$

$$\vee$$

$$(\widehat{x} = \widehat{p.f} \wedge \widehat{y} = \widehat{q.f} \wedge \widehat{p} \sqsubseteq \widehat{q}) \vee (\widehat{x} = \widehat{p[c]} \wedge \widehat{y} = \widehat{q[c]} \wedge \widehat{p} \sqsubseteq \widehat{q})$$

Intuitively, $\widehat{o_1} \sqsubseteq \widehat{o_2}$ holds when $\widehat{o_1}$ can be turned to $\widehat{o_2}$ by substituting any of its constant array indices with "$*$". Figure 8 gives an example of such ordering. The direction of the edges is from the less to the more general object.

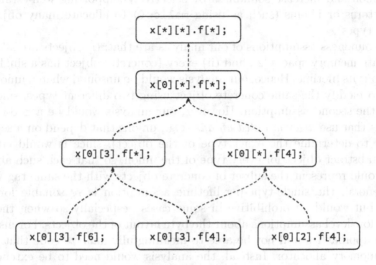

Fig. 8. Abstract object ordering – Example: nodes are abstract objects. An edge $(\widehat{s}, \widehat{t})$ denotes that object $\widehat{s}$ is generalized by object $\widehat{t}$ (i.e., $\widehat{s} \sqsubseteq \widehat{t}$).

Given this partial order, it suffices to add the two rules of Fig. 9 to account for possible index aliases. The first rule states that the points-to set of a (less general) object, such as $\widehat{o[c]}$, is a superset of the points-to set of any object that generalizes it, such as $\widehat{o[*]}$. The second rule modifies the treatment of load instructions, so that they may return anything in the points-to set of not just the object we load from (such as $\widehat{o[*]}$), but also of objects that it generalizes (such as $\widehat{o[c]}$). In this way, the general and specific points-to sets are kept distinct, while their subset relationship is maintained.

$$\textsc{Match} \quad \frac{\widehat{o_1} \sqsubseteq \widehat{o_2} \quad \widehat{o_2} \rightsquigarrow \widehat{o}}{\widehat{o_1} \rightsquigarrow \widehat{o}} \qquad \textsc{Load II} \quad \frac{i : \mathtt{p} = *\mathtt{q} \quad \mathtt{q} \mapsto \widehat{o_2} \quad \widehat{o_1} \sqsubseteq \widehat{o_2} \quad \widehat{o_1} \rightsquigarrow \widehat{o}}{\mathtt{p} \mapsto \widehat{o}}$$

Fig. 9. Associating array subobjects via their partial order.

3.4 Soundness

As stated by Avots et al. [2]: "*A C pointer alias analysis cannot be strictly sound, or else it would conclude that most locations in memory may point to any memory location.*" As in the PCP points-to analysis [2], our approach tries to maintain precision at all times, even if this means that the analysis is not sound in some cases. Instead of trying to be as conservative as possible, we choose to opt for precision and increase soundness by selectively supporting well-established code patterns or idioms (such as using `malloc()` to allocate many objects of different types).

The soundness assumptions of our analysis are that: (i) objects are allocated in separate memory spaces [2], and (ii) every (concrete) object has a single type throughout its lifetime. Hence, our analysis would be unsound when a union type is used to modify the same concrete object using two different types, since this violates the second assumption. However, our analysis would be a good fit for programs that use *discriminated unions* (e.g., unions that depend on a separate *tag* field to determine the exact type of the object), since it would create a different abstract object for every type of the union, so that each such abstract object would represent the subset of concrete objects with the same tag value.

In general, the single-type-per-lifetime assumption is reasonable for most objects, but would be prohibitive in some cases—especially so when the code relies on low-level assumptions about the byte layout of the objects. For instance, our base approach would not be able to meaningfully analyze code that uses a custom memory allocator. Instead, the analysis would need to be extended so that it models calls to the allocator by creating new abstract objects.

Finally, the analysis must be able to discover all associated types for any given object, to retain its soundness. For simplicity, we have only considered cast instructions as places where the analysis discovers new types, but it is easy to supply additional type hints by considering more candidates. For instance, an exception object of unknown type may be allocated and then thrown, by calling the `cxa::throw()` function in the C++ exception handling ABI, without any intervening cast. However, we can use the accompanying *typeinfo* object (always supplied as the second argument to `cxa::throw()`) to recover its true type and hence create a typed abstract exception object. To the best of our knowledge, such special treatment is needed only in rare cases, and the analysis can be easily extended to handle them.

4   Analyzing C++

LLVM bitcode is a representation well-suited for C. However, for OO languages such as C++, high-level features are translated to low-level constructs. A classic example is dynamic dispatch, through virtual methods. Virtual-tables are represented as constant arrays of function pointers, and virtual calls are, in turn, translated to a series of indirect access instructions.

Figure 10a presents (a simplified version of) the LLVM bitcode for such a translation. A virtual call has to (i) load the v-pointer of the class instance (at offset 0), (ii) index into the returned v-table (at the corresponding offset of the function being called), (iii) then load the returned function pointer to get the exact address of the function, and (iv) finally call the function. By employing

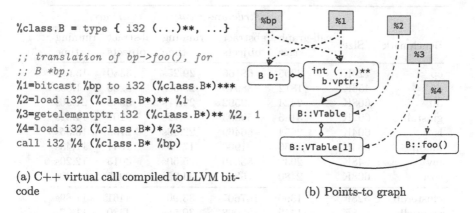

```
%class.B = type { i32 (...)**, ...}

;; translation of bp->foo(), for
;; B *bp;
%1=bitcast %bp to i32 (%class.B*)***
%2=load i32 (%class.B*)** %1
%3=getelementptr i32 (%class.B*)** %2, 1
%4=load i32 (%class.B*)* %3
call i32 %4 (%class.B* %bp)
```

(a) C++ virtual call compiled to LLVM bit-code

(b) Points-to graph

Fig. 10. C++ virtual call example

the techniques we have described so far, our structure-sensitive analysis is well-equipped to deal with such an involved pattern, and precisely resolve the function to be called.

Figure 10b shows what our analysis computes (assuming %bp points to variable b). Only a minor addition is required: anything that points to an object should also point to its first field (at byte offset 0). Hence, both %bp and %1 (after the cast) will point both to (stack-allocated) object $\widehat{b}$, and to its v-pointer field subobject $\widehat{b.vptr}$. The first load instruction will return the v-table. Indexing into the v-table will return the corresponding array element subobject, which will maintain its own independent (singleton) points-to set, due to array-sensitivity. Finally, the second load instruction will return the exact function that the v-table points to, at the given offset.

5 Evaluation

We compare our structure-sensitive analysis to a re-implementation of the Pearce et al. [20,21] analysis in cclyzer, that also operates over the full LLVM bitcode language. We will refer to this analysis as $Pearce^c$. Both analyses were implemented using Datalog, and include many enhancements to deal with various features (such as memcpy instructions, hidden copies of struct instances due to pass-by-value semantics, type compatibility rules, etc.) that arise in practice.

For our benchmark suite, we use the 8 largest programs (in terms of bitcode size) in *GNU Coreutils,*[2] and 14 executables from *PostgreSQL*. We use a 64-bit machine with two octa-core Intel Xeon E5-2667 (v2) CPUs at 3.30 GHz and 256 GB of RAM. The analysis is single-threaded and occupies a small portion of the RAM. We use the LogicBlox Datalog engine (v.3.10.14) and LLVM v.3.7.0.

---

[2] Our original selection included the 10 largest coreutils, but dir and vdir turned out to be identical to ls and are maintained mostly for backwards-compatibility reasons.

Benchmark	Size	call-graph edges	Structure-sensitive		Pearce^c	
			abstract objects	running time	abstract objects	running time
cp	720K	3205	68166	29.25s	3380	13.62s
df	456K	1812	38919	20.68s	2236	11.09s
du	608K	2424	49592	29.77s	3008	21.96s
ginstall	692K	3185	59893	25.12s	3207	14.32s
ls	604K	2654	66469	22.43s	2783	13.35s
mkdir	384K	1466	21900	17.35s	1641	11.43s
mv	648K	2932	55619	25.50s	3015	12.20s
sort	608K	2480	75360	34.25s	2955	21.40s
clusterdb	528K	1390	167605	33.90s	4461	11.89s
createdb	528K	1412	168068	30.58s	4480	11.07s
createlang	572K	1928	133869	25.67s	4275	12.68s
createuser	532K	1435	171115	31.07s	4569	9.31s
dropdb	524K	1361	165966	31.26s	4399	12.72s
droplang	572K	1936	133912	24.38s	4278	12.55s
dropuser	524K	1356	165615	30.45s	4386	12.15s
ecpg	1.2M	5713	59252	38.47s	5219	29.11s
pg-ctl	488K	1615	118689	23.36s	3655	9.14s
pg-dumpall	572K	2110	184276	32.18s	5153	11.95s
pg-isready	464K	1302	108622	21.54s	3343	11.25s
pg-rewind	556K	1943	136915	25.56s	4301	11.48s
pg-upgrade	604K	2501	151967	26.49s	4965	11.80s
psql	1.4M	5925	460522	67.76s	14025	25.28s

Fig. 11. Input and output metrics. The first column is benchmark bitcode size (in bytes). The second column is the number of call-graph edges (as computed by our analysis). The third (resp. fifth) column is the number of abstract objects created. The fourth (resp. sixth) column is the analysis running time.

Figure 11 presents some general metrics on the input and output of each analysis: (i) number of call-graph edges (allocation site to function), (ii) number of abstract objects created by the analysis, and (iii) running time (excluding constant overhead that bootstrap both analyses).

Figure 12 compares the two analyses in terms of the degree of resolving variable points-to targets. The first column of each analysis lists the percentage of fully resolved variables (virtual registers): *how many point to a single abstract object*. This is the main metric of interest for most analysis clients. The next two columns list the percentage of variables that point to two/three objects.

It is evident that our structure-sensitive analysis fares consistently better in fully resolving variable targets. Our analysis resolves many more variables than *Pearce^c* does, for any of the available benchmarks, with an average increase of 36 % across all coreutil benchmarks and 58 % in the PostgreSQL benchmarks. This is *despite using a finer-grained object abstraction than Pearce^c*:

Benchmark	Structure-sensitive			Pearce^c		
	(%) $|pt(v)| \to 1$	2	3	(%) $|pt(v)| \to 1$	2	3
cp	35.42	11.56	9.03	24.02	2.91	3.51
df	35.98	13.15	8.37	26.28	1.98	4.38
du	37.06	10.51	7.54	25.60	2.00	2.95
ginstall	36.31	14.24	8.28	27.15	7.44	3.14
ls	33.23	6.09	8.81	26.90	3.57	2.67
mkdir	36.11	8.43	9.65	23.02	2.00	4.35
mv	35.09	13.71	8.97	24.58	6.78	3.04
sort	29.20	5.25	9.65	22.37	1.47	2.53
average	34.49	9.51	8.79	25.37	3.53	3.19
clusterdb	40.86	8.42	7.93	24.46	2.79	3.85
createdb	40.82	9.11	7.95	24.54	2.83	4.31
createlang	42.72	8.87	11.89	25.62	4.10	4.78
createuser	40.33	8.85	8.75	24.07	3.18	4.44
dropdb	40.59	8.69	7.96	23.97	2.91	4.00
droplang	42.68	8.86	11.88	25.67	4.10	4.75
dropuser	40.36	8.72	8.01	23.86	2.86	4.02
ecpg	16.72	1.22	0.52	15.14	0.30	42.64
pg-ctl	41.31	8.46	8.50	25.31	3.31	4.05
pg-dumpall	40.52	7.10	7.21	27.74	3.10	4.61
pg-isready	39.89	8.12	7.87	23.59	2.92	4.03
pg-rewind	44.74	7.55	8.56	31.39	2.75	3.76
pg-upgrade	41.12	8.35	9.34	27.73	2.95	3.70
psql	38.62	5.81	9.33	25.61	2.31	3.20
average	39.38	7.72	4.55	24.91	2.89	6.87

Fig. 12. Variable points-to sets. Proportion of resolved variables (that point to one abstract object), as well as variables with two or three points-to targets.

The "abstract objects" column of Fig. 11 shows that our analysis abstraction has *one to two orders of magnitude more* abstract objects than *Pearce^c*. Yet it succeeds at resolving many more variables to a single (and much finer-grained) abstract object. (The only benchmark instance in which *Pearce^c* somewhat benefits from its coarse abstract object granularity is ecpg: a full 42.64 % of variables point to 3, much coarser than ours, abstract objects.) Note also that the *Pearce^c* analysis appears much better than it actually is for meaningful cases, due to large amounts of low-hanging fruit—e.g., global or address-taken variables, which are the single target of some virtual register, due to the SSA representation.

6   Related Work

We discussed some closely related work throughout the paper. Most C and C++ analyses in the past have focused on scalability, at the expense of precision.

Several (e.g., [7,14,25]) do not model more than a small fraction of the functionality of modern intermediate languages.

One important addition is the DSA work of Lattner et al. [13], which was the original points-to analysis in LLVM. The analysis is no longer maintained, so comparing experimentally is not possible. In terms of a qualitative comparison, the DSA analysis is a sophisticated but ad hoc mix of techniques, some of which add precision, while others sacrifice it for scalability. For instance, the analysis is field-sensitive using byte offsets, at both the source and the target of points-to edges. However, when a single abstract object is found to be used with two different types, the analysis reverts to collapsing all its fields. (Our analysis would instead create two abstract objects for the two different types.) Furthermore, the DSA analysis is unification-based (a Steensgaard analysis), keeping coarser abstract object sets and points-to sets than our inclusion-based analysis. Finally, the DSA analysis uses deep context-sensitivity, yet discards it inside a strongly connected component of methods.

The field-sensitive inclusion-based analysis of Avots et al. [2] uses type information to improve its precision. As in this work, they explicitly track the types of objects and their fields, and filter out field accesses whose base object has an incompatible type (which may arise due to analysis imprecision). However, their approach is array-insensitive and does not employ any kind of type back-propagation to create more (fine-grained) abstract objects for polymorphic allocation sites. Instead, they consider objects used with multiple types as possible type violations. Finally, they extend type compatibility with a form of structural equivalence to mark types with identical physical layouts as compatible. The implementation of cclyzer applies a more general form of type compatibility, which has been omitted from this paper for space reasons.

Miné [18] presents a highly precise analysis, expressed in the abstract interpretation framework, that translates any field and array accesses to pointer arithmetic. By relying on an external numerical interval analysis, this technique is able to handle arbitrary integer computations, and, thus, any kind of pointer arithmetic. However, the precision comes with scalability and applicability limitations: the technique can only analyze programs without dynamic memory allocation or recursion.

There are similarly other C/C++-based analyses that claim field-sensitivity [9,10], but it is unclear at what granularity this is implemented. Existing descriptions in the literature do not match the precision of our structure-sensitive approach, which maintains maximal structure information (with typed abstract objects and full distinction of subobjects), at both sources and targets of points-to relationships. Nystrom et al. [19] have a fine-grained heap abstraction that corresponds to standard use of "heap cloning" (a.k.a. "context-sensitive heap").

7   Conclusions

We presented a structure-sensitive points-to analysis for C and C++. The analysis attempts to always distinguish abstract objects and assign them a unique type (even when none is known at the point of object creation) as well as to discriminate between subobjects of a single object (array or structure instance). We describe the analysis in precise terms and show that its approach succeeds in maintaining precision when analyzing realistic programs. In our experience, the techniques we described are essential for analyzing C/C++ programs at the same level of precision as programs in higher-level languages.

Acknowledgments. We gratefully acknowledge funding by the European Research Council under grant 307334 (Spade). We thank Kostas Ferles and Eirini Psallida for their early contributions to `cclyzer`; and also the anonymous reviewers of this paper, for their insightful comments and suggestions.

References

1. Andersen, L.O.: Program analysis and specialization for the C programming language. Ph.d. thesis, DIKU, University of Copenhagen, May 1994
2. Avots, D., Dalton, M., Livshits, B., Lam, M.S.: Improving software security with a C pointer analysis. In: Proceedings of the 27th International Conference on Software Engineering, ICSE 2005, pp. 332–341. ACM, New York (2005)
3. Berndl, M., Lhoták, O., Qian, F., Hendren, L.J., Umanee, N.: Points-to analysis using BDDs. In: Proceedings of the 2003 ACM SIGPLAN Conference on Programming Language Design and Implementation, PLDI 2003, pp. 103–114. ACM, New York (2003)
4. Bravenboer, M., Smaragdakis, Y.: Strictly declarative specification of sophisticated points-to analyses. In: Proceedings of the 24th Annual ACM SIGPLAN Conference on Object Oriented Programming, Systems, Languages, and Applications, OOPSLA 2009. ACM, New York (2009)
5. Das, M.: Unification-based pointer analysis with directional assignments. In: Proceedings of the 2000 ACM SIGPLAN Conference on Programming Language Design and Implementation, PLDI 2000, pp. 35–46. ACM, New York (2000)
6. Emami, M., Ghiya, R., Hendren, L.J.: Context-sensitive interprocedural points-to analysis in the presence of function pointers. In: Proceedings of the 1994 ACM SIGPLAN Conference on Programming Language Design and Implementation, PLDI 1994, pp. 242–256. ACM, New York (1994)
7. Hardekopf, B., Lin, C.: The ant and the grasshopper: fast and accurate pointer analysis for millions of lines of code. In: Proceedings of the 2007 ACM SIGPLAN Conference on Programming Language Design and Implementation, PLDI 2007, pp. 290–299. ACM, New York (2007)
8. Hardekopf, B., Lin, C.: Exploiting pointer and location equivalence to optimize pointer analysis. In: Riis Nielson, H., Filé, G. (eds.) SAS 2007. LNCS, vol. 4634, pp. 265–280. Springer, Heidelberg (2007)
9. Hardekopf, B., Lin, C.: Semi-sparse flow-sensitive pointer analysis. In: Proceedings of the 36th ACM SIGPLAN-SIGACT Symposium on Principles of Programming Languages, POPL 2009, pp. 226–238. ACM, New York (2009)
10. Hardekopf, B., Lin, C.: Flow-sensitive pointer analysis for millions of lines of code. In: Proceedings of the 9th International Symposium on Code Generation and Optimization, CGO 2011, pp. 289–298. IEEE Computer Society (2011)

11. Heintze, N., Tardieu, O.: Ultra-fast aliasing analysis using CLA: a million lines of C code in a second. In: Proceedings of the 2001 ACM SIGPLAN Conference on Programming Language Design and Implementation, PLDI 2001, pp. 254–263. ACM, New York (2001)
12. Hind, M., Burke, M.G., Carini, P.R., Choi, J.: Interprocedural pointer alias analysis. ACM Trans. Program. Lang. Syst. **21**(4), 848–894 (1999)
13. Lattner, C., Lenharth, A., Adve, V.S.: Making context-sensitive points-to analysis with heap cloning practical for the real world. In: Proceedings of the 2007 ACM SIGPLAN Conference on Programming Language Design and Implementation, PLDI 2007, pp. 278–289. ACM, New York (2007)
14. Lhoták, O., Chung, K.C.A.: Points-to analysis with efficient strong updates. In: Proceedings of the 38th ACM SIGPLAN-SIGACT Symposium on Principles of Programming Languages, POPL 2011, pp. 3–16. ACM, New York (2011)
15. Li, Y., Tan, T., Sui, Y., Xue, J.: Self-inferencing reflection resolution for Java. In: Jones, R. (ed.) ECOOP 2014. LNCS, vol. 8586, pp. 27–53. Springer, Heidelberg (2014)
16. Livshits, B., Whaley, J., Lam, M.S.: Reflection analysis for Java. In: Yi, K. (ed.) APLAS 2005. LNCS, vol. 3780, pp. 139–160. Springer, Heidelberg (2005)
17. Milanova, A., Rountev, A., Ryder, B.G.: Parameterized object sensitivity for points-to and side-effect analyses for Java. In: Proceedings of the 2002 International Symposium on Software Testing and Analysis, ISSTA 2002, pp. 1–11. ACM, New York (2002)
18. Miné, A.: Field-sensitive value analysis of embedded C programs with union types and pointer arithmetics. In: Proceedings of the 2006 ACM SIGPLAN/SIGBED Conference on Languages, Compilers, and Tools for Embedded Systems, LCTES 2006, pp. 54–63. ACM (2006)
19. Nystrom, E.M., Kim, H., Hwu, W.W.: Importance of heap specialization in pointer analysis. In: Proceedings of the 5th ACM SIGPLAN-SIGSOFT Workshop on Program Analysis for Software Tools and Engineering, PASTE 2004, pp. 43–48. ACM, New York (2004)
20. Pearce, D.J., Kelly, P.H.J., Hankin, C.: Efficient field-sensitive pointer analysis for C. In: Proceedings of the 5th ACM SIGPLAN-SIGSOFT Workshop on Program Analysis for Software Tools and Engineering, PASTE 2004, pp. 37–42. ACM, New York (2004)
21. Pearce, D.J., Kelly, P.H.J., Hankin, C.: Efficient field-sensitive pointer analysis of C. ACM Trans. Program. Lang. Syst. **30**(1) (2007)
22. Rountev, A., Milanova, A., Ryder, B.G.: Points-to analysis for Java using annotated constraints. In: Proceedings of the 16th Annual ACM SIGPLAN Conference on Object Oriented Programming, Systems, Languages, and Applications, OOPSLA 2001, pp. 43–55. ACM, New York (2001)
23. Smaragdakis, Y., Balatsouras, G., Kastrinis, G., Bravenboer, M.: More sound static handling of Java reflection. In: Feng, X., et al. (eds.) APLAS 2015. LNCS, vol. 9458, pp. 485–503. Springer, Heidelberg (2015). doi:10.1007/978-3-319-26529-2_26
24. Whaley, J., Rinard, M.C.: Compositional pointer and escape analysis for Java programs. In: Proceedings of the 14th Annual ACM SIGPLAN Conference on Object Oriented Programming, Systems, Languages, and Applications, OOPSLA 1999, pp. 187–206. ACM, New York (1999)
25. Zheng, X., Rugina, R.: Demand-driven alias analysis for C. In: Proceedings of the 35th ACM SIGPLAN-SIGACT Symposium on Principles of Programming Languages, POPL 2008, pp. 197–208. ACM, New York (2008)

Bounded Abstract Interpretation

Maria Christakis[1](✉) and Valentin Wüstholz[2](✉)

[1] Microsoft Research, Redmond, USA
mchri@microsoft.com
[2] The University of Texas at Austin, Austin, USA
valentin@cs.utexas.edu

Abstract. In practice, software engineers are only able to spend a limited amount of resources on statically analyzing their code. Such resources may refer to their available time or their tolerance for imprecision, and usually depend on when in their workflow a static analysis is run. To serve these different needs, we propose a technique that enables engineers to interactively bound a static analysis based on the available resources. When all resources are exhausted, our technique soundly records the achieved verification results with a program instrumentation. Consequently, as more resources become available, any static analysis may continue from where the previous analysis left off. Our technique is applicable to any abstract interpreter, and we have implemented it for the .NET static analyzer Clousot. Our experiments show that bounded abstract interpretation can significantly increase the performance of the analysis (by up to 8x) while also increasing the quality of the reported warnings (more definite warnings that detect genuine bugs).

1 Introduction

Software engineers typically have very different resources to devote to checking correctness of their code by running a static program analysis. These resources refer to an engineer's available time, or their tolerance for imprecision and spurious errors. The availability of such resources may depend on several factors, like when in an engineer's workflow static analysis is run (for instance, in the editor, after every build, during code reviewing, or before a release), how critical their code is, or how willing they are to go through all warnings reported by the analysis.

As an example, consider that software engineers might choose to run a static analyzer for a very short amount of time (say, a few minutes) after every build, in which case they expect it to provide immediate feedback even if certain errors might be missed. In contrast, when waiting for code reviewers to sign off, engineers could take advantage of the wait and resume the analysis of their code from where it had previously left off (say, after the last build). However, this time, the analysis can run for a longer period of time since code reviews take at least a few hours to complete [28,29]. Engineers would now expect to find most errors in their code before making it available to others and are, therefore, more tolerant to spurious errors.

X. Rival (Ed.): SAS 2016, LNCS 9837, pp. 105–125, 2016.
DOI: 10.1007/978-3-662-53413-7_6

```
1  public void M() {
2    int c = 0;
3    while (*) {
4      if (c < 7) {
5        c++;
6      }
7    }
8    assert c < 585;
9    assert 7 < c;
10 }
```

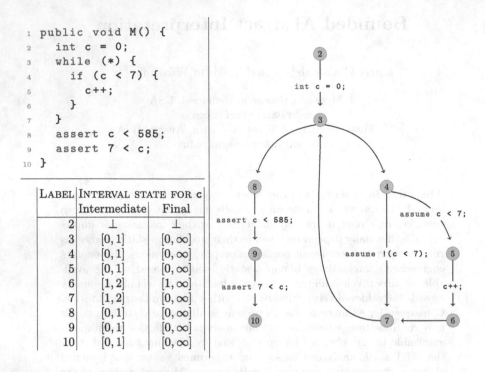

| Label | Interval state for c | |
	Intermediate	Final
2	$\perp$	$\perp$
3	$[0, 1]$	$[0, \infty]$
4	$[0, 1]$	$[0, \infty]$
5	$[0, 1]$	$[0, \infty]$
6	$[1, 2]$	$[1, \infty]$
7	$[1, 2]$	$[0, \infty]$
8	$[0, 1]$	$[0, \infty]$
9	$[0, 1]$	$[0, \infty]$
10	$[0, 1]$	$[0, \infty]$

Fig. 1. Example that demonstrates loss of precision in the analysis after performing a widening operation at program point 3 in method M. The source code for method M is shown on the top left. On the right, we show the control flow graph of the method (program points are depicted as nodes, and edges capture control flow and code). On the bottom left, we show the abstract interval state for variable c at an intermediate and the final state.

In this paper, we propose a technique that enables users to *interactively* adapt a static analysis to their available resources. We focus on static analysis in the form of abstract interpretation [11]. When there are no more resources, our technique *soundly* records, in the form of a program instrumentation, any correctness guarantees that have been achieved until that point in the analysis. Consequently, once more become available, the static analysis will not start from scratch; it will instead reuse these already collected verification results to continue from where it left off.

As an example, consider method M on the top left of Fig. 1. On line 2, we initialize a counter c, which is later incremented in the body of a non-deterministic while-loop (lines 3–7). After the loop, there are two assertions, the first of which (line 8) always holds, whereas the second one (line 9) constitutes an error.

When analyzing method M with the relatively imprecise interval domain [11], the abstract interpreter generates two warnings, one for each assertion in the code. Our technique allows software engineers to bound the analysis such that it runs faster and only reports the genuine error on line 9. Since the bounded analysis might miss errors, it is also possible to continue analyzing the code at a later point by reusing the verification results that have been previously collected.

Although bounded abstract interpretation is a general approach for bounding the analysis based on user resources, the possible analysis bounds that we discuss in this paper are time, imprecision, and the number of spurious errors. The bounded abstract interpreter is a verification tool until a bound is reached, at which point it switches to bug-finding while precisely recording its own unsoundness. This technique opens up a new way of building highly tunable abstract interpreters by soundly recording their intermediate verification results.

Our paper makes the following contributions. It presents:

- an algorithm for bounding a static analysis based on abstract interpretation according to the user's available resources,
- verification annotations and an instrumentation for soundly recording any intermediate verification results when a bound of the analysis is reached,
- three application scenarios for interactively tuning an analyzer to reduce the time, imprecision, and number of spurious errors of the analysis, and
- an experimental evaluation that explores the potential of bounded abstract interpretation when applied in a real, industrial analyzer.

Outline. The following section introduces the verification annotations that we use to record any intermediate verification results of the abstract interpreter. In Sects. 3 and 4, we present the algorithm for soundly recording these results and several application scenarios of our approach. In Sect. 5, we discuss our experimental results. We review related work in Sect. 6 and conclude in Sect. 7.

2   Verification Annotations

To soundly encode intermediate, partial verification results [30], we use two kinds of annotations. In our previous work, an *explicit assumption* of the form assumed P as a expresses that an analysis assumed property P to hold at this point in the code without checking it [5,6,8,30]. The unique *assumption identifier* a may be used to refer to this explicit assumption at other program points. In the context of bounded abstract interpretation, an assumed statement is used to express that the analyzer unsoundly assumes that a property P holds for all possible program states at a given program point. Actually, P holds only for those states that were explored by the analyzer within its limited resources, which is why the assumption is unsound.

As an example, consider that right before performing the widening operation at program point 3 of method M (see Fig. 1), the abstract interpreter runs out of user resources. At this stage of the analysis, we have learned that $c \in [0,1]$, as is also shown by the table in Fig. 1. Since all resources have been exhausted, the analyzer (unsoundly) assumes that $c \in [0,1]$ at this program point, even though a fixed point has not yet been reached. We capture this unsound assumption by introducing an assumed statement at the loop header, as shown on line 4 of Fig. 2.

```
 1  public void M() {
 2    int c = 0;
 3  LH:
 4    assumed 0 <= c && c <= 1 as a;              // label 3
 5    if (*) {
 6      assume 0 <= c && c <= 1 provided a;       // label 4
 7      if (c < 7) {
 8        assume 0 <= c && c <= 1 provided a;     // label 5
 9        c++;
10        assume 1 <= c && c <= 2 provided a;     // label 6
11      }
12      assume 1 <= c && c <= 2 provided a;       // label 7
13      goto LH;
14    }
15    assume 0 <= c && c <= 1 provided a;         // label 8
16    assume c < 585 provided a;
17    assert c < 585;                             // verified
18    assume 0 <= c && c <= 1 provided a;         // label 9
19    assume !(7 < c) provided a;
20    assert 7 < c;                               // falsified
21    assume 0 <= c && c <= 1 provided a;         // label 10
22  }
```

Fig. 2. Verification annotations (highlighted in gray) in method M for expressing the intermediate results achieved before performing the widening operation at program point 3 of Fig. 1.

To record intermediate, partial verification results, we introduce a new kind of verification annotations, namely, *partially-justified assumptions* of the form assume P provided A. These assumptions express that property P has been soundly derived (or inferred) by the analyzer provided that A holds. The condition A is a boolean expression over assumption identifiers, each of which is introduced in an assumed statement.

In Fig. 2, we use partially-justified assume statements to soundly record the verification results achieved by the analyzer within its bounds. At every program point, we introduce an assume statement to document what we have learned about variable c so far, also shown in the column for intermediate results of the table of Fig. 1. The properties of the assume statements are soundly inferred as long as explicit assumption a holds. Note that on line 16 we are also able to explicitly capture the fact that the first assertion in method M has been verified provided that a holds.

The concrete semantics of these verification annotations is defined in terms of assignments and standard assume statements, which are understood by most existing analyzers. For modular analyses, each assumption identifier corresponds to a local boolean variable, which is declared at the beginning of the enclosing method and initialized to true. A statement assumed P as a is encoded as:

$$a = a \ \&\& \ P;$$

This means that variable a accumulates the assumed properties for all executions of this statement. Note that this encoding ensures that any unsound assumption is captured at the program point at which it is made by the static analyzer, instead of where it is used.

A statement `assume` P `provided` A is encoded using a standard `assume` statement:

$$\texttt{assume } A \Rightarrow P\,;$$

This captures that the derived property P holds provided that the condition A holds, and it precisely reflects that P was soundly learned by the static analyzer under condition A. It also allows us to express that an analyzer found a program point to be unreachable if condition A holds. This can be achieved by instrumenting that program point with the following statement:

$$\texttt{assume false provided } A\,;$$

In some cases, an analyzer may even determine that an assertion P never holds at a given program point if condition A holds. We refer to this as a *definite warning*. This can be captured in the following way (line 19 of Fig. 2):

$$\texttt{assume } \neg P \texttt{ provided } A\,;$$

3 Sound Intermediate Verification Results

Abstract interpretation uses a fixed-point computation to converge on its verification results. Therefore, verification results only become valid once a fixed point has been reached. As a consequence, abstract interpreters cannot simply be interrupted at any point during the analysis when user-provided resources run out. In this section, we demonstrate a novel technique for soundly sharing verification results at intermediate states during an analysis.

3.1 Analysis

As a first step, we present an algorithm for analyzing a program such that the analysis can be interrupted at any point when a certain bound is reached. We give concrete examples of such bounds in the next section, but for now, the reader may assume that we refer to a user's available time, tolerance for imprecision, or for spurious errors. On a high level, our algorithm, Algorithm 1, uses abstract interpretation to analyze a program in the usual way until a bound is reached for a given program point. Now, the abstract state is *not* updated at this program point, and consequently, *no* change is propagated to subsequent program points, contrary to what is typically done. Instead, we only record that a bound is reached at the program point and continue the analysis without modifying the abstract state. As expected, this speeds up the fixed-point computation. Note that our algorithm is independent of a particular abstract domain.

As an example, consider an if-statement with a then- and an else-branch. Also, assume that, at a certain point in the analysis, the then-branch has already been analyzed and the program point right after the if-statement holds the post-state of the then-branch. After analyzing the else-branch of the if-statement, the program point right after the if-statement should be updated by joining the existing state with the state at the end of the else-branch. Now, imagine that a bound is reached at this point after the if-statement. Instead of performing the join and updating the state, we simply record this program point and continue.

As a result, the imprecision that may have been introduced by joining the states of both branches is avoided. In exchange for not losing precision, the analysis becomes unsound. In particular, any code after the if-statement is analyzed as if the else-branch did not exist. This, on one hand, potentially reduces the number of spurious errors of the analysis but, on the other hand, might make the analysis miss errors. The benefit for a user with limited resources is that the analysis becomes more precise within the allocated resources. Moreover, by recording at which program points unsoundness may have been introduced due to a bound, we soundly capture the verification results using the annotations from Sect. 2, as we explain in Sect. 3.2. This instrumentation achieves two additional goals: (1) the bounded abstract interpreter still provides definite correctness guarantees, and (2) the analysis of the program can still continue from where it left off at a later point, when user resources become available again.

Let us now describe our algorithm in more technical detail. In Algorithm 1, procedure ANALYZE takes as arguments the program p, l_{init}, which denotes the label or program point from which the analysis begins, and pre_{init}, which denotes the initial abstract state, that is, the pre-state of l_{init}. For example, if l_{init} is the first program point in a method body, then pre_{init} could refer to the state that expresses the precondition of the method.

On lines 2–5, we perform necessary initializations. Variable q is a work queue containing the labels that remain to be analyzed. Specifically, it contains tuples whose first element is a label and whose second element is a pre-state of that label. Initially, we push to q a tuple with l_{init} and its pre-state pre_{init}. Variable b is a set of labels for which a bound has been reached, and thus, whose state has not been updated as usual. Set b is initially empty. Variables pre and $post$ denote maps from a label to its computed pre- and post-state, respectively. Initially, these maps are also empty.

The loop on lines 6–20 iterates until q is empty. While q is not empty, we pop a label and its pre-state from the queue (line 7) and check whether a bound has been reached for this label. This is determined by the generic procedure BOUNDREACHED (line 8), which we instantiate in Sect. 4 for different application scenarios. If a bound has indeed been reached for a label l, then we add this label to set b (line 9). Otherwise, we determine the pre-state for l (lines 11–16).

Specifically, if the pre map already contains a previous pre-state for label l (line 12) and widening is desired (line 13), we perform widening of the previously computed pre-state of l, $pre(l)$, and its current pre-state (line 14). This current pre-state comes from the work queue and has been computed by performing earlier steps of the analysis, as we show next. If widening is not desired, we instead perform a join of the two pre-states of l (line 16).

Algorithm 1. Bounded analysis

```
 1  procedure ANALYZE(p, l_init, pre_init)
 2      q ← PUSH(⟨l_init, pre_init⟩, EMPTYQUEUE())
 3      b ← EMPTYSET()
 4      pre ← EMPTYMAP()
 5      post ← EMPTYMAP()
 6      while ¬ISEMPTY(q) do
 7          ⟨l, pre_l⟩, q ← POP(q)
 8          if BOUNDREACHED(pre, post, l, pre_l) then
 9              b ← ADD(b, l)
10          else
11              pre'_l ← pre_l
12              if l ∈ dom(pre) then
13                  if WIDENINGDESIRED(l, pre, pre'_l) then
14                      pre'_l ← ∇(pre(l), pre'_l)
15                  else
16                      pre'_l ← pre(l) ⊔ pre'_l
17              post_l ← STEP(p, pre'_l, l)
18              post(l), pre(l) ← post_l, pre'_l
19              foreach s in SUCCESSORS(p, l)
20                  q ← PUSH(q, ⟨s, post_l⟩)
21  return pre, post, b
```

On line 17, our algorithm performs one step of analysis for label l, that is, we compute the post-state of l by executing an abstract transformer, and on line 18, we update the pre and $post$ maps with the new pre- and post-states of l. For each successor s of l in program p (line 19), that is, for each program point immediately succeeding l, we push s and its new pre-state (line 20), $post_l$, to the work queue.

When the work queue becomes empty, procedure ANALYZE returns the information that has been learned during the analysis for each program point (stored in the pre and $post$ maps). We also return the set b, which is used in Sect. 3.2 for soundly expressing the intermediate verification results of the analysis, that is, the verification results that were achieved within the available resources.

To illustrate, let us explain Algorithm 1 on the example of Fig. 1. We assume that procedure BOUNDREACHED returns true whenever a widening operation would be used, in other words, the bound prevents any widening. This is the case at label 3 of method M (see graph of Fig. 1), right after the intermediate states shown in the table of Fig. 1 have been computed. As a result, label 3 is added to set b, and the interval state for variable c remains $[0, 1]$, which has earlier been stored to the pre and $post$ maps as $pre(3)$ and $post(2)$, respectively.

Similarly to abstract interpretation, many static analysis techniques, such as data flow analysis, or predicate abstraction [21], also perform a fixed-point computation in order to converge on their verification results. Therefore, our algorithm could also be applied to such analysis techniques that may progressively lose precision on examples like that of Fig. 1.

3.2   Instrumentation

Algorithm 2 shows how to instrument the program with intermediate verification results. In particular, procedure INSTRUMENT is run after ANALYZE to record, in the form of the verification annotations presented in Sect. 2, the information that has soundly been learned by the analysis at each program point.

On a high level, our algorithm concretizes the abstract states that have been computed for each program point by procedure ANALYZE and, after each point, inserts either an `assume` statement or an `assumed` statement, if a bound has been reached for the corresponding program point. Recall that an `assumed` statement denotes that at the corresponding program point the abstract interpreter unsoundly assumed that a property P holds for all possible program states, even though P actually holds only for those states that were explored by the analyzer within its limited resources. An `assume` statement expresses properties that have soundly been derived by the analyzer provided that an (unsound) assumption made by the analysis holds.

Procedure INSTRUMENT takes as arguments the program p, the map $post$ from a label to its computed post-state, and the set b of labels for which a bound has been reached. Note that $post$ and b are computed and returned by ANALYZE. For each label l in program p (line 2), we first concretize the bottom state and assign it to $post_l$ (line 3), which denotes the concrete post-state of l. If the $post$ map contains an entry for l (line 4), then we update $post_l$ with that entry (line 5). Finally, we check if a bound was reached at label l (line 6). In this case, we instrument the program to add an `assumed` statement for property $post_l$ right after program point l (line 7). We use label l as the unique assumption identifier in the `assumed` statement. In particular, the instrumentation added after program point l looks as follows:

$$\texttt{assumed } post_l \texttt{ as } l;$$

If label l is not in set b (line 8), we add an `assume` statement for property $post_l$, whose `provided` clause is a conjunction of all assumption identifiers (or labels) in set b (line 9). Assuming that set b contains n labels, the instrumentation in this case looks as follows:

$$\texttt{assume } post_l \texttt{ provided } l_0 \wedge l_1 \wedge ... \wedge l_{n-1};$$

Algorithm 2. Instrumentation of sound intermediate verification results

---

1 **procedure** INSTRUMENT$(p, post, b)$
2   **foreach** l **in** LABELS(p)
3          $post_l \leftarrow$ CONCRETIZE$(\bot)$
4   **if** $l \in dom(post)$ **then**
5              $post_l \leftarrow$ CONCRETIZE$(post(l))$
6   **if** $l \in b$ **then**
7   INSERTASSUMED$(p, l, post_l)$
8   **else**
9   INSERTASSUME$(p, l, post_l, b)$

This statement means that $post_l$ has been soundly learned by the abstract interpreter provided that the unsound assumptions made by the analysis at program points $l_0, ..., l_{n-1}$ hold. With this instrumentation, a partially-justified assumption might depend on identifiers of explicit assumptions made later in the code. However, note that the boolean variables corresponding to these identifiers are trivially true at the point of the partially-justified assumption due to their initialization (see Sect. 2).

Recall that for label 3 of method M, in Fig. 1, a bound was reached for the widening operation. Therefore, according to Algorithm 2, we introduce an **assumed** statement at that program point, as shown in Fig. 2. At all other program points, we insert an **assume** statement, as shown in the same figure. Note that the properties of these statements are the concretized, intermediate abstract states for variable c, which are shown in the table of Fig. 1. Also note that the **provided** clauses of the **assume** statements correspond to the unsound assumption made at program point 3. We added line 16 of Fig. 2 to show that the subsequent assertion is verified under assumption a. Similarly, we added line 20 of Fig. 2 to show that the subsequent assertion is found to never hold.

For simplicity, we record intermediate verification results for each program point in the code. However, an optimization could remove any **assume** statements that only contribute information that can easily be derived from the remaining ones.

Soundness Argument. In standard abstract interpretation, the inferred properties for labels that are not in the work queue are sound, given that the inferred properties for labels that are still in the queue hold. In bounded abstract interpretation, the inferred properties for labels that are not in the work queue are sound, given that the inferred properties for labels that are still in the queue *or in the set of labels for which a bound has been reached* hold. Our verification annotations precisely express these soundness guarantees since the work queue eventually ends up empty.

4   Applications

In this section, we discuss examples of user resources and the corresponding bounds that may be imposed during the analysis. In particular, we describe possible instantiations of procedure BOUNDREACHED from Algorithm 1 and an application scenario for each such instantiation.

4.1   Bounding Time

As a first example, consider running the computationally expensive polyhedra abstract domain [12]. In comparison to other simpler domains, it typically takes longer for the verification results of this domain to reach a fixed point. Simply imposing a timeout on such expensive analyses does not solve the problem for engineers who are often not willing to wait for long-running analyses to terminate. In case a timeout is hit before a fixed point is reached, all intermediate verification results are lost.

The implementation of procedure BOUNDREACHED for this scenario is very simple. For BOUNDREACHED to be deterministic, there needs to be a symbolic notion of time, instead of actual time that varies from machine to machine. Each symbolic time tick could, for example, refer to a step of the analysis in Algorithm 1 (line 17). For instance, this can be implemented using a shared counter of symbolic ticks, which is updated in procedure STEP, and a shared bound on the total number of ticks allowed to happen in the analysis, in other words, a symbolic timeout selected by the user. Note that, when reaching this bound, the number of explicit assumptions in the instrumentation is usually small as it is bounded by the size of queue q in Algorithm 1 at the point of the timeout.

4.2   Bounding Imprecision

We now consider as our limited resource a user's tolerance for imprecision. Specifically, three common sources of imprecision in abstract interpretation are joins, widenings, and calls. The motivation behind having a threshold on the amount of imprecision is the following: the analysis keeps accumulating imprecision while it runs, and after a certain point, many reported warnings are spurious and caused solely by the accumulated imprecision. Note that, for simplicity, we do not consider all possible sources of imprecision since accurately identifying them is an orthogonal issue; imprecision of the analysis generally depends on both the abstract domain and the analyzed program, and existing work [17,18] could be used to identify possible imprecision sources with more accuracy.

A join operation approximates the union of two sets of concrete program states in the abstract domain. In particular, it is often not possible to precisely express the union in a given abstract domain, thus, resulting in over-approximation. By bounding the number of joins, we are able to control the amount of imprecision that is caused by an abstract domain's inability to accurately express union (or disjunction) of states even though the join operation itself is known to be complete [17,18].

Algorithm 3 shows an implementation of BOUNDREACHED that counts the number of imprecise joins. On line 2, we check whether label l is in the domain of the *pre* map (storing the current pre-state for each label) and whether a join is desired. If this is the case, we compute the join of the current pre-state $pre(l)$ with the pre-state pre_l from the work queue on line 3. If its result pre_l', which may become the current pre-state for label l, is less than (not possible due to property of join) or equal to $pre(l)$, the join does not lead to additional imprecision and we do not increase the global counter *joins* for imprecise joins. Otherwise, we do (line 5). Note that, in this algorithm, we conservatively consider any join that generates a different result than $pre(l)$ as imprecise. This may include joins that are actually precise, but efficiently checking for imprecise joins is usually not possible within an abstract domain and the overhead would defeat the purpose.

Algorithm 3. Bounded imprecision due to joins

---

1 **procedure** BOUNDREACHED($pre, post, l, pre_l$)
2   **if** $l \in dom(pre) \land \neg$WIDENINGDESIRED($l, pre, pre_l$) **then**
3      $pre_l' \leftarrow pre(l) \sqcup pre_l$
4   **if** $\neg(pre_l' \sqsubseteq pre(l))$ **then**
5        $joins \leftarrow joins + 1$
6   **return** $maxJoins < joins$
7   **return** $false$

On line 6, we return whether the number of imprecise joins has exceeded the bound.

Similarly to joins, a widening operation is a source of imprecision as its result purposefully over-approximates its arguments in order to reach a fixed point more efficiently. The instantiation of procedure BOUNDREACHED in this case is similar to the one for joins in Algorithm 3. If widening is desired, we increase the global counter for imprecise widenings only if the result of performing the widening is different from the current pre-state in the map pre.

In modular abstract interpretation, calls also constitute a source of imprecision as the relation between a method's arguments and its return values is unknown. This relation is, in the best case, described by user-provided specifications, which however might not be precise enough to avoid some over-approximation in the analysis. To bound the amount of imprecision due to calls, BOUNDREACHED can be implemented such that the analysis simply terminates after analyzing a limited number of calls.

In addition to joins, widenings, and calls, our technique may be applied to any source of imprecision in a static analysis. For instance, we could bound the imprecision of certain abstract transformers, such as standard `assume` statements. Let us explain this concept through the following concrete example.

Consider an if-statement whose condition checks whether variable x is non-zero. Now, imagine that we are using an interval domain to learn the possible values of x. Right before the if-statement, we have inferred that $x \in [-1, 1]$. In the then-branch, even though we know that x cannot be zero (due to the condition of the if-statement), the analysis still derives that $x \in [-1, 1]$ since there is no way to express that x is either -1 or 1 in the interval domain. Therefore, assuming the condition of the if-statement in the then-branch is imprecise due to lack of expressiveness in this abstract domain. In such cases, our technique can restrict the imprecision that is introduced in the analysis because of such transformers by bounding their number, just like we do for calls.

More generally, one could imagine a slight generalization of Algorithm 1 that, in such cases, would execute an under-approximating abstract transformer and add the corresponding label to the set b of labels that have not been fully explored.

Note that, since we are making the analyzer aware of its sources of imprecision, our technique may also be used for ranking any warnings emitted by the analyzer. For example, warnings emitted when introducing fewer sources of imprecision in the analysis could be shown to the user first, before warnings that are emitted when more sources of imprecision may have affected the analysis.

4.3   Bounding Spurious Errors

The third scenario refers to bounding the number of spurious errors that are reported to the user. This acknowledges the fact that human time, required to identify spurious errors, is often more precious than analysis time. On the other hand, it is not always practical to use the most expensive and precise analysis for all code. To strike a good balance, we propose to only run a more precise analysis or one with higher bounds if the less expensive analysis will emit warnings. Before this switch happens, we record the verification results that have been collected until that point by the less expensive analysis so that they are not lost.

```
1  public void N() {
2    int c = 0;
3    if (*) {
4      while (c < 7) {
5        c++;
6      }
7    }
8    assert c != 5;
9  }
```

Fig. 3. Example for bounding spurious errors.

Let us consider the example in Fig. 3. When analyzing method N with the interval domain, we reach a point right before applying widening where the assertion holds. However, after widening, $c \in [0, \infty]$ is inferred right before the assertion and an error is reported. To avoid this spurious error, we can interrupt the analysis and record the results before the widening by marking the assertion as verified under an explicit assumption in the loop header, like in Fig. 2.

A second analysis can now take over. It could be the same analysis as before, an analysis with a more precise abstract domain, or one with higher bounds. It could even be dynamic test generation [5,8]. This second analysis can benefit from the existing verification results since the assertion has already been fully verified for the else-branch (the explicit assumption always holds on that branch). By applying a very inexpensive instrumentation from our previous work [5,8], we can prune away the fully-verified else-branch. This allows even an analysis of the same precision to verify the resulting instrumented program. In particular, $c \in [7, \infty]$ is derived right before the assertion, and method N is fully verified.

In other words, a subsequent analysis (static or dynamic) can analyze the instrumented program that is produced after running the previous analysis. As demonstrated in this section, the encoded intermediate results make it possible to ignore certain parts of the program state or even entire program paths. Our previous work has specifically shown that this instrumentation is suitable for subsequent analyses, in the context of dynamic test generation [6,8] and deductive verification [25].

5   Experimental Evaluation

Setup. We have implemented our technique and algorithms in the widely-used, commercial static analyzer Clousot [16], an abstract interpretation tool for .NET and Code Contracts [15].

For our experiments, we selected a large, popular, open-source C# project on GitHub, namely MSBuild, which is a platform for building applications and can be found at https://github.com/Microsoft/msbuild. The MSBuild project consists of five components, MSBuild, Microsoft.Build, Microsoft.Build.Framework, Microsoft.Build.Tasks, and Microsoft.Build.Utilities. We selected a project that has not been annotated with contracts in order not to depend on the quality of user-provided annotations.

We ran our version of Clousot, which we call *ClousotLight*, on one core assembly pertaining to each of MSBuild's components (in the bb10a5c change-set), MSBuild.exe, Microsoft.Build.dll, Microsoft.Build.Framework.dll, Microsoft.Build.Tasks.Core.dll, Microsoft.Build.Utilities.Core.dll. For our evaluation, we used Clousot's default settings, in addition to the configurations of ClousotLight that we describe in the rest of this section. Note that we did not use Clousot's contract inference in order to isolate the effect of bounds within individual methods; in practice however, contract inference can be useful as a complementary approach for reducing imprecision due to calls. We performed all experiments on a 64-bit machine with an Intel Xeon processor at 3.50 GHz and 32 GB of RAM.

Table 1. The number of potential imprecisions in the analysis of 11,990 methods (when no bounds are imposed), categorized as joins, widenings, and calls. Overall, 3,378,692 abstract transformers were executed during the analysis.

	Joins	Widenings	Calls
Potential imprecisions	199,354 (55.6 %)	3,251 (0.9 %)	155,990 (43.5 %)

Experiments. We used ClousotLight to analyze 11,990 methods, which are all the methods defined in the five core assemblies of MSBuild.

Table 1 summarizes the number of potential imprecisions in the analysis of these methods (when no bounds are imposed), categorized as joins, widenings, and calls. We observed that joins and calls account for the majority (99.1 %) of all these possible sources of imprecision. In total, the analysis executed 3,378,692 abstract transformers (that is, calls to procedure STEP from Algorithm 1). Note that we only counted joins and widenings that result in an update of the program state. For calls, we only counted those that modify any heap location or have a

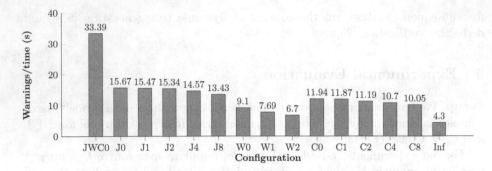

Fig. 4. The average number of warnings in 11,990 methods that were emitted per second of the analysis, for each configuration.

Table 2. The number of warnings (second column) emitted during the duration of the analysis in seconds (third column), for each configuration (first column).

Configuration	Warnings	Time (s)
JWC0	5,304	159
J0	11,777	752
J1	11,913	770
J2	12,008	783
J4	12,137	833
J8	12,240	911
W0	12,466	1,370
W1	12,467	1,621
W2	12,473	1,861
C0	5,214	437
C1	5,214	439
C2	7,195	643
C4	8,403	785
C8	9,683	963
Inf	12,480	2,902

return value. In other words, we did not count joins, widenings, and calls that definitely do not contribute any imprecision to the analysis.

For all experiments that we describe in the rest of this section, we used 15 different configurations of ClousotLight, namely JWC0, J0, J1, J2, J4, J8, W0, W1, W2, C0, C1, C2, C4, C8, and Inf. The configuration names denote the bounds that we imposed on the analysis. For instance, J0 indicates that we allow up to zero joins per method, W1 indicates that we allow up to one widening per method, and C2 that we allow up to two calls per method. JWC0 means that

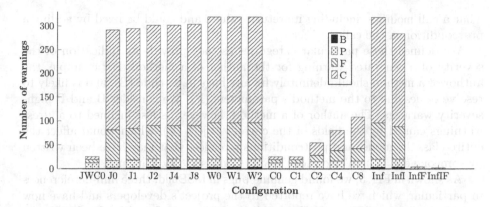

Fig. 5. Manual classification of warnings. We performed this classification for the ten methods that had the largest difference in the number of emitted warnings between configurations JWC0 and Inf. The warnings are classified into four categories: (1) B for genuine, confirmed bugs in the code of the method, (2) P for warnings that depend on the values of the method's parameters, (3) F for warnings that depend on the values of fields in the current object, and (4) C for warnings that depend on what a call modifies, including its return values.

we do not allow any joins, widenings, or calls, and Inf that we do not impose any bounds on the analysis (as in Table 1). These configurations emerged by choosing different bounds for each separate source of imprecision (e.g., J0, W1, C2) as well as the smallest bound for every source of imprecision (JWC0).

Figure 4 shows, for each configuration, the average number of warnings that were emitted per second of the analysis. Note that the fastest configuration is JWC0, with approximately 8x more warnings per second over Inf. The slowest configuration is W2, with 1.5x more warnings per second over Inf.

Table 2 shows the exact number of warnings (second column) emitted during the duration of the analysis (third column), for each configuration (first column). As shown in the table, configuration Inf generates 12,480 warnings in approximately 48 min. Configuration J0 generates approximately 94 % of these warnings in around 13 min. Configurations J8 and W0 generate almost all warnings in around 15 and 23 min, respectively.

We evaluate the impact of our technique on the number of genuine and spurious errors by manually classifying more than 300 warnings that were emitted by ClousotLight (see Fig. 5). We performed this classification for the ten methods (each consisting of hundreds of lines of code) that had the largest difference in the number of emitted warnings between configurations JWC0 and Inf. Since in a modular setting it is difficult to tell which warnings are spurious, we classify the warnings into four categories: (1) B for genuine, confirmed bugs in the code of the method, (2) P for warnings that depend on the values of the method's parameters and could be fixed by adding a precondition, (3) F for warnings that depend on the values of fields in the current object and could be fixed by adding a precondition or an object invariant, and (4) C for warnings that depend on what a call modifies, including its return values, and could be fixed by adding a postcondition in the callee.

We defined these particular categories as they provide an indication of the severity of a generated warning for the author of a method. For example, the author of a method should definitely fix any bugs in its code (B), and is likely to resolve issues due to the method's parameters (P). We consider B and P high-severity warnings. The author of a method, however, is less inclined to address warnings caused by the fields of the current object (F), which would affect the entire class, let alone, add postconditions to callees that may have been written by someone else (C). We consider F and C low-severity warnings.

As shown in Fig. 5, we found genuine bugs in MSBuild, three null-dereferences in particular, which we have reported to the project's developers and have now been fixed (issue #452 on GitHub). All three bugs are found by J2, J4, J8, the W configurations, and Inf. Configurations J0 and J1 detect only one of these errors, which happens to share its root cause with the other two. In other words, by addressing this one warning, all three errors could be fixed. Moreover, J0 and J1 report the warning as a definite one, that is, the analyzer proves that there is a null-dereference, which is made explicit by our annotations (see Sect. 2).

In general, the J configurations miss few warnings of high severity (between 15 % for J0 and 0 % for J8), as shown in the figure. The W configurations find exactly the same warnings as Inf. The C configurations perform very aggressive under-approximation of the state space and, consequently, miss all genuine bugs. This could be remedied by a less coarse under-approximation for calls.

As we observed in Fig. 5, the J and W configurations report a number of warnings very close to that reported by Inf. However, this is achieved with a significant speedup of the analysis. To further reduce the number of reported warnings in one run of a single analysis, a user may turn on orthogonal techniques, such as contract inference or filtering/ranking. For comparison, we include three variants of the Inf configuration with nearly identical running times: InfI (with Clousot's contract inference enabled), InfF (with Clousot's low-noise filtering enabled), and InfIF (with both of these options enabled). We observe that, by enabling Clousot's noise filtering, all high-priority warnings are missed and very few low-priority warnings are reported. We believe that a very fast configuration such as JWC0 strikes a much better balance as it reports 60 % of the high-priority warnings after a much shorter running time. We confirm that contract inference does help in reducing low-priority warnings noticeably. However, this complementary technique shows similar benefits when used with configurations that perform bounding and also benefits from their speedup.

To further evaluate whether our technique improves the detection of genuine bugs, we reviewed all definite warnings that were reported for MSBuild by configurations Inf, J0, and JWC0. Recall that the term "definite warnings" refers to messages that warn about an error that will definitely occur according to the analysis, instead of an error that *may* occur. Clousot prioritizes such warnings when reporting them to users. Inf reported 25 definite warnings, none of which corresponded to genuine bugs. JWC0 reported 15 definite warnings and detected one genuine bug, while J0 reported 44 definite warnings and detected two different and independent genuine bugs (including one of the three bugs from the manual classification). We have reported these bugs, which have been confirmed by the developers (issues #569 and #574 on GitHub). One of them has already been fixed, and the other will be addressed by deleting the buggy code.

This experiment suggests that a bounded analysis can significantly increase the number of definite warnings, which should be reported to the user first, as well as the number of genuine bugs detected by these warnings. For J0, the number of these warnings is increased by almost 2x. The aggressive JWC0 reports fewer definite warnings than Inf, however, a genuine bug is still detected by these warnings, whereas for Inf, it is missed.

Discussion. The experiments we have presented in this section demonstrate two beneficial aspects of bounded abstract interpretation: (1) it increases the performance of the analysis (by up to 8x) by interactively ignoring certain parts of the state space, and (2) when bounding imprecision, it can improve the quality of the reported warnings, either by increasing the number of definite warnings or the number of genuine bugs detected by these warnings, while only missing few high-severity warnings.

We have evaluated these aspects of bounded abstract interpretation in a modular analyzer, which is already highly scalable partly due to its modularity. We expect that the impact of our technique on the scalability of whole-program analysis should be even greater. Moreover, modular analysis is typically more prone to reporting spurious errors, which our technique alleviates with the second aspect that we described above.

For our experiments, we did not evaluate the first and third application scenarios, about bounding time and spurious errors, respectively. Bounding the time of the analysis is easy and very useful in practice, however, the analysis results are too unpredictable for us to draw any meaningful conclusions, for instance about the number of genuine bugs. We did not evaluate how the collaboration of multiple analyses helps reduce the number of spurious errors as we have experimented with several such scenarios in our previous work [5,6,8,30].

6 Related Work

Model Checking. Bounded model checking [4,9] is an established technique for detecting errors in specifications of finite state machines by only considering a bounded number of state transitions. This core idea has been extended in numerous tools, such as CBMC [10], for bug-finding in infinite state programs. In contrast, bounded abstract interpretation is based on a sound verification technique for infinite state programs [11]. It provides a way to terminate the analysis based on a chosen bound (e.g., the maximum number of joins) and to soundly capture the verification results as a program instrumentation, which can be understood by a wide range of other analyses. Furthermore, an advantage of our technique is that it can analyze an infinite number of paths even before a bound is hit.

Conditional model checking (CMC) [2,3] combines different model checkers to improve overall performance and state-space coverage. In particular, CMC aims at encoding verification results of model checkers right before a spaceout or timeout is hit, which are typical limitations of model checking techniques. A complementary model checker may then be used to continue the analysis from where the previous tool left off. A conditional model checker takes as input a program and its specification as well as a condition that describes the states that have previously been verified. It produces another such condition to encode the new verification results.

There are the following significant differences between CMC and our technique. CMC focuses on alleviating the effect of exhausting physical bounds, such as time or memory consumption. Our notion of bounds is more flexible and driven primarily by the user's resources. Moreover, the verification annotations that we use for representing partial static analysis results are suitable for modular analyses and relatively compact (there typically is a constant instrumentation overhead in terms of the original program size). Also, our annotations are universally understood by most program analyzers, as opposed to the verification condition of CMC.

Symbolic Execution. Our technique features the following significant differences over approaches based on symbolic execution [23]: (1) it produces sound results, (2) reasoning over abstract domains is typically more efficient than reasoning about logical domains (e.g., using SMT solvers), and (3) by relying on abstract interpretation, it inherently avoids path explosion and is more scalable.

Angelic Verification. There are two sources of spurious errors in static analysis: those that are generated in the presence of an unconstrained environment, and those that are caused by an imprecision of the analysis itself. Angelic verification [13] aims at constraining a verifier to report warnings only when no acceptable environment specification exists to prove a given property. In other words, angelic verification reduces the number of spurious errors generated due to an unconstrained environment, whereas our technique can address both sources of spurious errors.

Unsoundness. Our previous work on documenting any unsoundness in a static analyzer [5–8] focuses on making explicit fixed and deliberate unsound assumptions of the analysis, for example, that arithmetic overflow can never occur. Such *fixed* assumptions are used in most practical static analyzers and are deliberately introduced *by designers* (e.g., to reduce spurious errors). In contrast, this work focuses on providing users with a flexible way to interactively bound the analysis while soundly recording intermediate results such that the analysis can be resumed later on. Unsound assumptions are encountered *dynamically* during the analysis based on the *user-provided* bounds.

Ranking of Warnings. Work on ranking analysis warnings, for instance by using statistical measures [24], is orthogonal to ours. Such techniques typically constitute a post-analysis step that is not aware of the internal imprecision of the abstract interpreter, even though there is some work that considers sources of imprecision encountered during the analysis [22]. Instead of performing a post-analysis, we rely on bounding the analysis itself to suppress warnings.

Work on differential static analysis [1] and verification modulo versions [26] suppresses warnings based on another program or program version. Our work, on the other hand, does not require such a reference program or version.

An existing approach [17] makes it possible to prove completeness of an analysis for a given program. This provides a way to rank higher warnings for which the analysis is shown to be complete. Unlike our approach, it requires a dedicated proof system and input from the designer of the analysis, which makes it more difficult to apply in practice.

In addition, there are orthogonal approaches for controlling imprecision (e.g., due to joins [27], widenings [19,20], and generally incompleteness of abstract domains [14]) of an existing analysis. In contrast to our work, these approaches focus on refining the analysis to reduce imprecision while still reaching a fixed-point (usually at the cost of performance). The scenario described in Sect. 4.2 is just one possible application of our approach for bounding an analysis based on user resources. Even with approaches that refine the analysis, it can make sense to use our approach since they inherently cannot avoid every imprecision.

7   Conclusion

We have presented a technique for imposing different bounds on a static analysis based on abstract interpretation. Although such bounds make the analysis unsound, we are able to express its verification results in a sound way by instrumenting the program. This opens up a new way for building highly tunable (with respect to precision and performance) analyzers by soundly sharing intermediate analysis results early on. In our experiments, we evaluate several such bounds in an analyzer and show that the analysis time can be significantly reduced while increasing the quality of the reported warnings. The trade-off between analysis time and unsoundness is also beneficial in determining when in the workflow of a software engineer a static analysis should run and with which bounds.

Acknowledgments. We thank Rainer Sigwald for promptly confirming and helping us resolve the MSBuild bugs as well as the anonymous reviewers for their constructive feedback.

References

1. Ball, T., Hackett, B., Lahiri, S.K., Qadeer, S., Vanegue, J.: Towards scalable modular checking of user-defined properties. In: Leavens, G.T., O'Hearn, P., Rajamani, S.K. (eds.) VSTTE 2010. LNCS, vol. 6217, pp. 1–24. Springer, Heidelberg (2010)
2. Beyer, D., Henzinger, T.A., Keremoglu, M.E., Wendler, P.: Conditional model checking. CoRR, abs/1109.6926 (2011)
3. Beyer, D., Henzinger, T.A., Keremoglu, M.E., Wendler, P.: Conditional model checking: a technique to pass information between verifiers. In: FSE, pp. 57–67. ACM (2012)

4. Biere, A., Cimatti, A., Clarke, E., Zhu, Y.: Symbolic model checking without BDDs. In: Cleaveland, W.R. (ed.) TACAS 1999. LNCS, vol. 1579, pp. 193–207. Springer, Heidelberg (1999)
5. Christakis, M.: Narrowing the gap between verification and systematic testing. Ph.D. thesis, ETH Zurich (2015)
6. Christakis, M., Müller, P., Wüstholz, V.: Collaborative verification and testing with explicit assumptions. In: Giannakopoulou, D., Méry, D. (eds.) FM 2012. LNCS, vol. 7436, pp. 132–146. Springer, Heidelberg (2012)
7. Christakis, M., Müller, P., Wüstholz, V.: An experimental evaluation of deliberate unsoundness in a static program analyzer. In: D'Souza, D., Lal, A., Larsen, K.G. (eds.) VMCAI 2015. LNCS, vol. 8931, pp. 336–354. Springer, Heidelberg (2015)
8. Christakis, M., Müller, P., Wüstholz, V.: Guiding dynamic symbolic execution toward unverified program executions. In: ICSE. ACM (2016, to appear)
9. Clarke, E.M., Biere, A., Raimi, R., Zhu, Y.: Bounded model checking using satisfiability solving. FMSD **19**, 7–34 (2001)
10. Clarke, E., Kroning, D., Lerda, F.: A tool for checking ANSI-C programs. In: Jensen, K., Podelski, A. (eds.) TACAS 2004. LNCS, vol. 2988, pp. 168–176. Springer, Heidelberg (2004)
11. Cousot, P., Cousot, R.: Abstract interpretation: a unified lattice model for static analysis of programs by construction or approximation of fixpoints. In: POPL, pp. 238–252. ACM (1977)
12. Cousot, P., Halbwachs, N.: Automatic discovery of linear restraints among variables of a program. In: POPL, pp. 84–96. ACM (1978)
13. Das, A., Lahiri, S.K., Lal, A., Li, Y.: Angelic verification: precise verification modulo unknowns. In: Kroening, D., Păsăreanu, C.S. (eds.) CAV 2015. LNCS, vol. 9206, pp. 324–342. Springer, Heidelberg (2015)
14. D'Silva, V., Haller, L., Kroening, D.: Abstract conflict driven learning. In: POPL, pp. 143–154. ACM (2013)
15. Fähndrich, M., Barnett, M., Logozzo, F.: Embedded contract languages. In: SAC, pp. 2103–2110. ACM (2010)
16. Fähndrich, M., Logozzo, F.: Static contract checking with abstract interpretation. In: Beckert, B., Marché, C. (eds.) FoVeOOS 2010. LNCS, vol. 6528, pp. 10–30. Springer, Heidelberg (2011)
17. Giacobazzi, R., Logozzo, F., Ranzato, F.: Analyzing program analyses. In: POPL, pp. 261–273. ACM (2015)
18. Giacobazzi, R., Ranzato, F., Scozzari, F.: Making abstract interpretations complete. J. ACM **47**, 361–416 (2000)
19. Gopan, D., Reps, T.: Lookahead widening. In: Ball, T., Jones, R.B. (eds.) CAV 2006. LNCS, vol. 4144, pp. 452–466. Springer, Heidelberg (2006)
20. Gopan, D., Reps, T.: Guided static analysis. In: Riis Nielson, H., Filé, G. (eds.) SAS 2007. LNCS, vol. 4634, pp. 349–365. Springer, Heidelberg (2007)
21. Graf, S., Saïdi, H.: Construction of abstract state graphs with PVS. In: Grumberg, O. (ed.) CAV 1997. LNCS, vol. 1254, pp. 72–83. Springer, Heidelberg (1997)
22. Jung, Y., Kim, J., Shin, J., Yi, K.: Taming false alarms from a domain-unaware C analyzer by a Bayesian statistical post analysis. In: Hankin, C., Siveroni, I. (eds.) SAS 2005. LNCS, vol. 3672, pp. 203–217. Springer, Heidelberg (2005)
23. King, J.C.: Symbolic execution and program testing. CACM **19**, 385–394 (1976)
24. Kremenek, T., Engler, D.R.: Z-ranking: using statistical analysis to counter the impact of static analysis approximations. In: Cousot, R. (ed.) SAS 2003. LNCS, vol. 2694, pp. 295–315. Springer, Heidelberg (2003)

25. Leino, K.R.M., Wüstholz, V.: Fine-grained caching of verification results. In: Kroening, D., Păsăreanu, C.S. (eds.) CAV 2015. LNCS, vol. 9206, pp. 380–397. Springer, Heidelberg (2015)
26. Logozzo, F., Lahiri, S.K., Fähndrich, M., Blackshear, S.: Verification modulo versions: towards usable verification. In: PLDI, pp. 294–304. ACM (2014)
27. Mauborgne, L., Rival, X.: Trace partitioning in abstract interpretation based static analyzers. In: Sagiv, M. (ed.) ESOP 2005. LNCS, vol. 3444, pp. 5–20. Springer, Heidelberg (2005)
28. Do, L.N.Q., Ali, K., Bodden, E., Livshits, B.: Toward a just-in-time static analysis. Technical Report TUD-CS-2015-1167, Technische Universität Darmstadt (2015)
29. Sadowski, C., van Gogh, J., Jaspan, C., Söderberg, E., Winter, C., Tricorder: building a program analysis ecosystem. In: ICSE, pp. 598–608. IEEE Computer Society (2015)
30. Wüstholz, V.: Partial verification results. Ph.D. thesis, ETH Zurich (2015)

Completeness in Approximate Transduction

Mila Dalla Preda[1], Roberto Giacobazzi[1,2(✉)], and Isabella Mastroeni[1]

[1] University of Verona, Verona, Italy
[2] IMDEA Software Institute, Madrid, Spain
{mila.dallapreda,roberto.giacobazzi,isabella.mastroeni}@univr.it

Abstract. Symbolic finite automata (SFA) allow the representation of regular languages of strings over an infinite alphabet of symbols. Recently these automata have been studied in the context of abstract interpretation, showing their extreme flexibility in representing languages at different levels of abstraction. Therefore, SFAs can naturally approximate sets of strings by the language they recognise, providing a suitable abstract domain for the analysis of symbolic data structures. In this scenario, transducers model SFA transformations. We characterise the properties of transduction of SFAs that guarantee soundness and completeness of the abstract interpretation of operations manipulating strings. We apply our model to the derivation of sanitisers for preventing cross site scripting attacks in web application security. In this case we extract the code sanitiser directly from the backward (transduction) analysis of the program given the specification of the expected attack in terms of SFA.

Keywords: Abstract interpretation · Symbolic automata · Symbolic transducers

1 Introduction

Symbolic finite automata (SFA) have been introduced as an extension of traditional finite state automata for modelling languages with a potential infinite alphabet [28]. Transitions in SFA are modelled as constraints interpreted in a given Boolean algebra, providing the semantic interpretation of constraints, and therefore the (potentially infinite) structural components of the language recognised by the automaton. This extends the class of regular languages over potentially unbound alphabets, providing a number of applications, from code sanitisation [19] to verification (see [23] for an introductory account) to models for reasoning and comparing program analysis tools, such as in the case of similarity analysis of binary executables in [10]. Similarly, symbolic finite transducers (SFT) perform language transformation and correspond to operations performed over a language, e.g., the language recognised by an SFA (see for instance [3,4,11,13,26]).

Recently the abstract interpretation of SFAs has been considered with the aim of using these symbolic (finite) structures to reason about potentially infinite structures, such as the sequences of instructions of the possible executions

© Springer-Verlag GmbH Germany 2016
X. Rival (Ed.): SAS 2016, LNCS 9837, pp. 126–146, 2016.
DOI: 10.1007/978-3-662-53413-7_7

of a program [10]. In this case, SFA can be approximated by abstract interpretation of either its constraint part or of its interpretation, respectively leading to a syntactic or semantic abstraction. In both cases, the language recognised by the approximated (abstract) symbolic automation is an over approximation of the original (concrete) one, as usual in abstract interpretation. An abstract symbolic automaton is nothing else than a symbolic automaton over a modified (approximated) semantics or constraint structure.

Abstract symbolic automata can be used as the elements of an abstract domain of objects representing languages. This allows us to use standard results in SFA to reason about approximate regular languages parametrically on the level of abstraction chosen for interpreting or representing strings [10]. Predicate transformers in this domain require the abstract interpretation of language transformers. This is particularly important if we plan to use these symbolic structures to approximate the semantics of string manipulating programs, such as in code santizers examining an HTML document and producing a new and modified HTML file as output.

In this paper, we investigate the notion of approximate symbolic transduction. Transducers are Mealy automata that transform languages. The idea is to consider transductions as language transformers where languages are approximated by SFAs. If L is a language, an approximation of L, is a language $L^{\sharp}$ such that $L \subseteq L^{\sharp}$. These approximate languages can be obtained by considering regular approximations of, for instance, context free languages or by abstracting the concrete SFA representing some regular language over a possibly infinite alphabet. The operation of transduction transforms these (input) approximate languages into other (output) approximate languages, the so called transduced languages.

We prove that a notion of completeness, both in its forward ($\mathcal{F}$) and backward ($\mathcal{B}$) sense, can be formalised for the transduction of SFAs, similarly to what is known in Galois connection based abstract interpretation [8,16]. As in abstract interpretation, completeness formalizes the notion of precision of an approximation. Completeness is defined wrt a pair $\langle A, B \rangle$ with A and B being respectively the input and output SFA that approximate the languages of the transduction. Backward completeness means that no loss of precision is introduced by approximating the input language L of a transducer with respect to the approximation of the transduction of L. In this case the approximate transduction of L provides the same language as the approximate transduction of an approximation of L. Consider, for example, a transducer T that given, a string σ in Σ^* removes the symbols $s \in \Sigma$ by replacing them with ϵ. Consider an SFA A that recognises the language $\mathscr{L}(A) = \{a\sigma \mid \sigma \in \Sigma^*\}$ and an SFA B that recognises the language $\mathscr{L}(B) = \{(a+b)\sigma \mid \sigma \in (\Sigma \smallsetminus \{s\})^*\}$. Then, the pair of SFAs $\langle A, B \rangle$ is not $\mathcal{B}$-complete for the transduction T. Indeed, applying transduction T to the strings recognized by A and then projecting the output in B we obtain the set of strings $\{a\sigma \mid \sigma \in (\Sigma \smallsetminus \{s\})^*\}$, while applying transduction T to the (concrete) set of any possible strings and then projecting the output in B we obtain the set of strings $\{(a+b)\sigma \mid \sigma \in (\Sigma \smallsetminus \{s\})^*\}$. Forward completeness

[15] means instead that no loss of precision is introduced by approximating the output of the transaction of an approximate language $L^\sharp$ with respect to the concrete transaction of $L^\sharp$ itself. In the example above, if we consider an SFA B' recognizing $\mathscr{L}(B') = \{ab\sigma \mid \sigma \in (\Sigma \smallsetminus \{s\})^*\}$, we have that the pair of SFAs $\langle A, B' \rangle$ is not $\mathcal{F}$-complete for the transduction T. Indeed, applying transduction T to the strings recognized by A we obtain a set strictly containing $\mathscr{L}(B')$, namely the set containing all the strings without s starting with a (not only those starting with ab).

These two forms of completeness characterise the maximal precision achievable when transducing languages approximated by SFAs. We prove that it is possible to associate a pair of SFAs with any SFT (the input and output languages of the transducer) and conversely an SFT with any SFA. When $\mathcal{B}$-completeness is not satisfied, namely when the pair of SFAs $\langle A, B \rangle$ is not $\mathcal{B}$-complete for T, we characterize how to minimally expand the language recognized by the input SFA A or how to minimally reduce the language recognised by the output SFA B in order to achieve $\mathcal{B}$-completeness. For the example above, in order to achieve $\mathcal{B}$-completeness we can either add to $\mathscr{L}(A)$ the set of strings $\{b\sigma \mid \sigma \in \Sigma^*\}$ or remove from $\mathscr{L}(B)$ the strings in $\{b\sigma \mid \sigma \in (\Sigma \smallsetminus \{s\})^*\}$. A similar construction applies to $\mathcal{F}$-completeness. In the example, in order to achieve $\mathcal{F}$-completeness we can either remove from $\mathscr{L}(A)$ all those strings whose second symbol is not b, or add to $\mathscr{L}(B')$ all the strings (without s) starting with a. This result extends to symbolic transducers and symbolic automata the characterisation of complete abstractions in [16].

We apply our construction to the synthesis of sanitisers for cross-site scripting (XSS) and injection attack sanitisation in web application security. A script program manipulating strings P can be viewed as the combination T of transducers acting on a suitable language of allowed strings. If A is a language specifying a given attack, namely a set of strings that may lead the web application to bypass some access control, then whenever the inverse image of A by T is empty, then P is free from the attack specified in A. We extract the specification of a code sanitiser directly from the abstract interpretation of P viewed as an approximate transduction of a specification A of an expected attack in terms of SFA. Interestingly, this construction means that a script program P manipulating strings is unsafe with respect to the attack A if T is $\mathcal{B}$-incomplete with respect to A and an input SFA recognising the empty language. In this case, the extraction of the minimal sanitiser corresponds precisely to the expansion of the language of the SFA recognising the empty language towards $\mathcal{B}$-completeness with respect to A. This gives a minimality result with respect to language set inclusion, in the systematic derivation of script code sanitisation. We exemplify our idea with a simple example of sanitisation for a JavaScript-like pseudo code.

2   Background

Symbolic Finite Automata (SFA). We follow [12] in specifying symbolic automata in terms of effective Boolean algebra. Let $\mathcal{A} = \langle \mathfrak{D}_\mathcal{A}, \Psi_\mathcal{A}, \llbracket \cdot \rrbracket, \bot, \top, \wedge, \vee, \neg \rangle$ be an effective Boolean algebra, with domain elements in a r.e. set $\mathfrak{D}_\mathcal{A}$, a r.e. set of predicates $\Psi_\mathcal{A}$ closed under boolean connectives $\wedge$, $\vee$ and $\neg$. The semantics $[\![\cdot]\!] : \Psi_\mathcal{A} \longrightarrow \wp(\mathfrak{D}_\mathcal{A})$ is a partial recursive function such that $[\![\bot]\!] = \varnothing$, $[\![\top]\!] = \mathfrak{D}_\mathcal{A}$, and $\forall \varphi, \phi \in \Psi_\mathcal{A}$ we have that $[\![\varphi \vee \phi]\!] = [\![\varphi]\!] \cup [\![\phi]\!]$, $[\![\varphi \wedge \phi]\!] = [\![\varphi]\!] \cap [\![\phi]\!]$, and $[\![\neg\varphi]\!] = \mathfrak{D}_\mathcal{A} \smallsetminus [\![\varphi]\!]$. For $\varphi \in \Psi_\mathcal{A}$ we write $IsSat(\varphi)$ when $[\![\varphi]\!] \neq \varnothing$ and say that φ is *satisfiable*. $\mathcal{A}$ is decidable if $IsSat$ is decidable.

Definition 1 (Symbolic Finite Automata). *A SFA is $A = \langle \mathcal{A}, Q, q_0, F, \Delta \rangle$ where $\mathcal{A}$ is an effective Boolean algebra, Q is a finite set of states, $q_0 \in Q$ is the initial state, $F \subseteq Q$ is the set of final states and $\Delta \subseteq Q \times \Psi_\mathcal{A} \times Q$ is a finite set of transitions.*

A transition in $A = \langle \mathcal{A}, Q, q_0, F, \Delta \rangle$ labeled φ from state p to state q, $(p, \varphi, q) \in \Delta$ is often denoted $p \xrightarrow{\varphi} q$. φ is called the *guard* of the transition. An a-move of an SFA A is a transition $p \xrightarrow{\varphi} q$ such that $a \in [\![\varphi]\!]$, also denoted $p \xrightarrow{a} q$. The language recognized by a state $q \in Q$ in A is defined as:

$$\mathscr{L}_q(A) = \left\{ a_1, \ldots, a_n \in \mathfrak{D}_\mathcal{A}^* \,\middle|\, \forall 1 \leq i \leq n.\, p_{i-1} \xrightarrow{a_i} p_i, p_0 = q,\, p_n \in F \right\}$$

hence $\mathscr{L}(A) = \mathscr{L}_{q_0}(A)$. In the following we denote the string elements in bold. Moreover, given two strings $\mathbf{s}_1, \mathbf{s}_2 \in S^*$ then we write $\mathbf{s}_1 \preceq \mathbf{s}_2$ when $\mathbf{s}_1$ is a prefix of $\mathbf{s}_2$, we denote with $\mathbf{s}_1 \cdot \mathbf{s}_2$ the string concatenation $\mathbf{s}_1 \mathbf{s}_2$ and with $\mathbf{s}[n]$ the n-th symbol in $\mathbf{s}_1$. Consider $\mathbf{a} \in \mathcal{D}_\mathcal{A}^*$, we write $q \xrightarrow{\mathbf{a}} p$ to denote that state p is reachable from state q by reading the string $\mathbf{a}$.

The following terminology holds for SFA: A is *complete SFA* when all states hold an out-going a-move for any $a \in \mathfrak{D}$. A is *deterministic* whenever $p \xrightarrow{\varphi} q, p \xrightarrow{\beta} q' \in \Delta$: if $IsSat(\varphi \wedge \beta)$ then $q = q'$. A is *clean* if for all $p \xrightarrow{\varphi} q \in \Delta$: p is reachable from q_0 and $IsSat(\varphi)$. A is *normalized* if for all $p, q \in Q$: there is at most one move from p to q. A is *minimal* if it is deterministic, clean, normalized and for all $p, q \in Q$: $p = q \Leftrightarrow \mathscr{L}_q(A) = \mathscr{L}_p(A)$. In [12] the authors propose an efficient algorithm for SFA minimization. SFA can have ϵ-moves that can be eliminated in linear time [27]. Moreover, given two SFAs A and B it is possible to compute their union $A \oplus B$ such that $\mathscr{L}(A \oplus B) = \mathscr{L}(A) \cup \mathscr{L}(B)$, their product $A \times B$ such that $\mathscr{L}(A \times B) = \mathscr{L}(A) \cap \mathscr{L}(B)$, their difference $A - B$ such that $\mathscr{L}(A - B) = \mathscr{L}(A) \smallsetminus \mathscr{L}(B)$ [20].

Recently, it has been developed a general framework for abstracting SFAs [10]. Here SFAs form a domain ordered according to the language that they recognize, so an SFA is more concrete than another one if it recognizes a smaller language (with less noise). In particular, an SFA can be abstracted either by acting on the underlying Boolean algebra or on the automata. When abstracting at the level of Boolean algebra we can either approximate the domain of predicates (i.e., the syntax) or the domain of denotations (i.e., the semantics). In [10] there is a rigorous description of both syntactic and semantic abstraction of SFA and of their strong relation. The domain of SFA can be naturally used to represent properties of strings. As examples, consider the SFAs A and B in Fig. 1. In these SFAs the predicates are the label on the edges (we omit the label **true**), x denotes the following symbol read and the accepted language is the set

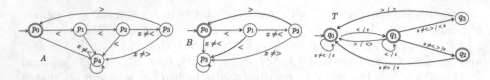

Fig. 1. An example of SFA A, SFA B and of SFT T.

of all the sequences of symbols, leading from the initial state p_0 to the final state (denoted with double line), such that each symbol satisfies the corresponding predicate. The SFA A, for instance, recognizes the language $\mathscr{L}(A) = \bigcup_{n \in \mathbb{N}} L_a^n$ where $L_a \triangleq \{<< x > \mid x \in \Sigma \smallsetminus \{<\}\}$, namely $\mathscr{L}(A)$ is a set of finite sequences of patterns of the form $<< x >$ with $x \in \Sigma$ is different from $<$. Similarly, $\mathscr{L}(B) = \bigcup_{n \in \mathbb{N}} L_b^n$, where $L_b \triangleq \{< x > \mid x \in \Sigma \smallsetminus \{<\}\}$.

Symbolic Finite Transducers (SFT). We follow [28] in the definition of SFT and of their background structure. Consider a background universe $\mathcal{U}$ which is a countable multi-carrier set equipped with a language of functions and relations with a fixed interpretation. We use σ, τ, γ to denote types, and $\mathcal{U}^\sigma$ to denote the elements of $\mathcal{U}$ that have type σ. In the following Σ refers to $\mathcal{U}^\sigma$ and Γ to $\mathcal{U}^\gamma$. We use $\mathbb{B}$ to denote the elements of boolean type, $\mathcal{U}^\mathbb{B} = \{true, false\}$, and $\mathbb{Z}$ for the integer type. Terms and formulas are defined by induction over the background language and are assumed to be well-typed. Terms of type $\mathbb{B}$ are treated as formulas. $t : \sigma$ denotes a term t of type σ, and $FV(t)$ denotes the set of its free variables. A term $t : \sigma$ is *closed* when $FV(t) = \emptyset$. Closed terms have a semantics $[\![t]\!]$. As usual $t[x/v]$ denotes the substitution of a variable $x : \tau$ with a term $v : \tau$. A λ-*term* f is an expression of the form $\lambda x.t$ where $x : \sigma$ is a variable and $t : \gamma$ is a term such that $FV(t) \subseteq \{x\}$. The λ-term f has type $\sigma \to \gamma$ and its semantics is a function $[\![f]\!] : \Sigma \to \Gamma$ that maps $a \in \Sigma$ to $[\![t[x/a]]\!] \in \Gamma$. Let f and g range over λ-terms. A λ-term of type $\sigma \to \mathbb{B}$ is called a σ-predicate. We use φ and ψ to denote σ-predicates. Given a σ-predicate φ, we write $a \in [\![\varphi]\!]$ for $[\![\varphi]\!](a) = \mathbf{true}$. Moreover, $[\![\varphi]\!]$ can be seen as the subset of Σ that satisfies φ. We sometimes use $\mathcal{P}^\sigma$ to refer to the set of σ-predicates. We assume implicit β-reduction, namely given a λ-term $f = (\lambda x.t : \sigma \to \gamma)$ and a term $u : \sigma$, $f(u)$ stands for $t[x/u]$. φ is *unsatisfiable* when $[\![\varphi]\!] = \emptyset$ and *satisfiable* otherwise.

Definition 2 (Label Theory). *A label theory for $\sigma \to \gamma$ is associated with a effectively enumerable set of λ-terms of type $\sigma \to \gamma$ and a effectively enumerable set of σ-predicates that is effectively closed under Boolean operations and relative difference, i.e., $[\![\varphi \wedge \psi]\!] = [\![\varphi]\!] \cap [\![\psi]\!]$, and $[\![\neg\varphi]\!] = \Sigma \smallsetminus [\![\varphi]\!]$.*

A label theory Ψ is *decidable* if $IsSat(\varphi)$ is decidable for $\varphi \in \Psi$. We use X^* to denote the Kleene closure of a set X, and τ^* to denote the type of sequences over τ. $\mathbf{x}$ or equivalently $[x_0, \dots, x_{k-1}]$ denote a sequence of length $|\mathbf{x}| = k \geq 0$, where $\mathbf{x}_i$ refers to the i-th element of $\mathbf{x}$ with $0 \leq i \leq k - 1$.

Definition 3 (Symbolic Finite Transducers). *A SFT T over $\sigma \to \gamma$ is a tuple $T = \langle Q, q_0, F, R \rangle$, where Q is a finite set of states, $q_0 \in Q$ is the initial state, $F \subseteq Q$ is the set of final states and R is a set of rules $(p, \varphi, \mathbf{f}, q)$ where $p, q \in Q$, φ is a σ-predicate and $\mathbf{f}$ is a sequence of λ-terms over a given label theory for $\sigma \to \gamma$.*

A rule $(p, \varphi, \mathbf{f}, q)$ of an SFT T is denoted as $p \xrightarrow{\varphi/\mathbf{f}}_T q$ where φ is called guard. We omit the index T when it is clear from the context. The sequence of λ-terms $\mathbf{f} : (\sigma \to \gamma)^*$ can be treated as a function $\lambda x.[\mathbf{f}_0(x), \ldots, \mathbf{f}_k(x)]$ where $k = |\mathbf{f}| - 1$. Concrete transitions are represented as rules. Consider $p, q \in Q$, $a \in \Sigma$ and $\mathbf{b} \in \Gamma^*$ then:

$$p \xrightarrow{a/\mathbf{b}}_T q \Leftrightarrow p \xrightarrow{\varphi/\mathbf{f}}_T q \in R : a \in [\![\varphi]\!] \wedge \mathbf{b} = [\![\mathbf{f}]\!](a)$$

Given two sequences $\mathbf{a} \in \Sigma^*$ and $\mathbf{b} \in \Gamma^*$, we write $q \xrightarrow{\mathbf{a}/\mathbf{b}} p$ when p is reachable from q reading $\mathbf{a}$ and producing in output $\mathbf{b}$. More specifically when there exists a path of transitions from q to p in T with input sequence $\mathbf{a}$ and output sequence $\mathbf{b}$, where $\mathbf{b} = \mathbf{b}^0 \cdot \mathbf{b}^1 \cdots \mathbf{b}^n$ with $n = |\mathbf{a}| - 1$ and $\mathbf{b}^i$ denoting a subseqeunce of $\mathbf{b}$, such that:

$$p = p_0 \xrightarrow{\mathbf{a}_0/\mathbf{b}^0} p_1 \xrightarrow{\mathbf{a}_1/\mathbf{b}^1} p_2 \ldots p_n \xrightarrow{\mathbf{a}_n/\mathbf{b}^n} p_{n+1} = q$$

SFTs can have ϵ-transitions and they can be eliminated following a standard procedure. We assume $p \xrightarrow{\epsilon/\epsilon} p$ for all $p \in Q$.

Definition 4 (Transduction). *The transduction of an SFT T over $\sigma \to \gamma$ is a function $\mathfrak{T}_T : \Sigma^* \to \wp(\Gamma^*)$ where: $\mathfrak{T}_T(\mathbf{a}) \triangleq \{\mathbf{b} \in \Gamma^* \mid \exists q \in F : q_0 \xrightarrow{\mathbf{a}/\mathbf{b}} q\}$.*

An SFT is *single-valued* when $|\mathfrak{T}_T(\mathbf{a})| \leq 1$ for all $\mathbf{a} \in \Sigma^*$. In [28] the authors define the notion of SFTs *equivalence* by saying that two SFTs T and R are equivalent $(T \equiv R)$ when $\{\mathbf{a} \in \Sigma^* \mid \mathfrak{T}_T(\mathbf{a}) \neq \emptyset\} = \{\mathbf{a} \in \Sigma^* \mid \mathfrak{T}_R(\mathbf{a}) \neq \emptyset\}$ (domain equivalence), and $\forall \mathbf{a} \in \mathscr{L}_I(T)$ we have $\mathfrak{T}_T(\mathbf{a}) = \mathfrak{T}_R(\mathbf{a})$ (partial equivalence). Equivalence of SFTs is decidable when SFTs are single-valued, [28] provides an algorithm for checking equivalence.

An example of SFT is given on the right, in Fig. 1. This SFT is a slight modification of an SFT from [28]. The considered SFT T reads a string of elements in Σ and returns the string of patterns $< x >$ and $<>$ that it contains, with $x \neq <, >$.

3 Approximating Transduction

Let us denote with SFA$^\sigma$ the set of SFAs that recognize sequences of symbols of type σ and with A^σ an element of SFA$^\sigma$. This means that given $A^\sigma \in$ SFA$^\sigma$ we have that $\mathscr{L}(A^\sigma) \in \wp(\Sigma^*)$, which means that the domain of denotations of the underlying Boolean algebra is Σ. Let SFT$^{\sigma/\gamma}$ be the set of SFTs over $\sigma \to \gamma$ and let us denote with $T^{\sigma/\gamma}$ an element of SFT$^{\sigma/\gamma}$. In the following we will omit the superscript denoting the type of SFA and SFT when it is not needed or when it is clear form the context. In this section, we want to show how the string transformation expressed by $T^{\sigma/\gamma}$ can been approximated as a transformation from SFA$^\sigma$ to SFA$^\gamma$. Indeed, the SFT $T^{\sigma/\gamma}$ is a language transformer that, given a language of strings over Σ^*, returns a language of strings over Γ^*. By approximating the input and output languages of strings manipulated by an SFT in the domain of SFAs, we can view SFTs as SFAs transformers, thus approximating the SFT computation on the domain of SFAs.

We associate with an SFT $T^{\sigma/\gamma}$ an input language and output language that collect respectively the input strings in Σ^* that produce an output when processed by T, and the output strings in Γ^* generated by T.

Definition 5 (Input/Output language of an SFT). *Given an SFT $T^{\sigma/\gamma} = \langle Q, q_0, F, R \rangle$, we define its input language $\mathscr{L}_\mathcal{I}(T)$ and output language $\mathscr{L}_\mathcal{O}(T)$ as:*

- $\mathscr{L}_\mathcal{I}(T) \triangleq \{ \mathbf{a} \in \Sigma^* \mid \mathfrak{T}_T(\mathbf{a}) \neq \emptyset \}$
- $\mathscr{L}_\mathcal{O}(T) \triangleq \{ \mathbf{b} \in \Gamma^* \mid \mathbf{b} \in \mathfrak{T}_T(\mathbf{a}), \mathbf{a} \in \mathscr{L}_\mathcal{I}(T) \}$

The proposed notion of input language corresponds to the notion of domain of an SFT introduced in [28]. Observe that, given an SFT T it is possible to build two SFA SFA$_\mathcal{I}(T)$ and SFA$_\mathcal{O}(T)$ that recognize respectively the input and output language of T.

Definition 6. *Given an SFT $T^{\sigma/\gamma} = \langle Q, q_0, F, R \rangle$ we define:*

- SFA$_\mathcal{I}(T) \triangleq \langle \mathcal{A}, Q, q_0, F, \Delta_{\text{SFA}_\mathcal{I}(T)} \rangle$, *where* $\mathcal{A} = \langle \Sigma, \mathcal{P}^\sigma, \llbracket \cdot \rrbracket, \bot, \top, \wedge, \vee, \neg \rangle$ *and rules defined as:* $\Delta_{\text{SFA}_\mathcal{I}(T)} \triangleq \{ (p, \varphi, q) \mid (p, \varphi, \mathbf{f}, q) \in R \}$.
- SFA$_\mathcal{O}(T) \triangleq \langle \mathcal{A}, Q, q_0, F, \Delta_{\text{SFA}_\mathcal{O}(T)} \rangle$, *where* $\mathcal{A} = \langle \Gamma^*, \mathcal{P}^{\gamma*}, \llbracket \cdot \rrbracket, \bot, \top, \wedge, \vee, \neg \rangle$ *and rules defined as:* $\Delta_{\text{SFA}_\mathcal{O}(T)} \triangleq \{ (p, \mathbf{f}(\varphi), q) \mid (p, \varphi, \mathbf{f}, q) \in R \}$, *where* $\llbracket \mathbf{f}(\varphi) \rrbracket \triangleq \{ \llbracket \mathbf{f} \rrbracket(a) \mid a \in \llbracket \varphi \rrbracket \}$.

Observe that the language of SFA$_\mathcal{O}(T)$ is an element of $\wp(\Gamma^{**})$ because at each step the SFA SFA$_\mathcal{O}(T)$ recognizes a string of Γ^*. We define function $seq : \wp(\Gamma^{**}) \to \wp(\Gamma^*)$ that transforms a set of strings of strings into a set of strings as the additive lift of:

$$seq(\mathbb{b}) \triangleq \begin{cases} \epsilon & \text{if } \mathbb{b} = \epsilon \\ \mathbf{b} \cdot seq(\mathbb{b}') & \text{if } \mathbb{b} = \mathbf{b}\mathbb{b}' \end{cases}$$

where $\mathbb{b}$ denotes a string in Γ^{**} and $\mathbf{b}$ a string in Γ^*. Consider for instance, again the SFT T in Fig. 1. Then we obtain the input SFA SFA$_\mathcal{I}(T)$, on the left in Fig. 2, simply by erasing the output function information (and minimizing if necessary). In particular, we can observe that SFA$_\mathcal{I}(T)$ accepts any possible string, namely is it equivalent to an SFA with only one final state with only one self edge labeled with **true**. The output SFA SFA$_\mathcal{O}(T)$ keeps only the output function transformation. The minimized output SFA of T is given in Fig. 2 (top-right). Note that, the accepted strings formally are sequences of strings, since

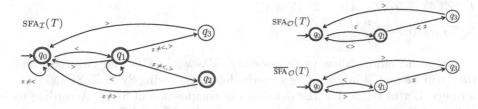

Fig. 2. The input and out SFA of the SFT T.

the edge connecting q_1 with q_3 accepts a string of two symbols instead of one single symbol. For this reason we need the function $seq(\mathbb{b})$ such that, for instance $seq(\mathbb{b})((<,s),>) = (<,s,>)$.

Lemma 1. *Given an SFT $T^{\sigma/\gamma}$, the followings hold:*

1. $\mathscr{L}_{\mathcal{I}}(T) = \mathscr{L}(\mathrm{SFA}_{\mathcal{I}}(T)) \in \wp(\Sigma^*)$
2. $\mathscr{L}_{\mathcal{O}}(T) = seq(\mathscr{L}(\mathrm{SFA}_{\mathcal{O}}(T))) \in \wp(\Gamma^*)$

For instance, if we consider again the SFT T in Fig. 1, $\mathscr{L}_{\mathcal{I}}(T) = \Sigma^*$ while $\mathscr{L}_{\mathcal{O}}(T) = \{(<,x,>) \mid x \neq '<'\}$.

Note that, by definition, the function **f** is a lambda term mapping each symbol in Σ satisfying the edge guard in a sequence of symbols in Γ, i.e., $\forall x \in [\![\varphi]\!] \subseteq \Sigma$ we have that $\mathbf{f}(x) = \mathbf{f}_0(x) \ldots \mathbf{f}_k(x)$ with $\forall i \in [0, k].\, \mathbf{f}_i(x) \in \Gamma$. This characteristic of transducers allows us to uniquely construct an equivalent SFA whose language is precisely $\mathscr{L}_{\mathcal{O}}(T)$.

Proposition 1. *Given a SFT T, we can always construct, starting from* $\mathrm{SFA}_{\mathcal{O}}(T)$ *the SFA* $\overline{\mathrm{SFA}}_{\mathcal{O}}(T) = \langle \overline{\mathcal{A}}, \overline{Q}, q_0, \overline{F}, \Delta_{\overline{\mathrm{SFA}}_{\mathcal{O}}(T)} \rangle$, *where* $\overline{\mathcal{A}} = \langle \Gamma, \mathcal{P}^\gamma, [\![\cdot]\!], \bot,$ $\top, \wedge, \vee, \neg \rangle$ *such that* $\mathscr{L}(\overline{\mathrm{SFA}}_{\mathcal{O}}(T)) = seq(\mathscr{L}(\mathrm{SFA}_{\mathcal{O}}(T)))$.

The idea of this transformation is that of splitting each edge labeled with a string $s_1 s_2 \ldots s_n \in \Gamma^*$ in n edges, each one labeled with one symbol $s_i \in \Gamma$, thus adding $n-1$ new states. In this transformation we do not change neither initial nor final states. For instance, in the example on the right in Fig. 2 we split the edge $q_1 \xrightarrow{<\,x} q_3$ in $q_1 \xrightarrow{<} q_1'$ and $q_1' \xrightarrow{x} q_3$. Then we erase ε-transition [27], when necessary (in this case we could change the set of final states), and we can finally minimize the resulting SFA, if possible [12]. In Fig. 2 (bottom-right) we have the SFA resulting by this transformation of $\mathrm{SFA}_{\mathcal{O}}(T)$.

We can also define how an SFA A can be associated with an SFT $\mathcal{T}_{\mathcal{O}}(A)$ whose input and output language is the one recognized by the SFA.

Definition 7. *Given an SFA $A^\sigma = \langle \mathcal{A}, Q, q_0, F, \Delta \rangle$ over $\mathcal{A} = \langle \Sigma, \mathcal{P}^\sigma, [\![\cdot]\!], \bot, \top,$ $\wedge, \vee, \neg \rangle$. We define the output SFT over $\sigma \to \sigma$ associated with A as $\mathcal{T}_{\mathcal{O}}(A) \triangleq$ $\langle Q, q_0, F, R^{id} \rangle$ where the set of rules is $R^{id} \triangleq \{(p, \varphi, id, q) \mid (p, \varphi, q) \in R\}$.*

Lemma 2. *Given an SFA A, the followings hold:*

1. $\mathscr{L}(A) = \mathscr{L}_I(\mathcal{T}_O(A)) = \mathscr{L}_O(\mathcal{T}_O(A))$
2. $\mathfrak{T}_{\mathcal{T}_O(A)}(\mathbf{a}) = \begin{cases} \mathbf{a} \ if \ \mathbf{a} \in \mathscr{L}(A) \\ \emptyset \ otherwise \end{cases}$

These definitions allow us to associate SFAs with SFTs and vice-versa and they will be usefull in providing a methodology for seeing SFTs as SFAs transformers. Let us recall that the definition of composition of SFTs. According to [28] we define the composition of two transductions $\mathfrak{T}_1$ and $\mathfrak{T}_2$ as:

$$\mathfrak{T}_1 \diamond \mathfrak{T}_2 \triangleq \lambda \mathbf{b}. \bigcup_{\mathbf{a} \in \mathfrak{T}_1(\mathbf{b})} \mathfrak{T}_2(\mathbf{a})$$

Observe that the composition $\diamond$ applies first $\mathfrak{T}_1$ and then $\mathfrak{T}_2$ and that single-value property is preserved by composition. Two label theories $\sigma \to \tau$ and $\tau \to \gamma$ are *composable* if there exists a label theory Ψ for $\sigma \to \gamma$ such that: (1) if $f : \sigma \to \tau$ and $g : \tau \to \gamma$ are λ-terms then $\lambda x.g(f(x))$ is a valid λ-term in Ψ, (2) if φ is a τ-predicate and $f : \sigma \to \tau$ is a λ-term then $\lambda x.\varphi(f(x))$ is a valid σ-predicate in Ψ. It has been proved that if T_1 and T_2 are SFTs over composable label theories, then there exists an SFT $T_1 \diamond T_2$ that is obtained effectively from T_1 and T_2 such that $\mathfrak{T}_{T_1 \diamond T_2} = \mathfrak{T}_1 \diamond \mathfrak{T}_2$ [28]. A constructive characterization of the composition of SFA can be found in [18]. We report in the following an algebra over SFTs that is obtained by extending the one in [28] with the association of SFAs to SFTs and vice versa.

σ, τ, γ ::= types
sfa^σ ::= explicit dfn of an SFA over σ
$sft^{\sigma/\gamma}$ ::= explicit dfn of an SFT over $\sigma \to \gamma$
A^σ ::= $sfa^\sigma \mid A^\sigma - A^\sigma \mid A^\sigma \times A^\sigma \mid A^\sigma \oplus A^\sigma \mid \text{SFA}_I(T^{\sigma/\gamma}) \mid \text{SFA}_O(T^{\gamma/\sigma}) \mid \overline{\text{SFA}}_O(T^{\gamma/\sigma})$
$T^{\sigma/\gamma}$ ::= $sft^{\sigma/\gamma} \mid T^{\sigma/\tau} \diamond T^{\tau/\gamma} \mid \mathcal{T}_O(A^\sigma)$

Now we have all we need for specifying SFTs as SFAs transformers. In order to use an SFT to transform an SFA we need that the two work on the same domain of elements. More specifically, an SFT $T^{\sigma/\gamma}$ transforms an SFA A^σ into an SFA B^γ. Intuitively, applying an SFT $T^{\sigma/\gamma}$ to the strings recognized by an SFA A^σ means to compute $\mathfrak{T}_T$ on the strings in $\mathscr{L}(A^\sigma)$. Interestingly this precisely corresponds to the following composition of SFTs: $\mathcal{T}_O(A^\sigma) \diamond T^{\sigma/\gamma}$. Indeed, in this composition the language recognized by the SFA A^σ becomes the input language of the SFT $T^{\sigma/\gamma}$. Observe that this composition is equivalent to the operation of domain restriction defined in [28].

Proposition 2. *The transduction of* $\mathcal{T}_O(A^\sigma) \diamond T^{\sigma/\gamma}$ *is:*

$$\mathfrak{T}_{\mathcal{T}_O(A^\sigma) \diamond T^{\sigma/\gamma}} = \lambda \mathbf{b}. \begin{cases} \mathfrak{T}_T(\mathbf{b}) \ if \ \mathbf{b} \in \mathscr{L}(A) \\ \emptyset \qquad otherwise \end{cases}$$

and $\mathscr{L}_I(\mathcal{T}_O(A^\sigma) \diamond T^{\sigma/\gamma}) = \mathscr{L}(A)$ *and* $\mathscr{L}_O(\mathcal{T}_O(A^\sigma) \diamond T^{\sigma/\gamma}) = \{\mathbf{b} \in \Gamma^* \mid \mathbf{b} \in \mathfrak{T}_T(\mathbf{a}), \mathbf{a} \in \mathscr{L}(A)\}$

Observe that by computing the SFA that recognizes the output language of $\mathcal{T}_O(A^\sigma) \diamond T^{\sigma/\gamma}$ we obtain the SFA obtained by transforming A^σ with $T^{\sigma/\gamma}$.

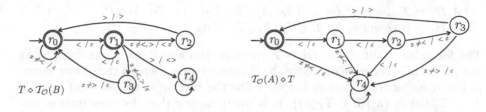

Fig. 3. Application of SFT $T^{\sigma/\sigma}$ to SFA A and to B

Proposition 3. $\mathscr{L}(\overline{\mathrm{SFA}}_{\mathcal{O}}(\mathcal{T}_{\mathcal{O}}(A^{\sigma}) \diamond T^{\sigma/\gamma})) = \{\mathbf{b} \in \Gamma^* \mid \mathbf{b} \in \mathfrak{T}_T(\mathbf{a}), \mathbf{a} \in \mathscr{L}(A)\}$

Thus, an SFT $T^{\sigma/\gamma}$ transforms an SFA A^{σ} into the SFA $\overline{\mathrm{SFA}}_{\mathcal{O}}(\mathcal{T}_{\mathcal{O}}(A^{\sigma}) \diamond T^{\sigma/\gamma})$, as shown in the following example where we consider the SFT $T^{\sigma/\sigma}$ and the SFA A^{σ} in Fig. 1. Now we compute the SFT $\mathcal{T}_{\mathcal{O}}(A^{\sigma})$ whose output language is exactly the language recognized by the SFA A^{σ}. Next, we apply the SFT to the SFA by computing the SFT given by the composition $\mathcal{T}_{\mathcal{O}}(A) \diamond T$, depicted (minimized) on the right of Fig. 3 (on the left we have another example of composition). Finally, we extract $\overline{\mathrm{SFA}}_{\mathcal{O}}(\mathcal{T}_{\mathcal{O}}(A) \diamond T)^{\sigma^*}$, which recognizes the output language of $\mathcal{T}_{\mathcal{O}}(A) \diamond T$. As expected, the output SFA is such that $\mathscr{L}(\overline{\mathrm{SFA}}_{\mathcal{O}}(\mathcal{T}_{\mathcal{O}}(A) \diamond T)^{\sigma^*})$ is the language $\bigcup_{n \in \mathbb{N}} L^n$ where we define $L \triangleq \{< x > \mid x \in \Sigma \smallsetminus \{<\}\}$.

4   Completeness

As in abstract interpretation-based static analysis, we wonder when the approximated computation of SFTs on the abstract domain of SFAs is precise, namely when computing on abstract values or abstracting the concrete computation provides the same loss of precision. In abstract interpretation theory, the ideal situation of no loss of precision between the concrete and abstract computation is called completeness [7,8]. There are two forms of completeness: *backward completeness* (denoted $\mathcal{B}$-completeness) and *forward completeness* (denoted $\mathcal{F}$-completeness). $\mathcal{B}$-completeness requires that the concrete and abstract computation are equivalent when we compare their outputs on the abstract domain, while $\mathcal{F}$-completeness requires that the concrete and abstract computation are equivalent when we consider abstractions of the inputs. It has been proved that, both forms of completeness, are properties of the abstract domain, and that it is possible to iteratively modify an abstract domain in order to make it complete for a given function [16]. In the following we introduce the notion of $\mathcal{B}$-completeness and $\mathcal{F}$-completeness of SFAs wrt a given SFT. When completeness is not satisfied we provide SFAs transformers that allow to achieve it by minimally modifying the language recognized by the SFAs. We consider the following notion of completeness:

Definition 8. *Let $T = \langle Q, q_0, F, R \rangle$ be an SFT and $A = \langle \mathcal{A}, Q, q_0, F, \Delta \rangle$ and $B = \langle \mathcal{A}', Q', q_0', F', \Delta' \rangle$ be SFAs.*

- $\langle A, B \rangle$ is $\mathcal{F}$-complete for T if $\mathcal{T}_{\mathcal{O}}(A) \diamond T \diamond \mathcal{T}_{\mathcal{O}}(B) \equiv \mathcal{T}_{\mathcal{O}}(A) \diamond T$
- $\langle A, B \rangle$ is $\mathcal{B}$-complete for T if $\mathcal{T}_{\mathcal{O}}(A) \diamond T \diamond \mathcal{T}_{\mathcal{O}}(B) \equiv T \diamond \mathcal{T}_{\mathcal{O}}(B)$.

The following result characterizes $\mathcal{F}$-completeness and $\mathcal{B}$-completeness of SFAs wrt SFTs. In order to characterize the $\mathcal{B}$-completeness we need the inverse image of the transduction function. Let us define the *inverse transduction* of an SFT T as $\mathfrak{T}_T^-(\mathbf{b}) \triangleq \{\mathbf{a} \mid \mathbf{b} \in \mathfrak{T}_T(\mathbf{a})\}$. It is worth noting that, by construction and definition, $\forall \mathbf{b} \in \mathscr{L}_{\mathcal{O}}(T)$ we have $\mathfrak{T}_T^-(\mathbf{b}) \subseteq \mathscr{L}_{\mathcal{I}}(T)$.

Theorem 1. *Let A, B be SFA and T an SFT*

1. *$\langle A, B \rangle$ is $\mathcal{F}$-complete for T iff $\forall \mathbf{a} \in \mathscr{L}(A). \mathfrak{T}_T(\mathbf{a}) \subseteq \mathscr{L}(B)$;*
2. *$\langle A, B \rangle$ is $\mathcal{B}$-complete for T iff $\forall \mathbf{b} \in \mathscr{L}(B). \mathfrak{T}_T^-(\mathbf{b}) \subseteq \mathscr{L}(A)$;*

Let us consider some examples of complete/incomplete SFAs for the SFT T depicted in Fig. 1. In particular, we consider the SFA S_0 and S_1 in Fig. 4. Let us verify whether the pair $\langle S_0, B \rangle$ is $\mathcal{B}$-complete for T. In this case, we observe that any string $\mathbf{b} = < x_1 > < x_2 > \ldots < x_n > \in \mathscr{L}(B)$ then $\mathfrak{T}_T^-(\mathbf{b})$ has the form $v_1 w_1 < x_1 > \ldots v_n w_n < x_n >$, where, for each $i \in [0, n]$, $v_i \in (\Sigma \setminus \{<\})^*$ is any sequence of symbols different from $<$, $w_i \in \{<\}^*$ is an arbitrarily long sequence of $<$, and $x_i \in \Sigma \setminus \{<\}$ is a symbol. It is immediate to observe that such strings are included in the language $\mathscr{L}(S_0)$, hence $\langle S_0, B \rangle$ is $\mathcal{B}$-complete for T. Let us consider now the SFA S_1, in this case we can observe that $\mathfrak{T}_T^-(\mathbf{b})$ is not contained in $\mathscr{L}(S_1)$, since if a strings starts with symbols different from $<$, then the string cannot be accepted by S_1. In this case, we have that $\langle S_1, B \rangle$ is not $\mathcal{B}$-complete for T, because the input language of $\mathcal{T}_{\mathcal{O}}(A) \diamond T \diamond \mathcal{T}_{\mathcal{O}}(B)$ is different from the input language of $T \diamond \mathcal{T}_{\mathcal{O}}(B)$.

Let us consider now $\mathcal{F}$-completeness, and let us check whether the pair $\langle A, S_1 \rangle$ is $\mathcal{F}$-complete for T. In particular, we observe that any string $\mathbf{a} = << x_1 > << x_2 \ldots << x_n > \in \mathscr{L}(A)$ is transformed by T in the sequence $\mathfrak{T}_T(\mathbf{a}) = < x_1 > < x_2 > \ldots < x_n >$, which is clearly accepted by S_1. Hence, we can say that $\langle A, S_1 \rangle$ is $\mathcal{F}$-complete for T. If we consider, instead, S_2, then we can observe that $\mathfrak{T}_T(\mathbf{a}) \notin \mathscr{L}(S_1)$ if there exists at least a value $i \in [0, n]$ such that $x_i \notin \mathbb{N}$, hence we can conclude that $\langle A, S_2 \rangle$ is not $\mathcal{F}$-complete for T because the output language of $\mathcal{T}_{\mathcal{O}}(A) \diamond T \diamond \mathcal{T}_{\mathcal{O}}(B)$ is different from the one of $\mathcal{T}_{\mathcal{O}}(A) \diamond T$.

Assume to have a pair of SFAs $\langle A, B \rangle$ that is not $\mathcal{B}(\mathcal{F})$-complete for an SFT T. In this case, as done in abstract-interpretation based static analysis [16], we would like to define SFAs transformers that force $\mathcal{B}(\mathcal{F})$-completeness of $\langle A, B \rangle$ for T. The idea is to transform either the input SFA A or the output SFA B in order to satisfy the completeness conditions. Consider a pair of SFAs $\langle A, B \rangle$ and an SFT T such that the $\mathcal{B}$-completeness condition is not satisfied: $\mathcal{T}_{\mathcal{O}}(A) \diamond T \diamond \mathcal{T}_{\mathcal{O}}(B) \not\equiv T \diamond \mathcal{T}_{\mathcal{O}}(B)$. By Theorem 1, this loss of $\mathcal{B}$-completeness happens iff $\exists \mathbf{b} \in \mathscr{L}(B) : \mathfrak{T}^{-1}(\mathbf{b}) \not\subseteq \mathscr{L}(A)$. We have to possible ways to force $\mathcal{B}$-completeness:

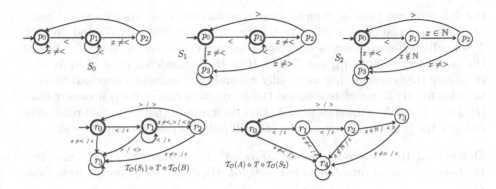

Fig. 4. Completeness examples.

- add to the language recognized by the SFA A the strings that $\mathfrak{T}_T$ maps to $\mathscr{L}(B)$,
- remove from the language recognized by the SFA B the strings obtained through $\mathfrak{T}_T$ from strings that do not belong to $\mathscr{L}(A)$.

Hence, in order to gain $\mathcal{B}$-completeness we can either expand the language of A or reduce the language of B. We would like to define a pair of SFA transformers that, given a pair of SFAs $\langle A, B \rangle$ and an SFT T for which $\mathcal{B}$-completeness does not hold, modify the input SFA A or the output SFA B in order to gain completeness by minimally expanding or reducing the language recognized respectively by A and B. Of course there are many SFAs over the same Boolean algebra that can recognize the same language. For this reason we consider the domain of SFAs up to language equivalence. More formally, we define a equivalence relation $\doteqdot$ over SFAs such that $A \doteqdot B \Leftrightarrow \mathscr{L}(A) = \mathscr{L}(B)$, and we denote an equivalence class as $[A]_{\doteqdot} = \{A \mid \mathscr{L}(A) = \mathscr{L}(B)\}$. We define the domain of SFAs up to language equivalence as follows: $\text{SFA}_{\doteqdot} \triangleq \{[A]_{\doteqdot} \mid A \in \text{SFA}\}$. We denote with $\text{SFA}_{\doteqdot}^{\sigma}$ the domain of SFAs over σ up to language equivalence. The following auxiliary functions define the language that has to be added or removed in order to gain $\mathcal{B}$-completeness.

Definition 9. *Let $T^{\sigma/\gamma}$ be an SFT we define the following functions:*

- $\mathfrak{s}_T^{\mathcal{B}} : \text{SFA}_{\doteqdot}^{\sigma} \to \wp(\Sigma^*)$ *such that* $\mathfrak{s}_T^{\mathcal{B}}([M]_{\doteqdot}) \triangleq \mathscr{L}_{\mathcal{I}}(T \diamond \mathcal{T}_{\mathcal{O}}(M))$
- $\mathfrak{c}_T^{\mathcal{B}} : \text{SFA}_{\doteqdot}^{\sigma} \to \wp(\Gamma^*)$ *such that* $\mathfrak{c}_T^{\mathcal{B}}([M]_{\doteqdot}) \triangleq \{s \in \Gamma^* \mid \mathfrak{T}_T^{-1}(s) \not\subseteq \mathscr{L}(M)\}$

The following result shows that the above definition is well-defined, namely that the computation of $\mathfrak{s}_T^{\mathcal{B}}$ and of $\mathfrak{c}_T^{\mathcal{B}}$ does not depend on the particular element chosen for representing the equivalence class.

Proposition 4. *Given $T^{\sigma/\gamma}$ and $[M]_{\doteqdot} \in \text{SFA}_{\doteqdot}^{\sigma}$ then $\forall M', M'' \in [M]_{\doteqdot}$ we have that $\mathfrak{s}_T^{\mathcal{B}}([M']_{\doteqdot}) = \mathfrak{s}_T^{\mathcal{B}}([M'']_{\doteqdot})$ and $\mathfrak{c}_T^{\mathcal{B}}([M']_{\doteqdot}) = \mathfrak{c}_T^{\mathcal{B}}([M'']_{\doteqdot})$.*

From Theorem 1 it is clear that the notion of completeness of SFA wrt a pair of SFAs depends on the languages recognized by the SFAs. For this reason in the following we provide completeness transformers that work on the domain of SFAs up to language equivalence. Given a pair of SFAs $\langle A, B \rangle$ and an SFT T for which $\mathcal{B}$-completeness does not hold, we define the $\mathcal{B}$-*complete shell* of the equivalence class $[A]_{\doteq}$ wrt T and B as the equivalence class of SFAs that recognize the language that minimally expand the language recognized by $[A]_{\doteq}$ in order to gain $\mathcal{B}$-completeness, and the $\mathcal{B}$-*complete core* of the equivalence class $[B]_{\doteq}$ wrt T and A as the class of SFAs that recognize the language that minimally reduces the language recognized by $[B]_{\doteq}$ in order to gain $\mathcal{B}$-completeness.

Definition 10. *Consider a pair of SFAs $\langle A^\sigma, B^\gamma \rangle$ and an SFT $T^{\sigma/\gamma}$ such that the $\mathcal{B}$-completeness condition is not satisfied. We define the following transformers:*

- $\mathcal{B}$-*complete shell transformer* $\mathcal{ST}^{\mathcal{B}}_{T,B} : \mathrm{SFA}^\sigma_{\doteq} \to \mathrm{SFA}^\sigma_{\doteq}$ *such that*

$$\mathcal{ST}^{\mathcal{B}}_{T,B}([A]_{\doteq}) \triangleq \{ M \in \mathrm{SFA}^\sigma \mid \mathscr{L}(M) = \mathscr{L}(A) \cup \mathfrak{s}^{\mathcal{B}}_T(B) \} \in \mathrm{SFA}^\sigma_{\doteq}$$

- $\mathcal{B}$-*complete core transformer* $\mathcal{CT}^{\mathcal{B}}_{T,A} : \mathrm{SFA}^\gamma_{\doteq} \to \mathrm{SFA}^\gamma_{\doteq}$ *such that*

$$\mathcal{CT}^{\mathcal{B}}_{T,A}([B]_{\doteq}) \triangleq \{ M \in \mathrm{SFA}^\gamma \mid \mathscr{L}(M) = \mathscr{L}(B) \smallsetminus \mathfrak{c}^{\mathcal{B}}_T(A) \} \in \mathrm{SFA}^\gamma_{\doteq}$$

Proposition 5. *Given a pair of SFAs $\langle A^\sigma, B^\gamma \rangle$ and an SFT $T^{\sigma/\gamma}$, we have that:*

- $\forall A', A'' \in [A]_{\doteq}$ *we have that* $\mathcal{ST}^{\mathcal{B}}_{T,B}([A']_{\doteq}) = \mathcal{ST}^{\mathcal{B}}_{T,B}([A'']_{\doteq})$
- $\forall B', B'' \in [B]_{\doteq}$ *we have that* $\mathcal{CT}^{\mathcal{B}}_{T,A}([B']_{\doteq}) = \mathcal{CT}^{\mathcal{B}}_{T,A}([B'']_{\doteq})$

The following result provides a characterization of an SFA in the equivalence class of $\mathcal{ST}^{\mathcal{B}}_{T,B}([A]_{\doteq})$ and of an SFA in the equivalence class $\mathcal{CT}^{\mathcal{B}}_{T,A}([B]_{\doteq})$ that proves that these classes are not empty, namely that in both cases there exists an SFA that precisely recognizes the desired language.

Proposition 6. *Consider a pair of SFAs $\langle A^\sigma, B^\gamma \rangle$ and an SFT $T^{\sigma/\gamma}$ we have that:*

- $A \oplus \mathrm{SFA}_{\mathcal{I}}(T \diamond \mathcal{T}_{\mathcal{O}}(B)) \in \mathcal{ST}^{\mathcal{B}}_{T,B}([A]_{\doteq})$
- $\mathrm{SFA}_{\mathcal{O}}(\mathcal{T}_{\mathcal{O}}(A) \diamond T \diamond \mathcal{T}_{\mathcal{O}}(B)) \in \mathcal{CT}^{\mathcal{B}}_{T,A}([B]_{\doteq})$

The following result proves that the complete shell and core transformers induce $\mathcal{B}$-completeness by minimally modifying the language of the input and output SFA.

Corollary 1. *Consider a pair of SFAs $\langle A^\sigma, B^\gamma \rangle$ and an SFT $T^{\sigma/\gamma}$ such that the $\mathcal{B}$-completeness condition is not satisfied:*

- $\forall A' \in \mathcal{ST}^{\mathcal{B}}_{T,B}([A]_{\doteq})$ *we have that* $\langle A', B \rangle$ *is $\mathcal{B}$-complete for T and $\mathscr{L}(A')$ minimally expands $\mathscr{L}(A)$ in order to gain $\mathcal{B}$-completeness*
- $\forall B' \in \mathcal{CT}^{\mathcal{B}}_{T,A}([B]_{\doteq})$ *we have that* $\langle A, B' \rangle$ *is $\mathcal{B}$-complete for T and $\mathscr{L}(B')$ minimally reduces $\mathscr{L}(B)$ in order to gain $\mathcal{B}$-completeness*

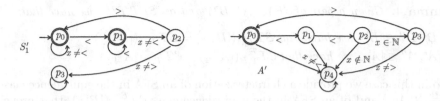

Fig. 5. $\mathcal{B}$-completeness shell example and $\mathcal{F}$-completeness core example.

Consider, for instance the pair $\langle S_1, B\rangle$ $\mathcal{B}$-incomplete for T (Fig. 4), in order to minimally transform S_1 for inducing $\mathcal{B}$-completeness we should add to $\mathscr{L}(S_1)$ the language $\mathscr{L}_\mathcal{I}(T \diamond \mathcal{T}_\mathcal{O}(B))$ (see Fig. 3), namely we fall in the equivalence class of an SFA such as S_1' accepting also strings starting with a sequence of symbols different from $<$ (on the left of Fig. 5). We can observe that $\mathscr{L}(S_1') \subset \mathscr{L}(S_0)$ since we minimally transform the language for gaining completeness. Unfortunately, in this case the core is not meaningful since the only $\mathcal{B}$-complete transformation of B reducing the language would take the empty language since any string in $\mathscr{L}(B)$ is obtained also as transformation of a string not in $\mathscr{L}(S_1)$, starting with symbols different from $<$. Dual reasoning holds for $\mathcal{F}$-completeness. Also in this case we can provide a pair of functions that define the languages that have to be either added or removed on order to gain $\mathcal{F}$-completeness.

Definition 11. *Let $T^{\sigma/\gamma}$ be an SFT we define the following functions:*

- $\mathfrak{s}_T^{\mathcal{F}} : \mathrm{SFA}_{\underline{\underline{\cong}}}^\sigma \to \wp(\Gamma^*)$ *such that* $\mathfrak{s}_T^{\mathcal{F}}([M]_{\underline{\underline{\cong}}}) \triangleq \mathscr{L}_\mathcal{O}(\mathcal{T}_\mathcal{O}(M) \diamond T)$
- $\mathfrak{c}_T^{\mathcal{F}} : \mathrm{SFA}_{\underline{\underline{\cong}}}^\sigma \to \wp(\Sigma^*)$ *such that* $\mathfrak{c}_T^{\mathcal{F}}([M]_{\underline{\underline{\cong}}}) \triangleq \{s \in \Sigma^* \mid \mathfrak{T}_T(s) \not\subseteq \mathscr{L}(M)\}$

Lemma 3. *Given $T^{\sigma/\gamma}$ and $[M]_{\underline{\underline{\cong}}} \in \mathrm{SFA}_{\underline{\underline{\cong}}}^\sigma$ then $\forall M', M'' \in [M]_{\underline{\underline{\cong}}}$ we have that $\mathfrak{s}_T^{\mathcal{F}}([M']_{\underline{\underline{\cong}}}) = \mathfrak{s}_T^{\mathcal{F}}([M'']_{\underline{\underline{\cong}}})$ and $\mathfrak{c}_T^{\mathcal{F}}([M']_{\underline{\underline{\cong}}}) = \mathfrak{c}_T^{\mathcal{F}}([M'']_{\underline{\underline{\cong}}})$.*

Given a pair of SFAs $\langle A, B\rangle$ and an SFT T for which $\mathcal{F}$-completeness does not hold, we define the $\mathcal{B}$-complete shell of the equivalence class $[B]_{\underline{\underline{\cong}}}$ wrt T and A as the equivalence class of SFAs that recognize the language that minimally expands the language recognized by $[B]_{\underline{\underline{\cong}}}$ in order to gain $\mathcal{F}$-completeness, and the $\mathcal{F}$-complete core of the equivalence class $[A]_{\underline{\underline{\cong}}}$ wrt T and B as the equivalence class of SFAs that recognize the language that minimally reduces the language recognized by $[A]_{\underline{\underline{\cong}}}$ in order to gain $\mathcal{F}$-completeness.

Definition 12. *Consider a pair of SFAs $\langle A^\sigma, B^\gamma\rangle$ and an SFT $T^{\sigma/\gamma}$ such that the $\mathcal{F}$-completeness condition is not satisfied. We define the following transformers:*

- *$\mathcal{F}$-complete shell transformer $ST_{T,A}^{\mathcal{F}} : \mathrm{SFA}_{\underline{\underline{\cong}}}^\gamma \to \mathrm{SFA}_{\underline{\underline{\cong}}}^\gamma$ such that*

$$ST_{T,A}^{\mathcal{F}}([B]_{\underline{\underline{\cong}}}) \triangleq \{M \in \mathrm{SFA}^\gamma \mid \mathscr{L}(M) = \mathscr{L}(B) \cup \mathfrak{s}_T^{\mathcal{F}}(A)\} \in \mathrm{SFA}_{\underline{\underline{\cong}}}^\gamma$$

- *$\mathcal{F}$-complete core transformer $CT_{T,B}^{\mathcal{F}} : \mathrm{SFA}_{\underline{\underline{\cong}}}^\sigma \to \mathrm{SFA}_{\underline{\underline{\cong}}}^\sigma$ such that*

$$CT_{T,B}^{\mathcal{F}}([A]_{\underline{\underline{\cong}}}) \triangleq \{M \in \mathrm{SFA}^\sigma \mid \mathscr{L}(M) = \mathscr{L}(A) \smallsetminus \mathfrak{c}_T^{\mathcal{F}}(B)\} \in \mathrm{SFA}_{\underline{\underline{\cong}}}^\sigma$$

Lemma 4. *Given a pair of SFAs $\langle A^\sigma, B^\gamma \rangle$ and an SFT $T^{\sigma/\gamma}$ we have that:*

- $\forall B', B'' \in [B]_{\doteq}$ we have that $\mathcal{ST}^{\mathcal{F}}_{T,A}([B']_{\doteq}) = \mathcal{ST}^{\mathcal{F}}_{T,A}([B'']_{\doteq})$
- $\forall A', A'' \in [A]_{\doteq}$ we have that $\mathcal{CT}^{\mathcal{F}}_{T,B}([A']_{\doteq}) = \mathcal{CT}^{\mathcal{F}}_{T,B}([A'']_{\doteq})$

Also in this case we provide a characterization of an SFA in the equivalence class $\mathcal{ST}^{\mathcal{B}}_{T,B}([A]_{\doteq})$ and of an SFA in the equivalence class $\mathcal{CT}^{\mathcal{B}}_{T,A}([B]_{\doteq})$, that proves that these classes are not empty.

Proposition 7. *Consider a pair of SFAs $\langle A^\sigma, B^\gamma \rangle$ and an SFT $T^{\sigma/\gamma}$ we have that:*

- $B \oplus \mathrm{SFA}_{\mathcal{O}}(\mathcal{T}_{\mathcal{O}}(A) \diamond T) \in \mathcal{ST}^{\mathcal{F}}_{T,A}([B]_{\doteq})$
- $\mathrm{SFA}_{\mathcal{I}}(\mathcal{T}_{\mathcal{O}}(A) \diamond T \diamond \mathcal{T}_{\mathcal{O}}(B)) \in \mathcal{CT}^{\mathcal{F}}_{T,B}([A]_{\doteq})$

The following result proves that the complete shell and core transformers induce $\mathcal{F}$-completeness by minimally modifying the language of the input and output SFA.

Proposition 8. *Consider a pair of SFAs $\langle A^\sigma, B^\gamma \rangle$ and an SFT $T^{\sigma/\gamma}$ such that the $\mathcal{F}$-completeness condition is not satisfied:*

- $\forall B' \in \mathcal{ST}^{\mathcal{F}}_{T,A}([B]_{\doteq})$ we have that $\langle A, B' \rangle$ is $\mathcal{F}$-complete for T and $\mathscr{L}(B')$ minimally expands $\mathscr{L}(B)$ in order to gain $\mathcal{F}$-completeness
- $\forall A' \in \mathcal{CT}^{\mathcal{F}}_{T,B}([A]_{\doteq})$ we have that $\langle A', B \rangle$ is $\mathcal{F}$-complete for T and $\mathscr{L}(A')$ minimally reduces $\mathscr{L}(A)$ in order to gain $\mathcal{F}$-completeness

Consider, for example the pair $\langle A, S_2 \rangle$ $\mathcal{F}$-incomplete for T. In this case, in order to gain completeness we should transform S_2 in order to add to $\mathscr{L}(S_2)$ the language $\mathscr{L}_{\mathcal{O}}(\mathcal{T}_{\mathcal{O}}(A) \diamond T)$ (see Fig. 3) which recognizes also the sequences involving $x \notin \mathbb{N}$ ($x \neq <$). We fall, in this way, in the equivalence class of the SFA B (Fig. 1), which is such that $\mathscr{L}(B) \subset \mathscr{L}(S_1)$, since we minimally enrich the language.

In this case, also the core is meaningful, since it erases from $\mathscr{L}(A)$ all the sequences leading to strings not belonging to $\mathscr{L}(S_2)$, which all those strings involving symbols not in $\mathbb{N}$, hence a representative of the resulting equivalence class is A' provided on the right of Fig. 5.

5   Code Sanitisation as Complete Approximate Transduction

Among the top ten most dangerous vulnerabilities we can find the code injection and the XSS vulnerabilities [1]. These attacks are mainly based on the evaluation (by means of a reflection operation) of a string containing code where code is not attended. Hence, following also the idea proposed in [24], we can characterize the language of the strings containing a possible attack. This language can be represented by regular expressions, CF grammars or SFA. For instance, in JavaScript, we can suppose that a string containing an attack can be any string containing " < script", which means that the string contains something that will be evaluated as code and therefore executed.

Characterising these attacks is difficult when we do expect code. In this case we need to discriminate between benign and malign code. The idea is that, once we have a specification of what we don't want to execute in output and a (potentially abstract) characterisation of how this output string is previously manipulated by the program, we can derive an approximation of the input language we can or cannot accept. As a consequence we have a specification of the kind of filter/sanitizer we have to implement in order to guarantee protection against the considered attacks. We contribute to this task as follows: (1) We characterize the transducer **T**, obtained by composing the different string manipulations in the program, focusing on the transformations of the strings of interest, finally evaluated in the reflection operation; (2) We consider an SFA **A** characterizing the attack language we want to avoid, i.e., the language of strings whose unexpected execution should be avoided. (3) If the language $\mathscr{L}_{\mathcal{I}}(\mathbf{T} \diamond \mathcal{T}_{\mathcal{O}}(\mathbf{A}))$ is empty it means that the transducer **T** does not produce in output any string recognized by **A**. In other words, the application is safe since no attack strings can be generated by the reflection operation. Otherwise, $\mathscr{L}_{\mathcal{I}}(\mathbf{T} \diamond \mathcal{T}_{\mathcal{O}}(\mathbf{A}))$ precisely describes the input strings leading to elements of the undesired output language, characterized by **A**.

```
1 : if (date₁.dd < 16)
2 :     src := display1₁.'vendor₁ :=' vendor1";
3 : if (date₁.dd > 15)                          Example of attack scenario in display1₁:
4 :     src := display2₁.'vendor₁ :=' vendor2";
5 : params_ħ := 'user = '.user_ħ.'and password = '.pwd_ħ      display1₁ =' Evil₁ := baseUrl'₁;
6 : baseUrl₁ := params_ħ;
7 : eval(src₁);
```

Fig. 6. Code with XSS vulnerable and example of attach.

Consider the example in Fig. 6[1], it is written in a simple pseudo JavaScript language (with the reflection operation **eval**). In this example we suppose to be on a site, e.g., mysite.com, where the user logs in providing a username and a password. In order to simulate a real web application, for instance written in JavaScript, we suppose that stores S are split in high level stores $\mathsf{S}_ħ$, representing, for instance, trusted sources such as web addresses, and low level stores $\mathsf{S}_\mathfrak{l}$, representing untrusted sources of data. In the following, we will use the pedix $ħ$ or $\mathfrak{l}$ for variables respectively in the high and low level store, i.e., $x_ħ$ or $x_\mathfrak{l}$. Hence, for instance, we can simulate in our language the action of sending information to a web server by saving the information on a low level variable. Moreover, suppose that date is a public object variable with fields dd, mm and yy. Hence, username and password are saved in the variable params_ħ (which is high level security). The page also loads two different third-party scripts (depending on the period of the month), which will be evaluated when the string is received from the network. The executed script is then followed by the setting of the vendor

---

[1] The JavaScript version of this example is inspired by an example in [6].

of the visualized add. The showed possible attack scenario corresponds to a bad network string `display1` sending, to an untrusted site represented by Evil_ι, the parameters. This is obtained by assigning the variable containing sensitive data to the evil site. In a real application, we could use a bad network string `display1.js`, returned by the malicious or compromised site, overwriting the pages settings. Then, by clicking the login button, username and password are sent to a bad site instead of to `mysite.com` [6].

Since we are interested only in the string executed by means of the **eval** statement, we need to characterize the transducer that transforms the **eval** input string, and this is obtained by composing the transducers corresponding to the different string manipulations in the program. A simplification of this transducer is given in Fig. 7, where φ_1 is the test on the date true when the day is less than 16, while φ_2 is the other condition, i.e., day greater or equal to 16. Moreover, by the notation $s.x.null$ we denote that x is the last symbol of the string `display1`. Suppose now that we aim at avoiding the attack showed in Fig. 6, in this case we could simply check whether the variable name `baseUrl` is in the string evaluated by the **eval** statement, since in this case the url may be arbitrarily modified. The SFA representing the language of strings containing `baseUrl` is given on the right of Fig. 7. At this point, in order to characterize the input language leading, through the execution of the transducer, to strings accepted by the SFA in Fig. 7, we first compute the composition $\mathbf{T} \diamond \mathcal{T}_{\mathcal{O}}(\mathbf{A})$ and then we extract the SFA recognizing its input language, i.e., $\text{SFA}_{\mathcal{I}}(\mathbf{T} \diamond \mathcal{T}_{\mathcal{O}}(\mathbf{A}))$, depicted in Fig. 8.

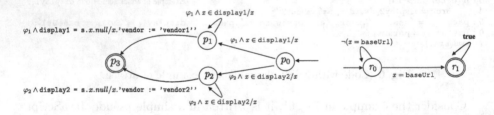

Fig. 7. Transducer manipulating the **eval** input string and SFA approximating the above attack scenario.

Note that this SFA can be used in order to specify a filter/sanitizer making the program safe, namely avoiding dangerous inputs. As far as our example is concerned, the following code is a possible filter avoiding the strings recongized by the SFA in Fig. 8:

```
1 : i := 0; temp_ι := display1_ι;
2 : while i < length(temp_ι)
3 :      {if temp_ι[i] = baseUrl then
4 :          {display1_ι := nil; i = length(temp); }
5 :      i := i + 1; }
```

This filter should be executed for both `display1`$_\iota$ and `display2`$_\iota$, before the rest of the program code. It is interesting to observe that the language of input

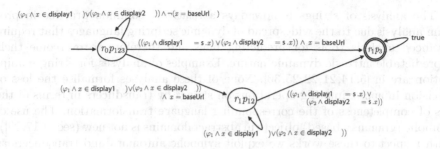

Fig. 8. Input SFA leading to the given attack.

strings to be avoid corresponds precisely to a $\mathcal{B}$-complete shell computation. In particular, consider an SFA recognizing the empty language $\mathbf{E}$, then if we have $\mathcal{T}_{\mathcal{O}}(\mathbf{E}) \diamond \mathbf{T} \diamond \mathcal{T}_{\mathcal{O}}(\mathbf{A}) \equiv \mathbf{T} \diamond \mathcal{T}_{\mathcal{O}}(\mathbf{A})$ it means that both the output languages are empty, which means, as said before, that the application is safe. So the property of being safe of a program (expressed as a transduction $\mathbf{T}$) wrt an attack (expressed as an SFA $\mathbf{A}$) can be expressed as a $\mathcal{B}$-completeness property. When we do not have $\mathcal{B}$-completeness, namely when $\mathcal{T}_{\mathcal{O}}(\mathbf{E}) \diamond \mathbf{T} \diamond \mathcal{T}_{\mathcal{O}}(\mathbf{A}) \not\equiv \mathbf{T} \diamond \mathcal{T}_{\mathcal{O}}(\mathbf{A})$, we can compute the $\mathcal{B}$-complete shell of $\mathbf{E}$ wrt $\mathbf{T}$ and $\mathbf{A}$ and obtain in this way a characterization of the smallest set of input strings that should be avoided in order to be sure that attack $\mathbf{A}$ cannot happen. Indeed, the $\mathcal{B}$-complete shell of $\mathbf{E}$ wrt $\mathbf{T}$ and $\mathbf{A}$ precisely corresponds to the computation of an SFA that recognizes the language $\mathscr{L}_{\mathcal{T}}(\mathbf{T} \diamond \mathcal{T}_{\mathcal{O}}(\mathbf{A}))$, as for example the SFA depicted in Fig. 8. It could also be interesting to compute the $\mathcal{B}$-complete core of $\mathbf{A}$ wrt $\mathbf{T}$ and $\mathbf{E}$, since this would provide a characterization of the attacks that can actually occur, which may in general be a subset of $\mathscr{L}(\mathbf{A})$.

6   Conclusion and Related Works

The main contribution of this paper is in introducing the notion of approximate transduction induced by abstract symbolic automata. We formalized the notion of $\mathcal{B}$ and $\mathcal{F}$-completeness of the approximate transduction on the abstract domain of SFAs. In particular, we gave necessary and sufficient conditions that guarantee the completeness of the approximate computation of transductions on SFAs, thus avoiding the increase of the loss of precision (viz., producing larger languages) when applied to approximate SFAs. Moreover we provided a formal characterization of the minimal modifications of the languages recognized by the SFAs that can guarantee $\mathcal{B}$ and $\mathcal{F}$-completeness (namely the $\mathcal{B}/\mathcal{F}$-complete shell and the $\mathcal{B}/\mathcal{F}$-complete core). An example of the computation of the $\mathcal{B}$-complete shell and of the $\mathcal{B}$-complete core has been given in the context of XSS attack prevention. Indeed, in this scenario the $\mathcal{B}$-complete shell of a SFA specification with respect to the corresponding approximate transduction can be used for the synthesis of a sanitiser from the symbolic specification of a given XSS attack. This provides an interesting bridge between the synthesis of a sanitiser and the completeness of the associated abstract interpretation in the domain of SFA.

The analysis of strings is nowadays a relatively common practice in program analysis due to the widespread of dynamic scripting languages that require advanced analysis tools for predicting bugs and therefore to overcome their unpredictable intrinsic dynamic nature. Examples of analyses for string manipulation are in [5,14,21,22,25,30]. None of these analyses formalise the loss of precision in approximating operations on strings by transducers in terms of the loss of completeness of the corresponding language transformation. The use of symbolic (grammar-based) objects in abstract domains is not new (see [9,17,29]). With respect to these works we exploit symbolic automata and transducers as abstract domain with a specific analysis of the completeness conditions for predicate transformers specified as symbolic transducers.

The use of transducers for script sanitisation is known in the literature (see for instance [19,30]). With respect to [19] we prove that by exploiting completeness it is possible to extract minimal sanitisers by a simple backward transduction. This better fits the assumption that sanitisers have to be small amount of code (possibly the smallest possible code for the task). Our application on XSS sanitisation is largely inspired from [30]. With respect to [30] the specification of the analysis in terms of abstract interpretation makes it suitable for being combined with other analyses, with a better potential in terms of tuning in accuracy and costs.

As future work, regular model checking [2] and the static analysis of dynamically generated code represent natural application fields for abstract symbolic automata and transducers. In the first case, sets of states and the transfer functions are respectively represented as automata and transducers. Our work provides completeness conditions for approximate (abstract) regular model checking. In the second case, the code dynamically generated in dynamic languages such as JavaScript and PHP can be approximated in the abstract domain of symbolic automata, and then further synthesised to statically extract the dynamic evolution of code as if it is a generic mutable data structure.

Acknowledgments. This work is partly supported by the MIUR FIRB project FACE (Formal Avenue for Chasing malwarE) RBFR13AJFT.

References

1. OWASP Top Ten Project (2013). https://www.owasp.org
2. Abdulla, P.A., Jonsson, B., Nilsson, M., Saksena, M.: A survey of regular model checking. In: Gardner, P., Yoshida, N. (eds.) CONCUR 2004. LNCS, vol. 3170, pp. 35–48. Springer, Heidelberg (2004)
3. Berstel, J.: Transductions and Context-Free Languages. Teubner-Verlag, Stuttgart (2009)
4. Bjørner, N., Veanes, M.: Symbolic transducers. Technical report MSR-TR-2011-3, Microsoft Research (2011)
5. Christensen, A.S., Møller, A.: Precise analysis of string expressions. In: Cousot, R. (ed.) SAS 2003. LNCS, vol. 2694, pp. 1–18. Springer, Heidelberg (2003)
6. Chugh, R., Meister, J.A., Jhala, R., Lerner, S.: Staged information flow for JavaScript. In: Hind, M., Diwan, A. (eds.) PLDI, pp. 50–62. ACM (2009)

7. Cousot, P., Cousot, R.: Abstract interpretation: a unified lattice model for static analysis of programs by construction or approximation of fixpoints. In: Conference Record of the 4th ACM Symposium on Principles of Programming Languages (POPL 1977), pp. 238–252. ACM Press (1977)

8. Cousot, P., Cousot, R.: Systematic design of program analysis frameworks. In: Conference Record of the 6th ACM Symposium on Principles of Programming Languages (POPL 1979), pp. 269–282. ACM Press (1979)

9. Cousot, P., Cousot, R.: Formal language, grammar and set-constraint-based program analysis by abstract interpretation. In: Proceedings of the Seventh ACM Conference on Functional Programming Languages and Computer Architecture, pp. 170–181. ACM Press, New York, 25–28 June 1995

10. Dalla Preda, M., Giacobazzi, R., Lakhotia, A., Mastroeni, I.: Abstract symbolic automata: mixed syntactic/semantic similarity analysis of executables. In: Rajamani, S.K., Walker, D. (eds.) Proceedings of the 42nd Annual ACM SIGPLAN-SIGACT Symposium on Principles of Programming Languages, POPL 2015, Mumbai, India, pp. 329–341. ACM, 15–17 January 2015

11. D'Antoni, L., Veanes, M.: Equivalence of extended symbolic finite transducers. In: Sharygina, N., Veith, H. (eds.) CAV 2013. LNCS, vol. 8044, pp. 624–639. Springer, Heidelberg (2013)

12. D'Antoni, L., Veanes, M.: Minimization of symbolic automata. In: Jagannathan, S., Sewell, P. (eds.) POPL, pp. 541–554. ACM (2014)

13. D'Antoni, L., Veanes, M.: Extended symbolic finite automata and transducers. Formal Methods Syst. Des. 47(1), 93–119 (2015)

14. Doh, K.-G., Kim, H., Schmidt, D.A.: Abstract parsing: static analysis of dynamically generated string output using LR-parsing technology. In: Palsberg, J., Su, Z. (eds.) SAS 2009. LNCS, vol. 5673, pp. 256–272. Springer, Heidelberg (2009)

15. Giacobazzi, R., Quintarelli, E.: Incompleteness, counterexamples, and refinements in abstract model-checking. In: Cousot, P. (ed.) SAS 2001. LNCS, vol. 2126, pp. 356–373. Springer, Heidelberg (2001)

16. Giacobazzi, R., Ranzato, F., Scozzari, F.: Making abstract interpretation complete. J. ACM 47(2), 361–416 (2000)

17. Heintze, N., Jaffar, J.: Set constraints and set-based analysis. In: Borning, A. (ed.) PPCP 1994. LNCS, vol. 874, pp. 281–298. Springer, Heidelberg (1994)

18. Hooimeijer, P., Livshits, B., Molnar, D., Saxena, P., Veanes, M.: Bek: Modeling imperative string operations with symbolic transducers. Technical report MSR-TR-2010-154, November 2010

19. Hooimeijer, P., Livshits, B., Molnar, D., Saxena, P., Veanes, M.: Fast and precise sanitizer analysis with BEK. In: Proceedings of the 20th USENIX Security Symposium, San Francisco, CA, USA, USENIX Association, August 8–12 2011

20. Hooimeijer, P., Veanes, M.: An evaluation of automata algorithms for string analysis. In: Jhala, R., Schmidt, D. (eds.) VMCAI 2011. LNCS, vol. 6538, pp. 248–262. Springer, Heidelberg (2011)

21. Kim, H., Doh, K.-G., Schmidt, D.A.: Static validation of dynamically generated HTML documents based on abstract parsing and semantic processing. In: Logozzo, F., Fähndrich, M. (eds.) Static Analysis. LNCS, vol. 7935, pp. 194–214. Springer, Heidelberg (2013)

22. Minamide, Y.: Static approximation of dynamically generated web pages. In: Ellis, A., Hagino, T. (eds.) Proceedings of the 14th International Conference on World Wide Web, WWW 2005, Chiba, Japan, pp. 432–441. ACM, 10–14 May 2005

23. Podelski, A.: Automata as proofs. In: Giacobazzi, R., Berdine, J., Mastroeni, I. (eds.) VMCAI 2013. LNCS, vol. 7737, pp. 13–14. Springer, Heidelberg (2013)

24. Ray, D., Ligatti, J.: Defining code-injection attacks. In: Field, J., Hicks, M. (eds.) POPL, pp. 179–190. ACM (2012)
25. Thiemann, P.: Grammar-based analysis of string expressions. In: Morrisett, J.G., Fähndrich, M. (eds.) Proceedings of TLDI 2005: 2005 ACM SIGPLAN International Workshop on Types in Languages Design and Implementation, Long Beach, CA, USA, pp. 59–70. ACM, 10 January 2005
26. Veanes, M.: Symbolic string transformations with regular lookahead and rollback. In: Voronkov, A., Virbitskaite, I. (eds.) PSI 2014. LNCS, vol. 8974, pp. 335–350. Springer, Heidelberg (2015)
27. Veanes, M., Halleux, P.d., Tillmann, N.: Rex: symbolic regular expression explorer. In: Proceedings of the 2010 Third International Conference on Software Testing, Verification and Validation, ICST 2010, Washington, DC, USA, pp. 498–507. IEEE Computer Society (2010)
28. Veanes, M., Hooimeijer, P., Livshits, B., Molnar, D., Bjørner, N.: Symbolic finite state transducers: algorithms and applications. In: Field, J., Hicks, M. (eds.) POPL, pp. 137–150. ACM (2012)
29. Venet, A.: Automatic analysis of pointer aliasing for untyped programs. Sci. Comput. Program. **35**(2), 223–248 (1999)
30. Yu, F., Alkhalaf, M., Bultan, T.: Patching vulnerabilities with sanitization synthesis. In: Taylor, R.N., Gall, H.C., Medvidovic, N. (eds.) Proceedings of the 33rd International Conference on Software Engineering, ICSE 2011, Waikiki, Honolulu, HI, USA, pp. 251–260. ACM, 21–28 May 2011

Relational Verification Through Horn Clause Transformation

Emanuele De Angelis[1]([✉]), Fabio Fioravanti[1], Alberto Pettorossi[2]([✉]),
and Maurizio Proietti[3]([✉])

[1] DEC, University 'G. D'Annunzio', Pescara, Italy
{emanuele.deangelis,fabio.fioravanti}@unich.it
[2] DICII, University of Rome Tor Vergata, Rome, Italy
pettorossi@disp.uniroma2.it
[3] IASI-CNR, Rome, Italy
maurizio.proietti@iasi.cnr.it

Abstract. We present a method for verifying relational program properties, that is, properties that relate the input and the output of two
programs. Our verification method is parametric with respect to the
definition of the operational semantics of the programming language in
which the two programs are written. That definition of the semantics
consists of a set *Int* of constrained Horn clauses (CHCs) that encode the
interpreter of the programming language. Then, given the programs and
the relational property we want to verify, we generate, by using *Int*, a
set of constrained Horn clauses whose satisfiability is equivalent to the
validity of the property. Unfortunately, state-of-the-art solvers for CHCs
have severe limitations in proving the satisfiability, or the unsatisfiability,
of such sets of clauses. We propose some transformation techniques that
increase the power of CHC solvers when verifying relational properties.
We show that these transformations, based on unfold/fold rules, preserve
satisfiability. Through an experimental evaluation, we show that in many
cases CHC solvers are able to prove the satisfiability (or the unsatisfiability) of sets of clauses obtained by applying the transformations we
propose, whereas the same solvers are unable to perform those proofs
when given as input the original, untransformed sets of CHCs.

1 Introduction

During the process of software development it is often the case that several
versions of the same program are produced. This is due to the fact that the programmer, for instance, may want to replace an old program fragment by a new
program fragment with the objective of improving efficiency, or adding a new
feature, or modifying the program structure. In these cases, in order to prove the
correctness of the whole program, it may be desirable to consider *relational properties* of those program fragments, that is, properties that relate the semantics
of the old fragments to the semantics of the new fragments. Among the many
examples of relational properties that can be considered in practice as indicated
in some papers [5,30], *program equivalence* has a prominent significance.

© Springer-Verlag GmbH Germany 2016
X. Rival (Ed.): SAS 2016, LNCS 9837, pp. 147–169, 2016.
DOI: 10.1007/978-3-662-53413-7_8

It has been noted that proving relational properties between two structurally similar program versions is often easier than directly proving the desired correctness property for the new program version [5, 20, 30]. Moreover, in order to automate the correctness proofs, it may be convenient to follow a transformational approach so that one can use the already available methods and tools for proving correctness of individual programs. For instance, various papers propose program composition and cross-product techniques such that, in order to prove that a given relation between program P_1 and P_2 holds, it is sufficient to show that suitable pre- and post-conditions for the composition of P_1 and P_2 hold [5, 30, 38]. The validity of these pre- and post-conditions is then checked by using state-of-the-art verification tools (e.g., BOOGIE [4] and WHY [21]). A different transformational approach is followed by Felsing et al. [20], who introduce a set of proof rules for program equivalence, and from these rules they generate *verification conditions* in the form of *constrained Horn clauses* (CHCs) which is a logical formalism recently suggested for program verification (see [7] for a survey of verification techniques that use CHCs). The satisfiability of the verification conditions, which guarantees that the relational property holds, can be checked by using CHC solvers, such as ELDARICA [26] and Z3 [17] (obviously, no complete solver exists because most properties of interest, and among them equivalence, are in general undecidable). Unfortunately, all the above mentioned approaches enable only a partial reuse of the available verification techniques, because one should develop specific transformation rules for each programming language and each proof system that has to be used.

In this paper we propose a method to achieve a higher parametricity with respect to the programming language and the class of relational properties considered, and this is done by pushing further the transformational approach. As a first step of our method, we formalize a relational property between two programs as a set of CHCs. This is done by using an interpreter for the given programming language written in clausal form [16, 34]. In particular, the properties of the data domain in use, such as the integers and the integer arrays, are formalized in the constraint theory of the CHCs. Now, it is very often the case that this first step is not sufficient to allow state-of-the-art CHC solvers to verify the properties of interest. Indeed, the strategies for checking satisfiability employed by those solvers deal with the sets of clauses encoding the semantics of each of the two programs in an independent way, thereby failing to take full advantage of the interrelations between the two sets of clauses. In this paper, instead of looking for a smarter strategy for satisfiability checking, we propose some transformation techniques for CHCs that compose together, in a suitable way, the clauses relative to the two programs, so that their interrelations may be better exploited. This transformational approach has the advantage that we can use existing techniques for CHC satisfiability as a final step of the verification process. Moreover, since the CHC encodings of the two programs do not explicitly refer to the syntax of the given programs, we are able to prove relations that would be difficult to infer by the above mentioned, syntax-driven approaches. Our approach has been proved to be effective in practice, as indicated in Sect. 5.

The main contributions of the paper are the following.

(1) We present a method for encoding as a set of CHCs a large class of relational properties of programs written in a simple imperative language. The only language-specific component of our method is a CHC interpreter that provides a formal definition of the semantics of the programming language in use.

(2) We propose an automatic transformation technique for CHCs, called *Predicate Pairing*, that combines together the clauses representing the semantics of each program with the objective of increasing the effectiveness of the subsequent application of the CHC solver in use. We prove that Predicate Pairing guarantees equisatisfiability between the initial and the final sets of clauses. The proof is based on the fact that this transformation can be expressed as a sequence of applications of the *unfolding* and *folding* rules [19,36].

(3) We report on an experimental evaluation performed by a proof-of-concept implementation (see Fig. 1) of our transformation technique by using the VERIMAP system [14]. The satisfiability of the transformed CHCs is then verified by using the solvers ELDARICA [26] and Z3 [17]. Our experiments show that the transformation is effective on a number of small, yet nontrivial examples. Moreover, our method is competitive with respect to other tools for checking relational properties [20].

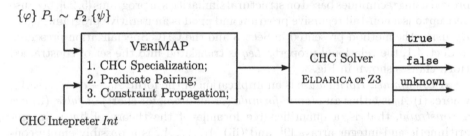

Fig. 1. The verification method. The VERIMAP system transforms CHCs, and the CHC solver checks the satisfiability of CHCs. VERIMAP takes as input: (i) the CHC encoding of a relational property $\{\varphi\} P_1 \sim P_2 \{\psi\}$ between programs P_1 and P_2, and (ii) the CHC interpreter that encodes the semantics of the programming language.

The paper is organized as follows. In Sect. 2 we present a simple introductory example. Then, in Sect. 3 we present the method for translating a relational property between two programs into constrained Horn clauses. In Sect. 4 we introduce the transformation techniques for CHCs and we prove that they preserve satisfiability (and unsatisfiability). The implementation of the verification method and its experimental evaluation are reported in Sect. 5. Finally, in Sect. 6, we discuss the related work.

2 An Introductory Example

In this section we present an example to illustrate the approach proposed in this paper. Let us consider the two imperative programs of Fig. 2. Program

```
/* -- Program sum_upto -- */        /* -- Program prod -- */
int x1, z1;                         int x2,y2,z2;
int f(int n1){                      int g(int n2, int m2){
  int r1;                             int r2;
  if (n1 <= 0) {                      r2 = 0;
    r1 = 0;                           while (n2 > 0) {
  } else {                             r2 += m2;
    r1 = f(n1 - 1) + n1; }             n2--; }
  return r1; }                       return r2; }
void sum_upto() {                   void prod() {
  z1 = f(x1); }                       z2 = g(x2,y2); }
```

Fig. 2. The programs sum_upto and prod.

sum_upto computes the sum of the first x1 non-negative integers and program prod computes the product of x2 by y2 by summing up x2 times the value of y2. We have that the following relational property holds:

Leq: $\{x1=x2,\ x2 \leq y2\}$ sum_upto $\sim$ prod $\{z1 \leq z2\}$

meaning that, if $x1=x2$ and $x2 \leq y2$ hold before the execution of sum_upto and prod, then $z1 \leq z2$ holds after their execution. Property Leq cannot directly be proved using techniques based on structural similarities of programs [5, 20], because sum_upto is a non-tail recursive program and prod is an iterative program.

By using the method presented in Sect. 3 and the CHC Specialization presented in Sect. 4.1, the relational property Leq is translated into the set of constrained Horn clauses shown in Fig. 3.

A *constrained Horn clause* is an implication of the form: $A_0 \leftarrow c, A_1, \ldots, A_n$, where: (i) A_0 is either an *atomic formula* (or an *atom*, for short) or *false*, (ii) c is a *constraint*, that is, a quantifier-free formula of the theory of linear integer arithmetic and integer arrays [9], and (iii) $A_1, \ldots, A_n$ is a possibly empty conjunction of atoms. A_0 is said to be the *head* of the clause, and the conjunction $c, A_1, \ldots, A_n$ is said to be the *body* of the clause. If the body is the empty conjunction of constraints and atoms (i.e., *true*), then the clause is called a *fact*. Clause 1 specifies the relational property Leq, where the logical variables $Z1$ and $Z2$ refer to the values of the imperative variables z1 and z2, respectively. Note that the constraint $Z1 > Z2$ in the body of clause 1 encodes the negation

---

1. $false \leftarrow X1=X2,\ X2 \leq Y2,\ Z1 > Z2,\ su(X1, Z1),\ pr(X2, Y2, Z2)$
2. $su(X, Z) \leftarrow f(X, Z)$
3. $f(N, Z) \leftarrow N \leq 0,\ Z=0$
4. $f(N, Z) \leftarrow N \geq 1,\ N1=N-1,\ Z=R+N,\ f(N1, R)$
5. $pr(X, Y, Z) \leftarrow W=0,\ g(X, Y, W, Z)$
6. $g(N, P, R, R) \leftarrow N \leq 0$
7. $g(N, P, R, R2) \leftarrow N \geq 1,\ N1=N-1,\ R1=P+R,\ g(N1, P, R1, R2)$

Fig. 3. Translation into constrained Horn clauses of the relational property Leq.

of the postcondition $z1 \leq z2$ we want to prove. Clauses 2–4 and 5–7 encode the input-output relations computed by programs sum_upto and prod, respectively. We have that the relational property Leq holds iff clauses 1–7 are satisfiable.

Unfortunately, state-of-the-art solvers for constrained Horn clauses with linear integer arithmetic (such as ELDARICA [26] and Z3 [17]) are unable to prove the satisfiability of clauses 1–7. This is due to the fact that those solvers act on the predicates su and pr separately, and hence, to prove that clause 1 is satisfiable (that is, its premise is unsatisfiable), they should discover quadratic relations among variables (in our case, $Z1 = X1 \times (X1-1)/2$ and $Z2 = X2 \times Y2$), and these relations cannot be expressed by linear arithmetic constraints.

In order to deal with this limitation one could extend constrained Horn clauses with solvers for the theory of non-linear integer arithmetic constraints [8]. However, this extension has to cope with the additional problem that the satisfiability problem for non-linear constraints is, in general, undecidable [31].

In this paper we propose an approach based on suitable transformations of the clauses that encode the property Leq into an equisatisfiable set of clauses, for which the satisfiability (or unsatisfiability) is hopefully easier to prove. In our example, the clauses of Fig. 3 are transformed into the ones shown in Fig. 4.

---

10. $false \leftarrow N \leq Y,\ W=0,\ Z1 > Z2,\ fg(N, Z1, Y, W, Z2)$
11. $fg(N, Z1, Y, Z2, Z2) \leftarrow N \leq 0,\ Z1 = 0$
13. $fg(N, Z1, Y, W, Z2) \leftarrow N \geq 1,\ N1 = N-1,\ Z1 = R+N,\ M = Y+W,$
$\qquad\qquad\qquad fg(N1, R, Y, M, Z2)$

Fig. 4. Transformed clauses derived from the clauses 1–7 in Fig. 3. Clause numbers are those indicated in the derivation of Sect. 4.2.

The predicate $fg(N, Z1, Y, W, Z2)$ is equivalent to the conjunction '$f(N, Z1)$, $g(N, Y, W, Z2)$'. The effect of this transformation is that it is possible to infer linear relations among a subset of the variables occurring in *conjunctions* of predicates, without having to use in an explicit way their non-linear relations with other variables. In particular, one can infer that, whenever $W = 0$, $fg(N, Z1, Y, W, Z2)$ enforces the constraint $(N > Y) \vee (Z1 \leq Z2)$, and hence the satisfiability of clause 10 of Fig. 4, without having to derive quadratic relations. Indeed, after this transformation, state-of-the-art solvers for CHCs with linear arithmetics are able to prove the satisfiability of the clauses of Fig. 4, which implies the validity of the relational property Leq (see Sect. 5).

3 Specifying Relational Properties Using CHCs

In this section we introduce the notion of a relational property relative to two programs written in a simple imperative language and we show how a relational property can be translated into CHCs.

3.1   Relational Properties

We consider a C-like imperative programming language manipulating integers and integer arrays via assignments, function calls, conditionals, while-loops, and jumps. A program is a sequence of labeled commands (or commands, for short). We assume that in each program there is a unique `halt` command that, when executed, causes program termination. We will feel free to write commands without their labels and programs without their `halt` commands, whenever those labels and commands are not needed for specifying the semantics of the programs.

The semantics of our language is defined by a binary *transition relation*, denoted by $\Longrightarrow$, between *configurations*. Each configuration is a pair $\langle\!\langle \ell : c, \delta \rangle\!\rangle$ of a labeled command $\ell : c$ and an *environment* δ. An environment δ is a function that maps a variable identifier x to its value v *either* in the integers (for integer variables) *or* in the set of finite sequences of integers (for array variables). Given an environment δ, $dom(\delta)$ denotes its domain. The definition of the relation $\Longrightarrow$ corresponds to the *multistep* operational semantics, that is: (i) the semantics of a command, different from a function call, is defined by a pair of the form $\langle\!\langle \ell : c, \delta \rangle\!\rangle \Longrightarrow \langle\!\langle \ell' : c', \delta' \rangle\!\rangle$, and (ii) the semantics of a function call is recursively defined in terms of the reflexive, transitive closure $\Longrightarrow^*$ of $\Longrightarrow$.

In particular, the semantics of an assignment is:

(R1) $\langle\!\langle \ell : x = e, \ \delta \rangle\!\rangle \ \Longrightarrow \ \langle\!\langle at(nextlab(\ell)), \ update(\delta, x, [\![e]\!] \delta) \rangle\!\rangle$

where: (i) $at(\ell)$ denotes the command whose label is ℓ, (ii) $nextlab(\ell)$ denotes the label of the command which is *immediately after* the command with label ℓ, (iii) $update(\delta, x, v)$ denotes the environment δ' that is equal to the environment δ, except that $\delta'(x) = v$, and (iv) $[\![e]\!] \delta$ is the value of the expression e in δ.

The semantics of a call to the function f is:

(R2) $\langle\!\langle \ell : x = f(e_1, \ldots, e_k), \ \delta \rangle\!\rangle \ \Longrightarrow \ \langle\!\langle at(nextlab(\ell)), update(\delta', x, [\![e]\!] \delta') \rangle\!\rangle$
$\qquad$ if $\langle\!\langle at(firstlab(f)), \ \overline{\delta} \rangle\!\rangle \ \Longrightarrow^* \ \langle\!\langle \ell_r : \texttt{return} \ e, \ \delta' \rangle\!\rangle$

where: (i) $firstlab(f)$ denotes the label of the first command in the definition of the function f, and (ii) $\overline{\delta}$ is the environment δ extended by the bindings for the formal parameters, say $x_1, \ldots, x_k$, and the local variables, say $y_1, \ldots, y_h$, of f (we assume that the identifiers x_i's and y_i's do not occur in $dom(\delta)$). Thus, we have that $\overline{\delta} = \delta \cup \{x_1 \mapsto [\![e_1]\!] \delta, \ldots, x_k \mapsto [\![e_k]\!] \delta, y_1 \mapsto v_1, \ldots, y_h \mapsto v_h\}$, for arbitrary values $v_1, \ldots, v_h$. We refer to [16] for a more detailed presentation of the multistep semantics.

A program P *terminates* for an initial environment δ, whose domain includes all global variables of P, and computes the final environment η, denoted $\langle P, \delta \rangle \Downarrow \eta$, iff $\langle\!\langle \ell_0 : c, \delta \rangle\!\rangle \Longrightarrow^* \langle\!\langle \ell_h : \texttt{halt}, \eta \rangle\!\rangle$, where $\ell_0 : c$ is the first labeled command of P. $\langle\!\langle \ell_0 : c, \delta \rangle\!\rangle$ and $\langle\!\langle \ell_h : \texttt{halt}, \eta \rangle\!\rangle$ are called the *initial configuration* and the *final configuration*, respectively. It follows from the definition of the operational semantics that also the domain of η includes all global variables of P.

Now, we can formally define a relational property as follows. Let P_1 and P_2 be two programs with global variables in $\mathcal{V}_1$ and $\mathcal{V}_2$, respectively, with $\mathcal{V}_1 \cap \mathcal{V}_2 = \emptyset$. Let φ and ψ be two first order formulas with variables in $\mathcal{V}_1 \cup \mathcal{V}_2$. Then, by using the notation of Barthe et al. [5], a relational property is specified by the 4-tuple $\{\varphi\} \, P_1 \sim P_2 \, \{\psi\}$. (See property *Leq* in Sect. 2 for an example.)

We say that $\{\varphi\}\, P_1 \sim P_2\, \{\psi\}$ is valid iff the following holds: if the inputs of P_1 and P_2 satisfy the *pre-relation* φ and the programs P_1 and P_2 both terminate, then upon termination the outputs of P_1 and P_2 satisfy the *post-relation* ψ. The validity of a relational property is formalized by Definition 1 below, where given a formula χ and an environment δ, by $\chi\,[\delta]$ we denote the formula χ where every free occurrence of a variable x in $dom(\delta)$ has been replaced by $\delta(x)$.

Definition 1. *A relational property* $\{\varphi\}\, P_1 \sim P_2\, \{\psi\}$ *is said to be* valid, *denoted* $\models \{\varphi\}\, P_1 \sim P_2\, \{\psi\}$, *iff for all environments* δ_1 *and* δ_2 *with* $dom(\delta_1) = \mathcal{V}_1$ *and* $dom(\delta_2) = \mathcal{V}_2$, *the following holds:*

if $\models \varphi\,[\delta_1 \cup \delta_2]$ *and* $\langle P_1, \delta_1 \rangle \Downarrow \eta_1$ *and* $\langle P_2, \delta_2 \rangle \Downarrow \eta_2$, *then* $\models \psi\,[\eta_1 \cup \eta_2]$.

3.2   Formal Semantics of the Imperative Language in CHCs

In order to translate a relational program property into CHCs, first we need to specify the operational semantics of our imperative language by a set of CHCs. We follow the approach proposed by De Angelis et al. [16] which now we briefly recall. The transition relation $\Longrightarrow$ between configurations and its reflexive, transitive closure $\Longrightarrow^*$ are specified by the binary predicates tr and $reach$, respectively. We only show the formalization of the semantic rules $R1$ and $R2$ above, consisting of the following clauses $D1$ and $D2$, respectively. For the other rules of the multistep operational semantics we refer to the original paper [16].

$(D1)$ $tr(cf(cmd(L, asgn(X, expr(E))), Env), cf(cmd(L1, C), Env1)) \leftarrow$
  $eval(E, Env, V), update(Env, X, V, Env1), nextlab(L, L1), at(L1, C)$
$(D2)$ $tr(cf(cmd(L, asgn(X, call(F, Es))), Env), cf(cmd(L2, C2), Env2)) \leftarrow$
  $fun\_env(Es, Env, F, FEnv), firstlab(F, FL), at(FL, C),$
  $reach(cf(cmd(FL, C), FEnv), cf(cmd(LR, return(E)), Env1)),$
  $eval(E, Env1, V), update(Env1, X, V, Env2), nextlab(L, L2), at(L2, C2)$

The predicate $reach$ is recursively defined by the following two clauses:

  $reach(C, C) \leftarrow$
  $reach(C, C2) \leftarrow tr(C, C1), reach(C1, C2)$

A program is represented by a set of facts of the form $at(L, C)$, where L and C encode a label and a command, respectively. For instance, program sum_upto of Fig. 2 is represented by the following facts:

$at(0, ite(lte(\mathbf{n1}, 0), 1, 2)) \leftarrow$ $at(4, return(\mathbf{r1})) \leftarrow$
$at(1, asgn(\mathbf{r1}, 0)) \leftarrow$ $at(5, asgn(\mathbf{z1}, call(\mathbf{f}, [\mathbf{x1}]))) \leftarrow$
$at(2, asgn(\mathbf{r1}, call(\mathbf{f}, [minus(\mathbf{n1}, 1)]))) \leftarrow$ $at(6, \mathbf{halt}) \leftarrow$
$at(3, asgn(\mathbf{r1}, plus(\mathbf{r1}, \mathbf{n1}))) \leftarrow$

In this representation of the program sum_upto the halt command and the labels of the commands, which were omitted in the listing of Fig. 2, have been explicitly shown. Configurations are represented by terms of the form $cf(cmd(L, C), Env)$, where: (i) $cmd(L, C)$ encodes a command C with label L, and (ii) Env encodes the environment. The term $asgn(X, expr(E))$ encodes the assignment of the value of the expression E to the variable X. The predicate $eval(E, Env, V)$ holds iff V is the value of the expression E in the environment Env. The term $call(F, Es)$ encodes the call of the function F with the list Es of the actual parameters. The predicate $fun\_env(Es, Env, F, FEnv)$ computes from Es and Env the list Vs of the values of the actual parameters of the function F and builds the new initial environment $FEnv$ for executing the body of F. In $FEnv$ the local variables of F are all bound to arbitrary values. The other terms and predicates occurring in clauses $D1$ and $D2$ have the obvious meaning which can be derived from the above explanation of the semantic rules $R1$ and $R2$ (see Sect. 3.1).

Given a program $Prog$, its input-output relation is represented by a predicate $prog$ defined as follows:

$$prog(X, X') \leftarrow initConf(C, X), \ reach(C, C'), \ finalConf(C', X')$$

where $initConf(C, X)$ and $finalConf(C', X')$ hold iff the tuples X and X' are the values of the global variables of $Prog$ in the initial and final configurations C and C', respectively.

3.3   Translating Relational Properties into CHCs

In any given a relational property $\{\varphi\}\, P_1 \sim P_2\, \{\psi\}$ between programs $P1$ and $P2$, we assume that φ and ψ are constraints, that is, as mentioned in Sect. 2, quantifier-free formulas of the theory of linear integer arithmetic and integer arrays [9]. Let $\mathcal{A}$ be the set of axioms of this theory. The set $\mathcal{C}$ of constraints is closed under conjunction and, when writing clauses, we will use comma to denote a conjunction of constraints.

More complex theories of constraints may be used for defining relational properties. For instance, one may consider theories with nested quantifiers [2]. Our approach is, to a large extent, parametric with respect to those theories. Indeed, the transformation rules on which it is based only require that satisfiability and entailment of constraints be decidable (see Sect. 4).

A set S of CHC clauses is said to be $\mathcal{A}$-*satisfiable* or, simply, *satisfiable*, iff $\mathcal{A} \cup S$ is satisfiable.

The relational property of the form $\{\varphi\}\, P_1 \sim P_2\, \{\psi\}$ is translated into the following CHC clause:

$(Prop)$ $false \leftarrow pre(X, Y), \ p1(X, X'), \ p2(Y, Y'), \ neg\_post(X', Y')$

where: (i) X and Y are the disjoint tuples of the global variables x_i's of program P_1 and the global variables y_i's of program P_2, respectively, rewritten in capital letters (so to comply with CHC syntax);
(ii) $pre(X, Y)$ is the formula φ with its variables replaced by the corresponding capital letters;
(iii) $neg\_post(X', Y')$ is the formula $\neg\psi$ with its variables replaced by the corresponding primed capital letters; and
(iv) the predicates $p1(X, X')$ and $p2(Y, Y')$ are defined by a set of clauses derived from program P_1 and P_2, respectively, by using the formalization of the operational semantics of the programming language presented in Sect. 3.2.

Note that we can always eliminate negation from the atoms $pre(X, Y)$ and $neg\_post(X', Y')$ by pushing negation inward and transforming negated equalities into disjunctions of inequalities. Moreover, we can eliminate disjunction from constraints and replace clause *Prop* by a *set* of two or more clauses with *false* in their head. Although these transformations are not strictly needed by the techniques described in the rest of the paper, they are useful when automating our verification method using constraint solving tools.

For instance, the relational property *Leq* of Sect. 2 is translated into the following clause (we moved all constraints to leftmost positions in the body):

$(Prop_{Leq})$ $false \leftarrow X1 = X2, X2 \leq Y2, Z1' > Z2',$
$$sum\_upto(X1, Z1, X1', Z1'), \ prod(X2, Y2, Z2, X2', Y2', Z2')$$

where predicates sum_upto and $prod$ are defined in terms of the predicate *reach* shown in Sect. 3.2. In particular, sum_upto is defined by the following clauses:

$sum\_upto(X1, Z1, X1', Z1') \leftarrow$
   $initConf(C, X1, Z1), reach(C, C'), finalConf(C', X1', Z1')$
$initConf(cf(cmd(5, asgn(\texttt{z1}, call(\texttt{f}, [\texttt{x1}]))), [(\texttt{x1}, X1), (\texttt{z1}, Z1)]), X1, Z1) \leftarrow$
$finalConf(cf(cmd(6, \texttt{halt}), [(\texttt{x1}, X1'), (\texttt{z1}, Z1')]), X1', Z1') \leftarrow$

where: (i) *initConf* holds for the initial configuration of the sum_upto program (that is, the pair of the assignment z1 = f(x1) and the initial environment), and (ii) *finalConf* holds for the final configuration of the sum_upto program (that is, the pair of the unwritten halt command silently occurring after the assignment z1 = f(x1) and the final environment).

Let *RP* be a relational property and T_{RP} be the set of CHCs generated from *RP* by the translation process described above, then T_{RP} is correct in the sense specified by the following theorem.

Theorem 1 (Correctness of the CHC Translation). *RP is valid iff T_{RP} is satisfiable.*

The proof of this theorem directly follows from the fact that the predicate *tr* is a correct formalization of the semantics of the programming language.

4   Transforming Specifications of Relational Properties

The reduction of the problem of checking whether or not $\{\varphi\} \ P_1 \sim P_2 \ \{\psi\}$ is valid, to the problem of verifying the satisfiability of a set T_{RP} of constrained Horn clauses allows us to apply reasoning techniques that are independent of the specific programming language in which programs P_1 and P_2 are written. Indeed, we can try to solve the satisfiability problem for T_{RP} by applying the available solvers for constrained Horn clauses. Unfortunately, as shown by the example in Sect. 2, it may be the case that these solvers are unable to prove satisfiability (or unsatisfiability). In Sect. 5 the reader will find an experimental evidence of this limitation. However, a very significant advantage of having to show the satisfiability of the set T_{RP} of constrained Horn clauses is that we can transform T_{RP} by applying any CHC satisfiability preserving algorithm, and then submit the transformed clauses to a CHC solver.

In this section we present two satisfiability preserving algorithms for transforming constrained Horn clauses that have the objective of increasing the effectiveness of the subsequent uses of CHC solvers. These algorithms, called *transformation strategies*, are: (1) the *CHC Specialization*, and (2) the *Predicate Pairing*.

These strategies are variants of techniques developed in the area of logic programming for improving the efficiency of program execution [18,35]. In Sect. 5 we will give an experimental evidence that these techniques are very effective for the verification of relational properties. The CHC Specialization and Predicate Pairing strategies are realized as sequences of applications of some elementary *transformation rules*, collectively called *unfold/fold rules*, proposed in the field of CLP a couple of decades ago [19]. Now we present the version of those rules we need in our context. This version allows us to derive from an old set *Cls* of constrained Horn clauses a new set *TransfCls* of constrained Horn clauses.

The *definition* rule allows us to introduce a new predicate symbol in *Cls* defined by a single clause.

Definition Rule. We introduce a *definition clause* D of the form $newp(X) \leftarrow c, G$, where *newp* is a new predicate symbol, X is a tuple of variables occurring in $\{c, G\}$, c is a constraint, and G is a non-empty conjunction of atoms. We derive the set of clauses $TransfCls = Cls \cup \{D\}$. We denote by *Defs* the set of definition clauses introduced in a sequence of application of the unfold/fold rules.

The *unfolding* rule consists in applying a resolution step with respect to an atom selected in the body of a clause in *Cls*.

Unfolding Rule. Let C be a clause in *Cls* of the form $H \leftarrow c, L, A, R$, where H is either *false* or an atom, A is an atom, c is a constraint, and L and R are (possibly empty) conjunctions of atoms. Let us consider the set $\{K_i \leftarrow c_i, B_i \mid i = 1, \ldots, m\}$ made out of the (renamed apart) clauses of *Cls* such that, for $i = 1, \ldots, m$, the following two conditions hold: (1) A is unifiable with K_i via the most general unifier ϑ_i, and (2) $\mathcal{A} \models \exists X (c, c_i) \vartheta_i$, where X is the tuple of variables in $(c, c_i) \vartheta_i$ (recall that by comma we denote conjunction). By unfolding C w.r.t. A using *Cls*, we derive the set of clauses $TransfCls = (Cls - \{C\}) \cup U(C)$, where the set $U(C)$ is $\{(H \leftarrow c, c_i, L, B_i, R) \vartheta_i \mid i = 1, \ldots, m\}$.

Since the definition rule introduces new predicates through a single definition clause, the head and the body of that clause are equivalent in the least $\mathcal{C}$-model of *Cls* [27]. The *folding* rule consists in replacing an instance of the body of a definition clause by the corresponding instance of its head.

Folding Rule. Let E be a clause in *Cls* of the form: $H \leftarrow e, L, Q, R$. Suppose that there exists a clause D in *Defs* of the form $K \leftarrow d, G$ such that: (1) for some substitution ϑ, $Q = G\vartheta$, and (2) $\mathcal{A} \models \forall X (e \rightarrow d\vartheta)$ holds, where X is the tuple of variables in $e \rightarrow d\vartheta$. Then, by folding E using D we derive the set of clauses $TransfCls = (Cls - \{E\}) \cup \{H \leftarrow e, L, K\vartheta, R\}$.

By using the results of Etalle and Gabbrielli [19], which ensure that the transformation rules preserve the least C-model of a set of constrained Horn clauses, if any, we get the following result.

Theorem 2 (Soundness of the Unfold/Fold Rules). *Suppose that from a set Cls of constrained Horn clauses we derive a new set TransfCls of clauses by a sequence of applications of the* unfold/fold *rules, where every definition clause used for folding is unfolded during that sequence. Then Cls is satisfiable iff TransfCls is satisfiable.*

Note that the applicability condition of Theorem 2 avoids that an unsatisfiable set of clauses is transformed into a satisfiable set. For instance, the unsatisfiable set of clauses $\{false \leftarrow p, \ p \leftarrow\}$ could be transformed into the satisfiable set of clauses (by taking q to be *false* and p to be *true*) $\{false \leftarrow q, \ q \leftarrow q, \ p \leftarrow\}$, by first introducing the new definition clause $q \leftarrow p$ and then folding both *false* $\leftarrow p$ and $q \leftarrow p$, using $q \leftarrow p$. This sequence of applications of the rules is avoided by the condition that the definition $q \leftarrow p$ must be unfolded, and hence replaced by the fact q.

4.1 CHC Specialization

Specialization is a transformation technique that has been proposed in various programming contexts to take advantage of static information for simplifying and customizing programs [28]. In the field of program verification it has been shown that the specialization of constrained Horn clauses can be very useful for transforming and simplifying clauses before checking their satisfiability [12,16,29].

We will use specialization of constrained Horn clauses, called *CHC Specialization*, for simplifying the set T_{RP} of clauses. In particular, starting from clause *Prop* (see Sect. 3.3):

$(Prop) \quad false \leftarrow pre(X,Y), \ p1(X,X'), \ p2(Y,Y'), \ neg\_post(X',Y')$

we introduce two new predicates $p1_{sp}$ and $p2_{sp}$, defined by the clauses:

$(S1) \ \ p1_{sp}(V,V') \leftarrow p1(X,X') \qquad\qquad (S2) \ \ p2_{sp}(W,W') \leftarrow p2(Y,Y')$

where V, V', W, W' are the sub-tuples of X, X', Y, Y', respectively, which occur in $pre(X,Y)$ or $neg\_post(X',Y')$. Then, by applying the folding rule to clause *Prop*, we can replace $p1$ and $p2$ by $p1_{sp}$ and $p2_{sp}$, respectively, thereby obtaining:

$(Prop_{sp}) \quad false \leftarrow pre(V,W), \ p1_{sp}(V,V'), \ p2_{sp}(W,W'), \ neg\_post(V',W')$

Now, by applying the specialization strategy proposed by De Angelis et al. [16], starting from the set $(T_{RP}-\{Prop\}) \cup \{Prop_{sp}, S1, S2\}$ of clauses, we will derive specialized versions of the clauses that define the semantics of programs P_1 and P_2. In particular, in the specialized clauses there will be references to neither the predicate *reach*, nor the predicate *tr*, nor the terms encoding configurations.

Let us illustrate the application of the specialization strategy [16] by considering again the example of Sect. 2. Starting from clause $Prop_{Leq}$ of Sect. 3.3, that is:

$(Prop_{Leq})$ $false \leftarrow X1 = X2,\ X2 \leq Y2,\ Z1' > Z2',$
$$sum\_upto(X1, Z1, X1', Z1'),\ prod(X2, Y2, Z2, X2', Y2', Z2')$$

we introduce two new predicates, namely su and pr, defined as follows:

$(S1_{Leq})\ su(X1, Z1') \leftarrow sum\_upto(X1, Z1, X1', Z1')$
$(S2_{Leq})\ pr(X2, Y2, Z2') \leftarrow prod(X2, Y2, Z2, X2', Y2', Z2')$

By applying the folding rule to $Prop_{Leq}$, we replace $sum\_upto(X1, Z1, X1', Z1')$ and $prod(X2, Y2, Z2, X2', Y2', Z2')$ by $su(X1, Z1')$ and $pr(X2, Y2, Z2')$, respectively, and we get (modulo variable renaming) clause 1 of Fig. 3.

Then, starting from $S1_{Leq}$ and $S2_{Leq}\}$ we get clauses 2–7 of Fig. 3 as we now show. We only illustrate the first few steps of the application of the specialization strategy, which consists in applying a sequence of the transformation rules presented in Sect. 4.

Unfolding: The strategy starts by unfolding $sum\_upto(X1, Z1, X1', Z1')$ occurring in the body of the clause $S1_{Leq}$, hence deriving:

$$su(X1, Z1') \leftarrow initConf(C, X1, Z1), reach(C, C'), finalConf(C', X1', Z1')$$

By unfolding the above clause w.r.t. *initConf*, *reach*, and *finalConf*, we get:

$$su(X1, Z1') \leftarrow tr(cf(cmd(5, asgn(\mathtt{z1}, call(\mathtt{f}, [\mathtt{x1}]))), [(\mathtt{x1}, X1),(\mathtt{z1}, Z1)]), C),$$
$$reach(C, cf(cmd(6, \mathtt{halt}, [(\mathtt{x1}, X1'),(\mathtt{z1}, Z1')])))$$

Then, by unfolding the above clause w.r.t. tr, we get:

$$su(X1, Z1') \leftarrow$$
$$reach(cf(cmd(0, ite(lte(\mathtt{n1}, 0), 1, 2), [(\mathtt{x1}, X1),(\mathtt{z1}, Z1), (\mathtt{n1}, N1),(\mathtt{r1}, R1)]),$$
$$cf(cmd(6, \mathtt{halt}, [(\mathtt{x1}, X1'),(\mathtt{z1}, Z1')])))$$

Definition and Folding: By the definition rule we introduce the following clause defining the new predicate f:

$$f(X1, Z1') \leftarrow$$
$$reach(cf(cmd(0, ite(lte(\mathtt{n1}, 0), 1, 2), [(\mathtt{x1}, X1),(\mathtt{z1}, Z1), (\mathtt{n1}, N1),(\mathtt{r1}, R1)]),$$
$$cf(cmd(6, \mathtt{halt}, [(\mathtt{x1}, X1'),(\mathtt{z1}, Z1')])))$$

Then, the new definition can used for folding, hence deriving (modulo variable renaming) clause 2 of Fig. 3.

Starting from the new definition for predicate f, after a similar sequence of applications of the unfolding, definition, and folding rules, we get clauses 3–4. Then, if we perform for the predicate pr the analogous transformation steps we have done for the predicate sum_upto, that is, if we start from clause $S2_{Leq}$, instead of $S1_{Leq}$, we eventually get the other clauses 5–7 of Fig. 3.

Since the CHC Specialization is performed by applying the unfold/fold rules, by Theorem 2 we have the following result.

Theorem 3. *Let T_{sp} be derived from T_{RP} by specialization. Then T_{RP} is satisfiable iff T_{sp} is satisfiable.*

Input: A set $Q \cup R \cup \{C\}$ of clauses where: (i) C is of the form *false* $\leftarrow c, q(X), r(Y)$, (ii) q and r occur in Q and R, respectively, and (iii) no predicate occurs in both Q and R.

Output: A set *TransfCls* of clauses.

INITIALIZATION: $InCls := \{C\}$; $Defs := \emptyset$; $TransfCls := Q \cup R$;

while there is a clause C in *InCls* *do*

 UNFOLDING: From clause C derive a set $U(C)$ of clauses by unfolding C with respect to every atom occurring in its body using $Q \cup R$;

 Perform *as long as possible* the following replacement: for every clause C' of the form: $H \leftarrow d, A_1, ..., A_k$ in $U(C)$, for every pair of (not necessarily distinct) atoms $A_i = p_i(...,X,...)$ and $A_j = p_j(...,Y,...)$, if $\mathcal{A} \models \forall (d \rightarrow (X = Y))$, then replace every occurrence of Y by X in C', thereby updating the set $U(C)$ of clauses.

 DEFINITION & FOLDING:

 $F(C) := U(C)$;

 for every clause $E \in F(C)$ of the form $H \leftarrow d, G_1, q(V), G_2, r(W), G_3$ where q and r occur in Q and R, respectively, *do*

  if in *Defs* there is no clause D of the form $newp(Z) \leftarrow q(V), r(W)$ (modulo variable renaming), where Z is the tuple of distinct variables in (V, W)

  then $InCls := InCls \cup \{D\}$; $Defs := Defs \cup \{D\}$;

   $F(C) := (F(C) - \{E\}) \cup \{H \leftarrow d, G_1, newp(Z), G_2, G_3\}$

 end-for

 $InCls := InCls - \{C\}$; $TransfCls := TransfCls \cup F(C)$;

end-while

Fig. 5. The *Predicate Pairing* transformation strategy.

4.2 Predicate Pairing

The second strategy which characterizes our verification method is the Predicate Pairing strategy (see Fig. 5). This strategy pairs together two predicates, say q and r into one new predicate t equivalent to their conjunction. As shown in the example of Sect. 2, Predicate Pairing may ease the discovery of relations among the arguments of the two distinct predicates, and thus it may ease the satisfiability test. Obviously, pairing may be iterated and more than two predicates may in general be tupled together.

Let us see the Predicate Pairing strategy in action by considering again the example of Sect. 2.

First Iteration of the while-loop of the Predicate Pairing strategy.

UNFOLDING: The strategy starts by unfolding $su(X1, Z1)$ and $pr(X2, Y2, Z2)$ in clause 1 of Fig. 3, hence deriving the following new clause:

8. *false* $\leftarrow N \leq Y$, $W = 0$, $Z1 > Z2$, $f(N, Z1)$, $g(N, Y, W, Z2)$

DEFINITION AND FOLDING: A new atom with predicate fg is introduced for replacing the conjunction of the atoms with predicates f and g in the body of clause 8:

9. $fg(N, Z1, Y, W, Z2) \leftarrow f(N, Z1)$, $g(N, Y, W, Z2)$

and that conjunction is folded, hence deriving:

10. $false \leftarrow N \leq Y,\ W=0,\ Z1 > Z2,\ fg(N, Z1, Y, W, Z2)$

Second Iteration of the while-loop of the Predicate Pairing strategy.

UNFOLDING: Now, the atoms with predicate f and g in the premise of the newly introduced clause 9 are unfolded, and the following new clauses are derived:

11. $fg(N, Z1, Y, Z2, Z2) \leftarrow N \leq 0,\ Z1 = 0$
12. $fg(N, Z1, Y, W, Z2) \leftarrow N \geq 1,\ N1 = N - 1,\ Z1 = R + N,\ M = Y + W,$
$\qquad f(N1, R),\ g(N1, Y, M, Z2)$

DEFINITION AND FOLDING: No new predicate is needed, as the conjunction of the atoms with predicate f and g in clause 12 can be folded using clause 9. We get:

13. $fg(N, Z1, Y, W, Z2) \leftarrow N \geq 1,\ N1 = N - 1,\ Z1 = R + N,\ M = Y + W,$
$\qquad fg(N1, R, Y, M, Z2)$

Clauses 10, 11, and 13, which are the ones shown in Fig. 4, constitute the final set of clauses we have derived.

The Predicate Pairing strategy always terminates because the number of the possible new predicate definitions is bounded by the number k of conjunctions of the form $q(V), r(W)$, where q occurs in Q and r occurs in R and, hence, the number of executions of the while-loop of the strategy is bounded by k.

Thus, from the fact that the unfold/fold transformation rules preserve satisfiability (see Theorem 2), we get the following result.

Theorem 4 (Termination and soundness of the Predicate Pairing strategy). *Let the set $Q \cup R \cup \{C\}$ of clauses be the input of the Predicate Pairing strategy. Then the strategy terminates and returns a set TransfCls of clauses such that $Q \cup R \cup \{C\}$ is satisfiable iff TransfCls is satisfiable.*

4.3 Verifying Loop Composition

Once the relational property has been translated into a set of CHCs, its verification is no longer dependent on the syntax of the source programs. Thus, as already mentioned in Sect. 2, we may be able to verify relations between programs that have different structure (e.g., relations between non-tail recursive programs and iterative programs). In this section we show one more example of a property that relates two programs that are not structurally similar (in particular, they are obtained by composing different numbers of while-loops).

Let us consider the programs sum1 and sum2 in Fig. 6. They both compute the sum of all integers up to m1 and m2, respectively. Program sum1 computes the result using a single while-loop, and sum2 consists of the composition of two while-loops: the first loop sums the numbers up to an integer n2, with $1 \leq n2 < m2$, and the second loop adds to the result of the first loop the sum of all numbers from n2+1 up to m2. We want to show the following relational property:

LeqS: $\{m1 = m2, 1 \leq n2 < m2\} sum1 \sim sum2 \{s1 \leq s2\}$

```
/* -- Program sum1 -- */          /* -- Program sum2 -- */
int m1, s1;                       int n2, m2, s2;
void sum1() {                     void sum2() {
    int i1 = 0;                       int i2 = 0;
    s1 = 0;                           s2 = 0;
    while (i1 <= m1) {                while (i2 <= n2) {
        s1 += i1;                         s2 += i2;
        i1++; }                           i2++; }
                                      while (i2 <= m2) {
                                          s2 += i2;
                                          i2++; } }
```

Fig. 6. The programs sum1 and sum2.

The relational property *LeqS* and the two programs are translated into the set of clauses shown in Fig. 7. Neither the solvers for CHCs with linear arithmetics (in particular, we tried ELDARICA and Z3) nor RÊVE, the tool for relational verification that implements the approach proposed by Felsing et al. [20], are able to prove the property *LeqS*.

$false \leftarrow M1 = M2, 1 \leq N2, N2 < M2, S1 > S2, sum1(M1, S1), sum2(M2, N2, S2)$

$sum1(M1, S1) \leftarrow S1i = 0, I1 = 0, s1(M1, S1i, I1, S1)$

$s1(M1, S1i, I1, S1) \leftarrow M1 < I1, S1i = S1$

$s1(M1, S1i, I1, S1) \leftarrow M1 \geq I1, T = S1i + I1, J = I1 + 1, s1(M1, T, J, S1)$

$sum2(M2, N2, S2) \leftarrow S2i = 0, I2 = 0, s2(M2, N2, S2i, I2, S2)$

$s2(M2, N2, S2i, I2, S2) \leftarrow M2 < I2, s3(N2, S2i, I2, S2)$

$s2(M2, N2, S2i, I2, S2) \leftarrow M2 \geq I2, U = S2i + I2, K = I2 + 1, s2(M2, N2, U, K, S2)$

$s3(N2, S2i, I2, S2) \leftarrow N2 < I2, S2i = S2$

$s3(N2, S2i, I2, S2) \leftarrow N2 \geq I2, U = S2i + I2, K = I2 + 1, s3(N2, U, K, S2)$

Fig. 7. Translation into constrained Horn clauses of the relational property *LeqS*.

The Predicate Pairing strategy transforms the clauses of Fig. 7 into the clauses of Fig. 8 (the variable names are automatically generated by our implementation). The strategy introduces the two new predicates $s1s2$ and $s1s3$, which stand for the conjunctions of $s1$ with $s2$, and $s1$ with $s3$, respectively.

The clauses of Fig. 8 can be further simplified. For instance, by propagating the constraints that occur in clause 1, we can discover that clause 2 can be removed, because it refers to values of the loop index for which sum1 has terminated and the second while-loop of sum2 is still in execution, and this is impossible with the given pre-relation. Similarly, clauses 3, 7, and 8 can be removed. This form of post-processing of the clauses obtained by Predicate Pairing can be performed by *Constraint Propagation*, through the use of CHC specialization [12]. In Sect. 5 we will demonstrate the positive effects of Constraint Propagation after Predicate Pairing, and indeed the satisfiability of the clauses of Fig. 8 is easily proved by ELDARICA and Z3 after Constraint Propagation.

1. $false \leftarrow 1 \leq E$, $E < A$, $D > F$, $B = 0$, $C = 0$, $s1s2(A, B, C, D, E, F)$
2. $s1s2(A, B, C, D, E, F) \leftarrow A < C$, $B = D$, $E < C$, $s3(A, B, C, F)$
3. $s1s2(A, B, C, D, E, F) \leftarrow A < C$, $B = D$, $E \geq C$, $G = B + C$, $H = C + 1$,
   $s2(E, A, G, H, F)$
4. $s1s2(A, B, C, D, E, F) \leftarrow A \geq C$, $E < C$, $G = B + C$, $H = C + 1$,
   $s1s3(A, G, H, D, B, C, F)$
5. $s1s2(A, B, C, D, E, F) \leftarrow A \geq C$, $E \geq C$, $G = B + C$, $H = C + 1$,
   $s1s2(A, G, H, D, E, F)$
6. $s1s3(A, B, C, D, E, F, G) \leftarrow A < C$, $B = D$, $A < F$, $E = G$
7. $s1s3(A, B, C, D, E, F, G) \leftarrow A < C$, $B = D$, $A \geq F$, $H = E + F$, $I = E + 1$, $s3(A, H, I, G)$
8. $s1s3(A, B, C, D, E, F, G) \leftarrow A \geq C$, $A < F$, $E = G$, $H = B + C$, $I = C + 1$, $s1(A, H, I, D)$
9. $s1s3(A, B, C, D, E, F, G) \leftarrow A \geq C$, $A \geq F$, $H = B + C$, $I = C + 1$, $J = E + F$, $K = F + 1$,
   $s1s3(A, H, I, D, J, K, G)$

Fig. 8. Output of the Predicate Pairing transformation for property *LeqS*.

5 Implementation and Experimental Evaluation

We have implemented the techniques presented in Sects. 3 and 4 as a part of the VERIMAP verification system [14], and we have used the SMT solvers ELDARICA and Z3 (collectively called CHC solvers) for checking the satisfiability of the CHCs generated by VERIMAP.

In particular, our implementation consists of the following three modules. (1) A front-end module, based on the C Intermediate Language (CIL) [33], that translates the given verification problem into the facts defining the predicates *at*, *initConf*, and *finalConf*, by using a custom implementation of the CIL visitor pattern. (2) A back-end module realizing the *CHC Specialization* and *Predicate Pairing* transformation strategies. (3) A module that translates the generated CHCs to the SMT-LIB format for the ELDARICA and Z3 solvers.

We have considered 100 problems[1] referring to relational properties of small, yet non-trivial, C programs mostly taken from the literature [5,6,20]. All programs act on integers, except the programs in the ARR category and 7 out of 10 in the CON category which act on integer arrays. The properties we have considered belong to the following categories. The ITE (respectively, REC) category consists of equivalence properties between pairs of iterative (respectively, recursive) programs, that is, we have verified that, for every pair of programs, the two programs in the pair compute the same output when given the same input. The I-R category consists of equivalence properties between an iterative and a recursive (non-tail recursive) program. For example, we have verified the equivalence of iterative and recursive versions of programs computing the greatest common divisor of two integers and the n-th triangular number $T_n = \sum_{i=1}^{n} i$. The ARR category consists of equivalence properties between programs acting on integer arrays. The LEQ category consists of inequality properties stating that if the inputs of two programs satisfy some given preconditions, then their outputs satisfy an inequality postcondition. For instance, we have

---

[1] The sources of the problems are available at http://map.uniroma2.it/relprop.

verified that, for all non-negative integers m and n: (i) if $n \leq m$, then $T_n \leq n \times m$ (see the example of Sect. 2), and (ii) $n^2 \leq n^3$. The MON (respectively, INJ) category consists of properties stating that programs, under some given preconditions, compute monotonically non-decreasing (respectively, injective) functions. For example, we have verified monotonicity and injectivity of programs computing the Fibonacci numbers, the square of a number, and the triangular numbers. The FUN category consists of properties stating that, under some given preconditions, some of the outputs of the given programs are functionally dependent on a *proper subset* of the inputs. The COMP category consists of equivalence and inequality properties relating two programs that contain compositions of different numbers of loops (see the example in Sect. 4.3).

The experimental process interleaves the application of a CHC transformation strategy (performed by VERIMAP) and a CHC satisfiability check (performed by ELDARICA and Z3). We have considered the following strategies: (i) the CHC Specialization, Sp for short, which is the strategy presented in Sect. 4.1 that transforms the set of CHCs encoding the relational property, (ii) the Predicate Pairing, PP for short, which is the strategy presented in Sect. 4.2, and (iii) the Constraint Propagation, CP for short, which is the strategy that propagates the constraints occurring in the clauses with the aim of discovering invariant constraints by means of the widening and convex-hull operators [12]. We have used the following CHC solvers for checking satisfiability of CHCs: (i) ELDARICA (v1.2-rc in standard mode[2]), and (ii) Z3 (version 4.4.2, master branch as of 2016-02-18) using the PDR engine [25] for programs acting on integers and the Duality engine [32] for programs acting on arrays.

The experimental process starts off by applying the Sp strategy. Then, it uses a CHC solver to check the satisfiability of the generated CHCs. If the CHC solver is unable to solve the considered problem, it applies the PP strategy. Finally, if the CHC solver is unable to solve a problem after PP, it applies the CP strategy. In some cases the CP strategy produces a set of CHCs without constrained facts (that is, without clauses of the form $A \leftarrow c$, where c is a constraint), and hence satisfiable, thereby solving the associated problems. In the other cases it applies the CHC solver on the CHCs obtained after constraint propagation.

The experimental process has been performed on a machine equipped with two Intel Xeon E5-2640 2.00 GHz CPUs and 64 GB of memory, running CentOS 7 (64 bit). A time limit of 5 min has been set for executing each step of the experimental process. The verification problems have been executed in parallel using 24 out of the 32 CPU threads. The results are summarized in Table 1.

The first two columns report the names of the categories and the number M of problems in each category, respectively. Columns Sp, PP, and CP report the average time taken for applying those CHC transformation strategies. The Sp and PP strategies terminate before the timeout for all problems, while the CP strategy does not terminate before the timeout for one problem belonging

---

[2] Using the options `-horn -hsmt -princess -i -abstract:oct`. Running ELDARICA in client-server mode could significantly improve its performance, but requires custom modifications for running multiple problems in parallel.

Table 1. M is the number of verification problems. N is the number of solved problems. Times are in seconds. The timeout is 5 min. Sp is CHC Specialization, PP is Predicate Pairing, CP is Constraint Propagation, Eld is ELDARICA. (∗) One problem in the category MON timed out.

Problem Category	M	Sp time	PP time	CP time	(1) Sp + Eld N	time	(2) Sp + Z3 N	time	(3) Sp + PP + Eld N	time	(4) Sp + PP + Z3 N	time	(5) Sp + PP+CP+Eld N	time	(6) Sp + PP+CP+Z3 N	time
ITE	21	0.10	5.32	0.46	9	23.94	6	0.88	15	19.09	12	17.00	18	16.83	21	11.36
REC	18	0.12	2.88	0.31	8	6.40	8	4.39	14	6.67	14	3.19	14	6.67	15	3.12
I-R	4	0.11	2.30	0.37	0	—	0	—	1	15.88	1	7.19	4	6.83	4	2.68
ARR	5	0.33	0.10	1.07	0	—	0	—	1	11.09	3	1.74	1	11.09	3	1.74
LEQ	6	0.10	0.80	0.17	0	—	0	—	0	—	0	—	2	6.32	3	1.11
MON	18	0.05	2.38	(∗) 0.15	6	9.62	4	0.25	11	9.77	8	0.97	11	9.77	14	1.43
INJ	11	0.05	1.31	0.15	2	11.38	0		6	55.80	5	1.89	6	55.80	10	1.70
FUN	7	0.05	3.62	0.10	5	4.52	5	0.24	7	5.23	7	0.59	7	5.23	7	0.59
COMP	10	0.26	0.65	19.61	0	—	0	—	3	24.40	6	4.51	6	16.15	9	3.70
Total number: avg. time:	100	0.11	2.67	2.24	30	12.32	23	1.85	58	16.53	56	5.53	69	14.83	86	4.41

to the MON category. In the remaining columns we report the number of problems solved by the ELDARICA and Z3 solvers after the application of our CHC transformation strategies. We also report the average time taken for each solved problem, which includes the time needed for applying the CHC transformation strategies. In the last two rows we indicate the total number of solved problems and the overall average time.

Columns 1 (Sp + Eld) and 2 (Sp + Z3) report the results for the problems that were solved by applying ELDARICA and Z3, respectively, on the CHCs generated by the Sp strategy. Columns 3 (Sp + PP + Eld) and 4 (Sp + PP + Z3) report the results obtained by applying ELDARICA and Z3, respectively, on the CHCs obtained by the Sp strategy, followed by the PP strategy in the cases where the CHC solvers were unable to produce an answer on the CHCs generated by the Sp strategy. Columns 5 (Sp + PP+ CP + Eld) and 6 (Sp + PP+ CP + Z3) report the results obtained by applying Eldarica and Z3, respectively, on the CHCs produced by the Sp strategy, followed by the PP and CP strategies.

The use of the PP and CP strategies significantly increases the number of problems that have been solved. In particular, the number of problems that can be solved by Eldarica increases from 30 (see Column 1) to 69 (Column 5). Similarly for Z3 from 23 (Column 2) to 86 (Column 6). We observe that the application of the PP strategy alone is very effective in increasing the number of solved problems. For instance, it allows Eldarica to solve 28 more problems (see Columns 1 and 3). Also the application of the CP strategy turns out to be very useful for solving additional problems. For instance, for Z3 the CP strategy allows the solution of 30 additional problems (see Columns 4 and 6).

Note that the set of CHCs produced as output by the PP and CP strategies can be larger than the set of CHCs provided as input. In our benchmark we have observed that the increase of size is, on average, about 1.88× for PP and 1.77× for CP (these numbers drop down to 1.77× for PP and 1.16× for CP when we remove from the benchmark 4 examples out of 100 for which the increase of size is very high). However, despite the increase of size, the PP and CP strategies are very effective at improving the efficacy of the considered CHC solvers.

Now, let us compare our experimental results with the ones obtained by RÊVE [20] (the most recent version of the tool is available on-line[3]). For the problems belonging to the ITE and REC categories, we have that if RÊVE succeeds, then also our tool succeeds by using the strategies presented in this paper. As regards the remaining problem categories, an exhaustive comparison with RÊVE is not possible because this tool needs a manual annotation of programs with 'marks', representing synchronization points between programs. Nevertheless, the categories MON, FUN, ARR, and LEQ consist of pairs of programs with a similar control structure (in particular, the programs in MON and FUN are mostly taken from the ITE and REC categories, but with different relational properties), and therefore the approach proposed by Felsing et al. [20] is generally expected to perform well. However, it is worth noting that the problems in I-R and COMP consist of pairs of programs that do *not* exhibit a similar control structure, and therefore the approach of RÊVE with marks cannot be directly applied for solving problems belonging to those categories.

6   Related Work

Several logics and methods have been presented in the literature for reasoning about various relations which may hold between two given programs. Their purpose is the formal, possibly automated, validation of program transformations and program analysis techniques.

A Hoare-like axiomatization of relational reasoning for simple while programs has been proposed by Benton [6], which however does not present any technique for automating proofs. In particular, *program equivalence* is one of the relational properties that has been extensively studied (see [5,10,11,20,23,37,38] for some recent work). Indeed, during software development it is often the case that one may want to modify the program text and then prove that its semantics has not been changed (this kind of proofs is sometimes called *regression verification* [20]).

The idea of reducing program equivalence to a standard verification task by using the *cross-product* construction was presented by Zaks and Pnueli [38]. However, this method only applies to structurally equivalent programs. A more refined notion of *program product* has been proposed by Barthe et al. [5] to partially automate general relational reasoning by reducing this problem, similarly to the method proposed by Zaks and Pnueli [38], to a standard program verification problem. The method requires human ingenuity: (i) for generating program products via suitable program refinements and also (ii) for providing suitable invariants to the program verifier. Also the *Differential Assertion Checking* technique proposed by Lahiri et al. [30] makes use of the notion of a *program*

---

[3] http://formal.iti.kit.edu/improve/reve/index.php.

composition to reduce the *relative correctness* of two programs to a suitable safety property of the composed program.

Among the various methods to prove relational properties, the one which is most related to ours is the method proposed by Felsing et al. [20], which presents proof rules for the equivalence of imperative programs that are translated into constrained Horn clauses. The satisfiability of these clauses which entails equivalence, is then checked by state-of-the-art CHC solvers. Although the proof rules are presented for the case of program equivalence, they can be extended to more general relational properties (and, indeed, the tool that implements the method supports a class of specifications comparable to the one presented in this paper). The main difference of our approach with respect to the one of Felsing et al. [20] is that we generate the translation of the relational properties into CHCs from the semantics of the language, and hence we do not need special purpose proof rules that depend on the programming language and the class of properties under consideration. Instead, we use general purpose transformation rules for CHCs. As demonstrated by our experimental evaluation, our approach gives results that are comparable with the ones by Felsing et al. when considering similar examples, but we are able to deal with a larger class of programs. Indeed, besides being more parametric and flexible, an advantage of our approach is that it is able to verify relations between programs that have different structure, because the transformation rules are independent of the syntax of the source programs (unlike the proof rules). For instance, we have shown that we are able to verify relations between while-loops and non-tail recursive functions without a preliminary conversion into tail-recursive form (see Sect. 2). We are also able to verify relations between programs consisting of the composition of two (or more) while-loops and programs with one while-loop only (see Sect. 4.3). The method presented by Felsing et al. is not able to deal with the above two classes of verification problems.

The idea of using program transformations to help the proof of relational properties relating higher-order functional programs has been explored by Asada et al. [3]. The main difference between this approach and ours is that, besides the difference of programming languages, we transform the logical representation of the property to be proved, rather than the two programs under analysis. Our approach allows higher parametricity with respect to the programming language, and also enables us to use very effective tools for CHC solving.

Our notion of the Predicate Pairing is related to that of the *mutual summaries* presented by Hawblitzel et al. [24]. Mutual summaries relate the summaries of two procedures, and can be used to prove relations between them, including relative termination (which we do not consider in our technique). Similarly to the already mentioned papers by Barthe et al. [5] and Lahiri et al. [30], this approach requires human ingenuity to generate suitable proof obligations, which can then be discharged by automated theorem provers. As regards reusing available verification techniques to prove program equivalence, we want also to mention the paper by Ganty et al. [22], where the authors identify a class of recursive programs for which it is possible to precisely compute summaries. This technique can be used to reduce the problem of checking the equivalence of two recursive programs to the problem of checking the equivalence of their summaries.

Finally, we want to mention that in the present paper we have used (variants and extensions of) transformation techniques for constrained Horn clauses proposed in the area of program verification in previous papers [1,12,13,15,16, 29,34]. However, the goal of those previous papers was the verification of the (partial and total) correctness of single programs, and not the verification of relations between two programs which has been the objective of our study here.

7 Conclusions

We have presented a method for verifying relational properties of programs written in a simple imperative language with integer and array variables. The method consists in: (i) translating the property to be verified into a set of constrained Horn clauses, then (ii) transforming these clauses to better exploit the interactions between the predicates that represent the computations evoked by the programs, and finally, (iii) using state-of-the-art constrained Horn clause solvers to prove satisfiability that enforces the property to be verified.

Although we have considered imperative programs, the only language-specific element of our method is the constrained Horn clause interpreter that we have used to represent in clausal form the program semantics and the property to be verified. Indeed, our method can also be applied to prove relations between programs written in different programming languages. Thus, our approach is basically independent of the programming language used.

Acknowledgements. We wish to thank A. Gurfinkel, V. Klebanov, Ph. Rümmer and the participants in the HCVS and VPT workshops at ETAPS 2016 for stimulating conversations. We also thank the anonymous referees for their very constructive comments. We acknowledge the financial support of INdAM-GNCS (Italy). E. De Angelis, F. Fioravanti, and A. Pettorossi are research associates at IASI-CNR.

References

1. Albert, E., Gómez-Zamalloa, M., Hubert, L., Puebla, G.: Verification of java byte-code using analysis and transformation of logic programs. In: Hanus, M. (ed.) PADL 2007. LNCS, vol. 4354, pp. 124–139. Springer, Heidelberg (2007)
2. Alberti, F., Ghilardi, S., Sharygina, N.: Decision procedures for flat array properties. In: Ábrahám, E., Havelund, K. (eds.) TACAS 2014 (ETAPS). LNCS, vol. 8413, pp. 15–30. Springer, Heidelberg (2014)
3. Asada, K., Sato, R., Kobayashi, N.: Verifying relational properties of functional programs by first-order refinement. In: Proceedings of PEPM 2015, pp. 61–72. ACM (2015)
4. Barnett, M., Chang, B.-Y.E., DeLine, R., Jacobs, B., M. Leino, K.R.: Boogie: a modular reusable verifier for object-oriented programs. In: de Boer, F.S., Bonsangue, M.M., Graf, S., de Roever, W.-P. (eds.) FMCO 2005. LNCS, vol. 4111, pp. 364–387. Springer, Heidelberg (2006)

5. Barthe, G., Crespo, J.M., Kunz, C.: Relational verification using product programs. In: Butler, M., Schulte, W. (eds.) FM 2011. LNCS, vol. 6664, pp. 200–214. Springer, Heidelberg (2011)
6. Benton, N.: Simple relational correctness proofs for static analyses and program transformations. In: Proceedings of POPL 2004, pp. 14–25. ACM (2004)
7. Bjørner, N., Gurfinkel, A., McMillan, K., Rybalchenko, A.: Horn clause solvers for program verification. In: Blass, A., Dershowitz, N., Finkbeiner, B., Schulte, W., Beklemishev, L.D., Beklemishev, L.D. (eds.) Gurevich Festschrift II 2015. LNCS, vol. 9300, pp. 24–51. Springer, Heidelberg (2015). doi:10.1007/978-3-319-23534-9_2
8. Borralleras, C., Lucas, S., Oliveras, A., Rodríguez-Carbonell, E., Rubio, A.: SAT modulo linear arithmetic for solving polynomial constraints. J. Autom. Reasoning 48(1), 107–131 (2012)
9. Bradley, A.R., Manna, Z., Sipma, H.B.: What's decidable about arrays? In: Emerson, E.A., Namjoshi, K.S. (eds.) VMCAI 2006. LNCS, vol. 3855, pp. 427–442. Springer, Heidelberg (2006)
10. Chaki, S., Gurfinkel, A., Strichman, O.: Regression verification for multi-threaded programs. In: Kuncak, V., Rybalchenko, A. (eds.) VMCAI 2012. LNCS, vol. 7148, pp. 119–135. Springer, Heidelberg (2012)
11. Ciobâcă, Ş., Lucanu, D., Rusu, V., Roşu, G.: A language-independent proof system for mutual program equivalence. In: Merz, S., Pang, J. (eds.) ICFEM 2014. LNCS, vol. 8829, pp. 75–90. Springer, Heidelberg (2014)
12. De Angelis, E., Fioravanti, F., Pettorossi, A., Proietti, M.: Program verification via iterated specialization. Sci. Comput. Program. 95(Part 2), 149–175 (2014)
13. De Angelis, E., Fioravanti, F., Pettorossi, A., Proietti, M.: A rule-based verification strategy for array manipulating programs. Fundamenta Informaticae 140(3–4), 329–355 (2015)
14. De Angelis, E., Fioravanti, F., Pettorossi, A., Proietti, M.: VeriMAP: a tool for verifying programs through transformations. In: Ábrahám, E., Havelund, K. (eds.) TACAS 2014 (ETAPS). LNCS, vol. 8413, pp. 568–574. Springer, Heidelberg (2014). http://map.uniroma2.it/VeriMAP
15. De Angelis, E., Fioravanti, F., Pettorossi, A., Proietti, M.: Proving correctness of imperative programs by linearizing constrained Horn clauses. Theor. Pract. Logic Program. 15(4–5), 635–650 (2015)
16. De Angelis, E., Fioravanti, F., Pettorossi, A., Proietti, M.: Semantics-based generation of verification conditions by program specialization. In: Proceedings of PPDP 2015, pp. 91–102. ACM (2015)
17. de Moura, L., Bjørner, N.S.: Z3: an efficient SMT solver. In: Ramakrishnan, C.R., Rehof, J. (eds.) TACAS 2008. LNCS, vol. 4963, pp. 337–340. Springer, Heidelberg (2008)
18. De Schreye, D., Glück, R., Jørgensen, J., Leuschel, M., Martens, B., Sørensen, M.H.: Conjunctive partial deduction: foundations, control, algorithms, and experiments. J. Logic Program. 41(2–3), 231–277 (1999)
19. Etalle, S., Gabbrielli, M.: Transformations of CLP modules. Theor. Comput. Sci. 166, 101–146 (1996)
20. Felsing, D., Grebing, S., Klebanov, V., Rümmer, P., Ulbrich, M.: Automating regression verification. In: Proceedings of ASE 2014, pp. 349–360 (2014)
21. Filliâtre, J.-C., Paskevich, A.: Why3 — where programs meet provers. In: Felleisen, M., Gardner, P. (eds.) ESOP 2013. LNCS, vol. 7792, pp. 125–128. Springer, Heidelberg (2013)

22. Ganty, P., Iosif, R., Konečný, F.: Underapproximation of procedure summaries for integer programs. In: Piterman, N., Smolka, S.A. (eds.) TACAS 2013 (ETAPS 2013). LNCS, vol. 7795, pp. 245–259. Springer, Heidelberg (2013)

23. Godlin, B., Strichman, O.: Regression verification: proving the equivalence of similar programs. Softw. Test. Verif. Reliab. **23**(3), 241–258 (2013)

24. Hawblitzel, C., Kawaguchi, M., Lahiri, S.K., Rebêlo, H.: Towards modularly comparing programs using automated theorem provers. In: Bonacina, M.P. (ed.) CADE 2013. LNCS, vol. 7898, pp. 282–299. Springer, Heidelberg (2013)

25. Hoder, K., Bjørner, N.: Generalized property directed reachability. In: Cimatti, A., Sebastiani, R. (eds.) SAT 2012. LNCS, vol. 7317, pp. 157–171. Springer, Heidelberg (2012)

26. Hojjat, H., Konečný, F., Garnier, F., Iosif, R., Kuncak, V., Rümmer, P.: A verification toolkit for numerical transition systems. In: Giannakopoulou, D., Méry, D. (eds.) FM 2012. LNCS, vol. 7436, pp. 247–251. Springer, Heidelberg (2012)

27. Jaffar, J., Maher, M.: Constraint logic programming: a survey. J. Logic Program. **19**(20), 503–581 (1994)

28. Jones, N.D., Gomard, C.K., Sestoft, P.: Partial Evaluation and Automatic Program Generation. Prentice Hall, Englewood Cliffs (1993)

29. Kafle, B., Gallagher, J.P.: Constraint specialisation in Horn clause verification. In: Proceedings of PEPM 2015, pp. 85–90. ACM (2015)

30. Lahiri, S.K., McMillan, K.L., Sharma, R., Hawblitzel, C.: Differential assertion checking. In: Proceedings of ESEC/FSE 2013, pp. 345–355. ACM (2013)

31. Matijasevic, Y.V.: Enumerable sets are diophantine. Doklady Akademii Nauk SSSR **191**, 279–282 (1970). in Russian

32. McMillan, K., Rybalchenko, A.: Computing relational fixed points using interpolation. Technical report MSR-TR-2013-6, Microsoft Research, January 2013

33. Necula, G.C., McPeak, S., Rahul, S.P., Weimer, W.: CIL: intermediate language and tools for analysis and transformation of C programs. In: Nigel Horspool, R. (ed.) CC 2002. LNCS, vol. 2304, pp. 213–265. Springer, Heidelberg (2002)

34. Peralta, J.C., Gallagher, J.P., Saglam, H.: Analysis of imperative programs through analysis of constraint logic programs. In: Levi, G. (ed.) SAS 1998. LNCS, vol. 1503, pp. 246–261. Springer, Heidelberg (1998)

35. Pettorossi, A., Proietti, M.: Transformation of logic programs: foundations and techniques. J. Logic Program. **19**(20), 261–320 (1994)

36. Tamaki, H., Sato, T.: Unfold/fold transformation of logic programs. In: Proceedings of ICLP 1984, pp. 127–138 (1984)

37. Verdoolaege, S., Janssens, G., Bruynooghe, M.: Equivalence checking of static affine programs using widening to handle recurrences. ACM Trans. Program. Lang. Syst. **34**(3), 11 (2012)

38. Zaks, A., Pnueli, A.: CoVaC: compiler validation by program analysis of the cross-product. In: Cuellar, J., Sere, K. (eds.) FM 2008. LNCS, vol. 5014, pp. 35–51. Springer, Heidelberg (2008)

Securing a Compiler Transformation

Chaoqiang Deng[1] and Kedar S. Namjoshi[2]([✉])

[1] New York University, New York City, USA
deng@cs.nyu.edu
[2] Bell Laboratories, Nokia, Murray Hill, USA
kedar@research.bell-labs.com

Abstract. A compiler can be correct and yet be insecure. That is, a compiled program may have the same input-output behavior as the original, and yet leak more information. An example is the commonly applied optimization which removes dead (i.e., useless) stores. It is shown that deciding *a posteriori* whether a new leak has been introduced as a result of eliminating dead stores is difficult: it is PSPACE-hard for finite-state programs and undecidable in general. In contrast, deciding the correctness of dead store removal is in polynomial time. In response to the hardness result, a sound but approximate polynomial-time algorithm for secure dead store elimination is presented and proved correct. Furthermore, it is shown that for several other compiler transformations, security follows from correctness.

1 Introduction

Compilers are essential to computing: without some form of compilation, it is not possible to turn a high level program description into executable code. Ensuring that a compiler produces correct code – i.e., the resulting executable has the same input-output behavior as the input program – is therefore important and a classic verification challenge. In this work, we assume correctness and investigate the *security* of a compiler transformation.

Compilers can be correct but insecure. The best-known example of this phenomenon is given by dead store elimination [7,10]. Consider the program on the left hand side of Fig. 1. It reads a password, uses it, then clears the memory containing password data, so that the password does not remain in the clear on the stack any longer than is necessary. Dead-store elimination, applied to this program, will remove the instruction clearing x, as its value is never used. In the resulting program, the password remains in the clear in the stack memory, as compilers usually implement a return from a procedure simply by moving the stack pointer to a different position, without erasing the procedure-local data. As a consequence, an attack elsewhere in the program which gains access to program memory may be able to read the password from the stack memory. Stated differently, the value of the password is leaked outside the function foo. The input-output behavior of the function is identical for the two programs, hence the dead-store removal is correct.

© Springer-Verlag GmbH Germany 2016
X. Rival (Ed.): SAS 2016, LNCS 9837, pp. 170–188, 2016.
DOI: 10.1007/978-3-662-53413-7_9

```
void foo()                        void foo()
{                                 {
    int x;                            int x;

    x = read_password();              x = read_password();
    use(x);                           use(x);
    x = 0; // clear password
    return;                           return;
}                                 }
```

Fig. 1. C programs illustrating the insecurity of dead-store elimination

There are workarounds which can be applied to this example to fix the problem. For example, x could be declared volatile in C, so the compiler will not remove any assignments to x. Specific compiler pragmas could be applied to force the compiler to retain the assignment to x. But these are all unsatisfactory, in several respects. First, they pre-suppose that the possibility of a compiler introducing a security leak is known to the programmer, which may not be the case. Next, they suppose that the programmer understands enough of the compiler's internal workings to implement the correct fix, which need not be the case either – compilation is a complex, opaque process. Furthermore, it supposes that the solution is portable across compilers, which need not be true. And, finally, the fix may be too severe: for instance, an assignment x:= 5 following the clearing of x can be removed safely, as the x:= 0 assignment already clears the sensitive data – marking x as volatile would prohibit this removal. A similar issue arises if a compiler inserts instructions to clear all potentially tainted data at the return point; as taint analysis is approximate, such instructions may incur a significant overhead. For these reasons, we believe it is necessary to find a fundamental solution to this problem.

One possible solution is to develop an analysis which, given an instance of a correct transformation, checks whether it is secure. This is a *Translation Validation* mechanism for security, similar to those developed in e.g., [12,15,18] for correctness. We show that translation validation for information leakage is undecidable for general programs and difficult (PSPACE-hard) for finite-state programs. This proof considers a dead store elimination transformation where the input and output programs as well as the location of the eliminated stores is supplied. On the other hand, given the same information, correctness can be determined in polynomial time. The large complexity gap suggests that translation validation for information leakage is likely to be much more difficult than the corresponding question for correctness.

Faced with this difficulty, we turn to algorithms that guarantee a *secure* dead-store elimination. Our algorithm takes as input a program P and a list of dead assignments, and prunes that list to those assignments whose removal is guaranteed not to introduce a new information leak. This is done by consulting the result of a control-flow sensitive taint analysis on the source program P. We formalize the precise notion of information leakage, present this algorithm, and the proof that it preserves security. Three important points should be noted. First, the algorithm is sub-optimal, given the hardness results. It may retain more stores than is strictly necessary. Second, the algorithm does not eliminate leaks that are originally in P; it only ensures that no new leaks are added during the transformation from P to Q. Thus, it shows that the transformation is secure in that it does not weaken the security guarantees of the original program. Finally, we assume correctness and focus on information leakage, which is but one aspect of security. There are other aspects, such as ensuring that a compiler does not introduce an undefined operation, e.g., a buffer overrun, which might compromise security. That is part of the correctness guarantee.

The difference between correctness and security is due to the fact that standard notions of refinement used for correctness do not necessarily preserve security properties. We develop a strong notion of refinement that does preserve security, and use it to show that other common optimizations, such as constant propagation, are secure.

To summarize, the main contributions of this work are (1) results showing that *a posteriori* verification of the security of compilation has high complexity, (2) a dead-store elimination procedure with security built in, along with a formal proof of the security guarantees that are provided, and (3) a general theorem which reduces security to correctness through a strong refinement notion. These are first steps towards the construction of a fully secure compiler.

2   Preliminaries

In this section, we define the correctness and the security of transformations on a small programming language. The programming language is deliberately kept simple, to more clearly illustrate the issues and the proof arguments.

Program Syntax and Semantics. For the formal development, we consider only **structured** programs whose syntax is given in the following. (Illustrative examples are, however, written in C.) For simplicity, all variables have Integer type. Variables are partitioned into input and state variables and, on a different axis, into sets H ("high security") and L ("low security"). All state variables are low security; inputs may be high or low security.

$$x \in \mathbb{X} \qquad\qquad\qquad\qquad\qquad\qquad\qquad\qquad\qquad \text{variables}$$
$$e \in \mathbb{E} := c \mid x \mid f(e_1, \ldots, e_n) \qquad \text{expressions: } f \text{ is a function, c a constant}$$
$$g \in \mathbb{G} \qquad\qquad\qquad\qquad\qquad\qquad\qquad \text{Boolean conditions on } \mathbb{X}$$
$$S \in \mathbb{S} := \mathsf{skip} \mid x := e \mid S_1; S_2 \mid \mathsf{if}\ g\ \mathsf{then}\ S_1\ \mathsf{else}\ S_2\ \mathsf{fi} \mid \mathsf{while}\ g\ \mathsf{do}\ S\ \mathsf{od}$$
$$\text{statements}$$

A program can be represented by its *control flow graph* (CFG). (We omit a description of this process, which is standard.) Each node of the CFG represents a program location, and each edge is labeled with a guarded command, of the form "$g \to x := e$" or "$g \to \mathsf{skip}$", where g is a Boolean predicate and e is an expression over the program variables. A special node, entry, with no incoming edges, defines the initial program location, while a special node, exit, defines the final program location. Values for input variables are specified at the beginning of the program and remain constant throughout execution.

The semantics of a program is defined in the standard manner. A *program state* s is a pair (m, p), where m is a CFG node (referred to as the *location* of s) and p is a function mapping each variable to a value from its type. The function p can be extended to evaluate an expression in the standard way (omitted). We suppose that a program has a fixed initial valuation for the state variables. An *initial state* is one located at the entry node, where the state variables have this fixed valuation. The *transition relation* is defined as follows: a pair of states, $(s = (m, p), t = (n, q))$ is in the relation if there is an edge $f = (m, n)$ of the CFG which connects the locations associated with s and t, and for the guarded command on that edge, either (i) the command is of the form $g \rightarrow x := e$, the guard g holds of p, and the function $q(y)$ is identical to $p(y)$ for all variables y other than x, while $q(x)$ equals $p(e)$; (ii) the command is of the form $g \rightarrow$ skip, the guard g holds of p, and q is identical to p. The guard predicates for all of the outgoing edges of a node form a partition of the state space, so that a program is *deterministic* and *deadlock-free*. A *execution trace* of the program (referred to in short as a trace) from state s is a sequence of states $s_0 = s, s_1, \ldots$ such that adjacent states are connected by the transition relation. A *computation* is a trace from the initial state. A computation is *terminating* if it is finite and the last state has the exit node as its location.

Post-domination in CFG. A set of nodes N *post-dominates* a node m if each path in the CFG from m to the exit node has to pass through at least one node from N.

Information Leakage. Information leakage is defined in a standard manner [3,6]. Input variables are divided into high security (H) and low security (L) variables. All state variables are low-security (L). A program P is said to *leak* information if there is a pair of H-input values $\{a, b\}$, with $a \neq b$, and an L-input c such that the computations of P on inputs $(H = a, L = c)$ and $(H = b, L = c)$ either (a) differ in the sequence of output values, or (b) both terminate, and differ in the value of one of the L-variables at their *final* states. We call (a, b, c) a *leaky triple* for program P.

Correct and Secure Transformations. For clarity, we consider program transformations which do not alter the set of input variables. A transformation from program P to program Q may alter the code of P or the set of state variables. The transformation is *correct* if, for every input value a, the sequence of output values for executions of P and Q from a is identical. (The return value from a function is considered to be an output.) The transformation is *secure* if the set of leaky triples for Q is a subset of the leaky triples for P. By the definition of leakage, for a correct transformation to be insecure, there must be a triple (a, b, c) for which the computations of Q with inputs $(H = a, L = c)$ and $(H = b, L = c)$ terminate with different L-values, and either one of the corresponding computations in P is non-terminating, or both terminate with the same L-values.

A correct transformation supplies the relative correctness guarantee that Q is at least as correct as P, it does not assure the correctness of either program with respect to a specification. Similarly, a secure transformation does not ensure the absolute security of either P or Q; it does ensure relative security, i.e., that Q is not more leaky than P.

This definition of a secure transformation does not distinguish between the "amount" of information that is leaked in the two programs. Consider, for instance, the case where both P and Q leak information about a credit card number. In program Q, the entire card number is made visible whereas, in P, only the last four digits are exposed. By the definition above, this transformation is secure, as both programs leak information about the credit card number. From a practical standpoint, though, one might consider Q to have a far more serious leak than P, as the last four digits are commonly revealed on credit card statements. It has proved difficult, however, to precisely define the notion of "amount of information" – cf. [16] for a survey. We conjecture, however, that the dead-store elimination procedure presented in this paper would not incur greater amount of information leakage than the original program; a justification for this conjecture is presented in Sect. 5.

3   The Hardness of Secure Translation Validation

One method of ensuring the security of a compiler transformation would be to check algorithmically, during compilation, that the result program Q obtained by the transformation on program P is at least as secure as P. This is akin to the Translation Validation approach [12,15,18] to compiler correctness. We show, however, that checking the security of a program transformation is hard and can be substantially more difficult than checking its correctness. Focusing on the dead store elimination procedure, we show that checking its security is undecidable in general, PSPACE-complete for finite-state programs, and co-NP-complete for loop-free, finite-state programs.

The precise setting is as follows. The input to the checker is a triple (P, Q, D), where P is an input program, Q is the output program produced after dead store elimination, and D is the list of eliminated assignments, which are known to be dead (i.e., with no useful effect) at their locations. The question is to determine whether Q is at most as leaky as P. To begin with, we establish that checking correctness is easy, in polynomial time, for arbitrary **while** programs.

Theorem 1. *The correctness of a dead store elimination instance* (P, Q, D) *can be checked in* PTIME.

Proof: The check proceeds as follows. First, check that P and Q have the same (identical, not isomorphic) graph. I.e., the set of node names is identical, and the transition relation is identical. Then check if Q differs from P only in the labeling of transitions in D, which are replaced by skip. Finally, check that every store in D is (syntactically) dead in P, by re-doing the liveness analysis on P. Each step is in polynomial time in the size of the programs. **EndProof.**

We now turn to the question of security, and show that it is substantially more difficult.

Theorem 2. *Checking the security of a dead store elimination given as a triple* (P, Q, D) *is* PSPACE-*complete for finite-state programs.*

Proof: Consider the complement problem of checking whether a transformation from P to Q is insecure. By definition, this is so if there exists a triple (a, b, c) which is leaky for Q but not for P. Determining whether (a, b, c) is leaky can be done in deterministic polynomial space, by simulating the program on the input pairs (a, c) and (b, c) independently in parallel. Checking the pairs sequentially does not work, as the computation from one of the pairs may not terminate. Non-termination is handled in a standard way by adding an n-bit counter, where 2^n is an upper bound on the size of the search space: the number n is linear in the number of program variables. A non-deterministic machine can guess the values a, b, c in polynomial time, and then check that (a, b, c) is leaky for Q but not leaky for P. Thus, checking insecurity is in non-deterministic PSPACE, which is in PSPACE by Savitch's theorem.

To show hardness, consider the problem of deciding whether a program with no inputs or outputs terminates, which is PSPACE-complete by a simple reduction from the IN-PLACE-ACCEPTANCE problem [13]. Given such a program R, let h be a fresh high security input variable and l a fresh low-security state variable, both Boolean, with l initialized to *false*. Define program P as: "R; $l := h$; $l := false$", and program Q as: "R; $l := h$". As the final assignment to l in P is dead, Q is a correct result of dead store elimination on P. Consider the triple $(h = true, h = false, \_)$. If R terminates, then Q has distinct final values for l for the two executions arising from inputs $(h = true, \_)$ and $(h = false, \_)$, while P does not, so the transformation is insecure. If R does not terminate, there are no terminating executions for Q, so Q has no leaky triples and the transformation is trivially secure. Hence, R is non-terminating if, and only if, the transformation from P to Q is secure. **EndProof.**

Theorem 3. *Checking the security of a dead store elimination given as a triple* (P, Q, D) *is undecidable for general programs.*

Proof: (Sketch) The PSPACE-hardness proof of Theorem 2 can be applied to general programs as well. Hence, the triple is insecure if, and only if, program R terminates. **EndProof.**

In the full version of the paper, we show that establishing security is difficult even for the very simple case of finite-state, loop-free programs.

Theorem 4. *Checking the security of a dead store elimination given as a triple* (P, Q, D) *is* co-NP-*complete for loop free programs.*

4 A Taint Proof System

In this section, we introduce a taint proof system for structured programs. It is similar to the security proof systems of [6,17] but explicitly considers per-variable, per-location taints. It is inspired by the taint proof system of [4], which is the basis of the STAC taint analysis plugin of the Frama-C compiler. There are some differences in the treatment of conditionals: in their system, assignments in a branch of an IF-statement with a tainted condition are tainted in an eager fashion while, in ours, the taint may be delayed to a point immediately after the statement.

The full version of this paper includes a proof of soundness for this system. Moreover, the key properties carry over to a more complex taint proof system for arbitrary CFGs. Although the focus here is on structured programs, this is done solely for clarity; the results carry over to arbitrary CFGs.

4.1 Preliminaries

Let $Taint$ be a Boolean set $\{untainted, tainted\}$ where $tainted = $ true and $untainted = $ false. A taint environment is a function $\mathcal{E} : Variables \rightarrow Taint$ which maps each program variable to a Boolean value. That is, for a taint environment $\mathcal{E}$, $\mathcal{E}(x)$ is true if x is tainted, and false if x is untainted. The taint environment $\mathcal{E}$ can be extended to terms as follows:

$\mathcal{E}(c) = $ false, if c is a constant
$\mathcal{E}(x) = \mathcal{E}(x)$, if x is a variable
$\mathcal{E}(f(t_1, \ldots, t_N)) = \bigvee_{i=1}^{N} \mathcal{E}(t_i)$

A pair of states $(s = (m, p), t = (n, q))$ satisfies a taint environment $\mathcal{E}$ if $m = n$ (i.e., s and t are at the same program location), and for every variable x, if x is untainted in $\mathcal{E}$ (i.e., $\mathcal{E}(x)$ holds), the values of x are equal in s and t.

Taint environments are ordered by component-wise implication: $\mathcal{E} \sqsubseteq \mathcal{F} \Leftrightarrow (\forall x : \mathcal{E}(x) \Rightarrow \mathcal{F}(x))$. If $\mathcal{E} \sqsubseteq \mathcal{F}$, then $\mathcal{F}$ taints all variables tainted by $\mathcal{E}$ and maybe more.

4.2 Basic Properties

Proposition 1 *(Monotonicity).* *If* $(s, t) \models \mathcal{E}$ *and* $\mathcal{E} \sqsubseteq \mathcal{F}$, *then* $(s, t) \models \mathcal{F}$.

For a statement S and states $s = (m, p)$ and $s' = (n, q)$, we write $s \xrightarrow{S} s'$ to mean that there is an execution trace from s to s' such that m denotes the program location immediately before S and n denotes the program location immediately after S; s' is the *successor* of s after executing S.

In addition, for taint environments $\mathcal{E}$ and $\mathcal{F}$, we write $\{\mathcal{E}\} S \{\mathcal{F}\}$ to mean that for any pair of states satisfying $\mathcal{E}$, their successors after executing S satisfy $\mathcal{F}$. Formally, $\{\mathcal{E}\} S \{\mathcal{F}\} \Leftrightarrow (\forall s, t : (s, t) \models \mathcal{E} \wedge s \xrightarrow{S} s' \wedge t \xrightarrow{S} t' : (s', t') \models \mathcal{F})$.

Proposition 2 *(Widening).* *If* $\{\mathcal{E}\} S \{\mathcal{F}\}, \mathcal{E}' \sqsubseteq \mathcal{E}$ *and* $\mathcal{F} \sqsubseteq \mathcal{F}'$, *then* $\{\mathcal{E}'\} S \{\mathcal{F}'\}$.

4.3   Proof System

We present a taint proof system for inferring $\{\mathcal{E}\}\, S\, \{\mathcal{F}\}$ for a structured program S. The soundness proof is by induction on program structure, following the pattern of the proof in [17].

$S\ is\ \text{skip:}\quad \{\mathcal{E}\}\ \text{skip}\ \{\mathcal{E}\}$

$S\ is\ an\ assignment\ x\ :=\ e\mathord{:}\quad \dfrac{\mathcal{F}(x) = \mathcal{E}(e) \qquad \forall y \neq x : \mathcal{F}(y) = \mathcal{E}(y)}{\{\mathcal{E}\}\, x\ :=\ e\, \{\mathcal{F}\}}$

$Sequence\mathord{:}\quad \dfrac{\{\mathcal{E}\}\, S_1\, \{\mathcal{G}\} \qquad \{\mathcal{G}\}\, S_2\, \{\mathcal{F}\}}{\{\mathcal{E}\}\, S_1; S_2\, \{\mathcal{F}\}}$

Conditional: For a statement S, we use $Assign(S)$ to represent a set of variables which over-approximates those variables assigned to in S. The following two cases are used to infer $\{\mathcal{E}\}\, S\, \{\mathcal{F}\}$ for a conditional:

Case A: $\dfrac{\mathcal{E}(c) = \text{false} \quad \{\mathcal{E}\}\, S_1\, \{\mathcal{F}\} \quad \{\mathcal{E}\}\, S_2\, \{\mathcal{F}\}}{\{\mathcal{E}\}\ \text{if } c \text{ then } S_1 \text{ else } S_2 \text{ fi } \{\mathcal{F}\}}$

Case B: $\dfrac{\begin{array}{c}\mathcal{E}(c) = \text{true} \quad \{\mathcal{E}\}\, S_1\, \{\mathcal{F}\} \quad \{\mathcal{E}\}\, S_2\, \{\mathcal{F}\} \\ \forall x \in Assign(S_1) \cup Assign(S_2) : \mathcal{F}(x) = \text{true}\end{array}}{\{\mathcal{E}\}\ \text{if } c \text{ then } S_1 \text{ else } S_2 \text{ fi } \{\mathcal{F}\}}$

While Loop: $\dfrac{\mathcal{E} \sqsubseteq \mathcal{I} \quad \{\mathcal{I}\}\ \text{if } c \text{ then } S \text{ else skip fi } \{\mathcal{I}\} \quad \mathcal{I} \sqsubseteq \mathcal{F}}{\{\mathcal{E}\}\ \text{while } c \text{ do } S \text{ od } \{\mathcal{F}\}}$

Theorem 5 *(Soundness). Consider a structured program P with a valid proof such that $\{\mathcal{E}\}\, P\, \{\mathcal{F}\}$ holds. For all initial states (s,t) such that $(s,t) \models E$: if there are terminating computations from s and t such that $s \xrightarrow{P} s'$ and $t \xrightarrow{P} t'$ hold, then $(s',t') \models F$.*

The proof system can be turned into an algorithm for calculating taints. The proof rule for each statement other than the while can be read as a monotone forward environment transformer. For while loops, the proof rule requires the construction of an inductive environment, I. This can be done through a straight-forward least fixpoint calculation for I based on the transformer for the body of the loop. Let I^k denote the value at the k'th stage. Each non-final fixpoint step from I^n to I^{n+1} must change the taint status of least one variable from untainted in I^n to tainted in I^{n+1}, while leaving all tainted variables in I^n tainted in I^{n+1}. Thus, the fixpoint is reached in a number of stages that is bounded by the number of variables. In a nested loop structure, the fixpoint for the inner loop must be evaluated multiple times, but this calculation does not have to be done from scratch; it can be started from the incoming environment E, which increases monotonically. The entire process is thus in polynomial time.

5   A Secure Dead Store Elimination Transformation

From the results of Sect. 3, checking the security of a program transformation after the fact is computationally difficult. A translation validation approach to security is, therefore, unlikely to be practical. The alternative is to build security into the program transformation. In this section, we describe a dead store elimination procedure built around taint analysis, and prove that it is secure.

1. Compute the control flow graph G for the source program S
2. Set each internal variable at the initial location as Untainted, each L-input as Untainted, and each H-input as Tainted
3. Do a taint analysis on G
4. Do a liveness analysis on G and obtain the set of dead assignments, DEAD
5. **while** DEAD *is not empty* **do**

   Remove an assignment, A, from DEAD, suppose it is "$x := e$"
   Let CURRENT be the set of all assignments to x in G except A
   if A *is post-dominated by* CURRENT **then** [Case 1]

   | Replace A with skip
   | Update the taint analysis for G

   else if x *is Untainted at the location immediately before A*
   and x is Untainted at the final location of G **then** [Case 2]

   | Replace A with skip

   else if x *is Untainted at the location immediately before A*
   and there is no path from A to CURRENT
   and A post-dominates the entry node **then** [Case 3]

   | Replace A with skip

   else

   | (* Do nothing *)

   end

   end
6. Output the result as program T

Fig. 2. Secure dead store elimination algorithm

The algorithm is shown in Fig. 2. It obtains the set of dead assignments and processes them using taint information to determine which ones are secure to remove. For the algorithm, we suppose that the control-flow graph is in a simplified form where each edge either has a guarded command with a skip action, or a trivial guard with an assignment. I.e., either $g \to$ skip or $true \to x := e$. The taint proof system is given for structured programs, so we suppose that the input program is structured, and the CFG obtained from it corresponds to that for a structured program. The "removal" of dead stores is done by replacing the store with a skip, so the CFG structure is unchanged. (The restriction to structured programs is for simplicity and may be relaxed, as discussed in Sect. 6.)

Removal of dead stores can cause previously live stores to become dead, so the algorithm should be repeated until no dead store can be removed. In Case 1 of the algorithm, it is possible for the taint proof to change as well, so the algorithm repeats the taint analysis. For cases 2 and 3, we establish and use the fact that removal does not alter the taint proof.

As the algorithm removes a subset of the known dead stores, the transformation is correct. In the following, we prove that it is also secure. We separately discuss each of the (independent) cases in the algorithm. For each case, we give an illustrative example followed by a proof that the store removal is secure.

5.1   Case 1: Post-domination

The example in Fig. 3 illustrates this case. In the program on the left, two dead assignments to x are redundant from the viewpoint of correctness. Every path to the exit from the first assignment, $x = 0$, passes through the second assignment to x. This is a simple example of the situation to which Case 1 applies. The algorithm will remove the first dead assignment, resulting in the program to the right. This is secure as the remaining assignment blocks the password from being leaked outside the function. The correctness of this approach in general is proved in the following lemmas.

```
void foo()                           void foo()
{                                    {
  int x;                               int x;

  x = read_password();                 x = read_password();
  use(x);                              use(x);
  x = 0;   // Dead Store               x = 5;   // Dead Store
  x = 5;   // Dead Store               return;
  return;                            }
}
```

Fig. 3. C programs illustrating Case 1 of the algorithm

Lemma 1 *(Trace Correspondence). Suppose that T is obtained from S by eliminating a dead store, $x := e$. For any starting state $s = (H = a, L = c)$, there is a trace in T from s if, and only if, there is a trace in S from s. The corresponding traces have identical control flow and, at corresponding points, have identical values for all variables other than x, and identical values for x if the last assignment to x is not removed.*

Proof: (Sketch) This follows from the correctness of dead store elimination, which can be established by showing that the following relation is a bisimulation. To set up the relation, it is easier to suppose that dead store $x := e$ is removed by replacing it with $x := \bot$, where $\bot$ is an "undefined" value, rather than by replacement with skip. The $\bot$ value serves to record that the value of x is not important. Note that the CFG is unaltered in the transformation. The relation connects states (m, s) of the source and (n, t) of the target if (1) $m = n$ (i.e., same CFG nodes); (2) $s(y) = t(y)$ for all y other than x; and (3) $s(x) = t(x)$ if $t(x) \neq \bot$. This is a bisimulation (cf. [11], where a slightly weaker relation is shown to be a bisimulation). From this the claim of the corresponding traces having identical control-flow follows immediately, and the data relations follow from conditions (2) and (3) of the relation. **EndProof.**

Lemma 2. *If α is a dead assignment to variable x in program S that is post-dominated by other assignments to x, it is secure to remove it from S.*

Proof: Let T be the program obtained from S by removing α. We show that any leaky triple for the transformed program T is already present in the source program S. Let (a, b, c) be a leaky triple for T. Let τ_a (resp. σ_a) be the trace in T (resp. S) from the initial state $(H = a, L = c)$. Similarly, let τ_b (resp. σ_b) be the trace in T (resp. S) from $(H = b, L = c)$. By trace correspondence (Lemma 1), σ_a and σ_b must also reach the exit point and are therefore terminating.

By the hypothesis, the last assignment to x before the exit point in σ_a and σ_b is not removed. Hence, by Lemma 1, τ_a and σ_a agree on the value of all variables at the exit point, including on the value of x. Similarly, τ_b and σ_b agree on all variables at the exit point. As (a, b, c) is a leaky triple for T, the L-values are different at the final states of τ_a and τ_b. It follows that the L-values are different at the final states for σ_a and σ_b, as well, so (a, b, c) is also a leaky triple for S. **EndProof.**

5.2 Case 2: Stable Untainted Assignment

An example of this case is given by the programs in Fig. 4. Assume user id to be public and password to be private, hence $read\_password()$ returns a H-input value while $read\_user\_id()$ returns a L-input value. There are two dead

```
int foo()                      int foo()
{                              {
  int x, y;                      int x, y;

  x = 0;  // Dead Store
  y = read_user_id();            y = read_user_id();
  if(is_valid(y)){               if(is_valid(y)){
    x = read_password();           x = read_password();
    log_in(x, y);                  log_in(x, y);
    x = 1; // Dead Store           x = 1; // Dead Store
  }else{                         }else{
    printf("Invalid ID");          printf("Invalid ID");
  }                              }
  return y;                      return y;
}                              }
```

Fig. 4. C programs illustrating Case 2 of the algorithm

assignments to x in the program on the left, and the algorithm will remove the first one, as x is untainted before that assignment and untainted at the final location as well. This is secure as in the program on the right x remains untainted at the final location, and no private information about the password will be leaked via x. The general correctness proof is given below.

Lemma 3. *Suppose that there is a taint proof for program S where (1) x is untainted at the final location and (2) x is untainted at the location immediately before a dead store, then it is secure to eliminate the dead store.*

Proof: The same proof outline is valid for the program T obtained by replacing the dead store "$x := e$ with "skip". Let $\{\mathcal{E}\}\, x := e\, \{\mathcal{F}\}$ be the annotation for the dead store in the proof outline. By the inference rule of assignment, we know that $\mathcal{F}(x) = \mathcal{E}(e)$ and that, for all other variables y, $\mathcal{F}(y) = \mathcal{E}(y)$.

Now we show that $\mathcal{E} \sqsubseteq \mathcal{F}$ is true. Consider any variable z. If z differs from x, then $\mathcal{E}(z) \Rightarrow \mathcal{F}(z)$, as $\mathcal{E}(z) = \mathcal{F}(z)$. If z is x, then by hypothesis (2), as x is untainted in $\mathcal{E}$, $\mathcal{E}(z) \Rightarrow \mathcal{F}(z)$ is trivially true, as $\mathcal{E}(z) = \mathcal{E}(x)$ is false.

The annotation $\{\mathcal{E}\}\, \text{skip}\, \{\mathcal{E}\}$ is valid by definition, therefore $\{\mathcal{E}\}\, \text{skip}\, \{\mathcal{F}\}$ is also valid by $\mathcal{E} \sqsubseteq \mathcal{F}$ and Proposition 2. Hence, the replacement of an assignment by skip does not disturb the proof. The only other aspect of the proof that can depend on the eliminated assignment is the proof rule for a conditional (Case B). However, this remains valid as well, as it is acceptable for the set of variables that are forced to be tainted to be an over-approximation of the set of assigned variables.

By hypothesis (1), x is untainted at the final location in S. As the proof remains unchanged in T, x is untainted at the final location in T. By the soundness of taint analysis, there is no leak in T from variable x. Hence, any leak in T must come from variable y different from x. By trace correspondence (Lemma 1), those values are preserved in the corresponding traces; therefore, so is any leak. **EndProof.**

5.3   Case 3: Final Assignment

The example in Fig. 5 illustrates this case. Assume the credit card number to be private, so that `credit_card_no()` returns an H-input value. In the program on the left, there are two dead assignments to x. The first one is post-dominated by the second one, while the second one is always the final assignment to x in every terminating computation, and x is untainted before it. By Case 1, the algorithm would remove the first one and keep the second one. Such a transformation is secure, as the source program and result program leaks same private information. But Case 3 of the algorithm would do a better job: it will remove the second dead assignment instead, resulting in the program on the right. We show that the result program is at least as secure as the source program (in this very example, it is actually more secure than the source program), as x becomes untainted at the final location and no private information can be leaked outside the function via x. The following lemma proves the correctness of this approach.

```
void foo()                          void foo()
{                                   {
  int x, y;                           int x, y;

  y = credit_card_no();               y = credit_card_no();
  x = y;                              x = y;
  use(x);                             use(x);
  x = 0; // Dead Store                x = 0; // Dead Store
  x = last_4_digits(y); // Dead Store y = 0; // Dead Store
  y = 0; // Dead Store                return;
  return;                           }
}
```

Fig. 5. C programs illustrating Case 3 of the algorithm

Lemma 4. *Suppose that there is a proof outline in the system above for program S where (1) x is untainted at the location immediately before a dead store, (2) no other assignment to x is reachable from the dead store, and (3) the store post-dominates the entry node, then it is secure to eliminate the dead store.*

Proof: Similar to Lemma 3, we can prove that the proof outline remains correct for the program T obtained by replacing the dead store "$x := e$" with skip. By hypothesis (1), x is still untainted at the same location in T.

By hypothesis (3), the dead store "$x := e$" is a top-level statement, i.e. it cannot be inside a conditional or while loop, thus the dead store (resp. the corresponding skip) occurs only once in every terminating computation of S (resp. T). Let $t_a, \ldots, t'_a, \ldots, t''_a$ be the terminating trace in T from the initial state ($H = a, L = c$), and $t_b, \ldots, t'_b, \ldots, t''_b$ be the terminating trace in T from the initial state ($H = b, L = c$) where t'_a and t'_b are at the location immediately before the eliminated assignment. By the soundness of taint analysis, x must have identical values in t'_a and t'_b.

By hypothesis (2), the value of x is not modified in the trace between t'_a and t''_a (or between t'_b and t''_b). Thus, the values of x in t''_a and t''_b are identical, and there is no leak in T from x. Hence, any leak in T must come from a variable y different from x. By trace correspondence (Lemma 1), those values are preserved in the corresponding traces; therefore, so is any leak. **EndProof.**

Theorem 6. *The algorithm for dead store elimination is secure.*

Proof: The claim follows immediately from the secure transformation properties shown in Lemmas 2, 3 and 4. **EndProof.**

Although the dead store elimination algorithm is secure, it is sub-optimal in that it may retain more dead stores than necessary. Consider the program "x = read_password(); use(x); x = read_password(); return;". The second store to x is dead and could be securely removed, but it will be retained by our heuristic procedure.

The case at the end of Sect. 2, in which the transformed program reveals the entire credit card number, cannot happen with dead store elimination. More generally, we conjecture that this algorithm preserves the amount of leaked information. Although there is not a single accepted definition of quantitative leakage, it appears natural to suppose that if two programs have identical computations with identical leaked values (if any) then the amounts should be the same. This is the case in our procedure. By Lemma 1, all variables other than x have identical values at the final location in the corresponding traces of S and T. From the proofs of Theorem 6, we know that at the final location of T, variable x has either the same value as in S (Case 1) or an untainted value (Cases 2 and 3) that leaks no information, thus T cannot leak more information than S.

6   Discussion

In this section, we discuss variations on the program and security model and consider the question of the security of other common compiler transformations.

6.1   Variations and Extensions of the Program Model

Unstructured While Programs. If the while program model is extended with goto statements, programs are no longer block-structured and the control-flow graph may be arbitrary. The secure algorithm works with CFGs and is therefore unchanged. An algorithm for taint analysis of arbitrary CFGs appears in [5,6]. This propagates taint from tainted conditionals to blocks that are solely under the influence of that conditional; such blocks can be determined using a graph dominator-based analysis. The full version of this paper contains a taint proof system for CFGs that is based on these ideas. It retains the key properties of the simpler system given here; hence, the algorithms and their correctness proofs apply unchanged to arbitrary CFGs.

Procedural Programs. An orthogonal direction is to enhance the programming model with procedures. This requires an extension of the taint proof system to procedures, but that is relatively straightforward: the effect of a procedure is summarized on a generic taint environment for the formal parameters and the summary is applied at each call site. A taint analysis algorithm which provides such a proof must perform a whole-program analysis.

A deeper issue, however, is that a procedure call extends the length of time that a tainted value from the calling procedure remains in memory. Hence, it may be desirable to ensure that all local variables are untainted before a long-running procedure invocation. This can be modeled by representing the location before a procedure invocation as a potential leak location, in addition to the exit point. We believe that the analysis and algorithms developed here can be adapted to handle multiple leak locations; this is part of ongoing work.

6.2   The Security of Other Compiler Transformations

Dead store elimination is known to be leaky. In the following, we show that, for several common compiler transformations, security follows from correctness.

The correctness of a transformation from program S to program T is shown using a refinement relation, R. For states u, v of a program P, define $u =_L v$ (u and v are "low-equivalent") to mean that u and v agree on the values of all Low-variables in program P. We say that R is a *strict refinement* if R is a refinement relation from T to S and, in addition:

(a) A final state of T is related by R only to a final state of S
(b) If $R(t_0, s_0)$ and $R(t_1, s_1)$ hold, then $t_0 =_L t_1$ (relative to T) if, and only if, $s_0 =_L s_1$ (relative to S). This condition needs to hold only when t_0 and t_1 are both initial states or are both final states of T.

Theorem 7. *Consider a transformation from program S to program T which does not change the set of high variables and is correct through a strict refinement relation R. Such a transformation is secure.*

Proof: Consider a leaky triple (a, b, c) for T. Let τ_a be the computation of T from initial state $(H = a, L_T = c)$, similarly let τ_b be the computation of T from initial state $(H = b, L_T = c)$. Let t_a, t_b be the final states of τ_a, τ_b, respectively. As the transformation is correct, one needs to consider only the case of a leak through the low variables at the final state. By assumption, there is a leak in T, so that $t_a =_L t_b$ is false. We show that there is a corresponding leak in S.

Let σ_a be the computation of S which corresponds to τ_a through R, such a computation exists as R is a refinement relation. Similarly let σ_b correspond to τ_b through R. By condition (a) of strictness, the state of σ_a (σ_b) that is related to the final state of τ_a (τ_b) must be final for S, hence, σ_a and σ_b are terminating computations. Apply condition (b) to the initial states of the corresponding computations τ_a, σ_a and τ_b, σ_b. As the initial τ-states are low-equivalent, condition (b) implies that the initial σ-states are low-equivalent. Applying condition (b) to the final states of the corresponding computations, and using the assumption that $t_a =_L t_b$ is false, the final σ-states are *not* low-equivalent. Hence, (a, b, c) is also a leaky triple for S. **EndProof.**

Informally, a functional definition of the refinement relation ensures condition (b) of strictness. Precisely, we say that a refinement relation R is functional if:

(a) Every low state variable x of S has an associated *1-1* function $f_x(Y_x)$, where $Y_x = (y_1, \ldots, y_k)$ is a vector of low state variables of T. We say that each y_i in Y_x *influences* x.
(b) Every low state variable z of T influences some low-state variable of S
(c) For every pair of states (t, s) related by R, $s(x)$ equals $f_x(t(y_1), \ldots, t(y_k))$

Lemma 5. *A functional refinement relation satisfies condition (b) of strictness.*

Proof: Suppose that $R(t_0, s_0)$ and $R(t_1, s_1)$ hold. By conditions (a) and (c) of the assumption, for every low state variable x of S, $s_0(x)$ equals $f_x(t_0(Y_x))$ and $s_1(x)$ equals $f_x(t_1(Y_x))$.

First, suppose that $t_0 =_L t_1$. As t_0 and t_1 agree on the values of all low variables in Y_x, $s_0(x)$ and $s_1(x)$ are equal. This holds for all x, so that $s_0 =_L s_1$. Next, suppose that $t_0 =_L t_1$ does not hold. Hence, $t_0(y) \neq t_1(y)$ for some low state variable y of T. By condition (b) of the assumption, y influences some low-state variable of S, say x. I.e., y is a component of the vector Y_x in the function $f_x(Y_x)$. Hence, $t_0(Y_x)$ and $t_1(Y_x)$ are unequal vectors. Since f_x is 1-1, it follows that $s_0(x) = f_x(t_0(Y_x))$ and $s_1(x) = f_x(t_1(Y_x))$ differ, so that $s_0 =_L s_1$ does not hold. **EndProof.**

The refinement relations for a number of transformations are defined functionally. For instance, constant propagation and control-flow simplifications do not alter the set of variables, and the refinement relation equates the values of each variable x in corresponding states of S and T. Hence, the relation meets the conditions of Lemma 5 and, therefore, condition (b) of strictness. These relations also satisfy condition (a), as the transformations do not change the termination behavior of the source program.

Dead-store removal *does not* does not have a functionally defined refinement relation. In the example from Fig. 1, the final value of x in the source (which is 0) cannot be expressed as a function of the final value of x in the result (which is arbitrary).

6.3 Insecurity of SSA

Another important transformation which *does not* meet the functionality assumption is the single static assignment (SSA) transformation. For instance, consider this transformation applied to the example of Fig. 1. In the program on the right of Fig. 6, the assignments to x have been replaced with single assignments to x1 and to x2. The final value of x in the source is the final value of x2; however, x1 does not influence x at all, violating condition (b) of functionality.

```
void foo()                      void foo()
{                               {
  int x;                          int x1,x2;

  x = read_password();            x1 = read_password();
  use(x);                         use(x1);
  x = 0; // clear password        x2 = 0;
  return;                         return;
}                               }
```

Fig. 6. C programs illustrating the insecurity of SSA transformation

As SSA transformation is crucial to the operation of modern compilers, the potential for a leak is particularly troubling. One possible resolution is to pass on taint information to the register allocation stage, forcing the allocator to add instructions to clear the memory reserved for x1, unless the memory has been re-allocated subsequently to an untainted variable. Investigation of such remedies is a topic for future work.

7   Related Work and Conclusions

The fact that correctness preservation is not the same as security preservation has long been known. Formally, the issue is that refinement in the standard sense, as applied for correctness, does not preserve security properties. Specifically, a low-level machine model may break security guarantees that are proved on a higher-level language model. Full abstraction has been proposed as a mechanism for preserving security guarantees across machine models in [1]. A transformation τ is fully abstract if programs P and Q are indistinguishable (to an attacker context) at level L_1 if and only if the transformed programs $P' = \tau(P)$ and $Q' = \tau(Q)$ are indistinguishable at level L_2. Recent work on this topic [2,8,14] considers various mechanisms for ensuring full abstraction. This work relates to the preservation of security across machine levels, while our work relates to the preservation of security within a single level. For a single level, one can show full abstraction by proving that P and $\tau(P)$ are indistinguishable. That is essentially the method followed in this paper.

The earliest explicit reference to the insecurity of dead store elimination that we are aware of is [10], but this issue has possibly been known for a longer period of time. Nevertheless, we are not aware of other constructions of a secure dead store elimination transformation. The complexity results in this paper on the difficulty of translation validation for security, in particular for the apparently simple case of dead store elimination, are also new to the best of our knowledge.

Theorem 7 in Sect. 6, which shows that strong refinement relations do pre-serve security is related to Theorem 10.5 in [2] which has a similar conclusion in a different formal setting. The new aspect in this paper is the application of Theorem 7 to reduce the security of several common compiler transformations to their correctness.

In a recent paper [7], the authors carry out a detailed study of possible ways in which compiler transformations can create information leaks. The authors point out that the correctness-security gap (their term) can be understood in terms of observables: establishing security requires more information about inter-nal state to be observable than that needed to establish correctness. (This is essentially the full abstraction property discussed above.) They describe several potential approaches to detecting security violations. The inherent difficulty of security checking has implications for translation validation and testing, two of the approaches considered in [7]. Our secure dead code elimination algorithm removes an important source of insecurity, while Theorem 7 reduces the secu-rity of several other transformations to establishing their correctness with strong refinement relations.

There is a considerable literature on type systems, static analyses and other methods for establishing (or testing) the security of a *single* program, which we will not attempt to survey here. In contrast, this paper treats the *relative security* question: is the program resulting from a transformation at least as secure as the original? This has been less studied, and it has proved to be an unexpectedly challenging question. Several new directions arise from these results. Securing the SSA transformation is an important concern, as is understanding the security of other common compiler transformations. A witnessing structure for security, analogous to the one for correctness in [11], might be a practical way to formally prove the security of compiler implementations. A different direction is to consider transformations that enhance security, rather than just preserve it; one such transformation is described in [9]. The ultimate goal is a compilation process that is both correct and secure.

Acknowledgements. We would like to thank Lenore Zuck, V.N. Venkatakrishnan and Sanjiva Prasad for helpful discussions and comments on this research. This work was supported, in part, by DARPA under agreement number FA8750-12-C-0166. The U.S. Government is authorized to reproduce and distribute reprints for Governmental purposes notwithstanding any copyright notation thereon. The views and conclusions contained herein are those of the authors and should not be interpreted as necessarily representing the official policies or endorsements, either expressed or implied, of DARPA or the U.S. Government.

References

1. Abadi, M.: Protection in programming-language translations. In: Larsen, K.G., Skyum, S., Winskel, G. (eds.) ICALP 1998. LNCS, vol. 1443, pp. 868–883. Springer, Heidelberg (1998)
2. de Amorim, A.A., Collins, N., DeHon, A., Demange, D., Hritcu, C., Pichardie, D., Pierce, B.C., Pollack, R., Tolmach, A.: A verified information-flow architecture. In: Jagannathan, S., Sewell, P. (eds.) The 41st Annual ACM SIGPLAN-SIGACT Symposium on Principles of Programming Languages, POPL 2014, San Diego, CA, USA, 20–21 January 2014, pp. 165–178. ACM (2014). http://doi.acm.org/10.1145/2535838.2535839
3. Bell, D., LaPadula, L.: Secure computer systems: Mathematical foundations, vol. 1-III. Technical report ESD-TR-73-278, The MITRE Corporation (1973)
4. Ceara, D., Mounier, L., Potet, M.: Taint dependency sequences: a characterization of insecure execution paths based on input-sensitive cause sequences. In: Third International Conference on Software Testing, Verification and Validation, ICST 2010, Paris, France, 7–9 April 2010. Workshops Proceedings, pp. 371–380 (2010). http://dx.doi.org/10.1109/ICSTW.2010.28
5. Denning, D.E.: Secure information flow in computer systems. Ph.D. thesis, Purdue University, May 1975
6. Denning, D.E., Denning, P.J.: Certification of programs for secure information flow. Commun. ACM **20**(7), 504–513 (1977). http://doi.acm.org/10.1145/359636.359712
7. D'Silva, V., Payer, M., Song, D.X.: The correctness-security gap in compiler optimization. In: 2015 IEEE Symposium on Security and Privacy Workshops, SPW 2015, San Jose, CA, USA, 21–22 May 2015, pp. 73–87. IEEE Computer Society (2015). http://dx.doi.org/10.1109/SPW.2015.33

8. Fournet, C., Swamy, N., Chen, J., Dagand, P., Strub, P., Livshits, B.: Fully abstract compilation to JavaScript. In: Giacobazzi, R., Cousot, R. (eds.) The 40th Annual ACM SIGPLAN-SIGACT Symposium on Principles of Programming Languages, POPL 2013, Rome, Italy, 23–25 January 2013, pp. 371–384. ACM (2013). http://doi.acm.org/10.1145/2429069.2429114

9. Gondi, K., Bisht, P., Venkatachari, P., Sistla, A.P., Venkatakrishnan, V.N.: SWIPE: eager erasure of sensitive data in large scale systems software. In: Bertino, E., Sandhu, R.S. (eds.) Second ACM Conference on Data and Application Security and Privacy, CODASPY 2012, San Antonio, TX, USA, 7–9 February 2012, pp. 295–306. ACM (2012). http://doi.acm.org/10.1145/2133601.2133638

10. Howard, M.: When scrubbing secrets in memory doesn't work (2002). http://archive.cert.uni-stuttgart.de/bugtraq/2002/11/msg00046.html. Also https://cwe.mitre.org/data/definitions/14.html

11. Namjoshi, K.S., Zuck, L.D.: Witnessing program transformations. In: Logozzo, F., Fähndrich, M. (eds.) Static Analysis. LNCS, vol. 7935, pp. 304–323. Springer, Heidelberg (2013)

12. Necula, G.: Translation validation of an optimizing compiler. In: Proceedings of the ACM SIGPLAN Conference on Principles of Programming Languages Design and Implementation (PLDI 2000), pp. 83–95 (2000)

13. Papadimitriou, C.H.: Computational Complexity. Addison-Wesley, Reading (1994)

14. Patrignani, M., Agten, P., Strackx, R., Jacobs, B., Clarke, D., Piessens, F.: Secure compilation to protected module architectures. ACM Trans. Program. Lang. Syst. 37(2), 6 (2015). http://doi.acm.org/10.1145/2699503

15. Pnueli, A., Shtrichman, O., Siegel, M.: The code validation tool (CVT)- automatic verification of a compilation process. Softw. Tools Technol. Transf. 2(2), 192–201 (1998)

16. Smith, G.: Recent developments in quantitative information flow (invited tutorial). In: 30th Annual ACM/IEEE Symposium on Logic in Computer Science, LICS 2015, Kyoto, Japan, 6–10 July 2015, pp. 23–31. IEEE (2015). http://dx.doi.org/10.1109/LICS.2015.13

17. Volpano, D.M., Irvine, C.E., Smith, G.: A sound type system for secure flow analysis. J. Comput. Secur. 4(2/3), 167–188 (1996). http://dx.doi.org/10.3233/JCS-1996-42-304

18. Zuck, L.D., Pnueli, A., Goldberg, B.: VOC: a methodology for the translation validation of optimizing compilers. J. UCS 9(3), 223–247 (2003)

Exploiting Sparsity
in Difference-Bound Matrices

Graeme Gange[1]([✉]), Jorge A. Navas[2], Peter Schachte[1],
Harald Søndergaard[1], and Peter J. Stuckey[1]

[1] Department of Computing and Information Systems,
The University of Melbourne, Melbourne, VIC 3010, Australia
gkgange@unimelb.edu.au
[2] NASA Ames Research Center, Moffett Field, CA 94035, USA

Abstract. Relational numeric abstract domains are very important in program analysis. Common domains, such as Zones and Octagons, are usually conceptualised with weighted digraphs and implemented using difference-bound matrices (DBMs). Unfortunately, though conceptually simple, direct implementations of graph-based domains tend to perform poorly in practice, and are impractical for analyzing large code-bases. We propose new DBM algorithms that exploit sparsity and closed operands. In particular, a new representation which we call split normal form reduces graph density on typical abstract states. We compare the resulting implementation with several existing DBM-based abstract domains, and show that we can substantially reduce the time to perform full DBM analysis, without sacrificing precision.

1 Introduction

Relational numeric abstract domains are an important and large class, ranging from the highly precise polyhedral domain [9] to cheaper but less expressive variants, such as Octagons [18], Zones (or difference-bound matrices, DBMs) [17], and others. They share the advantage over "non-relational" domains that they support the extraction of important runtime relationships between variables. However, for large code bases, even the cheaper relational domains tend to be too expensive to use [10,21], so the usual compromise is to use less expressive (and cheaper) non-relational domains or if possible weakly relational domains tailored to specific applications (e.g., pentagons [16]).

During program analysis there are, however, characteristics of typical program states that we would hope to take advantage of. For example, the relations among variables are often quite sparse, variables tend to settle into disjoint clusters, and many operations in the analysis change only a small subset of the overall set of relations. Moreover, knowledge about typical analysis workflow, which analysis operations are more frequent, which normally succeed which, and so on, can be exploited. Indeed, there have been previous attempts to capitalize on such observations. We discuss related work in Sect. 7.

X. Rival (Ed.): SAS 2016, LNCS 9837, pp. 189–211, 2016.
DOI: 10.1007/978-3-662-53413-7_10

We propose a better *Zones* implementation. With *zones*, program state descriptions take the form of conjunctions of constraints $y - x \leq k$ where x and y are variables and k is some constant. Our implementation is optimized for the commonly occurring case of sparse systems of constraints. We follow a well-established tradition of representing the constraints as weighted directed graphs, and so the analysis operations are reduced to various graph operations.

We assume the reader is familiar with abstract interpretation [6,7] and with graph concepts and algorithms, including the classical shortest-path algorithms. This paper offers the following novel contributions:

- We design new data structures and algorithms for Zones. These are based on refined shortest-path graph algorithms, including a specialised incremental variant of Dijkstra's algorithm, which we call Chromatic Dijkstra (Sect. 3).
- We identify an important source of waste inherent in the standard graph representations of difference constraints (namely, non-relational properties are treated on a par with relational properties, contributing unnecessary density). To fix this we introduce a *split normal form* for weighted digraphs, which preserves many of the properties of transitive closure while avoiding unwanted "densification". We show how to modify the previous algorithms to operate on this form (Sect. 4).
- We propose a graph representation that uses "sparse sets" [2], tailored for efficient implementation across all the abstract operations (Sect. 5).
- We present an experimental evaluation of our implementation of Zones (Sect. 6) and conclude that scalable relational analysis is achievable.

2 Zones, DBMs and Difference Logic

Much of what follows deals with weighted directed graphs. We use $x \xrightarrow{k} y$ to denote a directed edge from x to y with weight k, and $E(x)$ the set of outgoing edges from x in E. $wt_E(x, y)$ denotes the weight of the edge $x \rightarrow y$ in E (or ∞ if absent). This is generalized for a directed path $x_1 \xrightarrow{k_1} \ldots \xrightarrow{k_{n-1}} x_k$ as $wt_E(x_1, \ldots, x_k)$ denoting its path length (i.e., $\sum_{i=0}^{n-1} k_i$). We may write a graph as its set of edges.[1] When we take the union of two sets of edges E_1 and E_2, we take only the minimum-weight edge for each pair of end-points.

In many cases it will be useful to operate on a transformed *view* of a graph. $rev(E)$ denotes the graph obtained by reversing the direction of each edge in E (so $x \xrightarrow{k} y$ becomes $y \xrightarrow{k} x$). $E \setminus \{v\}$ is the graph obtained by removing from E all edges incident to v. Note that these graphs are never explicitly constructed; they merely define different interpretations of an existing graph.

Difference-bound matrices or *Zones* [17] approximate concrete states by predicates of the forms $x \leq k$, $x \geq k$, and $y - x \leq k$, where x and y are variables,

---

[1] For presentation purposes, we assume all program states share a fixed set V of variables. In practice, this is unnecessarily expensive—we instead maintain vertices for only the variables that are in scope, and add or remove vertices as needed.

and k some constant. Constraints $y - x \geq k$ can be translated to the $\leq$ form, and, assuming variables range over the integers[2], so can strict inequality.

The abstract states (systems of constraints) are typically represented as a weighted graph, where $v \in V \cup \{v_0\}$ is associated with a vertex, and a constraint $y - x \leq k$ is encoded as an edge $x \xrightarrow{k} y$. The added vertex v_0 represents the constant 0. Relations are composed by adding lengths along directed paths; transitive closure is obtained by computing all pairs of shortest paths in the graph. In the rest of the paper, the terms *closure* and *closed* will refer to transitive closure. G^* denotes the closure of some graph G.

Example 1. Consider the system of constraints $\{x \in [0, 1], y \in [1, 2], y - z \leq -3\}$. The corresponding constraint graph is shown in Fig. 1(a). Note that interval constraints $x \in [lo, hi]$ can be encoded as edges $v_0 \xrightarrow{hi} x$ and $x \xrightarrow{-lo} v_0$. □

We shall use $E_1 \oplus E_2$ and $E_1 \otimes E_2$ to denote the pointwise maximum and minimum over a pair of graphs. That is:

$$E_1 \oplus E_2 = \{x \xrightarrow{k} y \mid x \xrightarrow{k_1} y \in E_1 \wedge x \xrightarrow{k_2} y \in E_2 \wedge k = \mathbf{max}(k_1, k_2)\}$$

$$E_1 \otimes E_2 = \left\{ x \xrightarrow{k} y \left| \begin{array}{l} (x \xrightarrow{k} y \in E_1 \wedge k \leq wt_{E_2}(x, y)) \vee \\ (x \xrightarrow{k} y \in E_2 \wedge k < wt_{E_1}(x, y)) \end{array} \right. \right\}$$

In typical implementations of difference bound-based domains, the system of relations is encoded as a dense matrix, and closure is obtained by running the Floyd-Warshall algorithm.

The *language* of "difference logic" also appears in an SMT context: SMT(DL) problems query satisfiability over Boolean combinations of difference constraints. The problem of solving SMT(DL) instances is rather different to the problem of static analysis using DBMs, since the former does not compute *joins*—a major issue in the latter. Nevertheless, we take inspiration from SMT(DL) algorithms, in particular Cotton and Maler's approach to dealing with sparse systems of difference constraints [5]. In this approach the graph is augmented with a *potential function* π—a model of the constraint system. When an edge is added, π is revised to find a model of the augmented system. Given a valid potential function, the corresponding concrete state is $\{x \mapsto \pi(x) - \pi(v_0) \mid x \in V\}$. We extend π naturally: $\pi(e)$ denotes the value of expression e under assignment π.

Maintaining the potential function π allows the graph to be reformulated—for any constraint $y - x \leq k$, the *slack* (or *reduced cost* [5]) is given by $slack(y, x) = \pi(x) + k - \pi(y)$. As π is a model, this is non-negative; so shortest paths in the reformulated graph may be computed using Dijkstra's algorithm.

Example 2. Consider again the constraints captured in Fig. 1. Let the potential function $\pi = \{v_0 \mapsto 2, x \mapsto 3, y \mapsto 3, z \mapsto 9\}$. This corresponds to the concrete assignment $\{x \mapsto 1, y \mapsto 1, z \mapsto 7\}$ (as v_0 is adjusted to 0). The slack graph

---

[2] Our approach works for rational numbers as well. The implementation assumes 64-bit integers and does not currently take over-/under-flow into account.

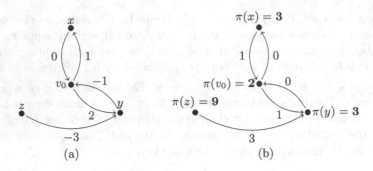

Fig. 1. (a) A graph representing the set of difference constraints $\{x \in [0,1], y \in [1,2], y-z \le -3\}$. (b) The *slack* graph (with all non-negative weights) under potential function $\pi = \{v_0 \mapsto 2, x \mapsto 3, y \mapsto 3, z \mapsto 9\}$.

under π is given in Fig. 1(b). As every constraint is satisfied by π, all weights in the reformulated graph are non-negative.

If we follow the shortest path from z to y in (b), we find the slack between z and y is 3. We can then invert the original transformation to find the corresponding constraint; in this case, we get $y - z \le \pi(y) - \pi(z) + slack(z,y) = -3$, which matches the original corresponding path in (a).   □

3   Zones Implemented with Sparse DBMs

A critical step for precise relational analysis is computing the closure of a system of relations, that is, finding all implied relations and making them explicit. Unfortunately, this also vastly dominates DBM runtimes [16,20,21]. Closure using Floyd-Warshall is $\Theta(|V|^3)$. In a sparse graph we can use Johnson's algorithm [13] to reduce this to $O(|V||E| + |V|^2 \log |V|)$, but this is still not ideal.

Typical manipulations during abstract interpretation are far from random. The operations we perform most frequently are assigning a fresh variable, forgetting a variable, adding a relation between two variables, and taking the disjunction of two states. Each of these exhibits some structure we can exploit to maintain closure more efficiently. On occasion we also need to perform conjunction or widening on abstract states; we discuss these at the end of this section.

In the following, an abstract state φ consists of a pair $\langle \pi, E \rangle$ of a potential function π, and a sparse graph of difference constraints E over vertices $V \cup \{v_0\}$. Potentials are initially 0. We assume the representation of E supports cheap initialization, and constant time insertion, lookup, removal and iteration; we discuss a suitable representation in Sect. 5.

3.1   Join

For $\langle \pi_1, E_1 \rangle \sqcup \langle \pi_2, E_2 \rangle$, both π_1 and π_2 are valid potentials, so we can choose either. We then collect the pointwise maximum $E_1 \oplus E_2$. If E_1 and E_2 are closed then so is $E_1 \oplus E_2$, and the overall result is simply $\langle \pi_1, E_1 \oplus E_2 \rangle$. Assuming we can lookup a specific edge in constant time, this takes worst case $O(\min(|E_1|, |E_2|))$.

3.2 Variable Elimination

To eliminate a variable, we simply remove all edges incident to it. Assuming a specific edge is removed in constant time, this takes $O(|V|)$ worst case time.

3.3 Constraint Addition

To add a single edge $x \xrightarrow{k} y$, we exploit an observation made by Cotton and Maler [5]: Any newly introduced shortest path must include $x \to y$. The potential repair step is unchanged, but our need to maintain closure means the rest of the algorithm differs somewhat. The closure process is given in Fig. 2.

The potential repair step has worst-case complexity $O(|V| \log |V| + |E|)$, and restoring closure is $O(|V|^2)$. This worst-case behaviour can be expected to be rare—in a sparse graph, a single edge addition usually affects few shortest paths.

```
add-edge(⟨π, E⟩, e)
    E' := E ∪ {e}
    π' := restore-potential(π, e, E')
    if π' = inconsistent
        return ⊥
    return ⟨π', E' ∪ close-edge(e, E')⟩


close-edge(x —k→ y, E)
    S := D := ∅
    δ := ∅
    for (s —k'→ x ∈ E)
        if k' + k < wt'_E(s, y)
            δ := δ ∪ {s —k'+k→ y}
            S := S ∪ {s}
    for (y —k'→ d ∈ E)
        if k + k' < wt'_E(y, d)
            δ := δ ∪ {x —k+k'→ d}
            D := D ∪ {d}
    for (s ∈ S, d ∈ D)
        if wt'_E(s, x, y, d) < wt'_E(s, d)
            δ := δ ∪ {s —wt'_E(s,x,y,d)→ d}
    return δ
```

Fig. 2. Algorithm for restoring closure after addition of $x \xrightarrow{k} y$.

3.4 Assignment

The key to efficient assignment is the observation that executing $[\![x := S]\!]$ can only introduce relationships between x and other variables; it cannot tighten any existing relation.[3] From the current state $\varphi = \langle \pi, G \rangle$, we can compute a valid potential for x simply by evaluating S under π.

We then need to compute the shortest distances to and from x (after adding edges corresponding to the assignment). As π is a valid potential function, we could simply run two passes of Dijkstra's algorithm to collect the consequences.

Example 3. Consider again the state shown in Fig. 1(a). Its closure is shown in Fig. 3(a). To evaluate $[\![w := x + z]\!]$ we compute a valid potential for w from potentials for x and z: $\pi(w) = \pi(v_0) + (\pi(x) - \pi(v_0)) + (\pi(z) - \pi(v_0)) = 10$. Replacing x and z with their bounds, we derive these difference constraints: $\{w \geq 4, x - w \leq -4, z - w \leq 0, w - z \leq 1\}$. These edges are shown in Fig. 3(b). Running a Dijkstra's algorithm to/from w, we also find the transitive $w \xrightarrow{-3} y$ edge (corresponding to $y - w \leq -3$). □

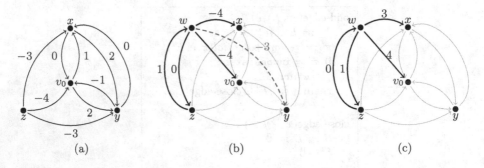

Fig. 3. (a) Closure of the state from Fig. 1(a). (b) Edges after evaluating $[\![w := z + y]\!]$. (c) Edges introduced in Example 4, re-cast in terms of slack.

But as G is closed we can do better. Assume a shortest path from x to z passes through $[x, u_1, \ldots, u_k, z]$. As G is closed there must be some edge (u_1, z) such that $wt_G(u_1, z) \leq wt_G(u_1, \ldots, u_k, z)$; thus, we never need to expand grand-children of x. The only problem is if we expand immediate children of x in the wrong order, and later discover a shorter path to a child we've already expanded.

However, recall that π allows us to reframe G in terms of slack, which is non-negative. If we expand children of x in order of increasing slack, we will never find a shorter path to an already expanded child. Thus we can abandon the priority queue entirely, simply expanding children of x by increasing slack, and collecting the minimum distance to each grandchild. The algorithm for restoring closure

---

[3] This assumes $\pi(S)$ is total. For a partial function like integer division we first close with respect to x, then enforce the remaining invariants.

after an assignment is given in Fig. 4. Its worst-case complexity is $O(|S| \log |S| + |E|)$. The assignment $[\![x := S]\!]$ generates at most $2|S|$ immediate edges, which we must sort. We then perform a single pass over the grandchildren of x. In the common case where $|S|$ is bounded by a small constant, this collapses to $O(|E|)$ (recall that $rev(E)$ is not explicitly computed).

$$
\begin{array}{l}
\textsf{close-assignment-fwd}(\langle \pi, E \rangle, x) \\
\quad reach(v) := 0 \ for \ all \ v \\
\quad reach(x) := 1; \ Dist(x) := 0; \ adj := \emptyset \\
\quad \textbf{for each } x \xrightarrow{k} y \in E(x) \ \text{by increasing } k - \pi(y) \\
\qquad \textbf{if } reach(y) \\
\qquad\quad Dist(y) := \mathbf{min}(Dist(y), k) \\
\qquad \textbf{else} \\
\qquad\quad adj := adj \cup \{y\} \\
\qquad\quad reach(y) := 1; \ Dist(y) := k \\
\qquad\quad \textbf{for } (y \xrightarrow{k'} z \in E(y)) \\
\qquad\qquad \textbf{if } reach(z) \\
\qquad\qquad\quad Dist(z) = \mathbf{min}(Dist(z), Dist(y) + k') \\
\qquad\qquad \textbf{else} \\
\qquad\qquad\quad adj := adj \cup \{z\} \\
\qquad\qquad\quad reach(z) := 1; \ Dist(z) := Dist(y) + k' \\
\quad \textbf{return } \{x \xrightarrow{Dist(y)} y \mid y \in adj, Dist(y) < wt_E(x, y)\} \\
\\
\textsf{close-assignment}(\langle \pi, E \rangle, x) \\
\quad \delta_f := \textsf{close-assignment-fwd}(\langle \pi, E \rangle, x) \\
\quad \delta_r := \textsf{close-assignment-fwd}(\langle -\pi, rev(E) \rangle, x) \\
\quad \textbf{return } \delta_f \cup rev(\delta_r) \\
\\
\textsf{eval-expr}(\pi, \mathsf{S}) \\
\quad \textbf{match } S \textbf{ with} \\
\qquad c: \textbf{return } c + \pi(v_0) \ \% \ \text{constant} \\
\qquad \mathsf{x}: \textbf{return } \pi(x) - \pi(v_0) \ \% \ \text{variable} \\
\qquad \mathsf{f}(\mathsf{s}_1, \ldots, \mathsf{s}_k): \ \% \ \text{arithmetic expression} \\
\qquad\quad \textbf{for } (i \in \{1, \ldots, k\}) \\
\qquad\qquad e_i := \textsf{eval-expr}(\pi, s_i) \\
\qquad\quad \textbf{return } f(e_1, \ldots, e_k) \\
\\
\textsf{assign}(\langle \pi, E \rangle, [\![\mathsf{x} := \mathsf{S}]\!]) \\
\quad \pi' := \pi[x \mapsto \pi(v_0) + \textsf{eval-expr}(\pi, S)] \\
\quad E' := E \cup \textsf{edges-of-assign}(E, [\![\mathsf{x} := \mathsf{S}]\!]) \\
\quad \delta := \textsf{close-assignment}(\langle \pi', E' \rangle, x) \\
\quad \textbf{return } \langle \pi', E' \otimes \delta \rangle
\end{array}
$$

Fig. 4. Updating the abstract state under an assignment

Example 4. Recall the assignment in Example 3. The slack graph, with respect to $\pi = \{v_0 \mapsto 2, x \mapsto 3, y \mapsto 3, z \mapsto 9, w \mapsto 10\}$, is shown in Fig. 3(c). Processing outgoing edges of w in order of increasing slack, we first reach z, marking v_0, x and y as reached, with $Dist(v_0) = -4, Dist(x) = -3$ and $Dist(y) = -3$. We then process x, which is directly reachable at distance $Dist(x) = -4$, but find no other improved distances. After finding no improved distances through v_0, we walk through the vertices that have been touched and collect any improved edges, returning $\{y - w \leq -3\}$ as expected.   □

3.5   Meet

The meet operation $\langle \pi_1, E_1 \rangle \sqcap \langle \pi_2, E_2 \rangle$ is more involved. We first collect each relation from $E_1 \cup E_2$, but we must then compute an updated potential function, and restore closure. The algorithm is outlined in Fig. 5.

$$
\begin{aligned}
&\mathsf{meet}(\langle \pi_1, E_1 \rangle, \langle \pi_2, E_2 \rangle) \\
&\quad E' := E_1 \otimes E_2 \\
&\quad \pi := \mathsf{compute\text{-}potential}(E', \pi_1) \\
&\quad \mathbf{if}\ \pi = \mathsf{inconsistent} \\
&\quad\quad \mathbf{return}\ \bot \\
&\quad \delta := \mathsf{close\text{-}meet}(\pi, E', E_1, E_2) \\
&\quad \mathbf{return}\ \langle \pi, E' \otimes \delta \rangle
\end{aligned}
$$

Fig. 5. Meet on sparse DBMs

The classic approach to computing valid potential functions is the Bellman-Ford [12] algorithm. Many refinements and variants have been described [4], any of which we could apply. We use the basic algorithm, with three refinements:

- π' is initialized from π_1 or π_2.
- Bellman-Ford is run separately on each strongly-connected component.
- We maintain separate queues for the current and next iteration.

Fig. 6 shows the modified algorithm. Note that if $\pi'(x)$ changes but x is still in Q, we do not need to add it to Q'—its successors will already have been updated at the end of the current iteration.

The direct approach to restoring closure of E' is to run Dijkstra's algorithm from each vertex (essentially running Johnson's algorithm). However, we can exploit the fact that E_1 and E_2 are already closed. When we collect the pointwise minimum $E_1 \otimes E_2$, we mark each edge as 1, 2 or both, according to its origin. Observe that if all edges reachable from some vertex v have the same mark, the subgraph from v is already closed.

Critically, consider the behaviour of Dijkstra's algorithm. We expand some vertex v, adding $v \xrightarrow{k} x$ to the queue. Assume the edge $v \xrightarrow{k} x$ originated from

```
compute-potential(E, π)
    π' := π
    for (scc ∈ components(E))
        Q := scc
        for (iter ∈ [1, |scc|])
            Q' := ∅
            while (Q ≠ ∅)
                x := Q.pop()
                for (x --k--> y ∈ E(x))
                    if π'(x) + k - π'(y) < 0
                        π'(y) := π'(x) + k
                        if (y ∈ scc ∧ y ∉ Q ∪ Q')
                            Q' := Q' ∪ {y}
            if Q' = ∅
                return π'
            Q := Q'
        while (Q ≠ ∅)
            x := Q.pop()
            for (x --k--> y ∈ E(x))
                if π'(x) + k - π'(y) < 0
                    return inconsistent
    return π'
```

Fig. 6. Warm-started Bellman-Ford; SCCs assumed to be ordered topologically.

the set E_1. At some point, we remove $v \xrightarrow{k} x$ from the queue. Let $x \xrightarrow{k'} y$ be some child of x. If $x \xrightarrow{k'} y$ *also* originated from E_1, we know that E_1 also contained some edge $v \xrightarrow{c} y$ with $c \le k + k'$ which will already be in the queue; thus there is no point exploring any outgoing E_1-edges from x.

We thus derive a specialized variant of Dijkstra's algorithm. The following assumes we can freely iterate through edges of specific colours—this index can be maintained during construction, or partitioning edges via bucket-sort between construction and closure.[4] This "chromatic" variant is given in Fig. 7. We run Dijkstra's algorithm as usual, except any time we find a minimum-length path to some node y, we mark y with the colour of the edge through which it was reached. Then, when we remove y from the priority queue we only explore edges where none of its colours are already on the vertex. Note that nodes in Q are ordered by slack $(\pi(x) + Dist(x) - \pi(y))$, rather than raw distance $Dist(x)$. The initialization of $Dist$ and $edge\text{-}col$ is performed only once and preserved between calls, rather than performed explicitly for each call.

Example 5. Consider the conjunction of closed states in Fig. 8(a). Running the closure-aware Dijkstra's algorithm from each vertex restores closure. Now taking

---

[4] It is not immediately clear how to extend this efficiently to an n-way meet, as a vertex may be reachable from some arbitrary subset of the operands.

```
chromatic-Dijkstra(⟨π, E⟩, x)
    Dist(v) := ∞ for all v
    δ := ∅
    for each x ─k→ y ∈ E(x)
        Dist(y) := k
        Q.add(y)
        reach-col(y) := edge-col(x, y)
    while (Q ≠ ∅)
        y := Q.remove-min()
        if Dist(y) < wtₑ(x, y))
            δ := δ ∪ {x ─Dist(y)→ y }
        % Iterate through edges of the other colour
        for (c ∈ {1, 2} \ reach-col(y))
            for each y ─k→ z in Eꟲ(y)
                dₓᵧᵤ := Dist(y) + k
                if dₓᵧᵤ = Dist(z)
                    reach-col(z) := reach-col(z) ∪ edge-col(y, z)
                if dₓᵧᵤ < Dist(z)
                    Dist(z) := dₓᵧᵤ
                    Q.update(z)
                    reach-col(z) := edge-col(y, z)
    return δ

close-meet(π, E, E₁, E₂)
    edge-col(x, y) := ∅  for all x, y
    for each i ∈ {1, 2}, x ─k→ y ∈ Eᵢ
        if wtₑ(x, y) = k
            edge-col(x, y) := edge-col(x, y) ∪ {i}
    δ := ∅
    for each vertex x
        δ := δ ∪ chromatic-Dijkstra(⟨π, E⟩, x)
    return δ
```

Fig. 7. Pseudo-code for Dijkstra's algorithm, modified to exploit closed operands.

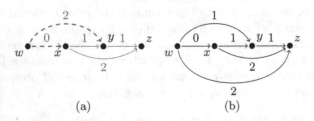

(a)   (b)

Fig. 8. (a) The conjunction of two closed graphs, $E_1 = \{x - w \le 0, y - w \le 2\}$ and $E_2 = \{y - x \le 1, z - y \le 1, z - x \le 2\}$, and (b) the closure $(E_1 \otimes E_2)^*$. (Color figure online)

x as the source, we add $x \xrightarrow{1} y$ and $x \xrightarrow{2} z$ to the priority queue, and mark y and z as reachable via blue (solid) edges. We then pop y from the queue. Variable y is marked as reachable via blue so we need only check purple (dashed) children, of which there are none. We finally pop z, finding the same.

Selecting w as source, we add $w \xrightarrow{0} x$ and $w \xrightarrow{2} y$ to the queue, both marked as reachable via purple (dashed) edges. We then process x. It is reachable via purple, so we must expand its blue children. The edges $x \xrightarrow{1} y$ and $x \xrightarrow{2} z$ respectively give an improved path to y and a path to z, so we update the distances and mark both y and z as reachable instead by blue. This places us in the same state we had before; we finish processing y and z as above. The resulting graph is shown in Fig. 8(b).   □

3.6 Widening

For widening we follow the usual practice of discarding *unstable* edges—any edges that were weakened in two successive iterates E_1 and E_2. (Note that for each edge $x \xrightarrow{k_2} y \in E_2$ there is an edge $x \xrightarrow{k_1} y \in E_1$ with $k_1 \le k_2$.)

To obtain the result $E = E_1 \triangledown E_2$, widening starts from an empty set E. It then considers each edge $x \xrightarrow{k_2} y \in E_2$ in turn and adds $x \xrightarrow{k_1} y$ to E iff $x \xrightarrow{k_1} y \in E_1$ *and* $k_2 \le k_1$. In the pseudo-code of Fig. 9, this is performed by remove-unstable-edges(E_1, E_2), which also returns a set is-stable containing those vertices which have lost no outgoing edges.

Figure 9 presents the complete pseudo-code for widening. The algorithm is, however, more complex than just removal of edges. The reason is that, unlike the join operation, the removal of edges may fail to preserve closure. Hence closure must be restored before subsequent operations, but at the same time, subsequent widenings must use the *un-closed* result. For this reason, widen produces both. The function close-after-widen is responsible for the restoration of closure. It uses a short-cut similar to the chromatic Dijkstra algorithm. Recall that $E(x)$ denotes the set $E' \subseteq E$ of edges that emanate from x. Consider again running Dijkstra's algorithm from v on $A \triangledown B$. At some point, we reach a vertex w with $A^*(w) = (A \triangledown B)(w)$—that is, all outgoing edges from w are stable in A^*. But since $A \sqsubseteq (A \triangledown B)$, we have $(A \triangledown B)(w) = A^*(w) \sqsubseteq (A \triangledown B)^*(w)$. Thus we do not need to further expand any children reached via w, as any such path is already in the queue. As such, we augment the left operand of the widening (the previous iterate) with a set S_E, threaded through successive widening steps, to indicate which vertices remain stable under closure. Details are provided in Fig. 9.

Dijkstra-restore-unstable($\langle \pi, E \rangle, x, is\text{-}stable$)
    $\delta := \emptyset, Dist(v) := \infty$ *for all* v
    for each $x \xrightarrow{k} y \in E(x)$
        $Dist(y) := k$
        $Q.\mathsf{add}(y)$
        $closed(y) := \mathtt{false}$
    while $Q \neq \emptyset$
        $y := Q.\mathsf{remove\text{-}min}()$
        if $Dist(y) < wt_E(x, y)$
            $\delta := \delta \cup \{x \xrightarrow{Dist(y)} y\}$
        if not $closed(y)$
            % Iterate through unstable successors
            for each $y \xrightarrow{k} z$ in $E(y)$
                $d_{xyz} := Dist(y) + k$
                if $d_{xyz} = Dist(z)$
                    $closed(z) := closed(z) \vee is\text{-}stable(y)$
                if $d_{xyz} < Dist(z)$
                    $Dist(z) := d_{xyz}$
                    $Q.\mathsf{update}(z)$
                    $closed(z) := is\text{-}stable(y)$
    return δ

close-after-widen($\langle \pi, E \rangle, is\text{-}stable$)
    $\delta := \emptyset, S_{E'} := is\text{-}stable$
    for each *vertex* x
        if not $is\text{-}stable(x)$
            $\delta_x := $ Dijkstra-restore-unstable($\langle \pi, E \rangle, x, is\text{-}stable$)
            if $delta_x = \emptyset$ **then** $S_{E'} := S_{E'} \cup \{x\}$
            $\delta := \delta \cup \delta_x$
    return $\delta, S_{E'}$

widen($\langle \pi_1, E_1 \rangle_{|S_E}, \langle \pi_2, E_2 \rangle$)
    $\langle E', is\text{-}stable \rangle := $ remove-unstable-edges(E_1, E_2)
    $un\text{-}closed := \langle \pi_2, E' \rangle$
    $\delta, S_{E'} := $ close-after-widen($un\text{-}closed, S_E \cap is\text{-}stable$)
    $closed := \langle \pi_2, E' \otimes \delta \rangle$
    return $\langle un\text{-}closed_{|S_{E'}}, closed \rangle$

Fig. 9. Widening on sparse DBMs

4   Zones as Sparse DBMs in Split Normal Form

So far we made the key assumption that abstract states are sparse. During the
later stages of analysis, this is typically the case. However, abstract states in early
iterations are often very dense; Singh, Püschel and Vechev [20] observed (in the
context of Octagon analysis) that the first 50 % of iterations were extremely

dense, with sparsity only appearing after widening. However, at a closer look this density turns out to be a mirage.

Recall the discussion in Sect. 2 on the handling of variable bounds: an artificial vertex v_0 is introduced, and bounds on x are encoded as relations between x and v_0. Unfortunately, this interacts badly with closure - if variables are given initial bounds, our abstract state becomes complete.

$$
\begin{array}{l}
0 : x_1, \ldots, x_k := 1, \ldots, k \\
1 : \mathbf{if}(*) \\
2 : \quad x_1 := x_1 + 1 \\
3 : \quad x_2 := x_2 + 1 \\
4 :
\end{array}
$$

Fig. 10. Small code fragment

This is regrettable, as it erodes the sparsity we want to exploit. It is only after widening that unstable variable bounds are discarded and sparsity arises, revealing the underlying structure of relations. Also, all these invariants are trivial—we only really care about relations *not* already implied by variable bounds.

Example 6. Consider the program fragment in Fig. 10. Variables $x_1, \ldots, x_k$ are initialised to constants at point 0. A direct implementation of DBM or Octagons will compute all $k(k-1)$ pairwise relations implied by these bounds. During the execution of lines 2 and 3, all these relations are updated, despite all inferred relations being simply the consequences of variable bounds.

At point 4 we take the join of the two sets of relations. In a direct implementation, this graph is complete, even though there is only one relation that is not already implied by bounds, namely $x_2 = x_1 + 1$. □

One can avoid this phantom density by storing the abstract state in a (possibly weakly) *transitively reduced* form, an approach that has been used to improve performance in SMT and constraint programming [5,11], and to reduce space consumption in model checking [14].[5] But we are hindered by the need to perform *join* operations. The join of two closed graphs is simply $E_1 \oplus E_2$. For transitively reduced graphs, we are forced to first *compute the closure*, perform the pointwise maximum, then restore the result to transitively reduced form. Algorithms exist to efficiently compute the transitive reduction and closure together, but we would still need to restore the reduction after joins.

Instead, we construct a modified normal form which distinguishes independent properties (edges to/from v_0) from strictly relational properties (edges

---

[5] This terminology may be confusing. The transitive reduction computes the greatest (by $\sqsubseteq$) equivalent representation of R, whereas the usual abstract-domain *reduction* corresponds to the transitive *closure*.

between program variable). An important property of this normal form is that *it preserves strongest invariants involving v_0.*

A graph $G = \langle V, E \rangle$ is in *split normal form* iff:

- $G \setminus \{v_0\}$ is closed, and
- for each edge $v_0 \xrightarrow{k} x$ (or $x \xrightarrow{k} v_0$) in G, the shortest path in G from v_0 to x (resp. x to v_0) has length k.

If G is in split normal form then any shortest path from x to y in G occurs either as an edge $x \xrightarrow{k} y$, or the path $x \xrightarrow{k_1} v_0, v_0 \xrightarrow{k_2} y$. We have $E_1 \sqsubseteq E_2$ iff, for every $x \xrightarrow{k} y \in E_2$, $\mathbf{min}(wt_{E_1}(x, y), wt_{E_1}(x, v_0, y)) \leq k$. Assuming constant-time lookups, this test takes $O(|E_2|)$ time.

Note that split normal form is *not* canonical: the graphs $\{x \xrightarrow{1} v_0, v_0 \xrightarrow{1} y\}$ and $\{x \xrightarrow{1} v_0, v_0 \xrightarrow{1} y, x \xrightarrow{2} y\}$ are both in split normal form, and denote the same set of relations. We could establish a canonical form by removing edges implied by variable bounds, then re-closing $G \setminus \{v_0\}$. But we gain nothing by doing so, as we already have an efficient entailment test.

An abstract state in the domain of *split DBMs* consists of a pair $\langle \pi, G \rangle$ of a graph G in split normal form, and a potential function π for G. We must now modify each abstract operation to deal with graphs in split normal form.

4.1   Abstract Operations for Split Normal Form

Variable elimination is unchanged—we simply discard edges touching x.

The modifications for variable assignment, constraint addition and meet are mostly straightforward. The construction of the initial (non-normalized) result and computation of potential function are performed exactly as in Sect. 3.

We then restore closure as before, but only over $G \setminus \{v_0\}$, yielding the set δ of changed edges. We then finish by walking over δ to restore variable bounds.

Widening is also straightforward. The construction of the *un-closed* component by removing *unstable* edges is done as in Sect. 3.6. For the closed result used in subsequent iterations, we restore closure as before but only over $G \setminus \{v_0\}$ and compute separately the closure for v_0.

Pseudo-code for constraint addition, assignment, meet, and widening are given in Fig. 11.

Computation of $E_1 \sqcup E_2$ for split normal graphs is more intricate. As before, either potential may be retained, and edges $v_0 \xrightarrow{k} x$ and $x \xrightarrow{k} v_0$ need no special handling. But direct application of the join used in Sect. 3 may lose precision.

Example 7. Consider the join at point 4 in Fig. 10. In split normal form, the abstract states are:

$$E_1 = \{x_1 \xrightarrow{-1} v_0, v_0 \xrightarrow{1} x_1, x_2 \xrightarrow{-2} v_0, v_0 \xrightarrow{2} x_2, \ldots\}$$
$$E_2 = \{x_1 \xrightarrow{-2} v_0, v_0 \xrightarrow{2} x_1, x_2 \xrightarrow{-3} v_0, v_0 \xrightarrow{3} x_2, \ldots\}$$

update-bounds$_F(E, \delta)$
$\qquad lb := \{v_0 \xrightarrow{k_0+k_e} d \mid v_0 \xrightarrow{k_0} s \in E \land s \xrightarrow{k_e} d \in \delta \land k_0 + k_e < wt_E(v_0, d)\}$
$\qquad ub := \{s \xrightarrow{k_0+k_e} v_0 \mid s \xrightarrow{k_e} d \in \delta \land d \xrightarrow{k_0} v_0 \in E \land k_0 + k_e \le wt_E(s, v_0)\}$
$\qquad$ **return** $\delta \cup lb \cup ub$

add-edge$_F(\langle \pi, E \rangle, e)$
$\qquad E' := E \cup \{e\}$
$\qquad \pi' := restore\text{-}potential(\pi, e, E')$
$\qquad$ **if** $\pi' = $ **inconsistent**
$\qquad\qquad$ **return** $\bot$
$\qquad \delta :=$ close-edge$(e, E' \setminus \{v_0\})$
$\qquad$ **return** $\langle \pi', E' \otimes$ update-bounds$_F(E, \delta) \rangle$

assign$_F(\langle \pi, E \rangle, [\![x := S]\!])$
$\qquad \pi' := \pi[x \mapsto eval\text{-}potential(\pi, S)]$
$\qquad E' := E \cup$ edges-of-assign$(E, [\![x := S]\!])$
$\qquad \delta :=$ close-assign$(\langle \pi', E' \setminus \{v_0\} \rangle, x)$
$\qquad$ **return** $\langle \pi', E' \otimes \delta \rangle$

meet$_F(\langle \pi_1, E_1 \rangle, \langle \pi_2, E_2 \rangle)$
$\qquad E' := E_1 \otimes E_2$
$\qquad \pi' :=$ compute-potential(E', π_1)
$\qquad$ **if** $\pi' = $ **inconsistent**
$\qquad\qquad$ **return** $\bot$
$\qquad \delta :=$ close-meet$(\pi', E' \setminus \{v_0\}, E_1, E_2)$
$\qquad$ **return** $\langle \pi, E' \otimes$ update-bounds$_F(E', \delta) \rangle$

widen$_F(\langle \pi_1, E_1 \rangle_{|S_E}, \langle \pi_2, E_2 \rangle)$
$\qquad \langle E', is\text{-}stable \rangle :=$ remove-unstable-edges(E_1, E_2)
$\qquad un\text{-}closed := \langle \pi_2, E' \rangle$
$\qquad \delta, S_{E'} :=$ close-after-widen$(\langle \pi_2, E' \setminus \{v_0\} \rangle, is\text{-}stable)$
$\qquad \delta := \delta \cup$ close-assignment$(un\text{-}closed, v_0)$
$\qquad closed := \langle \pi_2, E' \otimes \delta \rangle$
$\qquad$ **return** $\langle un\text{-}closed_{|S_{E'}}, closed \rangle$

Fig. 11. Modified algorithms for split normal graphs

In each case the relation $x_2 - x_1 = 1$ is implied by the paths $x_1 \xrightarrow{-1} v_0, v_0 \xrightarrow{2} x_2$ and $x_2 \xrightarrow{-2} v_0, v_0 \xrightarrow{1} x_1$. If we apply the join from Sect. 3, we obtain:

$$E' = \{x_1 \xrightarrow{-1} v_0, v_0 \xrightarrow{2} x_1, x_2 \xrightarrow{-2} v_0, v_0 \xrightarrow{3} x_2, \dots\}$$

This only supports the weaker relation $0 \le x_2 - x_1 \le 2$. $\qquad\qquad\square$

We could find the missing relations by computing the closures of E_1 and E_2; but this rather undermines our objective. Instead, consider the ways a relation might arise in $E_1 \sqcup E_2$:

1. $x \xrightarrow{k} y \in E_1, x \xrightarrow{k'} y \in E_2$
2. $x \xrightarrow{k} y \in E_1, \{x \xrightarrow{k'} v_0, v_0 \xrightarrow{k''} y\} \subseteq E_2$ (or the converse)
3. $\{x \xrightarrow{k_1} v_0, v_0 \xrightarrow{k_2} y\} \subseteq E_1, \{x \xrightarrow{k'_1} v_0, v_0 \xrightarrow{k'_2} y\} \subseteq E_2$, where

$$\mathbf{max}(k_1 + k_2, k'_1 + k'_2) < \mathbf{max}(k_1, k'_1) + \mathbf{max}(k_2, k'_2)$$

The join of Sect. 3 will collect only those relations which are explicit in both E_1 and E_2 (case 1). We can find relations of the second form by walking through E_1 and collecting any edges which are implicit in E_2. The final case is that illustrated in Example 7, where some invariant is implicit in both operands, but is no longer maintained in the result. The restriction on case 3 can only hold when $wt_{E_1}(x, v_0) < wt_{E_2}(x, v_0)$ and $wt_{E_2}(v_0, y) < wt_{E_1}(v_0, y)$ (or the converse).

We can collect suitable pairs by collecting the variables into buckets according to $sign(wt_{E_1}(v_0, x) - wt_{E_2}(v_0, x))$ and $sign(wt_{E_1}(x, v_0) - wt_{E_2}(x, v_0))$. We then walk through the compatible buckets and instantiate the resulting relations.

```
split-rels(E_I, E_R)
    E_IR := ∅
    for (x --k--> y ∈ (E_R − v_0))
        if(wt_{E_I}(x, v_0, y) < wt_{E_I}(x, y))
            E_IR := E_IR ∪ {x --wt_{E_I}(x,v_0,y)--> y}
    return E_IR

bound-rels(src, dest)
    E_II := ∅
    for ((x, k_1, k'_1) ∈ src, (y, k_2, k'_2) ∈ dest, x ≠ y)
        k_xy := max(k_1 + k_2, k'_1 + k'_2)
        E_II := E_II ∪ {x --k_xy--> y}
    return E_II

split-join(⟨π_1, E_1⟩, ⟨π_2, E_2⟩)
    π' := π_1
    E_I_1 := split-rels(E_1, E_2)
    E_I_2 := split-rels(E_2, E_1)
    E_1+ := close-meet(π_1, E_I_1 ⊗ E_1, E_I_1, E_1)
    E_2+ := close-meet(π_2, E_I_2 ⊗ E_2, E_I_2, E_2)
    for (s ∈ {+, −})
        src_s := {(x, wt_{E_1}(x, v_0), wt_{E_2}(x, v_0)) | sign(wt_{E_1}(x, v_0) − wt_{E_2}(x, v_0)) = s}
        dest_s := {(y, wt_{E_1}(v_0, y), wt_{E_2}(v_0, y)) | sign(wt_{E_1}(v_0, y) − wt_{E_2}(v_0, y)) = s}
    E_I_12 := bound-rels(src_+, dest_−) ∪ bound-rels(src_−, dest_+)
    return ⟨π', E_I_12 ⊗ (E_1+ ⊕ E_2+)⟩
```

Fig. 12. Pseudo-code for join of abstract states in split normal form. split-rels collects edges which are implicit in E_I but explicit in E_R. bound-rels collects relations implied by compatible bound changes.

This yields the join algorithm given in Fig. 12. Note the order of construction for E'. Each of the initial components E_1, E_{I_1}, E_2, E_{I_2} and $E_{I_{12}}$ are split-normal. Augmenting E_1 with implied properties E_{I_1} allows us to use the chromatic Dijkstra algorithm for normalization. There is no need to normalize when computing $E_{1+} \oplus E_{2+}$, as relations in classes (1) and (2) will be preserved, relations with v_0 are fully closed, and relations of class (3) will be imposed later.

Due to the construction of $E_{I_{12}}$, normalization of the result again comes for free. Assume $E_{I_{12}} \otimes (E_{1+} \oplus E_{2+})$ is *not* closed. Then there must be some path $x \xrightarrow{k} y \in E_{I_{12}}$, $y \xrightarrow{k'} z \in (E_{1+} \oplus E_{2+})$ such that $x \xrightarrow{k+k'} z$ is not in either operand. But that means there must be some path $x \xrightarrow{c_1} v_0, v_0 \xrightarrow{c_2} y, y \xrightarrow{c_3} z \in E_1$ such that $c_1 + c_2 \leq k$, $c_3 \leq k'$, so there must also be a path $x \xrightarrow{c_1} v_0, v_0 \xrightarrow{c'} z \in E_1$, with $c' \leq c_2 + c_3$. The same holds for E_2. Thus $x \xrightarrow{k+k'} z$ must be in $E_{I_{12}} \otimes (E_{1+} \oplus E_{2+})$.

5   Sparse Graph Representations

So far we avoided discussing the underlying graph representation. The choice is critical for performance. For $\sqcap$ or $\sqcup$, we must walk pointwise across the two graphs; during closure, it is useful to iterate over edges incident to a vertex, and to examine and update relations between arbitrary pairs of variables. On variable elimination, we must remove all edges to or from v. Conventional representations support only some of these operations efficiently. Dense matrices are convenient for updating specific entries but cannot iterate over only the non-trivial entries. $\sqcap$ and $\sqcup$ must walk across the entire matrix—even copying an abstract state is always a $O(|V|^2)$ operation. Adjacency lists support efficient iteration and handle sparsity gracefully, but we lose efficiency of insertion and lookup.

A representation which supports all the required operations is the *adjacency hash-table*, consisting of a hash-table mapping successors to weights for each vertex, and a hash-set of the predecessors of each vertex. This offers the asymptotic behaviour we want but is rather heavy-weight, with substantial overheads on operations. Instead we adopt a hybrid representation; weights are stored in a dense *but uninitialized* matrix, and adjacencies are stored using a "sparse-set" structure [2]. This improves the efficiency of primitive operations, for a reasonable space cost. It introduces an overhead of roughly 8 bytes per matrix element[6]—two bytes each for the *sparse* and *dense* entry for both predecessors and successors. For 64-bit weights, this doubles the overall memory requirements relative to the direct dense matrix.

A sparse-set structure consists of a triple (*dense*, *sparse*, *sz*) where *dense* is an array containing the elements currently in the set, *sparse* is an array mapping elements to the corresponding indices in *dense*, and *sz* the number of elements in the set. We can iterate through the set using $\{dense[0], \ldots, dense[sz - 1]\}$.

Fig. 13 shows the sparse-set operations. We preserve the invariant $\forall i \in [0, sz)$. $sparse[dense[i]] = i$. This means for any element k' outside the set,

---

[6] This assumes 16-bit vertex identifiers; if more than 2^{16} variables are in scope at a program point, any dense-matrix approach is already impractical.

```
elem((dense, sparse, sz), k)
    return sparse[k] < sz ∧ dense[sparse[k]] = k

add((dense, sparse, sz), k)
    sparse[k] := sz
    dense[sz] := k
    sz := sz + 1

remove((dense, sparse, sz), k)
    sz := sz - 1
    k' := dense[sz]
    dense[sparse[k]] := k'
    sparse[k'] := sparse[k]
```

Fig. 13. Sparse-set operations

either $sz \leq sparse[i]$, or $dense[sparse[k']]$ points to some element other than k'—without making any assumptions about the values in $sparse$ or $dense$. So we only need to allocate memory for $sparse$ and $dense$, and initialize sz.

The result is a representation with O(1) addition, removal, lookup and enumeration (with low constant factors) and $O(|V| + |E|)$ time to initialize/copy (we can reduce this to $O(|E|)$ by including an index of non-empty rows, but this adds an additional cost to each lookup).

While the sparse set incurs only a modest overhead (vs a dense matrix), this is still wasteful for extremely sparse graphs. So we choose an adaptive representation. Adjacency lists are initially allocated as unsorted vectors. When the length of a list exceeds a small constant (viz. 8) we allocate the $sparse$ array, turning the list into a sparse set. This yields equivalent performance (both asymptotically and in practice), with considerably smaller memory footprint for very sparse graphs.

6   Experimental Results

We have implemented the Zones abstract domain using both sparse DBMs and sparse DBMs in Split Normal Form. We now compare their performance, and we evaluate the major algorithmic choices discussed in Sects. 3, 4 and 5. All the DBM-based alternatives have been implemented and integrated in CRAB, a language-agnostic static analyzer based on abstract interpretation[7]. For the experiments we use 3753 programs from SV-COMP 2016 [1]. We focus on seven program categories that challenge numerical reasoning: Simple, ControlFlowInteger, Loops, Sequentialized, DeviceDrivers64, ECA, and ProductLines. Since

---

[7] Code is available from the authors upon request.

all programs are written in C they have first been translated[8] to LLVM [15] bit-code and then to a simple language consisting of assume, assignments, arithmetic operations, and goto statements understood by CRAB using the CRAB-LLVM tool. The ultimate goal of the analyzer is to infer inductive invariants at each basic block. All the experiments were carried out on a 2.1 GHz AMD Opteron processor 6172 with 32 cores and 64 GB on a Linux machine.

We first compare DBM-based implementations of Zones: dense-dbm [17] uses a dense matrix with incremental Floyd-Warshall ([3], Fig. 7, INCREMENTAL-DIFFERENCEV2) for both constraint addition and assignment; sparse-dbm uses sparse DBMs (Sect. 3); and split-dbm uses sparse DBMs but splits independent and relational invariants as described in Sect. 4. As performance baseline, we also compare with intervals, a classical implementation of intervals. Finally we add dense-dbm+pack which enhances dense-dbm with dynamic variable packing [21]. Note that dense-dbm, sparse-dbm, and split-dbm have the same expressiveness, so they infer the same invariants. The performance results of dense-dbm+pack are not really comparable with the other DBM implementations: the analysis is less precise since it only preserves relationships between variables in the same pack. For our benchmark suite, intervals inferred the same invariants as dense-dbm+pack in 19 % of the cases, whereas dense-dbm+pack infers the same as split-dbm in only 29 % of the cases.

Figure 14 shows the results, using an 8 GB memory limit and various timeouts ranging from 1 to 5 min. Five implementations are compared. Figure 14(a) shows, for each, the accumulated time in minutes. Figure 14(b) shows how many programs were analyzed without exceeding the timeout. If the analyzer exhausted the resources then the timeout value has been counted as analysis time. The comparison shows that sparse-dbm is significantly faster than dense-dbm (4.3x)

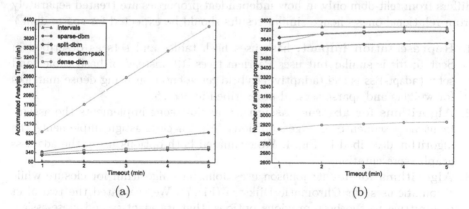

(a)   (b)

Fig. 14. Performance of several DBM-based implementations of *Zones* over 3753 SV-COMP'16 benchmarks with 8GB memory limit.

---

[8] We tried to stress test the DBM implementations by increasing the number of variables in scope through inlining. We inlined all function calls unless a called function was recursive or could not be resolved at compile time.

while being able to analyze many more programs (>500). Moreover, split-dbm outperforms sparse-dbm both in the number of analyzed programs (100 more) *and* analysis times ($2x$). Note that compared to the *far less precise* dense-dbm +pack, split-dbm can analyze almost the same number of programs while at the same time being faster ($1.1x$).

Table 1. Performance of different versions of split-dbm, applied to SV-COMP'16 programs, with a timeout of 60 s and a memory limit of 8 GB.

| | Graph Representation | | | | Assign | | Meet | |
| | Total: 3753 | | | | Total: 3753 | | Total: 4079 | |
	hash	trie	ss	adapt-ss	close-edge	close-assign	johnson	chromatic
Analyzed	3637	3545	3632	3662	3659	3662	4020	4028
TOs	116	208	68	91	91	91	91	48
MOs	0	0	53	0	3	0	0	3
Time	318	479	252	265	269	265	160	151

In another three experiments we have evaluated the major algorithmic and representation choices for split-dbm. Table 1 shows the results. Analyzed is the number of programs for which the analyzer converged without exhausting resources. TOs is the number of time-outs, MOs is the number of cases where memory limits were exceeded, and Time is the accumulated analysis time in minutes. Again, MOs instances were counted as time-outs for the computation of overall time. (We do not repeat these experiments with sparse-dbm since it differs from split-dbm only in how independent properties are treated separately from relational ones—hence similar results should be expected for sparse-dbm.)

1. **Representation impact:** hash uses hash tables and sets as described in Sect. 5; trie is similar but uses Patricia trees [19] instead of hash tables and sets; (adapt-) ss is the (adaptive) hybrid representation using dense matrices for weights and sparse sets, also described in Sect. 5.
2. **Algorithms for abstract assign** x:=e: close-edge implements the assignment as a sequence of edge additions (Fig. 2). close-assign implements the algorithm described in Fig. 4. We evaluated both options using the adapt-ss graph representation.
3. **Algorithms for meet:** johnson uses Johnson's algorithm for closure while chromatic uses our Chromatic Dijkstra (Fig. 7). We evaluated the two after committing to the best previous options, that is, adapt-ss and close-assign. NB: To increase the number of meets we did not inline programs here. This is the reason why the total number of programs has increased—LLVM can compile more programs in reasonable time when inlining is disabled.

These last three experiments justify the choices (adapt-ss, close-assign, and chromatic) used in the implementation whose performance is reported in Fig. 14.

7   Related Work

Much research has been motivated by the appeal, but ultimately lacking scalability, of program analyses based on relational domains. Attempts to improve the state of the art fall in three rough classes.

Approaches based on *dimensionality restriction* attempt to decrease the dimension k of the program abstract state by replacing the full space with a set of subspaces of lower-dimensional sub-spaces. Variables are separated into "buckets" or *packs* according to some criterion. *Variable packing* was first utilised in the Astree analyser [8]. A dynamic variant is used in the C Global Surveyor [21].

Others choose to sacrifice precision, establishing a new trade-off between performance and expressiveness. Some abandon the systematic transitive closure of relations (and work around the resulting lack a normal form for constraints). Constraints implied by closure may be discovered lazily, or not at all. Used with their Pentagon domain, Logozzo and Fähndrich [16] found that this approach established a happy balance between cost and precision. The Gauge domain proposed by Venet [22] can be seen as a combination of this approach and dimensionality restriction. In the Gauge domain, relations are only maintained between program variables and specially introduced "loop counter" variables.

Finally, one can focus on algorithmic aspects of classical abstract domains and attempt to improve performance without modifying the domain (as in this paper). Here the closest related work targets Octagons rather than Zones. Chawdhary, Robbins and King [3] present algorithmic improvements for the Octagon domain, assuming a standard matrix-based implementation (built on DBMs). They focus on the common use case where a single constraint is added/changed, that is, their goal is an improved algorithm for *incremental* closure.

8   Conclusion and Future Work

We have developed new algorithms for the Zones abstract domain and described a graph representation which is tailored for efficient implementation across the set of needed abstract operations. We have introduced *split normal form*, a new graph representation that permits separate handling of independent and relational properties. We have provided detailed descriptions of how to implement the necessary abstract operations for this representation. Performance results show that, despite having more involved operations (particularly the join operation), the resulting reduction in density is clearly worth the effort.

Evaluation on SV-COMP'16 instances shows that sparse-dbm and split-dbm are efficient, performing *full relational analysis* while being no more expensive than less expressive variable packing methods.

Standard implementations of Octagons are also based on DBMs [3,18]. A natural application of the algorithmic insights of the present paper is to adapt our ideas to Octagon implementation. This should be particularly interesting in the light of recent implementation progress based on entirely different ideas. For their improved Octagon implementation, Singh, Püschel and Vechev [20] commit to a (costly) dense matrix representation in order to enable abstract operations that are cleverly based on vectorization technology. (They also check for disconnected subgraphs, and decompose the matrix into smaller, packing-style, sub-components when this occurs.) In contrast we see Zone/Octagon types of program analysis as essentially-sparse graph problems. In Sect. 4 we have argued that the density observed elsewhere (including [20]) is artificial—it stems from a failure to separate independent properties from truly relational properties. Our approach is therefore almost diametrically opposite that of [20] as we choose to exploit the innate sparsity as best we can. A comparison should be interesting.

Acknowledgments. We acknowledge the support from the Australian Research Council through grant DP140102194. We would like to thank Maxime Arthaud for implementing the non-incremental version of dense difference-bound matrices as well as the variable packing technique.

References

1. Competition on software verification (SV-COMP) (2016). http://sv-comp.sosy-lab.org/2016/. Benchmarks https://github.com/sosy-lab/sv-benchmarks/c. Accessed 30 Mar 2016
2. Briggs, P., Torczon, L.: An efficient representation for sparse sets. ACM Lett. Program. Lang. Syst. **2**(1–4), 59–69 (1993)
3. Chawdhary, A., Robbins, E., King, A.: Simple and efficient algorithms for octagons. In: Garrigue, J. (ed.) APLAS 2014. LNCS, vol. 8858, pp. 296–313. Springer, Heidelberg (2014)
4. Cherkassky, B.V., Goldberg, A.V.: Negative-cycle detection algorithms. Math. Program. **85**(2), 277–311 (1999)
5. Cotton, S., Maler, O.: Fast and flexible difference constraint propagation for DPLL(T). In: Biere, A., Gomes, C.P. (eds.) SAT 2006. LNCS, vol. 4121, pp. 170–183. Springer, Heidelberg (2006)
6. Cousot, P., Cousot, R.: Abstract interpretation: a unified lattice model for static analysis of programs by construction or approximation of fixpoints. In: Proceedings of the Fourth ACM Symposium Principles of Programming Languages, pp. 238–252. ACM Press (1977)
7. Cousot, P., Cousot, R.: Systematic design of program analysis frameworks. In: Proceedings of the Sixth ACM Symposium Principles of Programming Languages, pp. 269–282. ACM Press (1979)
8. Cousot, P., Cousot, R., Feret, J., Mauborgne, L., Miné, A., Rival, X.: Why does Astrée scale up? Formal Methods Syst. Des. **35**(3), 229–264 (2009)
9. Cousot, P., Halbwachs, N.: Automatic discovery of linear constraints among variables of a program. In: Proceedings of the Fifth ACM Symposium Principles of Programming Languages, pp. 84–97. ACM Press (1978)
10. Fähndrich, M., Logozzo, F.: Static contract checking with abstract interpretation. In: Beckert, B., Marché, C. (eds.) FoVeOOS 2010. LNCS, vol. 6528, pp. 10–30. Springer, Heidelberg (2011)

11. Feydy, T., Schutt, A., Stuckey, P.J.: Global difference constraint propagation for finite domain solvers. In: Proceedings of the 10th International ACM SIGPLAN Conference Principles and Practice of Declarative Programming, pp. 226–235. ACM Press (2008)
12. Ford, L.R., Fulkerson, D.R.: Flows in Networks. Princeton University Press, Princeton (1962)
13. Johnson, D.B.: Efficient algorithms for shortest paths in sparse networks. J. ACM **24**(1), 1–13 (1977)
14. Larsen, K.G., Larsson, F., Pettersson, P., Yi, W.: Efficient verification of real-time systems: compact data structure and state-space reduction. In: Proceedings of the 18th International Symposium Real-Time Systems, pp. 14–24. IEEE Computer Society (1997)
15. Lattner, C., Adve, V.: LLVM: a compilation framework for lifelong program analysis and transformation. In: Proceedings of the International Symposium Code Generation and Optimization (CGO 2004), pp. 75–86. IEEE Computer Society (2004)
16. Logozzo, F., Fähndrich, M.: Pentagons: a weakly relational abstract domain for the efficient validation of array accesses. In: Proceedings of the 2008 ACM Symposium Applied Computing, pp. 184–188. ACM Press (2008)
17. Miné, A.: A new numerical abstract domain based on difference-bound matrices. In: Danvy, O., Filinski, A. (eds.) PADO 2001. LNCS, vol. 2053, pp. 155–172. Springer, Heidelberg (2001)
18. Miné, A.: The octagon abstract domain. High. Ord. Symbolic Comput. **19**(1), 31–100 (2006)
19. Okasaki, C., Gill, A.: Fast mergeable integer maps. In: Notes of the ACM SIGPLAN Workshop on ML, pp. 77–86, September 1998
20. Singh, G., Püschel, M., Vechev, M.: Making numerical program analysis fast. In: Proceedings of the 36th ACM SIGPLAN Conference Programming Language Design and Implementation, pp. 303–313. ACM (2015)
21. Venet, A., Brat, G.: Precise and efficient static array bound checking for large embedded C programs. In: Proceedings of the 25th ACM SIGPLAN Conference Programming Language Design and Implementation, pp. 231–242. ACM Press (2004)
22. Venet, A.J.: The gauge domain: scalable analysis of linear inequality invariants. In: Madhusudan, P., Seshia, S.A. (eds.) CAV 2012. LNCS, vol. 7358, pp. 139–154. Springer, Heidelberg (2012)

Flow- and Context-Sensitive Points-To Analysis Using Generalized Points-To Graphs

Pritam M. Gharat[1], Uday P. Khedker[1(✉)], and Alan Mycroft[2]

[1] Indian Institute of Technology Bombay, Mumbai, India
{pritamg,uday}@cse.iitb.ac.in
[2] University of Cambridge, Cambridge, UK
am@cl.cam.ac.uk

Abstract. Bottom-up interprocedural methods of program analysis construct summary flow functions for procedures to capture the effect of their calls and have been used effectively for many analyses. However, these methods seem computationally expensive for flow- and context-sensitive points-to analysis (FCPA) which requires modelling unknown locations accessed indirectly through pointers. Such accesses are commonly handled by using placeholders to explicate unknown locations or by using multiple call-specific summary flow functions. We generalize the concept of points-to relations by using the counts of indirection levels leaving the unknown locations implicit. This allows us to create summary flow functions in the form of *generalized points-to graphs* (GPGs) without the need of placeholders. By design, GPGs represent both memory (in terms of classical points-to facts) and memory transformers (in terms of generalized points-to facts). We perform FCPA by progressively reducing generalized points-to facts to classical points-to facts. GPGs distinguish between *may* and *must* pointer updates thereby facilitating strong updates within calling contexts.

The size of GPGs is linearly bounded by the number of variables and is independent of the number of statements. Empirical measurements on SPEC benchmarks show that GPGs are indeed compact in spite of large procedure sizes. This allows us to scale FCPA to 158 kLoC using GPGs (compared to 35 kLoC reported by liveness-based FCPA). Thus GPGs hold a promise of efficiency and scalability for FCPA without compromising precision.

1 Introduction

Points-to analysis discovers information about indirect accesses in a program and its precision influences the precision and scalability of other program analyses significantly. Computationally intensive analyses such as model checking are ineffective on programs containing pointers partly because of imprecision of pointer analyses [1,8].

We focus on exhaustive (as against demand driven [2,7,22]) points-to analysis with full flow- and context-sensitivity for precision. A top-down context sensitive

---

P.M. Gharat—Partially supported by a TCS Fellowship.

© Springer-Verlag GmbH Germany 2016
X. Rival (Ed.): SAS 2016, LNCS 9837, pp. 212–236, 2016.
DOI: 10.1007/978-3-662-53413-7_11

analysis propagates the information from callers to callees [28] thereby analyzing a procedure each time a new data flow value reaches its call(s). Some approaches in this category are: call strings method [21], its value-based variants [10,17] and the tabulation based functional method [18,21]. By contrast, bottom-up approaches avoid analyzing callees multiple times by constructing *summary flow functions* which are used at call sites to incorporate the effect of procedure calls [3,6,13,19,21,23–28].

It is prudent to distinguish between three kinds of summaries (see [4] for examples) that can be created for a procedure: *(a)* a bottom-up parameterized summary flow function which is context independent, *(b)* a top-down enumeration of summary flow function in the form of input-output pairs for the input values reaching a procedure, and *(c)* a bottom-up parameterless (and hence context-insensitive) summary information. Context independence (in *(a)* above), achieves context-sensitivity through parameterization and should not be confused with context-insensitivity (in *(c)* above).

We focus on summaries of the first kind. Their construction requires *composing* statement-level flow functions to represent a sequence of statements, and *merging* the composed functions to represent multiple control flow paths reaching a program point. These summaries should be compact and their size should be independent of the number of statements. This seems hard because of the presence of indirect pointees. The composition of the flow functions for a sequence of statements $x = *y; z = *x$ cannot be reduced to a flow function of the basic pointer assignments for 3-address code ($x = \&y$, $x = y$, $x = *y$, and $*x = y$).

Our Key Idea and Approach. We generalize the concept of points-to relations by using the counts of indirection levels leaving the unknown locations implicit. This allows us to create summary flow functions in the form of *generalized points-to graphs* (GPGs) whose size is linearly bounded by the number of variables (Sect. 2). By design, GPGs can represent both memory (in terms of classical points-to facts) and memory transformers (in terms of generalized points-to facts).

Example 1. Consider procedure g of Fig. 1 whose GPG is shown in Fig. 2(c). The edges in GPGs track indirection levels: indirection level 1 in the label $(1,0)$ indicates that the source is assigned the address (indicated by indirection level 0) of the target. Edge $a \xrightarrow{1,0} e$ is created for line 8. The indirection level 2 in edge $x \xrightarrow{2,1} z$ for line 10 indicates that the pointees of x are being defined; since z is read, its indirection level is 1. The combined effect of lines 13 (edge $y \xrightarrow{1,0} b$) and 17 (edge $y \xrightarrow{2,0} d$) results in the edge $b \xrightarrow{1,0} d$. However edge $y \xrightarrow{2,0} d$ is also retained because there is no information about the pointee of y along the other path reaching line 17.   □

The generalized points-to facts are composed to create new generalized points-to facts with smaller indirection levels (Sect. 3) whenever possible thereby converting them progressively to classical points-to facts. This is performed in

```
01 void f()        07 void g()        13    {  y = &b;      Procs. g and f are
02 {  x = &a;      08 {  a = &e;      14       z = &v;      used for illustrating
03    z = &w;      09    if (...) {   15    }                intraprocedural and
04    g();         10       *x = z;   16    x = &b;          interprocedural GPG
05    *x = z;      11       z = &u;   17    *y = &d;         construction
06 }               12    } else       18 }                   respectively.
```

Fig. 1. A program fragment used as a running example through the paper. All variables are global.

two phases: construction of GPGs, and use of GPGs to compute points-to information. GPGs are constructed flow-sensitively by processing pointer assignments along the control flow of a procedure and collecting generalized points-to facts (Sect. 4).

Function calls are handled context-sensitively by incorporating the effect of the GPG of a callee into the GPG of the caller (Sect. 5). Loops and recursion are handled using a fixed point computation. GPGs also distinguish between *may* and *must* pointer updates thereby facilitating strong updates.

Section 6 shows how GPGs are used for computing classical points-to facts. Section 7 presents the empirical measurements. Section 8 describes the related work. Section 9 concludes the paper. A detailed technical report [4] describes how we handle advanced issues (e.g. structures, heap memory, function pointers, arrays, pointer arithmetic) and also provides soundness proofs.

The Advantages of GPGs Over Conventional Summaries. Indirect accesses of unknown locations have been commonly modelled using *placeholders* (called extended parameters in [25] and external variables in [13]).

The *partial transfer function* (PTF) based method [25] uses placeholders to construct a collection of PTFs for a procedure for different aliasing patterns involving formal parameters and global variables accessed in the procedure.

Example 2. For procedure g of the program in Fig. 1, three placeholders ϕ_1, ϕ_2, and ϕ_3 have been used in the PTFs shown in Figs. 2(a) and (b). The possibility that x and y may or may not be aliased gives rise to two PTFs.   □

The number of PTFs could be combinatorial in the number of dereferences of globals and parameters. PTFs that do not correspond to actual aliasing patterns can be excluded by combining a top-down analysis for discovering aliasing patterns with the bottom-up construction of PTFs [25,28]. Yet, the number of PTFs could remain large.

An alternative approach makes no assumption about aliases in the calling context and constructs a single summary flow function for a procedure. In a degenerate case, it may require a separate placeholder for the same variable in different statements and the size of the summary flow functions may be proportional to the number of statements.

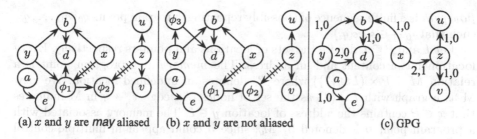

(a) x and y are *may* aliased   (b) x and y are not aliased   (c) GPG

Fig. 2. PTFs/GPG for proc. g of Fig. 1. Edges deleted due to flow-sensitivity are struck off.

Example 3. For the code snippet on the right, we need two different placeholders for y in statements s_1 and s_3 because statement s_2 could change the pointee of y depending upon whether $*z$ is aliased to y.

$$s_1: \quad x = *y;$$
$$s_2: \quad *z = q;$$
$$s_3: \quad p = *y;$$

□

Separate placeholders for different occurrences of a variable can be avoided if points-to information is not killed by the summary flow functions [13,23,24]. Another alternative is to use flow-insensitive summary flow functions [3]. However, both these cases introduces imprecision.

A fundamental problem with placeholders is that they explicate unknown locations by naming them, resulting in either a large number of placeholders (e.g., a GPG edge $\cdot \xrightarrow{i,j} \cdot$ would require $i + j - 1$ placeholders) or multiple summary flow functions for different aliasing patterns that exist in the calling contexts.

Since we use edges to track indirection levels leaving unknown locations implicit: *(a)* placeholders are not needed (unlike [13,23–25,28]), *(b)* aliasing patterns from calling contexts are not needed and a single summary per procedure is created (unlike [25,28]), *(c)* the size of summary is linearly bounded by the number of variables regardless of the number of statements (unlike [13,23,24]), and *(d)* updates can be performed in the calling contexts (unlike [3,13,23,24]). This facilitates the scalability of fully flow- and context-sensitive exhaustive points-to analysis.

2   Generalized Points-To Graphs (GPGs)

We define the basic concepts assuming scalars and pointers in the stack and static memory; see [4] for extensions to handle structures, heap, function pointers, etc.

2.1   Memory and Memory Transformer

We assume a control flow graph representation containing 3-address code statements. Program points t, u, v represent the points just before the execution of statements. The successors and predecessors of a program point are denoted by *succ* and *pred*; *succ* pred** denote their reflexive transitive closures. A *control* *flow path* is a finite sequence of (possibly repeating) program points $q_0, q_1, \ldots, q_m$ such that $q_{i+1} \in succ(q_i)$.

Let L and $P \subseteq L$ denote the sets of locations and pointers respectively. Every location has a content and an address. The *memory* at a program point is a relation $M \subseteq P \times (L \cup \{?\})$ where "?" denotes an undefined location. We view M as a graph with $L \cup \{?\}$ as the set of nodes. An edge $x \to y$ in M indicates that $x \in P$ contains the address of location $y \in L$. The memory associated with a program point u is denoted by M_u; since u could appear in multiple control flow paths and could also repeat in a control flow path, M_u denotes the memory associated with all occurrences of u.

The pointees of a set of pointers $X \subseteq P$ in M are computed by the application $M\,X = \{y \mid (x,y) \in M, x \in X\}$. A composition of degree i, $M^i\{x\}$ discovers the ith pointees of x which involves i transitive reads from x: first $i-1$ addresses are read followed by the content of the last address. For composability of M, we extend its domain to $L \cup \{?\}$ by inclusion map. By definition, $M^0\{x\} = \{x\}$.

For adjacent program points u and v, M_v is computed from M_u by incorporating the effect of the statement between u and v, $M_v = (\delta(u,v))(M_u)$ where $\delta(u,v)$ is a *statement-level flow function* representing a *memory transformer*. For $v \in succ^*(u)$, the effect of the statements appearing in all control flow paths from u to v is computed by $M_v = (\Delta(u,v))(M_u)$ where the memory transformer $\Delta(u,v)$ is a *summary flow function* mapping the memory at u to the memory at v. Definition 1 provides an equation to compute Δ without specifying a representation for it. Since control flow paths may contain cycles, Δ is the maximum fixed point of the equation where *(a)* the composition of Δs is denoted by $\circ$ such that $(g \circ f)(\cdot) = g(f(\cdot))$, *(b)* Δs are merged using $\sqcap$, *(c)* B captures the base case, and *(d)* Δ_{id} is the identity flow function. Hence-

---

Definition 1: Memory Transformer Δ

$$\Delta(u,v) := B(u,v) \; \sqcap \bigsqcap_{\substack{t \in succ^*(u) \\ v \in succ(t)}} \delta(t,v) \circ \Delta(u,t)$$

$$B(u,v) := \begin{cases} \Delta_{id} & v = u \\ \delta(u,v) & v \in succ(u) \\ \emptyset & \text{otherwise} \end{cases}$$

---

forth, we use the term memory transformer for a summary flow function Δ. The rest of the paper proposes GPG as a compact representation for Δ. Section 2.2 defines GPG and Sect. 2.3 defines its lattice.

2.2 Generalized Points-To Graphs for Representing Memory Transformers

The classical memory transformers explicate the unknown locations using placeholders. Effectively, they use a low level abstraction which is close to the memory defined in terms of classical points-to facts: Given locations $x, y \in L$, a classical points-to fact $x \to y$ in memory M asserts that x holds the address of y. We propose a higher level abstraction of the memory without explicating the unknown locations.

Pointer assignment	Pointers defined	Pointees	GPG edge	Pointers over-written	Effect on M after the assignment
$x = \&y$	$M^0\{x\}$	$M^0\{y\}$	$x \xrightarrow{1,0} y$	$M^0\{x\}$	$M^1\{x\} = M^0\{y\}$
$x = y$	$M^0\{x\}$	$M^1\{y\}$	$x \xrightarrow{1,1} y$	$M^0\{x\}$	$M^1\{x\} = M^1\{y\}$
$x = *y$	$M^0\{x\}$	$M^2\{y\}$	$x \xrightarrow{1,2} y$	$M^0\{x\}$	$M^1\{x\} = M^2\{y\}$
$*x = y$	$M^1\{x\}$	$M^1\{y\}$	$x \xrightarrow{2,1} y$	$M^1\{x\}$ or none	$M^2\{x\} \supseteq M^1\{y\}$

Fig. 3. GPG edges for basic pointer assignments in C.

Definition 2: *Generalized Points-to Graph (GPG).* Given locations $x, y \in L$, a *generalized points-to fact* $x \xrightarrow{i,j} y$ in a given memory M asserts that every location reached by $i - 1$ dereferences from x can hold the address of every location reached by j dereferences from y. Thus, $M^i\{x\} \supseteq M^j\{y\}$. A *generalized points-to graph* (GPG) is a set of edges representing generalized points-to facts. For a GPG edge $x \xrightarrow{i,j} y$, the pair (i, j) represents indirection levels and is called the *indlev* of the edge (i is the *indlev* of x, and j is the *indlev* of y).

Figure 3 illustrates the generalized points-to facts corresponding to the basic pointer assignments in C. Observe that a classical points-to fact $x \rightarrow y$ is a special case of the generalized points-to fact $x \xrightarrow{i,j} y$ with $i = 1$ and $j = 0$; the case $i = 0$ does not arise.

The generalized points-to facts are more expressive than the classical points-to facts because they can be composed to create new facts as shown by the example below. Section 3 explains the process of composing the generalized points-to facts through *edge composition* along with the conditions when the facts can and ought to be composed.

Example 4. Statements s_1 and s_2 to the right are represented by GPG edges $x \xrightarrow{1,0} y$ and $z \xrightarrow{1,1} x$ respectively. We can compose the two edges by creating a new edge $z \xrightarrow{1,0} y$ indicating that z points-to y. Effectively, this converts the generalized points-to fact for s_2 into a classical points-to fact. $\qquad\qquad\square$

$s_1: x = \&y;$
$s_2: z = x;$

Imposing an ordering on the set of GPG edges allows us to view it as a sequence to represent a flow-sensitive memory transformer. A reverse post order traversal over the control flow graph of a procedure dictates this sequence. It is required only at the interprocedural level when the effect of a callee is incorporated in its caller. Since a sequence is totally ordered but control flow is partially ordered, the GPG operations (Sect. 5) internally relax the total order to ensure that the edges appearing on different control flow paths do not affect each other.

While the visual presentation of GPGs as graphs is intuitively appealing, it loses the edge-ordering; we annotate edges with their ordering explicitly when it matters.

A GPG is a uniform representation for a memory transformer as well as (an abstraction of) memory. This is analogous to a matrix which can be seen both as a transformer (for a linear translation) and also as an absolute value. A points-to analysis using GPGs begins with generalized points-to facts $\cdot \xrightarrow{i,j} \cdot$ representing memory transformers which are composed to create new generalized points-to facts with smaller *indlev* s thereby progressively reducing them to classical points-to facts $\cdot \xrightarrow{1,0} \cdot$ representing memory.

2.3   The Lattice of GPGs

Definition 3 describes the meet semi-lattice of GPGs. For reasons described later in Sect. 5, we need to introduce an artificial ⊤ element denoted $\Delta_\top$ in the lattice. It is used as the initial value in the data flow equations for computing GPGs (Definition 5 which instantiates Definition 1 for GPGs).

The sequencing of edges is maintained externally and is explicated where required. This allows us to treat a GPG (other than $\Delta_\top$) as a pair of a set of nodes and a set of edges. The partial order is a point-wise super-set relation applied to the pairs. Similarly, the meet operation is a point-wise union of the pairs. It is easy

Definition 3: Lattice of GPGs
$\Delta \in \{\Delta_\top\} \cup \{(\mathcal{N}, \mathcal{E}) \mid \mathcal{N} \subseteq N, \mathcal{E} \subseteq E\}$
where
$N := L \cup \{?\}$
$E := \{x \xrightarrow{i,j} y \mid x \in P,\ y \in N,$ $\qquad 0 < i \le \lvert N \rvert,\ 0 \le j \le \lvert N \rvert\}$
$\Delta_1 \sqsubseteq \Delta_2 \Leftrightarrow (\Delta_2 = \Delta_\top) \vee (\mathcal{N}_1 \supseteq \mathcal{N}_2 \wedge \mathcal{E}_1 \supseteq \mathcal{E}_2)$
$\Delta_1 \sqcap \Delta_2 := \begin{cases} \Delta_1 & \Delta_2 = \Delta_\top \\ \Delta_2 & \Delta_1 = \Delta_\top \\ (\mathcal{N}_1 \cup \mathcal{N}_2,\ \mathcal{E}_1 \cup \mathcal{E}_2) & \text{otherwise} \end{cases}$

to see that the lattice is finite because the number of locations L is finite (being restricted to static and stack slots). When we extend GPGs to handle heap memory [4], explicit summarization is required to ensure finiteness. The finiteness of the lattice and the monotonicity of GPG operations guarantee the convergence of GPG computations on a fixed point; starting from $\Delta_\top$, we compute the maximum fixed point.

For convenience, we treat a GPG as a set of edges leaving the set of nodes implicit; the GPG nodes can always be inferred from the GPG edges.

2.4   A Hierarchy of GPG Operations

Figure 4 lists the GPG operations based on the concept of the generalized points-to facts. They are presented in two separate columns according to the two phases of our analysis and each layer is defined in terms of the layers below it. The operations are defined in the sections listed against them in Fig. 4.

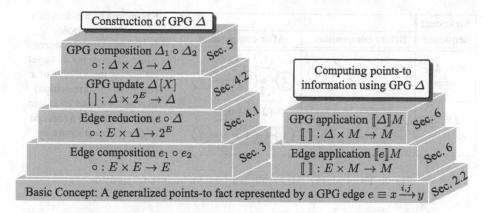

Fig. 4. A hierarchy of operations for points-to analysis using GPGs. Each operation is defined in terms of the layers below it. E denotes the set of GPG edges. By abuse of notation, we use M and Δ also as types to indicate the signatures of the operations. The operators "∘" and "[[ ]]" are overloaded and can be disambiguated using the types of the operands.

Constructing GPGs. An *edge composition* $e_1 \circ e_2$ computes a new edge e_3 equivalent to e_1 using the points-to information in e_2 such that the *indlev* of e_3 is smaller than that of e_1. An *edge reduction* $e_1 \circ \Delta$ computes a set of edges X by composing e_1 with the edges in Δ. A *GPG update* $\Delta_1 [X]$ incorporates the effect of the set of edges X in Δ_1 to compute a new GPG Δ_2. A *GPG composition* $\Delta_1 \circ \Delta_2$ composes a callee's GPG Δ_2 with GPG Δ_1 at a call point to compute a new GPG Δ_3.

Using GPGs for computing points-to information. An *edge application* $[[e]]M$ computes a new memory M' by incorporating the effect of the GPG edge e in memory M. A *GPG application* $[[\Delta]]M$ applies the GPG Δ to M and computes a new memory M' using edge application iteratively.

These operations allow us to build the theme of a GPG being a uniform representation for both memory and memory transformers.

3   Edge Composition

This section defines edge composition as a fundamental operation which is used in Sect. 4 for constructing GPGs. Some considerations in edge composition (explained in this section) are governed by the goal of including the resulting edges in a GPG Δ.

Let a statement-level flow function δ be represented by an edge $\boldsymbol{n}$ ("new" edge) and consider an existing edge $\boldsymbol{p} \in \Delta$ ("processed" edge). Edges $\boldsymbol{n}$ and $\boldsymbol{p}$ can be composed (denoted $\boldsymbol{n} \circ \boldsymbol{p}$) provided they have a common node called the *pivot* of composition (since a pivot can be the source or target of either of the edges, there are four possibilities as explained later). The goal is to *reduce* (i.e., simplify) $\boldsymbol{n}$ by using the points-to information from $\boldsymbol{p}$. This is achieved by using

Statement sequence	GPG	
	Before composition	After composition
$x = \&y$ $z = x$	$z \xrightarrow[1,1]{n} x \xrightarrow[1,0]{p} y$	$(1, 1-1+0)$ $z \xrightarrow{} x \to y$ $1,1 \quad 1,0$
$x = \&y$ $*x = z$	$z \xleftarrow[2,1]{n} x \xrightarrow[1,0]{p} y$	$(2-1+0, 1)$ $z \xleftarrow{} x \to y$ $2,1 \quad 1,0$

Regardless of the direction of an edge, i in *indlev* (i, j) represents its source while j represents its target. Balancing the *indlev*s of x (the pivot of composition) in p and n allows us to join y and z to create a reduced edge $r = n \circ p$ shown by dashed arrows.

Fig. 5. Examples of edge compositions for points-to analysis.

the pivot as a bridge to join the remaining two nodes resulting in a reduced edge r. This requires the *indlev*s of the pivot in both edges to be made the same. For example, given edges $n \equiv z \xrightarrow{i,j} x$ and $p \equiv x \xrightarrow{k,l} y$ with a pivot x, if $j > k$, then the difference $j - k$ can be added to the *indlev*s of nodes in p, to view p as $x \xrightarrow{j,(l+j-k)} y$. This balances the *indlev*s of x in the two edges allowing us to create a reduced edge $r \equiv z \xrightarrow{i,(l+j-k)} y$. Although this computes the transitive effect of edges, in general, it cannot be modelled using multiplication of matrices representing graphs as explained in our technical report [4].

Example 5. In the first example in Fig. 5, the *indlev*s of pivot x in both p and n is the same allowing us to join z and y through an edge $z \xrightarrow{1,0} y$. In the second example, the difference $(2-1)$ in the *indlev*s of x can be added to the *indlev*s of nodes in p viewing it as $x \xrightarrow{2,1} y$. This allows us to join y and z creating the edge $y \xrightarrow{1,1} z$. □

Let an edge n be represented by the triple $(S_n, (s_n^c, \tau_n^c), T_n)$ where S_n and T_n are the source and the target of n and (s_n^c, τ_n^c) is the *indlev*. Similarly, p is represented by $(S_p, (s_p^c, \tau_p^c), T_p)$ and the reduced edge $r = n \circ p$ by $(S_r, (s_r^c, \tau_r^c), T_r)$; (s_r^c, τ_r^c) is obtained by balancing the *indlev* of the pivot in p and n. The pivot of a composition, denoted $\mathbb{P}$, may be the source or the target of n and p. This leads to four combinations of $n \circ p$: SS, TS, ST, TT. Our implementation currently uses TS and SS compositions illustrated in Fig. 6; ST and TT compositions are described in the technical report [4].

- TS composition. In this case, $T_n = S_p$ i.e., the pivot is the target of n and the source of p. Node S_n becomes the source and T_p becomes the target of the reduced edge r.
- SS composition. In this case, $S_n = S_p$ i.e., the pivot is the source of both n and p. Node T_p becomes the source and T_n becomes the target of the reduced edge r.

Consider an edge composition $r = n \circ p, p \in \Delta$. For constructing a new Δ, we wish to include r rather than n: Including both of them is sound but may lead to imprecision; including only n is also sound but may lead to inefficiency because

Possible SS Compositions			Possible TS Compositions		
Statement sequence	Memory graph	GPG edges	Statement sequence	Memory graph	GPG edges
$s_n^c < s_p^c$			$\tau_n^c < s_p^c$		
Ex. ss1 $* x = \&y$ $x = \&z$	*(memory graph: x, y, z with ℓ_p, ℓ_n)*	$p: x \xrightarrow{2,0} y$ $n: x \xrightarrow{1,0} z$ *(irrelevant)*	**Ex. ts1** $* x = \&y$ $z = x$	*(memory graph: x, z, y with ℓ_n, ℓ_p)*	$p: x \xrightarrow{2,0} y$ $n: z \xrightarrow{1,1} x$ *(not useful)*
$s_n^c > s_p^c$ (Additionally $\tau_p^c \le s_p^c$)			$\tau_n^c > s_p^c$ (Additionally $\tau_p^c \le s_p^c$)		
Ex. ss2 $x = \&z$ $* x = \&y$	*(memory graph: x, z, y with ℓ_p, ℓ_n)*	$p: x \xrightarrow{1,0} z$ $n: x \xrightarrow{2,0} y$ $r: z \xrightarrow{1,0} y$	**Ex. ts2** $x = \&y$ $z = *x$	*(memory graph: x, y, z with ℓ_p, ℓ_n)*	$p: x \xrightarrow{1,0} y$ $n: z \xrightarrow{1,2} x$ $r: z \xrightarrow{1,1} y$
$s_n^c = s_p^c$			$\tau_n^c = s_p^c$ (Additionally $\tau_p^c \le s_p^c$)		
Ex. ss3 $* x = \&y$ $* x = \&z$	*(memory graph: x, y, z with ℓ_p, ℓ_n)*	$p: x \xrightarrow{2,0} y$ $n: x \xrightarrow{2,0} z$ *(irrelevant)*	**Ex. ts3** $x = \&y$ $z = x$	*(memory graph: x, y, z with ℓ_p, ℓ_n)*	$p: x \xrightarrow{1,0} y$ $n: z \xrightarrow{1,1} x$ $r: z \xrightarrow{1,0} y$

Fig. 6. Illustrating all exhaustive possibilities of SS and TS compositions (the pivot is x). Dashed edges are killed. Unmarked compositions are *relevant* and *useful* (Sect. 3); since the statements are consecutive, they are also *conclusive* (Sect. 3) and hence *desirable*.

it forsakes summarization. An edge composition is *desirable* if and only if it is *relevant*, *useful*, and *conclusive*. We define these properties below and explain them in the rest of the section.

(a) A composition $\boldsymbol{n} \circ \boldsymbol{p}$ is *relevant* only if it preserves flow-sensitivity.
(b) A composition $\boldsymbol{n} \circ \boldsymbol{p}$ is *useful* only if the *indlev* of the resulting edge does not exceed the *indlev* of $\boldsymbol{n}$.
(c) A composition $\boldsymbol{n} \circ \boldsymbol{p}$ is *conclusive* only when the information supplied by $\boldsymbol{p}$ used for reducing $\boldsymbol{n}$ is not likely to be invalidated by the intervening statements.

When the edge composition is *desirable*, we include $\boldsymbol{r}$ in the Δ being constructed, otherwise we include $\boldsymbol{n}$. In order to explain the *desirable* compositions, we use the following notation: Let ℓ_p denote a $(\mathbb{P}_p^c)^{th}$ pointee of pivot $\mathbb{P}$ accessed by $\boldsymbol{p}$ and ℓ_n denote a $(\mathbb{P}_n^c)^{th}$ pointee of $\mathbb{P}$ accessed by $\boldsymbol{n}$.

Relevant Edge Composition. An edge composition is *relevant* if it preserves flow-sensitivity. This requires the indirection levels in $\boldsymbol{n}$ to be reduced by using the points-to information in $\boldsymbol{p}$ (where $\boldsymbol{p}$ appears before $\boldsymbol{n}$ along a control flow path) but not vice-versa. The presence of a points-to path in memory (which is the transitive closure of the points-to edges) between ℓ_p and ℓ_n (denoted by $\ell_p \twoheadrightarrow \ell_n$ or $\ell_n \twoheadrightarrow \ell_p$) indicates that $\boldsymbol{p}$ can be used to resolve the indirection levels in $\boldsymbol{n}$.

Example 6. For $s_n^c < s_p^c$ in Fig. 6 (Ex. *ss1*), edge p updates the pointee of x and edge n redefines x. As shown in the memory graph, there is no path between ℓ_p and ℓ_n and hence y and z are unrelated rendering this composition *irrelevant*. Similarly, edge composition is *irrelevant* for $s_n^c = s_p^c$ (Ex. *ss3*).

For $s_n^c > s_p^c$ (Ex. *ss2*), $\ell_p \twoheadrightarrow \ell_n$ holds in the memory graph and hence this composition is *relevant*. For Ex. *ts1*, $\ell_n \twoheadrightarrow \ell_p$ holds; for *ts2*, $\ell_p \twoheadrightarrow \ell_n$ holds; for *ts3* both paths hold. Hence, all three compositions are *relevant*.   □

Useful Edge Composition. The *usefulness* of edge composition characterizes progress in conversion of the generalized points-to facts to the classical points-to facts. This requires the *indlev* (s_r^c, τ_r^c) of the reduced edge r to satisfy:

$$s_r^c \le s_n^c \wedge \tau_r^c \le \tau_n^c \tag{1}$$

Intuitively, this ensures that the *indlev* of the new source and the new target does not exceed the corresponding *indlev* in the original edge n.

Example 7. Consider Ex. *ts1* of Fig. 6, for $\tau_n^c < s_p^c$, $\ell_n \twoheadrightarrow \ell_p$ holds in the memory graph. Although this composition is *relevant*, it is not *useful* because the *indlev* of r exceeds the *indlev* of n. For this example, a *TS* composition will create an edge $z \xrightarrow{2,0} y$ whose *indlev* is higher than that of n ($z \xrightarrow{1,1} x$).   □

Thus, we need $\ell_p \twoheadrightarrow \ell_n$, and not $\ell_n \twoheadrightarrow \ell_p$, to hold in the memory graph for a *useful* edge composition. We can relate this with the *usefulness* criteria (Inequality 1). The presence of path $\ell_p \twoheadrightarrow \ell_n$ ensures that the *indlev* of edge r does not exceed that of n. The *usefulness* criteria (Inequality 1) reduces to $\tau_p^c \le s_p^c < s_n^c$ for *SS* composition and $\tau_p^c \le s_p^c \le \tau_n^c$ for *TS* composition.

From Fig. 6, we conclude that an edge composition is *relevant* and *useful* only if there exists a path $\ell_p \twoheadrightarrow \ell_n$ rather than $\ell_n \twoheadrightarrow \ell_p$. Intuitively, *such a path guarantees that the updates made by n do not invalidate the generalized points-to fact represented by p.* Hence, the two generalized points-to facts can be composed by using the pivot as a bridge to create a new generalized points-to fact represented by r.

Conclusive Edge Composition. Recall that $r = n \circ p$ is *relevant* and *useful* if we expect a path $\ell_p \twoheadrightarrow \ell_n$ in the memory. This composition is *conclusive* when location ℓ_p remains accessible from the pivot $\mathbb{P}$ in p when n is composed with p. Location ℓ_p may become inaccessible from $\mathbb{P}$ because of a combined effect of the statements in a calling context and the statements in the procedure being processed. Hence, the composition is *undesirable* and may lead to unsoundness if r is included in Δ instead of n.

Example 8. Line 6 in the code on the right indirectly defines a (because of the assignment on line 2) whereas line 7 directly defines a overwriting the value. Thus, x points to b and not c after line 8. When the GPG for procedure q is constructed, the relationship between y and a is not known. Thus, the composition of $n \equiv x \xrightarrow{1,2} y$ with $p \equiv y \xrightarrow{2,0} c$ results in $r \equiv x \xrightarrow{1,0} c$. Here ℓ_p is c, however it is not reachable from y anymore as the pointee of y is redefined by line 7.

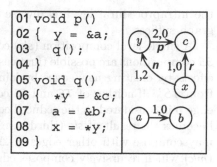

```
01 void p()
02 {   y = &a;
03     q();
04 }
05 void q()
06 {   *y = &c;
07     a = &b;
08     x = *y;
09 }
```

Since the calling context is not available during GPG construction, we are forced to retain edge n in the GPG, thereby missing an opportunity of reducing the *indlev* of n. Hence we propose the following condition for *conclusiveness*: The statements corresponding to p and n should be consecutive on every control flow *(a)* the intervening statements should not have an indirect assignment (e.g., $*x = \ldots$), and *(b)* the pointee of pivot $\mathbb{P}$ in edge p should have been found i.e., $\mathbb{P}_p^c = 1$.

In the example above, condition *(b)* is violated and hence we add $n \equiv x \xrightarrow{1,2} y$ to the GPG of procedure q instead of $r \equiv x \xrightarrow{1,0} c$. This avoids a greedy reduction of n when the available information is *inconclusive*.

4   Constructing GPGs at the Intraprocedural Level

In this section we define edge reduction, and GPG update; GPG composition is described in Sect. 5 which shows how procedure calls are handled.

4.1   Edge Reduction $n \circ \Delta$

Edge reduction $n \circ \Delta$ uses the edges in Δ to compute a set of edges whose *indlev*s do not exceed that of n (Definition 4). The results of SS and TS compositions are denoted by SS_Δ^n and TS_Δ^n which compute *relevant* and *useful* edge compositions; the *inconclusive* edge compositions are filtered out independently. The edge ordering is not required at

---

Definition 4: Edge reduction in Δ

$n \circ \Delta := mlc(\{n\}, \Delta)$

where

$$mlc(X, \Delta) := \begin{cases} X & slces(X, \Delta) = X \\ mlc(slces(X, \Delta), \Delta) & \text{Otherwise} \end{cases}$$

$$slces(X, \Delta) := \bigcup_{e \in X} slc(e, \Delta)$$

$$slc(n, \Delta) := \begin{cases} SS_\Delta^n \bowtie TS_\Delta^n & SS_\Delta^n \neq \emptyset, TS_\Delta^n \neq \emptyset \\ \{n\} & SS_\Delta^n = TS_\Delta^n = \emptyset \\ SS_\Delta^n \cup TS_\Delta^n & \text{Otherwise} \end{cases}$$

$$SS_\Delta^n := \{ n \circ p \mid p \in \Delta, S_n = S_p, T_p^c \leq s_p^c < s_n^c \}$$

$$TS_\Delta^n := \{ n \circ p \mid p \in \Delta, T_n = S_p, T_p^c \leq s_p^c \leq T_n^c \}$$

$$X \bowtie Y := \{ (S_n, (s_n^c, T_p^c), T_p) \mid n \in X, p \in Y \}$$

the intraprocedural level; a reverse post order traversal over the control flow graph suffices.

A single-level composition (slc) combines SS_Δ^n with TS_Δ^n. When both TS and SS compositions are possible (first case in slc), the join operator $\bowtie$ combines their effects by creating new edges by joining the sources from SS_Δ^n with the targets from TS_Δ^n. If neither of TS and SS compositions is possible (second case in slc), edge n is considered as the reduced edge. If only one of them is possible, its result becomes the result of slc (third case). Since the reduced edges computed by slc may compose with other edges in Δ, we extend slc to multi-level composition (mlc) which recursively composes edges in X with edges in Δ through function $slces$ which extends slc to a set of edges.

Example 9. When n represents a statement $x = *y$, we need multi-level compositions: The first-level composition identifies pointees of y while the second-level composition identifies the pointees of pointees of y. This is facilitated by function mlc. Consider the code snippet on the right. $\Delta = \{y \xrightarrow{1,0} a, a \xrightarrow{1,0} b\}$ for $n \equiv x \xrightarrow{1,2} y$ (statement s_3).

This involves two consecutive TS compositions. The first composition involves $y \xrightarrow{1,0} a$ as p resulting in $TS_\Delta^n = \{x \xrightarrow{1,1} a\}$ and $SS_\Delta^n = \emptyset$. This satisfies the third case of slc. Then, $slces$ is called with $X = \{x \xrightarrow{1,1} a\}$. The second TS composition between $x \xrightarrow{1,1} a$ (as a new n) and $a \xrightarrow{1,0} b$ (as p) results in a reduced edge $x \xrightarrow{1,0} b$. $slces$ is called again with $X = \{x \xrightarrow{1,0} b\}$ which returns X, satisfying the base condition of mlc. □

$$s_1 : y = \&a;$$
$$s_2 : a = \&b;$$
$$s_3 : x = *y;$$

Example 10. Single-level compositions are combined using $\bowtie$ when n represents $*x = y$.

For the code snippet on the right, SS_Δ^n returns $\{a \xrightarrow{1,1} y\}$ and TS_Δ^n returns $\{x \xrightarrow{2,0} b\}$ when n is $x \xrightarrow{2,1} y$ (for statement s_3). The join operator $\bowtie$ combines the effect of TS and SS compositions by combining the sources from SS_Δ^n and the targets from TS_Δ^n resulting in a reduced edge $r \equiv a \xrightarrow{1,0} b$. □

$$s_1 : x = \&a;$$
$$s_2 : y = \&b;$$
$$s_3 : *x = y;$$

4.2 Constructing GPGs $\Delta(u, v)$

For simplicity, we consider Δ only as a collection of edges, leaving the nodes implicit. Further, the edge ordering does not matter at the intraprocedural level and hence we treat Δ as a set of edges. The construction of Δ assigns sequence numbers in the order of inclusion of edges; these sequence numbers are maintained externally.

By default, the GPGs record the *may* information but a simple extension in the form of *boundary definitions* (described in the later part of this section) allows them to record the *must* information. This supports distinguishing between strong and weak updates and yet allows a simple set union to combine the information.

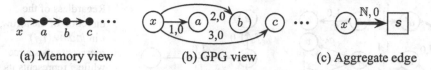

(a) Memory view   (b) GPG view   (c) Aggregate edge

Fig. 7. Aggregate edge for handling strong and weak updates. For this example, $s = \{a, b, c, \ldots\}$.

Definition 5 is an adaptation of Definition 1 for GPGs. Since Δ is viewed as a set of edges, the identity function Δ_{id} is $\emptyset$, meet operation is $\cup$, and $\Delta(\boldsymbol{u}, \boldsymbol{v})$ is the least fixed point of the equation in Definition 5. The com-

Definition 5: Construction of Δ

Assumption: $\boldsymbol{n}$ is $\delta(\boldsymbol{t}, \boldsymbol{v})$ and Δ is a set of edges

$$\Delta(\boldsymbol{u}, \boldsymbol{v}) := B(\boldsymbol{u}, \boldsymbol{v}) \ \cup \bigcup_{\substack{\boldsymbol{t}\, \in\, succ^+(\boldsymbol{u}) \\ \boldsymbol{v}\, \in\, succ(\boldsymbol{t})}} (\Delta(\boldsymbol{u}, \boldsymbol{t})) \,[\boldsymbol{n} \circ \Delta(\boldsymbol{u}, \boldsymbol{t})]$$

$$B(\boldsymbol{u}, \boldsymbol{v}) := \begin{cases} \boldsymbol{n} & \boldsymbol{v} \in succ(\boldsymbol{u}) \\ \emptyset & \text{otherwise} \end{cases}$$

where

$$\Delta[X] := (\Delta - conskill(X, \Delta)) \cup (X)$$
$$conskill(X, \Delta) := \{e_1 \mid e_1 \in match(e, \Delta), e \in X, |def(X)| = 1\}$$
$$match(e, \Delta) := \{e_1 \mid e_1 \in \Delta, \ S_e = S_{e_1}, \ s_e^c = s_{e_1}^c\}$$
$$def(X) := \{(S_e, s_e^c) \mid e \in X\}$$

position of a statement-level flow function ($\boldsymbol{n}$) with a summary flow function ($\Delta(\boldsymbol{u}, \boldsymbol{t})$) is performed by GPG update which includes all edges computed by edge reduction $\boldsymbol{n} \triangleright \Delta(\boldsymbol{u}, \boldsymbol{t})$; the edges to be removed are under-approximated when a strong update cannot be performed (described in the rest of the section). When a strong update is performed, we exclude those edges of Δ whose source and *indlev* match that of the shared source of the reduced edges (identified by $match(e, \Delta)$). For a weak update, $conskill(X, \Delta) = \emptyset$ and X contains reduced edges. For an *inconclusive* edge composition, $conskill(X, \Delta) = \emptyset$ and $X = \{\boldsymbol{n}\}$.

Extending Δ to Support Strong Updates. Conventionally, points-to information is killed based on the following criteria: An assignment $x = \ldots$ removes all points-to facts $x \rightarrow \cdot$ whereas an assignment $*x = \ldots$ removes all points-to facts $y \rightarrow \cdot$ where x *must*-points-to y; the latter represents a *strong update*. When x *may*-points-to y, no points-to facts can be removed representing a *weak update*.

Observe that the use of points-to information for strong updates is inherently captured by edge reduction. In particular, the use of edge reduction allows us to model both of the above criteria for edge removal uniformly as follows: the reduced edges should define the same pointer (or the same pointee of a given pointer) along every control flow path reaching the statement represented by $\boldsymbol{n}$. This is captured by the requirement $|def(X)| = 1$.

When $|def(X)| > 1$, the reduced edges define multiple pointers (or different pointees of the same pointer) leading to a weak update resulting in no removal of edges from Δ. When $|def(X)| = 1$, all reduced edges define the same pointer (or the same pointee of a given pointer). However, this is necessary but not sufficient

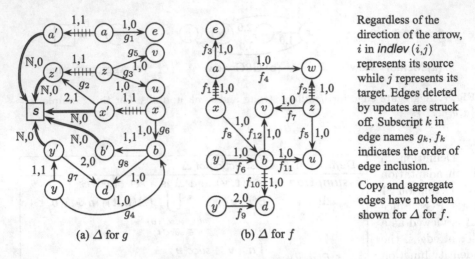

(a) Δ for g (b) Δ for f

Regardless of the direction of the arrow, i in *indlev* (i,j) represents its source while j represents its target. Edges deleted by updates are struck off. Subscript k in edge names g_k, f_k indicates the order of edge inclusion.

Copy and aggregate edges have not been shown for Δ for f.

Fig. 8. Δ for procedures f and g of Figure 1.

for a strong update because the pointer may not be defined along all the paths—there may be a path which does not contribute to $def(X)$. We refer to such paths as definition-free paths for that particular pointer (or some pointee of a pointer). The possibility of such a path makes it difficult to distinguish between strong and weak updates.

Since a pointer x or its transitive pointees may be defined along some control flow path from **u** to **v**, we eliminate the possibility of definition-free paths from **u** to **v** by introducing *boundary definitions* of the following two kinds at **u**: *(a)* a pointer assignment $x = x'$ where x' is a symbolic representation of the initial value of x at **u** (called the *upwards exposed* version of x), and *(b)* a set of assignments representing the relation between x' and its transitive pointees. They are represented by special GPG edges—the first, by a *copy edge* $x \xrightarrow{1,1} x'$ and the others, by an *aggregate* edge $x' \xrightarrow{N,0} s$ where $\mathbb{N}$ is the set of all possible *indlev* s and **s** is the summary node representing all possible pointees. As illustrated in Fig. 7, $x' \xrightarrow{N,0} s$ is a collection of GPG edges (Fig. 7(b)) representing the relation between x with it transitive pointees at **u** (Fig. 7(a)).

A reduced edge $x \xrightarrow{1,j} y$ along any path from **u** to **v** removes the copy edge $x \xrightarrow{1,1} x'$ indicating that x is redefined. A reduced edge $x \xrightarrow{i,j} y$, $i > 1$ modifies the aggregate edge $x' \xrightarrow{N,0} s$ to $x' \xrightarrow{(\mathbb{N}-\{i\}),0} s$ indicating that $(i-1)^{th}$ pointees of x are redefined.

The inclusion of aggregate and copy edges guarantees that $|def(X)| = 1$ only when the source is defined along every path. This leads to a necessary and sufficient condition for strong updates. Note that the copy and aggregate edges improve the precision of analysis and are not required for its soundness.

Example 11. Consider the construction of Δ_g as illustrated in Fig. 8(c). Edge g_1 created for line 8 of the program, kills edge $a \xrightarrow{1,1} a'$ because $|def(\{g_1\})| = 1$. For line 10, since the pointees of x and z are not available in g, edge g_2 is created from x' to z'; this involves composition of $x \xrightarrow{2,1} z$ with the edges $x \xrightarrow{1,1} x'$ and $z \xrightarrow{1,1} z'$. Edges g_3, g_4, g_5 and g_6 correspond to lines 11, 13, 14, and 16 respectively.

The $z \xrightarrow{1,1} z'$ edge is killed along both paths (lines 11 and 14) and hence is struck off in Δ_g, indicating z is *must*-defined. On the other hand, $y \xrightarrow{1,1} y'$ is killed only along one of the two paths and hence is retained by the control flow merge just before line 16. Similarly $x' \xrightarrow{2,0} s$ in the aggregate edge is retained indicating that pointee of x is not defined along all paths. Edge g_6 kills $x \xrightarrow{1,1} x'$. Line 17 creates edges g_7 and g_8; this is a weak update because y has multiple pointees ($|def(\{g_7, g_8\})| \neq 1$). Hence $b \xrightarrow{1,1} b'$ is not removed. Similarly, $y' \xrightarrow{2,0} s$ in the aggregate edge $y' \xrightarrow{N,0} s$ is not removed. □

5   Constructing GPGs at the Interprocedural Level

Definition 6 shows the construction of GPGs at the interprocedural level by handling procedure calls. Consider a procedure f containing a call to g between two consecutive program points **u** and **v**. Let $Start_g$ and End_g denote the start and the end points of g. Δ representing the control flow paths from $Start_f$ to **u** (i.e., just before the call to g) is $\Delta(Start_f, \boldsymbol{u})$; we denote it by Δ_f for brevity. Δ for the body of procedure g is $\Delta(Start_g, End_g)$; we denote it by Δ_g.

Since GPGs are sequences of edges, $\Delta_g \circ \Delta_f$ involves selecting an edge e in order from Δ_g and performing an update $\Delta_f[e \circ \Delta_f]$. We then update the resulting Δ with the next edge from Δ_g. This is repeated until all edges of Δ_g are exhausted. The update of Δ_f with an edge e from Δ_g involves the following: *(a)* substituting the callee's upwards exposed variable x' occurring in Δ_g by the caller's original variable x in Δ_f, *(b)* including the reduced edges $e \circ \Delta_f$, and *(c)* performing a strong or weak update.

A copy edge $x \xrightarrow{1,1} x' \in \Delta$ implies that x has not been defined along some path. Similarly, an aggregate edge $x' \xrightarrow{N,0} s \in \Delta$ implies that some $(i-1)^{th}$ pointees of x, $i > 1$ have not been defined along some path. We use these to define $mustdef(x \xrightarrow{i,j} y, \Delta)$ which asserts that the $(i-1)^{th}$ pointees of x, $i > 1$ are defined along every control flow path. We combine it with $def(x \xrightarrow{i,j} y \circ \Delta)$ to define *callsup* for identifying strong updates. Note that we need *mustdef* only at the interprocedural level and not at the intraprocedural level. This is because, when we use Δ_g to compute Δ_f, performing a strong update requires knowing whether the source of an edge in Δ_g has been defined along every control flow path in g. However, we do not have the control flow information of g when we analyze f. When a strong update is performed, we delete all edges in Δ_f that match $e \circ \Delta_f$. These edges are discovered by taking a union of $match(e_1, \Delta_f)$, $\forall e_1 \in (e \circ \Delta_f)$.

Definition 6: Δ for a call $g()$ in procedure f

/* let Δ_f denote $\Delta(Start_f, \boldsymbol{u})$ and Δ_g denote $\Delta(Start_g, End_g)$ */

$\Delta(Start_f, \boldsymbol{v}) := \Delta_g \circ \Delta_f$

$\Delta_g \circ \Delta_f := \Delta_f[\Delta_g]$
where /* let Δ_g be $\{e_1, e_2, \ldots e_k\}$ */

$\qquad \Delta_f[\Delta_g] := \Delta_f[e_1, \Delta_g][e_2, \Delta_g]\ldots[e_k, \Delta_g]$

$\qquad \Delta_f[e, \Delta_g] := (\Delta_f - callkill(e, \Delta_f, \Delta_g)) \cup (e \circ \Delta_f)$

$callkill(e, \Delta_f, \Delta_g) := \{e_2 \mid e_2 \in match(e_1, \Delta_f),\ e_1 \in e \circ \Delta_f,\ callsup(e, \Delta_f, \Delta_g)\}$

$callsup(e, \Delta_f, \Delta_g) := (|def(e \circ \Delta_f)| = 1) \wedge mustdef(e, \Delta_g)$

$mustdef(x \xrightarrow{i,j} y, \Delta) \Leftrightarrow (x \xrightarrow{i,k} z \in \Delta \Rightarrow k = j \wedge z = y) \wedge$
$\qquad\qquad\qquad\qquad\quad ((i > 1 \wedge x' \xrightarrow{i,0} s \notin \Delta) \vee (i = 1 \wedge x \xrightarrow{1,1} x' \notin \Delta))$

The total order imposed by the sequence of GPG edges is interpreted as a partial order as follows: Since the edges from Δ_g are added one by one, if the edge to be added involves an upwards exposed variable x', it should be composed with an original edge in Δ_f rather than a reduced edge included in Δ_f created by $e_1 \circ \Delta_f$ for some $e_1 \in \Delta_g$. Further, it is possible that an edge e_2 may kill an already added edge e_1 that coexisted with it in Δ_g. However, this should be prohibited because their coexistence in Δ_g indicates that they are *may* edges. This is ensured by checking the presence of multiple edges with the same source in Δ_g. For example, edge f_7 of Fig. 8(d) does not kill f_5 as they coexist in Δ_g.

Example 12. Consider the construction of Δ_f as illustrated in Fig. 8(d). Edges f_1 and f_2 correspond to lines 2 and 3. The call on line 4 causes the composition of $\Delta_f = \{f_1, f_2\}$ with Δ_g selecting edges in the order $g_1, g_2, \ldots, g_8$. The edges from Δ_g with their corresponding names in Δ_f (denoted name-in-g/name-in-f) are: g_1/f_3, g_3/f_5, g_4/f_6, g_5/f_7, g_6/f_8, g_7/f_9, and g_8/f_{10}. Edge f_4 is created by SS and TS compositions of g_2 with f_1 and f_2. Although x has a single pointee (along edge f_1), the resulting update is a weak update because the source of g_2 is *may*-defined indicated by the presence of $x' \xrightarrow{2,0} s$ in the aggregate edge $x' \xrightarrow{N,0} s$.

Edges g_3/f_5 and g_5/f_7 together kill f_2. Note that the inclusion of f_7 does not kill f_5 because they both are from Δ_g. Finally, the edge for line 5 $(x \xrightarrow{2,1} z)$ undergoes an SS composition (with f_8) and TS compositions (with f_5 and f_7). This creates edges f_{11} and f_{12}. Since $x \xrightarrow{2,1} z$ is accompanied by the aggregate edge $x' \xrightarrow{N-\{2\},0} s$ indicating that the pointee of x is *must*-defined, and x has a single pointee (edge f_8), this is a strong update killing edge f_{10}. Observe that all edges in Δ_f represent classical points-to facts except f_9. We need the pointees of y from the callers of f to reduce f_9. □

For recursive calls, the Δ for a callee may not have been computed because of a cycle in the call graph. This is handled in the usual manner [9,21] by over-approximating initial Δ that computes $\top$ for *may* points-to analysis (which is $\emptyset$). Such an initial GPG, denoted $\Delta_\top$ (Definition 3), kills all points-to relations and generates none. $\Delta_\top$ is not expressible as a GPG and is not a natural $\top$ element of the meet semi-lattice [9] of GPGs. The identity GPG Δ_{id} represents an empty set of edges because it does not generate or kill points-to information. For more details, please see [4].

6 Computing Points-To Information Using GPGs

Recall that the points-to information is represented by a memory M. We define two operations to compute a new memory M' using a GPG or a GPG edge from a given memory M.

- An *edge application* $[\![e]\!]M$ computes memory M' by incorporating the effect of GPG edge $e \equiv x \xrightarrow{i,j} y$ in memory M. This involves inclusion of edges described by the set $\left\{ w \xrightarrow{1,0} z \mid w \in M^{i-1}\{x\}, \ z \in M^j\{y\} \right\}$ in M' and removal of edges by distinguishing between a strong and a weak update. The edges to be removed are characterized much along the lines of *callkill*.
- A *GPG application* $[\![\Delta]\!]M$ applies the GPG Δ to M and computes the resulting memory M' using edge application iteratively.

Let PT_v denote the points-to information at program point v in procedure f. Then, PT_v can be computed by *(a)* computing *boundary information* of f (denoted BI_f) associated with $Start_f$, and *(b)* computing the points-to information at v from BI_f by incorporating the effect of all paths from $Start_f$ to v.

BI_f is computed as the union of the points-to information reaching f from all of its call points. For the main function, BI is computed from static initializations. In the presence of recursion, a fixed point computation is required for computing BI.

If v is $Start_f$, then $PT_v = BI_f$. For other program points, PT_v can be computed from BI_f in the following ways; both of them compute identical PT_v.

(a) *Using statement-level flow function (Stmt-ff):* Let $stmt(u, v)$ denote the statement between u and v. If it is a non-call statement, let its flow function $\delta(u, v)$ be represented by the GPG edge n. Then PT_v is computed as the least fixed point of the following data flow equations.

$$In_{u,v} = \begin{cases} [\![\Delta(Start_q, End_q)]\!]PT_u & stmt(u, v) = call\ q \\ [\![n]\!]PT_u & \text{otherwise} \end{cases}$$

$$PT_u = \bigcup_{u \in pred(v)} In_{u,v}$$

(b) *Using GPGs:* PT_v is computed using GPG application $[\![\Delta(Start_f, v)]\!]BI_f$. This approach of PT_v computation is oblivious to intraprocedural control flow and does not involve fixed point computation for loops.

Our measurements show that the *Stmt-ff* approach takes much less time than using GPGs for PT_v computation. This may appear surprising because the *Stmt-ff* approach requires an additional fixed point computation for handling loops which is not required in case of GPGs. However, using GPGs requires more time because the GPG at **v** represents a cumulative effect of the statement-level flow functions from *Start_f* to **v**. Hence the GPGs tend to become larger with the length of a control flow path. Thus computing PT_v using GPGs for multiple consecutive statements involves redundant computations.

Bypassing of *BI*. Our measurements show that using the entire *BI* of a procedure may be expensive because many points-to pairs reaching a call may not be accessed by the callee procedure. Thus the efficiency of analysis can be enhanced significantly by filtering out the points-to information which is irrelevant to a procedure but merely passes through it unchanged. This concept of *bypassing* has been successfully used for data flow values of scalars [15,16]. GPGs support this naturally for pointers with the help of upwards exposed versions of variables. An upwards exposed version in a GPG indicates that there is a use of a variable in the procedure which requires pointee information from the callers. Thus, the points-to information of such a variable is relevant and should be a part of *BI*. For variables that do not have their corresponding upwards exposed versions in a GPG, their points-to information is irrelevant and can be discarded from the *BI* of the procedure, effectively bypassing its calls.

7   Implementation and Measurements

We have implemented GPG based points-to analysis in GCC 4.7.2 using the LTO framework and have carried out measurements on SPEC CPU2006 benchmarks on a machine with 16 GB RAM with 8 64-bit Intel i7-4770 CPUs running at 3.40 GHz. Figure 9 provides the empirical data.

Our method eliminates local variables using the SSA form and GPGs are computed only for global variables. Eventually, the points-to information for local variables is computed from that of global variables and parameters. Our implementation over-approximates an array by treating it as a single variable and maintains its information flow-insensitively. Heap memory is approximated by maintaining indirection lists of field dereferences of length 2 (see [4]). Unlike the conventional approaches [25,27,28], our summary flow functions do not depend on aliasing at the call points. The actually observed number of aliasing patterns (column S in Fig. 9) suggests that it is undesirable to indiscriminately construct multiple PTFs for a procedure.

Columns A, B, P, and Q present the details of the benchmarks. Column C provides the time required for the first phase of our analysis i.e., computing GPGs. The computation of points-to information at each program point has four variants (using GPGs or *Stmt-ff* with or without bypassing). Their time measurements are provided in columns D, E, F, and G. Our data indicates

Table 1. Columns grouped as: *Time for GPG based approach (in seconds)* — GPG Constr. (C), *computing points-to info*: GPG NoByp (D), GPG Byp (E), Stmt-ff NoByp (F), Stmt-ff Byp (G); *Avg. # of pointees per pointer* — GPG: G/NoByp per stmt (H), G/Byp per stmt (I), L+Arr per proc (J); GCC: G+L+Arr per proc (K); LFCPA: G+L+Arr per stmt (L); *Avg. # of pointees per dereference* — GPG (M), GCC (N), LFCPA (O).

Program	kLoC	# of pointer stmts	GPG Constr.	GPG NoByp	GPG Byp	Stmt-ff NoByp	Stmt-ff Byp	G/NoByp	G/Byp	L+Arr	GCC G+L+Arr	LFCPA G+L+Arr	GPG	GCC	LFCPA
	A	B	C	D	E	F	G	H	I	J	K	L	M	N	O
lbm	0.9	370	0.10	0.22	0.21	0.26	0.28	1.31	1.42	2.21	17.74	0.05	1.09	2.25	1.50
mcf	1.6	480	75.29	33.73	30.05	1.25	0.91	18.73	6.10	10.48	34.74	1.22	4.25	2.57	0.62
libquantum	2.6	340	6.47	10.23	1.95	8.21	1.85	139.50	22.50	1.11	4.49	3.34	1.50	2.93	0.83
bzip2	5.7	1650	3.17	11.11	8.71	4.73	3.30	43.39	8.38	1.89	31.46	0.94	1.72	2.94	0.33
milc	9.5	2540	7.36	6.08	5.89	4.29	5.61	21.15	16.32	4.52	14.06	31.73	1.18	2.58	1.61
sjeng	10.5	700	9.36	39.66	25.75	14.75	7.56	445.22	64.81	3.07	2.68	-	0.98	2.71	-
hmmer	20.6	6790	38.23	51.73	14.86	31.32	13.50	43.49	5.85	6.05	59.35	1.56	1.04	3.62	0.91
h264ref	36.1	17770	208.47	1262.07	199.34	457.26	74.62	219.71	9.24	16.29	98.84	-	0.98	3.97	-
gobmk	158.0	212830	652.78	3652.99	1624.46	1582.62	1373.88	11.98	1.73	6.34	4.08	-	0.65	3.71	-

Table 2. Columns grouped as: # of call sites (P); # of procs. (Q); *Proc. count for different buckets of # of calls (reuse of GPGs)* — 2-5 (R), 5-10, 10-20, 20+; *# of procs. requiring different no. of PTFs based on the no. of aliasing patterns* — Actually observed: 2-5 (S), 6-10, 11-15, 15+; Predicted: 2-5 (T), 15+; *# of procs. for different sizes of GPG in terms of the number of edges* — 0 (U), 1-2, 3-4, 5-8, 9-50, 50+; *# of procs. for different % of context ind. info. (for non-empty GPGs)* — <20 (V), 20-40, 40-60, 60+; *# of inconclusive compositions* (W).

Program	# of call sites	# of procs.	2-5	5-10	10-20	20+	2-5	6-10	11-15	15+	2-5	15+	0	1-2	3-4	5-8	9-50	50+	<20	20-40	40-60	60+	W
	P	Q	R				S				T		U						V				W
lbm	30	19	5	0	0	0	8	0	0	0	13	0	13	4	2	0	0	0	0	0	3	3	0
mcf	29	23	11	0	0	0	0	0	0	0	4	4	10	5	2	3	2	1	1	5	1	6	1
libquantum	277	80	24	11	4	3	7	3	1	0	14	4	42	10	7	12	9	0	12	20	1	5	0
bzip2	288	89	35	7	2	1	22	0	0	0	28	2	62	13	4	5	5	0	0	26	0	1	1
milc	782	190	60	15	9	9	37	8	0	1	35	25	157	11	19	2	7	0	10	6	3	14	3
sjeng	726	133	46	20	5	6	14	3	1	3	10	14	99	20	6	3	5	0	4	3	10	17	0
hmmer	1328	275	93	33	22	11	62	5	3	4	88	32	167	56	20	15	15	2	20	54	11	23	4
h264ref	2393	566	171	60	22	16	85	17	5	3	102	46	419	76	23	15	30	3	13	54	27	53	8
gobmk	9379	2697	317	110	99	134	206	30	9	10	210	121	1374	93	8	1083	97	42	41	1192	39	51	0

Fig. 9. Time, precision, size, and effectiveness measurements for GPG Based Points-to Analysis. Byp (Bypassing), NoByp (No Bypassing), Stmt-ff (Statement-level flow functions), G (Global pointers), L (Local pointers), Arr (Array pointers).

that the most efficient method for computing points-to information is to use statement-level flow functions and bypassing (column G).

Our analysis computes points-to information flow-sensitively for globals. The following points-to information is stored flow-insensitively: locals (because they are in the SSA form) and arrays (because their updates are conservative). Hence, we have separate columns for globals (columns H and I) and locals+arrays (column J) for GPGs. GCC-PTA computes points-to information flow-insensitively (column K) whereas LFCPA computes it flow-sensitively (column L).

The second table provides measurements about the effectiveness of summary flow functions in terms of *(a)* compactness of GPGs, *(b)* percentage of context independent information, and *(c)* reusability. Column U shows that GPGs are empty for a large number of procedures. Besides, in six out of nine benchmarks, most procedures with non-empty GPGs have a significantly high percentage of context independent information (column V). Thus a top-down approach may involve redundant computations on multiple visits to a procedure whereas a bottom-up approach may not need much work for incorporating the effect of a callee's GPG into that of its callers. Further, many procedures are called multiple times indicating a high reuse of GPGs (column R).

The effectiveness of bypassing is evident from the time measurements (columns E and G) as well as a reduction in the average number of points-to pairs (column I).

We have compared our analysis with GCC-PTA and LFCPA [11]. The number of points-to pairs per function for GCC-PTA (column K) is large because it is partially flow-sensitive (because of the SSA form) and context-insensitive. The number of points-to pairs per statements is much smaller for LFCPA (column L) because it is liveness-based. However LFCPA which in our opinion represents the state of the art in fully flow- and context-sensitive exhaustive points-to analysis, does not seem to scale beyond 35 kLoC. We have computed the average number of pointees of dereferenced variables which is maximum for GCC-PTA (column N) and minimum for LFCPA (column O) because it is liveness driven. The points-to information computed by these methods is incomparable because they employ radically dissimilar features of points-to information such as flow- and context-sensitivity, liveness, and bypassing.

8   Related Work

Section 1 introduced two broad categories of constructing summary flow functions for pointer analysis. Some methods using placeholders require aliasing information in the calling contexts and construct multiple summary flow functions per procedure [25, 28]. Other methods do not make any assumptions about the calling contexts [12, 13, 20, 23, 24] but they construct larger summary flow functions causing inefficiency in fixed point computation at the intraprocedural level thereby prohibiting flow-sensitivity for scalability. Also, these methods cannot perform strong updates thereby losing precision.

Among the general frameworks for constructing procedure summaries, the formalism proposed by Sharir and Pnueli [21] is limited to finite lattices of data flow values. It was implemented using graph reachability in [14, 18, 19]. A general technique for constructing procedure summaries [5] has been applied to unary uninterpreted functions and linear arithmetic. However, the program model does not include pointers.

Symbolic procedure summaries [25, 27] involve computing preconditions and corresponding postconditions (in terms of aliases). A calling context is matched against a precondition and the corresponding postcondition gives the result. However, the number of calling contexts in a program could be unbounded hence constructing summaries for all calling contexts could lose scalability. This method requires statement-level transformers to be closed under composition; a requirement which is not satisfied by pointer analysis (as mentioned in Sect. 1). We overcome this problem using generalized points-to facts. Saturn [6] also creates summaries that are sound but may not be precise across applications because they depend on context information.

Some approaches use customized summaries and combine the top-down and bottom-up analyses to construct summaries for only those calling contexts that occur in a given program [28]. This choice is controlled by the number of times a procedure is called. If this number exceeds a fixed threshold, a summary is constructed using the information of the calling contexts that have been recorded for that procedure. A new calling context may lead to generating a new precondition and hence a new summary.

9   Conclusions and Future Work

Constructing bounded summary flow functions for flow and context-sensitive points-to analysis seems hard because it requires modelling unknown locations accessed indirectly through pointers—a callee procedure's summary flow function is created without looking at the statements in the caller procedures. Conventionally, they have been modelled using placeholders. However, a fundamental problem with the placeholders is that they explicate the unknown locations by naming them. This results in either *(a)* a large number of placeholders, or *(b)* multiple summary flow functions for different aliasing patterns in the calling contexts. We propose the concept of generalized points-to graph (GPG) whose edges track indirection levels and represent generalized points-to facts. A simple arithmetic on indirection levels allows composing generalized points-to facts to create new generalized points-to facts with smaller indirection levels; this reduces them progressively to classical points-to facts. Since unknown locations are left implicit, no information about aliasing patterns in the calling contexts is required allowing us to construct a single GPG per procedure. GPGs are linearly bounded by the number of variables, are flow-sensitive, and are able to perform strong updates within calling contexts. Further, GPGs inherently support bypassing of irrelevant points-to information thereby aiding scalability significantly.

Our measurements on SPEC benchmarks show that GPGs are small enough to scale fully flow and context-sensitive exhaustive points-to analysis to programs as large as 158 kLoC (as compared to 35 kLoC of LFCPA [11]). We expect to scale the method to still larger programs by *(a)* using memoisation, and *(b)* constructing and applying GPGs incrementally thereby eliminating redundancies within fixed point computations.

Observe that a GPG edge $x \xrightarrow{i,j} y$ in M also asserts an alias relation between $M^i\{x\}$ and $M^j\{y\}$ and hence GPGs generalize both points-to and alias relations.

The concept of GPG provides a useful abstraction of memory involving pointers. The way matrices represent values as well as transformations, GPGs represent memory as well as memory transformers defined in terms of loading, storing, and copying memory addresses. Any analysis that is influenced by these operations may be able to use GPGs by combining them with the original abstractions of the analysis. We plan to explore this direction in the future.

Acknowledgments. We are grateful to anonymous reviewers for incisive comments which helped in improving the paper significantly. The paper has benefited from the feedback of many people; in particular, Supratik Chakraborty and Sriram Srinivasan gave excellent suggestions for improving the accessibility of the paper. Our ideas have also benefited from discussions with Amitabha Sanyal, Supratim Biswas, and Venkatesh Chopella. The seeds of GPGs were explored in a very different form in the Master's thesis of Shubhangi Agrawal in 2010.

References

1. Beyer, D., Henzinger, T.A., Théoduloz, G.: Configurable software verification: concretizing the convergence of model checking and program analysis. In: Damm, W., Hermanns, H. (eds.) CAV 2007. LNCS, vol. 4590, pp. 504–518. Springer, Heidelberg (2007)
2. Dillig, I., Dillig, T., Aiken, A.: Sound, complete and scalable path-sensitive analysis. In: Proceedings of the 29th ACM SIGPLAN Conference on Programming Language Design and Implementation, PLDI 2008. ACM, New York (2008)
3. Feng, Y., Wang, X., Dillig, I., Dillig, T.: Bottom-up context-sensitive pointer analysis for Java. In: Feng, X., Park, S. (eds.) APLAS 2015. LNCS, vol. 9458, pp. 465–484. Springer, Heidelberg (2015). doi:10.1007/978-3-319-26529-2_25
4. Gharat, P.M., Khedker, U.P.: Flow and context sensitive points-to analysis using generalized points-to graphs. CoRR (2016). arXiv:1603.09597
5. Gulwani, S., Tiwari, A.: Computing procedure summaries for interprocedural analysis. In: De Nicola, R. (ed.) ESOP 2007. LNCS, vol. 4421, pp. 253–267. Springer, Heidelberg (2007)
6. Hackett, B., Aiken, A.: How is aliasing used in systems software? In: Proceedings of the 14th ACM SIGSOFT International Symposium on Foundations of Software Engineering, SIGSOFT 2006/FSE-14. ACM, New York (2006)
7. Heintze, N., Tardieu, O.: Demand-driven pointer analysis. In: Proceedings of the ACM SIGPLAN 2001 Conference on Programming Language Design and Implementation, PLDI 2001. ACM, New York (2001)
8. Jhala, R., Majumdar, R.: Software model checking. ACM Comput. Surv. **41**(4), 21:1–21:54 (2009)
9. Khedker, U.P., Sanyal, A., Sathe, B.: Data Flow Analysis: Theory and Practice. Taylor & Francis (CRC Press, Inc.), Boca Raton (2009)

10. Khedker, U.P., Karkare, B.: Efficiency, precision, simplicity, and generality in inter-procedural data flow analysis: Resurrecting the classical call strings method. In: Hendren, L. (ed.) CC 2008. LNCS, vol. 4959, pp. 213–228. Springer, Heidelberg (2008)

11. Khedker, U.P., Mycroft, A., Rawat, P.S.: Liveness-based pointer analysis. In: Miné, A., Schmidt, D. (eds.) SAS 2012. LNCS, vol. 7460, pp. 265–282. Springer, Heidelberg (2012)

12. Li, L., Cifuentes, C., Keynes, N.: Precise and scalable context-sensitive pointer analysis via value flow graph. In: Proceedings of the 2013 International Symposium on Memory Management, ISMM 2013. ACM, New York (2013)

13. Madhavan, R., Ramalingam, G., Vaswani, K.: Modular heap analysis for higher-order programs. In: Miné, A., Schmidt, D. (eds.) SAS 2012. LNCS, vol. 7460, pp. 370–387. Springer, Heidelberg (2012)

14. Naeem, N.A., Lhoták, O., Rodriguez, J.: Practical extensions to the IFDS algorithm. In: Gupta, R. (ed.) CC 2010. LNCS, vol. 6011, pp. 124–144. Springer, Heidelberg (2010)

15. Hakjoo, O., Heo, K., Lee, W., Lee, W., Yi, K.: Design and implementation of sparse global analyses for C-like languages. In: ACM SIGPLAN Conference on Programming Language Design and Implementation, PLDI 2012, Beijing, China, 11–16 June 2012

16. Hakjoo, O., Lee, W., Heo, K., Yang, H., Yi, K.: Selective context-sensitivity guided by impact pre-analysis. In: ACM SIGPLAN Conference on Programming Language Design and Implementation, PLDI 2014, Edinburgh, UK, 09–11 June 2014

17. Padhye, R., Khedker, U.P.: Interprocedural data flow analysis in SOOT using value contexts. In: Proceedings of the 2nd ACM SIGPLAN International Workshop on State Of the Art in Java Program Analysis, SOAP 2013. ACM, New York (2013)

18. Reps, T., Horwitz, S., Sagiv, M.: Precise interprocedural dataflow analysis via graph reachability. In: Proceedings of the 22nd ACM SIGPLAN-SIGACT Symposium on Principles of Programming Languages, POPL 1995. ACM, New York (1995)

19. Sagiv, M., Reps, T., Horwitz, S.: Precise interprocedural dataflow analysis with applications to constant propagation. In: Selected Papers from the 6th International Joint Conference on Theory and Practice of Software Development, TAPSOFT 1995. Elsevier Science Publishers B. V., Amsterdam (1996)

20. Shang, L., Xie, X., Xue, J.: On-demand dynamic summary-based points-to analysis. In: Proceedings of the Tenth International Symposium on Code Generation and Optimization, CGO 2012. ACM, New York (2012)

21. Sharir, M., Pnueli, A.: Two approaches to interprocedural data flow analysis. In: Muchnick, S.S., Jones, N.D. (eds.) Program Flow Analysis: Theory and Applications, Chap. 7 (1981)

22. Sridharan, M., Gopan, D., Shan, L., Bodík, R.: Demand-driven points-to analysis for Java. In: Proceedings of the 20th Annual ACM SIGPLAN Conference on Object-oriented Programming, Systems, Languages, and Applications, OOPSLA 2005. ACM, New York (2005)

23. Sălcianu, A., Rinard, M.: Purity and side effect analysis for Java programs. In: Cousot, R. (ed.) VMCAI 2005. LNCS, vol. 3385, pp. 199–215. Springer, Heidelberg (2005)

24. Whaley, J., Rinard, M.: Compositional pointer and escape analysis for Java programs. In: Proceedings of the 14th ACM SIGPLAN Conference on Object-oriented Programming, Systems, Languages, and Applications, OOPSLA 1999. ACM, New York (1999)

25. Wilson, R.P., Lam, M.S.: Efficient context-sensitive pointer analysis for C programs. In: Proceedings of the ACM SIGPLAN Conference on Programming Language Design and Implementation, PLDI 1995 (1995)
26. Yan, D., Guoqing, X., Rountev, A.: Rethinking SOOT for summary-based whole-program analysis. In: Proceedings of the ACM SIGPLAN International Workshop on State of the Art in Java Program Analysis, SOAP 2012. ACM, New York (2012)
27. Yorsh, G., Yahav, E., Chandra, S.: Generating precise and concise procedure summaries. In: Proceedings of the 35th Annual ACM SIGPLAN-SIGACT Symposium on Principles of Programming Languages, POPL 2008. ACM, New York (2008)
28. Zhang, X., Mangal, R., Naik, M., Yang, H.: Hybrid top-down and bottom-up interprocedural analysis. In: Proceedings of the 35th ACM SIGPLAN Conference on Programming Language Design and Implementation, PLDI 2014. ACM, New York (2014)

Learning a Variable-Clustering Strategy for Octagon from Labeled Data Generated by a Static Analysis

Kihong Heo[1]([✉]), Hakjoo Oh[2]([✉]), and Hongseok Yang[3]

[1] Seoul National University, Seoul, Korea
khheo@ropas.snu.ac.kr
[2] Korea University, Seoul, Korea
hakjoo_oh@korea.ac.kr
[3] University of Oxford, Oxford, UK
hongseok.yang@cs.ox.ac.uk

Abstract. We present a method for automatically learning an effective strategy for clustering variables for the Octagon analysis from a given codebase. This learned strategy works as a preprocessor of Octagon. Given a program to be analyzed, the strategy is first applied to the program and clusters variables in it. We then run a partial variant of the Octagon analysis that tracks relationships among variables within the same cluster, but not across different clusters. The notable aspect of our learning method is that although the method is based on supervised learning, it does not require manually-labeled data. The method does not ask human to indicate which pairs of program variables in the given codebase should be tracked. Instead it uses the impact pre-analysis for Octagon from our previous work and automatically labels variable pairs in the codebase as positive or negative. We implemented our method on top of a static buffer-overflow detector for C programs and tested it against open source benchmarks. Our experiments show that the partial Octagon analysis with the learned strategy scales up to 100KLOC and is 33x faster than the one with the impact pre-analysis (which itself is significantly faster than the original Octagon analysis), while increasing false alarms by only 2 %.

1 Introduction

Relational program analyses track sophisticated relationships among program variables and enable the automatic verification of complex properties of programs [3,8]. However, the computational costs of various operations of these analyses are high so that vanilla implementations of the analyses do not scale even to moderate-sized programs. For example, transfer functions of the Octagon analysis [8] have a cubic worst-case time complexity in the number of program variables, which makes it impossible to analyze large programs.

In this paper, we consider one of the most popular optimizations used by practical relational program analyses, called variable clustering [1,8,15,26]. Given a

© Springer-Verlag GmbH Germany 2016
X. Rival (Ed.): SAS 2016, LNCS 9837, pp. 237–256, 2016.
DOI: 10.1007/978-3-662-53413-7_12

program, an analyzer with this optimization forms multiple relatively-small sub-sets of variables, called variable clusters or clusters. Then, it limits the tracked information to the relationships among variables within each cluster, not across those clusters. So far strategies based on simple syntactic or semantic criteria have been used for clustering variables for a given program, but they are not sat-isfactory. They are limited to a specific class of target programs [1,26] or employ a pre-analysis that is cheaper than a full relational analysis but frequently takes order-of-magnitude more time than the non-relational analysis for medium-sized programs [15].

In this paper, we propose a new method for automatically learning a variable-clustering strategy for the Octagon analysis from a given codebase. When applied to a program, the learned strategy represents each pair of variables (x_i, x_j) in the program by a boolean vector, and maps such a vector to $\oplus$ or $\ominus$, where $\oplus$ signifies the importance of tracking the relationship between x_i and x_j. If we view such $\oplus$-marked (x_i, x_j) as an edge of a graph, the variant of Octagon in this paper decides to track the relationship between variables x and y only when there is a path from x to y in the graph. According to our experiments, running this strategy for all variable pairs is quick and results in a good clustering of variables, which makes the variant of Octagon achieve performance comparable to the non-relational Interval analysis while enjoying the accuracy of the original Octagon in many cases.

The most important aspect of our learning method is the automatic provision of labeled data. Although the method is essentially an instance of supervised learning, it does not require the common unpleasant involvement of humans in supervised learning, namely, labeling. Our method takes a codebase consisting of typical programs of small-to-medium size, and automatically generates labels for pairs of variables in those programs by using the impact pre-analysis from our previous work [15], which estimates the impact of tracking relationships among variables by Octagon on proving queries in given programs. Our method precisely labels a pair of program variables with $\oplus$ when the pre-analysis says that the pair should be tracked. Because this learning occurs offline, we can bear the cost of the pre-analysis, which is still significantly lower than the cost of the full Octagon analysis. Once labeled data are generated, our method runs an off-the-shelf classification algorithm, such as decision-tree inference [9], for inferring a classifier for those labeled data. This classifier is used to map vector representations of variable pairs to $\oplus$ or $\ominus$. Conceptually, the inferred classifier is a further approximation of the pre-analysis, which gets found automatically from a given codebase.

The experimental results show that our method results in the learning of a cost-effective variable-clustering strategy. We implemented our learning method on top of a static buffer overflow detector for C programs and tested against open source benchmarks. In the experiments, our analysis with the learned variable-clustering strategy scales up to 100KLOC within the two times of the analysis cost of the Interval analysis. This corresponds to the 33x speed-up of the selective relational analysis based on the impact pre-analysis [15] (which was already significantly faster than the original Octagon analysis). The price of speed-up was mere 2 % increase of false alarms.

We summarize the contributions of this paper below:

1. We propose a method for automatically learning an effective strategy for variable-clustering for the Octagon analysis from a given codebase. The method infers a function that decides, for a program P and a pair of variables (x, y) in P, whether tracking the relationship between x and y is important. The learned strategy uses this function to cluster variables in a given program.
2. We show how to automatically generate labeled data from a given codebase that are needed for learning. Our key idea is to generate such data using the impact pre-analysis for Octagon from [15]. This use of the pre-analysis means that our learning step is just the process of finding a further approximation of the pre-analysis, which avoids expensive computations of the pre-analysis but keeps its important estimations.
3. We experimentally show the effectiveness of our learning method using a realistic static analyzer for full C and open source benchmarks. Our variant of Octagon with the learned strategy is 33x faster than the selective relational analysis based on the impact pre-analysis [15] while increasing false alarms by only 2 %.

2 Informal Explanation

2.1 Octagon Analysis with Variable Clustering

We start with informal explanation of our approach using the program in Fig. 1. The program contains two queries about the relationships between i and variables a, b inside the loop. The first query i < a is always true because the loop condition ensures i < b and variables a and b have the same value throughout the loop. The second query i < c, on the other hand, may become false because c is set to an unknown input at line 2.

The Octagon analysis [8] discovers program invariants strong enough to prove the first query in our example. At each program point it infers an invariant of the form

$$\left(\bigwedge_{ij} L_{ij} \leq x_j + x_i \leq U_{ij}\right) \wedge \left(\bigwedge_{ij} L'_{ij} \leq x_j - x_i \leq U'_{ij}\right)$$

for $L_{ij}, L'_{ij} \in \mathbb{Z} \cup \{-\infty\}$ and $U_{ij}, U'_{ij} \in \mathbb{Z} \cup \{\infty\}$. In particular, at the first query of our program, the analysis infers the following invariant, which we present in the usual matrix form:

	a	−a	b	−b	c	−c	i	−i
a	0	∞	0	∞	∞	∞	−1	∞
−a	∞	0	∞	0	∞	∞	∞	∞
b	0	∞	0	∞	∞	∞	−1	∞
−b	∞	0	∞	0	∞	∞	∞	∞
c	∞	∞	∞	∞	0	∞	∞	∞
−c	∞	∞	∞	∞	∞	0	∞	∞
i	∞	∞	∞	∞	∞	∞	0	∞
−i	∞	−1	∞	−1	∞	∞	∞	0

$$(1)$$

```
1   int a = b;
2   int c = input();                // User input
3   for (i = 0; i < b; i++) {
4     assert (i < a);               // Query 1
5     assert (i < c);               // Query 2
6   }
```

Fig. 1. Example program

The ij-th entry m_{ij} of this matrix means an upper bound $e_j - e_i \leq m_{ij}$, where e_j and e_i are expressions associated with the j-th column and the i-th row of the matrix respectively and they are variables with or without the minus sign. The matrix records -1 and ∞ as upper bounds for $i - a$ and $i - c$, respectively. Note that these bounds imply the first query, but not the second.

In practice the Octagon analysis is rarely used without further optimization, because it usually spends a large amount of computational resources for discovering unnecessary relationships between program variables, which do not contribute to proving given queries. In our example, the analysis tracks the relationship between c and i, although it does not help prove any of the queries.

A standard approach for addressing this inefficiency is to form subsets of variables, called variable clusters or clusters. According to a pre-defined clustering strategy, the analysis tracks the relationships between only those variables within the same cluster, not across clusters. In our example, this approach would form two clusters $\{a, b, i\}$ and $\{c\}$ and prevent the Octagon analysis from tracking the unnecessary relationships between c and the other variables. The success of the approach lies in finding a good strategy that is able to find effective clusters for a given program. This is possible as demonstrated in the several previous work [1,15,26], but it is highly nontrivial and often requires a large amount of trial and error of analysis designers.

Our goal is to develop a method for automatically learning a good variable-clustering strategy for a target class of programs. This automatic learning happens offline with a collection of typical sample programs from the target class, and the learned strategy is later applied to any programs in the class, most of which are not used during learning. We want the learned strategy to form relatively-small variable clusters so as to lower the analysis cost and, at the same time, to put a pair of variables in the same cluster if tracking their relationship by Octagon is important for proving given queries. For instance, such a strategy would cluster variables of our example program into two groups $\{a, b, i\}$ and $\{c\}$, and make Octagon compute the following smaller matrix at the first query:

	a	$-a$	b	$-b$	i	$-i$
a	0	∞	0	∞	-1	∞
$-a$	∞	0	∞	0	∞	∞
b	0	∞	0	∞	-1	∞
$-b$	∞	∞	∞	0	∞	∞
i	∞	∞	∞	∞	0	∞
$-i$	∞	-1	∞	-1	∞	∞

$$(2)$$

2.2   Automatic Learning of a Variable-Clustering Strategy

In this paper we will present a method for learning a variable-clustering strategy. Using a given codebase, it infers a function $\mathcal{F}$ that maps a tuple $(P, (x, y))$ of a program P and variables x, y in P to $\oplus$ and $\ominus$. The output $\oplus$ here means that tracking the relationship between x and y is likely to be important for proving queries. The inferred $\mathcal{F}$ guides our variant of the Octagon analysis. Given a program P, our analysis applies $\mathcal{F}$ to every pair of variables in P, and computes the finest partition of variables that puts every pair (x, y) with the $\oplus$ mark in the same group. Then, it analyzes the program P by tracking relationships between variables within each group in the partition, but not across groups.

Our method for learning takes a codebase that consists of typical programs in the intended application of the analysis. Then, it automatically synthesizes the above function $\mathcal{F}$ in two steps. First, it generates labeled data automatically from programs in the codebase by using the impact pre-analysis for Octagon from our previous work [15]. This is the most salient aspect of our approach; in a similar supervised-learning task, such labeled data are typically constructed manually, and avoiding this expensive manual labelling process is considered a big challenge for supervised learning. Next, our approach converts labeled data to boolean vectors marked with $\oplus$ or $\ominus$, and runs an off-the-shelf supervised learning algorithm to infer a classifier, which is used to define $\mathcal{F}$.

Automatic Generation of Labeled Data. Labeled data in our case are a collection of triples $(P, (x, y), L)$ where P is a program, (x, y) is a pair of variables in P, and $L \in \{\oplus, \ominus\}$ is a label that indicates whether tracking the relationship between x and y is important. We generate such labeled data automatically from the programs $P_1, \ldots, P_N$ in the given codebase.

The key idea is to use the impact pre-analysis for Octagon [15], and to convert the results of this pre-analysis to labeled data. Just like the Octagon analysis, this pre-analysis tracks the relationships between variables, but it aggressively abstracts any numerical information so as to achieve better scalability than Octagon. The goal of the pre-analysis is to identify, as much as possible, the case that Octagon would give a precise bound for $\pm x \pm y$, without running Octagon itself. As in Octagon, the pre-analysis computes a matrix with rows and columns for variables with or without the minus sign, but this matrix $m^{\sharp}$ contains $\bigstar$ or $\top$, instead of any numerical values. For instance, when applied to our example program, the pre-analysis would infer the following matrix at the first query:

	a	−a	b	−b	c	−c	i	−i
a	$\bigstar$	$\top$	$\bigstar$	$\top$	$\top$	$\top$	$\bigstar$	$\top$
−a	$\top$	$\bigstar$	$\top$	$\bigstar$	$\top$	$\top$	$\top$	$\top$
b	$\bigstar$	$\top$	$\bigstar$	$\top$	$\top$	$\top$	$\bigstar$	$\top$
−b	$\top$	$\bigstar$	$\top$	$\bigstar$	$\top$	$\top$	$\top$	$\top$
c	$\top$	$\top$	$\top$	$\top$	$\bigstar$	$\top$	$\top$	$\top$
−c	$\top$	$\top$	$\top$	$\top$	$\top$	$\bigstar$	$\top$	$\top$
i	$\top$	$\top$	$\top$	$\top$	$\top$	$\top$	$\bigstar$	$\top$
−i	$\top$	$\bigstar$	$\top$	$\bigstar$	$\top$	$\top$	$\top$	$\bigstar$

$$(3)$$

Each entry of this matrix stores the pre-analysis's (highly precise on the positive side) prediction on whether Octagon would put a *finite* upper bound at the corresponding entry of its matrix at the same program point. ★ means likely, and ⊤ unlikely. For instance, the above matrix contains ★ for the entries for i − b and b − a, and this means that Octagon is likely to infer finite (thus informative) upper bounds of i − b and b − a. In fact, this predication is correct because the actual upper bounds inferred by Octagon are −1 and 0, as can be seen in (1).

We convert the results of the impact pre-analysis to labeled data as follows. For every program P in the given codebase, we first collect all queries $Q = \{q_1, \ldots, q_k\}$ that express legal array accesses or the success of assert statements in terms of upper bounds on $\pm x \pm y$ for some variables x, y. Next, we filter out queries $q_i \in Q$ such that the upper bounds associated with q_i are not predicted to be finite by the pre-analysis. Intuitively, the remaining queries are the ones that are likely to be proved by Octagon according to the prediction of the pre-analysis. Then, for all remaining queries $q'_1, \ldots, q'_l$, we collect the results $m_1^\sharp, \ldots, m_l^\sharp$ of the pre-analysis at these queries, and generate the following labeled data:

$$\mathcal{D}_P = \{(P, (x, y), L) \mid$$
$$L = \oplus \iff \text{at least one of the entries of some } m_i \text{ for } \pm x \pm y \text{ has } \bigstar\}.$$

Notice that we mark (x, y) with $\oplus$ if tracking the relationship between x and y is useful for some query q'_i. An obvious alternative is to replace some by all, but we found that this alternative led to the worse performance in our experiments.[1] This generation process is applied for all programs $P_1, \ldots, P_N$ in the codebase, and results in the following labeled data: $\mathcal{D} = \bigcup_{1 \leq i \leq N} \mathcal{D}_{P_i}$. In our example program, if the results of the pre-analysis at both queries are the same matrix in (3), our approach picks only the first matrix because the pre-analysis predicts a finite upper bound only for the first query, and it produces the following labeled data from the first matrix:

$$\{(P, t, \oplus) \mid t \in T\} \cup \{(P, t, \ominus) \mid t \notin T\}$$

where $T = \{(\mathsf{a}, \mathsf{b}), (\mathsf{b}, \mathsf{a}), (\mathsf{a}, \mathsf{i}), (\mathsf{i}, \mathsf{a}), (\mathsf{b}, \mathsf{i}), (\mathsf{i}, \mathsf{b}), (\mathsf{a}, \mathsf{a}), (\mathsf{b}, \mathsf{b}), (\mathsf{c}, \mathsf{c}), (\mathsf{i}, \mathsf{i})\}$.

Application of an Off-the-shelf Classification Algorithm. Once we generate labeled data $\mathcal{D}$, we represent each triple in $\mathcal{D}$ as a vector of $\{0, 1\}$ labeled with $\oplus$ or $\ominus$, and apply an off-the-shelf classification algorithm, such as decision-tree inference [9].

The vector representation of each triple in $\mathcal{D}$ is based on a set of so called features, which are syntactic or semantic properties of a variable pair (x, y) under a program P. Formally, a feature f maps such $(P, (x, y))$ to 0 or 1. For instance, f may check whether the variables x and y appear together in an assignment of the form $x = y + c$ in P, or it may test whether x or y is a global variable. Table 1

---

[1] Because the pre-analysis uses ★ cautiously, only a small portion of variable pairs is marked with $\oplus$ (that is, $5864/258, 165, 546$) in our experiments. Replacing "some" by "all" reduces this portion by half ($2230/258, 165, 546$) and makes the learning task more difficult.

lists all the features that we designed and used for our variant of the Octagon analysis. Let us denote these features and results of applying them using the following symbols:

$$\mathbf{f} = \{f_1, \ldots, f_m\}, \quad \mathbf{f}(P, (x, y)) = (f_1(P, (x, y)), \ldots, f_m(P, (x, y))) \in \{0, 1\}^m.$$

The vector representation of triples in $\mathcal{D}$ is the following set:

$$\mathcal{V} = \{(\mathbf{f}(P, (x, y)), L) \mid (P, (x, y), L) \in \mathcal{D}\} \in \wp(\{0, 1\}^m \times \{\oplus, \ominus\})$$

We apply an off-the-self classification algorithm to the set. In our experiments, the algorithm for learning a decision tree gave the best classifier for our variant of the Octagon analysis.

3   Octagon Analysis with Variable Clustering

In this section, we describe a variant of the Octagon analysis that takes not just a program to be analyzed but also clusters of variables in the program. Such clusters are computed according to some strategy before the analysis is run. Given a program and variable clusters, this variant Octagon analysis infers relationships between variables within the same cluster but not across different clusters. Section 4 presents our method for automatically learning a good strategy for forming such variable clusters.

3.1   Programs

A program is represented by a control-flow graph $(\mathbb{C}, \hookrightarrow)$, where $\mathbb{C}$ is the set of program points and $(\hookrightarrow) \subseteq \mathbb{C} \times \mathbb{C}$ denotes the control flows of the program. Let $Var_n = \{x_1, \ldots, x_n\}$ be the set of variables. Each program point $c \in \mathbb{C}$ has a primitive command working with these variables. When presenting the formal setting and our results, we mostly assume the following collection of simple primitive commands:

$$cmd ::= x = k \mid x = y + k \mid x = ?$$

where x, y are program variables, $k \in \mathbb{Z}$ is an integer, and $x = ?$ is an assignment of some nondeterministically-chosen integer to x. The Octagon analysis is able to handle the first two kinds of commands precisely. The last command is usually an outcome of a preprocessor that replaces a complex assignment such as non-linear assignment $x = y * y + 1$ (which cannot be analyzed accurately by the Octagon analysis) by this overapproximating non-deterministic assignment.

3.2   Octagon Analysis

We briefly review the Octagon analysis in [8]. Let $Var_n = \{x_1, \ldots, x_n\}$ be the set of variables that appear in a program to be analyzed. The analysis aims at finding the upper and lower bounds of expressions of the forms x_i, $x_i + x_j$ and $x_i - x_j$ for variables $x_i, x_j \in Var_n$. The analysis represents these bounds as a $(2n \times 2n)$ matrix m of values in $\mathbb{Z} \cup \{\infty\}$, which means the following constraint:

$$\bigwedge_{(1 \le i, j \le n)} \bigwedge_{(k, l \in \{0, 1\})} ((-1)^{l+1} x_j - (-1)^{k+1} x_i) \le m_{(2i-k)(2j-l)}$$

The abstract domain $\mathbb{O}$ of the Octagon analysis consists of all those matrices and $\bot$, and uses the following pointwise order: for $m, m' \in \mathbb{O}$,

$$m \sqsubseteq m' \iff (m = \bot) \vee (m \ne \bot \wedge m' \ne \bot \wedge \forall 1 \le i, j \le 2n. \ (m_{ij} \le m'_{ij})).$$

This domain is a complete lattice $(\mathbb{O}, \sqsubseteq, \bot, \top, \sqcup, \sqcap)$ where $\top$ is the matrix containing only ∞ and $\sqcup$ and $\sqcap$ are defined pointwise. The details of the lattice structure can be found in [8].

Usually multiple abstract elements of $\mathbb{O}$ mean constraints with the same set of solutions. If we fix a set S of solutions and collect in the set M all the abstract elements with S as their solutions, the set M always contains the least element according to the $\sqsubseteq$ order. There is a cubic-time algorithm for computing this least element from any $m \in M$. We write $m^{\bullet}$ to denote the result of this algorithm, and call it strong closure of m.

The abstract semantics of primitive commands $[\![cmd]\!] : \mathbb{O} \to \mathbb{O}$ is defined in Fig. 2. The effects of the first two assignments in the concrete semantics can be tracked precisely using abstract elements of Octagon. The abstract semantics of these assignments do such tracking. $[\![x_i = ?]\!]m$ in the last case computes the strong closure of m and forgets any bounds involving x_i in the resulting abstract element $m^{\bullet}$. The analysis computes a pre-fixpoint of the semantic function F :

$$[\![x_i = k]\!]m = m' \text{ when } m'_{pq} = \begin{cases} -2k & p = 2i - 1 \wedge q = 2i \\ 2k & p = 2i \wedge q = 2i - 1 \\ ([\![x_i = ?]\!]m)_{pq} & otherwise \end{cases}$$

$$[\![x_i = x_j + k]\!]m = m' \text{ when } m'_{pq} = \begin{cases} -k & p = 2i - 1 \wedge q = 2j - 1 \\ -k & p = 2j \wedge q = 2i \\ k & p = 2j - 1 \wedge q = 2i - 1 \\ k & p = 2i \wedge q = 2j \\ ([\![x_i = ?]\!]m)_{pq} & otherwise \end{cases}$$

$[\![x_i = ?]\!]m = \bot \text{ when } m^{\bullet} = \bot$

$$[\![x_i = ?]\!]m = m' \text{ when } m^{\bullet} \ne \bot \text{ and } m'_{pq} = \begin{cases} \infty & p \in \{2i - 1, 2i\} \wedge q \notin \{2i - 1, 2i\} \\ \infty & p \notin \{2i - 1, 2i\} \wedge q \in \{2i - 1, 2i\} \\ 0 & p = q = 2i - 1 \vee p = q = 2i \\ (m^{\bullet})_{pq} & otherwise \end{cases}$$

Fig. 2. Abstract semantics of some primitive commands in the Octagon analysis. We show the case that the input m is not $\bot$; the abstract semantics always maps $\bot$ to $\bot$. Also, in $x_i = x_j + k$, we consider only the case that $i \ne j$.

$(\mathbb{C} \to \mathbb{O}) \to (\mathbb{C} \to \mathbb{O})$ (i.e., X_I with $F(X_I)(c) \sqsubseteq X_I(c)$ for all $c \in \mathbb{C}$):

$$F(X)(c) = [\![cmd(c)]\!] (\bigsqcup_{c' \hookrightarrow c} X(c'))$$

where $cmd(c)$ is the primitive command associated with the program point c.

3.3 Variable Clustering and Partial Octagon Analysis

We use a program analysis that performs the Octagon analysis only partially. This variant of Octagon is similar to those in [8,15]. This partial Octagon analysis takes a collection Π of clusters of variables, which are subsets π of variables in Var_n such that $\bigcup_{\pi \in \Pi} \pi = Var_n$. Each $\pi \in \Pi$ specifies a variable cluster and instructs the analysis to track relationships between variables in π. Given such a collection Π, the partial Octagon analysis analyzes the program using the complete lattice $(\mathbb{O}_\Pi, \sqsubseteq_\Pi, \bot_\Pi, \top_\Pi, \sqcup_\Pi, \sqcap_\Pi)$ where

$$\mathbb{O}_\Pi = \prod_{\pi \in \Pi} \mathbb{O}_\pi \qquad (\mathbb{O}_\pi \text{ is the lattice of Octagon for variables in } \pi).$$

That is, $\mathbb{O}_\Pi$ consists of families $\{m_\pi\}_{\pi \in \Pi}$ such that each m_π is an abstract element of Octagon used for variables in π, and all lattice operations of $\mathbb{O}_\Pi$ are the pointwise extensions of those of Octagon. For the example in Sect. 2, if we use $\Pi = \{\{a, b, c, i\}\}$, the partial Octagon analysis uses the same domain as Octagon's. But if $\Pi = \{\{a, b, i\}, \{c\}\}$, the analysis uses the product of two smaller abstract domains, one for $\{a, b, i\}$ and the other for $\{c\}$.

The partial Octagon analysis computes a pre-fixpoint of the following F_Π:

$$F_\Pi : (\mathbb{C} \to \mathbb{O}_\Pi) \to (\mathbb{C} \to \mathbb{O}_\Pi), \qquad F_\Pi(X)(c) = [\![cmd(c)]\!]_\Pi (\bigsqcup_{c' \hookrightarrow c} X(c')).$$

Here the abstract semantics $[\![cmd(c)]\!]_\Pi : \mathbb{O}_\Pi \to \mathbb{O}_\Pi$ of the command c is defined in terms of Octagon's:

$$([\![x_i = ?]\!]_\Pi po)_\pi = \begin{cases} [\![x_i = ?]\!](po_\pi) & x_i \in \pi \\ po_\pi & otherwise \end{cases}$$

$$([\![x_i = k]\!]_\Pi po)_\pi = \begin{cases} [\![x_i = k]\!](po_\pi) & x_i \in \pi \\ po_\pi & otherwise \end{cases}$$

$$([\![x_i = x_j + k]\!]_\Pi po)_\pi = \begin{cases} [\![x_i = x_j + k]\!](po_\pi) & x_i, x_j \in \pi \\ [\![x_i = ?]\!](po_\pi) & otherwise \end{cases}$$

The abstract semantics of a command updates the component of an input abstract state for a cluster π if the command changes any variable in the cluster; otherwise, it keeps the component. The update is done according to the abstract semantics of Octagon. Notice that the abstract semantics of $x_i = x_j + k$ does not track the relationship $x_j - x_i = k$ in the π component when $x_i \in \pi$ but $x_j \notin \pi$. Giving up such relationships makes this partial analysis perform faster than the original Octagon analysis.

4   Learning a Strategy for Clustering Variables

The success of the partial Octagon analysis lies in choosing good clusters of variables for a given program. Ideally each cluster of variable should be relatively small, but if tracking the relationship between variables x_i and x_j is important, some cluster should contain both x_i and x_j. In this section, we present a method for learning a strategy that chooses such clusters. Our method takes as input a collection of programs, which reflects a typical usage scenario of the partial Octagon analysis. It then automatically learns a strategy from this collection.

In the section we assume that our method is given $\{P_1, \ldots, P_N\}$, and we let

$$\mathcal{P} = \{(P_1, Q_1), \ldots, (P_N, Q_N)\},$$

where Q_i means a set of queries in P_i. It consists of pairs (c, p) of a program point c of P_i and a predicate p on variables of P_i, where the predicate express an upper bound on variables or their differences, such as $x_i - x_j \leq 1$. Another notation that we adopt is Var_P for each program P, which means the set of variables appearing in P.

4.1   Automatic Generation of Labeled Data

The first step of our method is to generate labeled data from the given collection $\mathcal{P}$ of programs and queries. In theory the generation of this labeled data can be done by running the full Octagon analysis. For every (P_i, Q_i) in $\mathcal{P}$, we run the Octagon analysis for P_i, and collect queries in Q_i that are proved by the analysis. Then, we label a pair of variable (x_j, x_k) in P_i with $\oplus$ if (i) a nontrivial[2] upper or lower bound (x_i, x_k) is computed by the analysis at some program point c in P_i and (ii) the proof of some query by the analysis depends on this nontrivial upper bound. Otherwise, we label the pair with $\ominus$. The main problem with this approach is that we cannot analyze all the programs in $\mathcal{P}$ with Octagon because of the scalability issue of Octagon.

In order to lessen this scalability issue, we instead run the impact pre-analysis for Octagon from our previous work [15], and convert its results to labeled data. Although this pre-analysis is not as cheap as the Interval analysis, it scales far better than Octagon and enables us to generate labeled data from a wide range of programs. Our learning method then uses the generated data to find a strategy for clustering variables. The found strategy can be viewed as an approximation of this pre-analysis that scales as well as the Interval analysis.

Impact Pre-analysis. We review the impact pre-analysis from [15], which aims at quickly predicting the results of running the Octagon analysis on a given program P. Let $n = |Var_P|$, the number of variables in P. At each program point c of P, the pre-analysis computes a $(2n \times 2n)$ matrix $m^\sharp$ with entries in $\{\bigstar, \top\}$. Intuitively, such a matrix $m^\sharp$ records which entries of the matrix m computed by Octagon are likely to contain nontrivial bounds. If the ij-th entry

---

[2] By nontrivial, we mean finite bounds that are neither ∞ nor $-\infty$.

of $m^\sharp$ is $\bigstar$, the ij-th entry of m is likely to be non-∞ according to the prediction of the pre-analysis. The pre-analysis does not make similar prediction for entries of $m^\sharp$ with $\top$. Such entries should be understood as the absence of information.

The pre-analysis uses a complete lattice $(\mathbb{O}^\sharp, \sqsubseteq^\sharp, \bot^\sharp, \top^\sharp, \sqcup^\sharp, \sqcap^\sharp)$ where $\mathbb{O}^\sharp$ consists of $(2n \times 2n)$ matrices of values in $\{\bigstar, \top\}$, the order $\sqsubseteq^\sharp$ is the pointwise extension of the total order $\bigstar \sqsubseteq \top$, and all the other lattice operations are defined pointwise. There is a Galois connection between the powerset lattice $\wp(\mathbb{O})$ (with the usual subset order) and $\mathbb{O}^\sharp$:

$$\gamma : \mathbb{O}^\sharp \to \wp(\mathbb{O}), \qquad \gamma(m^\sharp) = \{\bot\} \cup \{m \in \mathbb{O} \mid \forall i, j.\ (m_{ij}^\sharp = \bigstar \implies m_{ij} \neq \infty)\},$$

$$\alpha : \wp(\mathbb{O}) \to \mathbb{O}^\sharp, \qquad \alpha(M)_{ij} = \bigstar \iff (\textstyle\bigsqcup M \neq \bot \implies (\textstyle\bigsqcup M)_{ij} \neq \infty).$$

The pre-analysis uses the abstract semantics $[\![cmd]\!]^\sharp : \mathbb{O}^\sharp \to \mathbb{O}^\sharp$ that is derived from this Galois connection and the abstract semantics of the same command in Octagon (Fig. 2). Figure 3 shows the results of this derivation.

$$[\![x_i = k]\!]^\sharp m^\sharp = m_1^\sharp \text{ when } (m_1^\sharp)_{pq} = \begin{cases} \bigstar & p = 2i - 1 \wedge q = 2i \\ \bigstar & p = 2i \wedge q = 2i - 1 \\ ([\![x_i = ?]\!]^\sharp m^\sharp)_{pq} & otherwise \end{cases}$$

$$[\![x_i = x_j + k]\!]^\sharp m^\sharp = m_1^\sharp \text{ when } (m_1^\sharp)_{pq} = \begin{cases} \bigstar & p = 2i - 1 \wedge q = 2j - 1 \\ \bigstar & p = 2j \wedge q = 2i \\ \bigstar & p = 2j - 1 \wedge q = 2i - 1 \\ \bigstar & p = 2i \wedge q = 2j \\ ([\![x_i = ?]\!]^\sharp m^\sharp)_{pq} & otherwise \end{cases}$$

$$[\![x_i = ?]\!]^\sharp m^\sharp = m_1^\sharp \text{ when } (m_1^\sharp)_{pq} = \begin{cases} \top & p \in \{2i - 1, 2i\} \wedge q \notin \{2i - 1, 2i\} \\ \top & p \notin \{2i - 1, 2i\} \wedge q \in \{2i - 1, 2i\} \\ \bigstar & p = q = 2i - 1 \vee p = q = 2i \\ ((m^\sharp)^\bullet)_{pq} & otherwise \end{cases}$$

Fig. 3. Abstract semantics of some primitive commands in the impact pre-analysis. In $x_i = x_j + k$, we show only the case that $i \neq j$.

Automatic Labeling. For every $(P_i, Q_i) \in \mathcal{P}$, we run the pre-analysis on P_i, and get an analysis result X_i that maps each program point in P_i to a matrix in $\mathbb{O}^\sharp$. From such X_i, we generate labeled data $\mathcal{D}$ as follows:

$$Q_i' = \{c \mid \exists p.\ (c, p) \in Q_i \wedge \text{the } jk \text{ entry is about the upper bound claimed in } p$$
$$\wedge X_i(c) \neq \bot \wedge X_i(c)_{jk} = \bigstar\},$$

$$\mathcal{D} = \bigcup_{1 \leq i \leq N} \{(P_i, (x_j, x_k), L) \mid L = \oplus \iff$$
$$\exists c \in Q_i'.\exists l, m \in \{0, 1\}.\ X_i(c)_{(2j-l)(2k-m)} = \bigstar\}.$$

Notice that we label (x_j, x_k) with $\oplus$ if tracking their relationship is predicted to be useful for *some* query according to the results of the pre-analysis.

4.2   Features and Classifier

The second step of our method is to represent labeled data $\mathcal{D}$ as a set of boolean vectors marked with $\oplus$ or $\ominus$, and to run an off-the-shelf algorithm for inferring a classifier with this set of labeled vectors. The vector representation assumes a collection of features $\mathbf{f} = \{f_1, \ldots, f_m\}$, each of which maps a pair $(P, (x, y))$ of program P and variable pair (x, y) to 0 or 1. The vector representation is the set $\mathcal{V}$ defined as follows:

$$\mathbf{f}(P, (x, y)) = (f_1(P, (x, y)), \ldots, f_m(P, (x, y))) \in \{0, 1\}^m,$$
$$\mathcal{V} = \{(\mathbf{f}(P, (x, y)), L) \mid (P, (x, y), L) \in \mathcal{D}\} \in \wp(\{0, 1\}^m \times \{\oplus, \ominus\}).$$

An off-the-shelf algorithm computes a binary classifier $\mathcal{C}$ from $\mathcal{V}$:

$$\mathcal{C} : \{0, 1\}^m \to \{\oplus, \ominus\}.$$

In our experiments, $\mathcal{V}$ has significantly more vectors marked with $\ominus$ than those marked with $\oplus$. We found that the algorithm for inferring a decision tree [9] worked the best for our $\mathcal{V}$.

Table 1 shows the features that we developed for the Octagon analysis and used in our experiments. These features work for real C programs (not just those in the small language that we have used so far in the paper), and they are all symmetric in the sense that $f_i(P, (x, y)) = f_i(P, (y, x))$. Features 1–6 detect good situations where the Octagon analysis *can* track the relationship between variables *precisely*. For example, $f_1(P, (x, y)) = 1$ when x and y appear in an assignment $x = y + k$ or $y = x + k$ for some constant k in the program P. Note that the abstract semantics of these commands in Octagon do not lose any information. The next features 7–11, on the other hand, detect bad situations where the Octagon analysis *cannot* track the relationship between variables *precisely*. For example, $f_7(P, (x, y)) = 1$ when x or y gets multiplied by a constant different from 1 in a command of P, as in the assignments $y = x * 2$ and $x = y * 2$. Notice that these assignments set up relationships between x and y that can be expressed only approximately by Octagon. We have found that detecting both good and bad situations is important for learning an effective variable-clustering strategy. The remaining features (12–30) describe various syntactic and semantics properties about program variables that often appear in typical C programs. For the semantic features, we use the results of a flow-insensitive analysis that quickly computes approximate information about pointer aliasing and ranges of numerical variables.

4.3   Strategy for Clustering Variables

The last step is to define a strategy that takes a program P, especially one not seen during learning, and clusters variables in P. Assume that a program P is given and let Var_P be the set of variables in P. Using features $\mathbf{f}$ and inferred classifier $\mathcal{C}$, our strategy computes the *finest* partition of Var_P,

$$\Pi = \{\pi_1, \ldots, \pi_k\} \subseteq \wp(Var_P),$$

Table 1. Features for relations of two variables.

i	Description of feature $f_i(P, (x, y))$. k represents a constant
1	P contains an assignment $x = y + k$ or $y = x + k$
2	P contains a guard $x \leq y + k$ or $y \leq x + k$
3	P contains a malloc of the form $x = \mathtt{malloc}(y)$ or $y = \mathtt{malloc}(x)$
4	P contains a command $x = \mathtt{strlen}(y)$ or $y = \mathtt{strlen}(x)$
5	P sets x to $\mathtt{strlen}(y)$ or y to $\mathtt{strlen}(x)$ indirectly, as in $t = \mathtt{strlen}(y); x = t$
6	P contains an expression of the form $x[y]$ or $y[x]$
7	P contains an expression that multiplies x or y by a constant different from 1
8	P contains an expression that multiplies x or y by a variable
9	P contains an expression that divides x or y by a variable
10	P contains an expression that has x or y as an operand of bitwise operations
11	P contains an assignment that updates x or y using non-Octagonal expressions
12	x and y are has the same name in different scopes
13	x and y are both global variables in P
14	x or y is a global variable in P
15	x or y is a field of a structure in P
16	x and y represent sizes of some arrays in P
17	x and y are temporary variables in P
18	x or y is a local variable of a recursive function in P
19	x or y is tested for the equality with ± 1 in P
20	x and y represent sizes of some global arrays in P
21	x or y stores the result of a library call in P
22	x and y are local variables of different functions in P
23	$\{x, y\}$ consists of a local var. and the size of a local array in different fun. in P
24	$\{x, y\}$ consists of a local var. and a temporary var. in different functions in P
25	$\{x, y\}$ consists of a global var. and the size of a local array in P
26	$\{x, y\}$ contains a temporary var. and the size of a local array in P
27	$\{x, y\}$ consists of local and global variables not accessed by the same fun. in P
28	x or y is a self-updating global var. in P
29	The flow-insensitive analysis of P results in a finite interval for x or y
30	x or y is the size of a constant string in P

such that for all $(x, y) \in Var_P \times Var_P$, if we let $\mathcal{F} = \mathcal{C} \circ \mathbf{f}$, then

$$\mathcal{F}(P, (x, y)) = \oplus \implies x, y \in \pi_i \text{ for some } \pi_i \in \Pi.$$

The partition Π is the clustering of variables that will be used by the partial Octagon analysis subsequently. Notice that although the classifier does not indicate the importance of tracking the relationship between some variables x

and z (i.e., $\mathcal{F}(P, (x, z)) = \ominus$), Π may put x and z in the same $\pi \in \Pi$, if $\mathcal{F}(P, (x, y)) = \mathcal{F}(P, (y, z)) = \oplus$ for some y. Effectively, our construction of Π takes the transitive closure of the raw output of the classifier on variables. In our experiments, taking this transitive closure was crucial for achieving the desired precision of the partial Octagon analysis.

5   Experiments

We describe the experimental evaluation of our method for learning a variable-clustering strategy. The evaluation aimed to answer the following questions:

1. **Effectiveness:** How well does the partial Octagon with a learned strategy perform, compared with the existing Interval and Octagon analyses?
2. **Generalization:** Does the strategy learned from small programs also work well for large unseen programs?
3. **Feature design:** How should we choose a set of features in order to make our method learn a good strategy?
4. **Choice of an off-the-shelf classification algorithm:** Our method uses a classification algorithm for inferring a decision tree by default. How much does this choice matter for the performance of our method?

   We conducted our experiments with a realistic static analyzer and open-source C benchmarks. We implemented our method on top of Sparrow, a static buffer-overflow analyzer for real-world C programs [25]. The analyzer performs the combination of the Interval analysis and the pointer analysis based on allocation-site abstraction with several precision-improving techniques such as fully flow-, field-sensitivity and selective context-sensitivity [15]. In our experiments, we modified Sparrow to use the partial Octagon analysis as presented in Sect. 3, instead of Interval. The partial Octagon was implemented on top of the sparse analysis framework [13,14], so it is significantly faster than the vanilla Octagon analysis [8]. For the implementation of data structures and abstract operations for Octagon, we tried the OptOctagons plugin [24] of the Apron framework [6]. For the decision tree learning, we used Scikit-learn [17]. We used 17 open-source benchmark programs (Table 2) and all the experiments were done on a Ubuntu machine with Intel Xeon clocked at 2.4 GHz cpu and 192 GB of main memory.

5.1   Effectiveness

We evaluated the effectiveness of a strategy learned by our method on the cost and precision of Octagon. We compared the partial Octagon analysis with a learned variable-clustering strategy with the Interval analysis and the approach for optimizing Octagon in [15]. The approach in [15] also performs the partial Octagon analysis in Sect. 3 but with a fixed variable-clustering strategy that uses the impact pre-analysis online (rather than offline as in our case): the strategy runs the impact pre-analysis on a given program and computes variable clusters of the program based on the results of the pre-analysis. Table 2 shows the results of our comparison with 17 open-source programs. We used the leave-one-out cross validation to evaluate our method; for each program P in the table, we applied our method to the other 16 programs, learned a variable-clustering strategy, and ran the partial Octagon on P with this strategy.

Table 2. Comparison of performance of the Interval analysis and two partial Octagon analyses, one with a fixed strategy based on the impact pre-analysis and the other with a learned strategy. **LOC** reports lines of code before preprocessing. **Var** reports the number of program variables (more precisely, abstract locations). **#Alarms** reports the number of buffer-overflow alarms reported by the interval analysis (**Itv**), the partial Octagon analysis with a fixed strategy (**Impt**) and that with a learned strategy (**ML**). **Time** shows the analysis time in seconds, where, in **X(Y)**, **X** means the total time (including that for clustering and the time for main analysis) and **Y** shows the time spent by the strategy for clustering variables.

Program	LOC	Var	#Alarms			Time(s)		
			Itv	Impt	ML	Itv	Impt	ML
brutefir-1.0f	103	54	4	0	0	0	0 (0)	0 (0)
consolcalculator-1.0	298	165	20	10	10	0	0 (0)	0 (0)
id3-0.15	512	527	15	6	6	0	0 (0)	1 (0)
spell-1.0	2,213	450	20	8	17	0	1 (1)	1 (0)
mp3rename-0.6	2,466	332	33	3	3	0	1 (0)	1 (0)
irmp3-0.5.3.1	3,797	523	2	0	0	1	2 (0)	3 (1)
barcode-0.96	4,460	1,738	235	215	215	2	9 (7)	6 (1)
httptunnel-3.3	6,174	1,622	52	29	27	3	35 (32)	5 (1)
e2ps-4.34	6,222	1,437	119	58	58	3	6 (3)	3 (0)
bc-1.06	13,093	1,891	371	364	364	14	252 (238)	16 (1)
less-382	23,822	3,682	625	620	625	83	2,354 (2,271)	87 (4)
bison-2.5	56,361	14,610	1,988	1,955	1,955	137	4,827 (4,685)	0237 (79)
pies-1.2	66,196	9,472	795	785	785	49	14,942 (14,891)	95 (43)
icecast-server-1.3.12	68,564	6,183	239	232	232	51	109 (55)	107 (42)
raptor-1.4.21	76,378	8,889	2,156	2,148	2,148	242	17,844 (17,604)	345 (104)
dico-2.0	84,333	4,349	402	396	396	38	156 (117)	51 (24)
lsh-2.0.4	110,898	18,880	330	325	325	33	139 (106)	251 (218)
Total			7,406	7,154	7,166	656	40,677 (40,011)	1,207 (519)

The results show that the partial Octagon with a learned strategy strikes the right balance between precision and cost. In total, the Interval analysis reports 7,406 alarms from the benchmark set.[3] The existing approach for partial Octagon [15] reduced the number of alarms by 252, but increased the analysis time by 62x. Meanwhile, our learning-based approach for partial Octagon reduced the number of alarms by 240 while increasing the analysis time by 2x.

---

[3] In practice, eliminating these false alarms is extremely challenging in a sound yet non-domain-specific static analyzer for full C. The false alarms arise from a variety of reasons, e.g., recursive calls, unknown library calls, complex loops, etc.

We point out that in some programs, the precision of our approach was incomparable with that of the approach in [15]. For instance, for `spell-1.0`, our approach is less precise than that of [15] because some usage patterns of variables in `spell-1.0` do not appear in other programs. On the other hand, for `httptunnel-3.3`, our approach produces better results because the impact pre-analysis of [15] uses ★ conservatively and fails to identify some important relationships between variables.

5.2 Generalization

Although the impact pre-analysis scales far better than Octagon, it is still too expensive to be used routinely for large programs (> 100 KLOC). Therefore, in order for our approach to scale, the variable-clustering strategy learned from a codebase of small programs needs to be effective for large unseen programs. Whether this need is met or not depends on whether our learning method generalize information from small programs to large programs well.

To evaluate this generalization capability of our learning method, we divided the benchmark set into small (< 60 KLOC) and large (> 60 KLOC) programs, learned a variable-clustering strategy from the group of small programs, and evaluated its performance on that of large programs.

Table 3. Generalization performance.

Program	LOC	Var	#Alarms			Time		
			Itv	All	Small	Itv	All	Small
pies-1.2	66,196	9,472	795	785	785	49	95 (43)	98 (43)
icecast-server-1.3.12	68,564	6,183	239	232	232	51	113 (42)	99 (42)
raptor-1.4.21	76,378	8,889	2,156	2,148	2,148	242	345 (104)	388 (104)
dico-2.0	84,333	4,349	402	396	396	38	61 (24)	62 (24)
lsh-2.0.4	110,898	18,880	330	325	325	33	251 (218)	251 (218)
Total			3,922	3,886	3,886	413	864 (432)	899 (432)

Table 3 shows the results. Columns labeled **Small** report the performance of our approach learned from the small programs. **All** reports the performance of the strategy used in Sect. 5.1 (i.e., the strategy learned with all benchmark programs except for each target program). In our experiments, **Small** had the same precision as **All** with negligibly increase in analysis time (4%). These results show that the information learned from small programs is general enough to infer the useful properties about large programs.

5.3 Feature Design

We identified top ten features that are most important to learn an effective variable-clustering strategy for Octagon. We applied our method to all the 17 programs so as to learn a decision tree, and measured the relative importance of features by computing their Gini index [2] with the tree. Intuitively, the Gini index shows how much each feature helps a learned decision tree to classify variable pairs as ⊕ or ⊖. Thus, features with high Gini index are located in the upper part of the tree.

According to the results, the ten most important features are 30, 15, 18, 16, 29, 6, 24, 23, 1, and 21 in Table 1. We found that many of the top ten features are negative and describe situations where the precise tracking of variable relationships by Octagon is unnecessary. For instance, feature 30 (size of constant string) and 29 (finite interval) represent variable pairs whose relationships can be precisely captured even with the Interval analysis. Using Octagon for such pairs is overkill. Initially, we conjectured that positive features, which describe situations where the Octagon analysis is effective, would be the most important for learning a good strategy. However, data show that effectively ruling out unnecessary variable relationships is the key to learning a good variable-clustering strategy for Octagon.

5.4   Choice of an Off-the-shelf Classification Algorithm

Our learning method uses an off-the-shelf algorithm for inferring a decision tree. In order to see the importance of this default choice, we replaced the decision-tree algorithm by logistic regression [10], which is another popular supervised learning algorithm and infers a linear classifier from labeled data. Such linear classifiers are usually far simpler than nonlinear ones such as a decision tree. We then repeated the leave-one-out cross validation described in Sect. 5.1.

In this experiment, the new partial Octagon analysis with linear classifiers proved the same number of queries as before, but it was significantly slower than the analysis with decision trees. Changing regularization in logistic regression from nothing to L_1 or L_2 and varying regularization strengths (10^{-3}, 10^{-4} and 10^{-5}) did not remove this slowdown. We observed that in all of these cases, inferred linear classifiers labeled too many variable pairs with ⊕ and led to unnecessarily big clusters of variables. Such big clusters increased the analysis time of the partial Octagon with decision trees by 10x–12x. Such an observation indicates that a linear classifier is not expressive enough to identify important variable pairs for the Octagon analysis.

6   Related Work

The scalability issue of the Octagon analysis is well-known, and there have been various attempts to optimize the analysis [14,24]. Oh et al. [14] exploited the data dependencies of a program and removed unnecessary propagation of information between program points during Octagon's fixpoint computation. Singh et al. [24] designed better algorithms for Octagon's core operators and implemented a new library for Octagon called OptOctagons, which has been incorporated in the Apron framework [6]. These approaches are orthogonal to our approach, and all of these three can be used together as in our implementation. We point out that although the techniques from these approaches [14,24] improve the performance of Octagon significantly, without additionally making Octagon partial with good variable clusters, they were not enough to make Octagon scale large programs in our experiments. This is understandable because the techniques keep the precision of the original Octagon while making Octagon partial does not.

Existing variable-clustering strategies for the Octagon analysis use a simple syntactic criterion for clustering variables [1] (such as selecting variable pairs that appear in particular kinds of commands and forming one cluster for each syntactic block), or a pre-analysis that attempts to identify important variable pairs for Octagon [15]. When applied to large general-purpose programs (not designed for embedded systems), the syntactic criterion led to ineffective variable clusters, which made the subsequent partial Octagon analysis slow and fail to achieve the desired precision [15]. The approach based on the pre-analysis [15], on the other hand, has an issue with the cost of the pre-analysis itself; it is cheaper than that of Octagon, but it is still expensive as we showed in the paper. In a sense, our approach automatically learns fast approximation of the pre-analysis from the results of running the pre-analysis on programs in a given codebase. In our experiments, this approximation (which we called strategy) was 33x faster than the pre-analysis while decreasing the number of proved queries by 2 % only.

Recently there have been a large amount of research activities for developing data-driven approaches to challenging program analysis problems, such as specification inference [18,20], invariant generation [4,11,19,21–23], acceleration of abstraction refinement [5], and smart report of analysis results [7,12,27]. In particular, Oh et al. [16] considered the problem of automatically learning analysis parameters from a codebase, which determine the heuristics used by the analysis. They formulated this parameter learning as a blackbox optimization problem, and proposed to use Bayesian optimization for solving the problem. Initially we followed this blackbox approach [16], and tried Bayesian optimization to learn a good variable-clustering strategy with our features. In the experiment, we learned the strategy from the small programs as in Sect. 5.2 and chose the top 200 variable pairs which are enough to make a good clustering as precise as our strategy; the learning process was too costly with larger training programs and more variable pairs. This initial attempt was a total failure. The learning process tried only 384 parameters and reduced 14 false alarms even during the learning phase for a whole week, while our strategy reduced 240 false alarms. Unlike the optimization problems for the analyses in [16], our problem was too difficult for Bayesian optimization to solve. We conjecture that this was due to the lack of smoothness in the objective function of our problem. This failure led to the approach in this paper, where we replaced the blackbox optimization by a much easier supervised-learning problem.

7   Conclusion

In this paper we proposed a method for learning a variable-clustering strategy for the Octagon analysis from a codebase. One notable aspect of our method is that it generates labeled data automatically from a given codebase by running the impact pre-analysis for Octagon [15]. The labeled data are then fed to an off-the-shelf classification algorithm (in particular, decision-tree inference in our implementation), which infers a classifier that can identify important variable pairs from a new unseen program, whose relationships should be tracked by the Octagon analysis. This classifier forms the core of the strategy that is returned by our learning method. Our experiments show that the partial Octagon analysis with the learned strategy scales up to 100KLOC and is 33x faster than the one with the impact pre-analysis (which itself is significantly faster than the original Octagon analysis), while increasing false alarms by only 2 %.

Acknowledgements. We thank the anonymous reviewers for their helpful comments. We also thank Kwangkeun Yi, Chung-Kil Hur, and all members of SoFA group members in Seoul National University for their helpful comments and suggestions. This work was supported by Samsung Research Funding Center of Samsung Electronics under Project Number SRFC-IT1502-07 and Institute for Information & communications Technology Promotion (IITP) grant funded by the Korea government (MSIP) (No. R0190-16-2011, Development of Vulnerability Discovery Technologies for IoT Software Security). This research was also supported by Basic Science Research Program through the National Research Foundation of Korea (NRF) funded by the Ministry of Science, ICT & Future Planning (NRF-2016R1C1B2014062).

References

1. Blanchet, B., Cousot, P., Cousot, R., Feret, J., Mauborgne, L., Miné, A., Monniaux, D., Rival, X.: A static analyzer for large safety-critical software. In: PLDI (2003)
2. Breiman, L.: Random forests. Mach. Learn. **45**, 5–32 (2001)
3. Cousot, P., Halbwachs, N.: Automatic discovery of linear restraints among variables of a program. In: POPL (1978)
4. Garg, P., Neider, D., Madhusudan, P., Roth, D.: Learning invariants using decision trees and implication counterexamples. In: POPL, pp. 499–512 (2016)
5. Grigore, R., Yang, H.: Abstraction refinement guided by a learnt probabilistic model. In: POPL (2016)
6. Jeannet, B., Miné, A.: APRON: a library of numerical abstract domains for static analysis. In: Bouajjani, A., Maler, O. (eds.) CAV 2009. LNCS, vol. 5643, pp. 661–667. Springer, Heidelberg (2009)
7. Mangal, R., Zhang, X., Nori, A.V., Naik, M.: A user-guided approach to program analysis. In: ESEC/FSE, pp. 462–473 (2015)
8. Miné, A.: The octagon abstract domain. Higher-order and symbolic computation (2006)
9. Mitchell, T.M.: Machine Learning. McGraw-Hill, Inc., New York (1997)
10. Murphy, K.P.: Machine Learning: A Probabilistic Perspective. Adaptive Computation and Machine Learning Series. MIT Press, Cambridge (2012)
11. Nori, A.V., Sharma, R.: Termination proofs from tests. In: FSE, pp. 246–256 (2013)
12. Octeau, D., Jha, S., Dering, M., McDaniel, P., Bartel, A., Li, L., Klein, J., Traon, Y.L.: Combining static analysis with probabilistic models to enable market-scale android inter-component analysis. In: POPL, pp. 469–484 (2016)
13. Oh, H., Heo, K., Lee, W., Lee, W., Park, D., Kang, J., Yi, K.: Global sparse analysis framework. ACM Trans. Program. Lang. Syst. **36**(3), 8:1–8:44 (2014)

14. Oh, H., Heo, K., Lee, W., Lee, W., Yi, K.: Design and implementation of sparse global analyses for C-like languages. In: PLDI (2012)
15. Oh, H., Lee, W., Heo, K., Yang, H., Yi, K.: Selective context-sensitivity guided by impact pre-analysis. In: PLDI (2014)
16. Oh, H., Yang, H., Yi, K.: Learning a strategy for adapting a program analysis via bayesian optimisation. In: OOPSLA (2015)
17. Pedregosa, F., Varoquaux, G., Gramfort, A., Michel, V., Thirion, B., Grisel, O., Blondel, M., Prettenhofer, P., Weiss, R., Dubourg, V., Vanderplas, J., Passos, A., Cournapeau, D., Brucher, M., Perrot, M., Duchesnay, É.: Scikit-learn: machine learning in Python. J. Mach. Learn. Res. **12**, 2825–2830 (2011)
18. Raychev, V., Bielik, P., Vechev, M.T., Krause, A.: Learning programs from noisy data. In: POPL, pp. 761–774 (2016)
19. Sankaranarayanan, S., Chaudhuri, S., Ivančić, F., Gupta, A.: Dynamic inference of likely data preconditions over predicates by tree learning. In: ISSTA, pp. 295–306 (2008)
20. Sankaranarayanan, S., Ivančić, F., Gupta, A.: Mining library specifications using inductive logic programming. In: ICSE, pp. 131–140 (2008)
21. Sharma, R., Gupta, S., Hariharan, B., Aiken, A., Liang, P., Nori, A.V.: A data driven approach for algebraic loop invariants. In: Felleisen, M., Gardner, P. (eds.) ESOP 2013. LNCS, vol. 7792, pp. 574–592. Springer, Heidelberg (2013)
22. Sharma, R., Gupta, S., Hariharan, B., Aiken, A., Nori, A.V.: Verification as learning geometric concepts. In: Logozzo, F., Fähndrich, M. (eds.) SAS 2013. LNCS, vol. 7935, pp. 388–411. Springer, Heidelberg (2013)
23. Sharma, R., Nori, A.V., Aiken, A.: Interpolants as classifiers. In: Madhusudan, P., Seshia, S.A. (eds.) CAV 2012. LNCS, vol. 7358, pp. 71–87. Springer, Heidelberg (2012)
24. Singh, G., Püschel, M., Vechev, M.: Making numerical program analysis fast. In: PLDI (2015)
25. Sparrow. http://ropas.snu.ac.kr/sparrow
26. Venet, A., Brat, G.: Precise and efficient static array bound checking for large embedded C programs. In: PLDI (2004)
27. Yi, K., Choi, H., Kim, J., Kim, Y.: An empirical study on classification methods for alarms from a bug-finding static C analyzer. Inf. Process. Lett. **102**(2–3), 118–123 (2007)

Static Analysis by Abstract Interpretation of the Functional Correctness of Matrix Manipulating Programs

Matthieu Journault[1]([⊠]) and Antoine Miné[2]

[1] Computer Science Department, ENS Cachan, Cachan, France
matthieu.journault@ens-cachan.fr
[2] Sorbonnes Universités, UPMC Univ Paris 6,
Laboratoire d'informatique de Paris 6 (LIP6), 4, pl. Jussieu, 75005 Paris, France
antoine.mine@lip6.fr

Abstract. We present new abstract domains to prove automatically the functional correctness of algorithms implementing matrix operations, such as matrix addition, multiplication, GEMM (general matrix multiplication), or more generally BLAS (Basic Linear Algebra Subprograms). In order to do so, we introduce a family of abstract domains parameterized by a set of matrix predicates and by a numeric domain. We show that our analysis is robust enough to prove the functional correctness of several versions of matrix addition and multiplication codes resulting from loop reordering, loop tiling, inverting the iteration order, line swapping, and expression decomposition. Finally, we extend our method to enable modular analysis on code fragments manipulating matrices by reference, and show that it results in a significant analysis speedup.

1 Introduction

Static analysis by abstract interpretation [7] allows discovering automatically properties about program behaviors. In order to scale up, it employs abstractions, which induce approximations. However, the approximation is sound, as it considers a super-set of all program behaviors; hence, any property proved in the abstract (such as the absence of run-time error, or the validation of some specification) also holds in all actual program executions. Static analysis by abstract interpretation has been applied with some success to the analysis of run-time errors [3]. More recently, it has been extended to proving functional properties, including array properties [1,6,8], such as proving that a sorting algorithm indeed outputs a sorted array. In this work, we consider functional properties of a different kind, not tackled before: properties on matrices. Consider as example Program 1.1 starting with the assumption $N > 0$. Our analyzer will automatically infer the following postcondition for the program: $\forall u, v \in [0, N-1]$, $C[u][v] = \sum_{w=0}^{N-1} A[u][w] \times B[w][v]$, i.e., the program indeed computes the product of matrices A and B into C.

This work is partially supported by the European Research Council under Consolidator Grant Agreement 681393 – MOPSA.

© Springer-Verlag GmbH Germany 2016
X. Rival (Ed.): SAS 2016, LNCS 9837, pp. 257–277, 2016.
DOI: 10.1007/978-3-662-53413-7_13

```
for (i=0; i<N; i++)
  for (j=0; j<N; j++) {
    C[i][j] = 0;
    for (k=0; k<N; k++)
      C[i][j] += A[i][k] * B[k][j];
}
```

Program 1.1. Matrix multiplication $C = A \times B$.

Introductory Example. To explain how our method works in more details, we focus on a simpler introductory example, the matrix addition from Program 1.2. Note that we will show later that our method is also successful on the multiplication from Program 1.1, as well as more complex, optimized variants of these algorithms, such as the tiled addition in Program 1.6.

```
1   /* N >= 5 */
2   i=0;
3   while (i<N) {
4     j=0;
5     while (j<N) {
6       C[i][j] = A[i][j] + B[i][j];
7       j++;
8     };
9     i++;
10  }
```

Program 1.2. Matrix addition $C \leftarrow A + B$.

We wish to design a sound analyzer capable of inferring that, at line 10, the addition of B and A has been stored into C. Note that the program is parametric in the size N of the matrix, and we want our analysis to be able to prove that it is correct independently from the precise value of N. Therefore, we would like to infer that the formula $\phi \triangleq \forall a, \forall b, (0 \leq a < N \wedge 0 \leq b < N) \Rightarrow C[a][b] = A[a][b] + B[a][b]$ holds for all the memory states reachable at line 10.

In order to do so, the static analyzer needs to first infer loop invariants for each of the while loops. For the outermost loop (line 3), we would infer: $\phi_i \triangleq \forall a, \forall b, (0 \leq a < i \wedge 0 \leq b < N) \Rightarrow C[a][b] = A[a][b] + B[a][b]$, and, for the innermost loop (line 5): $\phi_j \triangleq (\forall a, \forall b, (0 \leq a < i \wedge 0 \leq b < N) \Rightarrow C[a][b] = A[a][b] + B[a][b]) \wedge (\forall b, 0 \leq b < j \Rightarrow C[i][b] = A[i][b] + B[i][b])$. Note that the loop invariants are far more complex than the formula we expect at the end of the program. In particular, they depend on the local variables i and j. They express the fact that the addition has been performed only for some lines (up to i) and, for ϕ_j, only on one part of the last line (up to j). Every formula we need can be seen as a conjunction of one or several sub-formulas, where each sub-formula expresses that the addition has been performed on some rectangular sub-part of the matrix. Therefore, we introduce the following formula $Add(A, B, C, x, y, z, t)$ with which we will describe our matrices in the rest of the introductory example:

$$Add(A, B, C, x, y, z, t) \triangleq \forall a, \; \forall b, \; (x \leq a < z \wedge y \leq b < t)$$
$$\Rightarrow C[a][b] = A[a][b] + B[a][b]$$

The formulas ϕ_i, ϕ_j and ϕ can all be described as a conjunction of one or more instances of the fixed predicate Add, as well as numeric constraints relating only scalar variables, including program variables (i, j) and predicate variables (x, y, z, t). Abstract interpretation provides numeric domains, such as polyhedra [9], to reason on numeric relations. We will design a family of abstract domains combining existing numeric domains with predicates such as Add and show how, ultimately, abstract operations modeling assignments, tests, joins, etc. can be expressed as numeric operations to soundly reason about matrix contents. While the technique is similar to existing analyses of array operations [1,6,8], the application to matrices poses specific challenges: firstly, as matrices are bi-dimensional, it is less obvious how to update matrix predicates after assignments; secondly, matrix programs feature large levels of loop nesting, which may pose scalability issues.

Contribution. The article presents a new static analysis for matrix-manipulating programs, based on a combination of parametric predicates and numeric domains. The analysis has been proved sound and implemented in a prototype. We provide experimental results proving the functional correctness of a few basic matrix-manipulating programs, including more complex variants obtained by the PLUTO source to source loop optimizer [4,5]. We show that our analysis is robust against code modifications that leave the semantic of the program unchanged, such as loop tiling performed by PLUTO. In the context of full source to binary program certification, analyzing programs after optimization can free us from having to verify the soundness of the optimizer; therefore, our method could be used in combination with certified compilers, such as CompCert [14], while avoiding the need to certify optimization passes in Coq. The analysis we propose is modular: it is defined over matrix predicates that can be combined, and is furthermore parameterized by the choice of a numeric domain. Finally, the performance of our analyzer is reasonable.

The rest of the paper is organized as follows: Sect. 2 describes the programming language we aim to analyze; Sect. 3 formally defines the family of abstractions we are constructing. In Sect. 4, we introduce specific instances to handle matrix addition and multiplication. In Sect. 5, we briefly present a modular interprocedural version of our analysis. Some technical details about the implementation of our analyzer prototype and our experimental results can be found in Sect. 6. Section 7 discusses related works, while Sect. 8 concludes.

2 Syntax and Concrete Semantics

2.1 Programming Language Syntax

We consider a small imperative language, in Fig. 1, based on variables $X \in \mathbb{X}$, (bi-dimensional) array names $A \in \mathbb{A}$, and size variables denoting the width and height of arrays $\mathbb{S} \triangleq \{A.n \mid A \in \mathbb{A}\} \cup \{A.m \mid A \in \mathbb{A}\}$, with arithmetic expressions $E \in \mathbb{E}$, boolean expressions $B \in \mathbb{B}$, and commands $C \in \mathbb{C}$. The command Array A of $E_1 \ E_2$ denotes the definition of a matrix A of size $E_1 \times E_2$.

$$E ::= \mathbf{v} \in \mathbb{R} \mid X \in \mathbb{X} \mid E_1 + E_2 \mid E_1 \times E_2 \mid A[X_1][X_2] \mid A.n \mid A.m$$
$$B ::= E_1 < E_2 \mid E_1 \leq E_2 \mid E_1 = E_2 \mid \neg B \mid B_1 \vee B_2 \mid B_1 \wedge B_2$$
$$C ::= \mathtt{skip} \mid X := E \mid A[X_1][X_2] \leftarrow E \mid C_1 \ ; \ C_2 \mid$$
$$\mathtt{If} \ B \ \mathtt{then} \ C_1 \ \mathtt{else} \ C_2 \mid \mathtt{While} \ B \ \mathtt{do} \ C \ \mathtt{done} \mid \mathtt{Array} \ A \ \mathtt{of} \ E_1 \ E_2$$

Fig. 1. Syntax of the language.

2.2 Concrete Reachability

We define the concrete semantic of our programming language. It is the most precise mathematical expression describing the possible executions of the program and it will be given in terms of postconditions for commands. This concrete semantic is not computable; therefore, the rest of the article will propose computable approximations. The soundness property of Theorem 1 (Sect. 4.1) will hold with respect to this concrete semantic.

$\mathcal{D}$ is the domain of scalar values, and we assume from now on that $\mathcal{D} = \mathbb{R}$. $\mathcal{M}$ is the set of memory states, which are pairs in $\mathcal{M} \triangleq \mathcal{M}_\mathcal{V} \times \mathcal{M}_\mathcal{A}$ containing a scalar environment in $\mathcal{M}_\mathcal{V} \triangleq \mathcal{V} \to \mathcal{D}$ and a matrix contents environment in $\mathcal{M}_\mathcal{A} \triangleq \mathcal{A} \to (\mathbb{N} \times \mathbb{N}) \to \mathcal{D}$, where $\mathcal{V}$ (resp. $\mathcal{A}$) is any subset of $\mathbb{X} \cup \mathbb{S}$ (resp. $\mathbb{A}$). $\mathcal{E}[\![E]\!] \in \mathcal{M} \to \mathcal{D}$ is the semantic of an expression E (it is well-defined only on memory states that bind the variables and array names appearing in E). $\mathcal{B}[\![B]\!] \in \wp(\mathcal{M})$ defines the set of memory states in which B is true. $\mathbf{Post}[\![C]\!](S)$ denotes the set of states reachable from the set of states S after a command C. Finally, $\mathbf{var}(E)$, $\mathbf{var}(B)$, $\mathbf{var}(C)$ denote the variables appearing respectively in an arithmetic expression, a boolean expression, a command. Figures 2 and 3 describe the behavior of expressions and the state reachability of the program. The evaluation of boolean expressions was left out as it is standard.

- $\forall v \in \mathbb{R}, \mathcal{E}[\![\mathbf{v}]\!]m \triangleq v$
- $\mathcal{E}[\![X]\!]m \triangleq m_\mathcal{V}(X)$
- $\mathcal{E}[\![E_1 + E_2]\!]m \triangleq \mathcal{E}[\![E_1]\!]m + \mathcal{E}[\![E_2]\!]m$

- $\mathcal{E}[\![E_1 \times E_2]\!]m \triangleq \mathcal{E}[\![E_1]\!]m \times \mathcal{E}[\![E_2]\!]m$
- $\mathcal{E}[\![A.n]\!]m \triangleq m_\mathcal{V}(A.n)$
- $\mathcal{E}[\![A.m]\!]m \triangleq m_\mathcal{V}(A.m)$

- $\mathcal{E}[\![A[X_1][X_2]]\!]m \triangleq m_\mathcal{A}(A)(m_\mathcal{V}(X_1), m_\mathcal{V}(X_2))$ when $m_\mathcal{V}(X_1), m_\mathcal{V}(X_2) \in \mathbb{N}$

Fig. 2. Evaluation of expressions. m designates the pair $(m_\mathcal{V}, m_\mathcal{A})$.

Post$[\![C]\!](S) \triangleq$ match C with :

skip	$\to S$
$X := E$	$\to \{(m_\mathcal{V}[X \mapsto \mathcal{E}[\![E]\!]m], m_\mathcal{A}) \mid m \in S\}$
$A[X_1][X_2] \leftarrow E$	$\to \{(m_\mathcal{V}, m_\mathcal{A}[A \mapsto (m_\mathcal{V}(X_1), m_\mathcal{V}(X_2)) \mapsto \mathcal{E}[\![E]\!]m])$
	$\mid m \in S \wedge m_\mathcal{V}(X_1), m_\mathcal{V}(X_2) \in \mathbb{N}\}$
If B then C_1 else C_2	$\to$ **Post**$[\![C_1]\!](S \cap \mathcal{B}[\![B]\!]) \cup$ **Post**$[\![C_2]\!](S \cap \mathcal{B}[\![\neg B]\!])$
While B do C_1 done	$\to \mathrm{lfp}^{\subseteq}(\lambda S_0.S \cup$ **Post**$[\![C_1]\!](S_0 \cap \mathcal{B}[\![B]\!])) \cap \mathcal{B}[\![\neg B]\!]$
Array A of E_1 E_2	$\to \{(m_\mathcal{V}[A.\mathtt{m} \mapsto \mathcal{E}[\![E_1]\!]m, A.\mathtt{n} \mapsto \mathcal{E}[\![E_2]\!]m], m_\mathcal{A})$
	$\mid m \in S\}$
C_1 ; C_2	$\to$ **Post**$[\![C_2]\!]($**Post**$[\![C_1]\!](S))$

Fig. 3. Reachability semantics. m designates the pair $(m_\mathcal{V}, m_\mathcal{A})$.

3 Generic Abstract Semantics

3.1 Predicates

As suggested in Sect. 1, we define predicates to specify relations between matrices. The language of predicates is based on the expressions from our programming language, with added quantifiers. The predicate language is very general but we will only be using one fragment at a time to describe the behavior of our programs. In order to do so, we define terms $t \in \mathcal{T}$, using dedicated predicate variables $y \in \mathbb{Y}$ (such that $\mathbb{X} \cap \mathbb{Y} = \mathbb{Y} \cap \mathbb{S} = \emptyset$), atomic predicates $g \in \mathcal{G}$, and predicates $P \in \mathcal{P}$, as shown in Fig. 4. Their interpretation will be respectively: $\mathcal{I}_\mathcal{T}[\![t]\!]$, $\mathcal{I}_\mathcal{G}[\![g]\!]$, and $\mathcal{I}_\mathcal{P}[\![P]\!]$. Those interpretations are defined the same way as interpretations of expressions and booleans; therefore, they are not detailed.

$$t ::= A[x][y] \mid x \in \mathbb{Y} \mid t_1 + t_2 \mid t_1 \times t_2 \mid \mathbf{v} \in \mathbb{R} \mid \sum_{x=y}^{z} t$$

$$g ::= t_1 = t_2 \mid t_1 \leq t_2 \mid t_1 < t_2$$

$$P ::= \mathbf{tt} \mid \mathbf{ff} \mid g \in \mathcal{G} \mid \neg P_1 \mid P_1 \wedge P_2 \mid P_1 \vee P_2 \mid P_1 \Rightarrow P_2 \mid \forall x \in \mathbb{N}, P_1$$

Fig. 4. Terms, atomic predicates, and predicates.

Example 1. Modulo some syntactic sugar, we can define a predicate such as: $P_+(A, B, C, x, y, z, t) \triangleq \forall u \in [x, z-1], \forall v \in [y, t-1], A[u][v] = B[u][v] + C[u][v]$. The interpretation of such a predicate is the set of memory states in which the matrix A is the sum of two matrices B and C on some rectangle.

Finally, we introduce the following relation $P_1 =_S P_2$, meaning that $\exists \sigma \in \mathbf{var}(P_1) \to \mathbf{var}(P_2)$ a bijection such that $P_1\sigma = P_2$, i.e., P_1 and P_2 are syntactically equivalent modulo a renaming of the variables (e.g., $P_+(A, B, C, x, y, z,$

$t) =_S P_+(A, B, C, x', y', z', t'))$. This definition is extended to sets of predicates, $\mathfrak{P}_1 =_S \mathfrak{P}_2$, meaning that there is a one-to-one relation between the sets and every pair of elements in the relation are syntactically equivalent (e.g., $\{Q(A, B, C, x, y, z, t), P(A, u, v)\} =_S \{Q(A, B, C, x', y', z', t'), P(A, u', v')\}$).

3.2   Abstract States

We now assume we have an abstraction of the state $\mathcal{M}_\mathcal{V}$ of the scalar, numeric variables (e.g., the interval or polyhedra [9] domain) that we call $\mathcal{M}_\mathcal{V}^\sharp$, with concretization function $\gamma_\mathcal{V}$, join $\sqcup_\mathcal{V}$, widening $\triangledown_\mathcal{V}$, meet with a boolean constraint $\sqcap_{\mathcal{B},\mathcal{V}}$ or a family of boolean constraints $\sqcap_{\mathcal{B},\mathcal{V}}$, and a partial order relation $\sqsubseteq_\mathcal{V}$. The set of variables bound by an abstract variable memory state $\mathfrak{a} \in \mathcal{M}_\mathcal{V}^\sharp$ is noted $\mathbf{var}(\mathfrak{a}) \subset \mathbb{X} \cup \mathbb{Y} \cup \mathbb{S}$. In the following, we define an abstraction for the analysis of our programming language, this abstraction being built upon a set of predicates describing relations between matrices and a numeric domain. To simplify, without loss of generality, we forbid predicates from referencing program variables or array dimensions, hence $\mathbb{Y} \cap (\mathbb{X} \cup \mathbb{S}) = \emptyset$. We rely instead on the numeric domain to relate predicate variables with program variables, if needed.

We need abstract states to be disjunctions (expressing the different possible states a program can be in at some point) of conjunctions of predicates (that describe a possible state of the program, as a set of constraints and predicates that hold). The conjunctions are necessary as a predicate may hold on several rectangles; the disjunctions are necessary because, within the same loop, the number of predicates may vary from one loop iteration to another (a graphical illustration is given in Fig. 7). Hence, we will introduce a monomial as a conjunction of some predicates and a numeric abstract domain element; an abstract state will be a disjunction of such monomials. Moreover, we want our state to be a set of monomials as small as possible (and in all cases, bounded, to ensure termination); therefore, we would rather use the disjunctive features provided by the numeric domain, if any, than predicate-level disjunctions. We enforce this rule through a notion of well-formedness, explained below.

Definition 1 (*Monomial*). *We call a well-named monomial an element* $(\mathfrak{P}, \mathfrak{a}) \in \mathfrak{M} \triangleq \wp(\mathcal{P}) \times \mathcal{M}_\mathcal{V}^\sharp$ *such that* $\bigcup_{P \in \mathfrak{P}} \mathbf{var}(P) \subset \mathbf{var}(\mathfrak{a})$ *and* $\forall P_1 \neq P_2 \in \mathfrak{P}$, $\mathbf{var}(P_1) \cap \mathbf{var}(P_2) = \emptyset$.

Definition 2 (*Abstract memory state*). *We build an abstraction $\mathcal{M}^\sharp$ for memory states $\mathcal{M}$ that is $\mathcal{M}^\sharp \triangleq \wp(\mathfrak{M})$. We will say that an abstract memory state is well-named if every one of its monomials is well-named. The following concretization function is defined on every well-named abstract state as:*

$$\gamma_p(S^\sharp) = \bigcup_{(\mathfrak{P},\mathfrak{a}) \in S^\sharp} \{(m_{\mathcal{V}|\mathbb{X} \cup \mathbb{S}}, m_\mathcal{A}) \mid m_\mathcal{V} \in \gamma_\mathcal{V}(\mathfrak{a}) \wedge \forall P \in \mathfrak{P}, (m_\mathcal{V}, m_\mathcal{A}) \in \mathcal{I}_\mathcal{P}(P)\}$$

where $m_{\mathcal{V}|\mathbb{X} \cup \mathbb{S}}$ is the restriction of $m_\mathcal{V}$ to $\mathbb{X} \cup \mathbb{S}$.

Example 2. (P_+ is the predicate defined in Example 1). Let us consider an abstract state $\{(\mathfrak{P}, \mathfrak{a})\}$ where $\mathfrak{P} = \{P_+(A, B, C, x, y, z, t)\}$ and $\mathfrak{a}$ is a polyhedron defined by the set of equations $\{x = 0, y = 0, z = n, t = 1, i = 1, j = n,$ $A.n = n, B.n = A.n, C.n = A.n, C.m = B.m, B.m = A.m, A.m = n\}$. In this case: $\gamma_p(\{(\mathfrak{P}, \mathfrak{a})\})$ is the set of memory states in which the first column of the matrix A is the sum of the first columns of B and C.

Definition 3 (*Well-formed*). *We will say that an abstract state $S^\sharp$ is well-formed if $\forall (\mathfrak{P}_1, \mathfrak{a}_1), (\mathfrak{P}_2, \mathfrak{a}_2) \in S^\sharp, (\mathfrak{P}_1 =_S \mathfrak{P}_2) \Rightarrow (\mathfrak{P}_1, \mathfrak{a}_1) = (\mathfrak{P}_2, \mathfrak{a}_2)$, i.e., no two monomials in $S^\sharp$ can be made equal through variable renaming.*

Definition 4 (*Shape*). *We will say that two abstract states $S_1^\sharp, S_2^\sharp$ have the same shape, noted $S_1^\sharp =_F S_2^\sharp$, when $S_1^\sharp \subset_F S_2^\sharp \wedge S_2^\sharp \subset_F S_1^\sharp$ where $S_1^\sharp \subset_F S_2^\sharp \triangleq \forall (\mathfrak{P}_1, \mathfrak{a}_1) \in S_1^\sharp, \exists (\mathfrak{P}_2, \mathfrak{a}_2) \in S_2^\sharp, \mathfrak{P}_1 =_S \mathfrak{P}_2$.*

Remark 1. All the previous definitions amount to say that a well-named, well-formed abstract state is of the form:

(Mon_1 : numeric_constraints_1 $\wedge$ predicate_1_1 $\wedge$ predicate_1_2 $\wedge \dots$)
$$\vee$$
(Mon_2 : numeric_constraints_2 $\wedge$ predicate_2_1 $\wedge$ predicate_2_2 $\wedge \dots$)
$$\vee$$
$$\vdots$$
(Mon_n : numeric_constraints_n $\wedge$ predicate_n_1 $\wedge$ predicate_n_2 $\wedge \dots$)
where no two lines have the same multi-set of predicates.

Let us now define an algorithm $\mathbf{wf}_p$ that transforms any well-named abstract state into a well-named, well-formed abstract state, by transforming every pair of monomials $(\mathfrak{P}_1, \mathfrak{a}_1), (\mathfrak{P}_2, \mathfrak{a}_2) \in S_1^\sharp$ such that $\mathfrak{P}_1 =_S \mathfrak{P}_2$ into $(\mathfrak{P}_2, \mathfrak{a}_1 \sigma \cup_\mathcal{V} \mathfrak{a}_2)$ where $\mathfrak{P}_1 \sigma = \mathfrak{P}_2$ for some permutation σ. However, we only have $\gamma_p(S^\sharp) \subset \gamma_p(\mathbf{wf}_p(S^\sharp))$ in general and not the equality. Indeed, we transform a symbolic disjunction into a disjunction $\cup_\mathcal{V}$ on the numeric domain, therefore this transformation might not be exact. Figure 5 gives the basic operations on the sets of abstract states $\mathcal{M}^\sharp$: a join ($\sqcup_p$), a widening (∇_p),[1] a meet with booleans ($\sqcap_{p,\mathcal{B}}$), and an inclusion test of the numeric component with boolean expressions ($\sqsubseteq_{\mathcal{B}, \mathcal{V}}$).

$$\sqcap_{p,\mathcal{B}}: \quad S_1^\sharp \sqcap_{p,\mathcal{B}} B \triangleq \bigcup\nolimits_{(\mathfrak{P}, \mathfrak{a}) \in S_1^\sharp} \{(\mathfrak{P}, \mathfrak{a} \sqcap_{\mathcal{B}, \mathcal{V}} B)\}$$

$$\sqsubseteq_{\mathcal{B}, \mathcal{V}}: \quad \mathfrak{a} \in \mathcal{M}_\mathcal{V}^\sharp \sqsubseteq_{\mathcal{B}, \mathcal{V}} \bigwedge\nolimits_{i \in I} B_i \in B \triangleq \forall i \in I, \gamma_\mathcal{V}(\mathfrak{a}) \subseteq \mathcal{B}[\![B_i]\!]$$

Fig. 5. Operations on abstract states.

---

[1] ∇_p can not be used when the two abstract states do not have the same shape, in which case the analyzer will perform a join. However, ultimately, the shape will stabilize, thus allowing the analyzer to perform a widening. This widening technique is similar to the one proposed by [18] on cofibred domains.

3.3   Abstract Transfer Functions

We describe, in Fig. 6, how program commands are interpreted using the memory abstract domain to yield a computable over-approximation of the set of reachable states. We assume that the numeric domain provides the necessary transfer functions ($\mathbf{Post}_{\mathcal{V}}^{\sharp}[\![C]\!]$) for all instructions involving only scalar variables. When interpreting loops, the call to $\mathbf{fp}(f)(x)$ computes the fixpoint of f reached by successive iterations of f starting at x (terminating in finite time through the use of a widening).

$$\mathbf{Post}^{\sharp}[\![\mathtt{skip}]\!](S_1^{\sharp}) \triangleq S_1^{\sharp}$$

$$\mathbf{Post}^{\sharp}[\![X := E]\!](S_1^{\sharp}) \triangleq \bigcup_{(\mathfrak{P},\mathfrak{a})\in S_1^{\sharp}}\{(\mathfrak{P}, \mathbf{Post}_{\mathcal{V}}^{\sharp}[\![X := E]\!](\mathfrak{a}))\}$$

$$\mathbf{Post}^{\sharp}[\![A[X_1][X_2] \leftarrow E]\!](S_1^{\sharp}) \triangleq \mathbf{wf}_p(\bigcup_{(\mathfrak{P},\mathfrak{a})\in S_1^{\sharp}}\{\mathbf{Post}_{\mathfrak{M}}^{\sharp}(\mathfrak{P}, \mathfrak{a}, A, E, X_1, X_2)\})$$

$$\mathbf{Post}^{\sharp}[\![\mathtt{If}\ B\ \mathtt{then}\ C_1\ \mathtt{else}\ C_2]\!](S_1^{\sharp}) \triangleq$$
$$\quad \mathbf{Post}^{\sharp}[\![C_1]\!](S_1^{\sharp} \sqcap_{p,\mathcal{B}} B) \sqcup_p \mathbf{Post}^{\sharp}[\![C_2]\!](S_1^{\sharp} \sqcap_{p,\mathcal{B}} (\neg B))$$

$$\mathbf{Post}^{\sharp}[\![\mathtt{While}\ B\ \mathtt{do}\ C\ \mathtt{done}]\!](S_1^{\sharp}) \triangleq$$
$$\quad \mathbf{Res}(\mathbf{fp}(\lambda S^{\sharp} \to \mathtt{let}\ S_P^{\sharp} = S^{\sharp} \sqcup_p \mathbf{Post}^{\sharp}[\![C]\!](S^{\sharp} \sqcap_{p,\mathcal{B}} B)\ \mathtt{in}$$
$$\quad \mathtt{if}\ S_P^{\sharp} =_F S^{\sharp}\ \mathtt{then}\ S^{\sharp} \triangledown_p S_P^{\sharp}\ \mathtt{else}\ S_P^{\sharp})(S_1^{\sharp}) \sqcap_{p,\mathcal{B}} (\neg B))$$

$$\mathbf{Post}^{\sharp}[\![C_1\ ;\ C_2]\!](S_1^{\sharp}) \triangleq \mathbf{Post}^{\sharp}[\![C_2]\!](\mathbf{Post}^{\sharp}[\![C_1]\!](S_1^{\sharp}))$$

Fig. 6. Abstract postconditions.

Two functions are yet to be defined: $\mathbf{Post}_{\mathfrak{M}}^{\sharp}$ and $\mathbf{Res}$. Indeed, these functions will depend on our choice of predicates. For instance, Sect. 4.1 will introduce one version of $\mathbf{Post}_{\mathfrak{M}}^{\sharp}$, named $\mathbf{Post}_{+,\mathfrak{M}}^{\sharp}$, able to handle expressions of the form $A[X_1][X_2] \leftarrow B[X_1][X_2] + C[X_1][X_2]$ to analyze additions, while Sect. 4.2 will discuss multiplications. In practice, the developer will enrich the functions when adding new predicates to analyze new kinds of matrix algorithms in order to design a flexible, general-purpose analyzer. Depending on E and the predicates already existing in the abstract state, $\mathbf{Post}_{\mathfrak{M}}^{\sharp}(\ldots, E, \ldots)$ will either modify variables appearing in predicates, produce new predicates, or remove predicates. In the worst case, when $\mathbf{Post}_{\mathfrak{M}}^{\sharp}$ cannot handle some expression E, it yields the approximation $\top$, thus ensuring the correctness of the analyzer.

The function $\mathbf{Res}$ geometrically resizes the abstract state: it coalesces predicates describing adjacent matrix parts into a single part, as long as their join can be exactly represented in our domain (over-approximating the join would be unsound as our predicates employ universal quantifiers). An algorithm for $\mathbf{Res}$ for the case of the addition is proposed in Sect. 4.1. As expected, the problem of extending a bi-dimensional rectangle is slightly more complex than that of extending a segment, as done in traditional array analysis [6,8]. New rewriting rules are added to $\mathbf{Res}$ when new families of predicates are introduced.

Example 3. For example, we set $\mathbf{Post}_{\mathfrak{M}}^{\sharp}[\![A[0][0] \leftarrow B[0][0] + C[0][0]]\!](\emptyset, \emptyset) = (\{P_+(A, B, C, x, y, z, t)\}, \{x = y = 0, z = t = 1\})$ and $\mathbf{Res}(\{P_+(A, B, C, x, y,$

$z, t), P_+(A, B, C, a, b, c, d)\}, \{x = y = 0, z = 1, t = 10, a = 1, c = 2, b = 0, d = 10\}) = (\{P_+(A, B, C, x, y, z, t)\}, \{x = 0, z = 2, y = 0, t = 10\}).$

Maximum Number of Predicates. As widenings are used on pairs of abstract states with the same shape, we need to ensure that the shape will stabilize; therefore, we need to bound the number of possible shapes an abstract state can have. In order to do so, we only authorize a certain amount of each kind of predicates in a given abstract state. This number will be denoted as M_{pred}. This bound is necessary to ensure the termination of the analysis, but it can be set to an arbitrary value by the user. Note, however, that **Res** will naturally reduce the number of predicates without loss of precision, whenever possible. In practice, M_{pred} depends on the complexity of the loop invariant, which experimentally depends on the number of nested loops and is usually small ($M_{pred} = 4$ was enough to prove the correctness of all the programs considered here).

4   Abstraction Instances

4.1   Matrix Addition

We now consider the analysis of the assignment $E \triangleq A[X_1][X_2] \leftarrow B[X_1][X_2] + C[X_1][X_2]$, as part of proving that a matrix addition is correct. As suggested by the introductory example in Sect. 1, let us define the following predicate:

$$P_+(A, B, C, x, y, z, t) \triangleq \forall a, b \in [x, z-1] \times [y, t-1], \ A[a][b] = B[a][b] + C[a][b]$$

We define now versions $\mathbf{Post}^\sharp_{+,\mathfrak{M}}$ and $\mathbf{Res}_+$ to compute postconditions and possible resize over P_+. Even though the analyzer we implemented can handle predicates on arbitrary many matrices, we will make the description of the algorithms and the proof of correctness simpler by only allowing our analyzer to use predicates of the form P_+ such that $\exists A, B, C, \forall P_+(A', B', C', \dots) \in \mathfrak{P}, \ A' = A \wedge B' = B \wedge C' = C$ (i.e., the source and destination matrices are the same for all the addition predicates used in an abstract state).

$\mathbf{Post}^\sharp_{+,\mathfrak{M}}$. The computation of $\mathbf{Post}^\sharp_{+,\mathfrak{M}}(\mathfrak{P}, \mathfrak{a}, A, B, C, X_1, X_2)$ is described in Algorithm 1. It starts by looking whether one of the predicates stored in $\mathfrak{P}$ (the variables of which are bound by $\mathfrak{a}$) can be geometrically extended using the fact that the cell (X_1, X_2) (also bound by $\mathfrak{a}$) now also contains the addition of B and C. This helper function is detailed in Algorithm 3: we only have to test a linear relation among variables in the numerical domain. In this case, the variables in $\mathfrak{a}$ are rebound to fit the new rectangle. If no such predicate is found and $\mathfrak{P}$ already contains M_{pred} predicates then $\mathbf{Post}^\sharp_{+,\mathfrak{M}}$ gives back $(\mathfrak{P}, \mathfrak{a})$. If no such predicate is found but $\mathfrak{P}$ contains less than M_{pred} predicates, then a new predicate is added to $\mathfrak{P}$, stating that the square $(X_1, X_2, X_1 + 1, X_2 + 1)$ contains the addition of B and C. Finally, the other cases in the algorithm ensure that all predicates of the abstract state are describing the same matrices. The soundness of $\mathbf{Post}^\sharp_{+,\mathfrak{M}}$ comes from the fact that we extend a predicate only in the cell where an addition

---

Algorithm 1. $\text{Post}^\sharp_{+,\mathfrak{M}}$, computes the image by the transfer functions (associated to the expression $E = A[X_1][X_2] \leftarrow B[X_1][X_2] + C[X_1][X_2]$)

    Input : $(\mathfrak{P}, \mathfrak{a}), A, B, C, i, j$
    Output: $(\mathfrak{P}', \mathfrak{a}')$ the postcondition
1 **if** $\exists P_0 \in \mathfrak{P}$, $\text{FIND\_EXTENSION}((P_0, \mathfrak{a}), A, B, C, i, j) = res \neq \textit{None}$ **then**
2      $x', y', z', t' \leftarrow \textbf{fresh}()$;
3      $I \leftarrow \textbf{switch } res \textbf{ do}$
4   **case** *Some(Right)*
5            $\mid$ $(x = x' \wedge y = y' \wedge z + 1 = z' \wedge t = t')$
6   **case** *Some(Down)*
7            $\mid$ $(x = x' \wedge y = y' \wedge z = z' \wedge t + 1 = t')$
8   **case** *Some(Left)*
9            $\mid$ $(x = x' + 1 \wedge y = y' \wedge z = z' \wedge t = t')$
10   **case** *Some(Up)*
11           $\mid$ $(x = x' \wedge y = y' + 1 \wedge z = z' \wedge t = t')$
12   **endsw**
13   **return** $((\mathfrak{P} \setminus P_0) \cup \{P_+(A, B, C, x', y', z', t')\}, \mathfrak{a} \sqcap_{\mathcal{B}, \mathcal{V}} I)$
14 **else**
15   **if** $\forall P_+(A', B', C', \_, \_, \_, \_) \in \mathfrak{P}$, $A' = A \wedge B' = B \wedge C' = C$ **then**
16   **if** $\sharp\mathfrak{P} < M_{pred}$ **then**
17            $x', y', z', t' \leftarrow \textbf{fresh}()$;
18            $I \leftarrow (x' = i \wedge y' = j \wedge z' = i + 1 \wedge t' = j + 1)$;
19   **return** $(\mathfrak{P} \cup \{P_+(A, B, C, x', y', z', t')\}, \mathfrak{a} \sqcap_{\mathcal{B}, \mathcal{V}} I)$
20   **else**
21   **return** $(\mathfrak{P}, \mathfrak{a})$
22   **end**
23   **else**
24   **return** $(\emptyset, \mathfrak{a})$
25   **end**
26 **end**

Algorithm 2. $\text{Res}_{+,\mathfrak{M}}$, resizes possible predicate of a monomial

---

    Input : $(\mathfrak{P}, \mathfrak{a})$
    Output: $(\mathfrak{P}', \mathfrak{a}')$ resized state
1 $(\mathfrak{P}_o, \mathfrak{a}_o) \leftarrow (\mathfrak{P}, \mathfrak{a})$;
2 **while** $\exists (P_0, P_1) \in \mathfrak{P}_o$, $\text{FIND\_RESIZE}(P_0, P_1, \mathfrak{a}_o) \neq \textit{None}$ **do**
3      $P_+(A, B, C, x_0, y_0, z_0, t_0) = P_0$;
4      $P_+(A, B, C, x_1, y_1, z_1, t_1) = P_1$;
5      $x', y', z', t' \leftarrow \textbf{fresh}()$;
6      $I \leftarrow ((x' = x_0) \wedge (y' = y_0) \wedge (z' = z_1) \wedge (t' = t_1))$;
7      $(\mathfrak{P}_o, \mathfrak{a}_o) \leftarrow ((\mathfrak{P}_o \setminus \{P_0, P_1\}) \cup P_+(A, B, C, x', y', z', t'), \mathfrak{a}_o \sqcap_{\mathcal{B}, \mathcal{V}} I)$
8 **end**
9 **return** $(\mathfrak{P}_o, \mathfrak{a}_o)$

Algorithm 3. FIND_EXTENSION, finds possible extension of a monomial

Input : $(P, a), A, B, C, i, j$
Output: None $\|$ Some(dir): the direction in which the rectangle can be extended
1 $P_+(A', B', C', x, y, z, t) = P$;
2 **if** $A = A' \wedge B = B' \wedge C = C'$ **then**
3   **if** $a \sqsubseteq_{\mathcal{B}, \mathcal{V}} ((z = i) \wedge (y = j) \wedge (t = j + 1))$ **then**
4         $|$ Some(Right)
5   **else if** $a \sqsubseteq_{\mathcal{B}, \mathcal{V}} ((x = i) \wedge (z = i + 1) \wedge (t = j))$ **then**
6         $|$ Some(Down)
7   **else if** $a \sqsubseteq_{\mathcal{B}, \mathcal{V}} ((x = i + 1) \wedge (y = j) \wedge (t = j + 1))$ **then**
8         $|$ Some(Left)
9   **else if** $a \sqsubseteq_{\mathcal{B}, \mathcal{V}} ((x = i) \wedge (z = j) \wedge (y = j + 1))$ **then**
10        $|$ Some(Up)
11   **else**
12        $|$ None
13 **else**
14    $|$ None
15 **end**

Algorithm 4. FIND_RESIZE, finds possible resize among two predicates in a monomial

Input : P_0, P_1, a
Output: None $\|$ Some(dir): the direction in which the two rectangles can be
         merged
1 $P_+(A', B', C', x_0, y_0, z_0, t_0) = P_0$;
2 $P_+(A'', B'', C'', x_1, y_1, z_1, t_1) = P_1$;
3 **if** $A'' = A' \wedge B'' = B' \wedge C'' = C'$ **then**
4   **if** $a \sqsubseteq_{\mathcal{B}, \mathcal{V}} ((x_0 = x_1) \wedge (z_0 = z_1) \wedge (t_0 - y_1))$ **then**
5         $|$ Some(Right)
6   **else**
7   **if** $a \sqsubseteq_{\mathcal{B}, \mathcal{V}} ((y_0 = y_1) \wedge (t_0 = t_1) \wedge (z_0 = x_1))$ **then**
8            $|$ Some(Down)
9   **else**
10           $|$ None
11   **end**
12   **end**
13 **else**
14    $|$ None
15 **end**

has just been performed and from the test on line 15 in Algorithm 1 that ensures that if we start to store the sum of some newly encountered matrices in a matrix where some predicates held, then all the former predicates are removed.

Res$_+$. The function **Res$_+$** tries to merge two predicates when they correspond to two adjacent rectangles, the union of which can be exactly represented as a larger rectangle (the resize conditions are also given by linear relations). A description of a function **Res$_{+,\mathfrak{m}}$** can be found in Algorithm 2, with the help of Algorithm 4, and **Res$_+$** is the application of **Res$_{+,\mathfrak{m}}$** to every monomial in the abstract state considered. The soundness of **Res$_+$** comes from the soundness of the underlying numerical domain and the tests performed by FIND_RESIZE.

Theorem 1. *The analyzer defined by the* **Post$^\sharp$** *function is sound, in the sense that it over-approximates the reachable states of the program:*

$$\forall C \in \mathbb{C}, \forall S^\sharp, \mathbf{Post}[\![C]\!](\gamma_p(S^\sharp)) \subseteq \gamma_p(\mathbf{Post}^\sharp[\![C]\!](S^\sharp))$$

The idea of the proof is to show that the proposed functions **Post$^\sharp_{+,\mathfrak{m}}$** and **Res$_{+,\mathfrak{m}}$** are sound, and to underline that the termination of the analysis of the `while` loop is ensured by a convergence of the shape of the abstract states.

4.2   Matrix Multiplication

Consider Program 1.3 that implements a matrix multiplication. It employs two kinds of matrix assignments: $E_1 \triangleq A[X_1][X_2] \leftarrow c \in \mathbb{R}$ and $E_2 \triangleq A[X_1][X_2] \leftarrow A[X_1][X_2] + B[X_1][X_3] \times C[X_3][X_2]$, the first one being used as an initialization, and the other one to accumulate partial products. To achieve a modular design, we naturally associate to each kind of assignments a kind of predicates, and show how these predicates interact. More precisely, in our case, we consider the two predicates:

$$P_s(A, x, y, z, t, c) \triangleq \forall i, j \in [x, z-1] \times [y, t-1], A[i][j] = c$$

$$P_\times(A, B, C, x, y, z, t, u, v) \triangleq$$

$$\forall i, j \in [x, z-1] \times [y, t-1], A[i][j] = \sum_{k=u}^{v} B[i][k] \times C[k][j]$$

which state respectively that the matrix A has been set to c on some rectangle, and that the matrix A received a partial product of B and C.

```
1     n >= 1;
2     i := 0;
3     while (i < n) do
4        j := 0;
5        while (j < n) do
6           A[i][j] <- 0;
7           j := j +1
8        done;
9        i := i +1
10    done;
11    i := 0;
12    while (i < n) do
13       j := 0;
14       while (j < n) do
15          k := 0;
16          while (k < n) do
17             A[i][j]<-A[i][j]+
18                B[i][k]*C[k][j];
19             k := k + 1;
20          done
21          j := j + 1;
22       done
23       i := i + 1;
24    done
```

Program 1.3. Multiplication with inner loop on k.

Predicates can interact together in two ways. Firstly, in a non productive way, for example an addition is performed in a matrix A and then the matrix A is reset to 0. In order to ensure soundness, we need to remove the predicate stating that A received an addition. Secondly, in a productive way, meaning that a matrix A is set to 0 as a prerequisite to receiving the product of two matrices, by summation over k of the partial products $B[i][k] \times C[k][j]$.

Removing Predicates. The analysis suggested for the addition in terms of postconditions can be extended to the set predicate P_s the same way. Indeed, we add a function $\mathbf{Post}^{\sharp}_{s,\mathfrak{M}}$, that enlarges the predicates $P_s(A, x, y, z, t, c)$ and a function $\mathbf{Res}_{s,\mathfrak{M}}$, that resizes them when possible, and likewise $\mathbf{Post}^{\sharp}_{\times,\mathfrak{M}}$ and $\mathbf{Res}_{\times,\mathfrak{M}}$ for predicate $P_\times$ (it is done the same way as the addition predicate). However, for the analyzer to be sound, we need to ensure that $\mathbf{Post}^{\sharp}_{\times,\mathfrak{M}}$ and $\mathbf{Post}^{\sharp}_{s,\mathfrak{M}}$ check whether the matrix that was modified (A) by the evaluated command (resp. $A[X_1][X_2] \leftarrow B[X_1][X_2] + C[X_1][X_2]$ and $A[X_1][X_2] \leftarrow c$) appears in some other predicate P. If it is the case, then P is removed from the state, thus loosing information but ensuring soundness.

Splitting Predicates. In Program 1.3, matrix A is set to 0 before the main loop. This is necessary if we want to compute the product of B and C into A. Therefore, we can only assert $P_\times(A, B, C, i, j, i+1, j+1, 0, 1)$ after a com-

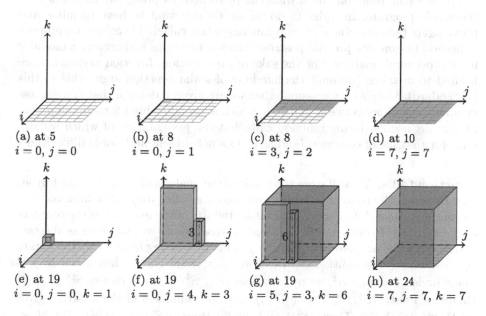

(a) at 5
$i = 0, j = 0$

(b) at 8
$i = 0, j = 1$

(c) at 8
$i = 3, j = 2$

(d) at 10
$i = 7, j = 7$

(e) at 19
$i = 0, j = 0, k = 1$

(f) at 19
$i = 0, j = 4, k = 3$

(g) at 19
$i = 5, j = 3, k = 6$

(h) at 24
$i = 7, j = 7, k = 7$

Fig. 7. Evolution of the predicates for Program 1.3. The predicates are, in order of apparition: $P_s(A, B, C, \dots)$ (in b, c, e, f, g), $P_s(A, B, C, \dots)$ (in c, d, e, f, g), $P_\times(A, B, C, \dots)$ (in e, f, g), $P_\times(A, B, C, \dots)$ (in f, g), $P_\times(A, B, C, \dots)$ (in g, h).

mand A[i][j] ← A[i][j] + B[i][k]*C[k][j] if some precondition states that
$A[i][j] = 0$ (e.g., a P_s predicate). Therefore the postcondition $\mathbf{Post}^{\sharp}_{\times,\mathcal{M}}$ checks
whether a predicate states that $A[i][j] = 0$. If no such predicate exists, we can
not produce a multiplication predicate. If it exists, then we can but we have
to split the zero predicates. In order to illustrate this case, Fig. 7 depicts the
evolution of the different predicates during the analysis of Program 1.3. Notice
that we have only drawn the evolution of predicates that will lead to a successful
result (meaning that, among all the possible states the matrix can be according
to the abstract state, Fig. 7 only depicts the most advanced one, i.e., the one
that is the most precise about the contents of the matrix). An abstract state is
the superposition of all possible states, hence not only those shown in Fig. 7.

Finally, we notice that the variables occuring in the $P_\times$ predicate mentioned
above do not have the same role. Indeed, x, y, z, t variables denote a localization
in the matrix while u, v variables depict the evolution of the multiplication.
To be able to analyze matrix multiplicating programs where loops on k and i
have been interchanged we had to introduce new predicates including existential
quantification over matrices, which we do not detail here for lack of space.

5   Function Calls

In this section, we extend our analysis to support analyzing function calls in
a modular way. Our goal is to be able to efficiently analyze larger programs,
where different functions need different predicates to prove the correctness of
the whole program. In order to do so, we do not want to have to inline and
prove again the correctness of each function when called. Therefore, we propose
a method to compute pre and postconditions of functions and achieve a modular
inter-procedural analysis. For the sake of presentation, function arguments are
limited to matrices (we omit the handling of scalar function arguments as this
is standard). Moreover, we assume that we are given a domain that can express
symbolic equalities between matrices, which is useful to bind formal and actual
matrix arguments during function calls, but the presentation of which we also
omit for the sake of concision (and as it does not present additional difficulties).

Function Calls. We will store the result of the analysis of a function for further
use. However, the context in which functions are called may differ from one call
to another. Those differences can be either the size of the matrices or the contents
of the matrices. In our analyzer, pre and postconditions are expressed as abstract
states: when the analysis of a function f is made, starting from an abstract state
$S^{\sharp}_i$ yielding a postcondition $S^{\sharp}_o$, we store $(f, S^{\sharp}_i, S^{\sharp}_o)$. Then, when a call to f is
made under a context $S^{\sharp}$, we test whether $S^{\sharp} \sqsubseteq S^{\sharp}_i$, in which case $\gamma(S^{\sharp}) \subseteq \gamma(S^{\sharp}_i)$
therefore $\mathbf{Post}(\gamma(S^{\sharp})) \subseteq \mathbf{Post}(\gamma(S^{\sharp}_i))$ and the soundness of the analyzer gives
us $\mathbf{Post}(\gamma(S^{\sharp})) \subseteq \gamma(\mathbf{Post}^{\sharp}(S^{\sharp}_i))$ and finally $\mathbf{Post}(\gamma(S^{\sharp})) \subseteq \gamma(S^{\sharp}_o)$. Therefore,
when $S^{\sharp} \sqsubseteq S^{\sharp}_i$ holds, a possible postcondition is $S^{\sharp}_o$, which enables us to avoid
reanalyzing the function. In order for this method to be efficient, we need to

store elements $(S_i^{\sharp}, S_o^{\sharp})$ such that $S_i^{\sharp}$ is the biggest possible, so that it covers many different calling contexts for the function, but small enough, so that the evaluation of the function produces an interesting state $S_o^{\sharp}$. To ensure this, in our implementation, we chose to enlarge the entry context $S_i^{\sharp}$ found at call sites in the following way:

- Conditions of the form $A.n = n \in \mathbb{N}^*$ stored in the ground domain $\mathfrak{a}$ are replaced with $A.n \geq 1$. But we keep (in)equalities between the sizes of matrices. That way, we generalize the precondition in order to be able to reuse the analysis on matrices of different sizes.
- Predicates on the matrices are forgotten.

These choices can prevent us from analyzing precisely programs we could analyze using the non-modular analysis of Sect. 4 by inlining functions; however, it makes the efficient and modular analysis easier to perform. Finding more clever abstractions of the calling context that are precise enough to enable the analysis and that maximize the possibility of reuse is a hard problem on which future work is required.

The Aliasing Problem. To present the aliasing problem, let us start by looking at Program 1.4. The analyzer proposed in Sect. 3.1 will not conclude that this program is storing in A the addition of the initial value of B and A (because when a command $A[X_1][X_2] \leftarrow B[X_1][X_2] + C[X_1][X_2]$ is encountered, it needs to check that $A \neq B \wedge A \neq C$). However, we would like our analyzer to conclude on Program 1.5 that at the end of function main we have $A = B + B + C$ where $+$ is the matrix addition. Firstly, let us note that the analyzer will reanalyze the code of a function each time it is called with a different aliasing. Indeed, the analysis made for a call add(A,B,C) is not the same as the analysis that will be made for add(A,B,A). Note that each aliasing is analyzed only once and there are a finite number of possible aliasing (i.e., partitions of $\{A, B, C\}$).

```
1   i := 0;
2   while (i < n) do
3     j := 0;
4     while (j < n) do
5       A[i][j] <- B[i][j] +
                A[i][j];
6       j := j + 1;
7     done
8     i := i + 1;
9   done
```

Program 1.4. Addition.

```
1   function add(A,B,C) {
2     i := 0;
3     while (i < A.n) do
4       j := 0;
5       while (j < A.n) do
6         A[i][j] <- B[i][j] + C[i][j];
7         j := j + 1;
8       done
9       i := i + 1;
10    done
11  }
12  function main () {
13    add(D,E,F)
14    add(A,B,C);
15    add(A,B,A)
16  }
```

Program 1.5. Addition with aliasing.

Callee Analysis. We consider new predicates, called equality predicates: $Eq(A, B, x, y, z, t) = \forall a, b \in [x, z-1] \times [y, t-1]$, $A[a][b] = B[a][b]$ that we will use in the analysis of the callee. In order to analyze a function call function $f(A_0, \ldots, A_{n-1}) = \{ C \}$, we perform two substitutions in the code C of the callee: a first one to match the semantic of the function call $((\lambda A.C)B \to C[B/A])$ and a second one which transforms every matrix name (B) in the body of the callee into an auxiliary name (B'). We add equality predicates stating that those two matrices are the same $(B = B')$ at the entry of the function. When a read is made in an auxiliary version (B') and the equality predicates specify that the two matrices are identical $(Eq(B, B', \ldots))$ we can state that the read was made in the original matrix (B). When a write is made to a matrix, we destroy the equality predicate in the corresponding cell. This method gives us:

- Input/Output relations between matrices (expressed as symbolic or predicate relations between matrices and their auxiliary versions).
- What matrices were unmodified by the function call (as matrices are passed by reference to the functions, knowing it was not modified is necessary if we want to ensure that relations existing in the caller before the function call are still holding).

Example 4. Let us consider Program 1.5. The function add is analyzed twice, because of the two different aliasing. A first analysis of add is performed on line 13, this concludes that add(G,H,I) stores the sum of H and I in G and leaves H and I unchanged. Therefore on line 14, no new analysis of add is performed as we are able to reuse the first analysis. However, on line 15, we need to perform a new analysis as no stored analysis result can be found to match the arguments. We are able to conclude at the end of the analysis of main that E,F,B,C were not modified, that A=B+B+C, and D=E+F.

The method proposed in this section can also be exploited to accelerate the analysis of nested loops. Traditional abstract interpretation by induction on the syntax requires reanalyzing inner loops completely for each iteration of outer loops, which is very costly for deeply nested loops. By considering each loop level as a module to be analyzed separately, we can compute pre and postconditions that are expressive enough, so that each evaluation of the loop body is reduced to a table lookup. This was used to improve the performance of our analyzer (Sect. 6).

6   Implementation

Results. We implemented the algorithms proposed above as well as various improvements to make the analysis more robust, notably symbolic equality domains [15] able to improve the pattern matching used in the assignment transfer function. Our prototype was able to prove the functional correctness of all the programs mentioned earlier (addition and multiplication). We also analyzed tiled versions of these algorithms, which is a classic optimization (performed by hand or automatically) that increases cache efficiency, but makes the algorithm more difficult to understand. Program 1.6 gives one example of optimized matrix addition, with a tiling factor of 32. Our method successfully analyzes the tiled algorithms, as long as the tiling size is a constant, which is the case for all the optimizers we know of. Note that the tiling transformation causes a doubling in the depth of nested loops and adds some complex conditionals to handle border cases (partially filled tiles), resulting in a more challenging program to analyze. Additionally, we analyzed alternate versions where loops are interchanged, or indices run in decreasing order (from $n - 1$ to 0). In all those cases, the analyzer still proves the functional correctness of the program. All of those programs were analyzed using only few predicates, thus showing that multiple versions of a program can be analyzed using a single predicate. Hence, the analysis is robust against all the following transformations: loop tiling, switching the loops (row-major or column-major iteration), reverting the loops (iterating downward instead of upward).

```
1     /* n >= 10 */;                        20            else
2     /* n = 32 * a + b */                  21              endj := b;
3     /* 1 <= b < 32 */                     22            while (jj < endj) do
4     Array A of n n;                       23              x = 32 * i + ii;
5     Array B of n n;                       24              y = 32 * j + jj;
6     Array C of n n;                       25              A[x][y] <- B[x][y] +
7     i := 0;                                                   C[x][y];
8     while (i <= a) do                     26              jj := jj + 1;
9       j := 0;                             27            done;
10      while (j <= a) do                   28            ii := ii + 1;
11        ii := 0;                          29          done;
12        if (i = a) then                   30          j := j + 1;
13          endi := 32                      31        done;
14        else                              32        i := i + 1;
15          endi := b;                      33      done
16        while (ii < endi) do
17          jj := 0;                        Program 1.6. Addition tiled with
18          if (j = b) then                 reminder.
19            endj := 32
```

Implementation. The implementation of the different analyzers has been written in Ocaml using the Apron module (for numerical domains). The final implementation using all proposed abstract domains is about 6000 line long (not counting the parser). It enables us to parse code written in a C like language and analyze this code using the previously mentioned abstractions. This analyzer computes the abstract reachability at every code point depending on the initial abstract states. The implementation has been tested mainly on programs performing additions, products, GEMM (general matrix multiplication: $C \leftarrow \alpha AB + \beta C$), scaling, with various optimizations and on every possible loop order. As examples, we mostly used programs optimized by PLUTO and programs we found in a BLAS library (Basic Linear Algebra Subprograms). Those programs are all successfully analyzed by the final implementation. Figure 8 gives the time it took for the analyzer to prove the functional correctness of programs proposed in this article. The number of loops indicated is the biggest number of interlocked while loops that can be found in the program (additions and multiplications require respectively 2 and 3 nested loops without tiling, and 4 and 6

	2 loops	3 loops	4 loops	6 loops
Set to 0	0.022			
Addition	0.042		0.772	50.9 (3.36 using §5)
Multiplication		0.232		110.0
Addition with rest			1.389	
GEMM		0.54		

Fig. 8. Analysis time in seconds.

nested loops with tiling enabled, addition tiled twice require 6 loops). For the (twice) tiled addition, we also show the benefit of the loop-modular analysis of Sect. 5.

Trace Partitioning. In order to make the analysis more precise, we used trace partitioning [17] to separate some monomials according to their history. We recall that abstract states are of the form $(\mathfrak{P}, \mathfrak{a})$ and that we ensured a finite number of possible shapes for monomials by bounding the number of predicates the analyzer can use. Hence, we modified abstract states to be of the form $(\mathfrak{i}, \mathfrak{P}, \mathfrak{a})$ where $\mathfrak{i} \in \mathbb{N}$ is called a *flag*. We now say that two monomials have the same shape if they have the same flag and they have the same shape according to the previous definition. We encode in a flag $\mathfrak{i}$ the program path taken by each monomial along the analysis (whether it has been through each loop or not and in which branch of a condition it has been).

Numerical Abstract Domain. The abstract states defined in this paper require an underlying numerical domain. Some of the numerical variables stored in the numerical domain are used to describe "zones" in a matrix where some relations hold. As we wanted our analyzer to be robust against operations such as tiling we needed relations such as $32i - j = 0$ and $32i - j \leq 0$ to be precise, therefore we chose the polyhedra domain [9]. As most of the operations performed by our analyzer are done on the numerical abstract domain, the cost of the analysis depends mainly on the cost of the operation in the underlying numerical domain. However for a different set of predicates (e.g., not describing rectangular shapes), a less expensive numerical domain could be used (such as intervals or octagons).

7 Related Work

A standard way to efficiently handle possibly unbounded arrays when a low level of precision is sufficient is to abstract arrays as a single cell containing a non-relational abstract value, using weak update. As the static analysis of array properties has drawn some significant attention lately, more precise methods have been devised. Gopan et al. [11] extend this standard method by allowing relational (but still uniform) abstractions. A class of analyses [8,12,13] dynamically partitions arrays, which allows expressing non-uniform properties of arrays as well as strong updates. Allamigeon has designed companion numeric domains specifically targeting array partition bounds [1]. String analysis for C programs can be seen as a special case of array analysis, and similar partitioning-based methods have been proposed [2]. All these methods differ on whether a partition or a covering is used, how partition bounds are expressed and inferred, the relationality between partition contents and partition bounds, etc. Fluid updates [10] address the problem of weak updates in a different way, by expressing array parts using constraints, manipulated by a SMT solver, instead of explicit partitions. Monniaux and Alberti [16] propose an original method by abstraction through ad-hoc Galois connections into purely scalar programs that are then analyzed with standard methods. Our work is much closer to parametric predicate abstraction [6], which also analyzes arrays using predicates of fixed shape conjoined with numeric properties. The large majority of these works only focus on properties of uni-dimensional arrays. Nevertheless some array abstractions are powerful enough to consider array elements of arbitrary types, and could be possibly nested to handle matrices as arrays of arrays of numbers (this is explicitly mentioned as a possibility in [8] but without details nor experiments) while the method of [16] can analyze matrix initialization (and possibly more) when parameterized with the correct predicate. As far as we know, none of these methods has been applied to prove matrix multiplication algorithms correct, nor do they address the problem of deeply nested loops in optimized matrix algorithms.

8 Conclusion

We have proposed new abstractions to prove the functional correctness of matrix-manipulating programs, such as addition and multiplication. They are parametric in a set of predicates (corresponding to the functional properties to prove) and classic relational numeric domains. Our prototype implementation provided encouraging experimental results, both in term of performance and precision. In particular, precision-wise, we could prove the correctness of several variants of additions and multiplications, including basic loop reordering but also versions generated from a source-to-source loop optimizer which introduces tiling (making the code significantly more complex, with in particular more nested loops). We also showed how our method can be embedded in a modular inter-procedural analysis, with clear benefits for the efficiency of the analysis.

Future work will include enriching our predicates in order to tackle a wider range of matrix and vector manipulations, such as Gauss elimination, LU decomposition, linear system resolution, eigenvectors, or eigenvalues computation, etc. Another direction for future work is to make the analysis robust against more varied program transformations and optimizations, such as instruction-level reordering, loop pipelining, or vectorization. Ultimately, we would like to be able to analyze the assembly or low-level representation output by a compiler, and prove that the functional correctness still holds despite compiler optimization, without the burden of certifying the optimizing part of the compiler itself. Our analysis currently assumes a real semantics, while actual implementations of matrix operations employ floating-point arithmetic. Hence, with respect to a float implementation, we prove that, e.g., a matrix addition program computes one float approximation of the matrix addition, but not that it does so while respecting the order of operations specified in the original, unoptimized program (and this may change the result due to rounding errors). While we believe that this already provides an interesting correctness criterion (especially because matrix libraries seldom guarantee an evaluation order), future work will include designing predicates reasoning on floats in order to take execution order and rounding into account. Finally, we have only demonstrated our method on a simple prototype for a toy language, but future work will consider more realistic C programs, such as actual BLAS libraries or scientific applications.

References

1. Allamigeon, X.: Non-disjunctive numerical domain for array predicate abstraction. In: Drossopoulou, S. (ed.) ESOP 2008. LNCS, vol. 4960, pp. 163–177. Springer, Heidelberg (2008)
2. Allamigeon, X., Godard, W., Hymans, C.: Static analysis of string manipulations in critical embedded C programs. In: Yi, K. (ed.) SAS 2006. LNCS, vol. 4134, pp. 35–51. Springer, Heidelberg (2006)
3. Blanchet, B., Cousot, P., Cousot, R., Feret, J., Mauborgne, L., Miné, A., Monniaux, D., Rival, X.: A static analyzer for large safety-critical software. In: Proceedings of PLDI 2003, pp. 196–207. ACM, June 2003
4. Bondhugula, U., Baskaran, M., Krishnamoorthy, S., Ramanujam, J., Rountev, A., Sadayappan, P.: Automatic transformations for communication-minimized parallelization and locality optimization in the polyhedral model. In: Hendren, L. (ed.) CC 2008. LNCS, vol. 4959, pp. 132–146. Springer, Heidelberg (2008)
5. Bondhugula, U., Hartono, A., Ramanujam, J., Sadayappan, P.: A practical automatic polyhedral parallelizer and locality optimizer. In: Proceedings of PLDI 2008, pp. 101–113. ACM (2008)
6. Cousot, P.: Verification by abstract interpretation. In: Dershowitz, N. (ed.) Verification: Theory and Practice. LNCS, vol. 2772, pp. 243–268. Springer, Heidelberg (2004)
7. Cousot, P., Cousot, R.: Abstract interpretation: a unified lattice model for static analysis of programs by construction or approximation of fixpoints. In: Proceedings of POPL 1977, pp. 238–252. ACM (1977)
8. Cousot, P., Cousot, R., Logozzo, F.: A parametric segmentation functor for fully automatic and scalable array content analysis. In: Proceedings of POPL 2011, pp. 105–118. ACM (2011)
9. Cousot, P., Halbwachs, N.: Automatic discovery of linear restraints among variables of a program. In: Proceedings of POPL 1978, pp. 84–96. ACM (1978)
10. Dillig, I., Dillig, T., Aiken, A.: Fluid updates: beyond strong vs. weak updates. In: Gordon, A.D. (ed.) ESOP 2010. LNCS, vol. 6012, pp. 246–266. Springer, Heidelberg (2010)
11. Gopan, D., DiMaio, F., Dor, N., Reps, T., Sagiv, M.: Numeric domains with summarized dimensions. In: Jensen, K., Podelski, A. (eds.) TACAS 2004. LNCS, vol. 2988, pp. 512–529. Springer, Heidelberg (2004)

12. Gopan, D., Reps, T.W., Sagiv, S.: A framework for numeric analysis of array operations. In: Proceedings of POPL 2005, pp. 338–350. ACM (2005)
13. Halbwachs, N., Péron, M.: Discovering properties about arrays in simple programs. SIGPLAN Not. **43**(6), 339–348 (2008)
14. Leroy, X.: Formal certification of a compiler back-end, or: programming a compiler with a proof assistant. In: Proceedings of POPL 2006, pp. 42–54. ACM (2006)
15. Miné, A.: Symbolic methods to enhance the precision of numerical abstract domains. In: Emerson, E.A., Namjoshi, K.S. (eds.) VMCAI 2006. LNCS, vol. 3855, pp. 348–363. Springer, Heidelberg (2006)
16. Monniaux, D., Alberti, F.: A simple abstraction of arrays and maps by program translation. In: Blazy, S., Jensen, T. (eds.) SAS 2015. LNCS, vol. 9291, pp. 217–234. Springer, Heidelberg (2015)
17. Rival, X., Mauborgne, L.: The trace partitioning abstract domain. ACM Trans. Program. Lang. Syst. **29**(5), 26 (2007)
18. Venet, A.: Abstract cofibered domains: application to the alias analysis of untyped programs. In: Cousot, R., Schmidt, D.A. (eds.) SAS 1996. LNCS, vol. 1145, pp. 366–382. Springer, Heidelberg (1996)

Generalized Homogeneous Polynomials for Efficient Template-Based Nonlinear Invariant Synthesis

Kensuke Kojima[1,2], Minoru Kinoshita[1,4], and Kohei Suenaga[1,3($\boxtimes$)]

[1] Kyoto University, Kyoto, Japan
ksuenaga@kuis.kyoto-u.ac.jp
[2] JST CREST, Kyoto, Japan
[3] JST PRESTO, Kyoto, Japan
[4] KLab Inc., Tokyo, Japan

Abstract. The *template-based* method is one of the most successful approaches to algebraic invariant synthesis. In this method, an algorithm designates a *template polynomial p* over program variables, generates constraints for $p = 0$ to be an invariant, and solves the generated constraints. However, this approach often suffers from an increasing template size if the degree of a template polynomial is too high.

We propose a technique to make template-based methods more efficient. Our technique is based on the following finding: If an algebraic invariant exists, then there is a specific algebraic invariant that we call a *generalized homogeneous* algebraic invariant that is often smaller. This finding justifies using only a smaller template that corresponds to a generalized homogeneous algebraic invariant.

Concretely, we state our finding above formally based on the abstract semantics of an imperative program proposed by Cachera et al. Then, we modify their template-based invariant synthesis so that it generates only generalized homogeneous algebraic invariants. This modification is proved to be sound. Furthermore, we also empirically demonstrate the merit of the restriction to generalized homogeneous algebraic invariants. Our implementation outperforms that of Cachera et al. for programs that require a higher-degree template.

1 Introduction

We consider the following *postcondition problem*: Given a program c, discover a fact that holds at the end of c regardless of the initial state. This paper focuses on a postcondition written as an *algebraic condition* $p_1 = 0 \wedge \cdots \wedge p_n = 0$, where $p_1, \ldots, p_n$ are polynomials over program variables; this problem is a basis for static verification of functional correctness.

One approach to this problem is *invariant synthesis*, in which we are to compute a family of predicates P_l indexed by program locations l such that P_l holds whenever the execution of c reaches l. The invariant associated with the end of c is a solution to the postcondition problem.

© Springer-Verlag GmbH Germany 2016
X. Rival (Ed.): SAS 2016, LNCS 9837, pp. 278–299, 2016.
DOI: 10.1007/978-3-662-53413-7_14

Because of its importance in static program verification, algebraic invariant synthesis has been intensively studied [4,16,19,20]. Among these proposed techniques, one successful approach is the constraint-based method in which invariant synthesis is reduced to a constraint-solving problem. During constraint generation, this method designates *templates*, which are polynomials over the program variables with unknown parameters at the coefficient positions [20]. The algorithm generates constraints that ensure that the templates are invariants and obtains the invariants by solving the constraints[1].

Example 1. The program c_{fall} in Fig. 1 models the behavior of a mass point with weight 1 and with a constant acceleration rate; the program takes friction between the mass point and air into account[2]. For this program, the postcondition $-gt + gt_0 - v + v_0 - x\rho + x_0\rho = 0$ holds regardless of the initial state.

We describe how a template-based method computes the postcondition in Example 1. The method described here differs from the one we explore in this paper; this explanation is intended to suggest the flavor of a template method.

A template-based method generates a *template polynomial* over the program variables that represent an invariant at Line 4.

```
1: x := x₀; v := v₀; t := t₀;
2: while t − a ≠ 0 do
3:     (x, v, t) := (x + vdt, v − gdt − ρvdt, t + dt);
4: end while
5:
```

Fig. 1. Program c_{fall}, which models a falling mass point. The symbols in the program represent the following quantities: x is the position of the point, v is its speed, t is time, x_0 is the initial position, v_0 is the initial speed, t_0 is the initial value of the clock t, g is the acceleration rate, ρ is the friction coefficient, and dt is the discretization interval. The simultaneous substitution in the loop body numerically updates the values of x, v, and t. The values of x, v, and t are numerical solutions of the differential equations $\frac{dx}{dt} = v$ and $\frac{dt}{dt} = 1$; notice that the force applied by the air to the mass point is $-\rho v$, which leads to the differential equation for $\frac{dv}{dt} = -g - \rho v$.

Suppose the generated polynomial $p(x_0, v_0, t_0, x, v, t, a, dt, g, \rho)$ is of degree 2 over the variables: $p(x_0, v_0, t_0, x, v, t, a, dt, g, \rho) := a_1 + a_{t_0}t_0 + a_{x_0}x_0 + \cdots + a_{g\rho}g\rho$, where a_w is the coefficient parameter associated with the power product w. The procedure then generates constraints such that $p(x_0, v_0, t_0, x, v, t, a, dt, g, \rho) = 0$ is indeed an invariant at Line 4. The method proposed by Sankaranarayanan et al. [20] based on the Gröbner basis [5] generates the constraints as an equations over the parameters; in this case, a solution to the constraints gives $-gt + ga - v + v_0 - x\rho + x_0\rho = 0$, which is indeed an invariant at the end of c_{fall}.

One of the drawbacks of the template-based method is excessive growth of the size of a template. Blindly generating a template of degree d for a

---

[1] The constraint-based method by Cachera et al. [4], which is the basis of the current paper, uses a template also for other purposes. See Sect. 6 for details.

[2] Although the guard condition $t - a \neq 0$ should be $t - a < 0$ in a real-world numerical program, we use the current example for presentation purposes.

degree parameter d makes the invariant synthesis less scalable for higher-degree invariants. For example, the program in Example 1 has an invariant $-gt^2 + gt_0^2 - 2tv + 2t_0v_0 + 2x - 2x_0 = 0$ at Line 4. This invariant requires a degree-3 template, which has $\binom{10+3}{3} = 286$ monomials in this case.

We propose a hack to alleviate this drawback in the template-based methods. Our method is inspired by a rule of thumb in physics called the *principle of quantity dimension*: A physical law should not add two quantities with different *quantity dimensions* [2]. If we accept this principle, then, at least for a physically meaningful program such as c_{fall}, an invariant (and therefore a template) should consist of monomials with the same quantity dimensions.

Indeed, the polynomial $-gt+gt_0-v+v_0-x\rho+x_0\rho$ in the invariant calculated in Example 1 consists only of quantities that represent velocities. (Notice that ρ is a quantity that corresponds to the inverse of a time quantity.) The polynomial $-gt^2+gt_0^2-2tv+2t_0v_0+2x-2x_0$ above consists only of quantities corresponding to the length. If we use the notation of quantity dimensions used in physics, the former polynomial consists only of monomials with the quantity dimension LT^{-1}, whereas the latter consists only of L, where L and T represent quantity dimensions for lengths and times, respectively.

By leveraging the quantity dimension principle in the template synthesis phase, we can reduce the size of a template. For example, we could use a template that consists only of monomials for, say, velocity quantities instead of the general degree-2 polynomial $p(x_0, v_0, x, v, t, a, dt, g, \rho)$ used above, which yields a smaller template.

The idea of the quantity dimension principle can be nicely captured by generalizing the notion of *homogeneous polynomials*. A polynomial is said to be *homogeneous* if it consists of monomials of the same degree; for example, the polynomial $x^3 + x^2y + xy^2 + y^3$ is a homogeneous polynomial of degree 3. We generalize this notion of homogeneity so that (1) a *degree* is an expression corresponding to a quantity dimension (e.g., LT^{-1}) and (2) each variable has its own degree in degree computation.

Let us describe our idea using an example, deferring formal definitions. Suppose we have the following *degree assignment* for each program variable: $\Gamma := \{x_0 \mapsto L, t_0 \mapsto T, g \mapsto LT^{-2}, t \mapsto T, dt \mapsto T, x \mapsto L, v \mapsto LT^{-1}, v_0 \mapsto LT^{-1}, \rho \mapsto T^{-1}, a \mapsto T\}$. This degree assignment intuitively corresponds to the assignment of the quantity dimension to each variable. With this degree assignment Γ, all of the monomials in $-gt + gt_0 - v + v_0 - x\rho + x_0\rho$ have the same degree; for example, the monomial $-gt$ has degree $\Gamma(g)\Gamma(t) = (LT^{-2})T = LT^{-1}$ and monomial $x\rho$ has degree $\Gamma(x)\Gamma(\rho) = LT^{-1}$, and so on. Hence, $-gt + gt_0 - v + v_0 - x\rho + x_0\rho$ is a homogeneous polynomial in the generalized sense. Such a polynomial is called a *generalized homogeneous (GH) polynomial*. We call an algebraic invariant with a GH polynomial a *generalized homogeneous algebraic (GHA) invariant*.

The main result of this paper is a formalization of this idea: If there is an algebraic invariant of a given program c, then there is a GHA invariant. This justifies the use of a template that corresponds to a GH polynomial in the template method. We demonstrate this result by using the abstract semantics of an imperative programming language proposed by Cachera et al. [4]. We also empirically show that the algorithm by Cachera et al. can be made more efficient using this idea.

As we saw above, the definition of GH polynomials is parameterized over a degree assignment Γ. The type inference algorithm for the *dimension type system* proposed by Kennedy [12,13] can be used to find an appropriate degree assignment; Γ above is inferred using this algorithm. The dimension type system was originally proposed for detecting a violation of the quantity-dimension principle in a numerical program. Our work gives an application of the dimension type system to invariant synthesis.

Although the method is inspired by the principle of quantity dimensions, it can be applied to a program that does not model a physical phenomenon because we abstract the notion of a quantity dimension using that of generalized homogeneity. All the programs used in our experiments (Sect. 7) are indeed physically nonsensical programs.

The rest of this paper is organized as follows. Section 2 sets up the basic mathematical definitions used in this paper; Sect. 3 defines the syntax and semantics of the target language and its abstract semantics; Sect. 4 defines GH polynomials; Sect. 5 defines the revised abstract semantics as the restriction of the original one to the set of GH polynomials and shows that the revised semantics is sound and complete; Sect. 6 gives a template-based invariant-synthesis algorithm and shows its soundness; Sect. 7 reports the experimental results; Sect. 8 discusses related work; and Sect. 9 presents the conclusions. Several proofs are given in the appendices.

2   Preliminaries

$\mathbb{R}$ is the set of real numbers and $\mathbb{N}$ is the set of natural numbers. We write $|S|$ for the cardinality of S if S is a finite set. We designate an infinite set of *variables* **Var**. K is a field ranged over by metavariable k; we use the standard notation for the operations on K. For $x_1, \ldots, x_n \in$ **Var**, we write $K[x_1, \ldots, x_n]$, ranged over by p and q, for the set of polynomials in $x_1, \ldots, x_n$ over K.

A subset $I \subseteq K[x_1, \ldots, x_n]$ is called an *ideal* if (1) I is an additive subgroup and (2) $pq \in I$ for any $p \in I$ and $q \in K[x_1, \ldots, x_n]$. A set $S \subseteq K[x_1, \ldots, x_n]$ is said to *generate* the ideal I, written $I = \langle S \rangle$, if I is the smallest ideal that contains S.

We call an expression of the form $x_1^{d_1} \ldots x_N^{d_N}$, where $d_1, \ldots, d_N \in \mathbb{N}$ and $x_1, \ldots, x_N \in$ **Var**, a *power product* over $x_1, \ldots, x_n$; w is a metavariable for power products. We call $\sum d_i$ the *degree* of this power product. A *monomial* is a term of the form kw; the degree of this monomial is that of w. We write $\mathbf{deg}(p)$, the degree of the polynomial p, for the maximum degree of the monomials in p.

A *state*, ranged over by σ, is a finite map from **Var** to K. We write **St** for the set of states. We use the metavariable S for a subset of **St**. We write $\sigma(p)$ for the evaluated value of p under σ. Concretely, $\sigma(p) := p(\sigma(x_1), \ldots, \sigma(x_n))$. The set $\mathcal{P}(\mathbf{St})$ constitutes a complete lattice with respect to the set-inclusion order.

3   Language

This section defines the target language, its concrete semantics, and its abstract semantics. We essentially follow the development by Cachera et al. [4]; we refer the interested reader to this paper.

The syntax of the target language is as follows:

$$c ::= \mathbf{skip} \mid x{:=}p \mid c_1; c_2 \mid \mathbf{if}\, p = 0\, \mathbf{then}\, c_1\, \mathbf{else}\, c_2 \mid \mathbf{while}\, p \bowtie 0\, \mathbf{do}\, c$$

where $\bowtie$ is either $=$ or $\neq$, and p is a polynomial over the program variables. We restrict the guard to a single-polynomial algebraic condition (i.e., $p = 0$) or its negation.

The semantics of this language is given by the following denotation function, which is essentially the same as that by Cachera et al.

$$\llbracket c \rrbracket : (\mathcal{P}(\mathbf{St}), \subseteq) \to (\mathcal{P}(\mathbf{St}), \subseteq)$$
$$\llbracket \mathbf{skip} \rrbracket(S) = S$$
$$\llbracket x{:=}p \rrbracket(S) = \{\sigma \mid \sigma[x \mapsto \sigma(p)] \in S\}$$
$$\llbracket c_1; c_2 \rrbracket(S) = \llbracket c_1 \rrbracket(\llbracket c_2 \rrbracket(S))$$
$$\llbracket \mathbf{if}\, p = 0\, \mathbf{then}\, c_1\, \mathbf{else}\, c_2 \rrbracket(S) = \{\sigma \in \llbracket c_1 \rrbracket(S) \mid \sigma(p) = 0\} \cup \{\sigma \in \llbracket c_2 \rrbracket(S) \mid \sigma(p) \neq 0\}$$
$$\llbracket \mathbf{while}\, p \bowtie 0\, \mathbf{do}\, c \rrbracket(S) = \nu(\lambda X.\{\sigma \in S \mid \sigma(p) \not\bowtie 0\} \cup \{\sigma \in \llbracket c \rrbracket(X) \mid \sigma(p) \bowtie 0\}),$$

where $\bowtie\, \in \{=, \neq\}$ and νF is the greatest fixed point of F. Intuitively, $\sigma \in \llbracket c \rrbracket(S)$ means that executing c from σ results in a state in S if the execution terminates; notice that σ should be in $\llbracket c \rrbracket(S)$ if c does not terminate. The semantics uses the greatest fixed point instead of the least fixed point in the **while** statement so that $\llbracket c \rrbracket(S)$ contains the states from which the execution of c does not terminate. If we used the least fixed point in the semantics of a while loop, then only the initial states from which the program terminates would be in the denotation of the loop. For example, consider the following program P that does not terminate for any initial state: **while** $0 = 0$ **do skip**. Then, $\llbracket P \rrbracket(S)$ should be **St**. However, if the denotation of a **while** loop were given by the least fixed point, then $\llbracket P \rrbracket(S)$ would be $\emptyset$.

Example 2. Recall the program c_{fall} in Fig. 1. Let p_1 be $-gt + gt_0 - v + v_0 - x\rho + x_0\rho$, p_2 be $-gt^2 + gt_0^2 - 2tv + 2t_0 v_0 + 2x - 2x_0$, p be $p_1 + p_2$, and S be $\{\sigma \in \mathbf{St} \mid \sigma(p) = 0\}$. We show that $\llbracket c_{fall} \rrbracket(S) = \mathbf{St}$. We write c_1 for $(x, v, t) := (x_0, v_0, t_0)$, and c_2 for $(x, v, t) := (x + v\,dt, v - g\,dt - \rho v\,dt, t + dt)$. We have $\llbracket c_{fall} \rrbracket(S) = \llbracket c_1 \rrbracket(\llbracket \mathbf{while}\, t - a \neq 0\, \mathbf{do}\, c_2 \rrbracket(S)) = \llbracket c_1 \rrbracket(\nu F)$ where $F(X) = \{\sigma \in S \mid \sigma(t - a) = 0\} \cup \{\sigma \in \llbracket c_2 \rrbracket(X) \mid \sigma(t - a) \neq 0\}$. It is easy to check that $\llbracket c_1 \rrbracket(S) = \mathbf{St}$, so it suffices to show that $\nu F \supseteq S$. This holds because S is a fixed point of F. Indeed, $F(S) = \{\sigma \in S \mid \sigma(t - a) = 0\} \cup \{\sigma \in \llbracket c_2 \rrbracket(S) \mid \sigma(t - a) \neq 0\} = \{\sigma \in S \mid \sigma(t - a) = 0\} \cup \{\sigma \in S \mid \sigma(t - a) \neq 0\} = S$ as desired. Note that $\llbracket c_2 \rrbracket(S) = S$ because c_2 does not change the value of p.

The abstract semantics is essentially the same as that given by Cachera et al. [4] with a small adjustment. The preorder $\sqsubseteq^\sharp \,\subseteq\, \mathcal{P}(K[x_1, \ldots, x_n]) \times$

$\mathcal{P}(K[x_1,\ldots,x_n])$ is defined by $S_1 \sqsubseteq^\sharp S_2 : S_2 \subseteq S_1{}^3$. Then $\mathcal{P}(K[x_1,\ldots,x_n])$ is a complete lattice, and the meet is given as the set unions: Given $H \in \mathcal{P}(K[x_1,\ldots,x_n])$ and $U \subseteq \mathcal{P}(K[x_1,\ldots,x_n])$, $H \sqsubseteq^\sharp G$ for all $G \in U$ if and only if $H \sqsubseteq^\sharp \bigcup U$.

The abstraction $\alpha(S)$ is defined by $\{p \in K[x_1,\ldots,x_n] | \forall \sigma \in S, \sigma(p) = 0\}$, the polynomials evaluated to 0 under all the states of S. The concretization $\gamma(G)$ is defined by $\{\sigma \in \mathbf{St} | \forall p \in G, \sigma(p) = 0\}$, the states that evaluate all the polynomials in G to 0. The pair of α and γ constitutes a Galois connection; indeed, both $\alpha(S) \sqsubseteq^\sharp G$ and $S \subseteq \gamma(G)$ are by definition equivalent to the following: $\forall p \in G, \forall \sigma \in S, \sigma(p) = 0$. For example, the set of a state $\{\{x_1 \mapsto 1, x_2 \mapsto 0\}\}$ is abstracted by the set $\{(x_1 - 1)p_1 + x_2 p_2 \mid p_1, p_2 \in K[x_1,\ldots,x_n]\}$; this set is equivalently $\langle x_1 - 1, x_2 \rangle$, the ideal generated by $x_1 - 1$ and x_2.

The definition of the abstract semantics is parameterized over a remainder-like operation $\mathbf{Rem}(f, p)$ that satisfies $\mathbf{Rem}(f, p) = f - qp$ for some q; we allow any $\mathbf{Rem}$ that satisfies this condition to be used. Note that this differs from the standard remainder operation where we require $\mathrm{LM}_{\preceq}(p)$ — the greatest monomial in p with respect to a monomial order $\preceq$ — not to divide any monomial in $\mathrm{LM}_{\preceq}(\mathbf{Rem}(f, p))$. We write $\mathbf{Rem}(G, p)$, where G is a set of polynomials, for the set $\{\mathbf{Rem}(f, p) | f \in G \setminus \{0\}\}$.

The abstract semantics $[\![c]\!]^\sharp_{\mathbf{Rem}}$ is defined as follows.

$$[\![c]\!]^\sharp_{\mathbf{Rem}} : (\mathcal{P}(K[x_1,\ldots,x_n]), \sqsubseteq^\sharp) \to (\mathcal{P}(K[x_1,\ldots,x_n]), \sqsubseteq^\sharp)$$
$$[\![\mathbf{skip}]\!]^\sharp_{\mathbf{Rem}}(G) = G$$
$$[\![x{:=}p]\!]^\sharp_{\mathbf{Rem}}(G) = G[x := p]$$
$$[\![c_1; c_2]\!]^\sharp_{\mathbf{Rem}}(G) = [\![c_1]\!]^\sharp_{\mathbf{Rem}}([\![c_2]\!]^\sharp_{\mathbf{Rem}}(G))$$
$$[\![\mathbf{if}\, p = 0\, \mathbf{then}\, c_1\, \mathbf{else}\, c_2]\!]^\sharp_{\mathbf{Rem}}(G) = p \cdot [\![c_2]\!]^\sharp_{\mathbf{Rem}}(G) \cup \mathbf{Rem}([\![c_1]\!]^\sharp_{\mathbf{Rem}}(G), p)$$
$$[\![\mathbf{while}\, p \neq 0\, \mathbf{do}\, c]\!]^\sharp_{\mathbf{Rem}}(G) = \nu(\lambda H. p \cdot [\![c]\!]^\sharp_{\mathbf{Rem}}(H) \cup \mathbf{Rem}(G, p))$$
$$[\![\mathbf{while}\, p = 0\, \mathbf{do}\, c]\!]^\sharp_{\mathbf{Rem}}(G) = \nu(\lambda H. p \cdot G \cup \mathbf{Rem}([\![c]\!]^\sharp_{\mathbf{Rem}}(H), p)).$$

In this definition, $G[x := p] = \{q[x := p] | q \in G\}$ and $q[x := p]$ is the polynomial obtained by replacing x with p in q. νF exists for an arbitrary monotone F because we are working in the complete lattice $\mathcal{P}(K[x_1,\ldots,x_n])$; concretely, we have $\nu F = \bigcup\{G | G \sqsubseteq^\sharp F(G)\}$.

$[\![c]\!]^\sharp_{\mathbf{Rem}}$ transfers backward a set of polynomials whose values are 0. Cachera et al. [4, Theorem 3] showed the soundness of this abstract semantics: For any program c and a set of polynomials G, we have $\gamma([\![c]\!]^\sharp_{\mathbf{Rem}}(G)) \subseteq [\![c]\!](\gamma(G))$. Although our abstract values are sets rather than ideals, we can prove this theorem in the same way (i.e., induction on the structure of c) as the original proof.

The highlight of the abstract semantics is the definition of $[\![\mathbf{if}\, p = 0$ $\mathbf{then}\, c_1\, \mathbf{else}\, c_2]\!]^\sharp_{\mathbf{Rem}}$. In order to explain this case, let us describe a part

---

[3] The original abstract semantics of Cachera et al. [4] is defined as a transformer on *ideals* of polynomials; however, we formulate it here so that it operates on *sets* of polynomials because their invariant-synthesis algorithm depends on the choice of a generator of an ideal.

of the soundness proof: We show $\gamma(\llbracket \text{if } p = 0 \text{ then } c_1 \text{ else } c_2 \rrbracket^\sharp_{\textbf{Rem}}(G)) \subseteq \llbracket \text{if } p = 0 \text{ then } c_1 \text{ else } c_2 \rrbracket(\gamma(G))$ assuming $\gamma(\llbracket c_1 \rrbracket^\sharp_{\textbf{Rem}}(G)) \subseteq \llbracket c_1 \rrbracket(\gamma(G))$ and $\gamma(\llbracket c_2 \rrbracket^\sharp_{\textbf{Rem}}(G)) \subseteq \llbracket c_2 \rrbracket(\gamma(G))$. Suppose $\sigma \in \gamma(\llbracket \text{if } p = 0 \text{ then } c_1 \text{ else } c_2 \rrbracket^\sharp_{\textbf{Rem}}(G))$. Our goal is to show $\sigma \in \llbracket \text{if } p = 0 \text{ then } c_1 \text{ else } c_2 \rrbracket(\gamma(G))$. Therefore, it suffices to show that (1) $\sigma(p) = 0$ implies $\sigma \in \llbracket c_1 \rrbracket(\gamma(G))$, and (2) $\sigma(p) \neq 0$ implies $\sigma \in \llbracket c_2 \rrbracket(\gamma(G))$.

- We first show that if $\sigma(p) = 0$ then $\sigma \in \llbracket c_1 \rrbracket(\gamma(G))$. By the induction hypothesis, we have $\gamma(\llbracket c_1 \rrbracket^\sharp_{\textbf{Rem}}(G)) \subseteq \llbracket c_1 \rrbracket(\gamma(G))$, so it suffices to show that $\sigma \in \gamma(\llbracket c_1 \rrbracket^\sharp_{\textbf{Rem}}(G))$. Take $f \in \llbracket c_1 \rrbracket^\sharp_{\textbf{Rem}}(G)$. Then there exists $r \in \textbf{Rem}(\llbracket c_1 \rrbracket^\sharp_{\textbf{Rem}}(G), p)$ and $q \in K[x_1, \ldots, x_n]$ such that $f = qp + r$. Because $\sigma(p) = 0$ and $r \in \textbf{Rem}(\llbracket c_1 \rrbracket^\sharp_{\textbf{Rem}}(G), p) \subseteq \llbracket \text{if } p = 0 \text{ then } c_1 \text{ else } c_2 \rrbracket^\sharp_{\textbf{Rem}}(G)$ and $\sigma \in \llbracket \text{if } p = 0 \text{ then } c_1 \text{ else } c_2 \rrbracket^\sharp_{\textbf{Rem}}(G)$, we have $\sigma(f) = \sigma(q)\sigma(p) + \sigma(r) = 0$. Since f is an arbitrary element of $\llbracket c_1 \rrbracket^\sharp_{\textbf{Rem}}(G)$, by definition of γ we conclude that $\sigma \in \gamma(\llbracket c_1 \rrbracket^\sharp_{\textbf{Rem}}(G))$.
- Next we show that $\sigma(p) \neq 0$ implies $\sigma \in \llbracket c_2 \rrbracket(\gamma(G))$. By the induction hypothesis, we have $\gamma(\llbracket c_2 \rrbracket^\sharp_{\textbf{Rem}}(G)) \subseteq \llbracket c_2 \rrbracket(\gamma(G))$, so it suffices to show that $\sigma \in \gamma(\llbracket c_2 \rrbracket^\sharp_{\textbf{Rem}}(G))$. Take $f \in \llbracket c_2 \rrbracket^\sharp_{\textbf{Rem}}(G)$. Then $pf \in p \cdot \llbracket c_2 \rrbracket^\sharp_{\textbf{Rem}}(G) \subseteq \llbracket \text{if } p = 0 \text{ then } c_1 \text{ else } c_2 \rrbracket^\sharp_{\textbf{Rem}}(G)$, thus $\sigma(pf) = 0$. From the assumption $\sigma(p) \neq 0$, this implies $\sigma(f) = 0$. Since f is arbitrary, we conclude that $\sigma \in \gamma(\llbracket c_2 \rrbracket^\sharp_{\textbf{Rem}}(G))$[4].

The abstract semantics is related to the postcondition problem as follows:

Theorem 1. *If* $\llbracket c \rrbracket^\sharp_{\textbf{Rem}}(G) = \{0\}$, *then* $\llbracket c \rrbracket(\gamma(G)) = \textbf{St}$ *(hence* $g = 0$ *is a solution of the postcondition problem for any* $g \in G$).

Proof. From the soundness above, $\gamma(\llbracket c \rrbracket^\sharp_{\textbf{Rem}}(G)) = \gamma(\{0\}) = \textbf{St} \subseteq \llbracket c \rrbracket(\gamma(G))$; therefore $\llbracket c \rrbracket(\gamma(G)) = \textbf{St}$ follows because $\textbf{St}$ is the top element in the concrete domain.

Example 3. We exemplify how the abstract semantics works using the program c_{fall} in Fig. 1. Set p, c_1, and c_2 as in Example 2. Define $\textbf{Rem}$ in this example by $\textbf{Rem}(f, p) = f$. First, let $F(H) := (t - a)\llbracket c_2 \rrbracket^\sharp_{\textbf{Rem}}(H) \cup \{p\}$, $g_0 := 1$, $g_{n+1} := (t - a)(t + dt - a) \ldots (t + ndt - a)$, and $G = \{g_n p \mid n \in \mathbb{N}\}$. Then $\nu F = G$. Indeed, by definition of $\sqsubseteq^\sharp$, we have $\top = \emptyset$, and it is easy to check that $F^n(\top) = \{g_k p \mid 0 \leq k < n\}$. Therefore we have $\nu F \sqsubseteq^\sharp G$, because G is the greatest lower bound of $(F^n(\top))_{n \in \mathbb{N}}$. By simple computation, we can see that G is a fixed point of F, so we also have $G \sqsubseteq^\sharp \nu F$; hence, $\nu F = G$. Therefore, $\llbracket c_{fall} \rrbracket^\sharp_{\textbf{Rem}}(\{p\}) = \{0\}$: $\llbracket c_{fall} \rrbracket^\sharp_{\textbf{Rem}}(\{p\}) = \llbracket c_1 \rrbracket^\sharp_{\textbf{Rem}}(\llbracket \text{while } t - a \neq 0 \text{ do } c_2 \rrbracket^\sharp_{\textbf{Rem}}(\{p\})) = \llbracket c_1 \rrbracket^\sharp_{\textbf{Rem}}(\nu(\lambda H.(t - a)\llbracket c_2 \rrbracket^\sharp_{\textbf{Rem}}(H) \cup \textbf{Rem}(\{p\}, t - a))) = \llbracket c_1 \rrbracket^\sharp_{\textbf{Rem}}(\nu(\lambda H.(t - a)\llbracket c_2 \rrbracket^\sharp_{\textbf{Rem}}(H) \cup \{p\})) = \llbracket c_1 \rrbracket^\sharp_{\textbf{Rem}}(\{g_n p \mid n \in \mathbb{N}\}) = \{(g_n p)[x := x_0, v := v_0, t := t_0] \mid n \in \mathbb{N}\} = \{0\}$.

---

[4] The soundness would still hold even if we defined $\llbracket \text{if } p = 0 \text{ then } c_1 \text{ else } c_2 \rrbracket^\sharp_{\textbf{Rem}}(G)$ by $\llbracket c_2 \rrbracket^\sharp_{\textbf{Rem}}(G) \cup \textbf{Rem}(\llbracket c_1 \rrbracket^\sharp_{\textbf{Rem}}(G), p)$ instead of $p \cdot \llbracket c_2 \rrbracket^\sharp_{\textbf{Rem}}(G) \cup \textbf{Rem}(\llbracket c_1 \rrbracket^\sharp_{\textbf{Rem}}(G), p)$. The multiplier p makes the abstract semantics more precise.

By Theorem 1, a set of polynomials G such that $[\![c]\!]_{\mathbf{Rem}}^{\sharp}(G) = \{0\}$ for *some* **Rem** constitutes a solution of the postcondition problem. The choice of **Rem** indeed matters in solving the postcondition problem: There are c and G such that $[\![c]\!]_{\mathbf{Rem}}^{\sharp}(G) = \{0\}$ holds for some **Rem** but not for others. The reader is referred to [4, Sect. 4.1] for a concrete example.

4   Generalized Homogeneous Polynomials

4.1   Definition

A polynomial p is said to be a homogeneous polynomial of degree d if the degree of every monomial in p is d [5]. As we mentioned in Sect. 1, we generalize this notion of homogeneity.

We first generalize the notion of the degree of a polynomial.

Definition 1. *The group of* generalized degrees (g-degrees) $\mathbf{GDeg}_B$, *ranged over by* τ, *is an Abelian group freely generated by the finite set* B; *that is,* $\mathbf{GDeg}_B := \{b_1^{n_1} \ldots b_m^{n_m} \mid b_1, \ldots, b_m \in B, n_1, \ldots, n_m \in \mathbb{Z}\}$. *We call* B *the set of the* base degrees. *We often omit* B *in* $\mathbf{GDeg}_B$ *if the set of the base degrees is clear from the context.*

For example, if we set B to $\{L, T\}$, then L, T, and LT^{-1} are all generalized degrees. By definition, $\mathbf{GDeg}_B$ has the multiplication on these g-degrees (e.g., $(LT) \cdot (LT^{-2}) = L^2 T^{-1}$ and $(LT^2)^2 = L^2 T^4$).

$$\Gamma \vdash \mathbf{skip} \qquad \text{(T-Skip)}$$

$$\frac{\Gamma \vdash c_1 \qquad \Gamma \vdash c_2}{\Gamma \vdash c_1; c_2} \quad \text{(T-Seq)}$$

$$\frac{\Gamma(x) = \mathbf{gdeg}_{\Gamma}(p)}{\Gamma \vdash x{:=}p}$$
$$\text{(T-Assign)}$$

$$\frac{\mathbf{gdeg}_{\Gamma}(p) = \tau \qquad \Gamma \vdash c_1 \qquad \Gamma \vdash c_2}{\Gamma \vdash \mathbf{if}\, p = 0\, \mathbf{then}\, c_1\, \mathbf{else}\, c_2}$$
$$\text{(T-If)}$$

$$\frac{\mathbf{gdeg}_{\Gamma}(p) = \tau \qquad \Gamma \vdash c}{\Gamma \vdash \mathbf{while}\, p \bowtie 0\, \mathbf{do}\, c}$$
$$\text{(T-While)}$$

Fig. 2. Typing rules

In the analogy of quantity dimensions, the set B corresponds to the base quantity dimensions (e.g., L for lengths and T for times); the set $\mathbf{GDeg}_B$ corresponds to the derived quantity dimensions (e.g., LT^{-1} for velocities and LT^{-2} for acceleration rates.); multiplication expresses the relationship among quantity dimensions (e.g., $LT^{-1} \cdot T = L$ for velocity $\times$ time = distance.)

Definition 2. *A g-degree assignment is a finite mapping from* **Var** *to* **GDeg**. *A metavariable* Γ *ranges over the set of g-degree assignments. For a power product* $w := x_1^{d_1} \ldots x_n^{d_n}$, *we write* $\mathbf{gdeg}_{\Gamma}(w)$ *for* $\Gamma(x_1)^{d_1} \ldots \Gamma(x_n)^{d_n}$ *and call it the* g-degree of w under Γ (*or simply* g-degree of w *if* Γ *is not important*); $\mathbf{gdeg}_{\Gamma}(kw)$, *the* g-degree of a monomial kw under Γ, *is defined by* $\mathbf{gdeg}_{\Gamma}(w)$.

For example, set Γ to $\{t \mapsto T, v \mapsto LT^{-1}\}$; then $\mathbf{gdeg}_\Gamma(2vt) = L$. In terms of the analogy with quantity dimensions, this means that the expression $2vt$ represents a length.

Definition 3. *We say p is a* generalized homogeneous (GH) *polynomial of g-degree τ under Γ if every monomial in p has the g-degree τ under Γ. We write $\mathbf{gdeg}_\Gamma(p)$ for the g-degree of p if it is a GH polynomial under Γ; if it is not, then $\mathbf{gdeg}_\Gamma(p)$ is not defined. We write $K[x_1,\ldots,x_n]_{\Gamma,\tau}$ for the set of the GH polynomials with g-degree τ under Γ. We write $K[x_1,\ldots,x_n]_\Gamma$ for $\bigcup_{\tau \in \mathbf{GDeg}} K[x_1,\ldots,x_n]_{\Gamma,\tau}$.*

Example 4. The polynomial $-gt^2 + gt_0^2 - 2tv + 2t_0v_0 + 2x - 2x_0$ (the polynomial p_2 in Example 2) is a GH-polynomial under

$$\Gamma := \left\{ \begin{array}{l} g \mapsto LT^{-2}, t \mapsto T, v \mapsto LT^{-1}, x \mapsto L, x_0 \mapsto L, \\ v_0 \mapsto LT^{-1}, \rho \mapsto T^{-1}, a \mapsto T \end{array} \right\}$$

because all the monomials in p_2 have the same g-degree in common; for example, $\mathbf{gdeg}_\Gamma(-gt^2) = \Gamma(g)\Gamma(t)^2 = (LT^{-2})T^2 = L$; $\mathbf{gdeg}_\Gamma(-2tv) = \Gamma(t)\Gamma(v) = T(LT^{-1}) = L$; $\mathbf{gdeg}_\Gamma(2x) = \Gamma(x) = L$; and $\mathbf{gdeg}_\Gamma(-2x_0) = \Gamma(x_0) = L$. Therefore, $\mathbf{gdeg}_\Gamma(p_2) = L$. We also have $\mathbf{gdeg}_\Gamma(p_1) = LT^{-1}$.

It is easy to see that any $p \in K[x_1,\ldots,x_n]$ can be uniquely written as the finite sum of GH polynomials as $p_{\Gamma,\tau_1} + \cdots + p_{\Gamma,\tau_m}$, where p_{Γ,τ_i} is the summand of g-degree τ_i under Γ in this representation. For example, the polynomial p in Example 2, can be written as $p_L + p_{LT^{-1}}$ where $p_L = p_1$ and $p_{LT^{-1}} = p_2$ from the previous example. We call $p_{\Gamma,\tau}$ the *homogeneous component of p with g-degree τ under Γ*, or simply *a homogeneous component of p*; we often omit Γ part if it is clear from the context.

The definitions above are parameterized over a g-degree assignment Γ. It is determined from the usage of variables in a given program, which is captured by the following type judgment.

Definition 4. *The judgment $\Gamma \vdash c$ is the smallest relation that satisfies the rules in Fig. 2. We say Γ is* consistent *with the program c if $\Gamma \vdash c$ holds.*

The consistency relation above is an adaptation of the *dimension type system* proposed by Kennedy [12,13] to our imperative language. A g-degree assignment Γ such that $\Gamma \vdash c$ holds makes every polynomial in c a GH one. In the rule T-ASSIGN, we require the polynomial p to have the same g-degree as that of x in Γ.

4.2   Automated Inference of the G-Degree Assignment

Kennedy also proposed a constraint-based automated type inference algorithm of his type system [12,13]. We adapt his algorithm so that, given a command c, it infers a g-degree assignment Γ such that $\Gamma \vdash c$. The algorithm is in three steps: (1) designating a template of the g-degree assignment, (2) generating constraints over g-degrees, and (3) solving the constraints. In order to make the current paper self-contained, we explain each step below.

Step 1: Designating a template of the g-degree assignment Let $S_c := \{x_1, \ldots, x_n\}$ be the set of the variables occurring in the given program c. Then, the algorithm first designates a template g-degree assignment $\Gamma_c := \{x_1 \mapsto \alpha_{x_1}, \ldots, x_n \mapsto \alpha_{x_n}\}$ where $\alpha_{x_1}, \ldots, \alpha_{x_n}$ are fresh unknowns taken from the set **GDegV** for the g-degrees of $x_1, \ldots, x_n$. For example, given the program c_{fall} in Fig. 1, the algorithm designates

$$\Gamma_{c_{fall}} := \left\{ \begin{matrix} g \mapsto \alpha_g, t \mapsto \alpha_t, dt \mapsto \alpha_{dt}, v \mapsto \alpha_v, x \mapsto \alpha_x, \\ x_0 \mapsto \alpha_{x_0}, v_0 \mapsto \alpha_{v_0}, \rho \mapsto \alpha_\rho, a \mapsto \alpha_a \end{matrix} \right\}$$

where $\alpha_g, \alpha_t, \alpha_{dt}, \alpha_v, \alpha_x, \alpha_{x_0}, \alpha_{v_0}, \alpha_\rho, \alpha_a$ are distinct unknowns for the g-degrees of the variables that are to be inferred.

Step 2: Generating constraints over g-degrees The algorithm then generates the constraints over the g-degrees. We first define the set of constraints. Let **GDeg'** be **GDeg**$_{\{\alpha_1, \ldots, \alpha_n\}}$ in the rest of this section, where $\alpha_1, \ldots, \alpha_n$ are the unknowns generated in the previous step. (Recall that **GDeg**$_S$ is the set of g-degrees generated by S. Therefore, **GDeg'** is the set of products of the form $\alpha_1^{k_1} \ldots \alpha_n^{k_n}$ for $k_1, \ldots, k_n \in \mathbb{Z}$.) The Γ_c generated in the previous step can be seen as a map from **Var** to **GDeg'**.

A *g-degree constraint* is an equation $\tau_1 = \tau_2$ where $\tau_1, \tau_2 \in$ **GDeg'**. We use a metavariable σ for maps from $\{\alpha_1, \ldots, \alpha_n\}$ to **GDeg**$_B$. This map can be naturally extended to take the elements of **GDeg'**. We say that σ is a *solution* of a constraint set C if it satisfies all the equations in C. For example, the map $\sigma := \{\alpha_v \mapsto LT^{-1}, \alpha_x \mapsto L, \alpha_t \mapsto T\}$ is a solution of the constraint set $\{\alpha_v = \alpha_x \alpha_t^{-1}\}$ since $\sigma(\alpha_v) = LT^{-1} = \sigma(\alpha_x \alpha_t^{-1}) = \sigma(\alpha_x)\sigma(\alpha_t)^{-1}$.

For a polynomial $p := a_1 w_1 + \cdots + a_n w_n$, we write **gdeg**$'_\Gamma(p)$ for the pair $(\textbf{gdeg}_\Gamma(w_1), C)$ where C is $\emptyset$ if $n = 1$ and $\{\textbf{gdeg}_\Gamma(w_1) = \textbf{gdeg}_\Gamma(w_2), \ldots, \textbf{gdeg}_\Gamma(w_{n-1}) = \textbf{gdeg}_\Gamma(w_n)\}$ otherwise. The intuition of **gdeg**$'_\Gamma(p) = (\tau, C)$ is that, for any solution σ of C, the polynomial p is generalized homogeneous and its g-degree is $\sigma(\tau)$.

For example, let Γ be $\{v \mapsto \alpha_v, g \mapsto \alpha_g, x \mapsto \alpha_x\}$ and p be $2v^2 + gx$; then, **gdeg**$'_\Gamma(p)$ is the pair (α_v^2, C) where C is $\{\alpha_v^2 = \alpha_g \alpha_x\}$. For a solution $\sigma := \{\alpha_v \mapsto LT^{-1}, \alpha_g \mapsto LT^{-2}, \alpha_x \mapsto L\}$ of C, $\sigma(\Gamma) = \{v \mapsto LT^{-1}, g \mapsto LT^{-2}, x \mapsto L\}$. The polynomial p is generalized homogeneous under $\sigma(\Gamma)$ since $\sigma(\Gamma)(v^2) = \sigma(\Gamma)(gx) = L^2T^{-2}$. This is equal to $\sigma(\alpha_v^2)$.

The function PT for the constraint generation is defined as follows:

$$PT(\Gamma, \textbf{skip}) := \emptyset$$
$$PT(\Gamma, c_1; c_2) := PT(\Gamma, c_1) \cup PT(\Gamma, c_2)$$
$$PT(\Gamma, x{:=}p) := \{\Gamma(x) = \tau\} \cup C$$
$$\text{where } (\tau, C) := \textbf{gdeg}'_\Gamma(p)$$
$$PT(\Gamma, \textbf{if } p = 0 \textbf{ then } c_1 \textbf{ else } c_2) := C \cup PT(\Gamma, c_1) \cup PT(\Gamma, c_2)$$
$$\text{where } (\tau, C) := \textbf{gdeg}'_\Gamma(p)$$
$$PT(\Gamma, \textbf{while } p \bowtie 0 \textbf{ do } c) := PT(\Gamma, c)$$
$$\text{where } (\tau, C) := \textbf{gdeg}'_\Gamma(p).$$

The constraints $PT(\Gamma, c)$ is defined so that its any solution σ satisfies $\sigma(\Gamma) \vdash c$. The definition essentially constructs the derivation tree of $\Gamma \vdash c$ following the rules in Fig. 2 and collects the constraints appearing in the tree.

Example 5. $PT(\Gamma_{c_{fall}}, c_{fall})$ generates the following constraints. From the commands in Line 1, the constraint set $\{\alpha_x = \alpha_{x_0}, \alpha_v = \alpha_{v_0}, \alpha_t = \alpha_{t_0}\}$ is generated; from the guard in Line 2, $\{\alpha_t = \alpha_a\}$ is generated; from the right-hand side of Line 3, the constraint set $\{\alpha_x = \alpha_v \alpha_{dt}, \alpha_v = \alpha_g \alpha_{dt}, \alpha_g \alpha_{dt} = \alpha_\rho \alpha_v \alpha_{dt}, \alpha_t = \alpha_{dt}\}$, which ensures the generalized homogeneity of each polynomial, is generated; PT also generates $\{\alpha_x = \alpha_x, \alpha_v = \alpha_v, \alpha_t = \alpha_t\}$, which ensures that the g-degrees of the left-hand side and the right-hand side are identical.

Step 3: Solving the constraints The algorithm then calculates a solution of the generated constraints. The constraint-solving procedure is almost the same as that by Kennedy [12, Section 5.2], which is based on Lankford's unification algorithm[5] [14].

The procedure obtains a solution σ from the given constraint set C by applying the following rewriting rules successively:

$$(\emptyset, \sigma) \rightarrow \sigma$$
$$(\{\alpha'^k \alpha^n = 1\} \cup C, \sigma) \rightarrow (\{\alpha' \mapsto \alpha^{-\frac{n}{k}}\}(C), \{\alpha' \mapsto \alpha^{-\frac{n}{k}}\} \circ \sigma)$$
$$\text{where } k \text{ is the exponent with least absolute value}$$
$$\text{(if } k \text{ divides all the integers in } n)$$
$$(\{\alpha'^k \alpha^n = 1\} \cup C, \sigma) \rightarrow (\{\omega^k \alpha^{n \bmod k} = 1\} \cup \sigma'(C), \sigma' \circ \sigma)$$
$$\text{where } k \text{ is the exponent with least absolute value,}$$
$$\sigma' = \{\alpha' \mapsto \omega \alpha^{-\lfloor \frac{n}{k} \rfloor}\},$$
$$\text{and } \omega \text{ is a fresh element of } \mathbf{GDegV}$$
$$\text{(if there is an integer in } n \text{ that is not divisible by } k)$$
$$(\{1 = 1\} \cup C, \sigma) \rightarrow (C, \sigma)$$
$$(\{\tau_1 = \tau_2\} \cup C, \sigma) \rightarrow (\{\tau_1 \tau_2^{-1} = 1\} \cup C, \sigma)$$
$$C \rightarrow (C, \emptyset).$$

The idea of the procedure is to construct a solution iteratively converting a constraint $\alpha'^k \alpha^n = 1$ to $\{\alpha' \mapsto \alpha^{-\frac{n}{k}}\}$ if k divides all the integers in n (i.e., the second case). If k does not (i.e., the third case)[6], the procedure (1) splits $\frac{n}{k}$ to the quotient $\lfloor \frac{n}{k} \rfloor$ and the remainder $n \bmod k$, (2) generates a fresh g-degree variable ω representing $\alpha^{-\frac{n \bmod k}{k}}$, and (3) sets α' in the solution to $\omega \alpha^{-\lfloor \frac{n}{k} \rfloor}$ which is equal to $\alpha^{-\frac{n}{k}}$.

After obtaining a solution with the procedure above, the inference algorithm assigns different base degree to each surviving g-degree variable.

Example 6. Consider the following constraint set C:

$$\left\{ \begin{array}{l} \alpha_x \alpha_{x_0}^{-1} = 1, \alpha_v \alpha_{v_0}^{-1} = 1, \alpha_t \alpha_{t_0}^{-1} = 1, \alpha_t \alpha_{dt}^{-1} = 1, \\ \alpha_x \alpha_v^{-1} \alpha_{dt}^{-1} = 1, \alpha_v \alpha_g^{-1} \alpha_{dt}^{-1} = 1, \alpha_g \alpha_{dt} \alpha_\rho^{-1} \alpha_v^{-1} \alpha_{dt}^{-1} = 1 \end{array} \right\}$$

---

[5] We do not discuss the termination of the procedure in this paper. See Kennedy [12, Section 5.2].

[6] We do not use this case in the rest of this paper.

which is equivalent to that of Example 5. After several steps of rewriting, the procedure obtains

$$\left(\left\{ \begin{array}{l} \alpha_{v_0}\alpha_g^{-1}\alpha_{dt}^{-1} = 1, \\ \alpha_g\alpha_\rho^{-1}\alpha_{v_0}^{-1} = 1 \end{array} \right\}, \left\{ \begin{array}{l} \alpha_x \mapsto \alpha_{v_0}\alpha_{dt}, \alpha_v \mapsto \alpha_{v_0}, \\ \alpha_t \mapsto \alpha_{dt}, \alpha_{t_0} \mapsto \alpha_{dt}, \\ \alpha_{x_0} \mapsto \alpha_{v_0}\alpha_{dt} \end{array} \right\} \right).$$

At the next step, suppose that the procedure picks up the constraint $\alpha_{v_0}\alpha_g^{-1}\alpha_{dt}^{-1} = 1$. By applying the second rule, the procedure generates the following state

$$\left(\left\{ \alpha_\rho^{-1}\alpha_{dt}^{-1} = 1 \right\}, \left\{ \begin{array}{l} \alpha_x \mapsto \alpha_g\alpha_{dt}^2, \alpha_v \mapsto \alpha_g\alpha_{dt}, \\ \alpha_t \mapsto \alpha_{dt}, \alpha_{t_0} \mapsto \alpha_{dt}, \\ \alpha_{x_0} \mapsto \alpha_g\alpha_{dt}^2, \alpha_{v_0} \mapsto \alpha_g\alpha_{dt} \end{array} \right\} \right).$$

Then, with the second and last rules, the procedure obtains the following solution:

$$\left\{ \begin{array}{l} \alpha_x \mapsto \alpha_g\alpha_{dt}^2, \alpha_v \mapsto \alpha_g\alpha_{dt}, \\ \alpha_t \mapsto \alpha_{dt}, \alpha_{t_0} \mapsto \alpha_{dt}, \\ \alpha_{x_0} \mapsto \alpha_g\alpha_{dt}^2, \alpha_{v_0} \mapsto \alpha_g\alpha_{dt}, \alpha_\rho \mapsto \alpha_{dt}^{-1} \end{array} \right\}.$$

By assigning the base degree A to α_g and T to α_{dt}, we have the following solution:

$$\left\{ \begin{array}{l} \alpha_x \mapsto AT^2, \alpha_v \mapsto AT, \alpha_t \mapsto T, \alpha_{t_0} \mapsto T, \\ \alpha_{x_0} \mapsto AT^2, \alpha_{v_0} \mapsto AT, \alpha_\rho \mapsto T^{-1} \end{array} \right\}.$$

Notice the set of base degrees is different from that we used in Example 4; in this example, the g-degree for the acceleration rates (A) is used as a base degree, whereas that for lengths (L) is used in Example 4. This happens because the order of the constraints chosen in an execution of the inference algorithm is nondeterministic. Our results in the rest of this paper do not depend on a specific choice of base degrees.

Limitation. A limitation of the current g-degree inference algorithm is that, even if a constant symbol in a program is intended to be of a g-degree other than 1, it has to be of g-degree 1 in the current type system. For example, consider the program c'_{fall} obtained by replacing g in c_{fall} with 9.81 and ρ with 0.24. Then, the g-degrees of v and dt are inferred to be 1 due to the assignment $v := v - 9.8dt - 0.24vdt$ in c'_{fall}: The constraints for this assignment generated by the inference algorithm is $\{\alpha_v = \alpha_{dt}, \alpha_{dt} = \alpha_v\alpha_{dt}, \alpha_v = \alpha_v\}$, whose only solution is $\{\alpha_v \mapsto 1, \alpha_{dt} \mapsto 1\}$. This degenerated g-degrees are propagated to the other variables during the inference of c'_{fall}, leading to the g-degree assignment in which all the variables have the g-degree 1. This g-degree assignment is not useful for the template-size reduction; any polynomial is a GH polynomial under this assignment.

As a workaround, our current implementation that will be described in Sect. 7 uses an extension that can assign a g-degree other than 1 to each occurrence of a constant symbol by treating a constant symbol as a variable. For example, for the following program sumpower_d: $(x, y, s) := (X + 1, 0, \underline{1})$; while $x \neq 0$ do if $y = 0$ then$(x, y) := (x - 1, x)$ else$(s, y) := (s + y^d, y - 1)$, the inference algorithm treats the underlined occurrence of 1 as a variable and assigns T^d to it; the other occurrences of 0 and 1 are given g-degree T. This g-degree assignment indeed produces a smaller template.

5 Abstract Semantics Restricted to GH Polynomials

This section gives the main result of this paper: If there is an algebraic invariant of c and $\Gamma \vdash c$, then there exists an algebraic invariant that consists of a GH polynomial under Γ.

To state this result formally, we revise our abstract semantics by restricting it to the domain of the GH polynomials. The domain is obtained by replacing the underlying set of the domain $\mathcal{P}(K[x_1, \ldots, x_n])$ with $\mathcal{P}(K[x_1, \ldots, x_n]_\Gamma)$. This is a subset of $\mathcal{P}(K[x_1, \ldots, x_n])$ that is closed under arbitrary meets. We can define the abstraction and the concretization in the same way as in Sect. 3.

The revised abstract semantics $[\![c]\!]^{\sharp H}_{\text{Rem}, \Gamma}$, which we hereafter call *GH abstract semantics*, is the same as the original one except that it is parameterized over the g-degree assignment Γ. In the following definition, we write $\mathbf{Rem}(G, p)$ for $\{\mathbf{Rem}(f, p) \mid f \in (G \cap K[x_1, \ldots, x_n]_\Gamma) \setminus \{0\}\}$, the set of the remainder obtained from a GH polynomial in G and p. We assume that our choice of $\mathbf{Rem}$ is a remainder operation such that whenever both f and p are GH polynomials, so is $\mathbf{Rem}(f, p)$.

$$[\![\mathbf{skip}]\!]^{\sharp H}_{\text{Rem}, \Gamma}(G) = G$$
$$[\![x := p]\!]^{\sharp H}_{\text{Rem}, \Gamma}(G) = G[x := p]$$
$$[\![c_1; c_2]\!]^{\sharp H}_{\text{Rem}, \Gamma}(G) = [\![c_1]\!]^{\sharp H}_{\text{Rem}, \Gamma}([\![c_2]\!]^{\sharp H}_{\text{Rem}, \Gamma}(G))$$
$$[\![\mathbf{if}\ p = 0\ \mathbf{then}\ c_1\ \mathbf{else}\ c_2]\!]^{\sharp H}_{\text{Rem}, \Gamma}(G) = p \cdot [\![c_2]\!]^{\sharp H}_{\text{Rem}, \Gamma}(G) \cup \mathbf{Rem}([\![c_1]\!]^{\sharp H}_{\text{Rem}, \Gamma}(G), p)$$
$$[\![\mathbf{while}\ p \neq 0\ \mathbf{do}\ c]\!]^{\sharp H}_{\text{Rem}, \Gamma}(G) = \nu(\lambda H. p \cdot [\![c]\!]^{\sharp H}_{\text{Rem}, \Gamma}(H) \cup \mathbf{Rem}(G, p))$$
$$[\![\mathbf{while}\ p = 0\ \mathbf{do}\ c]\!]^{\sharp H}_{\text{Rem}, \Gamma}(G) = \nu(\lambda H. p \cdot G \cup \mathbf{Rem}([\![c]\!]^{\sharp H}_{\text{Rem}, \Gamma}(H), p)).$$

The following theorem guarantees that the invariant found using the semantics $[\![c]\!]^{\sharp H}_{\text{Rem}, \Gamma}$ is indeed an invariant of c.

Theorem 2 (Soundness of the GH abstract semantics). *If $\Gamma \vdash c$ and G is a set of GH polynomials under Γ, then $[\![c]\!]^{\sharp H}_{\text{Rem}, \Gamma}(G) = [\![c]\!]^{\sharp}_{\text{Rem}}(G)$.*

Proof. By induction on c.

This theorem implies that if g is a GH polynomial under Γ and $[\![c]\!]^{\sharp H}_{\text{Rem}, \Gamma}(g) = \{0\}$, then g is indeed a solution of the postcondition problem.

Completeness of $[\![c]\!]^{\sharp H}_{\text{Rem}, \Gamma}$ is obtained as a corollary of the following lemma.

Lemma 1. *Suppose $\Gamma \vdash c$, $g_1', \ldots, g_m' \in K[x_1, \ldots, x_n]$, and g_i is a homogeneous component of g_i' (i.e., $g_i = g_{i\tau_i}'$ for some τ_i). If $h \in [\![c]\!]_{\mathbf{Rem}, \Gamma}^{\sharp H}(\{g_1, \ldots, g_m\})$, then there exists $h' \in [\![c]\!]_{\mathbf{Rem}}^{\sharp}(\{g_1', \ldots, g_m'\})$ such that h is a homogeneous component of h'.*

Proof. Let us say G is a homogeneous component of G' under Γ if, for any $p \in G$, there exists $p' \in G'$ such that $p = p_\tau'$ for some τ. By induction on c, we can prove that if G is a homogeneous component of G' under Γ, then $[\![c]\!]_{\mathbf{Rem}, \Gamma}^{\sharp H}(G)$ is a homogeneous component of $[\![c]\!]_{\mathbf{Rem}, \Gamma}^{\sharp H}(G')$ under Γ.

Theorem 3 (Completeness). *Let g_i and g_i' be the same as in Lemma 1. If $\Gamma \vdash c$ and $[\![c]\!]_{\mathbf{Rem}}^{\sharp H}(\{g_1', \ldots, g_m'\}) = \{0\}$, then $[\![c]\!]_{\mathbf{Rem}, \Gamma}^{\sharp H}(\{g_1, \ldots, g_m\}) = \{0\}$.*

Proof. Take $h \in [\![c]\!]_{\mathbf{Rem}, \Gamma}^{\sharp H}(\{g_1, \ldots, g_m\})$. Then there exists $h' \in [\![c]\!]_{\mathbf{Rem}}^{\sharp}(\{g_1', \ldots, g_m'\})$ such that $h_{\mathbf{gdeg}(h)}' = h$. By assumption, we have $h' = 0$; therefore $h = 0$.

Hence, if $g = 0$ is a solution of the postcondition problem, then so is $g' = 0$ for every homogeneous component g' of g.

Example 7. Recall Example 3. Theorem 3 and $[\![c_{fall}]\!]_{\mathbf{Rem}}^{\sharp}(\{p\}) = \{0\}$ guarantee $[\![c_{fall}]\!]_{\mathbf{Rem}, \Gamma}^{\sharp H}(\{p_1\}) = \{0\}$ and $[\![c_{fall}]\!]_{\mathbf{Rem}, \Gamma}^{\sharp H}(\{p_2\}) = \{0\}$ since p_1 and p_2 are homogeneous components of p.

6   Template-Based Algorithm

This section applies our idea to Cachera's template-based invariant-synthesis algorithm [4]. We hereafter use metavariable a for a *parameter* that represents an unknown value. We use metavariable A for a set of parameters. A *template* on A is an expression of the form $a_1 p_1 + \cdots + a_n p_n$ where $a_1, \ldots, a_n \in A$; we abuse the metavariable G for a set of templates. We denote the set of templates on A by $T(A)$. A *valuation* v on A is a map from A to K. We can regard v as a map from $T(A)$ to $K[x_1, \ldots, x_n]$ by $v(a_1 p_1 + \cdots + a_m p_m) = v(a_1)p_1 + \cdots + v(a_m)p_m$.

6.1   Algorithm Proposed by Cachera et al.

Cachera et al. proposed a sound template-based algorithm for the postcondition problem. Their basic idea is to express a fixed point by constraints on the parameters in a template in order to avoid fixed-point iteration.

To recall the algorithm of Cachera et al., we establish several definitions.

Definition 5. *An* equality constraint *on A is an expression of the form $\langle G \equiv G' \rangle$, where $G, G' \subseteq T(A)$. A* constraint set *on A, or simply* constraints, *is a set of equality constraints on A; a constraint set is represented by the metavariable C. We may write (A, C) for a constraint set C on A to make A explicit. A valuation v on A satisfies an equality constraint $\langle G \equiv G' \rangle$ on A, written $v \models \langle G \equiv G' \rangle$, if*

Algorithm 1. Inference of polynomial invariants.

1: **procedure** INVINF(c, d)
2:     $g \leftarrow$ the most general template of degree d
3:     $A_0 \leftarrow$ the set of the parameters occurring in g
4:     $(A, G, C) \leftarrow [\![c]\!]^{\sharp c}_{\mathrm{Rem}^{\mathrm{par}}}(A_0, \{g\}, \emptyset)$
5:     **return** $v(g)$ where v is a solution of $C \cup \{\langle G \equiv \{0\}\rangle\}$
6: **end procedure**

$v(G)$ and $v(G')$ generate the same ideal. A solution of a constraint set (A, C) is a valuation on A that satisfies all constraints in C. If v is a solution of (A, C), we write $v \models (A, C)$, or simply $v \models C$. A template $a_1 p_1 + \cdots + a_m p_m$ is a GH template of g-degree τ under Γ if $p_1, \ldots, p_m$ are GH polynomials of g-degree τ.

We extend the definition of the remainder computation to operate on templates.

Definition 6. $\mathbf{Rem}^{\mathrm{par}}(A, f, p)$ is a pair $(A', f - pq)$ where q is the most general template of degree $\mathbf{deg}(f) - \mathbf{deg}(p)$, the parameters of which are fresh; A' is the set of the parameters appearing in q. We write $\mathbf{Rem}^{\mathrm{par}}(A, \{p_1, \ldots, p_m\}, p)$ for (A', G'), where $(A_i, r_i) = \mathbf{Rem}^{\mathrm{par}}(A, p_i, p)$ and $A' = \bigcup A_i$ and $G' = \{r_1, \ldots, r_m\}$.

For example, if the set of variables is $\{x\}$, then $\mathbf{Rem}^{\mathrm{par}}(\emptyset, x^2, x + 1) = (\{a_1, a_2\}, x^2 - (a_1 x + a_2)(x + 1))$; the most general template of degree $\mathbf{deg}(x^2) - \mathbf{deg}(x + 1) = 1$ with variable x is $a_1 x + a_2$. By expressing a remainder using a template, we can postpone the choice of a remainder operator to a later stage; for example, if we instantiate (a_1, a_2) with $(1, -1)$, then we have the standard remainder operator on $\mathbb{R}[x]$.

We recall the constraint generation algorithm proposed by Cachera et al. We write (A_i, G_i, C_i) for $[\![c_i]\!]^{\sharp c}_{\mathrm{Rem}^{\mathrm{par}}}(A, G, C)$ in each case of the following definition.

$$[\![\mathbf{skip}]\!]^{\sharp c}_{\mathrm{Rem}^{\mathrm{par}}}(A, G, C) = (A, G, C)$$
$$[\![x := p]\!]^{\sharp c}_{\mathrm{Rem}^{\mathrm{par}}}(A, G, C) = (A, G[x := p], C)$$
$$[\![c_1; c_2]\!]^{\sharp c}_{\mathrm{Rem}^{\mathrm{par}}}(A, G, C) = [\![c_1]\!]^{\sharp c}_{\mathrm{Rem}^{\mathrm{par}}}([\![c_2]\!]^{\sharp c}_{\mathrm{Rem}^{\mathrm{par}}}(A, G, C))$$
$$[\![\mathbf{if}\ p = 0\ \mathbf{then}\ c_1\ \mathbf{else}\ c_2]\!]^{\sharp c}_{\mathrm{Rem}^{\mathrm{par}}}(A, G, C) = (A_3, p \cdot G_2 \cup G_3, C_1 \cup C_2)$$
$$\text{where}\ (A_3, G_3) = \mathbf{Rem}^{\mathrm{par}}(A_1 \cup A_2, G_1, p)$$
$$[\![\mathbf{while}\ p \bowtie 0\ \mathbf{do}\ c_1]\!]^{\sharp c}_{\mathrm{Rem}^{\mathrm{par}}}(A, G, C) = (A_1, G, C_1 \cup \{\langle G \equiv G_1\rangle\})$$

$[\![c]\!]^{\sharp c}_{\mathrm{Rem}^{\mathrm{par}}}(A, G, C)$ accumulates the generated parameters to A and the generated constraints to C. A is augmented by fresh parameters at the **if** statement where $\mathbf{Rem}^{\mathrm{par}}$ is called. At a **while** statement, $\langle G \equiv G_1\rangle$ is added to the constraint set to express the loop-invariant condition.

Algorithm 1 solves the postcondition problem with the constraint-generating subprocedure $[\![c]\!]^{\sharp c}_{\mathrm{Rem}^{\mathrm{par}}}$. This algorithm, given a program c and degree d, returns a set of postconditions that can be expressed by an algebraic condition with degree d or lower. The algorithm generates the most general template g of degree d for the postcondition and applies $[\![c]\!]^{\sharp c}_{\mathbf{Rem^{par}}}$ to g. For the returned set of polynomials G and the constraint set C, the algorithm computes a solution of $C \cup \langle G \equiv \{0\} \rangle$; the equality constraint $\langle G \equiv \{0\} \rangle$ states that $v(g) = 0$, where v is a solution of the constraint set $C \cup \langle G \equiv \{0\} \rangle$, has to hold at the end of c regardless of the initial state.

This algorithm is proved to be sound: If $p \in \mathrm{INVINF}(c, d)$, then $p = 0$ holds at the end of c for any initial states [4]. Completeness was not mentioned in their paper.

Remark 1. The algorithm requires a solver for the constraints of the form $\langle G \equiv G' \rangle$. This is the problem of finding v that equates $\langle G \rangle$ and $\langle G' \rangle$; therefore, it can be solved using a solver for the ideal membership problems [5]. To avoid high-cost computation, Cachera et al. proposed heuristics to solve an equality constraint.

Example 8. We explain how $\mathrm{INVINF}(c_{fall}, 3)$ works. The algorithm generates a degree-3 template $q(x, v, t, x_0, v_0, t_0, a, dt, g, \rho)$ over $\{x, v, t, x_0, v_0, t_0, a, dt, g, \rho\}$. The algorithm then generates the following constraints by $[\![c_{fall}]\!]^{\sharp cH}_{\mathbf{Rem^{par}}}$: $\langle\{ q(x, v, t, x_0, v_0, t_0, a, dt, g, \rho) \} \equiv \{ q(x + vdt, v - gdt - \rho vdt, t + dt, x_0, v_0, t_0, a, dt, g, \rho) \}\rangle$ (from the body of the loop) and $\langle\{ q(x_0, v_0, t_0, x_0, v_0, t_0, a, dt, g, \rho) \} \equiv \{ 0 \}\rangle$. By solving these constraints with a solver for ideal membership problems [5] or with the heuristics proposed by Cachera et al. [4], and by applying the solution to $q(x, v, t, x_0, v_0, t_0, a, dt, g, \rho)$, we obtain p in Example 2.

6.2 Restriction to GH Templates

We define a variation $[\![c]\!]^{\sharp cH}_{\mathbf{Rem^{parH}_{\Gamma}}, \Gamma}$ of the constraint generation algorithm in which we use only GH polynomial templates. $[\![c]\!]^{\sharp cH}_{\mathbf{Rem^{parH}_{\Gamma}}, \Gamma}$ differs from $[\![c]\!]^{\sharp c}_{\mathbf{Rem^{par}}}$ in that it is parameterized also over Γ, not only over the remainder operation used in the algorithm. The remainder operator $\mathbf{Rem^{parH}_{\Gamma}}H\Gamma(A, f, p)$ returns a pair $(A \cup A', f - pq)$ where q is the most general GH template with g-degree $\mathbf{gdeg}(f)\mathbf{gdeg}(p)^{-1}$, with degree $\mathbf{deg}(f) - \mathbf{deg}(p)$, and with fresh parameters; A' is the set of the parameters that appear in q. $\mathbf{Rem^{parH}_{\Gamma}}(A, G, p)$ is defined in the same way as Definition 6 for a set G of polynomials. We again write (A_i, G_i, C_i) for $[\![c_i]\!]^{\sharp c}_{\mathbf{Rem^{parH}_{\Gamma}}}(A, G, C)$ in each case of the following definition.

$$[\![\mathbf{skip}]\!]^{\sharp cH}_{\mathbf{Rem^{parH}_{\Gamma}}, \Gamma}(A, G, C) = (A, G, C)$$

$$[\![x:=p]\!]^{\sharp cH}_{\mathbf{Rem^{parH}_{\Gamma}}, \Gamma}(A, G, C) = (A, G[x := p], C)$$

$$[\![c_1; c_2]\!]^{\sharp cH}_{\mathbf{Rem^{parH}_{\Gamma}}, \Gamma}(A, G, C) = [\![c_1]\!]^{\sharp cH}_{\mathbf{Rem^{parH}_{\Gamma}}, \Gamma}([\![c_2]\!]^{\sharp cH}_{\mathbf{Rem^{parH}_{\Gamma}}, \Gamma}(A, G, C))$$

$$[\![\mathbf{if}\, p = 0\, \mathbf{then}\, c_1\, \mathbf{else}\, c_2]\!]^{\sharp cH}_{\mathbf{Rem^{parH}_{\Gamma}}, \Gamma}(A, G, C) = (A_3, p \cdot G_2 \cup G_3, C_1 \cup C_2)$$

$$\text{where } (A_3, G_3) = \mathbf{Rem^{parH}_{\Gamma}}H\Gamma(A_1 \cup A_2, G_1, p)$$

$$[\![\mathbf{while}\, p \bowtie 0\, \mathbf{do}\, c_1]\!]^{\sharp cH}_{\mathbf{Rem^{parH}_{\Gamma}}, \Gamma}(A, G, C) = (A_1, G, C_1 \cup \{\langle G \equiv G_1 \rangle\})$$

Algorithm 2. Inference of polynomial invariants (homogeneous version).

1: **procedure** $\text{INVINF}^{\text{H}}(c, d, \Gamma, \tau)$
2:     $g \leftarrow$ the most general template of g-degree τ and degree d
3:     $A_0 \leftarrow$ the set of the parameters occurring in g
4:     $(A, G, C) \leftarrow [\![c]\!]^{\sharp\text{cH}}_{\text{Rem}_\Gamma^{\text{parH}}, \Gamma}(A_0, \{g\}, \emptyset)$
5:     **return** $v(g)$ where v is a solution of $C \cup \{\langle G \equiv \{0\}\rangle\}$
6: **end procedure**

Algorithm 2 is a variant of Algorithm 1, in which we restrict a template to GH one.

The algorithm INVINF^{H} takes the input τ that specifies the g-degree of the invariant at the end of the program c. We have not obtained a theoretical result for τ to be passed to INVINF^{H} so that it generates a good invariant. However, during the experiments in Sect. 7, we found that the following strategy often works: *Pass the g-degree of the monomial of interest.* For example, if we are interested in a property related to x, then pass $\Gamma(x)$ (i.e., L) to INVINF^{H} for the invariant $-gt^2 + gt_0^2 - 2tv + 2t_0v_0 + 2x - 2x_0 = 0$. How to help a user to find such "monomial of her interest" is left as an interesting future direction.

The revised version of the invariant inference algorithm is sound; at the point of writing, completeness of INVINF^{H} with respect to INVINF is open despite the completeness of $[\![c]\!]^{\sharp\text{H}}_{\text{Rem}, \Gamma}$ with respect to $[\![c]\!]^{\sharp}_{\text{Rem}}$.

Theorem 4. (Soundness). *Suppose $\Gamma \vdash c$, $d \in \mathbb{N}$, and $\tau \in \mathbf{GDeg}$. Set P_1 to the set of polynomials that can be returned by $\text{INVINF}^{\text{H}}(c, d, \tau)$; set P_2 to those by $\text{INVINF}(c, d)$. Then, $P_1 \subseteq P_2$.*

7 Experiment

We implemented Algorithm 2 and conducted experiments. Our implementation Fastind_{dim} takes a program c, a maximum degree d of the template g in the algorithm, and a monomial w. It conducts type inference of c to generate Γ and calls $\text{INVINF}^{\text{H}}(c, d, \Gamma, \mathbf{gdeg}_\Gamma(w))$. The type inference algorithm is implemented with OCaml; the other parts (e.g., a solver for ideal-equality constraints) are implemented with Mathematica.

To demonstrate the merit of our approach, we applied this implementation to the benchmark used in the experiment by Cachera et al. [4] and compared our result with that of their implementation, which is called Fastind. The entire experiment was conducted on a MacBook Air 13-inch Mid 2013 model with a 1.7 GHz Intel Core i7 (with two cores, each of which has 256 KB of L2 cache) and 8 GB of RAM (1600 MHz DDR3). The modules written in OCaml were compiled with `ocamlopt`. The version of OCaml is 4.02.1. The version of Mathematica is 10.0.1.0. We refer the reader to [4,18,19] for detailed descriptions of each program in the benchmark. Each program contains a nested loop with a conditional branch (e.g., `dijkstra`), a sequential composition of loops (e.g., `divbin`), and nonlinear expressions (e.g., petter(n).) We generated a nonlinear invariant in each program.

Table 1 shows the result. The column deg shows the degree of the generated polynomial, t_{sol} shows the time spent by the ideal-equality solver (ms), $\#m$ shows the number of monomials in the generated template, t_{inf} shows the time spent by the dimension-type inference algorithm (ms), and $t_{inf} + t_{sol}$ shows the sum of t_{inf} and t_{sol}. By comparing $\#m$ for Fastind with that of Fastind$_{dim}$, we can observe the effect of the use of GH polynomials on the template sizes. Comparison of t_{sol} for Fastind with that of Fastind$_{dim}$ suggests the effect on the constraint reduction phase; comparison of t_{sol} for Fastind with $t_{inf} + t_{sol}$ for Fastind$_{dim}$ suggests the overhead incurred by g-degree inference.

Table 1. Experimental result.

Name	deg	Fastind		Fastind$_{dim}$			
		t_{sol}	$\#m$	t_{inf}	t_{sol}	$t_{inf} + t_{sol}$	$\#m$
dijkstra	2	9.29	21	0.456	8.83	9.29	21
divbin	2	0.674	21	0.388	0.362	0.750	8
freire1	2	0.267	10	0.252	0.258	0.510	10
freire2	3	2.51	35	0.463	2.60	3.06	35
cohencu	3	1.74	35	0.434	0.668	1.10	20
fermat	2	0.669	21	0.583	0.669	1.25	21
wensley	2	104	21	0.436	28.5	28.9	9
euclidex	2	1.85	45	1.55	1.39	2.94	36
lcm	2	0.811	28	0.513	0.538	1.05	21
prod4	3	31.6	84	0.149	2.78	2.93	35
knuth	3	137	220	4.59	136	141	220
mannadiv	2	0.749	21	0.515	0.700	1.22	18
petter1	2	0.132	6	0.200	0.132	0.332	6
petter2	3	0.520	20	0.226	0.278	0.504	6
petter3	4	1.56	35	0.226	0.279	0.505	7
petter4	5	7.15	56	0.240	0.441	0.681	8
petter5	6	17.2	84	0.228	0.326	0.554	9
petter10	11	485	364	0.225	0.354	0.579	14
sumpower1	3	2.20	35	0.489	2.31	2.80	35
sumpower5	7	670	330	0.469	89.1	89.6	140

Discussion. The size of the templates, measured as the number of monomials ($\#m$), was reduced in 13 out of 20 programs by using GH polynomials. The value of t_{sol} decreased for these 13 programs; it is almost the same for the other programs. $\#m$ did not decrease for the other seven programs because the extension of the type inference procedure mentioned above introduced useless auxiliary variables. We expect that such variables can be eliminated by using a more elaborate program analysis.

By comparing t_{sol} for Fastind and $t_{inf} + t_{sol}$ for Fastind$_{dim}$, we can observe that the inference of the g-degree assignment sometimes incurs an overhead for the entire execution time if the template generated by Fastind is sufficiently small; therefore, Fastind is already efficient. However, this overhead is compensated in the programs for which Fastind requires more computation time.

To summarize, our current approach is especially effective for a program for which (1) the existing invariant-synthesis algorithm is less efficient owing to the large size of the template and (2) a nontrivial g-degree assignment can be inferred. We expect that our approach will be effective for a wider range of programs if we find a more competent g-degree inference algorithm.

8 Related Work

The template-based algebraic invariant synthesis proposed to date [4,20] has focused on reducing the problem to constraint solving and solving the generated constraints efficiently; strategies for generating a template have not been the main issue. A popular strategy for template synthesis is to iteratively increase the degree of a template. This strategy suffers from an increase in the size of a template in the iterations when the degree is high.

Our claim is that prior analysis of a program effectively reduces the size of a template; we used the dimension type system for this purpose in this paper inspired by the principle of quantity dimensions in the area of physics. Of course, there is a tradeoff between the cost of the analysis and its effect on the template-size reduction; our experiments suggest that the cost of dimension type inference is reasonable.

Semialgebraic invariants (i.e., invariants written using *inequalities* on polynomials) are often useful for program verification. The template-based approach is also popular in semialgebraic invariant synthesis. One popular strategy in template-based semialgebraic invariant synthesis is to reduce this problem to one of semidefinite programming, for which many efficient solvers are widely available.

As of this writing, it is an open problem whether our idea regarding GH polynomials also applies to semialgebraic invariant synthesis; for physically meaningful programs, at least, we guess that it is reasonable to use GH polynomials because of the success of the quantity dimension principle in the area of physics. A possible approach to this problem would be to investigate the relationship between GH polynomials and Stengle's Postivstellensatz [22], which is the theoretical foundation of the semidefinite-programming approach mentioned above. There is a homogeneous version of the Stengle's Positivstellensatz [8, Theorem II.2]; because the notion of homogeneity considered there is equivalent to generalized homogeneity introduced in this paper, we conjecture that this theorem provides a theoretical foundation of an approach to semialgebraic invariant synthesis using GH polynomials.

Although the application of the quantity dimension principle to program verification is novel, this principle has been a handy tool for discovering hidden knowledge about a physical system. A well-known example in the field of hydrodynamics is the motion of a fluid in a pipe [2]. One fundamental result in this regard is that of Buckingham [3], who stated that *any physically meaningful relationship among n quantities can be rewritten as one among $n - r$ independent dimensionless quantities, where r is the number of the quantities of the base dimension*. Investigating the implications of this theorem in the context of our work is an important direction for future work.

The term "generalized homogeneity" appears in various areas; according to Hankey et al. [10], a function $f(x_1, \ldots, x_n)$ is said to be generalized homogeneous if there are $a_1, \ldots, a_n$ and a_f such that, for any positive λ, $f(\lambda^{a_1} x_1, \ldots, \lambda^{a_n} x_n) = \lambda^{a_f} f(x_1, \ldots, x_n)$. Barenblatt [2] points out that the essence of the quantity dimension principle is generalized homogeneity. Although we believe our GH polynomials are related to the standard definition, we have not fully investigated the relationship at the time of writing.

Our idea (and the quantity dimension principle) seems to be related to *invariant theory* [17] in mathematics. Invariant theory studies various mathematical structures using invariant polynomials. A well-known fact is that a ring of invariants is generated by homogeneous polynomials [5, Chap. 7]; GH polynomials can be seen as a generalization of the notion of degree.

The structure of $K[x_1, \ldots, x_n]$ resulting from the notion of the generalized degrees is an instance of *graded rings* from ring theory. Concretely, R is said to be *graded* over an Abelian group $\mathbb{G}$ if R is decomposed into the direct sum of a family of additive subgroups $\{R_g \mid g \in \mathbb{G}\}$ and these subgroups satisfy $R_g \cdot R_h \subseteq R_{gh}$ for all $g, h \in \mathbb{G}$. Then, an element $x \in R$ is said to be *homogeneous of degree g* if $x \in R_g$. We leave an investigation of how our method can be viewed in this abstract setting as future work.

9   Conclusion

We presented a technique to reduce the size of a template used in template-based invariant-synthesis algorithms. Our technique is based on the finding that, if an algebraic invariant of a program c exists, then there is a GH invariant of c; hence, we can reduce the size of a template by synthesizing only a GH polynomial. We presented the theoretical development as a modification of the framework proposed by Cachera et al. and empirically confirmed the effect of our approach using the benchmark used by Cachera et al. Although we used the framework of Cachera et al. as a baseline, we believe that we can apply our idea to the other template-based methods [1,4,7,16,19–21].

Our motivation behind the current work is safety verification of hybrid systems, in which the template method is a popular strategy. For example, Gulwani et al. [9] proposed a method of reducing the safety condition of a hybrid system to constraints on the parameters of a template by using Lie derivatives. We expect our idea to be useful for expediting these verification procedures.

In this regard, Suenaga et al. [11,23,24] have recently proposed a framework called *nonstandard static analysis*, in which one models the continuous behavior of a system as an imperative or a stream-processing program using an *infinitesimal* value. An advantage of modeling in this framework is that we can apply program verification tools without an extension for dealing with continuous dynamics. However, their approach requires highly nonlinear invariants for verification. This makes it difficult to apply existing tools, which do not handle nonlinear expressions well. We expect that the current technique will address this difficulty with their framework.

We are also interested in applying our idea to decision procedures and satisfiability modulo theories (SMT) solvers. Support of nonlinear predicates is an emerging trend in many SMT solvers (e.g., Z3 [15]). Dai et al. [6] proposed an algorithm for generating a semialgebraic Craig interpolant using semidefinite programming [6]. Application of our approach to these method is an interesting direction for future work.

Acknowledgment. We appreciate annonymous reviewers, Toshimitsu Ushio, Naoki Kobayashi and Atsushi Igarashi for their comments. This work is partially supported by JST PRESTO, JST CREST, KAKENHI 70633692, and in collaboration with the Toyota Motor Corporation.

A   Proof of Theorem 4

To prove Theorem 4, we define *renaming* of parameters and constraints.

Definition 7. *For an injection* $\iota : A \to A'$, *we write* $\iota : (A, G, C) \preceq (A', G', C')$ *if* $G' = \iota^*(G)$ *and* $C' = \iota^*(C)$ *where* ι^* *maps* $a' \in \iota(A)$ *to* $\iota^{-1}(a')$ *and* $a' \in \iota(A' \backslash \iota(A))$ *to* 0.

The injection ι gives a renaming of parameters. The relation $\iota : (A, G, C) \preceq (A', G', C')$ reads G and C are obtained from G' and C' by renaming the parameters in $\iota(A)$ using ι and substituting 0 to those not in $\iota(A)$.

Lemma 2. *If* $\iota : (A, G, C) \preceq (A', G', C')$, *then there exists* κ *such that (1)* $\kappa : [\![c]\!]_{\mathrm{Rem}^{\mathrm{par}}, \Gamma}^{\sharp\mathrm{cH}}(A, G, C) \preceq [\![c]\!]_{\mathrm{Rem}^{\mathrm{par}}}^{\sharp\mathrm{c}}(A', G', C')$ *and (2)* κ *is an extension of* ι.

Proof. Induction on the structure of c.   □

Proof of Theorem 4. Let $g \in T(A_0)$ be the most general template of generalized degree τ and degree d and $g' \in T(A_0')$ be the most general template of degree d. Without loss of generality, we assume $A_0 \subseteq A_0'$ and $g' = g + g_1$ for some $g_1 \in T(A_0' \backslash A_0)$. Let $(A, G, C) = [\![c]\!]_{\mathrm{Rem}^{\mathrm{par}}, \Gamma}^{\sharp\mathrm{cH}}(A_0, \{g\}, \emptyset)$ and $(A', G', C') = [\![c]\!]_{\mathrm{Rem}^{\mathrm{par}}}^{\sharp\mathrm{c}}(A_0', \{g'\}, \emptyset)$. Then, from Lemma 2, there exists κ such that $\kappa : (A, G, C) \preceq (A', G', C')$ and κ is an extension of the inclusion mapping $\iota : A_0 \to A_0'$. Suppose $v(g)$ is a result of $\mathrm{INVINF}^{\mathrm{H}}(c, d, \tau)$ where v is a solution to $C \cup \{\langle G \equiv \{0\}\rangle\}$. Define a valuation v' on A' by

$$v'(a') = \begin{cases} v(a) & a' = \kappa(a) \text{ for some } a \in A \\ 0 & \text{Otherwise.} \end{cases}$$

Then, $v'(g') = v'(g + g_1) = v'(g)$; the second equation holds because $v'(a')$ is constantly 0 on any $a' \in A' \backslash A$. All the parameters in g are in A_0 and κ is an identity on A_0. Therefore, $v'(g) = v(g)$. It suffices to show that $v' \models C' \cup \{\langle G' \equiv \{0\}\rangle\}$, which indeed holds from the definition of v' since $v \models C \cup \{\langle G \equiv \{0\}\rangle\}$ and C and G are renaming of C' and G'.   □

References

1. Adjé, A., Garoche, P.-L., Magron, V.: Property-based polynomial invariant generation using sums-of-squares optimization. In: Blazy, S., Jensen, T. (eds.) SAS 2015. LNCS, vol. 9291, pp. 235–251. Springer, Heidelberg (2015)
2. Barenblatt, G.I.: Scaling, Self-Similarity, and Intermediate Asymptotics: Dimensional Analysis and Intermediate Asymptotics, vol. 14. Cambridge University Press, Cambridge (1996)
3. Buckingham, E.: On physically similar systems; illustrations of the use of dimensional equations. Phys. Rev. **4**, 345–376 (1914)
4. Cachera, D., Jensen, T.P., Jobin, A., Kirchner, F.: Inference of polynomial invariants for imperative programs: a farewell to Gröbner bases. Sci. Comput. Program. **93**, 89–109 (2014)

5. Cox, D.A., Little, J., O'Shea, D.: Ideals, Varieties, and Algorithms: An Introduction to Computational Algebraic Geometry and Commutative Algebra. Undergraduate Texts in Mathematics, 3rd edn. Springer, New York (2007)

6. Dai, L., Xia, B., Zhan, N.: Generating non-linear interpolants by semidefinite programming. In: Sharygina, N., Veith, H. (eds.) CAV 2013. LNCS, vol. 8044, pp. 364–380. Springer, Heidelberg (2013)

7. Garg, P., Löding, C., Madhusudan, P., Neider, D.: ICE: a robust framework for learning invariants. In: Biere, A., Bloem, R. (eds.) CAV 2014. LNCS, vol. 8559, pp. 69–87. Springer, Heidelberg (2014)

8. Gonzalez-Vega, L., Lombardi, H.: Smooth parametrizations for several cases of the Positivstellensatz. Mathematische Zeitschrift **225**(3), 427–451 (1997). http://dx.doi.org/10.1007/PL00004620

9. Gulwani, S., Tiwari, A.: Constraint-based approach for analysis of hybrid systems. In: Gupta, A., Malik, S. (eds.) CAV 2008. LNCS, vol. 5123, pp. 190–203. Springer, Heidelberg (2008)

10. Hankey, A., Stanley, H.E.: Systematic application of generalized homogeneous functions to static scaling, dynamic scaling, and universality. Phys. Rev. B **6**(9), 3515 (1972)

11. Hasuo, I., Suenaga, K.: Exercises in nonstandard static analysis of hybrid systems. In: Madhusudan, P., Seshia, S.A. (eds.) CAV 2012. LNCS, vol. 7358, pp. 462–478. Springer, Heidelberg (2012)

12. Kennedy, A.: Dimension types. In: ESOP 1994, pp. 348–362 (1994)

13. Kennedy, A.: Programming languages and dimensions. Ph.D. thesis, St. Catharine's College, March 1996

14. Lankford, D., Butler, G., Brady, B.: Abelian group unification algorithms for elementary terms. Contemp. Math. **29**, 193–199 (1984)

15. de Moura, L., Bjørner, N.S.: Z3: an efficient SMT solver. In: Ramakrishnan, C.R., Rehof, J. (eds.) TACAS 2008. LNCS, vol. 4963, pp. 337–340. Springer, Heidelberg (2008)

16. Müller-Olm, M., Seidl, H.: Computing polynomial program invariants. Inf. Process. Lett. **91**(5), 233–244 (2004)

17. Neusel, M.D.: Invariant theory. The American Mathematical Society (2000)

18. Rodríguez-Carbonell, E.: Some programs that need polynomial invariants in order to be verified. http://www.cs.upc.edu/erodri/webpage/polynomial_invariants/list.html. Accessed 25 January 2016

19. Rodríguez-Carbonell, E., Kapur, D.: Generating all polynomial invariants in simple loops. J. Symb. Comput. **42**(4), 443–476 (2007)

20. Sankaranarayanan, S., Sipma, H., Manna, Z.: Non-linear loop invariant generation using Gröbner bases. In: POPL 2004, pp. 318–329 (2004)

21. Somenzi, F., Bradley, A.R.: IC3: where monolithic and incremental meet. In: FMCAD 2011, pp. 3–8 (2011)

22. Stengle, G.: A nullstellensatz and a positivstellensatz in semialgebraic geometry. Mathematische Annalen **207**(2), 87–97 (1974)

23. Suenaga, K., Hasuo, I.: Programming with infinitesimals: a while-language for hybrid system modeling. In: Aceto, L., Henzinger, M., Sgall, J. (eds.) ICALP 2011, Part II. LNCS, vol. 6756, pp. 392–403. Springer, Heidelberg (2011)

24. Suenaga, K., Sekine, H., Hasuo, I.: Hyperstream processing systems: nonstandard modeling of continuous-time signals. In: Giacobazzi, R., Cousot, R. (eds.) POPL 2013, pp. 417–430. ACM (2013)

On the Linear Ranking Problem for Simple Floating-Point Loops

Fonenantsoa Maurica[✉], Frédéric Mesnard, and Étienne Payet

Laboratoire d'Informatique et de Mathématiques, Université de La Réunion,
97490 Sainte-Clotilde, La Réunion, France
{fonenantsoa.maurica,frederic.mesnard,etienne.payet}@univ-reunion.fr

Abstract. Termination of loops can be inferred from the existence of
linear ranking functions. We already know that the existence of these
functions is PTIME decidable for simple rational loops. Since very
recently, we know that the problem is coNP-complete for simple integer loops. We continue along this path by investigating programs dealing with floating-point computations. First, we show that the problem
is at least in coNP for simple floating-point loops. Then, in order to
work around that theoretical limitation we present an algorithm which
remains polynomial by sacrificing completeness. The algorithm, based on
the Podelski-Rybalchenko algorithm, can also synthesize in polynomial
time the linear ranking functions it detects. To our knowledge, our work
is the first adaptation of this well-known algorithm to floating-points.

Keywords: Termination analysis · Linear ranking functions · Floating-
point numbers

1 Introduction

Termination analysis of programs is a research topic that has already produced
many remarkable results. This work is a continuation of a series of connected
results concerning simple loops. [24] first showed that termination of loops of
the form while $(Dx \leq d)$ do $x' = Vx + v$ done where the column vector of n
variables x ranges over $\mathbb{R}^{n \times 1}$ is decidable. Then, [7] showed that the problem is
also decidable when $x \in \mathbb{Q}^{n \times 1}$ and even when $x \in \mathbb{Z}^{n \times 1}$ for the homogeneous
case where $d = 0$. Followingly, [6] investigated the more general case of the non-
deterministic loops of the form while $(Dx \leq d)$ do $V (x\ x')^T \leq v$ done where
$(x\ x')^T = \begin{pmatrix} x \\ x' \end{pmatrix}$ denotes the column vector of $2n$ elements obtained by concate-
nating x with x'. Termination of such loops was proved to be undecidable when
$x, x' \in \mathbb{Z}^{n \times 1}$. The existence of *linear* ranking functions for such loops is however decidable and the problem is shown to be coNP-complete [4,5]. That result
applies even when the variables range over a finite set $E \subset \mathbb{Z}$ with $|E| \geq 2$,
like the case of machine integers. We now study in this paper the case where the

X. Rival (Ed.): SAS 2016, LNCS 9837, pp. 300–316, 2016.
DOI: 10.1007/978-3-662-53413-7_15

variables are of floating-point type. In addition to being a prolongation of these previous works, ours can also be seen as a part of the current efforts in analyzing bit-vector programs instead of purely mathematical ones with error-free computations. Indeed, the rounding errors inherent to floating-point arithmetic render invalid most of the results obtained for programs using real or rational variables.

The paper is organized as follows. Section 2 briefly introduces the prerequisites. Sections 3 and 4 expose our contribution. We first show that there is no polynomial algorithm that can decide the existence of linear ranking functions for simple floating-point loops as the problem is at least in coNP. Then, we work around that theoretical limitation by presenting a sufficient but not necessary condition, thus incomplete but checkable in polynomial time, that ensures the existence of these functions. Section 5 presents the related work. Section 6 concludes.

2 Preliminaries

In this section we introduce the notions and notations we use in the paper.

Definition 1 (Programs as transition systems). *We formalize a program $\mathcal{P}$ as a transition system $\langle \mathcal{X}, \mathcal{I}, \mathcal{R} \rangle$ where $\mathcal{X}$ is a set of states, $\mathcal{I} \subseteq \mathcal{X}$ is the set of initial states and $\mathcal{R} \subseteq \mathcal{X} \times \mathcal{X}$ is a transition relation between a state and its possible successors.*

```
rational x := 100;
while(x >= 0)
    x := x - 1;
```

Fig. 1. A simple program, $\mathcal{P}_{simple}$

Example 1. The program $\mathcal{P}_{simple}$ presented in Fig. 1 can be formalized as the transition system $\langle \mathcal{X}_{simple}, \mathcal{I}_{simple}, \mathcal{R}_{simple} \rangle$ where $\mathcal{X}_{simple} = \mathbb{Q}$, $\mathcal{I}_{simple} = \{100\}$ and $\mathcal{R}_{simple} = \{ \langle x, x' \rangle \in \mathbb{Q}^2 | x \geq 0 \wedge x' = x - 1 \}$.

Definition 2 (Sequences). *Given a set $\mathcal{X}$ of states X_i, we say that s is an $\mathcal{X}$-sequence if $s = X_1 X_2 \ldots$ A finite sequence will have a last index $last(s)$.*

Let $\mathcal{R} \subseteq \mathcal{X} \times \mathcal{X}$. A finite sequence s is said to be permitted by $\mathcal{R}$ if and only if $\forall i \in 1 \ldots last(s) - 1 : X_i \mathcal{R} X_{i+1}$. An infinite sequence s is permitted by $\mathcal{R}$ if and only if $\forall i : i > 0 \implies X_i \mathcal{R} X_{i+1}$.

Proposition 1 (Termination characterization, ranking functions). *A program $\mathcal{P} = \langle \mathcal{X}, \mathcal{I}, \mathcal{R} \rangle$, where $\mathcal{X}$ is a set of states X_i, terminates if and only if there exists a function f from $(\mathcal{X}, \mathcal{R})$ to a well-founded set $(\mathcal{W}, <)$ such that $\forall i : X_i \mathcal{R} X_{i+1} \implies f(X_i) > f(X_{i+1})$. The function f is called a ranking function for $\mathcal{P}$.*

By choosing $(\mathbb{Q}, <_{\delta_0, \delta}), \delta_0 \in \mathbb{Q}, \delta \in \mathbb{Q}_+^*$ such that $\forall x, x' \in \mathbb{Q} : x' <_{\delta_0, \delta} x \iff x \geq \delta_0 \wedge x \geq \delta + x'$ as well-founded set, a ranking function f is a function such that: $\forall X, X' \in \mathcal{X} : X \mathcal{R} X' \implies f(X) \geq \delta_0 \wedge f(X) \geq \delta + f(X')$.

Definition 3 (LRF). *A linear ranking function, that we shorten LRF, for a program having the column vector $X \in \mathbb{Q}^{n \times 1}$ as variables is a ranking function f of the form $f(X) = CX$ where $C \in \mathbb{Q}^{1 \times n}$ is a constant row vector.*

Definition 4 ($\mathbb{F}_{\beta, p, e_{min}, e_{max}}$). *A real number $x \in \mathbb{R}$ is said to be approximated by the floating-point number $\hat{x} \in \mathbb{F}_{\beta, p, e_{min}, e_{max}}$ if $x = (-1)^s m \beta^e$ and $\hat{x} = (-1)^s \hat{m} \beta^e$ where $s \in \{0, 1\}$ is the sign, $\beta \in \mathbb{N}$ such that $\beta \geq 2$ is the radix, $e \in \mathbb{N}$ such that $e_{min} \leq e \leq e_{max}$ is the exponent and $\hat{m}$ is the mantissa. The mantissa $\hat{m}$ is a fractional number approximating in $p \in \mathbb{N}^*$ digits the real number m and is such that $\hat{m} = \Diamond(\frac{m}{\beta^{-p+1}}) \beta^{-p+1}$ where $\Diamond$ is an approximation function that is defined according to the rounding mode $\square$. The number p is called precision.*

If $|x| \geq \beta^{e_{min}}$, $\hat{x}$ is called a normal floating-point number and $1 \leq \hat{m} < \beta$. Otherwise, $\hat{x}$ is called a subnormal floating-point number and $0 \leq \hat{m} < 1$.

Example 2. The floating-point type $\mathbb{F}_{simple} = \mathbb{F}_{\beta=10, p=2, e_{min}=-1, e_{max}=2}$ is presented in Fig. 2. Notice that the more we go away from zero, the more the distance between two consecutive floating-point numbers increases.

Using $\mathbb{F}_{simple}$, the real number $x = 10\pi = 31.4159\cdots = (-1)^s m \beta^e$ where $s = 0, m = \pi, \beta = 10$ and $e = 1$ is represented by $\hat{x} = (-1)^s \hat{m} \beta^e$ where $\hat{m} = 3.1$ or $\hat{m} = 3.2$ depending on the rounding mode $\square$ chosen.

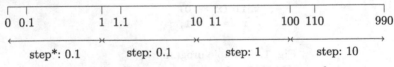

Fig. 2. A personalized floating-point type, $\mathbb{F}_{simple}$. Symmetry to the origin for the negatives.

We are addressing floating-point types that can be freely parameterized. This allows our result to be applied not only to programs using the IEEE-754 floating-point types, but also to programs using personalized ones like with the MPFR library [14].

Definition 5 (Rounding modes). *Given a real number x and the two floating-point numbers $\hat{x}_1$ and $\hat{x}_2$ adjacent to x such that $\hat{x}_1 \leq x \leq \hat{x}_2$, the rounding mode $\square$ defines the choice to make between $\hat{x}_1$ and $\hat{x}_2$ when approximating x.*

In the rounding mode to-nearest-ties-to-even, denoted o, we choose the one closest to x. In case of tie, we choose the one having the last digit in the mantissa even. In the rounding mode to-zero, denoted $\uparrow^0$, we choose the one closest to 0.

Definition 6 (Correct rounding). *Given a rounding mode $\square$, a real arithmetic operation $\star$, its floating-point equivalent $\circledast$ and 2 floating-point numbers $\hat{x}_1, \hat{x}_2$, we say that $\circledast$ is correctly rounded if $\hat{x}_1 \circledast \hat{x}_2 = \square(\hat{x}_1 \star \hat{x}_2)$.*

More details on floating-point computations can be found in [15].

Definition 7 (Simple rational loops). *We call simple rational loop a loop of the form while $(Dx \le d)$ do $V\left(x\ x'\right)^T \le v$. The column vector $x = \left(x_1 \dots x_n\right)^T \in \mathbb{Q}^{n \times 1}$ represents the variables at the beginning of an iteration. The primed equivalent x' represents the variables at the end of an iteration, when they have been updated. D, d, V, v are rational matrices of appropriate dimensions. The operations are done in the rationals.*

A simple rational loop can be viewed as the rational convex polyhedron described by the set of inequalities $A''\left(x\ x'\right)^T \le b$ obtained by conjuncting the loop condition with the update constraints.

Definition 8 (Simple floating-point loops). *Similarly to simple rational loops, simple floating-point loops are loops described by the set of inequalities $A'' \odot \left(x\ x'\right)^T \le b$ in which x and x' are column vectors of floating-point variables. The floating-point matrix multiplication $\odot$ is similar to the rational matrix multiplication with the difference that the operations are done within the set of the floating-point numbers, that is:*

$$
\begin{cases}
a_{11}\odot x_1 & \oplus & a_{12}\odot x_2 & \oplus & \dots & \oplus & a'_{1n}\odot x'_n & \le & b_1 \\
a_{21}\odot x_1 & \oplus & a_{22}\odot x_2 & \oplus & \dots & \oplus & a'_{2n}\odot x'_n & \le & b_2 \\
\dots \\
a_{m1}\odot x_1 & \oplus & a_{m2}\odot x_2 & \oplus & \dots & \oplus & a'_{mn}\odot x'_n & \le & b_m
\end{cases}
$$

where a_{ij}, x_i, x'_i and b_i are respectively elements of A'', x, x' and b. In absence of parenthesis, the order of operations is such that floating-point multiplications are performed before floating-point additions. Then, additions are performed from left to right.

We would like to note that simple rational loops, as we defined them, are named in multiple ways in the literature. With only slight differences, they are for example designated as Single-path Linear-Constraints loops in [4,5], Linear Simple Loops in [9] and Linear Arithmetic Simple While loops in [21]. In an attempt to have a uniform naming for both the rational and the floating-point case, we chose the denomination *simple loop* as floating-point operations are non-linear, making all the previous names inappropriate.

We also find interesting to note that any unnested loop, using rational variables and rational arithmetic operations, having sequential assignments in its body, can be described by a simple rational loop of Definition 7, as explained in [8, Sect. 3.1]. This result is not valid when dealing with floating-point numbers due to the non-associativity of the floating-point arithmetic operations. Generally, floating-point arithmetic expressions cannot be simplified like the rational ones and should be treated as-is. We chose to study the floating-point loops of Definition 8 to give general ideas that can be adapted to other form of floating-point loops.

Definition 9 (LinRF). *The decision problem of the existence of a LRF, denoted LinRF, is defined as follows. Its instance is a simple loop. The question it tries to answer is whether there exists a LRF for the simple loop. The decision problem is denoted by $LinRF(\mathbb{Q})$ and $LinRF(\mathbb{F})$ when the variables respectively range over rationals and floating-point numbers from any floating-point type $\mathbb{F}_{\beta,p,e_{min},e_{max}}$ (and any rounding mode $\square$) that could be defined. More generally, we denote by $LinRF(E)$ the decision problem when the variables range over E.*

In the same way, we define the more general problem of universal termination.

Definition 10 (Halt). *The decision problem of universal termination, denoted Halt, is defined as follows. Its instance is a simple loop. The question it tries to answer is whether the simple loop terminates for every possible input. We denote by $Halt(E)$ the decision problem when the variables range over E.*

3   Complexity of $LinRF(\mathbb{F})$

In this section, we show that there is no polynomial algorithm that can decide $LinRF(\mathbb{F})$. We start by studying the decidability of $Halt(\mathbb{F})$ and $LinRF(\mathbb{F})$.

Theorem 1. *Halt($\mathbb{F}$) is decidable.*

Proof. A program $\mathcal{P} = \langle \mathcal{X}, \mathcal{I}, \mathcal{R} \rangle$ terminates if and only if every possible $\mathcal{X}$-sequence permitted by $\mathcal{R}$ is finite. As the variables range over some finite set $\mathbb{F}_{\beta,p,e_{min},e_{max}}$, then for any given sequence $s = X_1 X_2 \ldots$, we can check whether or not it is finite.

If the last element $X_{last(s)}$ of s has no more successor with respect to $\mathcal{R}$, s is a finite sequence. If there exists an element X_i that appears in s at index i and that already appeared at an index j, $j < i$, then there exists a subsequence $X_j \ldots X_i$ that will be repeated infinitely, causing s to be infinite. $\square$

Theorem 2. *LinRF($\mathbb{F}$) is decidable.*

Proof. Recall the proof of Theorem 1. We reason similarly with the difference that in addition to checking the finiteness of all the sequences, we also check the existence of LRFs which are valid with respect to all of them.

We say that $f(X) = CX$ is a valid LRF with respect to a sequence $s = X_1 X_2 \ldots X_{last(s)}$ if and only if the following system of constraints Φ_s is satisfiable:

$$\begin{cases} CX_1 \geq \delta_0 \\ CX_1 \geq \delta + CX_2 \\ \ldots \\ CX_{last(s)-1} \geq \delta_0 \\ CX_{last(s)-1} \geq \delta + CX_{last(s)} \\ \delta > 0 \end{cases} \tag{1}$$

$\Phi = \bigwedge_{\text{all } s} \Phi_s$ is the system of constraints of validity of f with respect to all the sequences. If Φ is satisfiable, the space of all the valid LRFs is described by $f(X) = CX \wedge \Phi$. Otherwise, there is no valid LRF.   □

It is worth mentioning that the algorithms we just presented for deciding $Halt(\mathbb{F})$ and $LinRF(\mathbb{F})$ can be applied to any program using variables ranging over finite sets. In other words, they can be applied not only to simple loops using floating-point variables but also to any implementable program on machines. Indeed, machines all have a finite amount of memory forcing the variables to range over finite sets.

Let us now focus on $LinRF(\mathbb{F})$. We intuitively understand that the decision algorithm we proposed is highly costly. Indeed, if there are n variables in the program, that is $\mathcal{X} = \mathbb{F}^n_{\beta,p,e_{min},e_{max}}$, and if there are N floating-points numbers that can be taken as values, that is $|\mathbb{F}_{\beta,p,e_{min},e_{max}}| = N$, then in the very worst case, we need to build the system of constraints of validity Φ from the $|\mathcal{X}|! = n^N!$ possible $\mathcal{X}$-sequences.

The question now arises whether we can have a more efficient algorithm for deciding $LinRF(\mathbb{F})$. Notably, we would like to know if a polynomial one exists. For that purpose, we rely on a result presented in [5, Theorem 3.1] regarding the complexity of $LinRF(\mathbb{Z})$.

Lemma 1. $LinRF(\mathbb{Z})$ is coNP-hard. Even for a finite set $E \subset \mathbb{Z}$, $LinRF(E)$ is still coNP-hard.

Proof. The proof consists in reducing $LinRF(\mathbb{Z})$ to the well-known coNP-hard problem of deciding whether a rational convex polyhedron contains integer points.

Theorem 3. $LinRF(\mathbb{F})$ is at least in coNP.

Proof. The proof consists in showing that for some specific floating-point types $\mathbb{F}_{\beta,p,e_{min},e_{max}}$ and a rounding mode □, the problem is at least in coNP. As we are studying the worst case complexity, that gives us a lower bound for the complexity of the generalization for any possible floating-point type.

Consider the finite set $Z_M \subset \mathbb{Z}$ defined as $Z_M = \{z \in \mathbb{Z}| - M \leq z \leq M\}$. For all $M \in \mathbb{N}^*$, we can construct the floating-point type $\mathbb{F}_M$ defined by the parameters $\beta = M$, $p = 1$, $e_{min} = 0$ and $e_{max} = 1$ for which $Z_M = \mathbb{F}_M$. Both Z_M and $\mathbb{F}_M$ have the same elements. Moreover, if the rounding mode for the operations in $\mathbb{F}_M$ is to-zero, that is if □ $=\uparrow^0$, then the operations in both Z_M and $\mathbb{F}_M$ are performed identically.

Hence, $\forall M \in \mathbb{N}^*, LinRF(\mathbb{F}_M) = LinRF(Z_M)$. As $LinRF(Z_M)$ is at least in coNP by Lemma 1, so is $LinRF(\mathbb{F}_M)$.   □

As we already know [23], the coNP class contains problems that are at least as hard as the NP class. Indeed, the complement of an NP-complete problem, which is in coNP, admits a polynomial decision algorithm only if P = NP, implying P = coNP. Thus, by conjecturing that P $\neq$ NP, we derive the following corollary.

Corollary 1. *There is no polynomial algorithm for deciding LinRF($\mathbb{F}$).*

Although that theoretical limitation may be discouraging, it is important to note that it applies to the problem of finding *one* general algorithm for *all* the possible instances of *LinRF*($\mathbb{F}$). There may be special cases for which polynomial decision algorithms may exist. We could also have correct algorithms that are polynomial but not complete. In other words, we could have algorithms that detect in polynomial time only part of the space of the existing LRFs. We investigate this idea in the next section.

4   A Sufficient Condition for Inferring LRFs in Polynomial Time

In this section, we present a novel technique for inferring in polynomial time the existence of LRFs for simple floating-point loops. The idea is to adapt to *LinRF*($\mathbb{F}$) the well-known Podelski-Rybalchenko algorithm, that we shorten PR algorithm, which solves *LinRF*($\mathbb{Q}$) in polynomial time and which is complete. This is achieved by means of sound over-approximations, that we shorten approximations for simplicity.

Firstly, Sect. 4.1 studies from a termination analysis aspect the links between a program and its possible approximations. Secondly, Sect. 4.2 presents a floating-point version of the PR algorithm obtained by using the approximation by maximal absolute error. Lastly, Sect. 4.3 discusses the results obtained with other approximations.

4.1   Program Approximation and Termination

Definition 11 (Approximation). *We say that the program $\mathcal{P}^{\#} = \langle \mathcal{X}, \mathcal{I}^{\#}, \mathcal{R}^{\#} \rangle$ is an approximation of the program $\mathcal{P} = \langle \mathcal{X}, \mathcal{I}, \mathcal{R} \rangle$ if $\mathcal{I} \subseteq \mathcal{I}^{\#}$ and $\mathcal{R}^{\#}$ is such that $\forall X_1, X_2 \in \mathcal{X} : X_1 \mathcal{R} X_2 \implies X_1 \mathcal{R}^{\#} X_2$.*

Example 3. Consider the program $\mathcal{P}_{simple}$ presented in Example 1 and the program $\mathcal{P}_{simple}^{\#}$ presented in Fig. 3 in which :<= is a non-deterministic assignment. $\mathcal{P}_{simple}^{\#}$ can be formalized as the transition system $\langle \mathcal{X}_{simple}, \mathcal{I}_{simple}^{\#}, \mathcal{R}_{simple}^{\#} \rangle$ where $\mathcal{I}_{simple}^{\#} = \{x \in \mathbb{Q} | x \leq 1000\}$ and $\mathcal{R}_{simple}^{\#} = \{\langle x, x' \rangle \in \mathbb{Q}^2 | x \geq -1 \wedge x' \leq x - 0.5\}$. We can easily verify that $\mathcal{I}_{simple} \subseteq \mathcal{I}_{simple}^{\#}$ and $\forall x, x' \in \mathcal{X}_{simple} : x \mathcal{R}_{simple} x' \implies x \mathcal{R}_{simple}^{\#} x'$. Hence, $\mathcal{P}_{simple}^{\#}$ is an approximation of $\mathcal{P}_{simple}$.

We now study the link between the termination of a given program and the termination of one of its approximations.

Theorem 4. *Given a program $\mathcal{P}$ and a corresponding approximation $\mathcal{P}^{\#}$, if $\mathcal{P}^{\#}$ terminates, so does $\mathcal{P}$.*

```
rational x :<= 1000;
while(x  >= -1) {
    x :<= x - 0.5;
}
```

Fig. 3. An approximation of $\mathcal{P}_{simple}$, $\mathcal{P}_{simple}^{\#}$

Proof. Differently stated, if $(\mathcal{X}, \mathcal{R}^{\#})$ is well-founded, so is $(\mathcal{X}, \mathcal{R})$. In order to prove that, let us reason by contradiction.

Suppose $(\mathcal{X}, \mathcal{R}^{\#})$ is well-founded while $(\mathcal{X}, \mathcal{R})$ is not. There is an infinite $\mathcal{X}$-sequence s_{∞} permitted by $\mathcal{R}$: $s_{\infty} = X_0 \mathcal{R} X_1 \mathcal{R} \dots$ By definition of approximation (Definition 11), $X_i \mathcal{R} X_{i+1} \implies X_i \mathcal{R}^{\#} X_{i+1}$. Consequently, there exists $s_{\infty}^{\#} = X_0 \mathcal{R}^{\#} X_1 \mathcal{R}^{\#} \dots$ corresponding to s_{∞} which contradicts our hypothesis as an infinite sequence is permitted by $\mathcal{R}^{\#}$. □

Though Theorem 4 is already enough to infer termination of a program through one of its possible approximations, it gives no information about the termination argument. Notably, we would like to have the deeper knowledge of the link between the space of ranking functions, that we denote by SRF.

Theorem 5. *Given a program $\mathcal{P}$ and a corresponding approximation $\mathcal{P}^{\#}$, we have $SRF(\mathcal{P}^{\#}) \subseteq SRF(\mathcal{P})$.*

Proof. Let us reason by contradiction. Suppose $SRF(\mathcal{P}^{\#}) \not\subseteq SRF(\mathcal{P})$ which means that there exists a ranking function f for $\mathcal{P}^{\#}$ which is not one for $\mathcal{P}$.

As f is not a ranking function for $\mathcal{P}$, $\exists X_1, X_2 \in \mathcal{X} : X_1 \mathcal{R} X_2 \implies f(X_1) \not> f(X_2)$. However, by definition of approximation (Definition 11), $X_1 \mathcal{R} X_2 \implies X_1 \mathcal{R}^{\#} X_2$ and as f is a ranking function for $\mathcal{P}^{\#}$, $X_1 \mathcal{R}^{\#} X_2 \implies f(X_1) > f(X_2)$ which leads to a contradiction. □

Differently stated, Theorem 5 says that any ranking function for a given program is also a ranking function for any program it approximates. For our particular case of interest, we derive the following corollary regarding the space of LRFs, that we denote by $SLRF$.

Corollary 2. *Given a program $\mathcal{P}$ and a corresponding approximation $\mathcal{P}^{\#}$, we have $SLRF(\mathcal{P}^{\#}) \subseteq SLRF(\mathcal{P})$: if f is a LRF for $\mathcal{P}^{\#}$, then f is also a LRF for $\mathcal{P}$.*

Example 4. Consider the program $\mathcal{P}_{simple}$ presented in Example 1 and the corresponding approximation $\mathcal{P}_{simple}^{\#}$ presented in Example 3. The space of LRFs of $\mathcal{P}_{simple}^{\#}$ is described by $\rho(x) = ax, a > 0$. By Corollary 2, ρ also describes LRFs for $\mathcal{P}_{simple}$.

We point out that it is a misunderstanding of the previous results to deduce from them that all termination analysis based on approximations are doomed to be incomplete. It would be indeed the case if $SRF(\mathcal{P}^{\#}) \subset SRF(\mathcal{P})$. However, it is always possible to refine the approximation until having $SRF(\mathcal{P}^{\#}) = SRF(\mathcal{P})$. A way to do so for the particular case of floating-point loops is for example presented in [18].

Thus, in our search for LRFs for simple floating-point loops, it is always possible to find approximations that are precise enough to ensure completeness. However, due to Corollary 1, it cannot be achieved by any polynomial algorithm. In the technique we will now present, we trade completeness for complexity: the algorithm may fail at detecting all the possible LRFs, but it answers in polynomial time.

4.2 A Floating-Point Version of the Podelski-Rybalchenko Algorithm

Our technique is based on the well-known PR algorithm [21] which provides sufficient and necessary conditions, hence making the algorithm complete, for the existence of LRFs for simple rational loops. In addition to deciding the existence of LRFs, the algorithm can also synthesize them. It proceeds by reducing the decision/synthesizing problem to a linear programming problem which is long known to be solvable in polynomial time [17].

Theorem 6 (Podelski-Rybalchenko [21]). *Given a simple rational loop $\mathcal{L}_{\mathbb{Q}}$ described by $A'' \left(x \ x' \right)^T \leq b$ such that $A'' \in \mathbb{Q}^{m \times 2n}$, $b \in \mathbb{Q}^{m \times 1}$ and $x, x' \in \mathbb{Q}^{n \times 1}$, let $A'' = (A \ A')$ where $A, A' \in \mathbb{Q}^{m \times n}$. A LRF exists for $\mathcal{L}_{\mathbb{Q}}$ if and only if there exist $\lambda_1, \lambda_2 \in \mathbb{Q}^{1 \times m}$ such that:*

$$\begin{cases} \lambda_1, \lambda_2 \geq 0 \\ \lambda_1 A' = 0 \\ (\lambda_1 - \lambda_2)A = 0 \\ \lambda_2(A + A') = 0 \\ \lambda_2 b < 0 \end{cases}$$

The synthesized LRFs are of the form $f(x) = \mu x$ with $\mu = \lambda_2 A'$ and are such that for all x, x':

$$\begin{cases} f(x) \geq \delta_0, \delta_0 = -\lambda_1 b \\ f(x) \geq f(x') + \delta, \delta = -\lambda_2 b, \delta > 0 \end{cases}$$

Proof. Omitted as there are already various papers discussing it in various ways. Interested readers can find in-depth study of the PR algorithm in [1]. $\square$

Example 5. Consider the program $\mathcal{P}_{ilog37q}$ having $n = 2$ variables presented in Fig. 4. The loop of $\mathcal{P}_{ilog37q}$ can be expressed in the matrix form $\left(A_q \ A'_q \right) \left(x \ x' \right)^T \leq b$ by letting

$$A_q = \begin{pmatrix} -1 & 0 \\ 0 & -1 \\ -1 & 0 \\ 1 & 0 \\ 0 & 1 \\ 0 & -1 \end{pmatrix}, A_q' = \begin{pmatrix} 0 & 0 \\ 0 & 0 \\ 37 & 0 \\ -37 & 0 \\ 0 & -1 \\ 0 & 1 \end{pmatrix}, b = \begin{pmatrix} -37 \\ -1 \\ 0 \\ 0 \\ -1 \\ 1 \end{pmatrix} \tag{2}$$

The corresponding linear system given by PR is satisfiable and the row vectors $\lambda_1 = (\lambda_1^1 \ \lambda_1^2 \ \lambda_1^3 \ \lambda_1^4 \ \lambda_1^5 \ \lambda_1^6)$ and $\lambda_2 = (\lambda_2^1 \ \lambda_2^2 \ \lambda_2^3 \ \lambda_2^4 \ \lambda_2^5 \ \lambda_2^6)$ are such that:

$$\begin{cases} \lambda_1^1 = -\lambda_1^2 + \lambda_1^4 + \lambda_2^1 + \lambda_2^3 - \lambda_2^4 \\ \lambda_1^2 = -\lambda_2^5 + \lambda_2^6 \\ \lambda_1^3 = \lambda_1^4 \\ \lambda_1^4 \geq 0 \\ \lambda_1^5 \geq 0 \\ \lambda_1^6 = \lambda_1^5 \end{cases} \text{ and } \begin{cases} \lambda_2^1 = 36\lambda_2^3 - 36\lambda_2^4 \\ \lambda_2^2 = 0 \\ \lambda_2^3 > 0 \\ 0 \leq \lambda_2^4 < \lambda_2^3 \\ \lambda_2^5 \geq 0 \\ \lambda_2^5 \leq \lambda_2^6 < 1332\lambda_2^3 - 1332\lambda_2^4 \end{cases} \tag{3}$$

Thus, $SLRF(\mathcal{P}_{ilog37q})$ is completely described by $f(x_1, x_2) = \mu_1 x_1 + \mu_2 x_2$ such that $\mu_1 > 0$ and $0 \leq \mu_2 < 36\mu_1$.

```
rational x1 = input(), x2 = 1;
while(x1 >= 37 & x2 >=1) {
    x1 := x1 / 37;
    x2 := x2 + 1;
}
```

Fig. 4. A program that computes and stores in x2 the integer base-37 logarithm of x1, $\mathcal{P}_{ilog37q}$. A similar program with variables ranging over the integers is studied in [1].

Every time a LRF exists for a given simple rational loop, the PR algorithm *does* find it in polynomial time. Unfortunately, it cannot be applied to simple floating-point loops. Indeed, the rounding errors cause the floating-point operations to be non-associative, making invalid most of the mathematical results leading to the PR algorithm.

We work around that issue by means of rational approximations. These approximations must be linear and must be defined in a single piece so that the PR algorithm can be used. Detailed explanations for the need for these constraints are given in Sect. 4.3. An example of such approximation is the approximation by maximal absolute error, as used in various ways in various works [3,20].

Definition 12 (Absolute error). *The absolute error $\mathcal{A}(x)$ of the approximation of $x \in \mathbb{R}$ by $\hat{x} \in \mathbb{F}_{\beta, p, e_{min}, e_{max}}$ using a rounding mode $\square$ is defined as $\mathcal{A}(x) = |x - \hat{x}|$.*

Theorem 7 (Approximation by maximal absolute error). *Given a real arithmetic operation $\star$, its floating-point equivalent $\circledast$ and 2 floating-point numbers $\hat{x}_1, \hat{x}_2 \in \mathbb{F}_{\beta,p,e_{min},e_{max}}$, if we use the rounding mode to-nearest-ties-to-even and if no overflow occurs then the following holds:*

$$\hat{x}_1 \star \hat{x}_2 - \mathcal{A}_{max} \le \hat{x}_1 \circledast \hat{x}_2 \le \hat{x}_1 \star \hat{x}_2 + \mathcal{A}_{max}$$

where $\mathcal{A}_{max} = \frac{\beta^{e_{max}-p+1}}{2}$ is the maximal absolute error.

Proof. Recall that by property of correct rounding, as presented in Definition 6, $\hat{x}_1 \circledast \hat{x}_2 = o(\hat{x}_1 \star \hat{x}_2)$. Let $t = \hat{x}_1 \star \hat{x}_2$ and $\hat{t} = o(t) = \hat{x}_1 \circledast \hat{x}_2$, $t \in \mathbb{R}$ and $\hat{t} \in \mathbb{F}_{\beta,p,e_{min},e_{max}}$.

From the definition of the absolute error given in Definition 12, it can be easily derived that $t - \mathcal{A}(t) \le \hat{t} \le t + \mathcal{A}(t)$. In the worst case, t is located right in the middle of $\hat{t}$ and the nearest floating-point number $\hat{t}_a$ adjacent to $\hat{t}$. Thus we have $\mathcal{A}(t) \le \frac{|\hat{t}-\hat{t}_a|}{2}$. By writing $\hat{t}$ in standardized notation as presented in Definition 4, that is $\hat{t} = (-1)^s \hat{m} \beta^e$, we have $\hat{t}_a = (-1)^s (\hat{m} \pm \beta^{-p+1}) \beta^e$. Hence, in the worst case: $\mathcal{A}(t) \le \frac{\beta^{e-p+1}}{2}$. As $e \le e_{max}$, $\mathcal{A}(t) \le \mathcal{A}_{max}$ from which the theorem follows. $\qquad\square$

Example 6. Consider the floating-point type $\mathbb{F}_{simple}$ presented in Example 2. If the rounding mode to-nearest-ties-to-even is used, then for any arithmetic operation $\star$, its floating-point equivalent $\circledast$ and 2 floating-point numbers $\hat{x}_1, \hat{x}_2 \in \mathbb{F}_{simple}$, the following holds: $\hat{x}_1 \star \hat{x}_2 - 5 \le \hat{x}_1 \circledast \hat{x}_2 \le \hat{x}_1 \star \hat{x}_2 + 5$.

We now present an adaptation of the PR algorithm using the approximation by maximal absolute error.

Theorem 8 (General floating-point version of Podelski-Rybalchenko).
Consider the floating-point type $\mathbb{F}$ which has such parameters and which uses such rounding mode that $\mathcal{A}_{max}$ is the maximal absolute error. Consider also the simple floating-point loop $\mathcal{L}_\mathbb{F}$ described by $A'' \odot (x\ x')^T \le b$ such that $A'' \in \mathbb{F}^{m \times 2n}$, $b \in \mathbb{F}^{m \times 1}$ and $x, x' \in \mathbb{F}^{n \times 1}$. By letting $A'' = (A\ A')$ where $A, A' \in \mathbb{F}^{m \times n}$ and if no overflow occurs, a LRF exists for $\mathcal{L}_\mathbb{F}$ if there exist $\lambda_1, \lambda_2 \in \mathbb{Q}^{1 \times m}$ such that:

$$\begin{cases} \lambda_1, \lambda_2 \ge 0 \\ \lambda_1 A' = 0 \\ (\lambda_1 - \lambda_2)A = 0 \\ \lambda_2(A + A') = 0 \\ \lambda_2 c < 0 \end{cases}$$

where $c \in \mathbb{Q}^{m \times 1}$ and $c = b + colvect^m((4n-1)\mathcal{A}_{max})$. Here, $colvect^m(e)$ denotes the column vector of m elements, all elements equaling e.

The synthesized LRFs are of the form $f(x) = \mu x$ with $\mu = \lambda_2 A'$ and are such that for all x,x':

$$\begin{cases} f(x) \ge \delta_0, \delta_0 = -\lambda_1 c \\ f(x) \ge f(x') + \delta, \delta = -\lambda_2 c, \delta > 0 \end{cases}$$

Proof. Let us call l_k the first member of the k-th inequality, that is:

$$l_k = a_{k1} \odot x_1 \oplus a_{k2} \odot x_2 \oplus \ldots \oplus a'_{kn} \odot x'_n \qquad (4)$$
$$l_k \le b_k \qquad (5)$$

By approximating by below each operation using the approximation by maximal absolute error (Theorem 7) we get a linear lower bound for l_k:

$$(a_{k1}x_1 - \mathcal{A}_{max}) \oplus a_{k2} \odot x_2 \qquad \oplus \ldots \oplus a'_{kn} \odot x'_n \le l_k$$
$$a_{k1}x_1 \oplus (a_{k2}x_2 - \mathcal{A}_{max}) \qquad \oplus \ldots \oplus a'_{kn} \odot x'_n - \mathcal{A}_{max} \le l_k$$
$$(a_{k1}x_1 + a_{k2}x_2 - \mathcal{A}_{max}) \qquad \oplus \ldots \oplus a'_{kn} \odot x'_n - 2\mathcal{A}_{max} \le l_k$$
$$\cdots$$
$$a_{k1}x_1 + a_{k2}x_2 \qquad + \cdots + a'_{kn}x'_n - (4n-1)\mathcal{A}_{max} \le l_k \qquad (6)$$

Combining that result with the upper bound b_k of l_k as shown in (5), we get:

$$a_{k1}x_1 + a_{k2}x_2 + \ldots + a'_{kn}x'_n - (4n-1)\mathcal{A}_{max} \quad \le l_k \le b_k$$
$$a_{k1}x_1 + a_{k2}x_2 + \ldots + a'_{kn}x'_n - (4n-1)\mathcal{A}_{max} \quad \le b_k$$
$$a_{k1}x_1 + a_{k2}x_2 + \ldots + a'_{kn}x'_n \quad \le b_k + (4n-1)\mathcal{A}_{max} \qquad (7)$$

Hence, the floating-point loop $\mathcal{L}_{\mathbb{F}}$ described by $A'' \odot (x\ x')^T \le b$ is approximated by the rational loop $\mathcal{L}_{\mathbb{Q}}$ described by $A'' (x\ x')^T \le c$ where $c = b + colvect^m((4n-1)\mathcal{A}_{max})$.

By applying the PR algorithm presented in Theorem 6 on $\mathcal{L}_{\mathbb{Q}}$, if a LRF f is found, then f is also a LRF for $\mathcal{L}_{\mathbb{F}}$ by Corollary 2. $\qquad \square$

Example 7. Consider the program $\mathcal{P}_{ilog37q}$ presented in Example 5. We are interested in its floating-point version $\mathcal{P}_{ilog37f}$ in which variables are from the type $\mathbb{F}_{simple}$ presented in Example 2. The rounding mode used is to-nearest-ties-to-even.

As presented in Example 6, the maximal absolute error for any arithmetic floating-point operation $\circledast$ done in $\mathbb{F}_{simple}$ is $\mathcal{A}_{max} = 5$. Thus, $\mathcal{P}_{ilog37f}$ is approximated by the rational loop $\mathcal{P}^{\#}_{ilog37f}$ described by $(A_f\ A'_f) (x\ x')^T \le c$ such that:

$$A_f = A_q, A'_f = A'_q, c = b + colvect^6(35) = c_2 = (-2\ 34\ 35\ 35\ 34\ 36)^T \qquad (8)$$

By applying the PR algorithm, LRFs for $\mathcal{P}_{ilog37f}$ exist and are of the form $f(x_1, x_2) = \mu_1 x_1 + \mu_2 x_2$ such that $\mu_1 > 0$ and $0 \le \mu_2 < \frac{\mu_1}{36}$.

It is important to observe that this floating-point version of the PR algorithm applies only if no overflow occurs during the computation. Indeed, by using the approximation by maximal absolute error, we assumed that the results of the operations all laid in the authorized range. Thus, the initial ranges of the values of the variables that do not eventually lead to an overflow should be determined beforehand. It can be achieved for example using techniques from the framework of Abstract Interpretation [11].

As we already discussed in the Preliminaries section of the paper, floating-point expressions are to be studied as-is and our results are only general. For example, we can have a better approximation of $\mathcal{P}_{ilog37f}$ by noticing that there are less than $(4n - 1)$ operations per line. Moreover, by only approximating the operations that are not known to be exactly computed, we get the approximation $\mathcal{P}^{\#}_{ilog37f2}$ described by $\left(A_{f2}\ A'_{f2}\right)\left(x\ x'\right)^T \leq c_2$ such that:

$$A_{f2} = A_q, A'_{f2} = A'_q, c_2 = \left(-37\ -1\ 10\ 10\ 4\ 6\right)^T \tag{9}$$

By applying the PR algorithm, LRFs for $\mathcal{P}_{ilog37f2}$ exist and are of the form $f(x_1, x_2) = \mu_1 x_1 + \mu_2 x_2$ such that $\mu_1 > 0$ and $0 \leq \mu_2 < \frac{661\mu_1}{111}$. We easily verify that $SLRF(\mathcal{P}^{\#}_{ilog37f}) \subset SLRF(\mathcal{P}^{\#}_{ilog37f2})$, that is we detect a wider range of LRFs with $\mathcal{P}^{\#}_{ilog37f2}$.

4.3   Other Approximations

At this point of the paper, the reader may wonder why we specifically chose the approximation by maximal absolute error instead of another approximation. Indeed, the justification we proposed was that the approximation needed to be linear and defined in a single piece but we gave no further explanation. Now, we give more details.

Recall the proof for the general floating-point version of the PR algorithm (Theorem 8). It consisted in transforming the simple floating-point loop into a simple rational loop. Indeed, the PR algorithm works on loops described by linear systems, making the linearity of the approximation straightforward.

It remains to justify why the approximation needs to be defined in one piece. Indeed, we can have piecewise linear approximations having precisions that increase with the number of pieces, as shown in [18]. For example, the approximation defined in 3 pieces presented in Theorem 9 is better than the approximation by maximal absolute error. Indeed, the surface of the area enclosed between the upper and lower approximation functions is smaller in the approximation in 3 pieces, as illustrated in Fig. 5.

Theorem 9 (Approximation in 3 pieces). *Given a real arithmetic operation $\star$, its floating-point equivalent $\circledast$ and 2 floating-point numbers $\hat{x}_1, \hat{x}_2 \in \mathbb{IF}_{\beta,p,e_{min},e_{max}}$, if we use the rounding mode to-nearest-ties-to-even and if no overflow occurs then the following holds:*

$$\begin{cases} (1 - \mathcal{R}^n_{max})t \leq \hat{x}_1 \circledast \hat{x}_2 \leq (1 + \mathcal{R}^n_{max})t & \text{if} \quad n_{min} < t \leq n_{max} \\ t - \mathcal{A}^s_{max} \leq \hat{x}_1 \circledast \hat{x}_2 \leq t + \mathcal{A}^s_{max} & \text{if} \quad -n_{min} \leq t \leq n_{min} \\ 1 + \mathcal{R}^n_{max})t \leq \hat{x}_1 \circledast \hat{x}_2 \leq 1 - \mathcal{R}^n_{max})t & \text{if} \quad -n_{max} \leq t < -n_{min} \end{cases}$$

where $t = \hat{x}_1 \star \hat{x}_2$, $n_{min} = \beta^{e_{min}}$ is the smallest positive normal number, $n_{max} = (\beta - \beta^{-p+1})\beta^{e_{max}}$ is the biggest positive normal number, $\mathcal{A}^s_{max} = \frac{\beta^{e_{min}-p+1}}{2}$ is

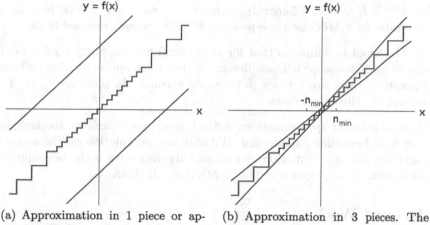

(a) Approximation in 1 piece or approximation by maximal absolute error

(b) Approximation in 3 pieces. The partitioning chosen here separates the normals from the subnormals.

Fig. 5. Piecewise linear approximations of $\hat{x}$ zoomed around the origin

the maximal absolute error for the subnormal numbers and $\mathcal{R}_{max}^{n} = \frac{\beta^{-p+1}}{2+\beta^{-p+1}}$ is the maximal relative error for the normal numbers.

Proof. For the case where $-n_{min} \leq t \leq n_{min}$, that is t is a subnormal number, the proof is similar to that for the approximation with maximal absolute error (Theorem 7). Only the value of the maximal absolute error differs.

For the case where $n_{min} \leq |t| \leq n_{max}$, that is t is a normal number, we use an approximation based on the maximal relative error. The relative error of the approximation of t is $\mathcal{R}(t) = \frac{|t-\hat{t}|}{|t|}$. From that definition, it can be easily derived that $(1 - \mathcal{R}(t))|t| \leq |\hat{t}| \leq (1 + \mathcal{R}(t))|t|$. As $\mathcal{R}(t) \leq \frac{\beta^{-p+1}}{2+\beta^{-p+1}}$ for the case of the normal numbers, as shown in [16], the theorem follows.   □

As another example of approximation, we can combine the bound for the absolute error for the subnormals with the bound for the relative error for the normals. It results in using approximation functions defined in 2 pieces as it distinguishes the positives from the negatives [18].

Using these piecewise linear approximations, a simple floating-point loop will be transformed into a set of simple rational loops, designated as *Multi-path Linear-Constraint* loops or MLC loops in [4,5]. The existence of LRFs in MLC loops are known to be also decidable in polynomial time [13,19]. However, the size of the obtained MLC loop is an exponential function in the size of the simple floating-point loop it approximates, as shown in the following theorem.

Theorem 10 (From simple floating-point loop to MLC loop). *Consider the floating-point type $\mathbb{F}$. Consider also the simple floating-point loop $\mathcal{L}_{\mathbb{F}}$ described by $A'' \odot (x \; x')^{T} \leq b$ such that $A'' \in \mathbb{F}^{m \times 2n}$, $b \in \mathbb{F}^{m \times 1}$ and*

$x, x' \in \mathbb{F}^{n \times 1}$. *If we use a linear approximation defined in k pieces, then $\mathcal{L}_{\mathbb{F}}$ is approximated by a MLC loop composed of $k^{(4n-1)m}$ simple rational loops.*

Proof. The proof is similar to that for the general floating-point version of the PR algorithm (Theorem 8). The difference is that when approximating by below one operation, there are k cases to take into account. As there are $(4n - 1)m$ operations, the theorem follows. □

Thus, only linear approximations defined in one piece preserve the transformations from becoming exponential. Without any information on the range of the variables, the approximation by maximal absolute error is the best approximation having these properties. That motivated our choice.

5   Related Work

To the best of our knowledge, there is only limited work on the termination of floating-point programs. One of the first work addressing that problem is [22] which is an extension of the adornments-based approach. It consists in transforming the logic program to analyze in a way that we can use techniques originally developed for analysis of numerical computations.

Recently, techniques have been developed for treating the case of bit-vector programs. These techniques belong to the family of Model Checking [2]. [10] presents several novel algorithms to generate ranking functions for relations over machine integers: a method based on a reduction to Presburger arithmetic, and a template-matching approach for predefined classes of ranking functions based on reduction to SAT- and QBF-solving. In a similar way, [12] reduces the termination problem for programs using machine integers or floating-point numbers to a second-order satisfiability problem. Both methods are complete but are highly costly.

A different approach is presented in [18]. It consists in translating the floating-point programs into rational ones by means of sound approximations. Hence, it bridges the gap between termination analysis of floating-point loops and rational loops. The floating-point expressions are approximated using piecewise linear functions that can be parameterized depending on the precision desired/required.

6   Conclusion

We have studied the hardness of termination proofs for simple loops when the variables are of floating-point type. We have focused on termination inferred from the existence of linear ranking functions and showed that the problem is at least in coNP. This is a very valuable information as it dissuades us from looking for a decision algorithm that is both polynomial and complete. The problem of deciding the existence of linear ranking functions for simple integer and machine integer loops was studied in depth very recently and was shown to be coNP-complete. To the best of our knowledge, our work is the first attempt at providing a similar result for the floating-points.

To design a polynomial algorithm, we have traded completeness for complexity. We have proposed the first adaptation of the Podelski-Rybalchenko algorithm for simple floating-point loops. This is achieved by means of linear approximations defined in one piece. We have suggested the use of the approximation by maximal absolute error. A possible improvement would be to use more precise linear approximations defined in one piece based on the ranges of the variables. As we have provided a sufficient but not necessary condition for inferring the existence of linear ranking functions, experimentations have yet to be conducted in order to get a practical evaluation of the technique.

References

1. Bagnara, R., Mesnard, F., Pescetti, A., Zaffanella, E.: A new look at the automatic synthesis of linear ranking functions. Inf. Comput. **215**, 47–67 (2012)
2. Baier, C., Katoen, J.: Principles of Model Checking. MIT Press, Cambridge (2008)
3. Belaid, M.S., Michel, C., Rueher, M.: Boosting local consistency algorithms over floating-point numbers. In: Milano, M. (ed.) CP 2012. LNCS, vol. 7514, pp. 127–140. Springer, Heidelberg (2012)
4. Ben-Amram, A.M.: Ranking functions for linear-constraint loops. In: Lisitsa, A., Nemytykh, A.P. (eds.) Proceedings of the 1st International Workshop on Verification and Program Transformation (VPT 2013). EPiC Series, vol. 16, pp. 1–8. EasyChair (2013)
5. Ben-Amram, A.M., Genaim, S.: Ranking functions for linear-constraint loops. J. ACM **61**(4), 26:1–26:55 (2014)
6. Ben-Amram, A.M., Genaim, S., Masud, A.N.: On the termination of integer loops. ACM Trans. Program. Lang. Syst. **34**(4), 16 (2012)
7. Braverman, M.: Termination of integer linear programs. In: Ball, T., Jones, R.B. (eds.) CAV 2006. LNCS, vol. 4144, pp. 372–385. Springer, Heidelberg (2006)
8. Chen, H.Y.: Program analysis: termination proofs for linear simple loops. Ph.D. thesis, Louisiana State University (2012)
9. Chen, H.Y., Flur, S., Mukhopadhyay, S.: Termination proofs for linear simple loops. Softw. Tools Technol. Transfer **17**(1), 47–57 (2015)
10. Cook, B., Kroening, D., Rümmer, P., Wintersteiger, C.M.: Ranking function synthesis for bit-vector relations. Formal Methods Syst. Des. **43**(1), 93–120 (2013)
11. Cousot, P., Cousot, R.: Abstract interpretation: a unified lattice model for staticanalysis of programs by construction or approximation of fixpoints. In: Graham, R.M., Harrison, M.A., Sethi, R. (eds.) Proceedings of the 4th ACM Symposium on Principles of Programming Languages (POPL 1977), pp. 238–252. ACM (1977)
12. David, C., Kroening, D., Lewis, M.: Unrestricted termination and non-termination arguments for bit-vector programs. In: Vitek, J. (ed.) ESOP 2015. LNCS, vol. 9032, pp. 183–204. Springer, Heidelberg (2015)
13. Feautrier, P.: Some efficient solutions to the affine scheduling problem. I. One-dimensional time. Int. J. Parallel Prog. **21**(5), 313–347 (1992)
14. Fousse, L., Hanrot, G., Lefèvre, V., Pélissier, P., Zimmermann, P.: MPFR: a multiple-precision binary floating-point library with correct rounding. ACM Trans. Math. Softw. **33**(2), 13 (2007)
15. Goldberg, D.: What every computer scientist should know about floating-point arithmetic. ACM Comput. Surv. **23**(1), 5–48 (1991)

16. Jeannerod, C.-P., Rump, S.M.: On relative errors of floating-point operations: optimal bounds and applications (2014). Preprint
17. Khachiyan, L.: Polynomial algorithms in linear programming. USSR Comput. Math. Math. Phys. **20**(1), 53–72 (1980)
18. Maurica, F., Mesnard, F., Payet, E.: Termination analysis of floating-point programs using parameterizable rational approximations. In: Proceedings of the 31st ACM Symposium on Applied Computing (SAC 2016) (2016)
19. Mesnard, F., Serebrenik, A.: Recurrence with affine level mappings is P-time decidable for CLP(R). Theory Pract. Logic Program. **8**(1), 111–119 (2008)
20. Miné, A.: Relational abstract domains for the detection of floating-point run-time errors. Computing Research Repository, abs/cs/0703077 (2007)
21. Podelski, A., Rybalchenko, A.: A complete method for the synthesis of linear ranking functions. In: Steffen, B., Levi, G. (eds.) VMCAI 2004. LNCS, vol. 2937, pp. 239–251. Springer, Heidelberg (2004)
22. Serebrenik, A., Schreye, D.D.: Termination of floating-point computations. J. Autom. Reasoning **34**(2), 141–177 (2005)
23. Sipser, M.: Introduction to the Theory of Computation. PWS Publishing Company, Boston (1997)
24. Tiwari, A.: Termination of linear programs. In: Alur, R., Peled, D.A. (eds.) CAV 2004. LNCS, vol. 3114, pp. 70–82. Springer, Heidelberg (2004)

Alive-FP: Automated Verification of Floating Point Based Peephole Optimizations in LLVM

David Menendez[1], Santosh Nagarakatte[1(✉)], and Aarti Gupta[2]

[1] Rutgers University, New Brunswick, USA
{davemm,santosh.nagarakatte}@cs.rutgers.edu
[2] Princeton University, Princeton, USA
aartig@cs.princeton.edu

Abstract. Peephole optimizations optimize and canonicalize code to enable other optimizations but are error-prone. Our prior research on Alive, a domain-specific language for specifying LLVM's peephole optimizations, automatically verifies the correctness of integer-based peephole optimizations and generates C++ code for use within LLVM. This paper proposes Alive-FP, an automated verification framework for floating point based peephole optimizations in LLVM. Alive-FP handles a class of floating point optimizations and fast-math optimizations involving signed zeros, not-a-number, and infinities, which do not result in loss of accuracy. This paper provides multiple encodings for various floating point operations to account for the various kinds of undefined behavior and under-specification in the LLVM's language reference manual. We have translated all optimizations that belong to this category into Alive-FP. In this process, we have discovered seven wrong optimizations in LLVM.

1 Introduction

Compilers perform numerous optimizations transforming programs through multiple intermediate representations to produce efficient code. Compilers are intended to preserve the semantics of source programs through such transformations and optimizations. However, modern compilers are error-prone similar to other large software systems. Recent random testing approaches [1,2] have found numerous bugs in mainstream compilers. These bugs range from compiler crashes to silent generation of incorrect programs. Among them, peephole optimizations are persistent source of compiler bugs [1,2].

Peephole optimizations perform local algebraic simplifications of code, clean up code produced by other stages, and canonicalize code to enable further optimizations. Any misunderstanding in the semantics of the instructions, overlooked corner cases, and the interaction of algebraic simplification with undefined behavior results in compiler bugs. Furthermore, modern compilers have numerous such peephole optimizations (*e.g.*, the LLVM compiler has more than a thousand such peephole optimizations performed by the InstCombine and the InstSimplify passes).

© Springer-Verlag GmbH Germany 2016
X. Rival (Ed.): SAS 2016, LNCS 9837, pp. 317–337, 2016.
DOI: 10.1007/978-3-662-53413-7_16

Our prior research on the Alive domain-specific language addresses a part of this problem of developing correct peephole optimizations in LLVM [3]. An Alive optimization is of the form *source* $\implies$ *target* with an optional precondition. The optimization checks the input code for a directed acyclic graph (DAG) of the form *source* and replaces it with the DAG specified by the *target* (see Sect. 2.1 for more details). Optimizations expressed in Alive are verified by encoding them as first-order logic formulae whose validity is checked using Satisfiability Modulo Theories (SMT) solvers. Further, the Alive interpreter generates C++ code for use within the LLVM compiler to provide competitive compilation time.

In our prior work, we restricted Alive to integer optimizations because floating point (FP) support with SMT solvers was either non-existent or not mature at that point in time. This paper proposes Alive-FP, an extension of Alive, that adds automated verification for a class of FP optimizations in LLVM. Alive-FP leverages the Floating Point Arithmetic (FPA) [4] theory in SMT-LIB, which has been supported by SMT solvers like Z3 [5], to perform automated reasoning.

A floating point number approximates a real number. The IEEE-754 standard [6] provides portability of FP operations across various hardware and software components by standardizing the representation and operations. Today, most processors support FP representation natively in hardware. To represent large and small values, floating point numbers in the IEEE-754 are represented in the form: $(-1)^s \times M \times 2^E$, where s determines the sign, significand M is a fractional binary number (ranges between $[1, 2)$ or $[0, 1)$), and E is the exponent that weights the value (see Sect. 2.2 for a background on FP numbers). The representation has normal values (the common case), denormal values (values close to zero), two zeros ($+0.0$ and -0.0), and special values such as positive infinity, negative infinity, and not-a-number (NaN). Further, the standard has specific rules on ordering and equality of numbers, and generation and propagation of special values. Most algebraic identities for real numbers are not accurate with FP numbers due to rounding errors (addition is associative with reals but is not with FP). Unfortunately, most programmers are not comfortable with these arcane details (see the seminal paper on FP [7] for more information).

Peephole optimizations in LLVM related to FP can be classified into two categories: optimizations that preserve bitwise precision (*i.e.*, there is no loss in accuracy with the optimization) and optimizations that do not preserve bit precision (*i.e.*, sacrifice some accuracy). The optimizations that preserve bit precision can further be classified into two categories: optimizations that are identities according to the IEEE-754 standard and optimizations that preserve bit precision in the absence of special values. LLVM, by default, enables optimizations that are identities according to the standard. LLVM enables bit-precise optimizations in the absence of special values with explicit fast-math attributes **nnan** (assume no NaNs), **nsz** (assume no distinction between two zeros), and **ninf** (assume no infinities). LLVM enables optimizations that are not bit-precise with fast-math attributes **arcp** (allow reciprocals) and **fast**.

In this paper, we are focused on verifying the correctness of bit-precise floating point based peephole optimizations in LLVM. We propose Alive-FP, a new domain-specific language, that extends Alive with FP instructions, types, and predicates (see Sect. 3) and allows the use of both integer and FP operations. Alive-FP proves the correctness of FP optimizations by encoding them into first-order logic formulae in the SMT-LIB theory of floating point arithmetic (FPA), whose validity is checked using Z3 [5]. We highlight the under-specification in the LLVM's language reference manual about undefined behavior and rounding modes with floating point operations. Given this under-specification about undefined behavior and rounding modes, we provide multiple encodings for the FP instructions and attributes (see Sect. 4) into FPA theory. We have translated 104 bit-precise FP peephole optimizations from LLVM into Alive-FP (see Sect. 5). In this process, Alive-FP has discovered seven previously unknown floating point bugs [8–12]. We have added new features to Alive-FP on request from developers (*e.g.*, bitcast with FP). Alive-FP is open source [13].

2   Background

This section provides background on Alive [3], which we build upon in this work. We also provide a quick primer on the FP representation in the IEEE standard.

2.1   Alive Domain-Specific Language

Alive [3] is a domain-specific language for specifying LLVM's peephole optimizations. The Alive interpreter automatically checks the correctness of an optimization by encoding it into a formula in first-order logic whose validity is checked using an SMT solver. It also generates C++ code for use within LLVM, which implements the optimization.

Syntax. Alive syntax is similar to the LLVM intermediate representation (IR), because LLVM developers are already familiar with it. Alive optimizations are specified as source ⇒ target, with an optional precondition. An Alive optimization is a directed, acyclic graph (DAG), with two *root* nodes, which have only outgoing edges. One root is the source, which is the instruction to be replaced, and the other is the target, which replaces it. To indicate that the source root replaces the target, they must have the same name. The leaves in the DAG are input variables, symbolic constants,

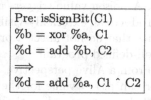

Pre: isSignBit(C1)
%b = xor %a, C1
%d = add %b, C2
⟹
%d = add %a, C1 ^ C2

Fig. 1. An Alive optimization. The predicate isSignBit(C1) is true when C1 is all zeros except for the sign bit.

or constant expressions. The target may refer to instructions defined in the source and create new instructions, which will be added when the source root is replaced. An example Alive optimization is shown in Fig. 1. The root %d in the source is replaced with the root in the target when the precondition is satisfied (*i.e.*, isSignBit(C1), where C1 is a symbolic constant). Alive preconditions consist of built-in predicates, equalities, signed/unsigned inequalities, and predicates representing the result of dataflow analyses. An Alive optimization is parametric over types and bit widths. Hence, the Alive interpreter checks the correctness of the optimization for feasible types and bit widths.

Undefined behavior and compiler optimizations. Most compiler bugs result from a misunderstanding in the semantics, especially regarding various kinds of undefined behavior [3]. The semantics of an instruction specifies when it is well-defined. LLVM optimizes the program with the assumption that the programmer never intends to have undefined behavior in the program [14–16].

To aggressively optimize well-defined programs, LLVM IR has undefined behavior with catch-fire semantics, the undef value, and poison values. Undefined behavior in LLVM is similar to undefined behavior in C/C++, where program can perform any action in the presence of undefined behavior. Typically, a program with undefined behavior will cause a fault/trap (*e.g.*, division by zero) at runtime.

The undef value indicates that the program reads an uninitialized memory location and the program is expected to be well-defined for any value chosen for the undef value. The undef value is equivalent to reading a hardware register at an arbitrary instant of time.

A *poison* value represents the fact that an instruction, which does not have side effects, has produced a condition that results in undefined behavior. Unlike undef values, there is no explicit way of representing a poison value in the IR. A poison value indicates ephemeral effects of certain incorrect operations (*e.g.*, signed overflow with an instruction expected not to have signed overflows). LLVM has instruction attributes such as nsw (no signed wrap), nuw (no unsigned wrap), and exact, which produce poison values on incorrect operations. An arithmetic instruction with the no signed wrap attribute produces a poison value on signed overflows [3]. Unlike undef values, poison propagates with dependencies. A poison value triggers undefined behavior with catch-fire semantics when it produces an externally-visible effect (*e.g.*, atomic loads/stores). Hence, poison values that do not affect a program's externally visible behavior are allowed in a well-defined program.

From a Alive perspective, when the source contains a undef value, the compiler can pick a value for the undef in the source that makes the optimization valid. In contrast, when the source produces a poison value, the compiler can replace the target with anything as the source is not well-defined.

Correctness of an Alive optimization. Alive's verification engine reasons about the correctness of optimizations taking into account various undefinedness conditions, which eases the job of the compiler writer. Given an optimization, the Alive interpreter instantiates candidate types for the optimization. The Alive interpreter encodes the Alive optimization with concrete types into first order logic formulae. The validity of the formulae imply the correctness of the optimization. The interpreter generates the following validity checks when the source template is well-defined, poison-free, and the precondition is satisfied: (1) the target is well-defined, (2) the target is poison-free, and (3) the source and target root of the DAG produce the same value, and (4) the memory states in the source and the target are equivalent (for optimizations involving memory operations). These checks are performed for each feasible type instantiation.

2.2 Floating Point Representation and Arithmetic

A floating point number is an approximation of a real number. Although many computer manufacturers had their own conventions for floating point earlier, IEEE-754 [6] has become the standard for floating point representation. The IEEE standard represents a floating point number in the form: $(-1)^s \times M \times 2^E$, where s determines the sign of the number, significand M is a fractional binary number ranging either between $[1, 2)$ or $[0, 1)$, and exponent E weights the value with a power of 2 (can be negative). The bit representation uses a single bit for sign s, k bits for the encoding the exponent E and n-bit fractional field for encoding the significand M (e.g., 32-bit float has 1 sign bit, $k = 8$, and $n = 23$). The value encoded by the bit representation is divided into three categories depending on the exponent field.

Normalized values. When the bit pattern for the exponent is neither all zeros nor all ones, the floating number is a normalized value. The exponent field is interpreted as a signed integer in biased form (i.e., $E = e - bias$), where e is the unsigned number from the bit pattern in the exponent field. The *bias* is $2^{k-1} - 1$. The significand M is $1.f$, where f is the fractional field in the representation. The normalized value is $(-1)^s \times 1.f \times 2^{(e-bias)}$.

Denormalized values. When the bit pattern in the exponent field is all zeros, then the number is a denormal value. In this case the exponent is $1 - bias$. The significand value is f, the fractional part without the leading 1. Denormal values are used to represent zero and values close to zero. When all the exponent bits and fractional bits in the bit pattern are zero, then it represents a zero. There is a positive zero and negative zero depending on value of the sign bit.

Special values. When the bit pattern in the exponent field is all ones, then it represents special values. There are three special values: positive-infinity, negative-infinity, and not-a-number (NaN). When the fractional field is all zeros, then the number is a positive-infinity or a negative infinity depending on the sign. When the fractional part is not all zeros, then it is a NaN. The standard provides specific rules for equality, generation, and propagation of these special values.

Rounding modes. The floating point number has limited range and precision compared to real numbers. Rounding modes specify a systematic method for finding the "closest" matching value that can be represented in a floating point format. The IEEE-754 standard specifies the following rounding modes: round toward nearest with ties going to the even value (RNE), round towards nearest with ties going away from zero (RNA), round towards positive (RTP), round towards negative (RTN), and round toward zero (RTZ). The rounding mode is described with respect to a program block in the standard. The FPA theory in SMT-LIB also includes these rounding modes, and parameterizes most operations with a rounding mode. In contrast, the LLVM language reference does not explicitly state the rounding mode for its FP operations.

3   Alive-FP Domain-Specific Language

Alive-FP is a domain-specific language that adds support for FP operations in LLVM to Alive. Alive-FP is a ground-up rewrite of Alive to simplify the addition of FP reasoning along with other extensible features. Alive-FP uses the FPA theory [4] in SMT-LIB to reason about the correctness of optimizations. An Alive-FP optimization may combine integer and FP operations. Figure 2 lists the new FP types, instructions, and attributes in Alive-FP.

$$
\begin{aligned}
prog &::= pre\ nl\ stmt \implies stmt \\
stmt &::= stmt\ nl\ stmt \mid reg = inst \mid reg = op \\
inst &::= binop\ \overline{attr}\ op, op \mid fpbop\ \overline{fmf}\ op, op \mid \\
&\quad conv\ op \mid select\ op, op, op \mid \\
&\quad icmp\ cond\ op, op \mid fcmp\ \overline{fmf}\ fcnd\ op, op \\
typ &::= isz \mid half \mid float \mid double \mid fp128 \mid \\
&\quad x86\_fp80 \\
binop &::= add \mid sub \mid mul \mid udiv \mid sdiv \mid \\
&\quad urem \mid srem \mid shl \mid lshr \mid ashr \mid \\
&\quad and \mid or \mid xor \\
attr &::= nsw \mid nuw \mid exact
\end{aligned}
$$

$$
\begin{aligned}
fpbop &::= fadd \mid fsub \mid fmul \mid fdiv \mid frem \\
fmf &::= nnan \mid ninf \mid nsz \mid arcp \mid fast \\
op &::= reg \mid constant \mid undef \mid \\
&\quad nan \mid inf \mid -inf \\
conv &::= zext \mid sext \mid trunc \mid fpext \mid fptrunc \mid \\
&\quad fptosi \mid fptoui \mid sitofp \mid uitofp \mid \\
&\quad bitcast \mid inttoptr \mid ptrtoint \\
cond &::= eq \mid ne \mid ugt \mid uge \mid ult \mid \\
&\quad ule \mid sgt \mid sge \mid slt \mid sle \\
fcnd &::= oeq \mid one \mid ogt \mid oge \mid olt \mid ole \mid ord \mid \\
&\quad ueq \mid une \mid ugt \mid uge \mid ult \mid ule \mid uno
\end{aligned}
$$

Fig. 2. Partial Alive-FP syntax. The new additions in Alive-FP when compared to Alive are shaded. $\overline{attr}$ represents a list of attributes with each instruction.

FP types. LLVM has six different floating point types: half, float, double, fp128, x86_fp80 (x86 extended float), and ppc_fp128 (PowerPC double double). Alive-FP supports five of the six floating point types. Alive-FP does not support ppc_fp128, as it uses a pair of double-precision values to represent a number and does not correspond directly to an SMT FP sort. Among the FP types supported by Alive-FP, half ($k=5$, $n=10$), float ($k=8$, $n=23$), double ($k=11$, $n=52$), and fp128 ($k=15$, $n=112$) correspond directly to SMT floating-point sorts, which are determined by the width in bits for the exponent and significand. We treat x86_fp80 as $k=15$, $n=64$, except when its exact bit representation is significant.

FP instructions. LLVM has twelve FP instructions in the LLVM IR. Alive-FP augments Alive with these twelve LLVM instructions dealing with FP values. The FP instructions can be classified into three categories: binary operators, conversion instructions, and a comparison instruction. All LLVM FP instructions are polymorphic over FP types, with the conversion operators imposing some additional constraints. Alive-FP's select instruction is polymorphic over all "first-class" types, which include integer and FP types.

Binary operators. Alive-FP supports the five binary arithmetic operators in LLVM for FP computation: fadd, fsub, fmul, fdiv, and frem, which implement addition, subtraction, multiplication, division, and taking the remainder, respectively. LLVM's frem instruction differs from fpRem in the IEEE standard and the FPA theory. LLVM's frem is similar to the fmod function in the C library. Given two floating-point values x and y, the `frem` instruction in LLVM (hence, Alive-FP) calculates x/y and truncates the fractional part. Let's call the resultant value n. Then, `frem x, y` returns $x - ny$.

Conversion operators. LLVM includes two instructions for converting between FP types, `fpext` and `fptrunc`, and four instructions for converting to or from signed and unsigned integers, `fptosi`, `fptoui`, `sitofp`, and `uitofp`. Alive-FP supports all these instructions. The `fpext` instruction promotes a value to a larger FP type, while `fptrunc` demotes a value to a smaller one. The `fptosi` and `fptoui` instructions first discard the fractional part of the input (*i.e.*, rounding to integer towards zero), then map the result to a signed or unsigned integer value, respectively. Similarly, `sitofp` and `uitofp` convert signed and unsigned integers to FP values. Alive-FP also supports the `bitcast` instruction between FP and integer types with the same representation size in bits.

Conversions to floating point can fail in two general ways: they may be inexact, meaning the value being converted falls between two finite values representable in the target type, or they may be out-of-range, meaning the value falls between the largest (or smallest) finite representable value and infinity. Further, LLVM does not specify rounding mode for all instructions.

Comparison instruction. LLVM provides a `fcmp` instruction for comparing FP values, which supports sixteen comparison predicates (see Fig. 2). An example is `fcmp uge %x, %y`, where `uge` is one of the sixteen comparison predicates in LLVM, `%x` and `%y` are operands to the `fcmp` instruction. The sixteen predicates are derived from four primitive predicates: *unordered*, which is true if either operand is NaN, and ordered equality, greater-than, and less-than, which are true when neither operand is NaN and the respective condition holds between `%x` and `%y`. The FP comparison predicate `uge` is true if the operands are unordered or equal or the first operand is greater than the second. All sixteen predicates can be translated using combinations of operations in FPA theory.

FP instruction attributes. LLVM defines five FP related instruction attributes that may appear on FP instructions. These are also called fast-math attributes. When present, the optimizer may make certain assumptions about the inputs to these instructions enabling more extensive code transformations.

The no-NaNs attribute, `nnan`, permits the optimizer to assume that the arguments and the result of an instruction will not be NaN. In particular, the LLVM language reference manual states that an operation with a NaN argument or that produces a NaN result is an undefined value (but not undefined behavior). However, it is unclear whether it is an `undef` value or a poison value.

The no-infinities attribute, `ninf`, is similar to `nnan`, except applying to ∞ and $-\infty$. The no-signed-zeros attribute, `nsz`, permits the optimizer to ignore the difference between positive and negative zero. The allow reciprocal attribute, `arcp`, permits the optimizer to assume that multiplying by the reciprocal is equivalent to division. Alive-FP does not handle this attribute as there is only one optimization that uses it. The final attribute, `fast`, implies all the others and permits the optimizer to perform optimizations that are possible with real numbers but can result in inaccurate computation with FP arithmetic (*e.g.*, reassociating arithmetic expressions). Alive-FP will report such optimizations to be incorrect, as they do not preserve bitwise precision. Handling `fast` attribute would require reasoning about accuracy loss [17,18].

FP constants and literals. Alive-FP supports expressing constant FP values in decimal representation. Alive-FP represents negative zero as `-0.0`, Not-a-Number as `nan`, positive-infinity as `inf`, and negative-infinity as `-inf`. Alive-FP also extends Alive's constant language to be polymorphic over integer and FP types, so that the expression `C+1` may describe an integer or a FP value, depending on the context. Alive-FP adds new constant functions to convert between FP types and to obtain information such as the bit width of an FP type's significand.

4   Verification with Alive-FP

The Alive-FP interpreter checks the correctness of an optimization by encoding FP operations into operations in FPA theory in SMT-LIB. Similar to Alive, integer operations are encoded with operations from the bitvector theory. The Alive-FP interpreter checks the correctness of an optimization for each feasible type. In contrast to Alive, Alive-FP enumerates all feasible types with a non-SMT based type checker to reduce the number of SMT queries.

4.1   Overview of Correctness Checking

Given a concrete type instantiation, the Alive-FP interpreter creates the following SMT expressions for each instruction in both the source and the target: (1) the expression v that represents the result of the instruction, (2) the expression δ that represents constraints for the instruction to have defined behavior, (3) the expression ρ that represents constraints for the instruction to produce a non-poison value. Further, to handle `undef` values, the interpreter also creates a set of quantified variables $\mathcal{U}$ for both the source and target. The validity checks will involve universal quantification for the variables from $\mathcal{U}$ in the target and existential quantification for the variables from $\mathcal{U}$ in the source. The definedness constraints and poison-free constraints propagate with data dependencies. Hence, the order of instructions in an Alive-FP optimization is not important. Instructions which do not introduce undefined behavior, poison, or `undef` values use these encodings by default:

$$\delta_x = \bigwedge_{a \in \mathsf{args}(x)} \delta_a, \qquad \rho_x = \bigwedge_{a \in \mathsf{args}(x)} \rho_a, \qquad \mathcal{U}_x = \bigcup_{a \in \mathsf{args}(x)} \mathcal{U}_a,$$

where δ_x, ρ_x, and $\mathsf{args}(x)$ are the definedness constraints, poison-free constraints, and arguments of instruction x, respectively.

The interpreter also generates SMT expressions corresponding to the precondition. Let $\psi \equiv \phi \wedge \delta^s \wedge \rho^s$ where ϕ represents constraints for the precondition,

δ^s represents constraints for the source root to be defined, and ρ^s represents the constraints for the source root to be poison-free. A transformation is correct if and only if all of the following constraints hold for the source and target roots.

1. $\forall_{\mathcal{I},\mathcal{U}^t} \exists_{\mathcal{U}^s} : \psi \implies \delta^t$
2. $\forall_{\mathcal{I},\mathcal{U}^t} \exists_{\mathcal{U}^s} : \psi \implies \rho^t$
3. $\forall_{\mathcal{I},\mathcal{U}^t} \exists_{\mathcal{U}^s} : \psi \implies v^s = v^t$

where $\mathcal{I}$ is the set of input variables in the DAG, $\mathcal{U}^t$ is the set of undef variables in the target, $\mathcal{U}^s$ is the set of undef variables in the source, δ^t represents the constraints for the target to be well-defined, ρ^t represents the constraints for the target to be poison-free, v^s is the value computed by the source, and v^t is the value computed by the target.

Next, we show how to encode three fast-math attributes (nnan, ninf, and nsz) into FPA theory and their interaction with various kinds of undefined behavior in LLVM. We also highlight the challenges in encoding that arise because the LLVM language reference is under-specified about what values are returned when an instruction is not well-defined. Finally, we provide the encoding for FP instructions in FPA theory and their interaction with fast-math attributes and rounding modes, as LLVM does not define rounding modes for all instructions.

4.2 Encoding Fast-Math Attributes

Fast-math attributes may occur on any of the five arithmetic instructions and the fcmp instruction. Optimizations are free to make certain assumptions when these attributes are present in an instruction, specifically:

nnan the arguments and result are not NaN
ninf the arguments and result are not positive or negative infinity
nsz there is no distinction between negative and positive zero

The challenging task in encoding these attributes is in their interaction with various kinds of undefined behavior in LLVM. When an instruction with an attribute violates the assumption, does it produce an undef value or a poison value? The key difference between the these two interpretations is that a poison value propagates through dependencies whereas an undef value does not. The LLVM language reference for FP operations predates the development of poison values and hence, there is no reference to it in the language reference. The LLVM language reference states that optimizations must "retain defined behavior for NaN (or infinite) inputs, but the value of the result is undefined".

Similar attributes for integer operations in LLVM, no-signed wrap (nsw), no-unsigned wrap (nuw), and exact, produce poison values. Given this under-specification in the LLVM language reference manual, we provide two encodings for nnan and ninf attributes: one using undef values and other with poison values. Both encodings have their own advantages and disadvantages. The encoding with poison values is the most permissive.

Encoding for nnan and ninf with undef values. In this interpretation, an instruction with nnan returns an undef value when an argument or the result is NaN. For an instruction z performing binary operation ($\oplus$) with arguments x and y, we create a fresh undef value and add it to the set of quantified variables if either of the operands or the result is NaN. These undef variables will be appropriately quantified depending on whether they occur in the source or the target in the validity checks.

$$\mathcal{U}_z = \{u\} \cup \mathcal{U}_x \cup \mathcal{U}_y$$
$$v_z = \begin{cases} u & \text{if isNaN}(v_x) \vee \text{isNaN}(v_y) \vee \text{isNaN}(v_x \oplus v_y) \\ v_x \oplus v_y & \text{otherwise} \end{cases}$$

where u is a fresh variable and isNaN predicate returns true if its argument is NaN. The encoding for infinities with undef values is similar except we use a different predicate (*i.e.*, isInf) with infinities.

Encoding nnan and ninf with poison values. In this interpretation, an instruction with nnan (or the ninf attribute) returns a poison value when either its arguments or the result is NaN (or infinity). We encode the fact that these result in poison values in the poison-free constraints for the instruction. The poison-free constraints for an instruction z performing a binary operation ($\oplus$) with arguments x and y are given below:

$$\rho_z = \neg(\text{isNaN}(v_x) \vee \text{isNaN}(v_y) \vee \text{isNaN}(v_x \oplus v_y)) \wedge \rho_x \wedge \rho_y$$
$$v_z = v_x \oplus v_y$$

There are multiple advantages in using the poison interpretation. First, the semantics of poison ensures that the poison value propagates along dependencies. In particular, if a value occurs in multiple instructions, some but not all of which have the nnan attribute, then an optimization is free to assume that value is not NaN everywhere. Second, it permits more optimizations and is consistent with the treatment of integer attributes, which use poison values. Third, the encoding does not use quantifiers and FPA theory solvers can check validity quickly. A disadvantage of this encoding is that this interpretation can arguably conflict with the LLVM language reference, which is ambiguous. The encoding for the ninf attribute with poison values is similar.

Encoding nsz attributes. The nsz attribute is used to indicate the assumption that the sign of zero does not matter. The LLVM language reference states that optimizations may "treat the sign of a zero argument or result as insignificant" when an instruction has the nsz attribute.

We encode the nsz attribute by giving zero-valued results an undef sign-bit (*i.e.*, the result is an undef value that is constrained to be from the set $\{+0, -0\}$).

For a non-division instruction z with arguments x and y performing the binary operation $\oplus$, we create a fresh undef variable and add it to the set of quantified variables. The result is constrained to choose either $+0.0$ or -0.0

based on the undef value. These variables to represent undef values will be appropriately quantified in the validity checks.

$$\mathcal{U}_z = \{b\} \cup \mathcal{U}_x \cup \mathcal{U}_y$$

$$v_z = \begin{cases} 0 \text{ if isZero}(v_x \oplus v_y) \wedge b \\ -0 \text{ if isZero}(v_x \oplus v_y) \wedge \neg b \\ v_x \oplus v_y \text{ otherwise} \end{cases}$$

where b is a fresh boolean variable. It is not necessary to examine the arguments of the instruction with the encoding for nsz as the sign of any input zero is only significant when the result is also zero.

The encoding is a bit more involved for the division instruction, as the sign of a zero input may affect a non-zero result. Given z = fdiv x, y, the result will be ± 0 if x is zero and y non-zero and $\pm \infty$ if y is zero and x non-zero. Other results are unaffected by signed zeros and can be calculated normally.

$$\mathcal{U}_z = \{b\} \cup \mathcal{U}_x \cup \mathcal{U}_y$$

$$v_z = \begin{cases} 0 \text{ if isZero}(v_x) \wedge \neg \text{isZero}(v_y) \wedge b \\ -0 \text{ if isZero}(v_x) \wedge \neg \text{isZero}(v_y) \wedge \neg b \\ \infty \text{ if } \neg \text{isZero}(v_x) \wedge \text{isZero}(v_y) \wedge b \\ -\infty \text{ if } \neg \text{isZero}(v_x) \wedge \text{isZero}(v_y) \wedge \neg b \\ v_x \div v_y \text{ otherwise} \end{cases}$$

where b is a fresh boolean variable.

Attributes with the fcmp instruction. Although fcmp accepts the same fast-math attributes as the binary operators, only nnan and ninf have any effect, because it does not return an FP value. Aside from the type of the undef value (for the undef encoding), attributes on fcmp can be encoded similarly to the binary operators.

4.3   Encoding FP Arithmetic Instructions

LLVM has five FP arithmetic instructions: fadd, fsub, fmul, fdiv, and frem. The first four translate directly to corresponding SMT FPA operations, aside from the presence of rounding modes. LLVM does not specify what rounding modes to use when performing arithmetic, nor does it provide any standard way for programs to access or determine the rounding mode.

Handling rounding mode with instructions. Alive-FP, by default, performs all arithmetic using a default rounding mode which is chosen by the user at the command line when the tool is run. In most cases, the choice of rounding mode does not affect correctness. Exceptions include optimizations involving zero-valued results, as the RTN (round-to-negative) rounding mode produces -0.0 for many operations that would produce 0.0 under other modes. The choice of rounding mode can also affect whether some out-of-range values round to the largest (or smallest) finite value, or to positive (or negative) infinity.

Alive-FP could also provide an option to make the rounding mode an **undef** value for each instruction, effectively returning a two-valued set (*i.e.*, round up or round down) for any imprecise operation. This interpretation of rounding rules out some existing optimizations as they produce different results depending on the rounding mode chosen. It is unclear whether the complexity of this interpretation is outweighed by any semantic benefit.

Handling the frem instruction. The **frem** instruction in LLVM does not correspond to the IEEE floating-point remainder operation, as it requires the remainder to have the same sign as the dividend. LLVM's **frem** corresponds to the **fmod** in the C library. In version 4.4.1, Z3's **fpRem** operation differs from the specification in the SMT-FPA theory and implements the **fmod** function in the C library, which we have reported as a bug [19]. Hence, we encode LLVM's **frem** directly using Z3's **fpRem** operation.

Implementing LLVM's **frem** using a correct SMT-FPA **fpRem** is relatively straightforward, involving some sign manipulation for negative dividends and addition.

$$frem(x,y) = \begin{cases} z \text{ if } \mathsf{isPos}(x) \wedge \mathsf{isPos}(z) \\ |y| + z \text{ if } \mathsf{isPos}(x) \wedge \mathsf{isNeg}(z) \\ -z \text{ if } \mathsf{isNeg}(x) \wedge \mathsf{isPos}(z) \\ -(|y| + z) \text{ if } \mathsf{isNeg}(x) \wedge \mathsf{isNeg}(z) \end{cases}$$
$$z = \mathsf{fpRem}(|x|, |y|)$$

4.4   Encoding Floating-Point Comparison

LLVM's **fcmp** instruction takes a condition code and two floating-point values, and returns a 1-bit integer, indicating whether the comparison is true. The condition code indicates which comparison is to be performed. LLVM includes ordered and unordered versions of the usual equality and inequality tests (see Fig. 2). The ordered tests always fail if one or more argument is NaN, and the unordered tests always succeed if one or more argument is NaN. These are encoded using SMT-FPA comparisons in the obvious manner.

4.5   Encoding Conversion Instructions

LLVM (hence, Alive-FP) has the following conversion instructions: **fpext**, **fptrunc**, **fptosi**, **fptoui**, **sitofp**, and **uitofp**. LLVM's language reference does not state whether these operations result in either an **undef** or a poison value in the case of imprecise conversions. Next, we describe our encoding of these operations.

Encoding fpext instruction. The **fpext** instruction promotes a floating-point value to a larger type. All floating-point types are strict supersets of smaller types, so **fpext** is always defined. Alive-FP encodes **fpext** as:

$$v_z = \mathsf{fpToFP}(r, v_x, \tau_z)$$

where r is the default rounding mode (the choice is irrelevant), τ_z is the target type, and fpToFP in the FPA theory converts either a FP value or a signed bitvector value to the specified FP type with the specified rounding mode.

Encoding fptrunc instruction. The fptrunc instruction demotes a floating-point value to a smaller type. Not all values in the larger type are exactly representable in the smaller type. These fall into two categories. A conversion is *imprecise* if the exponent can be represented in the target type, but least significant bits of the source significand are non-zero. LLVM requires the result of an imprecise conversion to be one of the two representable values closest to the source value, but leaves the choice undefined. This can be interpreted as rounding, according to (a) a fixed rounding mode (*e.g.*, RNE — round to the nearest representable number with ties to even), (b) an arbitrary rounding mode, or (c) an undefined choice between the two nearest values. By default, Alive-FP rounds using the current rounding mode in this case.

A conversion is *out of range* if the exponent cannot be represented in the target type. LLVM states that the result is undefined. This may be interpreted as an **undef** or a poison value. We provide encodings for both interpretations.

Encoding out-of-range truncations with undef values. In this interpretation, we handle out-of-range conversions by creating fresh **undef** variables that are appropriately quantified.

$$\mathcal{U}_z = \{u\} \cup \mathcal{U}_x$$

$$v_z = \begin{cases} \mathsf{fpToFP}(r, v_x, \tau_z) & \text{if } v_x \in \tau_z \\ u & \text{otherwise} \end{cases}$$

where r is the default rounding mode, τ_z is the target type, and u is a fresh variable. We write $v_x \in \tau_z$ to indicate that v_x is exactly representable in τ_z.

Encoding out-of-range truncations with poison values. In this interpretation, we encode out-of-range conversions in the poison-free constraints.

$$\rho_z = v_x \in \tau_z \wedge \rho_x$$
$$v_z = \mathsf{fpToFP}(r, v_x, \tau_z)$$

where τ_z is the target type, r is the current rounding mode, and ρ_x are the poison-free constraints for x.

Encoding fptosi instruction. The fptosi instruction converts a floating-point value to a bitvector, interpreted as a signed value. Any fractional part of the value is truncated (*i.e.*, rounded towards zero). If the resulting value is outside the range of the target type, the result is undefined. We provide encodings both as an **undef** value and a poison value to represent values outside the range of the target type.

Encoding out-of-range fptosi conversions with a undef value. We create a fresh **undef** variable, which will be appropriately quantified, when the value to be converted is beyond the range.

$$\mathcal{U}_z = \{u\} \cup \mathcal{U}_x$$

$$v_z = \begin{cases} \mathsf{fpToSBV}(\mathsf{RTZ}, v_x, \tau_z) \text{ if } smin(\tau_z) \leq v_x \leq smax(\tau_z) \\ u \qquad\qquad\qquad\qquad\quad \text{otherwise} \end{cases}$$

where u is a fresh variable, τ_z is the target type, and $\mathsf{fpToSBV}$ in the FPA theory converts a floating point number to signed bitvector similar to the semantics of $\mathtt{fptosi}$ instruction. Constant functions $smin(\tau_z)$ and $smax(\tau_z)$ return the largest and smallest signed values for a type τ_z. We use the rounding mode RTZ (round towards zero) because the LLVM language reference manual explicitly specifies it.

Encoding out-of-range $\mathtt{fptosi}$ conversions with a poison value. The encoding is similar to other instructions except the poison-free constraints use the constant functions $smin$ and $smax$.

$$\rho_z = smin(\tau_z) \leq v_x \leq smax(\tau_z) \wedge \rho_x$$

$$v_z = \mathsf{fpToSBV}(\mathsf{RTZ}, v_x, \tau_z)$$

where τ_z is the target type.

Encoding the $\mathtt{fptoui}$ instruction. The $\mathtt{fptoui}$ instruction converts a floating-point value to a bitvector, interpreted as an unsigned value. The encoding is similar to the $\mathtt{fptosi}$ instruction except we use the constant functions $umin$ and $umax$ (that return unsigned minimum and unsigned maximum value for a type), and $\mathsf{fpToUBV}$ in the FPA theory to convert the value to an unsigned bitvector.

Encoding the $\mathtt{sitofp}$ instruction. The $\mathtt{sitofp}$ instruction converts a bitvector, interpreted as a signed integer, to a floating-point value. As with $\mathtt{fptrunc}$, such a conversion may be exact, imprecise, or out-of-range. Alive-FP handles imprecise conversions by rounding according to the current rounding mode. Alive-FP provides both $\mathbf{undef}$ and poison interpretations for out-of-range conversions.

Encoding out-of-range $\mathtt{sitofp}$ conversions with $\mathbf{undef}$. The encoding is similar to $\mathtt{fptrunc}$ except we use the constant functions $fmin$ and $fmax$ that provide the largest and smallest finite values for a given floating point type.

$$\mathcal{U}_z = \{u\} \cup \mathcal{U}_x$$

$$v_z = \begin{cases} \mathsf{sbvToFP}(r, v_x, \tau_z) \text{ if } fmin(\tau_z) \leq v_x \leq fmax(\tau_z) \\ u \qquad\qquad\qquad\qquad\; \text{otherwise} \end{cases}$$

where u is a fresh variable, τ_z is the target type, and r is the current rounding mode.

Encoding out-of-range $\mathtt{sitofp}$ conversions with poison. Similar to the encoding for $\mathtt{fptrunc}$, we encode out-of-range conversions with $\mathtt{sitofp}$ as a poison value that result in an additional poison-free constraint.

$$\rho_z = fmin(\tau_z) \leq v_x \leq fmax(\tau_z) \wedge \rho_x$$

$$v_z = \mathsf{sbvToFP}(r, v_x, \tau_z)$$

```
%r = fmul nnan nsz %x, -1
=>
%r = fsub nnan nsz -0.0, %x
```

$P = \text{isNaN}(x) \vee \text{isNaN}(-1) \vee \text{isNaN}(x \times -1)$
$Q = \text{isNaN}(-0) \vee \text{isNaN}(x) \vee \text{isNaN}(-0 - x)$

(a) An example optimization

(b) The non-NaN conditions, used below

$\mathcal{U}^s = \{u_1, b_1\}$
$\delta^s = \top$
$\rho^s = \top$

$v^s = \begin{cases} u_1 \text{ if } P \\ 0 \text{ if } \neg P \wedge \text{isZero}(x \times -1) \wedge b_1 \\ -0 \text{ if } \neg P \wedge \text{isZero}(x \times -1) \wedge \neg b_1 \\ x \times -1 \text{ if } \neg P \wedge \neg \text{isZero}(x \times -1) \end{cases}$

$\mathcal{U}^t = \{u_2, b_2\}$
$\delta^t = \top$
$\rho^t = \top$

$v^t = \begin{cases} u_2 \text{ if } Q \\ 0 \text{ if } \neg Q \wedge \text{isZero}(-0 - x) \wedge b_2 \\ -0 \text{ if } \neg Q \wedge \text{isZero}(-0 - x) \wedge \neg b_2 \\ -0 - x \text{ if } \neg Q \wedge \neg \text{isZero}(-0 - x) \end{cases}$

value check: $\forall x \, u_2 \, b_2, \exists u_1 \, b_1, v^s = v^t$

(c) The **undef** encoding

$\mathcal{U}^s = \{b_1\}$
$\delta^s = \top$
$\rho^s = \neg P$

$v^s = \begin{cases} 0 \text{ if } \text{isZero}(x \times -1) \wedge b_1 \\ -0 \text{ if } \text{isZero}(x \times -1) \wedge \neg b_1 \\ x \times -1 \text{ if } \neg \text{isZero}(x \times -1) \end{cases}$

$\mathcal{U}^t = \{b_2\}$
$\delta^t = \top$
$\rho^t = \neg Q$

$v^t = \begin{cases} 0 \text{ if } \text{isZero}(-0 - x) \wedge b_2 \\ -0 \text{ if } \text{isZero}(-0 - x) \wedge \neg b_2 \\ -0 - x \text{ if } \neg \text{isZero}(-0 - x) \end{cases}$

poison check: $\forall x \, b_2, \exists b_1, \rho^s \implies \rho^t$

value check: $\forall x \, b_2, \exists b_1, \rho^s \implies v^s = v^t$

(d) The poison encoding

Fig. 3. Illustration of the encodings and the validity checks generated by Alive-FP for the optimization shown in (a). To simplify the exposition, we use the constraints in (b) in the examples. The constraints and the validity checks generated with the **undef** interpretation for **nnan** attribute is shown in (c). The constraints and the validity checks generated with the poison interpretation for the **nnan** attribute is shown in (d). The **fmul** instruction is always defined. Hence, the definedness condition (δ^s for source and δ^t for the target is true ($\top$). In the undef interpretation in (c), there are no poison values, hence poison-free conditions are set to true (*i.e.*, $\rho^s = \top$ and $\rho^t = \top$).

where r is the current rounding mode and τ_z is the target type.

Encoding the uitofp instruction. The **uitofp** instruction converts a bitvector, interpreted as an unsigned integer, to a floating-point value. This is handled analogously to **sitofp**, but using the corresponding unsigned conversion, ubvToFP in FPA theory.

Encoding bitcast instruction with floating point operations. The bitcast instruction converts a value from one type to another without changing any bits. Thus, its source and target types must have the same bit width. When converting an integer to a floating-point value, Alive-FP uses SMT-FPA's fpToFP, which converts a bit vector to a floating-point value directly when called with two arguments.

$$v_z = \text{fpToFP}(v_x, \tau_z)$$

When converting a floating-point value to an integer, we use Z3's fpToIEEEBV, a non-standard addition to the FPA theory.

$$v_z = \mathsf{fpToIEEEBV}(v_x, \tau_z)$$

This has the limitation of only producing one bit pattern for NaNs. An alternative would be returning an **undef** value restricted so that its conversion to floating point is equal to v_x.

Illustration of correctness checking. Figure 3(a) presents a simple Alive-FP optimization. Figures 3(c) and (d) present the encoding and the validity checks generated with the **undef** and poison encoding for the **nnan** attribute.

5   Evaluation

This section describes our prototype, the optimizations that we translated from LLVM to Alive-FP, new bugs discovered, and the time taken for verification.

Prototype. Alive-FP is a ground-up rewrite of the Alive infrastructure, designed with the goal of extending the language and the semantics. The Alive-FP interpreter is written in Python and uses Z3-4.4.1 for solving SMT queries. Alive-FP supports a subset of the features in Alive—enough to verify the Alive suite of optimizations—along with the new FP support. Specifically, Alive-FP does not support memory operations and cycle detection with composition [20]. Unlike Alive, which uses SMT queries to find feasible type instantiations, Alive-FP enumerates all feasible type models using an unification-based type checker.

When we were designing FP support in Alive-FP, we discovered that Alive's treatment of **undef** was incorrect in some scenarios where a single **undef** was referenced more than once [21]. Alive-FP addresses this problem by generating fresh quantified variables for each reference to an **undef** value or an instruction that may produce **undef** values. Alive-FP is open source [13].

Translation of LLVM optimizations to Alive-FP. We translated all the bit-precise FP optimizations, which do not result in loss of accuracy, in LLVM-3.8 to Alive-FP. In total, we generated a total of 104 Alive-FP optimizations. Among these 104 Alive-FP optimizations, 48 optimizations were from `InstSimplify`, 12 are FP mul/div/rem optimizations, 37 are FP compare optimizations, 1 is a cast optimization, and 6 are FP add/sub optimizations. Certain optimizations in LLVM are expressed as multiple Alive-FP optimizations, in particular optimizations involving `fcmp` conditions or conditional flags in the target.

New LLVM bugs reported with Alive-FP. We discovered and reported seven wrong FP optimizations in LLVM [8–12], which are listed in Fig. 4. Among these reported bugs, PR26746 [8] incorrectly changes the sign of zero and has already been fixed. The sign of the zero is important for complex elementary functions [22], where having a single zero can introduce discontinuities. After we reported bug PR26862-1 in Fig. 4, a developer pointed us to a discussion in LLVM developers mailing list [23] that alluded to the argument that an **undef**

```
Name: PR26746          Name: PR26862-1         Name: PR26863-1
Pre: C == 0.0          %r = fdiv undef, %x     %r = frem undef, %x
%1 = fsub -0.0, %x     =>                      =>
%r = fsub C, %1        %r = undef              %r = undef
=>
%r = %x                Name: PR26862-2         Name: PR26863-2
                       %r = fdiv %x, undef     %r = frem %x, undef
                       =>                      =>
                       %r = undef              %r = undef
```

```
Name: PR27151          Name: PR27153
Pre: C == 0.0          Pre: sitofp(CO) == C && \
%y = fsub nnan ninf C, %x   WillNotOverflowSignedAdd(%a, CO)
%z = fadd %y, %x       %x = sitofp %a
=>                     %r = fadd %x, C
%z = 0                 =>
                       CO = fptosi(C)
                       %y = add nsw %a, CO
                       %r = sitofp %y
```

Fig. 4. Seven wrong optimizations discovered by Alive-FP. In PR26746 [8], the optimization is wrong because when $x = -0.0$ and $C = 0$, the source always evaluates to 0 but target evaluates to -0. In PR26862-1 [9], the optimization is wrong because if $x = \pm 0$, the only possible return values for the source are $\pm\infty$ and NaN, but the target can produce any floating-point value. In PR26862-2 [9], the optimization is wrong because if $x = \pm 0$, the only possible return values for the source are ± 0 and NaN, but the target may return any value. In PR26863-1 [10], the optimization is wrong because if $x = \pm 0$, the only possible return value for the source is NaN, but the target may return any value. In fact, for any finite, positive x, we will have $r < x$ in the target. In PR26863-2 [10], the optimization is wrong because for a finite x we have $|r| < |x|$ for the source, but the target may return any value. The optimization in PR27151 [11] is wrong in the **undef** interpretation but correct in the **poison** interpretation for **nnan**. With **undef** interpretation, when x is NaN, then y will be an **undef** value. The value z in the source will always be NaN, because any value added to NaN is NaN but the target is 0. In the poison interpretation, we can assume x is not NaN, because that would result in z being a poison value. Because z can never be visibly used without causing undefined behavior, we are free to replace it with 0 in that case. The buggy optimization PR27153 [12] reassociates an integer-to-floating point conversion and a constant add, when LLVM can show that the constant C is exactly representable in the type of a and the sum $a + C$ is also representable in that type (i.e., computing it will not overflow). The optimization fails if a cannot be exactly represented in the target type but $a + C$ can be (this could occur if a and C have opposite signs). In such a case, the source will lose precision due to rounding, but the target will not, resulting in changed behavior.

value in the source can be a signaling NaN [6] and therefore the source likely exhibits undefined behavior. This argument is flawed because not all hardware supports traps for signaling NaNs, and because it effectively erases the distinction between **undef** and undefined behavior for FP values, which is explicit

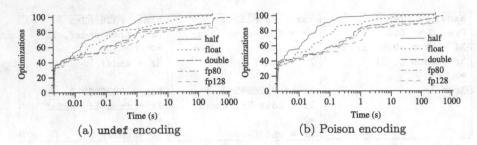

(a) **undef** encoding   (b) Poison encoding

Fig. 5. The number of optimizations solvable in a given time with the **undef** encoding and the poison encoding. The x-axis is in log-scale. We could not verify some of the optimizations with larger FP types because the solver returned **unknown** result, ran out of memory, or did not complete.

in the LLVM language reference. The optimization PR27151 [11] in Fig. 4 is wrong depending on the interpretation used for **nnan** and **ninf** attributes. The optimization is wrong under the **undef** interpretation but is correct under the poison interpretation. The optimization PR27153 [12] in Fig. 4 is wrong because the target has a higher precision than the source, which violates the expectation of bitwise similarity.

Time taken to verify optimizations. Figure 5 reports the number of optimizations that can be verified in a given amount of time for different FP types with the **undef** and the poison encoding. We conducted this experiment by specializing the FP type on a x86-64 2.6 GHz Haswell machine with 16 GB main memory. We were not able to verify 3 optimizations with any FP type because the solver did not complete. Figure 5 illustrates that the poison encoding is faster than the **undef** encoding. Further, the smaller FP types are verified quickly.

6   Related Work

There is significant prior research on checking, estimating, and/or improving the accuracy of FP operations [17,18,24–33], which is orthogonal to Alive-FP. Our work is also related to analyses and formal verification of bit-precise FP computations [30,34–36]. In the context of verified compilers, CompCert [37] provides semantics to FP operations and performs mechanized verification of bit-precise FP computations [38]. In contrast, Alive-FP performs automated verification by encoding into FPA theory and takes into account the undefined behavior in the LLVM compiler.

Alive-FP is also related to prior DSLs for specifying optimizations [39–41], which typically do not address FP operations. Alive-FP builds on our prior work Alive [3], which focused on integer optimizations. Concurrent to Alive-FP, LifeJacket [42] is initial work that also adds FP reasoning to Alive. In contrast to Alive-FP, LifeJacket does not explore the various semantic interpretations for attributes or instructions. LifeJacket primarily uses **undef** values for any undefined behavior. Its encoding for the `nsz` attribute is likely restrictive and can incorrectly rule out optimizations. Also, it does not support the `bitcast` instruction or the `x86_fp80` and `fp128` types.

7   Conclusion

We have presented Alive-FP, a domain-specific language to express and verify bit-precise FP optimizations in LLVM. We have proposed multiple encodings for FP operations and fast-math attributes (`nsz`, `nnan`, and `ninf`) to account for the ambiguity in the LLVM language reference. Alive-FP provides a comprehensive semantic treatment of FP operations and its interaction with undefined behavior in LLVM. Alive-FP is a first step in the automated verification of bit-precise FP computations in the LLVM compiler.

Acknowledgments. We thank Vinod Ganapathy, Thomas Wahl, and the reviewers for their feedback on this paper. This paper is based on work supported in part by NSF CAREER Award CCF-1453086, a sub-contract of NSF Award CNS-1116682, a NSF Award CNS-1441724, a Google Faculty Award, and gifts from Intel Corporation.

References

1. Yang, X., Chen, Y., Eide, E., Regehr, J.: Finding and understanding bugs in C compilers. In: Proceedings of the 32nd ACM SIGPLAN Conference on Programming Language Design and Implementation, PLDI, pp. 283–294. ACM (2011)
2. Le, V., Afshari, M., Su, Z.: Compiler validation via equivalence modulo inputs. In: Proceedings of the 35th ACM SIGPLAN Conference on Programming Language Design and Implementation, PLDI, pp. 216–226 (2014)
3. Lopes, N., Menendez, D., Nagarakatte, S., Regehr, J.: Provably correct peephole optimizations with Alive. In: Proceedings of the 36th ACM SIGPLAN Conference on Programming Language Design and Implementation, PLDI, pp. 22–32. ACM (2015)
4. Brain, M., Tinelli, C., Rümmer, P., Wahl, T.: An automatable formal semantics for IEEE-754 floating-point arithmetic. In: Proceedings of the 22nd IEEE Symposium on Computer Arithmetic, ARITH, pp. 160–167. IEEE, June 2015
5. de Moura, L., Bjørner, N.S.: Z3: an efficient SMT solver. In: Ramakrishnan, C.R., Rehof, J. (eds.) TACAS 2008. LNCS, vol. 4963, pp. 337–340. Springer, Heidelberg (2008)
6. IEEE standard for floating-point arithmetic. IEEE 754-2008. IEEE Computer Society, August 2008
7. Goldberg, D.: What every computer scientist should know about floating-point arithmetic. ACM Comput. Surv. **23**(1), 5–48 (1991)
8. Menendez, D.: LLVM bug 26746 InstructionSimplify turns 0.0 to −0.0. https://llvm.org/bugs/show_bug.cgi?id=26746. Accessed 16 Apr 2016
9. Menendez, D.: LLVM bug 26862 InstructionSimplify broadens undef when simplifying frem. https://llvm.org/bugs/show_bug.cgi?id=26862. Accessed 16 Apr 2016
10. Menendez, D.: LLVM bug 26863 InstructionSimplify broadens undef when simplifying fdiv. https://llvm.org/bugs/show_bug.cgi?id=26863. Accessed 16 Apr 2016

11. Menendez, D.: LLVM bug 27151 InstructionSimplify turns NaN to 0.0. https://llvm.org/bugs/show_bug.cgi?id=27151. Accessed 16 Apr 2016
12. Menendez, D.: LLVM bug 27153 InstCombine changes results by reassociating addition and sitofp. https://llvm.org/bugs/show_bug.cgi?id=27153. Accessed 16 Apr 2016
13. Menendez, D., Nagarakatte, S.: Alive-NJ. https://github.com/rutgers-apl/alive-nj. Accessed 16 Apr 2016
14. Lattner, C.: What every C programmer should know about undefined behavior, May 2011. http://blog.llvm.org/2011/05/what-every-c-programmer-should-know.html. Accessed 16 Apr 2016
15. Regehr, J.: A guide to undefined behavior in C and C++, July 2010. http://blog.regehr.org/archives/213. Accessed 16 Apr 2016
16. Wang, X., Zeldoivch, N., Kaashoek, M.F., Solar-Lezama, A.: Towards optimization-safe systems: analyzing the impact of undefined behavior. In: Proceedings of the 24th ACM Symposium on Operating Systems Principles, SOSP, pp. 260–275. ACM, November 2013
17. Panchekha, P., Sanchez-Stern, A., Wilcox, J.R., Tatlock, Z.: Automatically improving accuracy for floating point expressions. In: Proceedings of the 36th ACM SIGPLAN Conference on Programming Language Design and Implementation, PLDI, pp. 1–11. ACM, June 2015
18. Solovyev, A., Jacobsen, C., Rakamarić, Z., Gopalakrishnan, G.: Rigorous estimation of floating-point round-off errors with symbolic taylor expansions. In: Bjørner, N., Boer, F. (eds.) FM 2015. LNCS, vol. 9109, pp. 532–550. Springer, Heidelberg (2015)
19. Menendez, D.: FPA remainder does not match SMT-FPA semantics. https://github.com/Z3Prover/z3/issues/561. Accessed 16 Apr 2016
20. Menendez, D., Nagarakatte, S.: Termination-checking for LLVM peephole optimizations. In: Proceedings of the 38th International Conference of Software Engineering, ICSE, pp. 191–202, May 2016
21. Menendez, D.: Incorrect undef semantics. https://github.com/nunoplopes/alive/issues/31. Accessed 17 Apr 2016
22. Kahan, W.: Branch cuts for complex elementary functions, or much ado about nothing's sign bit. In: Proceedings of the Joint IMA/SIAM Conference on the State of the Art in Numerical Analysis Held at the UN, pp. 165–211 (1987)
23. Anderson, O.: Re: [llvmdev] bug 16257 - fmul of undef ConstantExpr not folded to undef, August 2014. http://lists.llvm.org/pipermail/llvm-dev/2014-August/076225.html. Accessed 17 Apr 2016
24. Ivančić, F., Ganai, M.K., Sankaranarayanan, S., Gupta, A.: Numerical stability analysis of floating-point computations using software model checking. In: Proceedings of the 8th IEEE/ACM International Conference on Formal Methods and Models for Codesign, MEMOCODE, pp. 49–58. IEEE, July 2010
25. Darulova, E., Kuncak, V.: Sound compilation of reals. In: Proceedings of the 41st ACM SIGPLAN-SIGACT Symposium on Principles of Programming Languages, POPL, pp. 235–248. ACM, New York (2014)
26. Kinsman, A.B., Nicolici, N.: Finite precision bit-width allocation using SAT-modulo theory. In: Proceedings of the Conference on Design, Automation and Test in Europe, DATE 2009, pp. 1106–1111. European Design and Automation Association, Leuven (2009)

27. Rubio-González, C., Nguyen, C., Nguyen, H.D., Demmel, J., Kahan, W., Sen, K., Bailey, D.H., Iancu, C., Hough, D.: Precimonious: tuning assistant for floating-point precision. In: Proceedings of the International Conference on High Performance Computing, Networking, Storage and Analysis, SC 2013, pp. 27:1–27:12. ACM, New York (2013)
28. Fu, Z., Bai, Z., Su, Z.: Automated backward error analysis for numerical code. In: Proceedings of the 2015 ACM SIGPLAN International Conference on Object-Oriented Programming, Systems, Languages, and Applications, OOPSLA 2015, pp. 639–654. ACM, New York (2015)
29. Barr, E.T., Vo, T., Le, V., Su, Z.: Automatic detection of floating-point exceptions. In: Proceedings of the 40th Annual ACM SIGPLAN-SIGACT Symposium on Principles of Programming Languages, POPL 2013, pp. 549–560. ACM, New York (2013)
30. Goubault, E.: Static analyses of the precision of floating-point operations. In: Cousot, P. (ed.) SAS 2001. LNCS, vol. 2126, pp. 234–259. Springer, Heidelberg (2001)
31. de Dinechin, F., Lauter, C.Q., Melquiond, G.: Assisted verification of elementary functions using Gappa. In: Proceedings of the 2006 ACM Symposium on Applied Computing, SAC, pp. 1318–1322. ACM (2006)
32. Brain, M., D'Silva, V., Griggio, A., Haller, L., Kroening, D.: Interpolation-based verification of floating-point programs with abstract CDCL. In: Logozzo, F., Fähndrich, M. (eds.) SAS 2013. LNCS, vol. 7935, pp. 412–432. Springer, Heidelberg (2013)
33. Goubault, E., Putot, S., Baufreton, P., Gassino, J.: Static analysis of the accuracy in control systems: principles and experiments. In: Leue, S., Merino, P. (eds.) FMICS 2007. LNCS, vol. 4916, pp. 3–20. Springer, Heidelberg (2008)
34. Monniaux, D.: The pitfalls of verifying floating-point computations. ACM Trans. Program. Lang. Syst. (TOPLAS) 30(3), 12:1–12:41 (2008)
35. Martel, M.: Semantics-based transformation of arithmetic expressions. In: Riis Nielson, H., Filé, G. (eds.) SAS 2007. LNCS, vol. 4634, pp. 298–314. Springer, Heidelberg (2007)
36. Harrison, J.: Floating point verification in HOL. In: Schubert, E.T., Windley, P.J., Alves-Foss, J. (eds.) Higher Order Logic Theorem Proving and Its Applications. LNCS, vol. 971, pp. 186–199. Springer, Heidelberg (1995)
37. Leroy, X.: Formal verification of a realistic compiler. Commun. ACM 52(7), 107–115 (2009)
38. Boldo, S., Jourdan, J.H., Leroy, X., Melquiond, G.: A formally-verified C compiler supporting floating-point arithmetic. In: Proceedings of the 21st IEEE Symposium on Computer Arithmetic, ARITH, pp. 107–115. IEEE, April 2013
39. Lerner, S., Millstein, T., Rice, E., Chambers, C.: Automated soundness proofs for dataflow analyses and transformations via local rules. In: Proceedings of the 32nd ACM SIGPLAN-SIGACT Symposium on Principles of Programming Languages, POPL, pp. 364–377 (2005)
40. Kundu, S., Tatlock, Z., Lerner, S.: Proving optimizations correct using parameterized program equivalence. In: Proceedings of the 30th ACM SIGPLAN Conference on Programming Language Design and Implementation, PLDI, pp. 327–337 (2009)
41. Buchwald, S.: OPTGEN: a generator for local optimizations. In: Franke, B. (ed.) CC 2015. LNCS, vol. 9031, pp. 171–189. Springer, Heidelberg (2015)
42. Nötzli, A., Brown, F.: LifeJacket: verifying precise floating-point optimizations in LLVM. http://arxiv.org/pdf/1603.09290v1.pdf. Accessed 04 Apr 2016

A Parametric Abstract Domain
for Lattice-Valued Regular Expressions

Jan Midtgaard$^{(\boxtimes)}$, Flemming Nielson, and Hanne Riis Nielson

DTU Compute, Technical University of Denmark, Kongens Lyngby, Denmark
mail@janmidtgaard.dk, fnie@dtu.dk, hrni@dtu.dk

Abstract. We present a lattice-valued generalization of regular expressions as an abstract domain for static analysis. The parametric abstract domain rests on a generalization of Brzozowski derivatives and works for both finite and infinite lattices. We develop both a co-inductive, simulation algorithm for deciding ordering between two domain elements and a widening operator for the domain. Finally we illustrate the domain with a static analysis that analyses a communicating process against a lattice-valued regular expression expressing the environment's network communication.

1 Introduction

As static analysis becomes more and more popular, so increases the need for reusable abstract domains. Within numerical abstract domains the past four decades have provided a range of such domains (signs, constant propagation, congruences, intervals, octagons, polyhedra, . . .) but for non-numerical domains the spectrum is less broad (notable exceptions include abstract cofibered domains [29] and tree schemata [23]). At the same time regular languages (regular expressions and finite automata) have enabled computer scientists to create models of software systems and to reason about them both with pen-and-paper and with model checking tools.

In this paper we recast and generalize regular expressions in an abstract interpretation setting. In particular we formulate a parametric abstract domain of lattice-valued regular expressions. We illustrate the domain by extending a traditional static analysis that infers properties of the variables of a communicating process to also analyze network activity. For example, when instantiating the regular expression domain with a domain of channel names and interval values, we can express values such as $(\mathtt{ask}![0; +\infty] + \mathtt{report}![0; +\infty] \cdot \mathtt{hsc}?[-\infty; +\infty])^*$ which describes an iterative communication pattern in which each iteration either outputs a non-negative integer on the $\mathtt{ask}$-channel, or outputs a non-negative integer on the $\mathtt{report}$-channel followed by reading *any value* on the $\mathtt{hsc}$-channel. As significant amounts of modern software depend critically on message-passing network protocols and the software's ability to behave according to certain communication policies, our illustration analysis serves as a first step towards enabling static analyses to address this challenge. The resulting abstract domain grew out of this development but certainly has other applications.

© Springer-Verlag GmbH Germany 2016
X. Rival (Ed.): SAS 2016, LNCS 9837, pp. 338–360, 2016.
DOI: 10.1007/978-3-662-53413-7_17

The contributions of this article are as follows:

- We develop a parametric regular expression domain over finite lattices including a co-inductive ordering algorithm and a widening operator (Sect. 2),
- we generalize the constructions to infinite lattices (Sect. 3),
- we illustrate the domain with a static analysis for analyzing a communicating process (Sect. 4), and
- we report on our prototype implementation (Sect. 5).

2 Regular Expressions over Complete Lattices

We first consider how to view lattice-valued regular expressions as a parametric abstract domain parameterized by an abstract domain A for its character literals. Let $\langle A; \sqsubseteq \rangle$ be a partially ordered set with a corresponding Galois insertion $\langle \wp(C), \subseteq \rangle \xrightleftharpoons[\alpha]{\gamma} \langle A, \sqsubseteq \rangle$ (i.e., a Galois connection in which $\alpha : \wp(C) \longrightarrow A$ is surjective [9]) connecting A to its concrete meaning (some set of characters C). We let ℓ range over the elements of A. An element a of a lattice A is an *atom* if $\bot \sqsubset a$ and there does not exist an ℓ such that $\bot \sqsubset \ell \sqsubset a$. We write $Atoms(A)$ for the set of A's atom elements and let a, b, c range over these. We furthermore require $\alpha : Atoms(\wp(C)) \longrightarrow Atoms(A)$, i.e., that α maps the atoms of $\wp(C)$ (the singleton sets) to atoms of A. These assumptions have a number of consequences:

- $\langle A; \sqsubseteq, \bot, \top, \sqcup, \sqcap \rangle$ is a complete lattice [9, Proposition 9],
- γ is strict ($\gamma(\bot) = \emptyset$),
- $\langle A; \sqsubseteq \rangle$ is an *atomic lattice* [10] (any non-bottom element has an atom less or equal to it),
- $\langle A; \sqsubseteq \rangle$ is an *atomistic* [15] (or atomically generated) lattice: it is atomic and any non-bottom element can be written as a join of atoms.
- $\alpha : Atoms(\wp(C)) \longrightarrow Atoms(A)$ is surjective,
- Atoms have no overlapping meaning: $a \neq a' \implies \gamma(a) \cap \gamma(a') = \emptyset$

Overall the Galois insertion assumption lets A inherit the complete lattice structure of $\wp(C)$. The further assumption of atom preservation lets A further inherit the atomic and atomistic structure of $\wp(C)$. These assumptions still permit a range of known base lattices, such as signs, parity, power sets, intervals, etc. For the rest of this section we will further assume that A is finite and later in Sect. 3 lift that restriction.

$$\mathcal{L}(\emptyset) = \emptyset \qquad \mathcal{L}(r^*) = \cup_{i \geq 0} \mathcal{L}(r)^i \qquad \mathcal{L}(r_1 + r_2) = \mathcal{L}(r_1) \cup \mathcal{L}(r_2)$$
$$\mathcal{L}(\epsilon) = \{\epsilon\} \qquad \mathcal{L}(r_1 \cdot r_2) = \mathcal{L}(r_1) \cdot \mathcal{L}(r_2) \qquad \mathcal{L}(r_1 \& r_2) = \mathcal{L}(r_1) \cap \mathcal{L}(r_2)$$
$$\mathcal{L}(\ell) = \{c \mid c \in \gamma(\ell)\} \qquad \mathcal{L}(\complement\, r) = \wp(C^*) \setminus \mathcal{L}(r)$$

Fig. 1. Denotation of lattice-valued regular expressions: $\mathcal{L} : \widehat{R}_A \longrightarrow \wp(C^*)$

The elements of A will play the role of the regular expression alphabet. Now the language of lattice-valued regular expressions is defined as follows:

$$\widehat{R}_A ::= \emptyset \mid \epsilon \mid \ell \mid \widehat{R}_A^* \mid \widehat{R}_A \cdot \widehat{R}_A \mid \complement \widehat{R}_A \mid \widehat{R}_A + \widehat{R}_A \mid \widehat{R}_A \,\&\, \widehat{R}_A \qquad \text{where } \ell \in A \setminus \{\bot\}$$

Notice how we include both complement $\complement$ and intersection $\&$ in the regular expressions [6] (the result is also referred to as *extended* or *generalized regular expressions*). Figure 1 lists our generalized denotation for the lattice-valued regular expressions. One significant difference from the traditional definition, is how we concretize lattice literals into one-element strings using the concretization function γ (traditionally, $\mathcal{L}(c) = \{c\}$ for a character c). We immediately get the traditional definition if we instantiate with $A = \wp(C)$ and the identity Galois insertion (and allow only atoms $\{c\}$ as literals). Both traditional regular expressions and lattice-valued regular expressions operate over a finite alphabet. However in contrast to traditional regular expressions where the finite alphabet carries through in the denoted language, γ may concretize a single 'lattice character' to an infinite set, e.g., $\mathcal{L}(even) = \{\ldots, -2, 0, 2, \ldots\}$ in a parity lattice. From the denotation it is also apparent how excluding $\bot \in A$ from lattice literals loses no generality, as bottom is expressible in the regular expressions as $\emptyset$ because γ is strict. Note that it is possible to express the same language in syntactically different ways: for example, $\emptyset$, $\emptyset \cdot even$, and $even \,\&\, odd$ all denote the same empty language. We therefore write $\approx$ to denote language equality in the regular expression domain.

The lattice-valued regular expressions are ordered under language inclusion: $r \sqsubseteq r' \iff \mathcal{L}(r) \subseteq \mathcal{L}(r')$. Note how we use a different symbol $\sqsubseteq$ to help distinguish the ordering of the lattice-valued regular expressions from $\sqsubseteq$, the ordering of the input domain A. The language inclusion ordering motivates our requirement for a Galois insertion: $\forall a, a' \in Atoms(A)$. $a \sqsubseteq a' \iff \mathcal{L}(a) \subseteq \mathcal{L}(a') \iff \gamma(a) \subseteq \gamma(a') \iff a = (\alpha \circ \gamma)(a) \sqsubseteq a'$, i.e., the two orderings are compatible. The ordering is not anti-symmetric: $\emptyset \sqsubseteq even \,\&\, odd$ and $even \,\&\, odd \sqsubseteq \emptyset$ but $\emptyset \neq even \,\&\, odd$. To regain a partial order we consider elements up to language equality. The resulting regular expression domain constitutes a lattice: the least and greatest elements (bottom and top) are $\emptyset$ and $\top^*$, respectively (with $\top$ being the top element from A). Furthermore, the least upper bound and the greatest lower bound of two elements r_1 and r_2 are given symbolically by $r_1 + r_2$ and $r_1 \,\&\, r_2$, respectively. However the regular expression domain does

$$\widehat{\mathcal{D}}_a(\emptyset) = \emptyset$$

$$\widehat{\mathcal{D}}_a(\epsilon) = \emptyset$$

$$\widehat{\mathcal{D}}_a(\ell) = \begin{cases} \epsilon & a \sqsubseteq \ell \\ \emptyset & a \not\sqsubseteq \ell \end{cases}$$

$$\widehat{\mathcal{D}}_a(r^*) = \widehat{\mathcal{D}}_a(r) \cdot r^*$$

$$\widehat{\mathcal{D}}_a(r_1 \cdot r_2) = \begin{cases} \widehat{\mathcal{D}}_a(r_1) \cdot r_2 + \widehat{\mathcal{D}}_a(r_2) & \epsilon \sqsubseteq r_1 \\ \widehat{\mathcal{D}}_a(r_1) \cdot r_2 & \epsilon \not\sqsubseteq r_1 \end{cases}$$

$$\widehat{\mathcal{D}}_a(\complement r) = \complement \widehat{\mathcal{D}}_a(r)$$

$$\widehat{\mathcal{D}}_a(r_1 + r_2) = \widehat{\mathcal{D}}_a(r_1) + \widehat{\mathcal{D}}_a(r_2)$$

$$\widehat{\mathcal{D}}_a(r_1 \,\&\, r_2) = \widehat{\mathcal{D}}_a(r_1) \,\&\, \widehat{\mathcal{D}}_a(r_2)$$

Fig. 2. Lattice-valued Brzozowski derivatives: $\widehat{\mathcal{D}} : Atoms(A) \longrightarrow \widehat{R}_A \longrightarrow \widehat{R}_A$

not constitute a *complete* lattice. For example, the least upper bound of the chain $\epsilon \sqsubseteq \epsilon + even \cdot odd \sqsubseteq \epsilon + even \cdot odd + even \cdot even \cdot odd \cdot odd \sqsubseteq \ldots$ is an infinite sum $\sum_n even^n odd^n$ which is not a regular language over A, but context-free and there is no least regular language containing it.

As a fundamental operation over the lattice-valued regular expressions, we consider the Brzozowski derivative [6]. A traditional Brzozowski derivative of a regular expression r with respect to some character c returns a regular expression denoting the suffix strings w resulting from having read a character c from r: $\mathcal{L}(\mathcal{D}_c(r)) = c \backslash \mathcal{L}(r) = \{w \mid c \cdot w \in \mathcal{L}(r)\}$. In Fig. 2 we define the generalized lattice-based derivatives. Note how we derive lattice-valued regular expressions only with respect to lattice atoms. Brzozowski's derivatives gave rise to a central equation, which also holds for the lattice-valued generalization: all regular expressions can be expressed as a sum of derivatives (modulo an optional epsilon):

Theorem 1 (Sum of derivatives [6])

$$\forall r \in \widehat{R}_A. \quad r \approx \sum_{a \in Atoms(A)} a \cdot \widehat{\mathcal{D}}_a(r) \; + \; \delta(r) \quad where \; \delta(r) = \begin{cases} \epsilon & \epsilon \sqsubseteq r \\ \emptyset & \epsilon \not\sqsubseteq r \end{cases}$$

The proof utilizes that atoms are non-overlapping. We can use the equation to characterize the lattice-valued Brzozowski derivatives. We first generalize the notation to account for sets in the denotations: $cs \backslash L = \{w \mid \forall c \in cs. \; c \cdot w \in L\}$ and then utilize this notation in the characterization.

Lemma 2 (Meaning of derivatives)

$$\forall r \in \widehat{R}_A, a \in Atoms(A). \quad \mathcal{L}(\widehat{\mathcal{D}}_a(r)) = \gamma(a) \backslash \mathcal{L}(r) = \{w \mid \forall c \in \gamma(a). \; c \cdot w \in \mathcal{L}(r)\}$$

Based on the inclusion ordering and Lemma 2 one can easily verify that $\widehat{\mathcal{D}}$ is monotone in the second, regular expression parameter.

Lemma 3 ($\widehat{\mathcal{D}}$ monotone). $\forall a \in Atoms(A), r, r' \in \widehat{R}_A. \; r \sqsubseteq r' \implies \widehat{\mathcal{D}}_a(r) \sqsubseteq \widehat{\mathcal{D}}_a(r')$

We test the side-condition $\epsilon \sqsubseteq r_1$ of Fig. 2 with a dedicated procedure, *nullable*, defined in Fig. 3. We can prove that *nullable* has the intended meaning:

Lemma 4 (*nullable* correct). $\forall r \in \widehat{R}_A. \quad \epsilon \sqsubseteq r \iff nullable(r)$

We can extend the definition of derivatives to sequences of derivatives. Sequences are defined inductively: $s ::= \epsilon \mid as$ and a derivation with respect to a sequence is defined structurally [6]: $\widehat{\mathcal{D}}_\epsilon(r) = r$ and $\widehat{\mathcal{D}}_{as}(r) = \widehat{\mathcal{D}}_s(\widehat{\mathcal{D}}_a(r))$ meaning that $\widehat{\mathcal{D}}_{a_1 \ldots a_n}(r) = \widehat{\mathcal{D}}_{a_n}(\ldots \widehat{\mathcal{D}}_{a_1}(r))$.

$$
\begin{aligned}
nullable(\emptyset) &= false & nullable(r_1 \cdot r_2) &= nullable(r_1) \wedge nullable(r_2) \\
nullable(\epsilon) &= true & nullable(\complement\, r) &= \neg nullable(r) \\
nullable(\ell) &= false & nullable(r_1 + r_2) &= nullable(r_1) \vee nullable(r_2) \\
nullable(r_1^*) &= true & nullable(r_1 \,\&\, r_2) &= nullable(r_1) \wedge nullable(r_2)
\end{aligned}
$$

Fig. 3. The *nullable* operation: $nullable : \widehat{R}_A \longrightarrow Bool$

2.1 Derivatives as Automata

One can view Brzozowski derivatives as a means for translating a regular expression to an automaton [6]. This view extends to the lattice-valued generalization: (1) Each state is identified with a regular expression denoting the language it accepts, (2) There is a transition consuming a from one state, r, to the state $\widehat{\mathcal{D}}_a(r)$, and (3) A state r is accepting if and only if $nullable(r)$. Consider the regular expression $odd + even^*$. Since $\widehat{\mathcal{D}}_{even}(odd + even^*) \approx even^*$ the corresponding automaton (depicted in Fig. 4) can transition from the former to the latter by consuming the atom $even$. The state corresponding to the root expression $odd + even^*$ furthermore acts as the initial state. As $odd + even^*$ is also *nullable* the corresponding state is also a final state.

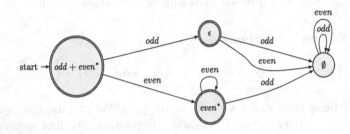

Fig. 4. Example automaton derived for $odd + even^*$

Brzozowski [6] proved that there are only a bounded number of different derivatives of a given regular expression up to associativity, commutivity, and idempotence (ACI) of $+$.[1] Intuitively, ACI of $+$ means that the terms of a sum act as a set: parentheses and term order are irrelevant and any term present is syntactically unique. For the lattice-valued generalization we can similarly establish an upper bound by structural induction on r as a counting argument on the number of syntactically unique term elements:

Lemma 5 (Number of dissimilar derivatives)

$$\forall r \in \widehat{R}_A.\ \exists n.\ |\{\widehat{\mathcal{D}}_s(r) \mid s \in Atoms(A)^*\}_{=_{ACI}}| \leq n$$

As a consequence a resulting automaton is guaranteed to have only a finite number of states. However a resulting automaton is not necessarily minimal. By incorporating additional *simplifying reductions* ($\epsilon \cdot r = r = r \cdot \epsilon$, $\emptyset + r = r$, ...) we can identify more equivalent states in a resulting automaton, thereby reducing its size further and thus making the approach practically feasible [25].

---

[1] It has later been pointed out [14,26,27] that Brzozowski's proof had a minor flaw, that could be fixed by patching the statement of the theorem [27] or by patching the definition of derivatives to avoid the syntactic occurrence of δ [26]. We have followed the latter approach in our generalization.

For example, there are five dissimilar derivatives (including the root expression) of $odd + even^*$ up to ACI of $+$:

$$\widehat{\mathcal{D}}_{even}(odd + even^*) = \emptyset + \epsilon \cdot even^* \qquad \widehat{\mathcal{D}}_{even}(\emptyset + \epsilon \cdot even^*) = \emptyset + \emptyset \cdot even^* + \epsilon \cdot even^*$$

$$\widehat{\mathcal{D}}_{odd}(odd + even^*) = \epsilon + \emptyset \cdot even^* \qquad \widehat{\mathcal{D}}_{even}(\epsilon + \emptyset \cdot even^*) = \emptyset + \emptyset \cdot even^*$$

Any remaining derivatives, e.g., $\widehat{\mathcal{D}}_{odd}(\emptyset + \epsilon \cdot even^*) = \emptyset + \emptyset \cdot even^* + \emptyset \cdot even^*$ is ACI equivalent to one of these: $\emptyset + \emptyset \cdot even^* + \emptyset \cdot even^* =_{ACI} \emptyset + \emptyset \cdot even^*$. By additional simplifying reductions, the five derivatives can be reduced to four: $odd + even^*$, $even^*$, ϵ, $\emptyset$ respectively. Collectively, these four derivatives represent the four states of Fig. 4 (including the explicit error state $\emptyset$). We stress that the results of this paper require only the ACI equivalences. For readability and to make the techniques practical, for the rest of the article we will incorporate the further simplifying reductions, which we denote $ACI+$.

2.2 An Ordering Algorithm

Both the least upper bound and the greatest lower bound of two regular expressions r_1 and r_2 can be symbolically represented as $r_1 + r_2$ and $r_1 \& r_2$, respectively. However a procedure for deciding domain ordering is not as easy: The language inclusion ordering $\sqsubseteq$ is ideal for pen-and-paper results, but it is not a tractable approach for algorithmically comparing elements on a computer. We will therefore develop an algorithm based on derivatives.

```
1   proc leq test(r₁, r₂)
2     memo tbl := {}
3     proc leq memo(r₁, r₂)
4       if (r₁, r₂) ∈_ACI memo tbl then return
5       memo tbl := memo tbl ∪ {(r₁, r₂)}
6       if nullable(r₁) ⟹ nullable(r₂)
7       then for all a ∈ Atoms(A), leq memo(𝒟̂ₐ(r₁), 𝒟̂ₐ(r₂))
8           return
9       else raise False
10      try leq memo(r₁, r₂) with False => return false
11      return true
```

Fig. 5. Ordering algorithm

With the "derivatives-as-automata-states" in mind, we formulate in Fig. 5 a procedure for computing a (constructive) simulation. Essentially, the algorithm corresponds to lazily exploring each state of the two regular expressions' automata using Brzozowski's construction, and computing a simulation (implemented as a hashtable) between these state pairs. Upon successful termination the algorithm will have computed in memo_tbl a simulation between the derivatives of r_1 and r_2. For example, if we invoke the algorithm with arguments $(\epsilon, even^*)$ it will compute a simulation memo_tbl $= \{(\epsilon, even^*), (\emptyset, \emptyset), (\emptyset, even^*)\}$

and ultimately return true. Underway, the first call to leq_memo with, e.g., arguments $(\emptyset, \emptyset)$ will memorize the pair and after ensuring that $false \implies false$ it will recursively call leq_memo with both $(\widehat{\mathcal{D}}_{odd}(\emptyset), \widehat{\mathcal{D}}_{odd}(\emptyset)) = (\emptyset, \emptyset)$ and $(\widehat{\mathcal{D}}_{even}(\emptyset), \widehat{\mathcal{D}}_{even}(\emptyset)) = (\emptyset, \emptyset)$ as arguments. These two invocations will immediately return successfully due to the memorization. By memorizing each pair of regular expressions and testing memo_tbl for membership up to ACI equivalence the algorithm is guaranteed to terminate. As such, the algorithm is an inclusion (or *containment*) analogue of Grabmayer's co-inductive axiomatization of regular expression equivalence [14, 17]. There are different opportunities for optimizing the ordering algorithm. By reflexivity, we can avoid derivatives when leq_memo is invoked with equal arguments r_1 and r_2. Another possibility is to utilize *hash consing* to avoid computing the same derivatives repeatedly.

We can show that the language inclusion ordering and the derivative-based ordering are in fact equivalent. The proof utilizes both Theorem 1, $\widehat{\mathcal{D}}$'s monotonicity (Lemma 3), and the correctness of *nullable* (Lemma 4). To prove equivalence we consider a simulation ordering which we will use as a stepping stone. We define a simulation $\preceq$ to be a relation that satisfies $r \preceq r'$ iff $nullable(r) \implies nullable(r')$ and for all atoms a: $\widehat{\mathcal{D}}_a(r) \preceq \widehat{\mathcal{D}}_a(r')$. We can view such a simulation $\preceq$ as a fixed point of a function $F : \wp(\widehat{R}_A \times \widehat{R}_A) \longrightarrow \wp(\widehat{R}_A \times \widehat{R}_A)$ defined as follows:

$$F(\preceq') = \{(r_1, r_2) \mid nullable(r_1) \implies nullable(r_2)\}$$
$$\cap \{(r_1, r_2) \mid \forall \text{ atoms } a : (\widehat{\mathcal{D}}_a(r_1), \widehat{\mathcal{D}}_a(r_2)) \in \preceq'\}$$

It is now straight-forward to verify that F is monotone. Since it is defined over a complete lattice (sets of regular expression pairs), the greatest fixed point is well-defined by Tarski's fixed-point theorem. In particular, for a fixed point $F(\preceq) = \preceq$, we then have $\preceq = \{(r_1, r_2) \mid nullable(r_1) \implies nullable(r_2)\} \cap \{(r_1, r_2) \mid \forall \text{ atoms } a : (\widehat{\mathcal{D}}_a(r_1), \widehat{\mathcal{D}}_a(r_2)) \in \preceq\}$. Write $\stackrel{.}{\preceq}$ for gfp F. We are now in position to prove equivalence of the language inclusion ordering and the derivative-based ordering. In the following lemma we do so in two steps:

Lemma 6 (Ordering equivalence)

(a) $\forall r, r' \in \widehat{R}_A$. leq_test$(r, r')$ *returns* true $\iff r \stackrel{.}{\preceq} r'$
(b) $\forall r, r' \in \widehat{R}_A$. $r \sqsubseteq r' \iff r \stackrel{.}{\preceq} r'$

Algorithms for testing inclusion (or containment) of two regular expressions r_1 and r_2 are well known [22]. The textbook algorithm tests $r_1 \,\&\, \complement r_2$ for emptiness [22]. In our generalized setting, this would correspond to invoking leq_test$(r_1 \,\&\, \complement r_2, \emptyset)$, for which all sub-derivatives of the second parameter $\emptyset$ passed around by leq_memo continue to be $\emptyset$ (which is clearly not *nullable*). The loop would thereby explore all paths from the first parameter's root expression $r_1 \,\&\, \complement r_2$ to a *nullable* derivative, corresponding to a search for a reachable acceptance state in a corresponding DFA under the derivatives-as-automata-view. As such, the textbook emptiness-testing algorithm can be viewed as a special case of our derivative-based algorithm.

2.3 Widening

A static analysis based on Kleene iteration over the regular expression domain is not guaranteed to terminate, as it contains infinite, strictly increasing chains: $\epsilon \sqsubseteq \epsilon + l \sqsubseteq \epsilon + l + (l \cdot l) \sqsubseteq \epsilon + l + (l \cdot l) + (l \cdot l \cdot l) \sqsubseteq \ldots$. For this reason we need a widening operator. From a high-level point of view the widening operator works by (a) formulating an equation system, (b) collapsing some of the equations in order to avoid infinite, strictly increasing chains, and (c) solving the collapsed equation system to get back a regular expression. Step (b) is inspired by a widening operator of Feret [11] and Le Gall, Jeannet, and Jéron [13], and step (c) uses a translation scheme due to Brzozowski [6].

Let us consider an example of widening *odd* and *even**. As a first step we form their sum: $odd + even^*$. We know from Sect. 2.1 that it has four different simplified derivatives: $\{odd + even^*, even^*, \epsilon, \emptyset\}$. By Theorem 1 we can characterize them as equations, where we name the four derivatives R_0, R_1, R_2, R_3 (R_0 denotes the root expression):

$$R_0 \approx even \cdot R_1 + odd \cdot R_2 + \epsilon$$
$$R_1 \approx even \cdot R_1 + odd \cdot R_3 + \epsilon$$
$$R_2 \approx even \cdot R_3 + odd \cdot R_3 + \epsilon$$
$$R_3 \approx even \cdot R_3 + odd \cdot R_3$$

We subsequently collect the coefficients of R_0, R_1, R_2, R_3 and state the resulting equation system as a matrix. For example, by collecting the coefficients to R_3 in the equation $R_2 \approx even \cdot R_3 + odd \cdot R_3 + \epsilon$ we obtain $R_2 \approx (even + odd) \cdot R_3 + \epsilon$. The resulting matrix describes the transitions of a corresponding finite automata as displayed in Fig. 4:

$$\begin{bmatrix} R_0 \\ R_1 \\ R_2 \\ R_3 \end{bmatrix} \approx \begin{bmatrix} \emptyset & even & odd & \emptyset \\ \emptyset & even & \emptyset & odd \\ \emptyset & \emptyset & \emptyset & even + odd \\ \emptyset & \emptyset & \emptyset & even + odd \end{bmatrix} \cdot \begin{bmatrix} R_0 \\ R_1 \\ R_2 \\ R_3 \end{bmatrix} + \begin{bmatrix} \epsilon \\ \epsilon \\ \epsilon \\ \emptyset \end{bmatrix}$$

The widening operator partitions the set of derivatives into a fixed, finite number of equivalence classes and works for any such partitioning. In the present case we will use a *coloring function*, $col : \widehat{R}_A \longrightarrow \widehat{R}_A \longrightarrow [1; 3]$ to partition a set of derivatives with respect to a given root expression r':

$$col_{r'}(r) = \begin{cases} 1 & \text{if } r =_{ACI} r' \\ 2 & \text{if } r \neq_{ACI} r' \text{ and } nullable(r) \\ 3 & \text{if } r \neq_{ACI} r' \text{ and } \neg nullable(r) \end{cases}$$

$col_{odd+even^*}$ will thus induce a partitioning: $\{\{\overbrace{odd + even^*}^{\text{color 1}}\}, \{\overbrace{even^*, \epsilon}^{\text{color 2}}\}, \overbrace{\{\emptyset\}}^{\text{color 3}}\}$. This partitioning can be expressed by equating R_1 and R_2. By adding the right-hand-sides of R_1 and R_2 into a combined right-hand-side for their combination R_{12}, we can be sure that the least solution to R_{12} in the resulting equation system is also a solution to the variables R_1 and R_2 in the original equation system. For example, the equation $R_0 \approx even \cdot R_1 + odd \cdot R_2 + \epsilon$ becomes $R_0 \approx (even + odd) \cdot R_{12} + \epsilon$ in the collapsed system. The resulting equation system now reads:

$$\begin{bmatrix} R_0 \\ R_{12} \\ R_3 \end{bmatrix} \approx \begin{bmatrix} \emptyset & even + odd & \emptyset \\ \emptyset & even & even + odd \\ \emptyset & \emptyset & even + odd \end{bmatrix} \cdot \begin{bmatrix} R_0 \\ R_{12} \\ R_3 \end{bmatrix} + \begin{bmatrix} \epsilon \\ \epsilon \\ \emptyset \end{bmatrix}$$

This particular step of the algorithm represents a potential information loss, as the coefficients of each of R_1 and R_2 are merged into joint coefficients for R_{12}. We can now solve these by combining (a) elimination of variables and (b) Arden's lemma [3] (which states that an equation of the form $X \approx A \cdot X + B$ has solution $X \approx A^* \cdot B$). The equation $R_3 \approx (even + odd) \cdot R_3 + \emptyset$ therefore has solution $R_3 \approx (even + odd)^* \cdot \emptyset =_{ACI+} \emptyset$, and we can thus eliminate the variable R_3 by substituting this solution in (and simplifying):

$$\begin{bmatrix} R_0 \\ R_{12} \end{bmatrix} \approx \begin{bmatrix} \emptyset & even + odd \\ \emptyset & even \end{bmatrix} \cdot \begin{bmatrix} R_0 \\ R_{12} \end{bmatrix} + \begin{bmatrix} \epsilon \\ \epsilon \end{bmatrix}$$

Now $R_{12} \approx even \cdot R_{12} + \epsilon$ has solution $R_{12} \approx even^* \cdot \epsilon =_{ACI+} even^*$ by Arden's lemma. Again we eliminate the variable:

$$[R_0] \approx [\emptyset] \cdot [R_0] + [(even + odd) \cdot even^* + \epsilon]$$

From this we read off the result: $R_0 \approx (even + odd) \cdot even^* + \epsilon$. which clearly includes both arguments odd and $even^*$ to the widening operator as well as some additional elements, such as $odd \cdot even$.

ALGORITHM WIDENING(r, r')

1. Form $r_0 = r + r'$
2. Derive the characteristic equations over variables R_i:
   $R_i \approx \sum_{a_j \in Atoms(A)} a_j \cdot R_j + \delta(r_i)$
3. For each equation collect the coefficients for each variable R_i
4. Compute equivalence classes for R_i
5. Collapse equations based on equivalence classes and solve the collapsed equations
6. Return the solution to (the equivalence class containing) R_0

Fig. 6. The widening algorithm

We summarize the widening algorithm in Fig. 6 where we write R_i for the variable corresponding to the derivative regular expression r_i. We can furthermore prove that the procedure indeed is a widening operator.

Theorem 7. *The widening algorithm constitutes a widening operator:*

(a) *the result is greater or equal to any of the arguments and*

(b) *given an increasing chain $r_0 \sqsubseteq r_1 \sqsubseteq r_2 \sqsubseteq \ldots$ the resulting widening sequence defined as $\overline{r}_0 = r_0$ and $\overline{r}_{k+1} = \overline{r}_k \triangledown r_{k+1}$ stabilizes after a finite number of steps.*

The widening algorithm in Fig. 6 works for any partitioning into a fixed number of equivalence classes. The above example illustrates the setting (level 0) in which a coloring function is used directly to partition the derivatives into three equivalence classes. Inspired by Feret [11] and Le Gall, Jeannet, and Jéron [13], we generalize this pattern to distinguish two regular expressions at level $k + 1$ if their derivatives can be distinguished at level k:

$$r_1 \approx_0^{col_r} r_2 \text{ iff } col_r(r_1) = col_r(r_2)$$

$$r_1 \approx_{k+1}^{col_r} r_2 \text{ iff } r_1 \approx_k^{col_r} r_2 \wedge \forall \text{ atoms } a. \ \widehat{\mathcal{D}}_a(r_1) \approx_k^{col_r} \widehat{\mathcal{D}}_a(r_2)$$

The resulting partitioning $\approx_k^{col_r}$ essentially expresses bisimilarity up to some bound k. With this characterization in mind, we define an extensive, idempotent operator $\rho_k^{col_r}$ that quotients the language of the underlying languages with respect to $\approx_k^{col_r}$: $r \triangledown r' = \rho_k^{col_{r+r'}}(r+r')$. Collectively, $\rho_k^{col_{r+r'}}$ represents a family of widening operators (one for each choice of k).

In our example of widening *odd* and *even** the coloring function assigns the error state R_3 (representing $\emptyset$) to a different equivalence class than any non-error states, thereby preventing them from being collapsed. Such collapsing will result in a severe precision loss, as the self-loops of error states such as R_3 are inherited by a resulting collapsed state, thereby leading to spurious self-loops in the result. After having identified the issue on a number of examples, we designed a refined coloring function $col_{alt} : \widehat{R}_A \longrightarrow \widehat{R}_A \longrightarrow [1; 4]$ that gives a separate color 4 to "error states": regular expressions from which a *nullable* expression is unreachable under any sequence of derivatives. In the matrix representation such expressions can be identified by their complement: we can find all non-error states by a depth-first marking of all R_i (representing r_i) reachable from a *nullable* state under a reverse ordering of the derivative transitions.[2]

3   From Finite to Infinite Lattices

The Brzozowski identity and the algorithms utilizing it are only tractable up to a certain point: For example, even for a finite interval lattice over 32-bit integers, there are 2^{32} atoms of the shape $[i; i]$ making a sum (and loops iterating) over all such atoms unrealistic to work with. In fact, many derivatives are syntactically identical, which allow us to consider only a subset of "representative" atoms. For example, consider a derivative over interval-valued regular expressions: $\widehat{\mathcal{D}}_{[1;1]}([1; 10] + [20; 22]) = \epsilon + \emptyset$. Clearly the result is identical for atoms

---

[2] Solving the equations for such error states before step 5 (collapsing) has the same effect: their collective solution is $\emptyset$ in the matrix, and substituting the solution in removes any transitions to and from them, and thereby any observable effect of grouping an error state and a non-error state in the same equivalence class.

$[2; 2], \ldots, [10; 10]$.[3] To this end we seek to partition a potentially infinite set of atoms into a finite set of equivalence classes $[a_1], \ldots, [a_n]$ with identical derivatives. We represent a partition as an abstract type $\widehat{equiv}_A$ suitably instantiated for each lattice A. One operation $\widehat{to\_equivs} : A \longrightarrow \widehat{equiv}_A$ computes a partition for a given lattice literal and a second operation $\widehat{overlay} : \widehat{equiv}_A \longrightarrow \widehat{equiv}_A \longrightarrow \widehat{equiv}_A$ combines two partitions into a refined one. The computed partition should satisfy the following two properties:

$$\forall \ell \in A, [a_i] \in \widehat{to\_equivs}(\ell), a, a' \in Atoms(A).$$
$$a, a' \in [a_i] \implies (a \sqsubseteq \ell \wedge a' \sqsubseteq \ell) \vee (a \not\sqsubseteq \ell \wedge a' \not\sqsubseteq \ell) \quad (1)$$

$$\forall \overline{[b]}, \overline{[c]} \in \widehat{equiv}_A, [a_i] \in \widehat{overlay}(\overline{[b]}, \overline{[c]}), a, a' \in Atoms(A).$$
$$a, a' \in [a_i] \implies \exists j, k.\ a, a' \in [b_j] \wedge a, a' \in [c_k] \quad (2)$$

$$\widehat{range}(\emptyset) = \widehat{to\ equivs}(\top) \qquad \widehat{range}(r_1 \cdot r_2) = \begin{cases} \widehat{overlay}(\widehat{range}(r_1), \widehat{range}(r_2)) & \epsilon \sqsubseteq r_1 \\ \widehat{range}(r_1) & \epsilon \not\sqsubseteq r_1 \end{cases}$$

$$\widehat{range}(\epsilon) = \widehat{to\ equivs}(\top)$$
$$\widehat{range}(\complement\, r) = \widehat{range}(r)$$
$$\widehat{range}(\ell) = \widehat{to\ equivs}(\ell)$$
$$\widehat{range}(r_1 + r_2) = \widehat{overlay}(\widehat{range}(r_1), \widehat{range}(r_2))$$
$$\widehat{range}(r^*) = \widehat{range}(r)$$
$$\widehat{range}(r_1 \,\&\, r_2) = \widehat{overlay}(\widehat{range}(r_1), \widehat{range}(r_2))$$

Fig. 7. Generic $\widehat{range}$ function for partitioning A's atoms: $\widehat{range} : \widehat{R}_A \longrightarrow \widehat{equiv}_A$

where $\overline{[b]}, \overline{[c]}$ range over partitions of A's atoms. Based on $\widehat{to\_equivs}$ and $\widehat{overlay}$ we can formulate in Fig. 7 a generic $\widehat{range}$ function, that computes an atom partition for a given regular expression. Assuming that $\widehat{to\_equivs}$ produces a partition and that $\widehat{overlay}$ preserves partitions the result of $\widehat{range}$ will also be a partition. Specifically, $\widehat{range}$ computes a partition over A's atoms for the equivalence relation $\widehat{\mathcal{D}}_a(r) = \widehat{\mathcal{D}}_{a'}(r)$. We can verify this property by structural induction over r:

Lemma 8. $\forall r \in \widehat{R}_A, [a_i] \in \widehat{range}(r), a, a' \in Atoms(A).\, a, a' \in [a_i] \implies \widehat{\mathcal{D}}_a(r) = \widehat{\mathcal{D}}_{a'}(r)$

As a consequence we can optimize the ordering algorithm in Fig. 5. For all atoms a, a' such that $[a_1], \ldots, [a_n] = \widehat{overlay}(\widehat{range}(r_1), \widehat{range}(r_2))$ and $a, a' \in [a_i]$ for some $1 \leq i \leq n$, by Lemma 8 and Property 2 we have both $\widehat{\mathcal{D}}_a(r_1) = \widehat{\mathcal{D}}_{a'}(r_1)$ and $\widehat{\mathcal{D}}_a(r_2) = \widehat{\mathcal{D}}_{a'}(r_2)$ and can therefore just check one representative from each equivalence class. We thus replace line number 7 in Fig. 5 with:

---

[3] The result is also $\epsilon + \emptyset$ for $[20; 20], [21; 21], [22; 22]$ up to ACI of $+$, but that just constitutes a refinement identifying even more equivalent atoms.

then for all $[a_i] \in \widehat{overlay}(\widehat{range}(r_1), \widehat{range}(r_2))$, leq_memo($\widehat{\mathcal{D}}_{\widehat{repr}([a_i])}(r_1), \widehat{\mathcal{D}}_{\widehat{repr}([a_i])}(r_2)$)

where the function $\widehat{repr}$ returns a representative atom a_i from the equivalence class $[a_i]$.

Corollary 9 (Correctness of modified ordering algorithm)

$$\forall r, r' \in \widehat{R}_A. \text{ leq\_test}'(r, r') \text{ returns true} \iff r \sqsubseteq r'$$

Similarly we can adjust step 2 of the widening algorithm in Fig. 6 to form finite characteristic equations. We do so by limiting the constructed sums to one term per equivalence class in $\widehat{range}$'s partition of $Atoms(A)$: $R_i \approx \sum_{[a_j] \in \widehat{range}(r_i)}$ $\widehat{project}([a_j]) \cdot R_j + \delta(r_i)$ where $\widehat{project}([a_j])$ returns a lattice value from A accounting for all atoms in the equivalence class $[a_j]$: $\forall a \in [a_j]. \ a \sqsubseteq \widehat{project}([a_j])$.[4] For infinite lattices A not satisfying ACC, we cannot ensure stabilization over, e.g., $\emptyset \sqsubset [0;0] \sqsubset [0;1] \sqsubset \dots$ (injected as character literals into $\widehat{R}_{Interval}$), as the widening algorithm does not incorporate widening over A. However, when limited to chains with only a finite number of different lattice literals the operator constitutes a widening:

$$to\_\widehat{equivs}([l;u]) = \begin{cases} [-\infty;+\infty] & l=-\infty \wedge u=+\infty \\ [-\infty;u], [u+1;+\infty] & l=-\infty \wedge u \neq +\infty \\ [-\infty;l-1], [l;+\infty] & l \neq -\infty \wedge u=+\infty \\ [-\infty;l-1], [l;u], [u+1;+\infty] & l \neq -\infty \wedge u \neq +\infty \end{cases}$$

$$\widehat{overlay}([l_1;+\infty], [l_2;+\infty]) = [l_1;+\infty] \quad l_1 = l_2 \text{ holds as an invariant}$$

$$\widehat{overlay}([l_1;u_1] :: R'_1, [l_2;u_2] :: R'_2) = \begin{cases} [l_1;u_1] :: \widehat{overlay}(R'_1, R'_2) & l_1=l_2 \wedge u_1=u_2 \\ [l_1;u_1] :: \widehat{overlay}(R'_1, [u_1+1;u_2] :: R'_2) & l_1=l_2 \wedge u_1 < u_2 \\ [l_2;u_2] :: \widehat{overlay}([u_2+1;u_1] :: R'_1, R'_2) & l_1=l_2 \wedge u_1 > u_2 \end{cases}$$

Fig. 8. $to\_\widehat{equivs}$ and $\widehat{overlay}$ for the interval lattice

Corollary 10. *The modified widening algorithm constitutes a widening operator over increasing chains containing only finitely many lattice literals from A.*

The widening operator over the lattice-valued regular expressions does not incorporate a widening operator over A. As such there may be infinite, strictly increasing chains of values from A that flow into $\widehat{R}_A$ (when such values are injected as character literals). Furthermore there may be a complex flow of values from A and into $\widehat{R}_A$ and back again from $\widehat{R}_A$ and into A via $\widehat{project}$. Following abstract interpretation tradition [4], any such cyclic flows of values (be it over A or $\widehat{R}_A$) should cross at least one widening operator, e.g., on loop headers, to guarantee termination. An analysis component over A (e.g., for interval analysis

---

[4] Generally the solution to this equation is an over-approximation but so is the result of widening.

of variables) that supplies $\widehat{R}_A$ with injected values from A will therefore itself have to incorporate widening over A at these points. In this situation, thanks to A's widening operator only a finite number of different values from A can flow to (the chains of) the regular expressions. We thereby satisfy Corollary 10's condition and ensure overall termination by "delegating the termination responsibility" to each of the participating abstract domains. Next, we turn to specific instances for A.

3.1   Small, Finite Instantiations

Simple finite lattices such as the parity lattice can meet the above interface by letting each atom a represent a singleton equivalence class $[a]$. We can then represent $\widehat{equiv}_A$ as a constant list of such atoms. For example, for the parity lattice we can implement $\widehat{to\_equivs}$ and $\widehat{overlay}$ as constant functions, returning $[even], [odd]$. It follows that $\widehat{to\_equivs}$ produces a partition, that $\widehat{overlay}$ preserves it, and that the definitions satisfies Properties 1,2.

3.2   The Interval Lattice

For an interval lattice [7] we can represent each equivalence class as an interval and the entire partition as a finite set of non-overlapping intervals: $\widehat{equiv}_{Interval} = \wp(Interval)$. We can formulate $\widehat{to\_equivs}$ in Fig. 8 as a case dispatch that takes into account the limit cases $-\infty$ and $+\infty$ of an interval literal $[l; u]$. As an example, $\widehat{to\_equivs}([0; 2])$ returns the partition $[-\infty; -1], [0; 2], [3; +\infty]$ of the atoms $[i; i]$. By sorting the equivalence classes (intervals) we can $\widehat{overlay}$ two partitions in linear time. In Fig. 8 we formulate $\widehat{overlay}$ as a recursive function over two such sorted partitions. The implementation satisfies the invariant that at a recursive invocation (a) neither of its arguments are empty, (b) the two leftmost lower bounds are identical, and (c) the two rightmost upper bounds are $+\infty$. As such each recursive invocation of $\widehat{overlay}$ combines two partitions from (their common) leftmost lower bound to $+\infty$. As an example, $\widehat{overlay}$ of $[-\infty; -1], [0; 2], [3; +\infty]$ and $[-\infty; -3], [-2; 1], [2; +\infty]$ returns the partition $[-\infty; -3], [-2; -1], [0; 1], [2; 2], [3; +\infty]$. We prove that the definitions have the desired properties. For $\widehat{overlay}$ they follow by well-ordered induction under the termination measure "number of overlapping interval pairs".

Lemma 11. *(a) $\widehat{to\_equivs}$ computes a partition and (b) $\widehat{overlay}$ preserves partitions*

Lemma 12. *$\widehat{to\_equivs}$ and $\widehat{overlay}$ satisfy Properties 1, 2*

3.3   Product Lattices

We can combine partitions to form partitions over product lattices of either of the two traditional forms: Cartesian products and reduced/smash products.

The Cartesian Product Lattice. Given two potentially infinite lattices A, B and their product lattice $A \times B$ ordered componentwise, we can partition their atoms in a compositional manner. Assuming the product lattice $A \times B$ satisfies the requirements of Sect. 2, this implicitly means we work over a domain where for all $\ell_A \in A \setminus \{\bot\}$. $\gamma(\langle \ell_A, \bot \rangle) \neq \emptyset$ and for all $\ell_B \in B \setminus \{\bot\}$. $\gamma(\langle \bot, \ell_B \rangle) \neq \emptyset$ since either would mean that, e.g., $\gamma(\langle \ell_A, \bot \rangle) = \emptyset = \gamma(\bot)$ and thereby break the Galois insertion requirement. With this implicit assumption in place, the atoms of the product lattice must be of the shape $\langle a, \bot \rangle \in Atoms(A) \times B$ and $\langle \bot, b \rangle \in A \times Atoms(B)$. Given representations $\widehat{equiv}_A$ and $\widehat{equiv}_B$ partitioning A's and B's atoms, we can partition the atoms of $A \times B$ with a partition $\widehat{equiv}_A \times \widehat{equiv}_B$ where the first component partitions atoms in $Atoms(A) \times \{\bot\}$ and the second component partitions atoms in $\{\bot\} \times Atoms(B)$. Based on operations $\widehat{to\_equivs}_A$ and $\widehat{to\_equivs}_B$ we can therefore write $\widehat{to\_equivs}(\ell_A, \ell_B) = (\widehat{to\_equivs}_A(\ell_A), \widehat{to\_equivs}_B(\ell_B))$. For example, for a Cartesian product of intervals $\widehat{to\_equivs}([-1; 2], [0; 1])$ returns the partition $(([-\infty; -2], [-1; 2], [3; +\infty]), ([-\infty; -1], [0; 1], [2; +\infty]))$. Let $\overline{[a]}$ and $\overline{[b]}$ range over partitions of A's and B's atoms. We can also write $\widehat{overlay}$ compositionally: $\widehat{overlay}((\overline{[a]}, \overline{[b]}), (\overline{[a']}, \overline{[b']})) = (\widehat{overlay}_A(\overline{[a]}, \overline{[a']}), \widehat{overlay}_B(\overline{[b]}, \overline{[b']}))$.

The Reduced/smash Product Lattice. If for two lattices A and B, for all $\ell_A \in A \setminus \{\bot\}$. $\gamma(\langle \ell_A, \bot \rangle) = \emptyset$ and for all $\ell_B \in B \setminus \{\bot\}$. $\gamma(\langle \bot, \ell_B \rangle) = \emptyset$ we can instead consider the reduced/smash product: $A * B = \{\langle \bot, \bot \rangle\} \cup (A \setminus \{\bot\}) \times (B \setminus \{\bot\})$ where atoms are of the shape $\langle a, b \rangle \in Atoms(A) \times Atoms(B)$. Again we can partition the atoms of $A * B$ with a product $\widehat{equiv}_A \times \widehat{equiv}_B$ this time interpreting an equivalence class $([a], [b]) \in \widehat{equiv}_A \times \widehat{equiv}_B$ as all atoms (a', b') where $a' \in [a]$ and $b' \in [b]$. Despite the different interpretation, we define $\widehat{to\_equivs}$ and $\widehat{overlay}$ as in Cartesian products.

Coarser partitions are possible. For the reduced/smash product we have experimented with a functional partition $[Atoms(A)] \longrightarrow \widehat{equiv}_B$ maintaining individual partitions of B for each equivalence class of $Atoms(A)$. For example, for a interval pair literal $\langle [1; 1], [0; 2] \rangle$ the coarser functional partition will have only 5 equivalence classes (both the $[-\infty; 0]$ and $[2; +\infty]$ entries map to the partition $[-\infty; +\infty]$ and the atom partition for $[0; 2]$ at entry $[1; 1]$ has three entries) whereas the finer partition will have $3 \times 3 = 9$ equivalence classes. A coarser partition leads to fewer iterations in the algorithms and ultimately shorter, more readable regular expressions output to the end user.

For both products we summarize our partition results in the following lemmas.

Lemma 13. *If $\widehat{to\_equivs}_A$ and $\widehat{to\_equivs}_B$ computes partitions and $\widehat{overlay}_A$ and $\widehat{overlay}_B$ preserves partitions then (a) $\widehat{to\_equivs}_{A \times B}$ computes a partition, (b) $\widehat{overlay}_{A \times B}$ preserves partitions, (c) $\widehat{to\_equivs}_{A * B}$ computes a partition, and (d) $\widehat{overlay}_{A * B}$ preserves partitions*

Lemma 14. *If to_equivs_A and $\widehat{overlay}_A$ and to_equivs_B and $\widehat{overlay}_B$ satisfy Properties 1, 2 then (a) $to\_equivs_{A \times B}$ and $\widehat{overlay}_{A \times B}$ also satisfy Properties 1, 2 and (b) $to\_equivs_{A * B}$ and $\widehat{overlay}_{A * B}$ satisfy Properties 1, 2*

For presentational purposes we have stated the results in terms of a Cartesian pair and a reduced/smashed pair, but the results hold for a general Cartesian product $\Pi_i A_i$ and for a general reduced/smashed product $\Pi_i(A_i \backslash \{\bot\}) \cup \{\bot\}$.

4   An Example Language and Analysis

With the regular expression domain in place we are now in position to illustrate it with a static analysis. To this end we first study a concurrent, imperative programming language. Our starting point is a core imperative language structured into three syntactic categories of arithmetic expressions (e), Boolean expressions (b), and statements (s):

$$E \ni e ::= n \mid x \mid ? \mid e_1 + e_2 \mid e_1 - e_2$$
$$B \ni b ::= \mathtt{tt} \mid \mathtt{ff} \mid x_1 < x_2$$
$$S \ni s ::= \mathtt{skip} \mid x := e \mid s\,;s \mid \mathtt{if}\ b\ \mathtt{then}\ s\ \mathtt{else}\ s \mid \mathtt{while}\ b\ \mathtt{do}\ s\ \mathtt{end}$$
$$\ \mid s \oplus s \mid ch?x \mid ch!e \mid \mathtt{stop}$$
$$P \ni p ::= pid_1 : s_1 \parallel \ \ldots \ \parallel pid_n : s_n$$

For presentational purposes we keep the arithmetic and Boolean expressions minimal. The slightly non-standard arithmetic expression '?' non-deterministically evaluates to *any* integer. The statements of the core language have been extended with primitives for non-deterministic choice ($\oplus$), for reading and writing messages from/to a named channel ($ch?x$ and $ch!e$), and for terminating a process (stop). The two message passing primitives are synchronous. To build systems of communicating processes, we extend the language further with a syntactic category of programs (p), consisting of a sequence of named processes.

As an example, consider a server communicating with a client as illustrated in Fig. 9. The server and the client each keep track of a 'highscore'. The client may

```
spawn server() {                        spawn client() {
    highscore = 0;                          id = 0;
    while (true) {                          best = 0;
        choose {                            while (true) {
            { ask? cid                          ask! id;
              hsc! highscore; }                 hsc? best;
            | { report? new                     new = ?;
              if (highscore < new)              if (best < new)
                { highscore = new; } } } } }        { best = new;
                                                      report! best; } } }
```

Fig. 9. A server and client sharing a high score

query the server on the `ask`-channel and subsequently receive the server's current highscore on the `hsc`-channel. The client may also submit a new highscore to the server, using the `report`-channel. The example client performs an indefinite cycle consisting of a query followed by a subsequent response and a potential new highscore report. We can express this example as a program of our core process language.

$$\widehat{\mathcal{P}}[\![\mathtt{skip}^\ell]\!] = \lambda(\widehat{\rho}, f).(\widehat{\rho}, f)$$

$$\widehat{\mathcal{P}}[\![x :=^\ell e]\!] = \lambda(\widehat{\rho}, f).(\widehat{assign}(\widehat{\rho}, x, \widehat{\mathcal{A}}(e, \widehat{\rho})), f)$$

$$\widehat{\mathcal{P}}[\![s_1 ;^\ell s_2]\!] = \widehat{\mathcal{P}}[\![s_2]\!] \circ \widehat{\mathcal{P}}[\![s_1]\!]$$

$$\widehat{\mathcal{P}}[\![\mathtt{if}^\ell\ b\ \mathtt{then}\ s_1\ \mathtt{else}\ s_2]\!] = \lambda(\widehat{\rho}, f).\widehat{\mathcal{P}}[\![s_1]\!](\widehat{true}(b, \widehat{\rho}), f) \sqcup \widehat{\mathcal{P}}[\![s_2]\!](\widehat{false}(b, \widehat{\rho}), f)$$

$$\widehat{\mathcal{P}}[\![\mathtt{while}^\ell\ b\ \mathtt{do}\ s\ \mathtt{end}]\!] = \lambda(\widehat{\rho}, f).(\widehat{false}(b, \widehat{\rho}''), f'')$$

$$\text{where } (\widehat{\rho}'', f'') = \lim_i F^i(\widehat{\rho}, f) \text{ and } F(\widehat{\rho}', f') = (\widehat{\rho}', f') \triangledown \widehat{\mathcal{P}}[\![s]\!](\widehat{true}(b, \widehat{\rho}'), f')$$

$$\widehat{\mathcal{P}}[\![s_1 \oplus^\ell s_2]\!] = \lambda(\widehat{\rho}, f).\widehat{\mathcal{P}}[\![s_1]\!](\widehat{\rho}, f) \sqcup \widehat{\mathcal{P}}[\![s_2]\!](\widehat{\rho}, f)$$

$$\widehat{\mathcal{P}}[\![ch?^\ell x]\!] = \lambda(\widehat{\rho}, f). \bigsqcup_{\substack{[ch!v_a]\in\widehat{range}(f) \\ ch!v=project([ch!v_a]) \\ \widehat{\mathcal{D}}_{\widehat{repr}([ch!v_a])}(f)\not\sqsubseteq\emptyset}} (\widehat{assign}(\widehat{\rho}, x, v), \widehat{\mathcal{D}}_{\widehat{repr}([ch!v_a])}(f))$$

$$\widehat{\mathcal{P}}[\![ch!^\ell e]\!] = \lambda(\widehat{\rho}, f). \bigsqcup_{\substack{[ch?v_a]\in\widehat{overlay}(\widehat{range}(f),to\_equivs(ch?v')) \\ ch?v=project([ch?v_a]) \\ v\sqcap v'\neq\bot \\ \widehat{\mathcal{D}}_{\widehat{repr}([ch?v_a])}(f)\not\sqsubseteq\emptyset}} (\widehat{\rho}, \widehat{\mathcal{D}}_{\widehat{repr}([ch?v_a])}(f)) \text{ where } v' = \widehat{\mathcal{A}}(e, \widehat{\rho})$$

$$\widehat{\mathcal{P}}[\![\mathtt{stop}^\ell]\!] = \lambda(\widehat{\rho}, f).(\bot, f)$$

Fig. 10. Analysis of the process language: $\widehat{\mathcal{P}} : S \longrightarrow \widehat{Store} \times \widehat{R}_{\widehat{Ch(Val)}} \longrightarrow \widehat{Store} \times \widehat{R}_{\widehat{Ch(Val)}}$

We formulate in Fig. 10 a static analysis $\widehat{\mathcal{P}}$ which analyzes a process in isolation against an invariant for the context's communication. The analysis is formulated for a general abstract domain of values $\widehat{Val}$, e.g., intervals. To capture communication over a particular channel, we reuse an interval lattice (assuming the channels have been enumerated). This leads to a reduced product $Interval * \widehat{Val}$ for characterizing reads and an identical product for characterizing writes. We can then formulate a channel lattice for capturing both reads and writes: $\widehat{Ch(Val)} = (Interval * \widehat{Val}) \times (Interval * \widehat{Val})$. This product should not be reduced, as we do not wish to exclude processes that, e.g., only perform writes (with the read half of the channel domain being bottom). Finally we can plug the channel lattice into the regular expression domain: $\widehat{R}_{\widehat{Ch(Val)}}$. In the static analysis in Fig. 10, f (for future) ranges over this domain. Intuitively, $\widehat{\rho}$ over-approximates the store (as traditional), whereas f over-approximates the signals of the environment (it is *consumed* by the analysis). The sequential analysis furthermore relies on an auxiliary function $\widehat{\mathcal{A}}$ for analyzing arithmetic expressions and two filter functions $\widehat{true}$ and $\widehat{false}$ to pick up additional information from variable comparisons (their definitions are available in the full version of this paper). Finally, the auxiliary function $\widehat{assign}$ defined as $\widehat{assign}(\widehat{\rho}, x, v) = \widehat{\rho}[x \mapsto v]$ models the effect of an assignment.

In the two cases for network read and write we utilize the shorthand notation $[ch!v_a]$ and $[ch?v_a]$ to denote equivalence classes $[\langle(\perp, \perp), ([ch; ch], [v_a; v_a])\rangle]$ and $[\langle([ch; ch], [v_a; v_a]), (\perp, \perp)\rangle]$ over atom writes and atom reads in $\widehat{Ch}(\widehat{Val})$, respectively. Both of these cases utilize the Brzozowski derivative $\widehat{\mathcal{D}}$ of f to anticipate all possible writes and reads from the network environment. For example, if we analyze a read statement in?x in an abstract store $\widehat{\rho}$ and in a network environment described by in!$[1; 1000] \cdot r$ (for some $r \not\sqsubseteq \emptyset$) we first assume channel names have been numbered, e.g., mapping channel name 'in' to 0. For readability, we therefore write in!$[1; 1000] \cdot r$ instead of $\langle(\perp, \perp), ([0; 0], [1; 1000])\rangle \cdot r$ where the channel name in should be understood as 0 (which we can capture precisely with the intervals as $[0; 0]$) and where we similarly utilize the above shorthand notation. Now $\widehat{range}(\text{in}![1; 1000] \cdot r) = \widehat{range}(\text{in}![1; 1000]) = \widehat{to\_equivs}(\text{in}![1; 1000])$ returns a partition that includes the equivalence class $[\text{in}![1; 1000]]$. Furthermore $\widehat{project}([\text{in}![1; 1000]]) = \text{in}![1; 1000]$ and $\widehat{repr}([\text{in}![1; 1000]])$ returns an atom in this equivalence class, e.g., in!$[1; 1]$ such that $\widehat{\mathcal{D}}_{\text{in}![1;1]}([\text{in}![1; 1000]] \cdot r) = \epsilon \cdot r =_{ACI+} r \not\sqsubseteq \emptyset$. The analysis therefore includes $(\widehat{assign}(\widehat{\rho}, \text{x}, [1; 1000]), r) = (\widehat{\rho}[\text{x} \mapsto [1; 1000]], r)$ as an approximate post-condition for the read statement. When the analysis attempts to derive wrt. atoms from other equivalence classes, e.g., the atom in!$[1001; 1001]$ we get $\widehat{\mathcal{D}}_{\text{in}![1001;1001]}([0![1; 1000]] \cdot r) = \emptyset \cdot r =_{ACI+} \emptyset$ and such contributions are therefore disregarded. As usual, the analysis can incur some information loss, e.g., if each branch of a conditional statement contains a read into the same variable. These values will then be over-approximated by the join of the underlying value domain.

For the interval domain of values, we stick to the traditional widening operator [7]. For the abstract stores, we perform a traditional pointwise lift $\dot{\nabla}$ of the interval widening for each store entry. For regular expressions, the situation is more interesting: In the search for a while-loop invariant, new futures can only appear as derivatives of the loop's initial future. Since there are only a finite number of these up to ACI of $+$, an upward Kleene iteration is bounded and hence does not require widening. The resulting widening operator over analysis pairs can therefore be expressed as follows: $(\widehat{\rho}_1, f_1) \nabla (\widehat{\rho}_2, f_2) = (\widehat{\rho}_1 \dot{\nabla} \widehat{\rho}_2, f_1 + f_2)$.

For example, under the worst-case assumption of *any* context communication ($\top^*$), the analysis will determine the following server invariant for the highscore example, expressed as an abstract store and a regular expression over channel-labeled intervals: $[\text{cid} \mapsto [-\infty; +\infty]; \text{highscore} \mapsto [0; +\infty]; \text{new} \mapsto [-\infty; +\infty]]$ and $\top^*$. When analyzed under the erroneous policy of receiving (non-negative payload) messages in the wrong order $(\text{ask}![0; +\infty] + \text{report}![0; +\infty] \cdot \text{hsc}?[-\infty; +\infty])^*$

the analysis infers the following stronger invariant for the server: [highscore ↦ [0; +∞]; new ↦ [0; +∞]] and (ask![0; +∞]+report![0; +∞]·hsc?[−∞; +∞])* and that hsc! highscore in line number 6 cannot execute successfully.

5 Implementation

We have implemented a prototype of the analysis in OCaml. Currently the prototype spans approximately 5000 lines of code. Each lattice (intervals, abstract stores, ...) is implemented as a separate module, with suitable parameterization using functors, e.g., for the generic regular expression domain. The partition of lattice atoms is implemented by requiring that a parameter lattice A implements to_equivs and $overlay$ with signatures as listed in Sect. 3. To gain confidence in the implementation, we have furthermore performed randomized, property-based testing (also known as 'quickchecking') of the prototype. The QuickCheck code takes an additional ∼ 650 lines of code. We quickchecked the individual lattices for typical lattice properties (partial order properties, associativity and commutivity of join and meet, etc.) and the lattice operations ($\widehat{\mathcal{D}}$, ·, etc.) for monotonicity, using the approach of Midtgaard and Møller [24]. This approach was fruitful in designing and testing the suggested ordering algorithm (and its implementation) and in our implementations of to_equivs and $overlay$. To increase our confidence in the suggested widening operator, we furthermore extended the domain-specific language of Midtgaard and Møller [24] with the ability to test whether lattice-functions are increasing, when applied to arbitrarily generated input. We then used this ability to test all involved widening operators. QuickCheck immediately found a bug in an earlier version of our widening algorithm, which was not increasing in the second argument on the input $(\epsilon, (\top^* \cdot odd \cdot odd)$ & $\complement\epsilon)$ (here again listed over the parity domain). The corresponding automaton computed for this counterexample turns out to have a strongly connected component, which led us to find and patch an early erroneous attempt to identify and remove explicit error states.

With the domain and analysis implemented and tested, we can apply it to the example program from Sect. 4 and we obtain the reported results. We have also analyzed a number of additional example programs, including several from the literature: two CSP examples from Cousot and Cousot [8], a simple math server adapted from Vasconcelos, Gay, and Ravara [28], and a simple authentication protocol from Zafiropulo et al. [31]. For each of these examples, the analysis prototype completes in less than 0.003 s on a lightly loaded laptop with a 2.8 Ghz Intel Core i5 processor and 8 GB RAM. While this evaluation is encouraging it is also preliminary. We leave a proper empirical evaluation of the approach for future work. The source code of the prototype, the corresponding QuickCheck code, and our examples are available as downloadable artifacts.[5] Our proofs are available in the full version of this paper.[6]

---

[5] https://github.com/jmid/regexpanalyser.

[6] http://janmidtgaard.dk/papers/Midtgaard-Nielson-Nielson:SAS16-full.pdf.

6   Related Work

Initially Cousot and Cousot developed a static analysis for Hoare's Communicating Sequential Processes (CSP) [8]. Our example analysis also works for a CSP-like language, but differs in the means to capture communication, where we have opted for lattice-valued regular expressions. A line of work has since developed static analyses for predicting the *communication topology* of mobile calculi. For example, Venet [30] developed a static analysis framework for π-calculus and Rydhof Hansen et al. [16] develop a control-flow analysis and an occurrence counting analysis for mobile ambients. Whereas the communication topology is apparent from the program text of our process programs, we instead focus on analyzing the *order* and the *content* of such communication by means of lattice-valued regular expressions.

Historically, the Communicating Finite State Machines (CFSMs) [5] have been used to model and analyze properties of protocols. CFSMs express a distributed computation as a set of finite state automata that communicate via (buffered) message passing over channels. We refer to Le Gall, Jeannet, and Jéron [13] for an overview of (semi-)algorithms and decidability results within CFSMs. Le Gall, Jeannet, and Jéron [13] themselves developed a static analysis for analyzing the communication patterns of FIFO-queue models in CFSMs. In a follow-up paper, Le Gall and Jeannet [12] developed the abstract domain of *lattice automata* (parameterized by an atomic value lattice), thereby lifting a previous restriction to finite lattices. Our work differs from Le Gall and Jeannet's in that it starts from the language-centric, lattice-valued regular expressions, as opposed to the decision-centric, lattice-valued finite automata (one can however translate one formalism to the other). The two developments share a common dependency on atomistic lattices:[7] Lattice automata require atoms (and partitions over these) as its labels, whereas our co-inductive ordering algorithm relies on Brzozowski derivatives wrt. atoms (and partitions over these). We see advantages in building on Brzozowski derivatives: (a) we can succinctly express both intersection (meet) and complement symbolically in the domain, (b) we immediately inherit a "one-step normal form" from the underlying equation (Theorem 1), whereas Le Gall and Jeannet develop a class of 'normalized lattice automata', and (c) our ordering algorithm lazily explores the potentially exponential space of derivatives (states) and bails early upon discovering a mismatch.

Our work has parallels to previous work by Lesens, Halbwachs, and Raymond (LHR) on inferring *network invariants* for a linear network of synchronously communicating processes [20]. Similar to us, they use a regular language to capture network communication. They furthermore allow *network observers* to monitor network communication and emit disjoint *alarms* if a desired property is not satisfied. They primarily consider a greatest fixed point expressing satisfiability of a desired network invariant, which they under-approximate by an analysis over a regular domain using a *dual widening* operator, that starts above and

---

[7] These are however referred to as 'atomic lattices' contradicting standard terminology [10,15].

finishes below the greatest fixed point. Our work differs in that LHR abstract away from the concrete syntax of processes whereas we instead attempt to lift existing analysis approaches. As a consequence, LHR target a fixed communication topology, whereas in our case, which process that reads another process' output depend on their inner workings. As pointed out by LHR, widening operators have to balance convergence speed and precision. They discuss possible design choices and settle on a (dual) operator that makes an extreme tradeoff, by being very precise but sacrificing guaranteed convergence. On the contrary we opt for a convergence guarantee at the cost of precision. On the other hand, their *delayed widening* technique to further improve precision, is likely to also improve our present widening further. Whereas our widening operator is less precise, we believe LHR's automata with powersets of signals fits immediately our atomistic Galois insertion condition. Finally LHR's approach depends on determinising automata which incurs a worst case exponential blow up. They therefore seek to avoid such determinization in future work. Since lattice-valued regular expressions require less determinization (writing out the equations in steps 2,3 of Fig. 6 before collapsing them in step 5 requires determinization), they represent a step in that direction.

Our process analysis approach is inspired by an approach of Logozzo [21] for analyzing classes of object-oriented programs. Logozzo devises a modular analysis of class invariants using contexts approximated by a lattice-valued regular expression domain to capture calling policies. Like us, Logozzo builds on a language inclusion ordering but he does not develop an algorithm for computing it. Before developing the current widening operator we experimented with his structural widening operator based on symbolic pattern matching of two given regular expressions. QuickCheck found an issue with the definition: The original definition [21, Fig. 3] allows $(odd \cdot even) \triangledown_r odd = (odd \triangledown_r odd) \cdot even = odd \cdot even$ which is not partially ordered with respect to its second argument under a language inclusion ordering.

Owens, Reppy, and Turon [25] report on using derivatives over extended regular expressions (EREs) for building a scanner generator. In doing so, they revisit Brzozowski's original constructions in a functional programming context. To handle large alphabets such as Unicode, they extend EREs (conservatively) with *character sets*, allowing a subset of characters of the input alphabet as letters of their regular expressions. From our point of view, the extension can be seen as EREs with characters over a powerset lattice. Overall their experiments show that a well-engineered scanner generator will explore only a fraction of all possible derivatives, and in many cases compute the minimal automaton. Our implementation is inspired by that of Owens, Reppy, and Turon [25], in that it uses (a) an internal syntax tree representation that maps ACI-equivalent regular expressions to the same structure and (b) an interface of *smart constructors*, e.g., to perform simplifying reductions.

A line of work has concerned axiomatizing equivalence (and containment) of regular expressions (REs) and of the more general Kleene algebras [14,17,19,27]. We refer to Henglein and Nielsen [17] for a historical account of such developments. Grabmayer [14] gave a co-inductive axiomatization of RE equivalence based on Brzozowski derivatives and connects it to an earlier axiomatization of Salomaa [27]. In particular, our *nullable* function corresponds to Grabmayer's o-function, and his COMP/FIX proof system rule concludes that two REs E and F are equivalent if $o(E) = o(F)$ and if all derivatives $\mathcal{D}_a(E) = \mathcal{D}_a(F)$ are equivalent much like our co-inductive leq_test for deciding containment checks for *nullable* and queries all derivatives for containment. In fact, we can turn Fig. 5 into an equivalence algorithm akin to Grabmayer [14] by simply replacing the implication in line number 6 with if $nullable(r_1) \iff nullable(r_2)$. Kozen's axiomatization of Kleene algebras and his RE completeness proof of these [19] have a number of parallels to the current work: (a) the axiomatization contains a conditional inclusion axiom similar to Arden's lemma, (b) our k-limited partitioning $\approx_k^{col_r}$ can be viewed as an approximation of Kozen's *Myhill-Nerode equivalence relation* that algebraically expresses state minimization, and (c) the completeness proof involves solving matrices over REs (which themselves form a Kleene algebra) in a manner reminiscent of Brzozowski's translation scheme. To synthesize a regular expression from the collapsed equations we could alternatively have used Kozen's approach that partitions the matrix into sub-matrices with square sub-matrices on the diagonal and recursively solves these. Henglein and Nielsen [17] themselves gave a co-inductive axiomatization of RE containment, building on strong connections to type inhabitation and sub-typing.

Our work also has parallels to Concurrent Kleene Algebra (CKA) [18]. In particular, CKA is based on a set-of-traces ordering—a language inclusion ordering—in which a set of possible traces describes program event histories, akin to our example analysis. Furthermore, CKA's extension over Kleene algebra to include a parallelism operator could be a viable path forward to extend the proposed example analysis from a single process in a network environment to support arbitrary process combinations.

Within model checking over timed automata [1], there are parallels between partitioning clock interpretations over timed transition tables into regions and our partitioning of lattice atoms into equivalence classes. The two developments however differ in that timed Büchi and Muller automata naturally target liveness properties (by their ability to recognize ω-regular languages), whereas we for now target safety properties with lattice-valued regular expressions. The extension to parametric timed automata [2] allow for enriching the expressible relations on transitions. In the current framework this would correspond to instantiating the lattice-valued regular expressions with a relational abstract domain. In future work we would like to investigate the degree to which such instantiations are possible.

7   Conclusion

We have developed lattice-valued regular expressions as an abstract domain for static analysis including a co-inductive ordering algorithm and a widening operator. As an illustration of the parametric domain we have presented a static analysis of communication properties of a message-passing process program against a given network communication policy. Lattice-valued regular expressions constitute an intuitive and well-known formalism for expressing such policies. We plan to reuse the domain for further message-passing analysis in the future.

References

1. Alur, R., Dill, D.L.: A theory of timed automata. TCS **126**(2), 183–235 (1994)
2. Alur, R., Henzinger, T.A., Vardi, M.Y.: Parametric real-time reasoning. In: STOC 1993, pp. 592–601 (1993)
3. Arden, D.N.: Delayed-logic and finite-state machines. In: 2nd Annual Symposium on Switching Circuit Theory and Logical Design, pp. 133–151. IEEE Computer Society (1961)
4. Bourdoncle, F.: Abstract debugging of higher-order imperative languages. In: PLDI 1993, pp. 46–55 (1993)
5. Brand, D., Zafiropulo, P.: On communicating finite state machines. JACM **30**, 323–342 (1983)
6. Brzozowski, J.A.: Derivatives of regular expressions. JACM **11**(4), 481–494 (1964)
7. Cousot, P., Cousot, R.: Static determination of dynamic properties of programs. In: ISOP 1976, pp. 106–130. Dunod, Paris (1976)
8. Cousot, P., Cousot, R.: Semantic analysis of communicating sequential processes. In: de Bakker, J., van Leeuwen, J. (eds.) ICALP 1980. LNCS, vol. 85, pp. 119–133. Springer, Heidelberg (1980)
9. Cousot, P., Cousot, R.: Abstract interpretation and application to logic programs. J. Logic Program. **13**(2–3), 103–179 (1992)
10. Davey, B.A., Priestley, H.A.: Introduction to Lattices and Order, 2nd edn. Cambridge University Press, Cambridge (2002)
11. Feret, J.: Abstract interpretation-based static analysis of mobile ambients. In: Cousot, P. (ed.) SAS 2001. LNCS, vol. 2126, pp. 412–430. Springer, Heidelberg (2001)
12. Le Gall, T., Jeannet, B.: Lattice automata: a representation for languages on infinite alphabets, and some applications to verification. In: Riis Nielson, H., Filé, G. (eds.) SAS 2007. LNCS, vol. 4634, pp. 52–68. Springer, Heidelberg (2007)
13. Le Gall, T., Jeannet, B., Jéron, T.: Verification of communication protocols using abstract interpretation of FIFO queues. In: Johnson, M., Vene, V. (eds.) AMAST 2006. LNCS, vol. 4019, pp. 204–219. Springer, Heidelberg (2006)
14. Grabmayer, C.: Using proofs by coinduction to find "Traditional" proofs. In: Fiadeiro, J.L., Harman, N.A., Roggenbach, M., Rutten, J. (eds.) CALCO 2005. LNCS, vol. 3629, pp. 175–193. Springer, Heidelberg (2005)
15. Grätzer, G.: General Lattice Theory. Academic Press, New York (1978)
16. Rydhof Hansen, R., Jensen, J.G., Nielson, F., Riis Nielson, H.: Abstract interpretation of mobile ambients. In: Cortesi, A., Filé, G. (eds.) SAS 1999. LNCS, vol. 1694, pp. 134–148. Springer, Heidelberg (1999)
17. Henglein, F., Nielsen, L.: Regular expression containment: coinductive axiomatization and computational interpretation. In: POPL 2011, pp. 385–398 (2011)

18. Hoare, T., van Staden, S., Möller, B., Struth, G., Villard, J., Zhu, H., O'Hearn, P.: Developments in concurrent Kleene Algebra. In: Höfner, P., Jipsen, P., Kahl, W., Müller, M.E. (eds.) RAMiCS 2014. LNCS, vol. 8428, pp. 1–18. Springer, Heidelberg (2014)

19. Kozen, D.: A completeness theorem for Kleene algebras and the algebra of regular events. Inf. Comput. **110**(2), 366–390 (1994)

20. Lesens, D., Halbwachs, N., Raymond, P.: Automatic verification of parameterized linear networks of processes. In: POPL 1997, pp. 346–357 (1997)

21. Logozzo, F.: Separate compositional analysis of class-based object-oriented languages. In: Rattray, C., Maharaj, S., Shankland, C. (eds.) AMAST 2004. LNCS, vol. 3116, pp. 334–348. Springer, Heidelberg (2004)

22. Martin, J.C.: Introduction to Languages and the Theory of Computation. McGraw-Hill, New York (1997)

23. Mauborgne, L.: Tree schemata and fair termination. In: Palsberg, J. (ed.) SAS 2000. LNCS, vol. 1824, pp. 302–319. Springer, Heidelberg (2000)

24. Midtgaard, J., Møller, A.: Quickchecking static analysis properties. In: ICST 2015, pp. 1–10. IEEE Computer Society (2015)

25. Owens, S., Reppy, J., Turon, A.: Regular-expression derivatives re-examined. J. Funct. Program. **19**(2), 173–190 (2009)

26. Rosu, G., Viswanathan, M.: Testing extended regular language membership incrementally by rewriting. In: Nieuwenhuis, R. (ed.) RTA 2003. LNCS, vol. 2706, pp. 499–514. Springer, Heidelberg (2003)

27. Salomaa, A.: Two complete axiom systems for the algebra of regular events. JACM **13**(1), 158–169 (1966)

28. Vasconcelos, V.T., Gay, S., Ravara, A.: Typechecking a multithreaded functional language with session types. TCS **368**(1–2), 64–87 (2006)

29. Venet, A.: Abstract cofibered domains: application to the alias analysis of untyped programs. In: Cousot, R., Schmidt, D.A. (eds.) SAS 1996. LNCS, vol. 1145, pp. 366–382. Springer, Heidelberg (1996)

30. Venet, A.: Automatic determination of communication topologies in mobile systems. In: Levi, G. (ed.) SAS 1998. LNCS, vol. 1503, pp. 152–167. Springer, Heidelberg (1998)

31. Zafiropulo, P., West, C.H., Rudin, H., Cowan, D.D., Brand, D.: Towards analyzing and synthesizing protocols. IEEE Trans. Commun. **Com–28**(4), 651–661 (1980)

Cell Morphing: From Array Programs to Array-Free Horn Clauses

David Monniaux[1,2] and Laure Gonnord[3(✉)]

[1] University of Grenoble Alpes, VERIMAG, 38000 Grenoble, France
[2] CNRS, VERIMAG, 38000 Grenoble, France
david.monniaux@imag.fr
[3] University of Lyon, LIP (UMR CNRS/ENS Lyon/UCB Lyon1/Inria),
69000 Lyon, France
laure.gonnord@ens-lyon.fr

Abstract. Automatically verifying safety properties of programs is hard. Many approaches exist for verifying programs operating on Boolean and integer values (e.g. abstract interpretation, counterexample-guided abstraction refinement using interpolants), but transposing them to array properties has been fraught with difficulties. Our work addresses that issue with a powerful and flexible abstraction that morphes concrete array cells into a finite set of abstract ones. This abstraction is parametric both in precision and in the back-end analysis used.

From our programs with arrays, we generate nonlinear Horn clauses over scalar variables only, in a common format with clear and unambiguous logical semantics, for which there exist several solvers. We thus avoid the use of solvers operating over arrays, which are still very immature.

Experiments with our prototype VAPHOR show that this approach can prove automatically and without user annotations the functional correctness of several classical examples, including *selection sort, bubble sort, insertion sort*, as well as examples from literature on array analysis.

1 Introduction

In this article, we consider programs operating over arrays, or, more generally, *maps* from an index type to a value type (in the following, we shall use "array" and "map" interchangeably). Such programs contain read (e.g. $v := a[i]$) and write ($a[i] := v$) operations over arrays, as well as "scalar" operations.[1] We wish to fully automatically verify properties on such programs; e.g. that a sorting algorithm outputs a sorted permutation of its input.

The research leading to these results has received funding from the European Research Council under the European Union's Seventh Framework Programme (FP/2007-2013) / ERC Grant Agreement nr. 306595 "STATOR".

[1] In the following, we shall lump as "scalar" operations all operations not involving the array under consideration, e.g. $i := i + 1$. Any data types (integers, strings etc.) are supported if supported by the back-end solver.

X. Rival (Ed.): SAS 2016, LNCS 9837, pp. 361–382, 2016.
DOI: 10.1007/978-3-662-53413-7_18

Universally Quantified Properties. Very often, desirable properties over arrays are universally quantified; e.g. sortedness may be expressed as $\forall k_1, k_2 \; k_1 < k_2 \implies a[k_1] \leq a[k_2]$. However, formulas with universal quantification and linear arithmetic over integers and at least one predicate symbol (a predicate being a function to the Booleans) form an undecidable class [20], of which some decidable subclasses have however been identified [8]. There is therefore no general algorithm for checking that such invariants hold, let alone inferring them. Yet, there have been several approaches proposed to infer such invariants (see Sect. 7).

We here propose a method for inferring such universally quantified invariants, given a specification on the output of the program. This being undecidable, this approach may fail to terminate in the general case, or may return "unknown". Experiments however show that our approach can successfully and automatically verify nontrivial properties (e.g. the output from selection sort is sorted and is a permutation of the input).

Our key insight is that if there is a proof of safety of an array-manipulating program, it is likely that there exists a proof that can be expressed with simple steps over properties relating only a small number N of (parametric) array cells, called "distinguished cells". For instance, all the sorting algorithms we tried can be proved correct with $N = 2$, and simple array manipulations (copying, reversing. . .) with $N = 1$.

Horn Clauses. We convert the verification problem to Horn clauses, a common format for program verification problems [36] supported by a number of tools. Usual conversions [18] map variables and operations from the program to variables of the same type and the same operations in the Horn clause problem:[2] an integer is mapped to an integer, an array to an array, etc. If arrays are not supported by the back-end analysis, they may be abstracted away (reads replaced by nondeterministic choices, writes discarded) at the expense of precision. In contrast, our approach abstracts programs much less violently, with tunable precision, even though the result is still a Horn clause problem without arrays. Section 3 explains how many properties (e.g. initialization) can be proved using one "distinguished cell" ($N = 1$), Sect. 4 explains how properties such as sortedness can be proved using two cells; completely discarding arrays corresponds to using zero of them.

An interesting characteristic of the Horn clauses we produce is that they are nonlinear[3], even though a straightforward translation of the semantics of a control-flow graph into Hoare triples expressed as clauses yields a linear system (whose unfoldings correspond to abstract execution traces). If a final property to prove (e.g. "all values are 0") queries one cell position, this query may morph, by

---

[2] With the exception of pointers and references, which need special handling and may be internally converted to array accesses.

[3] A nonlinear clause is of the form $P_1(\ldots) \wedge P_2(\ldots) \wedge \cdots \wedge P_n(\ldots) \wedge$ *arithmetic condition* $\implies Q(\ldots)$, with several antecedent predicates $P_1, P_2, \ldots$. Unfolding such rules yields a tree. In contrast a linear rule $P(\ldots) \wedge$ *arithmetic condition* $\implies Q(\ldots)$ has only one antecedent predicate, and unfolding a system of such rules yields a linear chain.

the backward unfolding of the clauses, into a tree of queries at other locations, in contrast to some earlier approaches [31].

We illustrate this approach with automated proofs of several examples from the literature: we apply Sects. 3, 4 or 5 to obtain a system of Horn clauses without arrays. This system is then fed to the Z3, ELDARICA or SPACER solver, which produces a model of this system, meaning that the postcondition (e.g. sortedness or multiset of the output equal to that of the input) truly holds.[4]

Previous approaches [31] using "distinguished cells" amounted (even though not described as such) to linear Horn rules; on contrast, our abstract semantics uses non-linear Horn rules, which leads to higher precision (Sect. 7.1).

Contributions. Our main contribution is a system of rules for transforming the atomic program statements in a program operating over arrays or maps, as well as (optionally) the universally quantified postcondition to prove, into a system of non-linear Horn clauses over scalar variables only. The precision of this transformation is tunable using a Galois connection parameterized by the number of "distinguished cells"; e.g. properties such as sortedness need two distinguished cells (Sect. 4) while simpler properties need only one (Sect. 3). Statements operating over non-arrays variables are mapped (almost) identically to their concrete semantics. This system over-approximates the behavior of the program. A solution of that system can be mapped to inductive invariants over the original programs, including universal properties over arrays.

A second contribution, based on the first, is a system of rules that also keeps track of array/map contents (Sect. 5) as a multiset. This system is suitable for showing content properties, e.g. that the output of a sorting algorithm is a permutation of the input, even though the sequence of operations is not directly a sequence of swaps.

We implemented our approach and benchmarked it over several classical examples of array algorithms (Sect. 6), comparing it favorably to other tools.

2   Program Verification as Solving Horn Clauses

A classical approach to program analysis is to consider a program as a control-flow graph and to attach to each vertex p_i (control point) an *inductive invariant* I_i: a set of possible values $\mathbf{x}$ of the program variables (and memory stack and heap, as needed) so that (i) the set associated to the initial control point p_{i_0} contains the possible initialization values S_{i_0} (ii) for each edge $p_i \rightarrow_c p_j$ (c for *concrete*), the set I_j associated to the target control point p_j should include all the states reachable from the states in the set I_i associated to the source control point p_i according to the transition relation $\tau_{i,j}$ of the edge. Inductiveness is thus defined by *Horn clauses*[5]:

$$\forall \mathbf{x}, \; S_{i_0}(\mathbf{x}) \implies I_{i_0}(\mathbf{x}) \tag{1}$$

$$\forall \mathbf{x}, \mathbf{x}', \; I_i(\mathbf{x}) \wedge \tau_{i,j}(\mathbf{x}, \mathbf{x}') \implies I_j(\mathbf{x}') \tag{2}$$

---

[4] Z3 and ELDARICA can also occasionally directly solve Horn clauses over arrays; we also compare to that.

[5] Classically, we denote the sets using predicates: $I_{i_0}(\mathbf{x})$ means $\mathbf{x} \in I_{i_0}$.

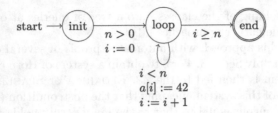

Fig. 1. Compact control-flow graph for Program 1

For proving safety properties, in addition to inductiveness, one requires that error locations $p_{e_1}, \ldots, p_{e_n}$ are proved to be unreachable (the associated set of states is empty): this amounts to Horn clauses implying false: $\forall \mathbf{x}, I_{e_i}(\mathbf{x}) \Rightarrow \bot$.

Various tools can solve such systems of Horn clauses, that is, can synthesize suitable predicates I_i, which constitute *inductive invariants*. In this article, we tried Z3[6] with the PDR fixed point solver [22], Z3 with the SPACER solver [24,25],[7] and ELDARICA [35].[8] Since program verification is undecidable, such tools, in general, may fail to terminate, or may return "unknown".

For the sake of simplicity, we shall consider, in this article, that all integer variables in programs are mathematical integers ($\mathbb{Z}$) as opposed to machine integers[9] and that arrays are infinite. Again, it is easy to modify our semantics to include systematic array bound checks, jumps to error conditions, etc.

In examples, instead of writing I_{stmt} for the name of the predicate (inductive invariant) at statement *stmt*, we shall write *stmt* directly, for readability's sake: thus we write e.g. *loop* for a predicate at the head of a loop. Furthermore, for readability, we shall sometimes coalesce several successive statements into one.

Example 1 (Motivating example). Consider the program:

```
void array_fill1(int n, int a[n]) {
    for(int i=0; i<n; i++) a[i]=42;
    /* assert ∀0 ≤ k < n, a[k] = 42 */
}
```

We would like to prove that this program truly fills array a[] with value 42. The flat encoding into Horn clauses assigns a predicate (set of states) to each of the control nodes (Fig. 1), and turns each transition into a Horn rule with variables ranging in $Arr(A, B)$, the type of arrays of B indexed by A [26, Chap. 7]:

$$\forall n \in \mathbb{Z} \ \forall a \in Arr(\mathbb{Z}, \mathbb{Z}) \ n > 0 \implies loop(n, 0, a) \quad (3)$$

$$\forall n, i \in \mathbb{Z} \ \forall a \in Arr(\mathbb{Z}, \mathbb{Z}) \ i < n \land loop(n, i, a) \implies loop(n, i + 1, store(a, i, 42)) \quad (4)$$

---

[6] https://github.com/Z3Prover hash 7f6ef0b6c0813f2e9e8f993d45722c0e5b99e152; due to various problems we preferred not to use results from later versions.

[7] https://bitbucket.org/spacer/code hash 7e1f9af01b796750d9097b331bb66b752ea0ee3c.

[8] https://github.com/uuverifiers/eldarica/releases/tag/v1.1-rc.

[9] A classical approach is to add overflow checks to the intermediate representation of programs in order to be able to express their semantics with mathematical integers even though they operate over machine integers.

$$\forall n, i \in \mathbb{Z} \; \forall a \in Arr\,(\mathbb{Z}, \mathbb{Z}) \;\; i \geq n \wedge loop(n, i, a) \implies end(n, i, a) \quad (5)$$

$$\forall x, n, i \in \mathbb{Z} \; \forall a \in Arr\,(\mathbb{Z}, \mathbb{Z}) \;\; 0 \leq x < n \wedge end(n, i, a) \implies select(a, x) = 42 \quad (6)$$

where $store(a, i, v)$ is array a where the value at index i has been replaced by v and $select(a, x)$ denotes $a[x]$.

None of the tools we have tried (Z3, SPACER, ELDARICA) has been able to solve this system, presumably because they cannot infer universally quantified invariants over arrays.[10] Indeed, here the loop invariant needed is

$$0 \leq i \leq n \wedge (\forall k \; 0 \leq k < i \implies a[k] = 42) \quad (7)$$

While $0 \leq i \leq n$ is inferred by a variety of approaches, the rest is tougher. We shall also see (Example 6) that a slight alteration of this example also prevents some earlier abstraction approaches from checking the desired property.

Most software model checkers attempt constructing invariants from *Craig interpolants* obtained from refutations [9] of the accessibility of error states in local [22] or global [29] unfoldings of the problem. However, interpolation over array properties is difficult, especially since the goal is not to provide any interpolant, but interpolants that generalize well to invariants [1,2]. This article instead introduces a way to derive universally quantified invariants from the analysis of a system of Horn clauses on scalar variables (without array variables).

3 Getting Did of the Arrays

To use the power of Horn solvers, we soundly abstract problems with arrays to problems without arrays. In the Horn clauses for Example 1, we attached to each program point p_ℓ a predicate I_ℓ over $\mathbb{Z} \times \mathbb{Z} \times Arr\,(\mathbb{Z}, \mathbb{Z})$ when the program variables are two integers i, n and one integer-value, integer-indexed array a.[11] In any solution of the system of clauses, if the valuation (i, n, a) is reachable at program point p_ℓ, then $I_\ell(i, n, a)$ holds. Instead, in the case of Example 1, we will consider a predicate $I_\ell^\sharp$ over $\mathbb{Z} \times \mathbb{Z} \times \mathbb{Z} \times \mathbb{Z}$ (the array *key* $\rightarrow$ *value* has been replaced by a pair $(key, value)$) such that $I_\ell^\sharp(i, n, k, a_k)$[12] holds for each reachable state (i, n, a) satisfying $a[k] = a_k$. This is the same Galois connection [11] as some earlier works [31] [13, Sect. 2.1]; yet, as we shall see, our abstract transformers are more precise.

Definition 1. *The "one distinguished cell" abstraction of $I \subseteq \chi \times Arr\,(\iota, \beta)$ is $\alpha(I) = \{(\mathbf{x}, i, a[i]) \mid \mathbf{x} \in \chi, i \in \iota\}$. The concretization of $I^\sharp \subseteq \chi \times (\iota \times \beta)$ is $\gamma(I^\sharp) = \{(\mathbf{x}, a) \mid \forall i \in \iota \; (\mathbf{x}, i, a[i]) \in I^\sharp\}$.*

Theorem 1. $\mathcal{P}\,(\chi \times Arr\,(\iota, \beta)) \xrightleftharpoons[\alpha]{\gamma} \mathcal{P}\,(\chi \times (\iota \times \beta))$ *is a Galois connection.*

---

[10] Some of these tools can however infer some simpler array invariants.

[11] For instance, $I_{loop} = loop(n, i, a)$, $I_{end} = end(n, i, a)$.

[12] also denoted by $I_\ell^\sharp((i, n), (k, a_k))$ for sake of readability.

To provide the abstract transformers, we will suppose in the sequel that any statement in the program (*control flow graph*) will be: (i) either an array read to a fresh variable, v=a[i]; in C syntax, $v := a[i]$ in pseudo-code; the variables of the program are $(\mathbf{x}, i, v)$ where $\mathbf{x}$ is a vector of arbitrarily many variables; (ii) either an array write, a[i]=v; (where v and i are variables) in C syntax, $a[i] := v$ in pseudo-code; the variables of the program are $(\mathbf{x}, i, v)$ before and after the statement; (iii) or a scalar operation, including assignments and guards over scalar variables. More complex statements can be transformed to a sequence of such statements, by introducing temporary variables if needed: for instance, $a[i] := a[j]$ is transformed into $temp := a[j]$; $a[i] := temp$.

Definition 2 (Read statement). *Let* v *be a variable of type* β, i *be a variable of type* ι, *and* a *be an array of values of type* β *with an index of type* ι. *Let* $\mathbf{x}$ *be the other program variables, taken in* χ. *The concrete "next state" relation for the read statement* v=a[i]; *between locations* p_1 *and* p_2 *is* $(\mathbf{x}, i, v, a) \rightarrow_c (\mathbf{x}, i, a[i], a)$.

Its forward abstract semantics is encoded into two Horn clauses:

$$\forall \mathbf{x} \in \chi \ \forall i \in \iota \ \forall v, a_i \in \beta \ \forall k \in \iota \ \forall a_k \in \beta$$
$$k \neq i \wedge I_1^\sharp((\mathbf{x}, i, v), (k, a_k)) \wedge I_1^\sharp((\mathbf{x}, i, v), (i, a_i)) \implies I_2^\sharp((\mathbf{x}, i, a_i), (k, a_k)) \tag{8}$$

$$\forall \mathbf{x} \in \chi \ \forall i \in \iota \ \forall v, a_i \in \beta \ \forall k \in \iota \ \forall a_k \in \beta$$
$$I_1^\sharp((\mathbf{x}, i, v), (i, a_i)) \implies I_2^\sharp((\mathbf{x}, i, a_i), (i, a_i)) \tag{9}$$

The tuple (k, a_k) now represents a "distinguished cell". While rule 9 is straightforward (a_i is assigned to the variable v), the nonlinear rule 8 may be more difficult to comprehend. The intuition is that, to have both $a_i = a[i]$ and $a_k = a[k]$ at the read instruction with a given valuation $(\mathbf{x}, i)$ of the other variables, both $a_i = a[i]$ and $a_k = a[k]$ had to be reachable with the same valuation.

Remark 1. We use two separate rules for $k = i$ and $k \neq i$ for better precision. A single rule $I_1^\sharp((\mathbf{x}, i, v), (k, a_k)) \wedge I_1^\sharp((\mathbf{x}, i, v), (i, a_i)) \implies I_2^\sharp((\mathbf{x}, i, a_i), (k, a_k))$ would not enforce that if $i = k$ then $a_i = a_k$ in the consequent.

From now on, we shall omit all universal quantifiers inside rules, for readability.

Definition 3 (Write statement). *The concrete "next state" relation for the write statement* a[i]=v; *is* $(\mathbf{x}, i, v, a) \rightarrow_c (\mathbf{x}, i, v, store(a, i, v))$. *Its forward abstract semantics is encoded into two Horn clauses, depending on whether the distinguished cell is* i *or not:*

$$I_1^\sharp((\mathbf{x}, i, v), (k, a_k)) \wedge i \neq k \implies I_2^\sharp((\mathbf{x}, i, v), (k, a_k)) \tag{10}$$

$$I_1^\sharp((\mathbf{x}, i, v), (i, a_i)) \implies I_2^\sharp((\mathbf{x}, i, v), (i, v)) \tag{11}$$

Example 2 (Example 1, cont.). The $a[i] := 42$ statement of Example 1 is translated into (the *loop* control point is divided into *loop/write/incr*, all predicates of arity 4):

$$i \neq k \wedge write(n, i, k, a_k) \implies incr(n, i, k, a_k) \tag{12}$$

$$write(n, i, i, a_i) \implies incr(n, i, i, 42) \tag{13}$$

Definition 4 (Initialization). *The creation of an array variable with nondeterministically chosen initial content is abstracted by* $I_1^\sharp(\mathbf{x}) \implies I_2^\sharp(\mathbf{x}, k, a_k)$.

Definition 5 (Scalar statements). *With the same notations as above, we consider a statement (or sequence thereof) operating only on scalar variables:* $\mathbf{x} \to_s \mathbf{x}'$ *if it is possible to obtain scalar values* $\mathbf{x}'$ *after executing the statement on scalar values* $\mathbf{x}$. *The concrete "next state" relation for that statement is* $(\mathbf{x}, i, v, a) \to_c (\mathbf{x}', i, v, a)$. *Its forward abstract semantics is encoded into:*

$$I_1^\sharp(\mathbf{x}, k, a_k) \wedge \mathbf{x} \to_s \mathbf{x}' \implies I_2^\sharp(\mathbf{x}', k, a_k) \tag{14}$$

Example 3. A test $x \neq y$ gets abstracted as

$$I_1^\sharp(x, y, k, a_k) \wedge x \neq y \implies I_2^\sharp(x, y, k, a_k) \tag{15}$$

Definition 6. *The scalar operation* $kill(v_1, \dots, v_n)$ *removes variables* $v_1, \dots, v_n$: $(\mathbf{x}, v_1, \dots, v_n) \to \mathbf{x}$. *We shall apply it to get rid of dead variables, sometimes, for the sake of brevity, without explicit note, by coalescing it with other operations.*

Our Horn rules are of the form $\forall \mathbf{y} \ I_1^\sharp(\mathbf{f_1}(\mathbf{y})) \wedge \cdots \wedge I_1^\sharp(\mathbf{f_m}(\mathbf{y})) \wedge P(\mathbf{y}) \implies I_2^\sharp(\mathbf{g}(\mathbf{y}))$ ($\mathbf{y}$ is a vector of variables, $\mathbf{f_1}, \dots, \mathbf{f_m}$ vectors of terms depending on $\mathbf{y}$, P an arithmetic predicate over $\mathbf{y}$). In other words, they impose in $I_2^\sharp$ the presence of $\mathbf{g}(\mathbf{y})$ as soon as certain $\mathbf{f_1}(\mathbf{y}), \dots, \mathbf{f_m}(\mathbf{y})$ are found in $I_1^\sharp$. Let $I_{2-}^\sharp$ be the set of such imposed elements. This Horn rule is said to be *sound* if $\gamma(I_{2-}^\sharp)$ includes all states $(\mathbf{x}', a')$ such that there exists $(\mathbf{x}, a)$ in $\gamma(I_1^\sharp)$ and $(\mathbf{x}, a) \to_c (\mathbf{x}', a')$.

Lemma 1. *The forward abstract semantics of the read statement (Definition 2), of the write statement (Definition 3), of array initialization (Definition 4), of the scalar statements (Definition 5) are sound w.r.t the Galois connection.*

Remark 2. The scalar statements include "killing" dead variables (Definition 6). Note that, contrary to many other abstractions, in ours, removing some variables may cause irrecoverable loss of precision on other variables [31, Sect. 4.2]: if v is live, then one can represent $\forall k, \ a[k] = v$, which implies $\forall k_1, k_2 \ a[k_1] = a[k_2]$ (constantness), but if v is discarded, the constantness of a is lost.

Theorem 2. *If* $I_1^\sharp, \dots, I_m^\sharp$ *are a solution of a system of Horn clauses sound in the above sense, then* $\gamma(I_1^\sharp), \dots, \gamma(I_m^\sharp)$ *are inductive invariants w.r.t the concrete semantics* $\to_c$.

Definition 7 (Property conversion). *A property "at program point* p_ℓ, *for all* $\mathbf{x} \in \chi$ *and all* $k \in \iota$, $\phi(\mathbf{x}, k, a[k])$ *holds" (where* ϕ *is a formula, say over arithmetic) is converted into a Horn query* $\forall \mathbf{x} \in \chi \ \forall k \in \iota \ I_\ell^\sharp(\mathbf{x}, k, a_k) \implies \phi(\mathbf{x}, k, a_k)$.

Our method for converting a scalar program into a system of Horn clauses over scalar variables is thus:

Algorithm 1 (Abstraction into Horn constraints). *Given the control-flow graph of the program:*

1. *To each control point p_ℓ, with vector of scalar variables $\mathbf{x}_\ell$, associate a predicate $I_\ell^\sharp(\mathbf{x}_\ell, k, a_k)$ in the Horn clause system (the vector of scalar variables may change from control point to control point).*
2. *For each transition of the program, generate Horn rules according to Definitions 2, 3, 5 as applicable (an initialization node has no antecedents in its rule).*
3. *Generate Horn queries from desired properties according to Definition 7.*

Example 4 (Example 1, continued). Let us now apply the Horn abstract semantics from Definitions 3 and 5 to Program 1; in this case, $\beta = \mathbb{Z}$, $\iota = \{0, \ldots, n-1\}$ (thus we always have $0 \le k < n$), $\chi = \mathbb{Z}$. After slight simplification, we get:

$$0 \le k < n \implies loop(n, 0, k, a_k) \tag{16}$$

$$0 \le k < n \wedge i < n \wedge loop(n, i, k, a_k) \implies write(n, i, k, a_k) \tag{17}$$

$$0 \le k < n \wedge i \ne k \wedge write(n, i, k, a_k) \implies incr(n, i, k, a_k) \tag{18}$$

$$write(n, i, i, a_i) \implies incr(n, i, i, 42) \tag{19}$$

$$0 \le k < n \wedge incr(n, i, k, a_k) \implies loop(n, i+1, k, a_k) \tag{20}$$

$$0 \le k < n \wedge i \ge n \wedge loop(n, i, k, a_k) \implies end(n, i, k, a_k) \tag{21}$$

Finally, we add the postcondition (using Definition 7):

$$0 \le k < n \wedge end(n, i, k, a_k) \Rightarrow a_k = 42 \tag{22}$$

A solution to the resulting system of Horn clauses can be found by e.g. Z3.

Our approach can also be used to establish relationships between several arrays, or between the initial values in an array and the final values: arrays $a[i]$ and $b[j]$ can be abstracted by a quadruple (i, a_i, j, b_j).[13]

Example 5. Consider the problem of finding the minimum of an array slice $a[d \ldots h-1]$, with value $b = a[p]$:

```
void find_minimum(int n, int a[n], int d, int h){
  int p = d, b = a[d], i = d+1;
  while(i < h) {
    if (a[i] < b) {
      b = a[i];
      p = i;
    }
    i = i+1;
  }
}
```

---

[13] If one is sure that the only relation that matters between a and b are between cells of same index, then one can use triples (i, a_i, b_i).

Again, we encode the abstraction of the statements (Definitions 2, 3, 5) as Horn clauses. We obtained a predicate $end(d, h, p, b, k, a_k)$ constrained as follows:

$$end(d, h, p, b, p, a_p) \implies b = a_p \qquad (23)$$

$$d \leq k < h \wedge end(d, h, p, b, k, a_k) \implies b \leq a_k \qquad (24)$$

Rule 23 imposes the postcondition $b = a[p]$, Rule 24 imposes the postcondition $\forall k \; d \leq k < h \implies b \leq a[k]$. This example is again solved by Z3.

Earlier approaches based on translation to programs [31], thus transition systems, are equivalent to translating into *linear* Horn clauses where $x_1, \ldots, x_p$ are the same in the antecedent and consequent:

$$I_1(\ldots, x_1, a_1, \ldots, x_p, a_p) \wedge condition \to I_2(\ldots, x_1, a'_1, \ldots, x_p, a'_p) \qquad (25)$$

In contrast, in this article we use a much more powerful translation to non-linear Horn clauses (Sect. 7.1) where $x''_1, \ldots, x''_p$ differ from $x_1, \ldots, x_p$:

$$I_1(\ldots, x_1, a_1, \ldots, x_p, a_p) \wedge \cdots \wedge I_1(\ldots, x''_1, a''_1, \ldots, a''_p, x''_p) \wedge condition$$
$$\to I_2(\ldots, x_1, a'_1, \ldots, x_p, a'_p) \qquad (26)$$

Example 6 (Motivating example, altered). The earlier work [31] could successfully analyze Example 1. However a slight modification of the program prevents it from doing so:

```
int tab[n];
for (int i=0; i<n; i++) tab[i]=42;
M: f = 0;
for (int i=0; i<n; i++) { if (tab[i] != 42) f=1; }
assert(f == 0);
```

For this particular example, the array tab would be abstracted *all over the program* using a *fixed* number of cells $tab[x_1], \ldots, tab[x_p]$, where $x_1, \ldots, x_p$ are symbolic constants.

The second loop is then analyzed as though it were[14].

```
for (int i=0; i<n; i++) {
    r = random();
    if (i == x₁) r = a₁;
    ⋮
    if (i == xₚ) r = aₚ;
T: if (r != 42) f=1;
}
```

---

[14] It would still be possible to proceed by first analyzing the first loop, getting the scalar invariant $tab_x = 42$ at location M, quantifying it universally as $\forall x \; tab[x]$, then analyzing the second loop. Such an approach would however fail if this program was itself included in an outer loop.

One easily sees that if $p < n$, there must be a loop iteration where i $\notin$ $\{x_1, \ldots, x_p\}$ and thus at location T, r takes any value and f may take value 1. The output of our translation process in this example is the same until the M control point, then[15] it is:

$$end(n, i, k, a_k) \implies loop2(n, 0, x, k, a_k, 0) \tag{27}$$

$$loop2(n, i, x, k, a_k, f) \wedge i < n \implies rd2(n, i, x, k, a_k, f) \tag{28}$$

$$rd2(n, i, x, k, a_k, f) \wedge i \neq k \wedge \mathbf{rd2(n, i, x, i, a_i, f)} \implies test2(n, i, a_i, k, a_k, f) \tag{29}$$

$$rd2(n, i, x, i, a_i, f) \implies test2(n, i, a_i, i, a_i, f) \tag{30}$$

$$test2(n, i, x, k, a_k, f) \wedge x \neq 42 \implies loop2(n, i+1, k, a_k, 1) \tag{31}$$

$$test2(n, i, x, k, a_k, f) \wedge x = 42 \implies loop2(n, i+1, k, a_k, f) \tag{32}$$

$$loop2(n, i, x, k, a_k, f) \wedge i \geq n \implies end2(f) \tag{33}$$

$$end2(f) \Rightarrow f = 0 \quad \text{(property to prove)} \tag{34}$$

This abstraction is precise enough to prove the desired property, thanks to the **bold** antecedent (multiples cell indices occur within the same unfolding). Without this nonlinear rule (removing this antecedent yields a sound abstraction equivalent to [31]), the unfoldings of the system of rules all carry the same k (index of the distinguished cell) between predicates: the program is analyzed with respect to one single $a[k]$, with k symbolic, leading to insufficient precision.

No Restrictions on Domain Type and Relationships, and Matrices. The kind of relationship that can be inferred between loop indices, array indices and array contents is limited only by the capabilities of the Horn solver. For instance, invariants of the form $\forall i \ i \equiv 0 \pmod 2 \implies a[i] = 0$ may be inferred if the Horn solver supports numeric invariants involving divisibility. Similarly, we have made no assumption regarding the nature of the indexing variable: we used integers because arrays indexed by an integer range are a very common kind of data structure, but really it can be any type supported by the Horn clause solver, e.g. rationals or strings. For instance, *matrices* (resp. *n-tensors*) are specified by having pairs of integers (resp. *n*-tuples) as indices.

4   Sortedness and Other N-ary Predicates

The Galois connection of Definition 1 expresses relations of the form $\forall k \in \iota \ \phi(\mathbf{x}, k, a[k])$ where $\mathbf{x}$ are variables from the program, a a map and k an index into the map a; in other words, relations between each array element individually and the rest of the variables. It cannot express properties such as sortedness, which link *two* array elements: $\forall k_1, k_2 \in \iota \ k_1 < k_2 \implies a[k_1] \leq a[k_2]$.

For such properties, we need two "distinguished cells", with indices k_1 and k_2. For efficiency, we break this symmetry between indices k_1 and k_2 by imposing $k_1 < k_2$ for some total order.

---

[15] The statement if tab[i]!=42 is decomposed into x:=a[i];if(x!=42).

Definition 8. *The abstraction with indices $k_1 < k_2$ is*

$$\gamma_{2<}(I^\sharp) = \{(\mathbf{x}, a) \mid \forall k_1 < k_2 \in \iota \ (\mathbf{x}, k_1, a[k_1], k_2, a[k_2]) \in I^\sharp\} \tag{35}$$

$$\alpha_{2<}(I) = \{(\mathbf{x}, k_1, a[k_1], k_2, a[k_2]) \mid x \in \chi, k_1 \le k_2 \in \iota\} \tag{36}$$

Theorem 3. $\alpha_{2<}$ *and* $\gamma_{2<}$ *form a Galois connection:*

$$\mathcal{P}\left(\chi \times Arr\left(\iota, \beta\right)\right) \xrightleftharpoons[\alpha_{2<}]{\gamma_{2<}} \mathcal{P}\left(\{(x, k_1, v_1, k_2, v_2) \mid x \in \chi, \ k_1 < k_2 \in \iota, \ v_1, v_2 \in \beta\}\right)$$

These constructions easily generalize to arbitrary N indices $k_1, \ldots, k_N$.

Definition 9 (Read, two indices $k_1 < k_2$). *The abstraction of $v := a[i]$ is:*

$$I_1^\sharp(\mathbf{x}, i, v, k_1, a_{k_1}, k_2, a_{k_2}) \wedge I_1^\sharp(\mathbf{x}, i, v, i, a_i, k_2, a_{k_2}) \wedge \\ I_1^\sharp(\mathbf{x}, i, v, i, a_i, k_1, a_{k_1}) \wedge i < k_1 < k_2 \implies I_2^\sharp(\mathbf{x}, i, a_i, k_1, a_{k_1}, k_2, a_{k_2}) \tag{37}$$

$$I_1^\sharp(\mathbf{x}, i, v, i, a_i, k_2, a_{k_2}) \wedge I_1^\sharp(\mathbf{x}, i, v, k_1, a_{k_1}, k_2, a_{k_2}) \wedge \\ I_1^\sharp(\mathbf{x}, i, v, k_1, a_{k_1}, i, a_i) \wedge k_1 < i < k_2 \implies I_2^\sharp(\mathbf{x}, i, a_i, k_1, a_{k_1}, k_2, a_{k_2}) \tag{38}$$

$$I_1^\sharp(\mathbf{x}, i, v, k_2, a_{k_2}, i, a_i) \wedge I_1^\sharp(\mathbf{x}, i, v, k_1, a_{k_1}, i, a_i) \wedge \\ I_1^\sharp(\mathbf{x}, i, v, k_1, a_{k_1}, k_2, a_{k_2}) \wedge k_1 < k_2 < i \implies I_2^\sharp(\mathbf{x}, i, a_i, k_1, a_{k_1}, k_2, a_{k_2}) \tag{39}$$

$$I_1^\sharp(\mathbf{x}, i, v, i, a_i, k_2, a_{k_2}) \wedge i < k_2 \implies I_2^\sharp(\mathbf{x}, i, a_i, i, a_i, k_2, a_{k_2}) \tag{40}$$

$$I_1^\sharp(\mathbf{x}, i, v, k_1, a_{k_1}, i, a_i) \wedge k_1 < i \implies I_2^\sharp(\mathbf{x}, i, a_i, k_1, a_{k_1}, i, a_i) \tag{41}$$

This generalizes to N-ary abstraction by considering all orderings of i inside $k_1 < \cdots < k_N$, and for each ordering taking all sub-orderings of size N.

Definition 10 (Write statement, two indices $k_1 < k_2$). *The abstraction of $a[i] := v$ is:*

$$I_1^\sharp(\mathbf{x}, i, v, k_1, a_{k_1}, k_2, a_{k_2}) \wedge i \ne k_1 \wedge i \ne k_2 \implies I_2^\sharp(\mathbf{x}, i, v, k_1, a_{k_1}, k_2, a_{k_2}) \tag{42}$$

$$I_1^\sharp(\mathbf{x}, i, v, i, a_i, k_2, a_{k_2}) \wedge i < k_2 \implies I_2^\sharp(\mathbf{x}, i, v, i, v, k_2, a_{k_2}) \tag{43}$$

$$I_1^\sharp(\mathbf{x}, i, v, k_1, a_{k_1}, i, a_i) \wedge k_1 < i \implies I_2^\sharp(\mathbf{x}, i, v, k_1, a_{k_1}, i, v) \tag{44}$$

Lemma 2. *The abstract forward semantics of the read statement (Definition 9) and of the write statement (Definition 10) are sound w.r.t the Galois connection.*

Example 7 (Selection sort). Selection sort finds the least element in $a[d \ldots h-1]$ (using Program 5 as its inner loop) and swaps it with $a[d]$, then sorts $a[d+1, h-1]$. At the end, $a[d_0 \ldots h-1]$ is sorted, where d_0 is the initial value of d.

```
int d = d0;
while (d < h−1) {
    int p = d, b = a[d], f = b, i = d+1;
    while(i < h) { //find_mini
        if (a[i] < b) {
            b = a[i]; p = i;
        }
        i = i+1;
    }
}
```

```
a[d] = b; a[p] = f;    // swap
d = d+1;
}
```

Using the rules for the read (Definition 9) and write (Definition 10) statements, we write the abstract forward semantics of this program as a system of Horn clauses.

We wish to prove that, at the end, $a[d_0, h-1]$ is sorted: at the *exit* node,

$$\forall d_0 \leq k_1 < k_2 < h, \ a[k_1] \leq a[k_2] \tag{45}$$

This is expressed as the final condition:

$$d_0 \leq k_1 < k_2 < h \wedge exit(d_0, h, k_1, a_{k_1}, k_2, a_{k_2}) \implies a_{k_1} \leq a_{k_2} \tag{46}$$

By running a solver on these clauses, we show that the output of selection sort is truly sorted[16] Let us note that this proof relies on nontrivial invariants:[17]

$$\forall k_1, k_2, \ d_0 \leq k_1 < d \wedge k_1 \leq k_2 < h \implies a[k_1] \leq a[k_2] \tag{47}$$

This invariant can be expressed in our Horn clauses as:

$$d_0 \leq k_1 < d \wedge k_1 < k_2 < h \wedge outerloop(d_0, d, h, k_1, a_{k_1}, k_2, a_{k_2}) \implies a_{k_1} \leq a_{k_2} \tag{48}$$

If this invariant is added to the problem as an additional query to prove, solving time is reduced from 6 min to 1 s. It may seem counter-intuitive that a solver takes less time to solve a problem with an additional constraint; but this constraint expresses an invariant necessary to prove the solution, and thus nudges the solver towards the solution.

Our approach is therefore flexible: if a solver fails to prove the desired property on its own, it is possible to help it by providing partial invariants. This is a less tedious approach than having to provide full invariants at every loop header, as common in assisted Floyd-Hoare proofs.

5 Sets and Multisets

Our abstraction for maps may be used to abstract (multi)sets. Let us see for instance how to abstract the multiset of elements of an array, so as to show that the output of a sorting algorithm is a permutation of the input.

In Example 7, we showed how to prove that the output of selection sort is sorted. This is not enough for functional correctness: we also have to prove that the output is a permutation of the input, or, equivalently, that the multiset of elements in the output array is the same as that in the input array.

---

[16] In Example 8 we shall see how to prove that the multiset of elements in the output is the same as in the input.

[17] Nontrivial in the sense that a human user operating a Floyd-Hoare proof assistant typically does not come up with them so easily.

Let us remark that it is easy to keep track, in an auxiliary map, of the number $\#a(x)$ of elements of value x in the array $a[]$. Only write accesses to $a[]$ have an influence on $\#a$: a write $a[i] := v$ is replaced by a sequence:

$$\#a(a[i]) := \#a(a[i]) - 1; \quad a[i] := v; \quad \#a(v) := \#a(v) + 1 \qquad (49)$$

(that is, in addition to the array write, the count of elements for the value that gets overwritten is decremented, and the count of elements for the new value is incremented).

This auxiliary map $\#a$ can itself be abstracted using our approach! Let us now see how to implement this in our abstract forward semantics expressed using Horn clauses. We enrich our Galois connection (Definition 1) as follows:

Definition 11. *The concretization of* $I^\sharp \subseteq \chi \times (\iota \times \beta) \times (\beta \times \mathbb{N})$ *is*

$$\gamma_\#(I^\sharp) = \left\{ (\mathbf{x}, a) \mid \forall i \in \iota \; \forall v \in \beta \; (\mathbf{x}, (i, a[i]), (v, \operatorname{card}\{j \in \iota \mid a[j] = v\})) \in I^\sharp \right\} \qquad (50)$$

where $\operatorname{card} X$ *denotes the number of elements in the set* X.

The abstraction of $I \subseteq \chi \times Arr(\iota, \beta)$ *is*

$$\alpha_\#(I) = \left\{ (\mathbf{x}, (i, a[i]), (v, \operatorname{card}\{j \in \iota \mid a[j] = v\})) \; \middle| \; x \in \chi, i \in \iota \right\} \qquad (51)$$

Theorem 4. $\mathcal{P}\left(\chi \times Arr(\iota, \beta)\right) \xrightleftharpoons[\alpha_\#]{\gamma_\#} \mathcal{P}\left(\chi \times (\iota \times \beta) \times (\beta \times \mathbb{N})\right)$

The Horn rules for array reads and for scalar operations are the same as those for our first abstraction, except that we carry over the extra two components identically.

Definition 12 (Read statement). *Same notations as Definition 2:*

$$k \neq i \wedge I_1^\sharp((\mathbf{x}, i, v), (k, a_k), (z, a_{\#z})) \wedge$$
$$I_1^\sharp((\mathbf{x}, i, v), (i, a_i), (z, a_{\#z})) \implies I_2^\sharp((\mathbf{x}, i, a_i), (k, a_k), (z, a_{\#z}))$$
$$I_1^\sharp((\mathbf{x}, i, v), (i, a_i), (z, a_{\#z})) \implies I_2^\sharp((\mathbf{x}, i, a_i), (i, a_i), (z, a_{\#z}))$$

Lemma 3. *The abstract forward semantics of the read statement (Definition 12) is a sound abstraction of the concrete semantics given in Definition 2.*

The abstraction of the write statement is more complicated (see the sequence of instructions in Formula 49). To abstract a write $a[i] := v$ between control points p_1 and p_2, we execute a read of the old value from the cell abstraction of the array, decrement the number of cells with this value, execute the write to the cell abstraction, and increment the number of cells with the new value.

Definition 13 (Write statement). *With the same notations in Definition 3:*

Step	translation
`e:=a[i]; #a[e]--; kill(e)`	$a_i \neq z \wedge I_1^{\sharp}((\mathbf{x}, i, v), (k, a_k), (z, a_{\#z})) \wedge I_1^{\sharp}((\mathbf{x}, i, v), (i, a_i), (z, a_{\#z}))$ $\implies I_a^{\sharp}((\mathbf{x}, i, v), (k, a_k), (z, a_{\#z}))$ $I_1^{\sharp}((\mathbf{x}, i, v), (k, a_k), (a_i, a_{\#z})) \wedge I_1^{\sharp}((\mathbf{x}, i, v), (i, a_i), (a_i, a_{\#z}))$ $\implies I_a^{\sharp}((\mathbf{x}, i, v), (k, a_k), (a_i, a_{\#z} - 1))$
`#a[v]++`	$v \neq z \wedge I_a^{\sharp}((\mathbf{x}, i, v), (k, a_k), (z, a_{\#z})) \implies I_b^{\sharp}((\mathbf{x}, i, v), (k, a_k), (z, a_{\#z}))$ $I_a^{\sharp}((\mathbf{x}, i, v), (k, a_k), (v, a_{\#z})) \implies I_b^{\sharp}((\mathbf{x}, i, v), (k, a_k), (v, a_{\#z} + 1))$
`a[i]=v`	$i \neq k \wedge I_1^{\sharp}((\mathbf{x}, i, v), (k, a_k), (z, a_{\#z})) \implies I_2^{\sharp}((\mathbf{x}, i, v), (k, a_k), (z, a_{\#z}))$ $I_1^{\sharp}((\mathbf{x}, i, v), (i, a_i), (z, a_{\#z})) \implies I_2^{\sharp}((\mathbf{x}, i, v), (i, v), (z, a_{\#z}))$

Lemma 4. *The abstract forward semantics of the write statement (Definition 13) is a sound abstraction of the concrete semantics given in Definition 3.*

If we want to compare the multiset of the contents of an array a at the end of a procedure to its contents at the beginning of the procedure, one needs to keep a copy of the old multiset. It is common that the property sought is a relation between the number of occurrences $\#a(z)$ of an element z in the output array a and its number of occurrences $\#a_0(z)$ in the input array a^0. In the above formulas, one may therefore replace the pair $(z, a_{\#z})$ by $(z, a_{\#z}, a_{\#z}^0)$, with $a_{\#z}^0$ always propagated identically.

Example 8. Consider again selection sort (Program 7). We use the abstract semantics for read (Definition 12) and write (Definition 13), with an additional component $a_{\#z}^0$ for tracking the original number of values z in the array a.

We specify the final property as the query

$$exit(l_0, h, k, a_k, z, a_{\#z}, a_{\#z}^0) \implies a_{\#z} = a_{\#z}^0 \tag{52}$$

6   Experiments

Implementation. We implemented our prototype VAPHOR in 2k lines of OCAML. VAPHOR takes as input a mini-Java program (a variation of WHILE with array accesses, and assertions) and produces a SMTLIB2 file[18]. The core analyzer implements the translation for one and two-dimensional arrays described in Sects. 3 and 4, and also the direct translation toward a formula with array variables.

Experiments. We have tested our analyzer on several examples from the literature, including the array benchmark proposed in [15] also used in [3] (Table 1); and other classical array algorithms including *selection sort*, *bubble sort* and *insertion sort* (Table 2). We compared our approach to existing Horn clause solvers capable of dealing with arrays. All these files are available on the webpage https://hal.archives-ouvertes.fr/hal-01206882

---

[18] http://smtlib.cs.uiowa.edu/.

Table 1. Comparison on the array benchmarks of [15]. (Average) timing are in seconds, CPU time. Abstraction with $N = 1$. "sat" means the property was proved, "unsat" that it could not be proved. "hints" means that some invariants had to be manually supplied to the solver (e.g. even/odd conditions). A star means that we used another version of the solver. Timeout was 5 mn unless otherwise noted. The machine has 32 i3-3110M cores, 64 GiB RAM, C/C++ solvers were compiled with gcc 4.8.4, the JVM is OpenJDK 1.7.0-85.

Benchmark	Z3/PDR		Z3/Spacer		Eldarica		Comment
	Res	Time	Res	Time	Res	Time	
Correct problems, "sat" expected							
append	sat	2.11	sat	0.85	sat	22.61	
copy	sat	4.66	sat	0.44	timeout(300 s)		
find	sat	0.20	sat	0.14	sat	12.93	
findnonnull	sat	0.50	sat	0.34	sat	12.04	
initcte	sat	0.16	sat	0.26	sat	13.28	
init2i	sat	0.31	sat	0.16	sat	14.67	
partialcopy	sat	1.88	sat	0.34	timeout(300 s)		
reverse	sat	40.70	sat	2.19	timeout(300 s)		
strcpy	sat	0.92	sat	0.37	sat*	66.69	
strlen	sat	0.24	sat	0.22	sat	36.69	
swapncopy	sat	71.16	timeout(300 s)		timeout(300 s)		
memcpy	sat	3.54	sat	0.39	timeout(300 s)		
initeven	sat	1.32	sat	0.71	timeout(300 s)		"hints"
mergeinterleave	sat	39.49	sat	4.61	timeout	322.39	"hints"
Incorrect problems, "unsat" expected							
copyodd_buggy	unsat	0.08	unsat	0.04	unsat	7.42	
initeven_buggy	unsat	0.06	unsat	0.06	unsat	6.28	
reverse_buggy	unsat	1.88	unsat	1.28	unsat	58.96	
swapncopy_buggy	unsat	3.13	unsat	0.74	unsat	27.54	
mergeinterleave_buggy	unsat	1.16	unsat	0.56	unsat	31.22	

Limitations. Our tool does not currently implement the reasoning over array contents (multiset of values). Experiments for these were thus conducted by manually applying the transformations described in this article in order to obtain a system of Horn clauses. For this reason, because applying rules manually is tedious and error-prone, the only sorting algorithm for which we have checked that the multiset of the output is equal to the multiset of the inputs is selection sort. We are however confident that the two other algorithms would go through, given that they use similar or simpler swapping structures.

Some examples from Dillig et al. [15] involve invariants with even/odd constraints. The Horn solvers we tried do not seem to be able to infer invariants involving divisibility predicates unless these predicates were given by the user. For these cases we added these even/odd properties as additional invariants to prove.

Efficiency caveats. Our tool does not currently simplify the system of Horn clauses that it produces. We have observed that, in some cases, manually simplifying the clauses (removing useless variables, inlining single antecedents by substitution...) dramatically reduces solving times. Also, precomputing some

Table 2. Other array-manipulating programs, including various sorting algorithms. A star means that we used another version of the solver, R1 means random_seed=1. The ~~striked-out~~ result is likely a bug in Z3; the alternative is a bug in Spacer, since the same system cannot be satisfiable and unsatisfiable at the same time.

Benchmark	N	Z3/PDR		Z3/Spacer		Eldarica		Comment
		Res	Time	Res	Time	Res	Time	
bin_search_check	1	sat	0.71	sat	0.34	Crash		
find_mini_check	1	sat	4.22	sat	0.82	sat	110.58	
revrefill1D_check_buggy	1	unsat	0.03	unsat	0.07	unsat	9.21	
array_init_2D	1	sat	0.46	sat	0.22	sat	12.76	
array_sort_2D	1	sat	0.78	sat	0.30	sat	26.68	
selection_sort (sortedness)	2	sat*	99.04	timeout(300 s)		timeout(300 s)		
selection_sort (sortedness)	2	~~unsat~~	83	sat	48	timeout	334	manual translation
selection_sort (permutation)	1	timeout	600	sat	9.24	timeout	336	manual translation
bubble_sort_simplified	2	sat	5.98	sat	2.77	sat	158.70	
insertion_sort	2	sat(R1)	53.83	timeout(300 s)		timeout(300 s)		

simple scalar invariants on the Horn clauses (e.g. $0 \leq k < i$ for a loop from k to $i - 1$) and asserting them as assertions to prove in the Horn system sometimes reduces solving time.

We have observed that the execution time of a Horn solver may dramatically change depending on minor changes in the input, pseudo-random number generator seed, or version of the solver. For instance, the same version of Z3 solves the same system of Horn clauses (proving the correctness of selection sort) in 3 min 40 s or 3 h 52 min depending on whether the random seed is 1 or 0.[19]

Furthermore, we have run into numerous problems with solvers, including one example that, on successive versions of the same solver, produced "sat" then "unknown" and finally "unsat", as well as crashes.

For all these reasons, we believe that solving times should not be regarded too closely. The purpose of our experimental evaluation is not to benchmark solvers relative to each other, but to show that our abstraction, even though it is incomplete, is powerful enough to lead to fully automated proofs of functional correctness of nontrivial array manipulations, including sorting algorithms. Tools for solving Horn clauses are still in their infancy and we thus expect performance and reliability to increase dramatically.

7   Related Work

7.1   Cell-Based Abstractions

Smashing. The simplest abstraction for an array is to "smash" all cells into a single one — this amounts to removing the k component from our first Galois connection (Definition 1). The weakness of that approach is that all writes are treated as "may writes" or *weak updates*: $a[i] := x$ adds the value x to the values

---

[19] We suspect that different choices in SAT lead to different proofs of unsatisfiability, thus different interpolants and different refinements in the PDR algorithm.

possibly found in the array a, but there is no way to remove any value from that set. Such an approach thus cannot treat initialization loops (e.g. Program 1) precisely.

Exploding. At the other extreme, for an array of statically known finite length N (which is common in embedded safety-critical software), one can distinguish all cells $a[0], \ldots, a[N-1]$ and treat them as separate variables $a_0, \ldots, a_{N-1}$. This is a good solution when N is small, but a terrible one when N is large: (i) many analyses scale poorly with the number of active variables (ii) an initialization loop will have to be unrolled N times to show it initializes all cells. Both smashing and exploding have been used with success in the Astrée static analyzer [4,5].

Slices. More sophisticated analyses [12,17,19,32,33] distinguish *slices* or *segments* in the array; their boundaries depend on the index variables. For instance, in array initialization (Program 1), one slice is the part already initialized (indices $< i$), the other the part yet to be initialized (indices $\geq i$). In the simplest case, each slice is "smashed" into a single value, but more refined analyses express relationships between slices. Since the slices are segments $[a, b]$ of indices, these analyses generalize poorly to multidimensional arrays. Also, there is often a combinatorial explosion in analyzing how array slices may or may not overlap.

Cornish et al. [10] similarly apply a program-to-program translation over the LLVM intermediate representation, followed by a scalar analysis.

To our best knowledge, all these approaches factor through our Galois connections $\xrightarrow[\alpha]{\gamma}$, $\xrightarrow[\alpha_{2<}]{\gamma_{2<}}$ or combinations thereof: that is, their abstraction can be expressed as a composition of our abstraction and further abstraction — even though our implementation of the abstract transfer functions is completely different from theirs. Our approach, however, separates the concerns of (i) abstracting array problems to array-less problems (ii) abstracting the relationships between different cells and indices.

Fluid updates. Dillig et al. [15] extend the slice approach by introducing "fluid updates" to overcome the dichotomy between strong and weak updates. They specifically exclude sortedness from the kind of properties they can study.

Array removal by program transformation. Monniaux and Alberti [31] analyze array programs by transforming them into array-free programs, which are sent to a back-end analyzer. The resulting invariants contain extra index variables, which can be universally quantified away, similar to the Skolem constants of earlier invariant inference approaches [16,27]. We have explained (p. 3) why these approaches are less precise than ours.

Another difficulty they obviously faced was the limitations of the back-end solvers that they could use. The integer acceleration engine FLATA severely limits the kind of transition relations that can be considered and scales poorly. The abstract interpreter CONCURINTERPROC can infer disjunctive properties (necessary to distinguish two slices in an array) only if given case splits using observer

Boolean variables; but the cost increases greatly (exponentially, in the worst case) with the number of such variables.

7.2 Horn Clauses

Transformations. De Angelis et al. [14] start from a system of Horn clauses over array variables and apply a sequence of transformation rules that (i) either yield the empty set of clauses, meaning the program is correct (ii) either yield the "false" fact, meaning the program is incorrect (iii) either fails to terminate. These rules are based on the axioms of arrays and on a generalization scheme for arithmetic predicates using widening and convex hull.

In contrast to theirs, our approach (i) does not require a target property to prove (though the backend solver may need one) (ii) does not mix concerns about arrays and arithmetic constraints (iii) can prove the correctness of the full insertion sort algorithm (they can prove only the inner loop).

Instantiation. Bjørner et al. [3] propose an approach for solving universally quantified Horn clauses: a Horn clause $(\forall x\ P(x, y)) \to Q(y)$, not handled by current solvers, is abstracted by $P(x_1(y)) \wedge \cdots \wedge P(x_n(y)) \to Q(y)$ where the x_i are heuristically chosen instantiations. Our approach can be construed as an application of their approach to the axioms of arrays, with specific instantiation heuristics.

We improve on their interesting contribution in several ways. (i) Instead of presenting our approach as a heuristic instantiation scheme, we show that it corresponds to specific Galois connections, which clarifies what abstraction is done and what kind of properties can or cannot be represented. (ii) We handle sortedness properties. None of their examples deal with sortedness and it is unclear how their instantiation heuristics would behave on them. (iii) We handle multisets (and thus permutation properties) by reduction to arrays. It is possible that our approach in this respect can be described as an instantiation scheme over the axioms for arrays (including the multiset of array contents), but, again, it is unclear how their instantiation heuristics would behave in this respect.

Their approach has not been implemented except in private research prototypes; we could not run a comparison.[20]

7.3 Predicate Abstraction, CEGAR and Array Interpolants

There exist a variety of approaches based on counterexample-guided abstraction refinement using *Craig interpolants* [28–30]. In a nutshell, Craig interpolants are predicates suitable for proving, using Hoare triples, that some unfolding of the execution cannot lead to an error state. They are typically processed from the proof of unsatisfiability of the unfolding produced by an SMT solver.

Generating good interpolants from purely arithmetic problems is already a difficult problem, and generating good universally quantified interpolants on array properties has proved even more challenging [1, 2, 23].

---

[20] Their approach is *not* implemented in Z3 (personal communication from N. Bjørner).

7.4 Acceleration

Bozga et al. [7] have proposed a method for accelerating certain transition relations involving actions over arrays, outputting the transitive closure in the form of a *counter automaton*. Translating the counter automaton into a first-order formula expressing the array properties however results in a loss of precision.

8 Conclusion and Perspectives

We have proposed a generic approach to abstract programs and universal properties over arrays (or arbitrary maps) by syntactic transformation into a system of Horn clauses without arrays, which is then sent to a solver. This transformation is powerful enough to prove, fully automatically and within minutes, that the output of selection sort is sorted and is a permutation of the input.

While some solvers have difficulties with the kind of Horn systems that we generate, some (e.g. SPACER) are capable of solving them quite well. We have used the stock version of the solvers, without tuning or help from their designers, thus higher performance is to be expected in the future. If the solver cannot find the invariants on its own, it can be helped by partial invariants from the user.

As experiments show, our approach significantly improves on the procedures currently in array-capable Horn solvers, as well as earlier approaches for inferring quantified array invariants: they typically cannot prove sorting algorithms.

Our rules are for forward analysis: a solution to our Horn clauses defines a super-set of all states reachable from program initialization, and the desired property is proved if this set is included in the property. We intend to investigate *backward analysis*: find a super-set of the set of all states reachable from a property violation, not intersecting the initial states.

One advantage of some of the approaches (the abstract interpretation ones from Sect. 7.1 and the transformation from [31]) is that they are capable of inferring what a program does, or at least a meaningful abstraction of it (e.g. "at the end of this program all cells in the array a contains 42") as opposed to merely proving a property supplied by the user. Our approach can achieve this as well, *provided it is used with a Horn clause solver that provides interesting solutions without the need of a query*. This Horn clause solver should however be capable of generating disjunctive properties (e.g. $(k < i \wedge a_k = 0) \vee (k \geq i \wedge a_k = 42)$); thus a simple approach by abstract interpretation of the Horn clauses in, say, a sub-class of the convex polyhedra, will not do. We know of no such Horn solver; designing one is a research challenge. Maybe certain partitioning approaches used in sequential program verification [21,34] may be transposed to Horn clauses.

We have considered simple programs operating over arrays or maps, as opposed to a real-life programming language with *objects*, references or, horror, pointer arithmetic. Yet, our approach can be adapted to such languages, following methods that view memory as arrays [6], whose disjointness is proved by typing (e.g. two values of different types can never be aliased, two fields of different types can never be aliased) or by alias analysis.

Acknowledgments. We wish to thank the anonymous referees for their careful reading and helpful comments.

References

1. Alberti, F., Monniaux, D.: Polyhedra to the rescue of array interpolants. In: Symposium on applied computing (Software Verification & Testing), pp. 1745–1750. ACM (2015). doi:10.1145/2695664.2695784
2. Alberti, F., Bruttomesso, R., Ghilardi, S., Ranise, S., Sharygina, N.: An extension of lazy abstraction with interpolation for programs with arrays. Formal Methods Syst. Des. **45**(1), 63–109 (2014). doi:10.1007/s10703-014-0209-9
3. Bjørner, N., McMillan, K., Rybalchenko, A.: On solving universally quantified Horn clauses. In: Logozzo, F., Fähndrich, M. (eds.) SAS 2013. LNCS, vol. 7935, pp. 105–125. Springer, Heidelberg (2013). doi:10.1145/2695664.2695784
4. Blanchet, B., Cousot, P., Cousot, R., Feret, J., Mauborgne, L., Miné, A., Monniaux, D., Rival, X.: Design and implementation of a special-purpose static program analyzer for safety-critical real-time embedded software. In: Mogensen, T.Æ., Schmidt, D.A., Sudborough, I.H. (eds.) The Essence of Computation. LNCS, vol. 2566, pp. 85–108. Springer, Heidelberg (2002). doi:10.1007/3-540-36377-7_5
5. Blanchet, B., Cousot, P., Cousot, R., Feret, J., Mauborgne, L., Miné, A., Monniaux, D., Rival, X.: A static analyzer for large safety-critical software. In: Programming Language Design and Implementation (PLDI), pp. 196–207. ACM (2003). doi:10.1145/781131.781153
6. Bornat, R.: Proving pointer programs in Hoare logic. In: Backhouse, R.C., Oliveira, J.N. (eds.) MPC 2000. LNCS, vol. 1837, pp. 102–126. Springer, Heidelberg (2000). doi:10.1007/10722010_8
7. Bozga, M., Habermehl, P., Iosif, R., Konečný, F., Vojnar, T.: Automatic verification of integer array programs. In: Bouajjani, A., Maler, O. (eds.) CAV 2009. LNCS, vol. 5643, pp. 157–172. Springer, Heidelberg (2009). doi:10.1007/978-3-642-02658-4_15
8. Bradley, A.R., Manna, Z., Sipma, H.B.: What's decidable about arrays? In: Emerson, E.A., Namjoshi, K.S. (eds.) VMCAI 2006. LNCS, vol. 3855, pp. 427–442. Springer, Heidelberg (2006). doi:10.1007/11609773_28
9. Christ, J.: Interpolation Modulo Theories. Ph.D thesis, University of Freiburg (2015)
10. Cornish, J.R.M., Gange, G., Navas, J.A., Schachte, P., Søndergaard, H., Stuckey, P.J.: Analyzing array manipulating programs by program transformation. In: Proietti, M., Seki, H. (eds.) LOPSTR 2014. LNCS, vol. 8981, pp. 3–20. Springer, Heidelberg (2015). doi:10.1007/978-3-319-17822-6_1
11. Cousot, P., Cousot, R.: Abstract interpretation frameworks. J. Log. Comput. **2**(4), 511–547 (1992). doi:10.1093/logcom/2.4.511
12. Cousot, P., Cousot, R., Logozzo, F.: A parametric segmentation functor for fully automatic and scalable array content analysis. In: Principles of Programming Languages (POPL), pp. 105–118. ACM (2011). doi:10.1145/1926385.1926399
13. Cousot, P., Cousot, R.: Invited talk: higher order abstract interpretation. In: IEEE International Conference on Computer Languages, pp. 95–112. IEEE (1994)
14. De Angelis, E., Fioravanti, F., Pettorossi, A., Proietti, M.: A rule-based verification strategy for array manipulating programs. Fundamenta Informaticae **140**(3–4), 329–355 (2015). doi:10.3233/FI-2015-1257

15. Dillig, I., Dillig, T., Aiken, A.: Fluid updates: beyond strong vs. weak updates. In: Gordon, A.D. (ed.) ESOP 2010. LNCS, vol. 6012, pp. 246–266. Springer, Heidelberg (2010). doi:10.1007/978-3-642-11957-6_14

16. Flanagan, C., Qadeer, S.: Predicate abstraction for software verification. In: POPL, pp. 191–202 (2002)

17. Gopan, D., Reps, T.W., Sagiv, S.: A framework for numeric analysis of array operations. In: Principles of Programming Languages (POPL), pp. 338–350 (2005) doi:10.1145/1040305.1040333

18. Gurfinkel, A., Kahsai, T., Komuravelli, A., Navas, J.A.: The seahorn verification framework. In: Kroening, D., Păsăreanu, C.S. (eds.) CAV 2015. LNCS, vol. 9206, pp. 343–361. Springer, Heidelberg (2015)

19. Halbwachs, N., Péron, M.: Discovering properties about arrays in simple programs. In: Programming language design and implementation (PLDI), pp. 339–348. ACM (2008) doi:10.1145/1375581.1375623

20. Halpern, J.Y.: Presburger arithmetic with unary predicates is Π_1^1 complete. J. Symbolic Logic **56**(2), 637–642 (1991). doi:10.2307/2274706. ISSN 0022–4812

21. Henry, J., Monniaux, D., Moy, M.: Succinct representations for abstract interpretation. In: Miné, A., Schmidt, D. (eds.) SAS 2012. LNCS, vol. 7460, pp. 283–299. Springer, Heidelberg (2012). doi:10.1007/978-3-642-33125-1_20

22. Hoder, K., Bjørner, N.: Generalized property directed reachability. In: Cimatti, A., Sebastiani, R. (eds.) SAT 2012. LNCS, vol. 7317, pp. 157–171. Springer, Heidelberg (2012). doi:10.1007/978-3-642-31612-8_13. ISBN 978-3-642-31611-1

23. Jhala, R., McMillan, K.L.: Array abstractions from proofs. In: Damm, W., Hermanns, H. (eds.) CAV 2007. LNCS, vol. 4590, pp. 193–206. Springer, Heidelberg (2007). doi:10.1007/978-3-540-73368-3_23

24. Komuravelli, A., Gurfinkel, A., Chaki, S., Clarke, E.M.: Automatic abstraction in SMT-based unbounded software model checking. In: Sharygina, N., Veith, H. (eds.) CAV 2013. LNCS, vol. 8044, pp. 846–862. Springer, Heidelberg (2013). doi:10.1007/978-3-642-39799-8_59. ISBN 978-3-642-39798-1

25. Komuravelli, A., Gurfinkel, A., Chaki, S.: SMT-based model checking for recursive programs. In: Biere, A., Bloem, R. (eds.) CAV 2014. LNCS, vol. 8559, pp. 17–34. Springer, Heidelberg (2014). doi:10.1007/978-3-319-08867-9_2. ISBN 978-3-319-08866-2

26. Kroening, D., Strichman, O.: Decision Procedures. Springer, Heidelberg (2008). ISBN 978-3-540-74104-6

27. Lahiri, S.K., Bryant, R.E.: Indexed predicate discovery for unbounded system verification. In: Alur, R., Peled, D.A. (eds.) CAV 2004. LNCS, vol. 3114, pp. 135–147. Springer, Heidelberg (2004). doi:10.1007/978-3-540-27813-9_11

28. McMillan, K.L.: Applications of craig interpolation to model checking. In: Ciardo, G., Darondeau, P. (eds.) ICATPN 2005. LNCS, vol. 3536, pp. 15–16. Springer, Heidelberg (2005). doi:10.1007/11494744_2

29. McMillan, K.L.: Lazy abstraction with interpolants. In: Ball, T., Jones, R.B. (eds.) CAV 2006. LNCS, vol. 4144, pp. 123–136. Springer, Heidelberg (2006). doi:10.1007/11817963_14

30. McMillan, K.L.: Interpolants from Z3 proofs. In: Formal Methods in Computer-Aided Design (FMCAD), pp. 19–27 (2011). ISBN 978-0-9835678-1-3

31. Monniaux, D., Alberti, F.: A simple abstraction of arrays and maps by program translation. In: Blazy, S., Jensen, T. (eds.) SAS 2015. LNCS, vol. 9291, pp. 217–234. Springer, Heidelberg (2015). doi:10.1007/978-3-662-48288-9_13. ISBN 978-3-662-48288-9

32. Péron, M.: Contributions to the Static Analysis of Programs HandlingArrays. Theses, Université de Grenoble, September 2010. https://tel.archives-ouvertes.fr/tel-00623697

33. Perrelle, V.: Analyse statique de programmes manipulant des tableaux. Theses, Université de Grenoble, February 2013. https://tel.archives-ouvertes.fr/tel-00973892

34. Rival, X., Mauborgne, L.: The trace partitioning abstract domain. ACM Trans. Program. Lang. Syst., **29**(5) (2007). doi:10.1145/1275497.1275501

35. Rümmer, P., Hojjat, H., Kuncak, V.: Disjunctive interpolants for horn-clause verification. In: Sharygina, N., Veith, H. (eds.) CAV 2013. LNCS, vol. 8044, pp. 347–363. Springer, Heidelberg (2013). doi:10.1007/978-3-642-39799-8_24. ISBN 978-3-642-39798-1

36. Rümmer, P., Hojjat, H., Kuncak, V.: Classifying and solving horn clauses for verification. In: Cohen, E., Rybalchenko, A. (eds.) VSTTE 2013. LNCS, vol. 8164, pp. 1–21. Springer, Heidelberg (2014). doi:10.1007/978-3-642-54108-7_1

Loopy: Programmable and Formally Verified Loop Transformations

Kedar S. Namjoshi[1] and Nimit Singhania[2][(✉)]

[1] Bell Laboratories, Nokia, Murray Hill, USA
kedar@research.bell-labs.com
[2] University of Pennsylvania, Philadelphia, USA
nimits@seas.upenn.edu

Abstract. This paper presents a system, Loopy, for programming loop transformations. Manual loop transformation can be tedious and error-prone, while fully automated methods do not guarantee improvements. Loopy takes a middle path: a programmer specifies a loop transformation at a high level, which is then carried out automatically by Loopy, and formally verified to guard against specification and implementation mistakes. Loopy's notation offers considerable flexibility with assembling transformations, while automation and checking prevent errors. Loopy is implemented for the LLVM framework, building on a polyhedral compilation library. Experiments show substantial improvements over fully automated loop transformations, using simple and direct specifications.

1 Introduction

Restructuring loops in programs to match a target architecture can yield dramatic improvements in run-time, e.g., by exploiting parallelism, by matching the pattern of memory accesses to cache sizes and memory layout, and through judicious placement of prefetching instructions. Re-structuring a loop is, however, a difficult task to do manually – it is tedious and error-prone, and the resulting code is difficult to understand and to maintain. This problem has long been recognized, and it has led to decades of work on sophisticated algorithms which automatically optimize loops. An *optimal* transformation algorithm remains out of reach, though, as the underlying optimization questions are computationally difficult, having to balance a number of potentially conflicting objectives such as code size, parallelism, and cache locality. Performance gains are, therefore, quite variable, even with state-of-the-art compilers.

A remedy to these problems is a semi-automatic optimization approach, where the work is split between the programmer and the compiler: the transformation is *specified* at a high level by the programmer, but the task of *implementing* it falls to the compiler and is done fully automatically. We explore this approach in our work. The approach has multiple benefits. In comparison with manual optimization, first, the programmer is relieved from the manual effort of rewriting the program and the possibility of introducing errors. Second, the specification or parts of it can be re-used, resulting in a library of transformations

© Springer-Verlag GmbH Germany 2016
X. Rival (Ed.): SAS 2016, LNCS 9837, pp. 383–402, 2016.
DOI: 10.1007/978-3-662-53413-7_19

which further reduces manual effort. Third, the specification acts as a certificate for the transformation, it can be verified during application by the compiler, and even checked independently as a further guarantee of correctness.

In comparison with automatic optimization, significant performance gains can be achieved using fairly simple specifications, as we observe in our experiments, and has also been observed previously [6,9,12]. An alternate approach often used to optimize programs is via calls to hand-optimized libraries like Intel's MKL [13] and ATLAS [28]. A semi-automatic optimization approach can complement these approaches and be useful when they do not produce the desired performance improvement.

An effective semi-automatic optimization framework must (1) provide source-code level semantics for the specifications, so that a programmer can easily describe and reason about a transformation, and (2) automatically check the correctness of a specification, so that incorrect transformations are not implemented. Most existing works fall short on at least one of these. CHiLL [6,23], POET [29], Orio [12] and X Language [7] allow program-level transformations, but do not check correctness. On the other hand, URUK [9] verifies transformations, but the specification is on the underlying mathematical representation, which can be too abstract for a programmer. Our work ensures both, by exposing a small set of basic operators, which can be combined together to form complex transformations, and by associating a formal declarative semantics to each operator, which is used for automation and checking.

A transformation in our language is specified as a composition of (instances of) primitive, building-block operations. The language supports four basic operations, which allow arbitrary affine transformations on loop nests and flexible ways of splitting and merging loops. Programmers label loops and sections of loops with loop tags, which are used as handles to describe focused piece-wise transformations on the loop components. The combination of powerful primitive operations with piece-wise application makes it easy for a programmer to assemble a complex loop transformation.

We define formal semantics for each of the basic operations via polyhedral representation of programs. These semantics are used to implement the transformations on the source program, and to ensure that the transformed program is semantically equivalent to the original program.

We have implemented a prototype tool, Loopy[1], building on a polyhedral library for the LLVM compiler framework. Loopy is essentially an interpreter for the specification language, it carries out the specified transformation and verifies its correctness. We have evaluated Loopy on Polybench, a benchmark suite for polyhedral model based tools. The experiments show significant improvements in performance over fully automated methods, with simple specifications.

---

[1] The name is an obvious pun on 'loop' transformation. Moreover, "loopy" is slang for "crazy", which we hope is **not** how this work strikes the reader!

```
for(i=0;i<N;i++){
  for(j=0;j<N;j++){
  {
    Init: C[i][j] = 0;
  }
  for(k=0;k<N;k++){
    Mult:
      C[i][j] += A[i][k]*B[k][j];      for(i=1;i<N;i++){
  }                                      Div:
  }                                        A[i] = A[i]/A[i-1];
}                                        }
```

(a) C++ matrix multiplication fragment   (b) Correctness Checking

Fig. 1. Illustrative Programs to compare Loopy with URUK and CHiLL

2   Illustrative Example

We use simple C/C++ programs, shown in Fig. 1, to illustrate capabilities of Loopy as compared to two other semi-automatic optimization approaches, CHiLL [6] and URUK [9]. CHiLL is representative of systems that specify transformations at source program level, however do not provide any correctness guarantees. URUK is representative of the systems that provide correctness guarantees but operate on alternate representations of programs.

We first focus on improving cache usage on a single-core machine for a matrix multiplication program, shown in Fig. 1a. A multidimensional array in a C/C++ program is stored in row-major order and thus, accesses to elements of array B exhibit poor spatial locality as consecutive accesses occur along the column. Also, accesses to both A and B exhibit poor temporal locality, as each element is accessed repeatedly in different iterations of the outer loops. We would like to reorder these accesses to improve locality. A sequence of loop transformations that would achieve this is: the loop is first split into its component sections, Init and Mult, the loop indices j and k are interchanged in Mult and finally, the resulting loop is tiled. The first transformation enables the subsequent operations on Mult, the second operation improves spacial locality for B and the last operation improves temporal locality for arrays A and B.

We present optimization scripts in Loopy and URUK to implement these loop transformations. Figure 2a shows the Loopy script. The first operation, *realign*, readjusts the number of common loops between two adjacent loop components. Here, the number of common loops is set to 0, which results in complete splitting of the loops. The second one, *affine*, applies the specified affine transformation to the iterators of a loop component. As is well known, affine transformations can be used to represent common transformations such as loop permutations, loop reversal, loop shifting, loop scaling, and loop tiling. For this example, the affine transformations permute loop indices and tile the loop.

```
realign(Init, Mult, 0)                          FISSION([0], [0], [1])
affine(Mult, {[i,j,k] -> [i,k,j]})              INTERCHANGE([1, 0])
affine(Mult, {[i,j,k] -> [i1,j1,k1,i2,j2,k2]:   TILE([1, 0], 64, 64)
        i1 = [i/64] and i2 = i%64 and           STRIPMINE([1], 64)
        j1 = [j/64] and j2 = j%64 and           INTERCHANGE([1, 0])
        k1 = [k/64] and k2 = k%64})             INTERCHANGE([1, 0, 0])
```

(a) Loopy script   (b) URUK script

Fig. 2. Optimization scripts for program in Fig. 1a.

In URUK, the transformations are applied on a polyhedral representation of programs, where each statement is represented by a vector of integers (we refer to this representation in more detail in Sect. 3.2). Figure 2b shows a script that is input to URUK. The FISSION operation splits the loop into component sections. The first INTERCHANGE operation interchanges loop indices. The remaining operations implement tiling. The TILE operation tiles the two inner loops, while STRIPMINE sections the outermost loop. The INTERCHANGE operations are used to permute loop indices in correct order. In our view, the script for Loopy is simpler and more direct than that for URUK. Loop tags Init and Mult make it possible to focus the transformations on specific parts of the loop, without referring to cryptic representations of statements.

We now use a sample loop, shown in Fig. 1b, to illustrate requirements for verifying correctness of transformations. It is easy to see that reversing the loop Div is incorrect. Suppose the loop is executed with A initialized to $[1, 2, 3, 4]$. On executing the loop, A is updated to $[1, 2, 3/2, 8/3]$. However, on executing the reverse loop, A is updated to a different array $[1, 2, 3/2, 4/3]$. Hence, a transformation that reverses this loop is incorrect. Our experiment with CHiLL shows that it implements this transformation without complaint. Loopy, on the other hand, does not carry out the transformation, it generates a violation that points to the execution order dependency that is not preserved. As mistakes such as this are easy to make when complex transformations are involved, correctness checking is essential.

3 Design

We describe the design of Loopy. The tool represents a point in the trade-off between manual optimization (much effort for good performance) and automatic optimization (little manual effort but variable performance).

Loopy may be viewed as a compiler extension that reads in and interprets a transformation script. A script is a sequence of (instances of) primitive building-block transformations. Loopy's interpreter carries out the transformation defined by the composition of the sequence of operations in the script. Loopy contains a verifier, which checks the script and informs the user of an error if carrying it out may result in a program with differing semantics.

In more detail, the transformation process works as follows. Initially, the polyhedral model (parameterized statements, iteration domains, initial schedules and dependency maps) is constructed from the program. Loop components and their domains are identified and computed from the loop tags in the program. Following that step, the transformation script is read in, one operation at a time, and interpreted. The interpretation of each operation results in a new schedule and (possibly) the update of existing loop components and the creation of new loop components. After all of the transformations are completed, the final program schedule is checked by the verifier against the execution order dependency maps, and any dependency violations are reported to the programmer.

This section presents the specification language (Sect. 3.1) with the formal semantics for the building blocks (Sect. 3.2). Verification of transformations is described in Sect. 4.

3.1 Specification Language

We give an overview of the operations available to a programmer to identify loop components and specify transformations.

Loop Tagging. Users may label loops or loop sections with tags and use those as handles in a script. With tags, transformations can be focused on specific portions of a loop. We re-use the idea of scope blocks from C and C++, and define a block of code surrounded by curly braces ({ }) as a *loop component*. We also assign a label to the first statement of the component and use it as the loop tag and a handle in the optimization script. Labels Init and Mult in Fig. 1a are examples of loop tags. This re-purposing of scope blocks and labels avoids the need for modifications to the source language.

Building-Block Operations. Next, we define the primitive operators currently supported in Loopy. (We expect to add more as we gain experience with the tool.) The operators are illustrated by the examples in Fig. 3.

Realign. The realign operator, written as $\mathsf{realign}(l_1, l_2, n)$, is used to split or merge two adjacent loop components l_1 and l_2. This operator realigns the loop components so that the number of common loops in the loop nests of l_1 and l_2 is n. Consider the program in Fig. 3a which consists of loops $L1$ and $L2$ with indices i and j sharing one common loop. The result of applying the operators $\mathsf{realign}(L1, L2, 0)$ and $\mathsf{realign}(L1, L2, 2)$ are shown in Figs. 3b and c respectively. The first splits the components into independent loop nests, while the second merges them into a single loop nest.

Lift. The lift operator, written as $l_2 = \mathsf{lift}(l_1, n)$, returns a handle l_2 to the nth level loop in the loop nest of l_1. It does not transform the program schedule. The ability to select a sub-loop is useful when a subsequent operator is to be applied to an outer loop of the component. For example, applying the operator

```
                        for(i=0;i<N;i++){
                          for(j=0;j<N;j++){
for(i=0;i<N;i++){           L1:  ....
  for(j=0;j<N;j++){              ....
    L1:  ....             }                          for(i=0;i<N;i++){
         ....             }                            for(j=0;j<N;j++){
  }                       for(i=0;i<N;i++){              L1: ....
  for(j=0;j<N;j++){         for(j=0;j<N;j++){                ....
    L2: ....                  L2: ....                    L2: ....
       ....                      ....                        ....
  }                         }                          }
}                         }                          }
```

            (a) P   (b) Q   (c) R

```
                                                     for(i=0;i<N;i++){
                                                       for(j=0;j<N/2;j++){
for(i=0;i<N;i++){    for(i=0;i<N1;i+=2){    L3:  ....
  for(j=0;j<N;j++){    for(j=i/2;j<N2;j++){      ....
    L:  ....             L:  ....               }
       ....                ....               for(j=N/2;j<N;j++){
       ....                ....                 L4:  ....
  }                    }                           ....
}                    }                          }
                                              }
```

            (d) S   (e) T   (f) U

Fig. 3. Examples of basic operations: (a) P: original program (b) Q: realign($L1, L2, 0$) on P (c) R: realign($L1, L2, 2$) on P (d) S: $L = \text{lift}(L1, 2)$ on R (e) T: affine($L, \{[i,j] \to [2i, i+j]\}$) on S (where, $N1 = 2N$ and $N2 = N+i/2$) (f) U: ($L3, L4$) = isplit($L, \{[i,j] : j < N/2\}, 1$) on S.

$L = \text{lift}(L1, 2)$ to the program in Fig. 3c returns handle L to the merged loop as shown in Fig. 3d, which is used for further transformations.

Affine. The affine operator, written as affine(l, f), is used to restructure the loop nest of l according to a general affine function f. A new set of iterators is defined, and each new iterator is assigned an affine function of old iterators, which is given by the function f. As is well known, affine functions can be used to represent a number of useful transformations, such as loop reversal (with $\{[i,j] \to [-i,j]\}$), loop permutation (with $\{[i,j,k] \to [j,k,i]\}$), loop scaling and shifting (with $\{[i,j] \to [2i+1,j]\}$) and loop rotation (with $\{[i,j] \to [i+j, i-j]\}$). Further, we also allow integer division by a constant which further enables loop tiling (as in $\{[i,j] \to [i/32, j/32, i\%32, j\%32]\}$). Figure 3e shows an affine transformation of program S in Fig. 3d.

Isplit. The isplit operator, written as $(l_1, l_2) = \mathsf{isplit}(l, p, n)$, is used to split the index set of the loop nest of l to create two new loop nests given by handles l_1 and l_2, such that the indices in l_1 satisfy the predicate p and those in l_2 satisfy $\neg p$. The value n specifies the loop nest level at which the splitting occurs or the number of common loops after the splitting. For example, consider the operator $(L3, L4) = \mathsf{isplit}(L, \{[i, j] : j < N/2\}, 1)$ on program S in Fig. 3d. The result is shown in Fig. 3f, where $L3$ consists of iterations of j with values less than $N/2$ and $L4$ consists of those with values greater than $N/2$.

3.2   Formal Semantics

We use the polyhedral model of programs to define the semantics of these operators. The polyhedral model represents a program as a collection of statements each of which is parameterized by the iterators of its enclosing loop nest. This model is easy to manipulate via algorithms and hence, is widely used in automated analysis and optimization tools. It allows a rich class of transformations, including the ones expressed in our specification language. We briefly describe the model and follow that with a precise formulation of each operator.

Polyhedral Model. The polyhedral model represents a program as a collection of statement instances, S, defined over an *iteration space* formed by the possible values of iteration variables. A statement instance has the form $s[i_1, i_2, \ldots, i_M]$, where s is a statement in the program, and $i = (i_1, \ldots, i_M)$ is a vector of integer variables representing the iterators of the loop nest which contains s. The set of valid instances of statement s is given by constraining i, in terms of affine inequalities on the iterators and the external parameters of the program; the set of valid vectors is called the *iteration domain* of the statement.

A partial *schedule* function, denoted θ, maps a statement and a point in the iteration space to a linearly ordered (abstract) "time" domain. The time value given by $\theta(s, i)$ is referred to as the *schedule vector* of instance $s[i]$. We use a schedule vector of the following shape: for statement instance $s[i]$,

$$\theta(s, i) = (p_0, j_1, p_1, \ldots, j_M, p_M)$$

The p-entries represent positions, the j-entries the iteration number, as explained next. For convenience, we sometimes separate the position and iteration entries in a vector, representing this as the pair of vectors (p, j).

Consider the abstract syntax tree of a loop nest. Each node represents a basic program statement or a loop; its children (if any) represent nested sub-statements of that statement, and are ordered by their sequence in the program. The natural number p_0 identifies a top-level loop or statement; the number p_1 identifies one of the sub-statements of the p_0'th statement. Thus, the sequence of numbers $p_0, p_1, p_2, \ldots$ fixes a path from root to leaf in the abstract syntax tree of the outermost loop. The integer j_{k+1} fixes a particular iteration of the loop statement at position $p_0, p_1, \ldots p_k$.

To simplify manipulation, we fix the dimension of the schedule vector to the length of the longest root-to-leaf path in the abstract syntax tree, filling missing entries with 0's. As a convenient notation, let $pos_\theta(s, i)$ denote the position vector $(p_0, p_1, \ldots, p_M)$, and let $it_\theta(s, i)$ denote the iteration vector $(j_1, j_2, \ldots, j_M)$ in the schedule vector $\theta(s, i)$.

Let $u = \theta(s, i)$ and $v = \theta(t, j)$ be schedule vectors for statement instances $s[i]$ and $t[j]$ in the current schedule θ. If u is lexicographically smaller than v i.e. $u \prec v$ then $s[i]$ is executed before $t[j]$. Every loop transformation alters only the schedule θ; the original set of statement instances and iteration domains remains unchanged. I.e., only the execution order of the same set of statement instances is rearranged.

As an example, consider the program in Fig. 1a. The program consists of statements $s_{Init}[i, j]$ and $s_{Mult}[i, j, k]$. The iteration domains of these statements are $0 \leq i < N \wedge 0 \leq j < N$ and $0 \leq i < N \wedge 0 \leq j < N \wedge 0 \leq k < N$ and their initial schedule is $(0, i, 0, j, 0, 0, 0)$ and $(0, i, 0, j, 1, k, 0)$ respectively. The corresponding position vectors in the initial schedule are $[0, 0, 0, 0]$ and $[0, 0, 1, 0]$. The execution order of the program is implicitly captured in the schedule vectors: for an iteration $[i_0, j_0]$, $s_{Init}[i_0, j_0]$ is executed before $s_{Mult}[i_0, j_0, k]$ since, $[0, 0, 0, 0] \prec [0, 0, 1, 0]$ and similarly, for two iterations $[i_0, j_0]$ and $[i_1, j_1]$ if $[i_0, j_0] \prec [i_1, j_1]$, then $s_{Init}[i_0, j_0]$ is executed before $s_{Init}[i_1, j_1]$.

Consider program A in Fig. 4a. Each statement is annotated with its position vector. For example, statement s_4 is annotated with vector $[1, 1, 0]$, as the outermost loop with iterator i is at position 1, the second loop with iterator j is again at position 1, while the statement itself is at position 0.

Loop Component. Let $\mathcal{L}$ denote the set of loop components in the program. Let $P(l)$ be the set of positions represented by component l. I.e., $P(l)$ is the set of positions of statements in the subtree rooted at l. Given P and schedule θ, let $D_\theta(l)$ denote the set of statement instances contained in the scope block of the component. I.e., $s[i]$ is in $D_\theta(l)$ if and only if its position vector $pos_\theta(s, i)$ is in $P(l)$. In Fig. 4a, for loop component $L1$, $P(L1) = \{[0, 0, 0], [0, 0, 1]\}$, and $D_\theta(L1) = \{s_0[i, j], s_1[i, j]\}$ for the implied schedule θ.

Basic Transformations. Now, we define the semantics of each basic operation. This is defined as a change of the schedule of the program. I.e., a basic transformation only rearranges the execution order of statements, it does not change the set of statements. In each case, we specify the semantics of an operation as a map from a current schedule θ to the new schedule θ'.

Realign. In a realign(l_1, l_2, n) operation, the position vector of statements in loop component l_2 is updated so that, statements in l_1 and l_2 share the first n loops, and l_2 is next to l_1 in the nth loop after the update. To define this, we first compute the current gap between the positions of statements in l_1 and l_2. Let the lexicographically largest position in l_1 be p_1 i.e. $p_1 = max(q), q \in P(l_1)$ and the lexicographically smallest position in l_2 be p_2 i.e. $p_2 = min(q), q \in P(l_2)$

```
                                                    for(i=0;i<N;i++){
                                                     for(j=0;j<N;j++){
for(i=0;i<N;i++){                                    L1:  <s0>[0,0,0,0]
 for(j=0;j<N;j++){                                        <s1>[0,0,1,0]
  L1:  <s0>[0,0,0]                                   }
       <s1>[0,0,1]                                  }
 }                     for(i=0;i<N;i++){           for(i=0;i<N;i++){
}                       for(j=0;j<N;j++){            for(j=0;j<N1;j++){
for(i=0;i<N;i++){        L1:  <s0>[0,0,0]             for(k=0;k<N2;k++){
 for(j=0;j<N;j++){            <s1>[0,0,1]              L2:  <s2>[1,0,0,0]
  L2:  <s2>[1,0,0]       L2:  <s2>[0,0,2]                  <s3>[1,0,0,1]
       <s3>[1,0,1]            <s3>[0,0,3]             }
 }                      }                           }
}                      }                            }
 for(j=0;j<N;j++){      for(j=0;j<N;j++){            for(j=0;j<N;j++){
  L3:  <s4>[1,1,0]       L3:  <s4>[0,1,2]            L3:  <s4>[1,1,0,0]
       <s5>[1,1,1]            <s5>[0,1,3]                 <s5>[1,1,1,0]
 }                      }                            }
}                      }                            }

      (a) A                   (b) B                         (c) C
```

Fig. 4. Examples illustrating semantics of basic operations (a) A: original program with statements labeled with position vectors (b) B: realign$(L1, L2, 2)$ on A (c) C: affine$(L2, \{[i,j] \rightarrow [i, j/32, j\%32]\})$ on A (where $N1 = N/32 + 1, N2 = \min\{32, N - j * 32\}$). Note the change in position vectors in programs B and C.

and let gap, g be their difference, i.e. $g = p_2 - p_1$. For example, in Fig. 4a, the largest position in $L1$ is $[0, 0, 1]$ and the smallest position in $L2$ is $[1, 0, 0]$ and their gap is $[1, 0, -1]$. Now, to get the desired update, this gap should be removed, and thus, g must be subtracted from position vectors of statements in l_2. To position statements in l_2 next to those in l_1 at the nth loop, the nth value in their position vectors must be incremented by 1. Therefore, for a statement $s[i] \in D(l_2)$, the new position vector, $pos_{\theta'}(s, i)$ is $pos_\theta(s, i) - g + I(n)$, where $I(n)$ is an indicator vector with component $I_j(n) = 1$ if $j = n$ and 0 otherwise.

In a realign operation, the positions of statements with positions *after* those in l_2 must also be updated by the same amount as statements in l_2. This is because, the relative difference between the positions of statements in l_2 and those after l_2 must remain same. For example, consider the operation realign$(L1, L2, 2)$ on program A in Fig. 4a. The resulting program is shown in Fig. 4b. To preserve the relative position with respect to $L2$, the statements in $L3$ must also be moved inside the loop with iterator i.

The overall transformation is:

$$\phi_{\text{realign}}(\boldsymbol{p}, \boldsymbol{j}) = \begin{cases} (\boldsymbol{p} + \boldsymbol{p}_1 - \boldsymbol{p}_2 + I(n), \boldsymbol{j}) & \boldsymbol{p} \succeq \boldsymbol{p}_2 \\ (\boldsymbol{p}, \boldsymbol{j}) & \text{otherwise} \end{cases}$$

Note that, $\boldsymbol{p} \succeq \boldsymbol{p}_2$ denotes all position vectors lexicographically greater than or equal to p_2 and thus, represents all statements in l_2 or those after l_2 in the syntax tree. Now, the new schedule $\theta' = \phi_{\text{realign}} \circ \theta$ and for each component $l \in \mathcal{L}$, $P'(l) = \phi_{\text{realign}}(P(l))$.

Lift. The operation $l_2 = \text{lift}(l_1, n)$ is different from the others in that it is only definitional, it does not alter schedules. This operation adds a new component l_2 to $\mathcal{L}$. This component consists of all statements within the nth outer loop of l_1. These are precisely the statements in the program for which the position vectors match those in $P(l_1)$ on the first n values. Hence, the operation returns a loop component l_2 such that,

$$P(l_2) = \{q : (q_0, q_1, \ldots, q_{n-1}) \equiv (p_0, p_1, \ldots, p_{n-1}) \text{ for some } p \in P(l_1)\}$$

Affine. The operation $\text{affine}(l, f)$ applies function f to the iteration vector of statements in l. As f may increase the number of iterators, it may be required to update the position vectors of statements as well. Let f take a iterators and generate b iterators as output, i.e. $f : Z^a \to Z^b, b \geq a$. First, the number of dimensions of position vectors must be increased by $b - a$ dimensions to account for the additional iterators. Next, the dimensions of old position vectors must be mapped to the new set of dimensions, such that the relative position difference between statements in l and those outside l remains the same and also, the statements in l are contained inside the new iteration set.

The position of statements outside l remains the same with only zeros padded in the end. However, the position vectors of statements within l is updated as follows. To preserve the relative position difference, we map the first a dimensions of old position vector to the a dimensions of the new one. To contain the statements inside the new iteration set, every subsequent dimension is shifted to the right by $b - a$ positions and thus, kth dimension of old position vector is mapped to $(k + b - a)$th dimension in the new position vector. The remaining dimensions are filled with zeros. For example, Fig. 4c shows the result of operation $\text{affine}(L2, \{[i, j] \to [i, j/32, j\%32]\})$ on program in Fig. 4a. As can be seen, for statements in $L1$ and $L3$, a zero is added in the last dimension, while for $L2$, zero is added in the third dimension of the position vector.

The overall transformation is:

$$\phi_{\text{affine}}(p, j) = \begin{cases} ((p_0, \ldots, p_a, \overbrace{0, \ldots, 0}^{(b-a)}, p_{a+1}, \ldots, p_M), f(j)) & p \in P(l) \\ \qquad\quad \underbrace{\quad}_{(b-a)} \qquad\quad \underbrace{\quad}_{(b-a)} \\ ((p, \overbrace{0, \ldots, 0}^{(b-a)}), (j, \overbrace{0, \ldots, 0}^{(b-a)})) & \text{otherwise} \end{cases}$$

As in the case of realign, $\theta' = \phi_{\text{affine}} \circ \theta$ and for each component $l \in \mathcal{L}$, $P'(l) = \phi_{\text{affine}}(P(l))$.

Isplit. The operation $(l_1, l_2) = \text{isplit}(l, pred, n)$ splits the iteration domain of the loop component l into two new components, l_1 and l_2. Component l_1 consists of statements in l whose current iteration vector satisfies the predicate $pred$, i.e. $pred(it_\theta(s, i)) = true$, while l_2 consists of the remaining statements. Note that the first component l_1 takes the place of l, while l_2 is inserted after l_1 in the nth loop. To accommodate this, statements in l_2 and all subsequent statements must be moved down by one position. This is done just as in the case of realign operation. Let the lexicographically smallest schedule vector in $P(l)$ be $\boldsymbol{p_m}$. The transformation here is

$$\phi_{\mathsf{isplit}}(\boldsymbol{p}, \boldsymbol{j}) = \begin{cases} (\boldsymbol{p}, \boldsymbol{j}) & \boldsymbol{p} \prec \boldsymbol{p_m} \vee \boldsymbol{p} \in P(l) \wedge pred(\boldsymbol{j}) \\ (\boldsymbol{p} + \boldsymbol{I}(n), \boldsymbol{j}) & \text{otherwise} \end{cases}$$

As in the previous cases, $\theta' = \phi_{\mathsf{isplit}} \circ \theta$ and for each component $l \in \mathcal{L}$, $P'(l) = \phi_{\mathsf{isplit}}(P(l))$. Further, the new components l_1 and l_2 are defined as follows:

$$P'(l_1) = \{(\boldsymbol{p}) : \boldsymbol{p} \in P(l)\}$$

$$P'(l_2) = \{(\boldsymbol{p} + \boldsymbol{I}(n)) : \boldsymbol{p} \in P(l)\}$$

Note that, ϕ_{isplit} ensures that statements in l_1 and l_2 correspond to those at locations in $P'(l_1)$ and $P'(l_2)$ respectively.

4 Verification

The loop transformation operates in three stages. First, the program text is turned into a polyhedral model. Then the model is transformed according to the specified script. Finally, the resulting model is turned back into a program text. The first (and more important in practice) check is to ensure that an incorrect script specified by a programmer is never executed. We do so by verifying certain conditions at the polyhedral level. The second is to ensure consistency between the execution semantics of the polyhedral model and its associated program. In our experience with Loopy, the first check has proved to be invaluable, preventing us from performing transformations that seemed correct but violated dependencies in subtle ways. The second check is not yet implemented.

4.1 Verifying the Polyhedral Transformation

Programmers have full freedom to specify transformations and may, therefore, specify incorrect ones. An incorrect specification will lead to a schedule that suffers from one of two possible problems:

- The schedule may not be a one-to-one map. I.e., more than one statement instance could be mapped to the same time in the new schedule.
- The new schedule may not respect execution order dependencies between statement instances. A transformation is guaranteed to be correct if it rearranges execution order only for independent statement instances. (Two statement instances are independent if they refer to disjoint variables, or if all common references are reads.)

The verifier in Loopy checks the correctness of a transformation by checking that it is a one-to-one map, and that it preserves dependencies. We assume that the original schedule is one-to-one and Loopy only checks one-to-oneness of the overall transformation function ϕ. Since ϕ is a linear transformation, Loopy uses a linear algebra library, ISL [27] to do this check. Loopy relies on the polyhedral model to supply the original execution order dependency maps between statement instances. If there is a dependency $s[i] \to t[j]$, then $s[i]$ must be executed before $t[j]$; a transformation that does not preserve this dependency is likely to be faulty. Let the final schedule of the transformed program be given by the function θ'. Loopy checks that $\theta'(s, i) \prec \theta'(t, j)$ holds for all dependencies $s[i] \to t[j]$. If this check fails, the violated dependencies are reported to the user as a source of potential incorrectness.

The checks are performed only after composing the sequence of transformations in the specification. This is because dependencies can be temporarily violated in the middle of a sequence but established at the end. A check performed after every transformation would (incorrectly) mark such sequences as invalid. The situation is similar to that commonly encountered in establishing an inductive loop invariant, which may be temporarily violated within the loop body while being re-established at the start of the next iteration.

4.2   Verifying the Program-Model Correspondence

We formulate the consistency question as follows. A program has a natural operational semantics, where the program is represented by a state transition system. The state is a map from variables to values, while a transition corresponds to execution of a statement instance. In the polyhedral model, on the other hand, statement instances are executed according to the specified schedule. The question is to formulate conditions under which the scheduled ordering coincides with the natural ordering. As will be apparent, the conditions have a strong similarity to invariants and ranking functions. This analysis is valid only for sequential programs, checking parallelizing transformations is a topic for future work.

As formulated in the previous section, polyhedral execution is defined over an iteration space I (the set of all valid iteration vectors). Each statement is associated over a subset of that space, called its domain (denoted dom(s), for statement s). The schedule function, $\theta : stmt \times I \to T$, maps a statement and a point of the space to an element of a totally ordered set, T ("time"). The schedule function is partial; however, for a statement s it is defined for all points in dom(s). The operational model executes statement instances in the order defined by the schedule. I.e., in a computation following the schedule, instance $t[j]$ occurs after instance $s[i]$ if $\theta(s, i) \prec \theta(t, j)$.

As programs are sequential, one must rule out the possibility of concurrent execution. This is done by checking that the schedule is a one-to-one map, so that different instances are not mapped to the same time.. I.e., the following is valid:

$$[(s \neq t) \wedge (i \neq j) \wedge i \in \mathsf{dom}(s) \wedge j \in \mathsf{dom}(t) \Rightarrow \theta(s, i) \neq \theta(t, j)]$$

Next, we present conditions which ensure that every natural execution is a scheduled execution. To simplify the presentation, we suppose that there are empty statements, entry and exit, at the start and end of the loop, with scheduled time $\perp$ (the minimum of the time domain) and $\top$ (the maximum of the time domain) respectively. Let $p_{s,t}$ represent the path transition relation from the state before statement s to the state before statement t.

(**Inv**) If an instance of t follows an instance of s in the program semantics, its iteration vector should belong to the domain of t. The following validity expresses the constraint.

$$[p_{s,t}(i,j) \wedge i \in \mathrm{dom}(s) \Rightarrow j \in \mathrm{dom}(t)]$$

Note that this implies that the collection of statement domains is a mutual inductive invariant.

(**Rank1**) The instance of t must have a scheduled time after that of the instance of s. I.e., the following should be valid:

$$[p_{s,t}(i,j) \wedge i \in \mathrm{dom}(s) \Rightarrow \theta(s,i) \prec \theta(t,j)]$$

(**Rank2**) The instance of t must have the *minimum* scheduled time after that of the instance of s. I.e., the following should be valid:

$$[p_{s,t}(i,j) \wedge i \in \mathrm{dom}(s) \wedge u \neq t \wedge k \in \mathrm{dom}(u) \wedge \theta(s,i) \prec \theta(u,k)$$
$$\Rightarrow \theta(t,j) \prec \theta(u,k)]$$

These are implicitly universally quantified expressions in the free variables. As the domain and schedule functions are given by affine expressions, if the path conditions can be represented in an SMT-supported logic, the validity checks can be carried out automatically using an SMT solver.

To illustrate this further, consider the program in Fig. 1a. As noted in the previous section, it has two statements, $s_{Init}[i,j]$ and $s_{Mult}[i,j,k]$. The iteration domains of these statements are $0 \leq i < N \wedge 0 \leq j < N$ and $0 \leq i < N \wedge 0 \leq j < N \wedge 0 \leq k < N$ and their initial schedule θ is $(0,i,0,j,0,0,0)$ and $(0,i,0,j,1,k,0)$ respectively. Now consider a path from $s_{Init}[i,j]$ to $s_{Mult}[i,j,0]$:

- Inv: For each $(i,j) \in \mathrm{dom}(s_{Init})$, $(i,j,0) \in \mathrm{dom}(s_{Mult})$
- Rank1: $\theta(s_{Init},(i,j)) = (0,i,0,j,0,0,0) \prec (0,i,0,j,1,0,0) = \theta(s_{Mult},(i,j,0))$
- Rank2: $s_{Mult}[i,j,0]$ has the minimum scheduled time after $s_{Init}[i,j]$

We similarly check paths entry to $s_{Init}[0,0]$, $s_{Mult}[i,j,k]$ to $s_{Mult}[i,j,k+1]$, $k < N-1$, $s_{Mult}[i,j,N-1]$ to $s_{Init}[i,j+1]$, $j < N-1$, and $s_{Mult}[N,N,N]$ to exit.

Theorem 1. *For a schedule meeting the conditions above, the scheduled computations are precisely the program computations.*

For any natural program computation, conditions (Inv), (Rank1) and (Rank2) ensure that there is a corresponding scheduled computation with the same sequence of actions. The other direction follows by determinism, non-blocking, and the 1-1 nature of θ. A detailed proof is presented in [19].

5   Implementation

We have implemented Loopy in Polly [10], a polyhedral library for LLVM [17]. LLVM is a popular compiler framework used to generate optimized code for various front-end high level languages and back-end platforms. LLVM converts the high-level program into an intermediate representation, known as the LLVM IR, that goes through a sequence of compiler analysis and transformations and is then converted into an executable for a back-end platform. Polly is a sophisticated library of transformations used to extract polyhedral models from LLVM IR, transform the extracted model, and convert it back to LLVM IR. Loopy is implemented as an optimization phase within Polly that transforms the polyhedral model of the program provided by Polly. Polyhedral models can be extracted for a wide variety of programs containing structured and unstructured loops [4]. Code is generated from the polyhedral model for various kinds of schedules [11]. By basing itself on Polly, Loopy becomes immediately applicable to a large class of programs and transformations.

ISL [27] is a library for representing and manipulating integer sets and relations; it supports various operations and decision procedures on these. This library is used to represent the components of polyhedral model, such as the set of statements, their iteration domains, and schedules. We further use ISL to implement the basic transformations, apply them on the polyhedral model, and to verify the final model for correctness. Verification checks the polyhedral transformation; the program-model correspondence is not yet implemented. Most of the operations used in defining our transformations can be mapped directly to an operation in ISL, which simplifies the implementation.

The optimization script is stored in a separate file, which is read in through a parser that extracts the type and inputs for each transformation to be applied on the program. Further, we rely on the ISL parser to parse the affine transformation and predicate representations for the *affine* and *isplit* operators.

To implement loop tags and extract domains of loop components in the polyhedral model, we do the following. The front-ends for LLVM do not necessarily preserve scope blocks while generating LLVM IR from the source code. Therefore, we surround a loop component block with a dummy `for` loop containing a single iteration, if there is not one already present. This helps identify the block of tagged code in the corresponding LLVM IR. While we currently perform this manually as needed, this will be automated in the future. The label of the first statement in a loop block is read during the construction of polyhedral model in Polly to get the desired loop component handle. We augment the polyhedral construction phase to construct a map from the handle to the initial schedule of all statements contained within the loop component, which gives the required domain of the loop component. This works well in general. However, we did find a few cases where prior optimization to LLVM IR either modified the label of the loop component or the loop itself and thus, domains could not be constructed for some of the loop components. We plan to resolve this issue in future.

6   Evaluation

In this section, we present a preliminary evaluation of Loopy. We had multiple goals while evaluating Loopy. First, we wanted to understand the amount of speed-up that can be achieved using Loopy as compared to state-of-the-art optimizing compilers. Second, we wanted to assess the amount of effort that is required to achieve these significant speed-ups. Third, we wanted to understand what kind of optimizations are applicable and which basic transformations get used most often. Lastly, we wanted to understand the overall experience of using this tool. We present our observations here.

We evaluated Loopy on Polybench 4.1 [20], a benchmark suite maintained by the polyhedral compilation community. This is a collection of 30 programs from various domains, which provides a diverse set of benchmark programs. The programs expose only the kernels that need to be optimized and thus, are easy to work with. We optimize these programs for performance on single cores, focusing on improving cache usage. We compare Loopy with the PLUTO [5] based optimizer in Polly (LLVM version 3.7.0), with LLVM/Clang (version 3.7.0), and with the Intel C++ Compiler (version 16.0.2) under -O3 optimization.

For each program in the suite, we labeled the program with loop tags, and wrote an optimization script. We experimented with different combinations of transformations to improve performance of the programs, selecting those which showed significant improvements. All scripts together were written and analyzed in a *week's time*. They required combining specifications of loop splitting, loop merging, loop interchange, loop shifting and loop tiling. The specifications are included in [19]. Most of the programs have simple optimization scripts.

The experimental setup used is as follows. We ran experiments on a Macbook Pro with Intel i5 processor (2.6 GHz, 3 MB L3 Cache, 256 KB L2 Cache) and 8 GB 1600 MHz DDR3 RAM. Polybench comes with data sets of different sizes, we use the standard data set here. We report execution times that are average of 3 runs of the programs, though we found them to be fairly consistent. The verification step does not noticeably influence the compilation time, therefore, we do not report the compilation times here.

The results of the experiments are shown in Fig. 5. The benchmarks are split into different categories, with a sub-plot for each category. Each sub-plot shows the speed up achieved using Loopy-specified optimizations as compared to those performed by ICC, Polly and LLVM/clang, respectively. The number of basic transformations used by Loopy is annotated on top of the bars, for each benchmark.

As can be seen from the figure, we achieve significant speedups for Linear Algebra Kernels and Solvers and Data Mining applications. We found that most of these programs were variants of matrix multiplication program from Fig. 1a, and similar ideas worked to improve the performance. In particular, improving spatial locality of data accesses resulted in a significant speed up. Tiling the iteration space was also useful in improving the temporal locality, although it improved the performance only slightly. In this class, the optimization scripts were fairly small and involved realigning loops followed by affine transformations.

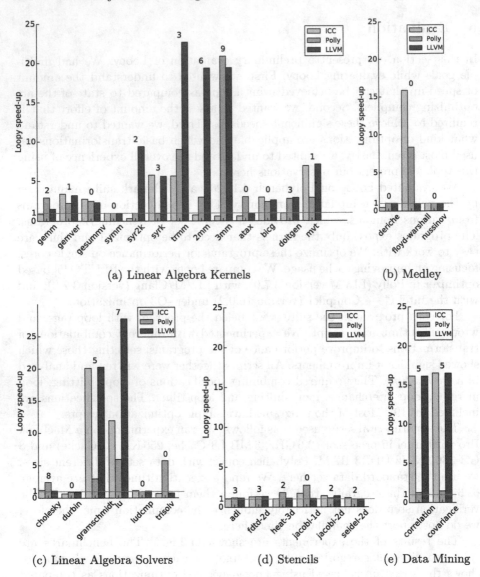

Fig. 5. Speed-ups with Loopy vs ICC, Polly, and LLVM/clang on Polybench programs. The number of basic transformations used by Loopy is annotated on top of the bars, for each benchmark. Speed-ups are ratios of execution times of the kernels: e.g., speedup in Loopy vs ICC is given by (ICC optimized execution time)/(Loopy optimized execution time).

We did not achieve significant speedups for Stencils, as the data-accesses were already aligned well and hence exhibited good spatial locality. Most of the speed up came from shifting loops and then merging adjacent loops that led to reuse of data elements across loops and hence improved temporal locality.

In some cases, it is possible to tile the loops; however, this required complex skewing transformations, which we found hard to specify manually. Specifically, in `seidel-2d`, it took multiple iterations to find the right transformation and verification came handy in this search. We plan to experiment with new operators which address loop skewing directly, which should simplify this process in future.

Lastly, for some benchmarks, we did not find any transformation (in the limited time spent optimizing the scripts) that improved the performance of the application. In Fig. 5, those are applications where the number of transformations is 0. Note that in all cases, our performance is almost equivalent or better than the other compilers. This indicates that those programs were difficult to optimize automatically as well. Further in certain cases, automatic optimization deteriorated performance. For example in linear algebra kernels `gesummv` and `bicg`, Polly tiles a key loop in the program which already exhibits good spatial and temporal locality. This transformation, therefore, only adds an overhead of additional checks and leads to poor performance.

We now detail some of experiences with using the tool. First, we found verification to be helpful in finding bugs in our optimizations. In particular, while optimizing `lu`, we received an error on merging adjacent loops, which we had thought initially was possible. On further inspection, we realized that Polly normalizes iterators to start from 0 and increment by 1, which caused the problem with our strategy. After modifying the transformation to take this into account, we obtained a correct optimization. The feedback about which dependencies were violated in the initial strategy was helpful in understanding the source of the mistake. For programs `3mm` and `ludcmp`, we found that Polly does not produce dependency maps between statements, which prevents Polly from optimizing the program. For Loopy, on the other hand, dependency maps are only necessary to check correctness at the final step, and are not needed for the actual transformation. We were able to transform those programs and achieved significant speedup for `3mm`. Lastly, for `durbin` and `ludcmp`, we found that some of the loop tags in the source program are not preserved in the conversion to LLVM IR. This prevented us from applying certain optimizations.

7 Related Work

Our system builds upon a considerable body of work on automated loop transformation methods, which is covered in a number of excellent books [1–3, 18], papers and tools. In particular, we build upon the theory of polyhedral loop transformation (cf. [8, 14]) – which grew out of earlier work on algebraic representations of iteration spaces [16] and other influences – and its implementation in the Polly system for LLVM [10]. A well studied means for automated optimization (e.g., followed in PLUTO [5]) is to convert the problem into an integer linear programming (ILP) formulation and optimize an objective function. A different approach (cf. [9, 15, 25, 26, 29]) is a search through the space of sequences of transformations: the search process generates sequences of transformations formed from a basis set and chooses those which maximize performance based on run-time tests. These automatic approaches work well in a variety of situations, though not *all* situations, primarily due to the computational hardness of the underlying problems. Loopy relies on programmers to specify transformations and programmer insight can often supersede these sophisticated algorithms.

A few domain specific works have also been developed along similar lines: SPIRAL [21] for digital signal processing, Halide [22] for image processing pipelines and BLAC [24] for linear algebra expressions. However, first, they are specific to a domain, and second, they require programmers to express computation in a new language which might be a steep learning curve.

Other systems have been developed with goals similar to ours. CHiLL [6,23] is a system which makes available a rich set of affine transformations to the programmer. POET [29], Orio [12] and X Language [7] also provide similar facilities. However, as noted in Sect. 2, these systems do not guard programmers against incorrect specifications, which may hinder usability. Another system from ALCHEMY group, URUK [9] provides transformation primitives that operate on polyhedral representation of loops and also checks transformations for correctness. However, polyhedral representation can be too abstract for a programmer to use efficiently. In fact, the primary motive of this work was to provide a structured transformation space for automatic methods to search efficient implementations, and not direct usage by programmers. Loopy represents the best of both worlds with clean programmer semantics and strong correctness guarantees.

8   Conclusion and Future Work

The Loopy framework gives full freedom to a programmer's ingenuity while ensuring that every transformation is correctly implemented. The key insight is that the combination of flexibility, automation and checking ("trust but verify"!) is powerful and enjoyable to work with. Our experiments show that simple, direct specifications can result in significant improvements over fully automated methods. In future work, we plan to explore this combination for the *parallelization* of loops for multi-core and GPU platforms. Here, verification becomes even more essential, in order to catch subtle errors that can arise from weak memory models. We hope to be able to make use of the considerable literature on weak memory model verification to ensure correct transformations.

Acknowledgements. We would like to thank our colleagues at Bell Labs and at the University of Pennsylvania for their helpful comments on this research. This work was supported, in part, by DARPA under agreement number FA8750-12-C-0166. The U.S. Government is authorized to reproduce and distribute reprints for Governmental purposes notwithstanding any copyright notation thereon. The views and conclusions contained herein are those of the authors and should not be interpreted as necessarily representing the official policies or endorsements, either expressed or implied, of DARPA or the U.S. Government.

References

1. Aho, A.V., Lam, M.S., Sethi, R., Ullman, J.D.: Compilers: Principles, Techniques, and Tools. Addison Wesley, Boston (2006)
2. Allen, R., Kennedy, K.: Optimizing Compilers for Modern Architectures: A Dependence-Based Approach. Morgan Kaufmann, San Francisco (2001)
3. Banerjee, U.: Loop Transformations for Restructuring Compilers: Dependence analysis. Kluwer (1997)
4. Benabderrahmane, M., Pouchet, L., Cohen, A., Bastoul, C.: The polyhedral model is more widely applicable than you think. In: Compiler Construction, 19th International Conference, CC 2010, Held as Part of the Joint European Conferences on Theory and Practice of Software, ETAPS 2010, Paphos, Cyprus, 20–28 March 2010, Proceedings, pp. 283–303 (2010). http://dx.doi.org/10.1007/978-3-642-11970-5_16
5. Bondhugula, U., Hartono, A., Ramanujam, J., Sadayappan, P.: A practical automatic polyhedral parallelizer and locality optimizer. In: Proceedings ofthe ACM SIGPLAN 2008 Conference on Programming Language Design and Implementation, Tucson, AZ, USA, 7–13 June 2008, pp. 101–113 (2008). http://doi.acm.org/10.1145/1375581.1375595
6. Chen, C., Chame, J., Hall, M.: CHiLL: A framework for composing high-level loop transformations. Technical Report 08–897, University of Southern California (2008)
7. Donadio, S., Brodman, J., Roeder, T., Yotov, K., Barthou, D., Cohen, A., Garzarán, M.J., Padua, D.A., Pingali, K.K.: A language for the compact representation of multiple program versions. In: Ayguadé, E., Baumgartner, G., Ramanujam, J., Sadayappan, P. (eds.) LCPC 2005. LNCS, vol. 4339, pp. 136–151. Springer, Heidelberg (2006)
8. Feautrier, P.: Some efficient solutions to the affine scheduling problem. Part II. Multidimensional time. Int. J. Parallel Program. **21**(6), 389–420 (1992). http://dx.doi.org/10.1007/BF01379404
9. Girbal, S., Vasilache, N., Bastoul, C., Cohen, A., Parello, D., Sigler, M., Temam, O.: Semi-automatic composition of loop transformations for deep parallelism and memory hierarchies. Int. J. Parallel Program. **34**(3), 261–317 (2006). http://dx.doi.org/10.1007/s10766-006-0012-3
10. Grosser, T., Größlinger, A., Lengauer, C.: Polly-performing polyhedral optimizations on a low-level intermediate representation. Parallel Process. Lett. **22**(4) (2012). http://dx.doi.org/10.1142/S0129626412500107
11. Grosser, T., Verdoolaege, S., Cohen, A.: Polyhedral AST generation is more than scanning polyhedra. ACM Trans. Program. Lang. Syst. **37**(4) (2015). http://dx.doi.org/10.1145/2743016. Article no. 12
12. Hartono, A., Norris, B., Sadayappan, P.: Annotation-based empirical performance tuning using Orio. In: 23rd IEEE International Symposium on Parallel and Distributed Processing, IPDPS 2009, Rome, Italy, 23–29 May 2009, pp. 1–11 (2009). http://dx.doi.org/10.1109/IPDPS.2009.5161004
13. Intel: Intel Math Kernel Library (MKL) (2016). https://software.intel.com/en-us/intel-mkl/
14. Kelly, W., Pugh, W.: A framework for unifying reordering transformations. Technical Report UMIAS-TR-92-126.1, Univ. of Maryland, College Park, MD, USA (1993)
15. Khan, M.M., Basu, P., Rudy, G., Hall, M.W., Chen, C., Chame, J.: A script-based autotuning compiler system to generate high-performance CUDA code. TACO **9**(4), 31 (2013). http://doi.acm.org/10.1145/2400682.2400690

16. Lamport, L.: The parallel execution of DO loops. Commun. ACM **17**(2), 83–93 (1974). http://doi.acm.org/10.1145/360827.360844

17. Lattner, C., Adve, V.S.: LLVM: A compilation framework for lifelong program analysis & transformation. In: CGO, pp. 75–88 (2004). llvm.org

18. Muchnick, S.S.: Advanced Compiler Design and Implementation. Morgan Kaufmann, San Francisco (1997)

19. Namjoshi, K.S., Singhania, N.: Loopy: programmable and formally verified loop transformations. Technical Report MS-CIS-16-04, Department of Computer and Information Science, University of Pennsylvania (2016)

20. Pouchet, L.N.: Polybench, the polyhedral benchmark suite (2015). http://polybench.sourceforge.net/

21. Püschel, M., Moura, J.M.F., Johnson, J., Padua, D., Veloso, M., Singer, B., Xiong, J., Franchetti, F., Gacic, A., Voronenko, Y., Chen, K., Johnson, R.W., Rizzolo, N.: SPIRAL: code generation for DSP transforms. Proc. IEEE **93**(2), 232–275 (2005). Program Generation, Optimization, and Adaptation

22. Ragan-Kelley, J., Barnes, C., Adams, A., Paris, S., Durand, F., Amarasinghe, S.: Halide: a language and compiler for optimizing parallelism, locality, and recomputation in image processing pipelines. In: Proceedings of the 34th ACMSIGPLAN Conference on Programming Language Design and Implementation, pp. 519–530, PLDI 2013. ACM, New York (2013). http://doi.acm.org/10.1145/2491956.2462176

23. Rudy, G., Khan, M.M., Hall, M.W., Chen, C., Chame, J.: A programming language interface to describe transformations and code generation. In: Languages and Compilers for Parallel Computing - 23rd International Workshop, LCPC 2010, Houston, TX, USA, 7–9 October 2010, Revised Selected Papers, pp. 136–150 (2010). http://dx.doi.org/10.1007/978-3-642-19595-2_10

24. Spampinato, D.G., Püschel, M.: A basic linear algebra compiler. In: Proceedings of Annual IEEE/ACM International Symposium on Code Generation and Optimization, pp. 23:23–23:32, CGO 2014. ACM, New York (2014). http://doi.acm.org/10.1145/2544137.2544155

25. Steuwer, M., Fensch, C., Lindley, S., Dubach, C.: Generating performance portable code using rewrite rules: from high-level functional expressions to high-performance OpenCL code. SIGPLAN Not. **50**(9), 205–217 (2015). http://doi.acm.org/10.1145/2858949.2784754

26. Tiwari, A., Chen, C., Chame, J., Hall, M.W., Hollingsworth, J.K.: A scalable autotuning framework for compiler optimization. In: 23rd IEEE International Symposium on Parallel and Distributed Processing, IPDPS 2009, Rome, Italy, 23–29 May 2009, pp. 1–12 (2009). http://dx.doi.org/10.1109/IPDPS.2009.5161054

27. Verdoolaege, S.: *isl*: an integer set library for the polyhedral model. In: Mathematical Software - ICMS 2010, Third International Congress on Mathematical Software, Kobe, Japan, 13–17 September 2010, Proceedings, pp. 299–302 (2010). http://dx.doi.org/10.1007/978-3-642-15582-6_49

28. Whaley, R.C., Dongarra, J.J.: Automatically tuned linear algebra software. In: Proceedings of the 1998 ACM/IEEE Conference on Supercomputing, pp. 1–27, SC 1998. IEEE Computer Society, Washington, DC (1998). http://dl.acm.org/citation.cfm?id=509058.509096

29. Yi, Q.: POET: a scripting language for applying parameterized source-to-source program transformations. Softw. Pract. Exper. **42**(6), 675–706 (2012). http://dx.doi.org/10.1002/spe.1089

Abstract Interpretation of Supermodular Games

Francesco Ranzato[✉]

Dipartimento di Matematica, University of Padova, Padova, Italy
francesco.ranzato@unipd.it

Abstract. Supermodular games are a well known class of noncooperative games which find significant applications in a variety of models, especially in operations research and economic applications. Supermodular games always have Nash equilibria which are characterized as fixed points of multivalued functions on complete lattices. Abstract interpretation is here applied to set up an approximation framework for Nash equilibria of supermodular games. This is achieved by extending the theory of abstract interpretation in order to cope with approximations of multivalued functions and by providing some methods for abstracting supermodular games, thus obtaining approximate Nash equilibria which are shown to be correct within the abstract interpretation framework.

1 Introduction

Supermodular Games. Games may have so-called strategic complementarities, which encode, roughly speaking, a complementarity relationship between own actions and rivals' actions, i.e., best responses of players have monotonic reactions. Games with strategic complementarities occur in a large array of models, especially in operations research and economic applications of noncooperative game theory—a significant sample of them is described in the book [14]. For example, strategic complementarities arise in economic game models where the players are competitive firms that must each decide how many goods to produce and an increase in the production of one firm increases the marginal revenues of the others, because this gives the other firms an incentive to produce more too. Pioneered by Topkis [13] in 1978, this class of games is formalized by so-called supermodular games, where the payoff functions of each player have the lattice-theoretical properties of supermodularity and increasing differences. In a supermodular game, the strategy space of every player is partially ordered and is assumed to be a complete lattice, while the utility in playing a higher strategy increases when the opponents also play higher strategies. It turns out that pure strategy Nash equilibria of supermodular games form a complete lattice w.r.t. the ordering relation of the strategy space, thus exhibiting the least and greatest Nash equilibria. Furthermore, since the best response correspondence of a supermodular game turns out to satisfy a monotonicity condition, its least and greatest equilibria can be characterized and calculated (under assumptions of finiteness) as least and greatest fixed points by Knaster-Tarski fixed point theorem, which provides the theoretical basis for the so-called Robinson-Topkis algorithm [14].

X. Rival (Ed.): SAS 2016, LNCS 9837, pp. 403–423, 2016.
DOI: 10.1007/978-3-662-53413-7_20

Battle of the sexes [16] is a popular and simple example of two-player (non)supermodular game. Assume that a couple, Alice and Bob, argues over what do on the weekend. Alice would prefer to go to the opera O, Bob would rather go to the football match F, both would prefer to go to the same place rather than different ones, in particular than the disliked ones. Where should they go? The following matrix with double-entry cells provides a model for this problem.

Bob

		O	F
Alice	O	3, 2	1, 1
	F	0, 0	2, 3

Alice chooses a row (either O or F) while Bob chooses a column (either O or F). In each double-entry cell, the first and second numbers represent, resp., Alice's and Bob's utilities, i.e., preferences. Hence, $u_A(O,O) = 3 = u_B(F,F)$ is the greatest utility for both Alice and Bob, for two different strategies ((O,O) for Alice and (F,F) for Bob), while $u_A(F,O) = 0 = u_B(F,O)$ is the least utility for both Alice and Bob. This game has two pure strategy Nash equilibria: one (O,O) where both go to the opera and another (F,F) where both go to the football game. If the ordering between O and F is either $O < F$ or $F < O$ for both Alice and Bob then this game turns out to be supermodular. If $O < F$ then (O,O) and (F,F) are, resp., the least and greatest equilibria, while their roles are exchanged when $F < O$. Instead, if $F < O$ for Alice and $O < F$ for Bob then, as expected, this game is not supermodular: the two equilibria (O,O) and (F,F) are uncomparable so that least and greatest equilibria do not exist.

Motivation. Since the breakthrough on the PPAD-completeness of finding mixed Nash equilibria [7], the question of approximating Nash equilibria emerged as a key problem in algorithmic game theory [8,10]. In this context, approximate equilibrium refers to ϵ-approximation, with $\epsilon > 0$, meaning that, for each player, all the strategies have a payoff which is at most ϵ more (or less) than the precise payoff of the given strategy. On the other hand, the notion of (correct or sound) approximation is central in static program analysis. In particular, the abstract interpretation approach to static analysis relies on an order-theoretical model of the notion of approximation. Here, program properties are modelled by a (collecting) domain endowed with a partial order $\leq$ which plays the role of logical relation where $x \leq y$ means that the property x is logically stronger than y. Also, the fundamental principle of abstract interpretation is to provide an approximate interpretation of a program for a given abstraction of the properties of its concrete semantics. This leads to the key notion of abstract domain, defined as an ordered collection of abstract program properties which can be inferred by static analysis, where approximation is modeled by the ordering relation. Furthermore, program semantics are typically defined using fixed points and a basic result of abstract interpretation tells us that correctness of approximations is preserved from functions to their least/greatest fixed points.

Goal. The similarities between supermodular games and program semantics should be clear, since they both rely on order-theoretical models and on computing extremal fixed points of suitable functions on lattices. However, while static analysis of program semantics based on order-theoretical approximations is a well-established area since forty years, to the best of our knowledge, no attempt has been made to apply standard techniques used in static program analysis for defining a corresponding notion of approximation in supermodular games. The overall goal of this paper is to investigate whether and how abstract interpretation can be used to define and calculate approximate Nash equilibria of supermodular games, where the key notion of approximation will be modeled by a partial ordering relation similarly to what happens in static program analysis. This appears to be the first contribution to make use of an order-theoretical notion of approximation for equilibria of supermodular games, in particular by resorting to the abstract interpretation framework.

Contributions. Abstract interpretation essentially relies on: (1) abstract domains A which encode approximate program properties; (2) abstract functions $f^{\sharp}$ which must correctly approximate on A the behavior of some concrete operations f; (3) results of correctness for the abstract interpreter using A and $f^{\sharp}$, such as the correctness of extremal fixed points of abstract functions, e.g. $\mathrm{lfp}(f^{\sharp})$ correctly approximates $\mathrm{lfp}(f)$; (4) widening/narrowing operators tailored for the abstract domains A to ensure and/or accelerate the convergence in iterative fixed point computations of abstract functions. We contribute to set up a general framework for designing abstract interpretations of supermodular games which encompasses the above points (1)-(3), while widening/narrowing operators are not taken into account since their definition is closely related to some specific abstract domain. Our main contributions can be summarized as follows.

Abstract interpretation is typically used for approximating single-valued functions on complete lattices. For supermodular games, best responses are multivalued functions of type $B : S_1 \times \cdots \times S_N \to \wp(S_1 \times \cdots \times S_N)$. A game strategy $s \in S_1 \times \cdots \times S_N$ is called a fixed point of B when $x \in B(x)$, and these fixed points turn out to characterize Nash equilibria of this game. As a preliminary step, we first show how abstractions of strategy spaces can be composed in order to define an abstraction of the product $S_1 \times \cdots \times S_N$, and, on the other hand, an abstraction of the product $S_1 \times \cdots \times S_N$ can be decomposed into abstract domains of the individual S_i's. Next, we provide a short and direct constructive proof ensuring the existence of fixed points for multivalued functions and we show how abstract interpretation can be generalized to cope with multivalued functions.

Then, we investigate how to define an "abstract interpreter" of supermodular games. The first approach consists in defining a supermodular game on an abstract strategy space. Given a supermodular game Γ with strategy spaces S_i and utility functions $u_i : S_1 \times \cdots \times S_N \to \mathbb{R}$, this means that we assume a family of abstractions A_i, one for each S_i, that gives rise to an abstract strategy space $A = A_1 \times \cdots \times A_N$, and a suitable abstract restriction of the utility functions $u_i^A : A_1 \times \cdots \times A_N \to \mathbb{R}$. This defines what we call an abstract game Γ^A, which, under some conditions, has abstract equilibria which correctly approximate the equilibria of Γ. This abstraction technique provides a generalization of an efficient algorithm by Echenique [9] for finding all the equilibria in a finite game with strategic complementarities. Moreover, we put forward a second notion of abstract game where the strategy spaces are subject to a kind of partial approximation, meaning that, for any utility function u_i for the player i, we consider approximations of the strategy spaces of the "other players", i.e., correct approximations of the functions $u_i(s_i, \cdot) : S_1 \times \cdots S_{i-1} \times S_{i+1} \times \cdots \times S_N \to \mathbb{R}$, for any given strategy $s_i \in S_i$. This abstraction technique gives rise to games having an abstract best response correspondence. This approach is inspired and somehow generalizes the implicit methodology of approximate computation of equilibria considered in Carl and Heikkilä's book [1, Chap. 8].

Our results are illustrated on some examples of supermodular games. In particular, a couple of examples of Bertrand oligopoly models are taken from the book [1].

2 Background on Games

2.1 Order-Theoretical Notions

Given a function $f : X \to Y$ and a subset $S \in \wp(X)$ then $f(S) \triangleq \{f(s) \in Y \mid s \in S\}$ while its powerset lifting $f^s : \wp(X) \to \wp(Y)$ is defined by $f^s(S) \triangleq f(S)$. A multivalued function, also called correspondence in game theory terminology, is any mapping $f : X \to \wp(X)$. An element $x \in X$ is called a fixed point of a multivalued function f when $x \in f(x)$ while $\mathrm{Fix}(f) \triangleq \{x \in X \mid x \in f(x)\}$ denotes the corresponding set of fixed points. Let $\langle C, \leq, \wedge, \vee, \bot, \top \rangle$ be a complete lattice, compactly denoted by $\langle C, \leq \rangle$. Given a function $f : C \to C$, with a slight abuse of notation, $\mathrm{Fix}(f) \triangleq \{x \in C \mid x = f(x)\}$ denotes its set of fixed points of f, while $\mathrm{lfp}(f)$ and $\mathrm{gfp}(f)$ denote, resp., the least and greatest fixed points of f, when they exist (recall that least and greatest fixed points always exist for monotone functions). If $f : C \to C$ then for any ordinal $\alpha \in \mathbb{O}$, the α-power $f^\alpha : C \to C$ is defined by transfinite induction as usual: for any $x \in C$, (1) if $\alpha = 0$ then $f^0(x) \triangleq x$; (2) if $\alpha = \beta+1$ then $f^{\beta+1}(x) \triangleq f(f^\beta(x))$; (3) if $\alpha = \vee\{\beta \in \mathbb{O} \mid \beta < \alpha\}$ then $f^\alpha(x) \triangleq \bigvee_{\beta < \alpha} f^\beta(x)$. If $f, g : X \to C$ then $f \sqsubseteq g$ denotes the standard pointwise ordering relation between functions, that is, $f \sqsubseteq g$ if for any $x \in X$, $f(x) \leq g(x)$.

Let us recall the following relations on the powerset $\wp(C)$: for any $X, Y \in \wp(C)$,

$$\text{(Smyth)} \quad X \preceq_S Y \overset{\triangle}{\Longleftrightarrow} \forall y \in Y. \exists x \in X.\, x \leq y$$

$$\text{(Hoare)} \quad X \preceq_H Y \overset{\triangle}{\Longleftrightarrow} \forall x \in X. \exists y \in Y.\, x \leq y$$

$$\text{(Egli-Milner)} \; X \preceq_{EM} Y \overset{\triangle}{\Longleftrightarrow} X \preceq_S Y \;\&\; X \preceq_H Y$$

$$\text{(Veinott)} \quad X \preceq_V Y \overset{\triangle}{\Longleftrightarrow} \forall x \in X. \forall y \in Y.\, x \wedge y \in X \;\&\; x \vee y \in Y$$

Smyth $\preceq_S$, Hoare $\preceq_H$ and Egli-Milner $\preceq_{EM}$ relations are reflexive and transitive (i.e., preorders), while the Veinott relation $\preceq_V$ (also called strong set relation) is transitive and antisymmetric [15]. A multivalued function $f : C \to \wp(C')$

is S-monotone if for any $x, y \in C$, $x \leq y$ implies $f(x) \preceq_S f(y)$. H-, EM- and V-monotonicity are defined analogously. We also use the following notations:

$$\wp^\wedge(C) \triangleq \{X \in \wp(C) \mid \wedge X \in X\}$$
$$\wp^\vee(C) \triangleq \{X \in \wp(C) \mid \vee X \in X\}$$
$$\wp^\circ(C) \triangleq \wp^\wedge(C) \cap \wp^\vee(C)$$
$$\mathrm{SL}(C) \triangleq \{X \in \wp(C) \mid X \neq \varnothing, X \text{ subcomplete sublattice of } C\}$$

Observe that if $X, Y \in \wp^\wedge(C)$ then $X \preceq_S Y \Leftrightarrow \wedge X \leq \wedge Y$. Similarly, if $X, Y \in \wp^\vee(C)$ then $X \preceq_H Y \Leftrightarrow \vee X \leq \vee Y$ and if $X, Y \in \wp^\circ(C)$ then $X \preceq_{EM} Y \Leftrightarrow \wedge X \leq \wedge Y \ \& \ \vee X \leq \vee Y$.

Supermodularity. Given a family of $N > 0$ sets $(S_i)_{i=1}^N$, $s \in \times_{i=1}^N S_i$ and $i \in [1, N]$ then $S_{-i} \triangleq S_1 \times \cdots \times S_{i-1} \times S_{i+1} \times \cdots S_N$, while $s_{-i} \triangleq (s_1, \ldots, s_{i-1}, s_{i+1}, \ldots, s_N) \in S_{-i}$. Let $\langle \mathbb{R}^N, \leq \rangle$ denote the product poset of real numbers, where for $s, t \in \mathbb{R}^N$, $s \leq t$ iff for any $i \in [1, N]$, $s_i \leq t_i$, while $s + t \triangleq (s_i + t_i)_{i=1}^N$ ($s - t$ is analogously defined).

Supermodular games rely on (quasi)supermodular functions (we refer to [1,14] for in-depth studies). Given a complete lattice C, a function $u : C \to \mathbb{R}^N$ is *supermodular* if for any $c_1, c_2 \in C$, $u(c_1 \vee c_2) + u(c_1 \wedge c_2) \geq u(c_1) + u(c_2)$, while u is *quasisupermodular* if for any $c_1, c_2 \in C$, $u(c_1 \wedge c_2) \leq u(c_1) \Rightarrow u(c_2) \leq u(c_1 \vee c_2)$ and $u(c_1 \wedge c_2) < u(c_1) \Rightarrow u(c_2) < u(c_1 \vee c_2)$. Note that supermodularity implies quasisupermodularity (the converse is not true). Let us recall that if $u : C \to \mathbb{R}^N$ is quasisupermodular then $\mathrm{argmax}(f) \triangleq \{x \in C \mid \forall y \in C. \ f(y) \leq f(x)\}$ turns out to be a sublattice of C.

A function $u : C_1 \times C_2 \to \mathbb{R}^N$ has *increasing differences* when for any $(x, y) \leq (x', y')$, we have that $u(x', y) - u(x, y) \leq u(x', y') - u(x, y')$, or, equivalently, the functions $u(x', \cdot) - u(x, \cdot)$ and $u(\cdot, y') - u(\cdot, y)$ are monotone. Moreover, a function $u : C_1 \times C_2 \to \mathbb{R}^N$ has the *single crossing property* when for any $(x, y) \leq (x', y')$, $u(x, y) \leq u(x', y) \Rightarrow u(x, y') \leq u(x', y')$ and $u(x, y) < u(x', y) \Rightarrow u(x, y') < u(x', y')$. Notice that if u has increasing differences then u has the single crossing property, while the converse does not hold.

Supermodularity on product complete lattices and increasing differences are related as follows: a function $u : C_1 \times C_2 \to \mathbb{R}^N$ is supermodular if and only if u has increasing differences and, for any $c_i \in C_i$, $u(c_1, \cdot) : C_2 \to \mathbb{R}^N$ and $u(\cdot, c_2) : C_1 \to \mathbb{R}^N$ are supermodular.

2.2 Noncooperative Games

Let us recall some basic notions on noncooperative games, which can be found, e.g., in the books [1,14].

A *noncooperative game* $\Gamma = \langle S_i, u_i \rangle_{i=1}^n$ for players $i = 1, \ldots, n$ (with $n \geq 2$) consists of a family of feasible strategy spaces $(S_i, \leq_i)_{i=1}^n$ which are assumed to be complete lattices, so that the strategy space $S \triangleq \times_{i=1}^n S_i$ is a complete lattice for the componentwise order $\leq$, and of a family of utility (or payoff) functions $u_i : S \to \mathbb{R}^{N_i}$, with $N_i \geq 1$. The i-th *best response correspondence* $B_i : S_{-i} \to \wp(S_i)$ is defined as

$$B_i(s_{-i}) \triangleq \operatorname{argmax}(u_i(\cdot, s_{-i})) = \{x_i \in S_i \mid \forall s_i \in S_i.\ u_i(s_i, s_{-i}) \leq u_i(x_i, s_{-i})\}$$

while the best response correspondence $B : S \to \wp(S)$ is defined by the product $B(s) \triangleq \times_{i=1}^n B_i(s_{-i})$. A strategy $s \in S$ is a *pure Nash equilibrium* for Γ when s is a fixed point of B, i.e., $s \in B(s)$, meaning that in s there is no feasible way for any player to strictly improve its utility if the strategies of all the other players remain unchanged. We denote by $\mathrm{Eq}(\Gamma) \in \wp(S)$ the set of Nash equilibria for Γ, so that $\mathrm{Eq}(\Gamma) = \mathrm{Fix}(B)$.

A noncooperative game $\Gamma = \langle S_i, u_i \rangle_{i=1}^n$ is *supermodular* when: (1) for any i, for any $s_{-i} \in S_{-i}$, $u_i(\cdot, s_{-i}) : S_i \to \mathbb{R}^{N_i}$ is supermodular; (2) for any i, $u_i(\cdot, \cdot) : S_i \times S_{-i} \to \mathbb{R}^{N_i}$ has increasing differences. Also, Γ is *quasisupermodular* (or, with *strategic complementarities*) when: (1) for any i, for any $s_{-i} \in S_{-i}$, $u_i(\cdot, s_{-i}) : S_i \to \mathbb{R}^{N_i}$ is quasisupermodular; (2) for any i, $u_i(\cdot, \cdot) : S_i \times S_{-i} \to \mathbb{R}^{N_i}$ has the single crossing property. In these cases, it turns out (cf. [14, Theorems 2.8.1 and 2.8.6]) that the i-th best response correspondence $B_i : S_{-i} \to \wp(S_i)$ is *EM*-monotone, as well as the best response correspondence $B : S \to \wp(S)$.

Let us recall that, given a complete lattice C, a function $f : C \to \mathbb{R}^N$ is order upper semicontinuous if for any chain $Y \subseteq C$,

$$\limsup_{x \in Y, x \to \vee Y} f(x) \leq f(\vee C) \quad \text{and} \quad \limsup_{x \in Y, x \to \wedge Y} f(x) \leq f(\wedge C).$$

It turns out (cf. [14, Lemma 4.2.2]) that if each $u_i(\cdot, s_{-i}) : S_i \to \mathbb{R}^{N_i}$ is order upper semicontinuous then, for each $s \in S$, $B_i(s_{-i}) \in \mathrm{SL}(S_i)$, i.e., $B_i(s_{-i})$ is a nonempty subcomplete sublattice of S_i, so that $B(s) \in \mathrm{SL}(S)$ also holds. In particular, we have that $\wedge_i B_i(s_{-i}), \vee_i B_i(s_{-i}) \in B_i(s_{-i})$ as well as $\wedge B(s), \vee B(s) \in B(s)$, namely, $B_i(s_{-i}) \in \wp^\diamond(S_i)$ and $B(s) \in \wp^\diamond(S)$. It also turns out [17, Theorem 2] that $\langle \mathrm{Eq}(\Gamma), \leq \rangle$ is a complete lattice—although, in general, it is not a subcomplete sublattice of S—and therefore Γ admits the least and greatest Nash equilibria, which are denoted, respectively, by $\mathrm{leq}(\Gamma)$ and $\mathrm{geq}(\Gamma)$. It should be remarked that the hypothesis of upper semicontinuity for $u_i(\cdot, s_{-i})$ holds for any finite-strategy game, namely for those games where each strategy space S_i is finite. In the following, we will consider (quasi)supermodular games which satisfy this hypothesis of upper semicontinuity.

If, given any $s_i \in S_i$, the function $u_i(s_i, \cdot) : S_{-i} \to \mathbb{R}^{N_i}$ is monotone then it turns out [1, Propositions 8.23 and 8.51] that $\mathrm{geq}(\Gamma)$ majorizes all equilibria, i.e., for all i and $s \in \mathrm{Eq}(\Gamma)$, $u_i(\mathrm{geq}(\Gamma)) \geq u_i(s)$, while $\mathrm{leq}(\Gamma)$ minimizes all equilibria.

Computing Game Equilibria. Consider a (quasi)supermodular game $\Gamma = \langle S_i, u_i \rangle_{i=1}^n$ and let us define the functions $B_\wedge, B_\vee : S \to S$ as follows: $B_\wedge(s) \triangleq \wedge B(s)$ and $B_\vee(s) \triangleq \vee B(s)$. As recalled above, we have that $B_\wedge(s), B_\vee(s) \in B(s)$. When the image of the strategy space S for $B_\wedge$ turns out to be finite, the standard algorithm [14, Algorithm 4.3.2] for computing $\mathrm{leq}(\Gamma)$ consists in applying the constructive Knaster-Tarski fixed point theorem to the function $B_\wedge$ so that $\mathrm{leq}(\Gamma) = \bigvee_{k \geq 0} B_\wedge^k(\bot_S)$. Dually, we have that

$$\langle s_1, ..., s_n \rangle := \langle \perp_1, ..., \perp_n \rangle; \quad // \langle s_1, ..., s_n \rangle := \langle \top_1, ..., \top_n \rangle;$$
$$\textbf{do } \{\langle t_1, ..., t_n \rangle := \langle s_1, ..., s_n \rangle;$$
$$s_1 := \wedge_1 B_1(s_{-1}); \qquad // s_1 := \vee_1 B_1(s_{-1});$$
$$...$$
$$s_n := \wedge_n B_n(s_{-n}); \qquad // s_n := \vee_n B_n(s_{-n});$$
$$\} \textbf{ while } \neg(\langle s_1, ..., s_n \rangle = \langle t_1, ..., t_n \rangle)$$

Fig. 1. Robinson-Topkis (RT) algorithm.

$\text{geq}(\Gamma) = \bigwedge_{k \geq 0} B_\vee^k(\top_S)$. In particular, this procedure can be always used for finite games. The application of the chaotic iteration strategy in this fixed point computation yields the Robinson-Topkis (RT) algorithm [14, Algorithm 4.3.1] in Fig. 1, also called round-robin optimization, which is presented in its version for least fixed points, while the statements in comments provide the version for calculating greatest fixed points.

Let us provide a running example of supermodular finite game.

Example 2.1. Consider a two players finite game Γ represented in so-called normal form by the following double-entry payoff matrix:

	1	2	3	4	5	6
6	-1,-3	-1,-1	2,4	5,6	6,5	6,5
5	0,0	0,2	3,4	6,6	7,5	6,5
4	3,1	3,3	3,5	5,6	5,5	4,4
3	2,2	2,4	2,6	4,5	4,4	3,2
2	6,4	6,6	6,7	6,4	5,2	4,-1
1	6,4	5,6	5,6	4,2	3,0	2,-3

Here, S_1 and S_2 are both the finite chain of integers $C = \langle \{1, 2, 3, 4, 5, 6\}, \leq \rangle$ and $u_1(x, y), u_2(x, y) : S_1 \times S_2 \to \mathbb{R}$ are, respectively, the first and second entry in the payoff matrix element determined by row x and column y. For example, $u_1(2, 6) = 4$ and $u_2(2, 6) = -1$. It turns out that both u_1 and u_2 have increasing differences, so that, since S_1 and S_2 are finite (chains), Γ is a finite supermodular game. The two best response correspondences $B_1, B_2 : C \to \text{SL}(C)$ are as follows:

$$B_1(1) = \{1, 2\}, B_1(2) = B_1(3) = \{2\}, B_1(4) = \{2, 5\}, B_1(5) = \{5\}, B_1(6) = \{5, 6\};$$

$$B_2(1) = \{2, 3\}, B_2(2) = B_2(3) = \{3\}, B_2(4) = B_2(5) = B_2(6) = \{4\}.$$

Thus, $\text{Eq}(\Gamma) = \{(2, 3), (5, 4)\}$, since this is the set $\text{Fix}(B)$ of fixed points of the best response correspondence $B = B_1 \times B_2$: indeed, $(2, 3) \in B(2, 3) = \{(2, 3)\}$ and $(5, 4) \in B(5, 4) = \{(2, 4), (5, 4)\}$. We also notice that $u_1(\cdot, s_2), u_2(s_1, \cdot) : C \to \mathbb{R}$ are neither monotone nor antimonotone. The fixed point computations of the least and greatest equilibria through the RT algorithm in Fig. 1 proceed as follows:

$$(\perp_1, \perp_2) = (1,1) \mapsto (\wedge B_1(1,1), 1) = (1,1) \mapsto (1, \wedge B_2(1,1)) = (1,2) \mapsto$$
$$(2,2) \mapsto (2,3) \mapsto (2,3) \mapsto (2,3) \quad \text{(lfp)}$$

$$(\top_1, \top_2) = (6,6) \mapsto (\vee B_1(6,6), 6) = (6,6) \mapsto (6, \vee B_2(6,6)) = (6,4) \mapsto$$
$$(5,4) \mapsto (5,4) \mapsto (5,4) \quad \text{(gfp)} \quad \square$$

3   Abstractions on Product Domains

Background on Abstract Interpretation. In standard abstract interpretation [2,3], abstract domains (also called abstractions), are specified by Galois connections/insertions (GCs/GIs for short). Concrete and abstract domains, $\langle C, \leq_C \rangle$ and $\langle A, \leq_A \rangle$, are assumed to be complete lattices which are related by abstraction and concretization maps $\alpha : C \to A$ and $\gamma : A \to C$ that give rise to a GC (α, C, A, γ), i.e., for all $a \in A$ and $c \in C$, $\alpha(c) \leq_A a \Leftrightarrow c \leq_C \gamma(a)$. Recall that a GC is a GI when $\alpha \circ \gamma = \text{id}$. A GC is (finitely) disjunctive when γ preserves all (finite) lubs. We use $\text{Abs}(C)$ to denote all the possible abstractions of C, where $A \in \text{Abs}(C)$ means that A is an abstract domain of C specified by some GC/GI. Let us recall that a map $\rho : C \to C$ is a (upper) closure operator when: (i) $x \leq y \Rightarrow \rho(x) \leq \rho(y)$; (ii) $x \leq \rho(x)$; (iii) $\rho(\rho(x)) = \rho(x)$. We denote by $\text{uco}(\langle C, \leq \rangle)$ the set of all closure operators on the complete lattice $\langle C, \leq_C \rangle$. We will make use of some well known properties of a GC (α, C, A, γ): (1) α is additive; (2) γ is co-additive; (3) $\gamma \circ \alpha : C \to C$ is a closure operator; (4) if $\rho : C \to C$ is a closure operator then $(\rho, C, \rho(C), \text{id})$ is a GI; (5) (α, C, A, γ) is a GC iff $\gamma(A)$ is the image of a closure operator on C; (6) a GC (α, C, A, γ) is (finitely) disjunctive iff $\gamma(A)$ is meet- and (finitely) join-closed.

Example 3.1. Let us consider a concrete domain $\langle C, \leq \rangle$ which is a finite chain. Then, it turns out that (α, C, A, γ) is a GC iff $\gamma(A)$ is the image of a closure operator on C iff $\gamma(A)$ is any subset of C which contains the top element $\top_C$. Hence, for the game Γ in Example 2.1, where S_i is the chain of integers $\{1,2,3,4,5,6\}$, we have that $A_1 = \{3,5,6\}$ and $A_2 = \{2,6\}$ are two abstractions of C. $\square$

Example 3.2. Let us consider the ceil function on real numbers $\lceil \cdot \rceil : \mathbb{R} \to \mathbb{R}$, that is, $\lceil x \rceil$ is the smallest integer not less than x. Let us observe that $\lceil \cdot \rceil$ is a closure operator on $\langle \mathbb{R}, \leq \rangle$ because: (1) $x \leq y \Rightarrow \lceil x \rceil \leq \lceil y \rceil$; (2) $x \leq \lceil x \rceil$; (3) $\lceil \lceil x \rceil \rceil = \lceil x \rceil$. Therefore, the ceil function allows us to view integer numbers $\mathbb{Z} = \lceil \mathbb{R} \rceil$ as an abstraction of real numbers. The ceil function can be generalized to any finite fractional part of real numbers: given any integer number $N \geq 0$, $\text{cl}_N : \mathbb{R} \to \mathbb{R}$ is defined as follows: $\text{cl}_N(x) = \frac{\lceil 10^N x \rceil}{10^N}$. For $N = 0$, $\text{cl}_N(x) = \lceil x \rceil$, while for $N > 0$, $\text{cl}_N(x)$ is the smallest rational number with at most N fractional digits not less than x. For example, if $x \in \mathbb{R}$ and $1 < x \leq 1.01$ then $\text{cl}_2(x) = 1.01$. Clearly, it turns out that cl_N is a closure operator which permits to cast rational numbers with at most N fractional digits as an abstraction of real numbers. $\square$

Let us show how abstractions of different concrete domains C_i can be composed in order to define an abstract domain of the product domain $\times_i C_i$, and, on the other hand, an abstraction of a product $\times_i C_i$ can be decomposed into abstract domains of the component domains C_i. In the following, we consider a finite family of complete lattices $\langle C_i, \leq_i \rangle_{i=1}^n$, while product domains are considered with the componentwise ordering relation.

Product Composition of Abstractions. As shown by Cousot and Cousot in [6, Sect. 4.4], given a family of GCs $(\alpha_i, C_i, A_i, \gamma_i)_{i=1}^n$, one can easily define a componentwise abstraction $(\alpha, \times_{i=1}^n C_i, \times_{i=1}^n A_i, \gamma)$ of the product complete lattice $\times_{i=1}^n C_i$, where $\times_{i=1}^n C_i$ and $\times_{i=1}^n A_i$ are both complete lattices w.r.t. the componentwise partial order and for any $c \in \times_{i=1}^n C_i$ and $a \in \times_{i=1}^n A_i$,

$$\alpha(c) \triangleq (\alpha_i(c_i))_{i=1}^n, \qquad \gamma(a) \triangleq (\gamma_i(a_i))_{i=1}^n.$$

For any i, we also use the function $\gamma_{-i} : A_{-i} \to C_{-i}$ to denote $\gamma_{-i}(a_{-i}) = \gamma(a)_{-i} = (\gamma_j(a_j))_{j \neq i}$.

Lemma 3.3. $(\alpha, \times_{i=1}^n C_i, \times_{i=1}^n A_i, \gamma)$ *is a GC. Moreover, if each* $(\alpha_i, C_i, A_i, \gamma_i)$ *is a (finitely) disjunctive GC then* $(\alpha, \times_{i=1}^n C_i, \times_{i=1}^n A_i, \gamma)$ *is a (finitely) disjunctive GC.*

Let us observe that $(\alpha, \times_{i=1}^n C_i, \times_{i=1}^n A_i, \gamma)$ is a so-called nonrelational abstraction since the product abstraction $\times_{i=1}^n A_i$ does not take into account any relationship between the different concrete domains C_i.

Decomposition of Product Abstractions. Let us show that any GC $(\alpha, \times_{i=1}^n C_i, A, \gamma)$ for the concrete product domain $\times_{i=1}^n C_i$ induces a family of corresponding abstractions $(\alpha_i, C_i, A_i, \gamma_i)$ of the components C_i as follows:

- $A_i \triangleq \{c_i \in C_i \mid \exists a \in A . \gamma(a)_i = c_i\} \subseteq C_i$, endowed with the partial order $\leq_i$ of C_i;
- for any $c_i \in C_i$, $\alpha_i(c_i) \triangleq \gamma(\alpha(c_i, \perp_{-i}))_i$; for any $x_i \in A_i$, $\gamma_i(x_i) \triangleq x_i$.

Lemma 3.4. $(\alpha_i, C_i, A_i, \gamma_i)$ *is a GC. Moreover, this GC is (finitely) disjunctive when* $(\alpha, \times_{i=1}^n C_i, A, \gamma)$ *is (finitely) disjunctive.*

A GC $(\alpha, \times_{i=1}^n C_i, A, \gamma)$ is defined to be *nonrelational* when it is isomorphic to the product composition, according to Lemma 3.3, of its component GCs as obtained by Lemma 3.4. Otherwise, $(\alpha, \times_{i=1}^n C_i, A, \gamma)$ is called *relational*. Of course, according to this definition, the product composition by Lemma 3.3 of abstract domains is trivially nonrelational. It is worth remarking that if A is relational then A cannot be obtained as a product of abstractions of C. As a consequence, the property of being relational for an abstraction A prevents the definition of a standard noncooperative game over the strategy space A since A cannot be obtained as a product domain.

Example 3.5. Let us consider the game Γ in Example 2.1 whose finite strategy space is $C \times C$, where $C = \{1, 2, 3, 4, 5, 6\}$ is a chain. Consider the subset $A \subseteq C \times C$ as depicted by the following diagram where the ordering is induced from $C \times C$:

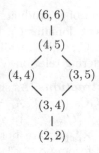

Since A is meet- and join-closed and includes the greatest element $(6,6)$ of $C \times C$, we have that A is a disjunctive abstraction of $C \times C$, where $\alpha : C \times C \to A$ is the closure operator induced by A and $\gamma : A \to C \times C$ is the identity. Observe that A is relational since its decomposition by Lemma 3.4 provides $A_1 = \{2,3,4,6\}$ and $A_2 = \{2,4,5,6\}$, and the product composition $A_1 \times A_2$ by Lemma 3.3 yields a more expressive abstraction than A, for example $(2,4) \in (A_1 \times A_2) \smallsetminus A$. On the other hand, for the abstractions $A_1 = \{3,5,6\}$ and $A_2 = \{2,6\}$ of Example 3.1, by Lemma 3.3, the product domain $A_1 \times A_2$ is a nonrelational abstraction of $C \times C$. □

4   Approximation of Multivalued Functions

Let $f : C \to C$ be some concrete monotone function and let $f^\sharp : A \to A$ be a corresponding monotone abstract function defined on some abstraction $A \in \mathrm{Abs}(C)$ specified by a GC (α, C, A, γ). Then, $f^\sharp$ is a correct (or sound) approximation of f on A when $f \circ \gamma \sqsubseteq \gamma \circ f^\sharp$ holds. If $f^\sharp$ is a correct approximation of f then recall that we also have fixed point correctness, i.e., $\mathrm{lfp}(f) \leq_C \gamma(\mathrm{lfp}(f^\sharp))$ and $\mathrm{gfp}(f) \leq_C \gamma(\mathrm{gfp}(f^\sharp))$. Let us also recall that $f^A \triangleq \alpha \circ f \circ \gamma : A \to A$ is the best correct approximation of f on A, because it turns out that any abstract function $f^\sharp$ is correct iff $f^A \sqsubseteq f^\sharp$. Let us show how to lift these standard notions in order to approximate least/greatest fixpoints of multivalued functions.

4.1   Constructive Results for Fixed Points of Multivalued Functions

Let $f : C \to \wp(C)$ be a multivalued function and $f_\wedge, f_\vee : C \to C$ be the functions defined as: $f_\wedge(c) \triangleq \wedge f(c)$ and $f_\vee(c) \triangleq \vee f(c)$. The following constructive result ensuring the existence of least fixed points for a multivalued function is given by Straccia et al. in [12, Propositions 3.10 and 3.24]. We provide a shorter and more direct constructive proof than in [12] which is based on the constructive version of Tarski's fixed point theorem given by Cousot and Cousot [4].

Lemma 4.1. *If $f : C \to \wp^\wedge(C)$ is S-monotone then f has the least fixed point $\mathrm{lfp}(f)$. Moreover, $\mathrm{lfp}(f) = \bigvee_{\alpha \in \mathbb{O}} f_\wedge^\alpha(\bot)$.*

Proof. By hypothesis, $f(x) \in \wp^\wedge(C)$, so that $f_\wedge(x) \in f(x)$. If $x, y \in C$ and $x \leq y$ then, by hypothesis, $f(x) \preceq_S f(y)$. Therefore, since $f_\wedge(y) \in f(y)$, there exists some $z \in f(x)$ such that $z \leq f_\wedge(y)$, and, in turn, $f_\wedge(x) \leq z \leq f_\wedge(y)$. Hence, since $f_\wedge$ is a monotone function on a complete lattice, by Tarski's theorem, its least fixed point $\mathrm{lfp}(f_\wedge) \in C$ exists. Furthermore, by the constructive version of Tarski's theorem [4, Theorem 5.1], $\mathrm{lfp}(f_\wedge) = \bigvee_{\alpha \in \mathbb{O}} f_\wedge^\alpha(\bot)$. We have that $\mathrm{lfp}(f_\wedge) = f_\wedge(\mathrm{lfp}(f_\wedge)) \in f(\mathrm{lfp}(f_\wedge))$, hence $\mathrm{lfp}(f_\wedge) \in \mathrm{Fix}(f)$. Consider any $z \in \mathrm{Fix}(f)$. We prove by transfinite induction that for any $\alpha \in \mathbb{O}$, $f_\wedge^\alpha(\bot) \leq z$. If $\alpha = 0$ then $f_\wedge^0(\bot) = \bot \leq z$. If $\alpha = \beta + 1$ then $f_\wedge^\alpha(\bot) = f_\wedge(f_\wedge^\beta(\bot))$, and, since, by inductive hypothesis, $f_\wedge^\beta(\bot) \leq z$, then, by monotonicity of $f_\wedge$, $f_\wedge(f_\wedge^\beta(\bot)) \leq f_\wedge(z) = \wedge f(z) \leq z$. If $\alpha = \vee\{\beta \in \mathbb{O} \mid \beta < \alpha\}$ is a limit ordinal then $f_\wedge^\alpha(\bot) = \bigvee_{\beta < \alpha} f_\wedge^\beta(\bot)$; since, by inductive hypothesis, $f_\wedge^\beta(\bot) \leq z$ for any $\beta < \alpha$, we obtain that $f_\wedge^\alpha(\bot) \leq z$. This therefore shows that f has the least fixed point $\mathrm{lfp}(f) = \mathrm{lfp}(f_\wedge)$. $\qquad\square$

By duality, as consequences of the above result, we obtain the following characterizations, where point (3) coincides with Zhou's theorem (see [17, Theorem 1] and [12, Proposition 3.15]), which is used for showing that pure Nash equilibria of a supermodular game form a complete lattice.

Corollary 4.2
(1) If $f : C \to \wp^\vee(C)$ is H-monotone then f has the greatest fixed point $\mathrm{gfp}(f) = \bigwedge_{\alpha \in \mathbb{O}} f_\vee^\alpha(\top)$.
(2) If $f : C \to \wp^\circ(C)$ is EM-monotone then f has the least and greatest fixed points, where $\mathrm{lfp}(f) = \bigvee_{\alpha \in \mathbb{O}} f_\wedge^\alpha(\bot)$ and $\mathrm{gfp}(f) = \bigwedge_{\alpha \in \mathbb{O}} f_\vee^\alpha(\top)$.
(3) If $f : C \to \mathrm{SL}(C)$ is EM-monotone then $\langle \mathrm{Fix}(f), \leq \rangle$ is a complete lattice.
(4) If $f, g : C \to \mathrm{SL}(C)$ are EM-monotone and, for any $c \in C$, $f(c) \preceq_{EM} g(c)$ then $\mathrm{Fix}(f) \preceq_{EM} \mathrm{Fix}(g)$.

4.2 Concretization-Based Approximations

As argued by Cousot and Cousot in [5], a minimal requirement for defining an abstract domain consists in specifying the meaning of its abstract values through a concretization map. Let $\langle A, \leq_A \rangle$ be an abstraction of a concrete domain C specified by a monotone concretization map $\gamma : A \to C$. Let us observe that the powerset lifting $\gamma^s : \wp(A) \to \wp(C)$ is S-monotone, meaning that if $Y_1 \preceq_S Y_2$ then $\gamma^s(Y_1) \preceq_S \gamma^s(Y_2)$: in fact, if $\gamma(y_2) \in \gamma^s(Y_2)$ then there exists $y_1 \in Y_1$ such that $y_1 \leq_A y_2$, so that $\gamma(y_1) \in \gamma^s(Y_1)$ and $\gamma(y_1) \leq_C \gamma(y_2)$, i.e., $\gamma^s(Y_1) \preceq_S \gamma^s(Y_2)$. Analogously, γ^s is H- and EM-monotone. Then, consider a concrete S-monotone multivalued function $f : C \to \wp^\wedge(C)$, whose least fixed point exists by Lemma 4.1.

Definition 4.3 (Correct Approximation of Multivalued Functions). An abstract multivalued function $f^\sharp : A \to \wp(A)$ over A is a S-correct approximation of f when:

(1) $f^\sharp : A \to \wp^\wedge(A)$ and $f^\sharp$ is S-monotone   (fixed point condition)
(2) for any $a \in A$, $f(\gamma(a)) \preceq_S \gamma^s(f^\sharp(a))$ (soundness condition)

H- and EM-correct approximations are defined by replacing in this definition S-with, respectively, H- and EM-, and $\wp^\wedge$ with, respectively, $\wp^\vee$ and $\wp^\circ$.   □

Let us point out that the soundness condition (2) in Definition 4.3 is close to the standard correctness requirement used in abstract interpretation: the main technical difference is that we deal with mere preorders $\langle \wp^\wedge(C), \preceq_S \rangle$ and $\langle \wp^\wedge(A), \preceq_S \rangle$ rather than posets. However, this is enough for guaranteeing a correct approximation of least fixed points.

Theorem 4.4 (Correct Least Fixed Point Approximation). *If $f^\sharp$ is a S-correct approximation of f then $\mathrm{lfp}(f) \leq_C \gamma(\mathrm{lfp}(f^\sharp))$.*

Dual results hold for H- and EM-correct approximations.

Corollary 4.5
(1) *If $f^\sharp$ is a H-correct approximation of f then $\mathrm{gfp}(f) \leq_C \gamma(\mathrm{gfp}(f^\sharp))$.*
(2) *If $f^\sharp$ is a EM-correct approximation of f then $\mathrm{Fix}(f) \preceq_{EM} \gamma^s(\mathrm{Fix}(f^\sharp))$, in particular, $\mathrm{lfp}(f) \leq_C \gamma(\mathrm{lfp}(f^\sharp))$ and $\mathrm{gfp}(f) \leq_C \gamma(\mathrm{gfp}(f^\sharp))$.*

The approximation of least/greatest fixed points of multivalued functions can also be easily given for an abstraction map $\alpha : C \to A$. In this case, a S-monotone map $f^\sharp : A \to \wp^\wedge(A)$ is a called a correct approximation of a concrete S-monotone map $f : C \to \wp^\wedge(C)$ when, for any $c \in C$, $\alpha^s(f(c)) \preceq_S f^\sharp(\alpha(c))$, where $\alpha^s : \wp(C) \to \wp(A)$. Here, fixed point approximation states that $\alpha(\mathrm{lfp}(f)) \leq_A \mathrm{lfp}(f^\sharp)$.

4.3 Galois Connection-Based Approximations

Let us now consider the ideal case where best approximations of concrete objects in an abstract domain A always exist, that is, A is specified by a GC (α, C, A, γ). However, recall that here $\preceq_S$ is a mere preorder and not a partial order. Then, given two preorders $\langle X, \preceq_X \rangle$ and $\langle Y, \preceq_Y \rangle$, we say that two functions $\beta : X \to Y$ and $\delta : Y \to X$ specify a *preorder-GC* (β, X, Y, δ) when δ and β are monotone (meaning, e.g. for β, that $x \preceq_X x' \Rightarrow \beta(x) \preceq_Y \beta(x')$) and the equivalence $\beta(x) \preceq_Y y \Leftrightarrow x \preceq_X \delta(y)$ holds. As expected, it turns out that GCs induce preorder-GCs for Smyth, Hoare and Egli-Milner preorders.

Lemma 4.6. *Let (α, C, A, γ) be a GC. Then, $(\alpha^s, \langle \wp^\wedge(C), \preceq_S \rangle, \langle \wp^\wedge(A), \preceq_S \rangle, \gamma^s)$, $(\alpha^s, \langle \wp^\vee(C), \preceq_H \rangle, \langle \wp^\vee(A), \preceq_H \rangle, \gamma^s)$, $(\alpha^s, \langle \wp^\circ(C), \preceq_{EM} \rangle, \langle \wp^\circ(A), \preceq_{EM} \rangle, \gamma^s)$ are all preorder-GCs.*

The Galois connection-based framework allows us to define best correct approximations of multivalued functions. If $f : C \to \wp(C)$ and (α, C, A, γ) is a GC then its *best correct approximation* on the abstract domain A is the multifunction $f^A : A \to \wp(A)$ defined as follows: $f^A(a) \triangleq \alpha^s(f(\gamma(a)))$. In particular, if $f : C \to \wp^\wedge(C)$ is S-monotone then $f^A : A \to \wp^\wedge(A)$ turns out to be S-monotone. Analogously for Hoare and Egli-Milner preorders. Similarly to standard abstract interpretation [3], f^A turns out to be the best S-correct approximation of f, as stated by the following result.

Lemma 4.7. *A S-monotone correspondence $f^\sharp : A \to \wp^\wedge(A)$ is a S-correct approximation of f iff for any $a \in A$, $f^A(a) \preceq_S f^\sharp(a)$. Also, analogous characterizations hold for H- and EM-correct approximations.*

Hence, it turns out that the fixed point approximations given by Theorem 4.4 and Corollary 4.5 apply to the best correct approximations f^A.

4.4 Approximations of Best Response Correspondences

The above abstract interpretation framework for multivalued functions can be then applied to (quasi)supermodular games by approximating their best response correspondences. In particular, one can abstract both the i-th best response correspondences $B_i : S_{-i} \to \mathrm{SL}(S_i)$ and the overall best response $B : S \to \mathrm{SL}(S)$.

Example 4.8. Let us consider the game Γ in Example 2.1 and the abstraction A of its strategy space $C \times C$ defined in Example 3.5. Then, one can define the best correct approximation B^A in A of the best response function $B : C \times C \to \mathrm{SL}(C \times C)$, that is, $B^A : A \to \wp(A)$ is defined as $B^A(a) \triangleq \alpha^s(B(\gamma(a)) = \alpha^s(B(a)) = \{\alpha(s_1, s_2) \in A \mid (s_1, s_2) \in B(a)\}$. We therefore have that:

$$B^A(2,2) = \alpha^s(\{(2,3)\}) = \{(3,4)\}, \ B^A(3,4) = \alpha^s(\{(2,3),(5,3)\}) = \{(3,4),(6,6)\},$$

$$B^A(4,4) = \alpha^s(\{(2,4),(5,4)\}) = \{(3,4),(6,6)\}, \ B^A(3,5) = \alpha^s(\{(5,3)\}) = \{(6,6)\},$$

$$B^A(4,5) = \alpha^s(\{((5,4)\}) = \{(6,6)\}, \ B^A(6,6) = \alpha^s(\{(5,4),(6,4)\}) = \{(6,6)\}.$$

Hence, $\mathrm{Fix}(B^A) = \{(3,4),(6,6)\}$. Therefore, by Theorem 4.4 and Corollary 4.5, here we have that $\mathrm{leq}(\Gamma) = \mathrm{lfp}(B) = (2,3) \leq (3,4) = \mathrm{lfp}(B^A)$ and $\mathrm{geq}(\Gamma) = \mathrm{gfp}(B) = (5,4) \leq (6,6) = \mathrm{gfp}(B^A)$. □

5 Games with Abstract Strategy Spaces

Consider a game $\Gamma = \langle S_i, u_i \rangle_{i=1}^n$ and a corresponding family $\mathcal{G} = (\alpha_i, S_i, A_i, \gamma_i)_{i=1}^n$ of GCs of the strategy spaces S_i. By Lemma 3.3, $(\alpha, \times_{i=1}^n S_i, \times_{i=1}^n A_i, \gamma)$ defines a nonrelational product abstraction of the whole strategy space $\times_{i=1}^n S_i$. We define the i-th utility function $u_i^{\mathcal{G}} : \times_{i=1}^n A_i \to \mathbb{R}^{N_i}$ on the abstract strategy space $\times_{i=1}^n A_i$ simply by restricting u_i on $\gamma(\times_{i=1}^n A_i)$ as follows: $u_i^{\mathcal{G}}(a) \triangleq u_i(\gamma(a))$. We point out that this definition is a kind of generalization of the restricted games considered by Echenique [9, Sect. 2.3].

Lemma 5.1. *If $u_i(\cdot, s_{-i})$ is (quasi)supermodular and all the GCs in $\mathcal{G}$ are finitely disjunctive then $u_i^{\mathcal{G}}(\cdot, a_{-i}) : A_i \to \mathbb{R}^{N_i}$ is (quasi)supermodular. Also, if $u_i(s_i, \cdot)$ is monotone then $u_i^{\mathcal{G}}(a_i, \cdot) : A_{-i} \to \mathbb{R}^{N_i}$ is monotone.*

Let us also observe that if $u_i(s_i, s_{-i})$ has increasing differences (the single crossing property), $X \subseteq \times_{i=1}^n S_i$ is any subset of the strategy space and $u_{i/X} : X \to \mathbb{R}^{N_i}$ is the mere restriction of u_i to the subset X then $u_{i/X}$ still has increasing differences (the single crossing property). Hence, in particular, this holds for $u_i^{\mathcal{G}} : \times_{i=1}^n A_i \to \mathbb{R}$. As a consequence of this and of Lemma 5.1, we obtain the following class of *abstract (quasi)supermodular games*.

Corollary 5.2. *Let $\Gamma = \langle S_i, u_i \rangle_{i=1}^n$ be a (quasi)supermodular game and let $\mathcal{G} = (\alpha_i, S_i, A_i, \gamma_i)_{i=1}^n$ be a family of finitely disjunctive GCs. Then, $\Gamma^{\mathcal{G}} \triangleq \langle A_i, u_i^{\mathcal{G}} \rangle_{i=1}^n$ is a (quasi)supermodular game.*

Let us see an array of examples of abstract games.

Example 5.3. Consider the supermodular game Γ in Example 2.1 and the product abstraction $A_1 \times A_2 \in \mathrm{Abs}(S_1 \times S_2)$ as defined in Example 3.5. The restricted game $\Gamma^{\sharp}$ of Lemma 5.1 on the abstract space $\{3, 5, 6\} \times \{2, 6\}$ is thus specified by the following payoff matrix:

	2	6
6	-1,-1	6,5
5	0,2	6,5
3	2,4	3,2

Since both A_1 and A_2 are trivially disjunctive abstractions, by Corollary 5.2, it turns out that $\Gamma^{\sharp}$ is supermodular. The best response correspondences $B_i^{\sharp}$: $A_{-i} \to \mathrm{SL}(A_i)$ for the supermodular game $\Gamma^{\sharp}$ are therefore as follows:

$$B_1^{\sharp}(2) = \{3\}, B_1^{\sharp}(6) = \{5, 6\}, B_2^{\sharp}(3) = \{2\}; B_2^{\sharp}(5) = \{6\}, B_2^{\sharp}(6) = \{6\}.$$

We observe that $B_2^{\sharp}$ is not a S-correct approximation of B_2 because: $B_2(3) = \{3\} \not\leq_S \{2\} = B_2^{\sharp}(3)$. Indeed, it turns out that $\mathrm{Eq}(\Gamma^{\sharp}) = \{(3, 2), (5, 6), (6, 6)\}$, so that $\mathrm{leq}(\Gamma) = (2, 3) \not\leq (3, 2) = \mathrm{leq}(\Gamma^{\sharp})$. Thus, in this case, the solutions of the abstract game $\Gamma^{\sharp}$ do not correctly approximate the solutions of Γ.

Instead, following the approach in Sect. 4.4 and analogously to Example 4.8, one can define the best correct approximation $B^A : A \to \mathrm{SL}(A)$ in $A \triangleq A_1 \times A_2$ of the best response correspondence B of Γ. Thus, $B^A(a_1, a_2) = \{(\alpha_1(s_1), \alpha_2(s_2)) \in A \mid (s_1, s_2) \in B(a_1, a_2)\}$ acts as follows:

$$B^A(3, 2) = \{(3, 6)\}, \quad B^A(3, 6) = \{(5, 6), (6, 6)\}, \quad B^A(5, 2) = \{(3, 6)\},$$
$$B^A(5, 6) = \{(5, 6), (6, 6)\}, \quad B^A(6, 2) = \{(3, 6)\}, \quad B^A(6, 6) = \{(5, 6), (6, 6)\}.$$

Here, we have that $\mathrm{Fix}(B^A) = \{(5, 6), (6, 6)\}$, so that $\mathrm{leq}(\Gamma) = \mathrm{lfp}(B) = (2, 3) \leq (5, 6) = \mathrm{lfp}(B^A)$ and $\mathrm{geq}(\Gamma) = \mathrm{gfp}(B) = (5, 4) \leq (6, 6) = \mathrm{gfp}(B^A)$. □

Example 5.4. In Example 5.3, let us consider the abstraction $A_2 = \{4, 6\} \in \mathrm{Abs}(S_2)$, so that the restricted supermodular game $\Gamma^{\sharp}$ is defined by the following payoff matrix:

	4	6
6	5,6	6,5
5	6,6	6,5
3	4,5	3,2

while the best response correspondences $B_i^\sharp$ turn out to be defined as:

$$B_1^\sharp(4) = \{5\},\ B_1^\sharp(6) = \{5,6\},\ B_2^\sharp(3) = \{4\};\ B_2^\sharp(5) = \{4\},\ B_2^\sharp(6) = \{4\}.$$

Thus, here we have that $\mathrm{Eq}(\Gamma^\sharp) = \{(5,4)\}$. In this case, it turns out that $B_i^\sharp$ is a *EM*-correct approximation of B_i, so that, by Corollary 4.5 (2), $\mathrm{Eq}(\Gamma) = \mathrm{Fix}(B) = \{(2,3),(5,4)\} \preceq_{EM} \{(5,4)\} = \mathrm{Fix}(B^\sharp) = \mathrm{Eq}(\Gamma^\sharp)$ holds. □

Example 5.5. Here, we consider the disjunctive abstractions $A_1 = \{4,5,6\} \in \mathrm{Abs}(S_1)$ and $A_2 = \{3,4,5,6\} \in \mathrm{Abs}(S_2)$, so that we have the following abstract supermodular game $\Gamma^\sharp$ over $A_1 \times A_2$:

	3	4	5	6
6	2,4	5,6	6,5	6,5
5	3,4	6,6	7,5	6,5
4	3,5	5,6	5,5	4,4

Best response functions $B_i^\sharp$ are therefore as follows:

$$B_1^\sharp(3) = \{4,5\},\ B_1^\sharp(4) = \{5\},\ B_1^\sharp(5) = \{5\},\ B_1^\sharp(6) = \{5,6\};$$
$$B_2^\sharp(4) = \{4\},\quad B_2^\sharp(5) = \{4\},\ B_2^\sharp(6) = \{4\}.$$

In this case, it turns out that $B_i^\sharp$ is a *EM*-correct approximation of B_i, so that the abstract best response $B^\sharp : A_1 \times A_2 \to \mathrm{SL}(A_1 \times A_2)$ is a *EM*-correct approximation of B. Then, by Corollary 4.5 (2), we have that $\mathrm{Eq}(\Gamma) = \mathrm{Fix}(B) = \{(2,3),(5,4)\} \preceq_{EM} \{(5,4)\} = \mathrm{Fix}(B^\sharp) = \mathrm{Eq}(\Gamma^\sharp)$. □

Thus, for the concrete supermodular game Γ of Example 2.1, the abstract games of Examples 5.4 and 5.5 can be viewed as correct approximations of the game Γ since

$$\mathrm{Eq}(\Gamma) \preceq_{EM} \gamma^s(\mathrm{Eq}(\Gamma^\mathcal{G}))$$

holds. This means that any Nash equilibrium of Γ is approximated by some Nash equilibrium of the abstract game $\Gamma^\mathcal{G}$ and, conversely, any Nash equilibrium of $\Gamma^\mathcal{G}$ approximates some Nash equilibrium of the concrete game Γ. In particular, $\mathrm{leq}(\Gamma) \leq \gamma^s(\mathrm{leq}(\Gamma^\mathcal{G}))$ and $\mathrm{geq}(\Gamma) \leq \gamma^s(\mathrm{geq}(\Gamma^\mathcal{G}))$. Instead, this approximation condition does not hold for the abstract game in Example 5.3. The following results provide conditions that justify these different behaviors.

Theorem 5.6 (Correctness of Games with Abstract Strategy Spaces). Let $\mathcal{G} = (\alpha_i, S_i, A_i, \gamma_i)_{i=1}^n$ be a family of finitely disjunctive GIs, $S = \times_{i=1}^n S_i$, $A = \times_{i=1}^n A_i$ and (α, S, A, γ) be the nonrelational product composition of $\mathcal{G}$. Let $\Gamma = \langle S_i, u_i \rangle_{i=1}^n$ be a (quasi)supermodular game, with best response B, and $\Gamma^\mathcal{G} = \langle A_i, u_i^\mathcal{G} \rangle_{i=1}^n$ be the corresponding abstract (quasi)supermodular game, with best response $B^\mathcal{G}$. Assume that for any $a \in A$,

$$\bigvee_S B(\gamma(a)) \vee_S \gamma(\bigwedge_A B^\mathcal{G}(a)) \in \gamma(A) \qquad (*)$$

Then, $\mathrm{Eq}(\Gamma) \preceq_{EM} \gamma^s(\mathrm{Eq}(\Gamma^\mathcal{G}))$ and, in particular, $\mathrm{leq}(\Gamma) \leq \gamma^s(\mathrm{leq}(\Gamma^\mathcal{G}))$ and $\mathrm{geq}(\Gamma) \leq \gamma^s(\mathrm{geq}(\Gamma^\mathcal{G}))$.

This result depends on the condition (∗) which allows us to obtain a generalization of Echenique's result [9, Lemma 4] which is the basis for designing the efficient algorithm in [9, Sect. 4] that computes all the Nash equilibria in a finite game with strategic complementarities. Let us call (α, C, A, γ) a *principal filter GC* when the image $\gamma(A)$ is the principal filter at $\gamma(\perp_A)$, that is, $\gamma(A) = \{c \in C \mid \gamma(\perp_A) \leq c\}$ holds.

Corollary 5.7. *Let* $\mathcal{G} = (\alpha_i, S_i, A_i, \gamma_i)_{i=1}^n$ *be principal filter GCs. Then,* $\mathrm{Eq}(\Gamma) \preceq_{EM} \gamma^s(\mathrm{Eq}(\Gamma^{\mathcal{G}}))$.

Example 5.8. Let us consider the following finite supermodular game Δ taken from [1, Example 8.11], which is an example of the well known Bertrand oligopoly model [14]. Players $i \in \{1, 2, 3\}$ stand for firms which sell substitute products p_i (e.g., a can of beer), whose feasible selling prices (e.g., in euros) s_i range in $S_i \triangleq [a, b]$, where the smallest price shift is 5 cents. The payoff function $u_i : S_1 \times S_2 \times S_3 \rightarrow \mathbb{R}$ models the profit of the firm i:

$$u_i(s_1, s_2, s_3) \triangleq d_i(s_1, s_2, s_3)(s_i - c_i)$$

where $d_i(s_1, s_2, s_3)$ gives the demand of p_i, i.e., how many units of p_i the firm i sells in a given time frame, while c_i is the unit cost of p_i so that $(s_i - c_i)$ is the profit per unit. Following [1, Example 8.11], let us assume that:

$$u_1(s_1, s_2, s_3) = (370 + 213(s_2 + s_3) + 60s_1 - 230s_1^2)(s_1 - 1.10)$$
$$u_2(s_1, s_2, s_3) = (360 + 233(s_1 + s_3) + 55s_2 - 220s_2^2)(s_2 - 1.20)$$
$$u_3(s_1, s_2, s_3) = (375 + 226(s_1 + s_2) + 50s_3 - 200s_3^2)(s_3 - 1.25)$$

As shown in general in [1, Corollary 8.9], it turns out that each payoff function u_i has increasing differences and $u_i(s_i, \cdot)$ is monotone, so that the game Δ has the least and greatest price equilibria $\mathrm{leq}(\Delta)$ and $\mathrm{geq}(\Delta)$, and $\mathrm{geq}(\Delta)$ ($\mathrm{leq}(\Delta)$) provides the best (least) profits among all equilibria. It should be noted that [1, Example 8.11] considers as payoff functions the integer part of u_i, namely $\lfloor u_i(s_1, s_2, s_3) \rfloor$. However, we notice that this definition of payoff function does not have increasing differences, so that [1, Corollary 8.9], which assumes the hypothesis of increasing differences, cannot be correctly applied. Indeed, [1, Example 8.11] considers $S_i = \{x/20 \mid x \in [26, 42]_{\mathbb{Z}}\}$ and with $(1.3, 1.3, 1.8) \leq (1.35, 1.3, 1.85)$, we would have that

$$\lfloor u_1(1.35, 1.3, 1.8) \rfloor - \lfloor u_1(1.3, 1.3, 1.8) \rfloor = \lfloor 173.03125 \rfloor - \lfloor 143.92 \rfloor = 30 >$$
$$\lfloor u_1(1.35, 1.3, 1.85) \rfloor - \lfloor u_1(1.3, 1.3, 1.85) \rfloor = \lfloor 175.69375 \rfloor - \lfloor 146.05 \rfloor = 29$$

meaning that u_1 does not have increasing differences. By contrast, we consider here $S_i \triangleq \{x/20 \mid x \in [20, 46]_{\mathbb{Z}}\}$, namely the feasible prices range from 1 to 2.3 euros with a 0.05 shift. Using the standard RT algorithm in Fig. 1 (we made a simple C++ implementation of RT), one obtains $\mathrm{leq}(\Delta) = (1.80, 1.90, 1.95) = \mathrm{geq}(\Delta)$, namely, the game Δ admits a unique Nash equilibrium. It turns out that the algorithm RT calculates $\mathrm{leq}(\Delta)$ starting from the bottom $(1.0, 1.0, 1.0) \in S_1 \times S_2 \times S_3$

through 12 calls to $\bigwedge B_i(s_{-i})$, while it may output the same equilibrium as $\text{geq}(\Delta)$ beginning from the top $(2.3, 2.3, 2.3)$ through 9 calls to $\bigvee B_i(s_{-i})$. Let us consider the following abstractions $A_i \in \text{Abs}(S_i)$:

$$A_1 \triangleq \{x/20 \mid x \in [35, 38]_{\mathbb{Z}} \cup [42, 46]_{\mathbb{Z}}\},$$
$$A_2 \triangleq \{x/20 \mid x \in [36, 46]_{\mathbb{Z}}\},$$
$$A_3 \triangleq \{x/20 \mid x \in [38, 46]_{\mathbb{Z}}\}.$$

Notice that A_2 and A_3 are principal filter abstractions, while this is not the case for A_1, so that Corollary 5.7 cannot be applied. We observe that:

$$\{\textstyle\bigvee_1 B_1(a_{-1}) \in S_1 \mid a_{-1} \in A_2 \times A_3\} = \{36/20, 37/20, 38/20\},$$
$$\{\textstyle\bigvee_2 B_2(a_{-2}) \in S_2 \mid a_{-2} \in A_1 \times A_3\} = \{38/20, 39/20, 40/20\},$$
$$\{\textstyle\bigvee_3 B_3(a_{-3}) \in S_3 \mid a_{-3} \in A_1 \times A_2\} = \{39/20, 40/20, 41/20, 42/20\}.$$

The condition $(*)$ of Theorem 5.6 is therefore satisfied, because for any $a_{-i} \in A_{-i}$, we have that $\bigvee B_i(a_{-i}) \in A_i$. Hence, by Corollary 5.2, we consider the abstract supermodular game Δ^A on the abstract strategy spaces A_i. By exploiting the RT algorithm in Fig. 1 for Δ^A, we still obtain a unique equilibrium $\text{leq}(\Delta^A) = (1.80, 1.90, 1.95) = \text{geq}(\Delta^A)$, so that in this case no approximation of equilibria occurs. Here, RT calculates $\text{leq}(\Delta^A)$ starting from the bottom $(1.8, 1.8, 1.9)$ of $A_1 \times A_2 \times A_3$ through 6 calls to $\bigwedge B_i^A(a_{-i})$ and any call $\bigwedge B_i^A(a_{-i})$ scans the smaller abstract strategy space A_i instead of S_i. On the other hand, $(1.80, 1.90, 1.95) = \text{geq}(\Delta)$ can be also calculated from the top $(2.3, 2.3, 2.3)$ still with 9 calls to $\bigvee B_i^A(a_{-i})$, each scanning the reduced abstract strategy spaces A_i. $\square$

6   Games with Abstract Best Response

In the following, we put forward a notion of abstract game where the strategy spaces are subject to a form of partial approximation by abstract interpretation, meaning that we consider approximations of the strategy spaces of the "other players" for any utility function, i.e., correct approximations of the functions $u_i(s_i, \cdot)$, for any given s_i. This approach gives rise to games having an abstract best response correspondence. Here, we aim at providing a systematic abstraction framework for the implicit methodology of approximate computation of equilibria considered by Carl and Heikkilä [1] in their Examples 8.58, 8.63 and 8.64.

Given a game $\Gamma = \langle S_i, u_i \rangle_{i=1}^n$, we consider a family $\mathcal{G} = (\alpha_i, S_i, A_i, \gamma_i)_{i=1}^n$ of GCs and, by Lemma 3.3, their nonrelational product $(\alpha, \times_{i=1}^n S_i, \times_{i=1}^n A_i, \gamma)$, where we denote by $\rho \triangleq \gamma \circ \alpha \in \text{uco}(\times_{i=1}^n S_i)$ the corresponding closure operator and, for any i, by $\rho_{-i} \in \text{uco}(S_{-i})$ the closure operator corresponding to the $(n-i)$-th nonrelational product $(\alpha_{-i}, \times_{j \neq i} S_j, \times_{j \neq i} A_j, \gamma_{-i})$. The utility function $u_{i,\mathcal{G}} : \times_{i=1}^n S_i \to \mathbb{R}$ is then defined as follows: for any $s \in \times_{i=1}^n S_i$, $u_{i,\mathcal{G}}(s_i, s_{-i}) \triangleq u_i(s_i, \rho_{-i}(s_{-i}))$.

Lemma 6.1. *If $u_i(s_i, s_{-i})$ has increasing differences (the single crossing property) then $u_{i,\mathcal{G}}(s_i, s_{-i})$ has increasing differences (the single crossing property). Also, if $u_i(s_i, \cdot)$ is monotone then $u_{i,\mathcal{G}}(s_i, \cdot)$ is monotone.*

Let us also point out that if $u_i(\cdot, s_{-i})$ is (quasi)supermodular then $u_{i,\mathcal{G}}(\cdot, s_{-i})$ remains (quasi)supermodular as well, so that by defining the game $\Gamma_{\mathcal{G}} \triangleq \langle S_i, u_{i,\mathcal{G}} \rangle_{i=1}^{n}$ we obtain the following consequence.

Corollary 6.2. *If Γ is (quasi)supermodular then $\Gamma_{\mathcal{G}}$ is (quasi)supermodular.*

$\Gamma_{\mathcal{G}}$ is called a *game with abstract best response* because the i-th best response correspondence $B_{i,\mathcal{G}} : S_{-i} \to \mathrm{SL}(S_i)$ is such that $B_{i,\mathcal{G}}(s_{-i}) = \{s_i \in S_i \mid \forall x_i \in S_i . u_i(x_i, \rho_{-i}(s_{-i})) \leq u_i(x_i, \rho_{-i}(s_{-i}))\} = B_i(\rho_{-i}(s_{-i}))$, and, in turn, $B_{\mathcal{G}}(s) = B_{\mathcal{G}}(\rho(s)) = B(\rho(s))$ holds, namely, $B_{\mathcal{G}}$ can be viewed as the restriction of B to the abstract strategy space $\rho(S)$.

Corollary 6.3 (Correctness of Games with Abstract Best Response).
Let us consider a family $\mathcal{G} = (\alpha_i, S_i, A_i, \gamma_i)_{i=1}^{n}$ of GCs. Then, $\mathrm{Eq}(\Gamma) \preceq_{EM} \mathrm{Eq}(\Gamma_{\mathcal{G}})$ and, in particular, $\mathrm{leq}(\Gamma) \leq \mathrm{leq}(\Gamma_{\mathcal{G}})$ and $\mathrm{geq}(\Gamma) \leq \mathrm{geq}(\Gamma_{\mathcal{G}})$.

Example 6.4. Let us consider the two-player game $\Gamma = \langle S_i, u_i \rangle_{i=1}^{2}$ in [1, Example 8.53], which is a further example of Bertrand oligopoly, where: $S_1 = S_2 = [\frac{3}{2}, \frac{5}{2}] \times [\frac{3}{2}, \frac{5}{2}]$ and the utility functions $u_i : S_1 \times S_2 \to \mathbb{R}^2$ are defined by $u_i((s_{i1}, s_{i2}), s_{-i}) = (u_{i1}(s_{i1}, s_{-i}), u_{i2}(s_{i2}, s_{-i})) \in \mathbb{R}^2$ with

$$u_{11}(s_{11}, s_{21}, s_{22}) \triangleq \left(52 - 21 s_{11} + s_{21} + 4 s_{22} + 8 \operatorname{sgn}(s_{21} s_{22} - 4)\right)(s_{11} - 1)$$

$$u_{12}(s_{12}, s_{21}, s_{22}) \triangleq$$
$$\left(51 - 21 s_{12} - \operatorname{sgn}(s_{12} - \tfrac{11}{5}) + 2 s_{21} + 3 s_{22} + 4 \operatorname{sgn}(s_{21} + s_{22} - 4)\right)(s_{12} - \tfrac{11}{10})$$

$$u_{21}(s_{21}, s_{11}, s_{12}) \triangleq$$
$$\left(50 - 20 s_{21} - \operatorname{sgn}(s_{21} - \tfrac{11}{5}) + 3 s_{11} + 2 s_{12} + 2 \operatorname{sgn}(s_{11} + s_{12} - 4)\right)(s_{21} - \tfrac{11}{10})$$

$$u_{22}(s_{22}, s_{11}, s_{12}) \triangleq \left(49 - 20 s_{22} + 4 s_{11} + s_{12} + \operatorname{sgn}(s_{11} s_{12} - 4)\right)(s_{22} - 1)$$

Since any utility function $u_{ij}(s_{ij}, s_{-i})$ does not depend on $s_{i,-j}$ (e.g., u_{11} and u_{12} do not depend, resp., on s_{12} and s_{11}), let us observe that $u_i(\cdot, s_{-i}) : S_i \to \mathbb{R}^2$ is supermodular. Moreover, by [1, Propositions 8.56, 8.57], we also have that $u_i(s_1, s_2)$ has the single crossing property, so that Γ is indeed quasisupermodular. Also, since S_i is a compact (for the standard topology) complete sublattice of $\mathbb{R}^2$, we also have that $u_i(\cdot, s_{-i})$ is order upper semicontinuous, so that, for any $s \in S_1 \times S_2$, the best response correspondence B satisfies $B(s) \in \mathrm{SL}(S_1 \times S_2)$. Indeed, as observed in [1, Example 8.53], it turns out that the utility functions $u_{ij}(\cdot, s_{-i}) : [\frac{3}{2}, \frac{5}{2}] \to \mathbb{R}$ have unique maximum points denoted by $f_{ij}(s_{-i})$ which are the solutions of the equations $\frac{d}{ds} u_{ij}(s, s_{-i}) = 0$. An easy computation then provides:

$$f_{11}(s_{21}, s_{22}) \triangleq \tfrac{73}{42} + \tfrac{1}{42}s_{21} + \tfrac{2}{21}s_{22} + \tfrac{4}{21}\operatorname{sgn}(s_{21}s_{22} - 4)$$

$$f_{12}(s_{21}, s_{22}) \triangleq \tfrac{247}{140} + \tfrac{1}{42}s_{21} + \tfrac{1}{14}s_{22} + \tfrac{2}{21}\operatorname{sgn}(s_{21} + s_{22} - 4)$$

$$f_{21}(s_{11}, s_{12}) \triangleq \tfrac{9}{5} + \tfrac{3}{40}s_{11} + \tfrac{1}{20}s_{12} + \tfrac{1}{20}\operatorname{sgn}(s_{11} + s_{12} - 4)$$

$$f_{22}(s_{11}, s_{12}) \triangleq \tfrac{69}{40} + \tfrac{1}{10}s_{11} + \tfrac{1}{40}s_{12} + \tfrac{1}{40}\operatorname{sgn}(s_{11}s_{12} - 4)$$

so that the best response B can be simplified as follows:

$$B(s_{11}, s_{12}, s_{21}, s_{22}) = \left\{ \left(f_{11}(s_{21}, s_{22}), f_{12}(s_{21}, s_{22}), f_{21}(s_{11}, s_{12}), f_{22}(s_{11}, s_{12}) \right) \right\}.$$

As shown in [1, Example 8.53], least and greatest equilibria of Γ can be obtained by solving a linear system of four equations with four real variables:

$$\operatorname{leq}(\Gamma) = \left(\tfrac{4940854}{2778745}, \tfrac{5281784}{2778745}, \tfrac{5497457}{2778745}, \tfrac{10699993}{5557490} \right),$$

$$\operatorname{geq}(\Gamma) = \left(\tfrac{6033654}{2778745}, \tfrac{5848294}{2778745}, \tfrac{5885617}{2778745}, \tfrac{11224753}{5557490} \right).$$

Carl and Heikkilä [1, Example 8.58] describe how to algorithmically derive approximate solutions of Γ by approximating the fractional part of real numbers through the floor function, namely, the greatest rational number with N fractional digits which is not more than a given real number. In this section we gave an abstract interpretation-based methodology for systematically designing this kind of approximate solutions which generalizes this approach by Carl and Heikkilä in [1, Example 8.58]. Here, we use the ceil abstraction of real numbers already described in Example 3.2. Thus, we consider the closure operator $cl_3 : [\tfrac{3}{2}, \tfrac{5}{2}] \to [\tfrac{3}{2}, \tfrac{5}{2}]$, that is, $cl_3(x)$ is the smallest rational number with at most 3 fractional digits not less than x. With a slight abuse of notation, cl_3 is also used to denote the corresponding componentwise function $cl_3 : [\tfrac{3}{2}, \tfrac{5}{2}]^2 \to [\tfrac{3}{2}, \tfrac{5}{2}]^2$, namely, $cl_3(s_{i1}, s_{i2}) = (cl_3(s_{i1}), cl_3(s_{i1}))$. Let A_{cl_3} be the following domain

$$A_{cl_3} \triangleq \{ \tfrac{y}{10^3} \in \mathbb{Q} \mid y \in [1500, 2500]_{\mathbb{Z}} \} = \{ cl_3(x) \mid x \in [\tfrac{3}{2}, \tfrac{5}{2}] \}$$

and $A \triangleq A_{cl_3} \times A_{cl_3}$. Then, $(cl_3, [\tfrac{3}{2}, \tfrac{5}{2}], A_{cl_3}, \mathrm{id})$ is a GC, so that, by Lemma 3.3, $\mathcal{G}_3 = (cl_3, S_i, A, \mathrm{id})_{i=1}^2$ is a pair of GCs. Let us denote by $\Gamma_{\mathcal{G}_3}$ the corresponding game with abstract best response as defined in Corollary 6.2, so that $u_{i, \mathcal{G}_3}(s_i, s_{-i}) = u_i(s_i, cl_3(s_{-i}))$. Thus, it turns out that the abstract best response correspondence $B_{\mathcal{G}_3}$ is defined as follows:

$$B(s_1, s_2) = \left\{ \left(f_{11}(cl_3(s_2)), f_{12}(cl_3(s_2)), f_{21}(cl_3(s_1)), f_{22}(cl_3(s_1)) \right) \right\}$$

so that $B_{\mathcal{G}_3}$ can be restricted to the finite domain $A \times A$ and therefore has a finite range. This allows us to compute the least and greatest equilibria of $\Gamma_{\mathcal{G}_3}$ by the standard RT algorithm in Fig. 1. By relying on a simple C++ program, we obtained the following solutions:

$$\operatorname{leq}(\Gamma_{\mathcal{G}_3}) = \left(\tfrac{10669}{6000}, \tfrac{6653}{3500}, \tfrac{79139}{40000}, \tfrac{77017}{40000} \right), \quad \operatorname{geq}(\Gamma_{\mathcal{G}_3}) = \left(\tfrac{91199}{42000}, \tfrac{14733}{7000}, \tfrac{42363}{20000}, \tfrac{80793}{40000} \right).$$

By Corollary 6.3, we know that these are correct approximations, i.e., $\mathrm{leq}(\Gamma) \leq \mathrm{leq}(\Gamma_{\mathcal{G}_3})$ and $\mathrm{geq}(\Gamma) \leq \mathrm{geq}(\Gamma_{\mathcal{G}_3})$. Both fixed point calculations $\mathrm{leq}(\Gamma_{\mathcal{G}_3})$ and $\mathrm{geq}(\Gamma_{\mathcal{G}_3})$ need 16 calls to the abstract functions $f_{ij}(a_{-i})$, for some $a_{-i} \in A_{-i}$, which provide the unique maximum points for $u_{ij}(\cdot, a_{-i})$. It is worth noting that, even with the precision of 3 fractional digits of cl_3, the maximum approximation for these abstract solutions turns out to be quite small: $\mathrm{leq}(\Gamma_{\mathcal{G}_3})_{22} - \mathrm{leq}(\Gamma)_{22} = \frac{2148733}{22229960000} = 0.00009665932822$.   □

7   Further Work

We investigated whether and how the abstract interpretation technique can be applied to define and calculate approximate Nash equilibria of supermodular games, thus showing how a notion of approximation of equilibria can be modeled by an ordering relation analogously to what happens in static program analysis. To our knowledge, this is the first contribution towards the goal of approximating solutions of supermodular games by relying on an order-theoretical approach. We see a number of interesting avenues for further work on this subject. First, our notion of correct approximation of a multivalued function relies on a naive pointwise lifting of an abstract domain, as specified by a Galois connection, to Smyth, Hoare, Egli-Milner and Veinott preorder relations on the powerset, which is the range of best response correspondences in supermodular games. It is worth investigating whether abstract domains can be lifted through different and more sophisticated ways to this class of preordered powersets, in particular by taking into account that, for a particular class of complete lattices (that is, complete Heyting and co-Heyting algebras), the Veinott ordering gives rise to complete lattices [11]. Secondly, it could be interesting to investigate some further conditions which can guarantee the correctness of games with abstract strategy spaces (cf. Theorem 5.6). The goal here would be that of devising a notion of simulation between games whose strategy spaces are related by some form of abstraction, in order to prove that if Γ' simulates Γ then the equilibria of Γ are approximated by the equilibria of Γ'. Finally, while this paper set up the abstraction framework by using very simple abstract domains, the general task of designing useful and expressive abstract domains, possibly endowed with widening operators for efficient fixed point computations, for specific classes of supermodular games is left as an open issue.

Acknowledgements. The author has been partially supported by the University of Padova under the PRAT project "ANCORE" no. CPDA148418.

References

1. Carl, S., Heikkilä, S.: Fixed Point Theory in Ordered Sets and Applications. Springer, New York (2011)
2. Cousot, P., Cousot, R., Abstract interpretation: a unified lattice model for static analysis of programs by construction or approximation of fixed points. In: Proceedings of the 4th ACM Symposium on Principles of Programming Languages (POPL 1977), pp. 238–252, ACM Press (1977)
3. Cousot, P., Cousot, R.: Systematic design of program analysis frameworks. In: Proceedings of the 6th ACM Symposium on Principles of Programming Languages (POPL 1979), pp. 269–282, ACM Press (1979)
4. Cousot, P., Cousot, R.: Constructive versions of Tarski's fixed point theorems. Pac. J. Math. **82**(1), 43–57 (1979)
5. Cousot, P., Cousot, R.: Abstract interpretation frameworks. J. Logic Comput. **2**(4), 511–547 (1992)
6. Cousot, P., Cousot, R.: Higher-order abstract interpretation (and application to comportment analysis generalizing strictness, termination, projection and PER analysis of functional languages) (Invited Paper). In: Proceedings of the IEEE International Conference on Computer Languages (ICCL 1994), pp. 95–112. IEEE Computer Society Press (1994)
7. Daskalakis, C., Goldberg, P.W., Papadimitriou, C.H.: The complexity of computing a Nash equilibrium. SIAM J. Comput. **39**(1), 195–259 (2009)
8. Daskalakis, C., Mehta, A., Papadimitriou, C.H.: Progress in approximate Nash equilibria. In: Proceedings of the 8th ACM Conference on Electronic Commerce (EC 2007), pp. 355–358, ACM Press (2007)
9. Echenique, F.: Finding all equilibria in games of strategic complements. J. Econ. Theor. **135**(1), 514–532 (2007)
10. Hazan, E., Krauthgamer, R.: How hard is it to approximate the best Nash equilibrium? SIAM J. Comput. **40**(1), 79–91 (2011)
11. Ranzato, F.: A new characterization of complete Heyting, co-Heyting algebras. Preprint arXiv:1504.03919v1 (2015)
12. Straccia, U., Ojeda-Aciego, M., Damásio, C.V.: On fixed-points of multivalued functions on complete lattices and their application to generalized logic programs. SIAM J. Comput. **38**(5), 1881–1911 (2008)
13. Topkis, D.M.: Minimizing a submodular function on a lattice. Oper. Res. **26**(2), 305–321 (1978)
14. Topkis, D.M.: Supermodularity and Complementarity. Princeton University Press, Princeton (1998)
15. Veinott, A.F.: Lattice Programming. Unpublished notes from lectures at Johns Hopkins University (1989)
16. Wikipedia. Battle of the sexes. https://en.wikipedia.org/wiki/Battle_of_the_sexes_(game_the_ory)
17. Zhou, L.: The set of Nash equilibria of a supermodular game is a complete lattice. Games Econ. Behav. **7**(2), 295–300 (1994)

Validating Numerical Semidefinite Programming Solvers for Polynomial Invariants

Pierre Roux[1(✉)], Yuen-Lam Voronin[2], and Sriram Sankaranarayanan[2]

[1] ONERA – The French Aerospace Lab, Toulouse, France
pierre.roux@onera.fr
[2] University of Colorado, Boulder, CO, USA

Abstract. Semidefinite programming (SDP) solvers are increasingly used as primitives in many program verification tasks to synthesize and verify polynomial invariants for a variety of systems including programs, hybrid systems and stochastic models. On one hand, they provide a tractable alternative to reasoning about semi-algebraic constraints. However, the results are often unreliable due to "numerical issues" that include a large number of reasons such as floating-point errors, ill-conditioned problems, failure of strict feasibility, and more generally, the specifics of the algorithms used to solve SDPs. These issues influence whether the final numerical results are trustworthy or not. In this paper, we briefly survey the emerging use of SDP solvers in the static analysis community. We report on the perils of using SDP solvers for common invariant synthesis tasks, characterizing the common failures that can lead to unreliable answers. Next, we demonstrate existing tools for guaranteed semidefinite programming that often prove inadequate to our needs. Finally, we present a solution for verified semidefinite programming that can be used to check the reliability of the solution output by the solver and a padding procedure that can check the presence of a feasible nearby solution to the one output by the solver. We report on some successful preliminary experiments involving our padding procedure.

1 Introduction

Program analysis techniques using abstract interpretation, especially numerical domain program analysis, rely fundamentally on the ability to reason about constraints expressed in a suitable logic that stems from the abstract domain. Typical *reasoning tasks* include the problem of checking satisfiability of an assertion in the logic used in emptiness and inclusion checks, and characterizing elements of the cone of consequences of an assertion used to compute the transfer function and join operations [16]. The process of using basic solver primitives has led to many constraint-based approaches to synthesizing and verifying

This work was supported by the US National Science Foundation (NSF) under CNS-0953941 and CCF-1527075. All opinions expressed are those of the authors and not necessarily of the NSF.

© Springer-Verlag GmbH Germany 2016
X. Rival (Ed.): SAS 2016, LNCS 9837, pp. 424–446, 2016.
DOI: 10.1007/978-3-662-53413-7_21

invariants for programs [2,15,25–27,52]. Initial approaches that focused on linear systems [25,26,52] have been generalized to address nonlinear (polynomial) systems [2,4,28,42]. Other extensions to hybrid systems and stochastic systems have also been proposed [12,17,47].

However, extensions to polynomial systems necessarily face the challenge of reasoning about polynomial inequality constraints. While the problem of checking satisfiability of these constraints is well-studied, precise solutions to this problem are as yet intractable for large problems. Likewise, computing the cone of consequences precisely is also prohibitively expensive in practice, requiring quantifier elimination. A more tractable alternative uses a convex relaxation from the given polynomial system to a *semidefinite programming problem* (SDP) using the *sum of squares* (SOS) relaxation [36,43,55]. Such a relaxation guarantees soundness when used in invariant checking/synthesis tasks, and has been shown to have nice theoretical guarantees. However, in practice, the approach requires us to use SDP solvers. It is well-known that precise solutions of SDPs is a hard and open research question. For instance, there are SDPs which have a feasible solution but no rational feasible solutions. Therefore, most solvers seek an approximate solution. At the same time, it is well known (but not well documented) that numerical SDP solvers are also hard to use in practice. The presence of "numerical issues" leads to unreliable answers from the SDP solvers, that in turn lead to unsound results when employed in program analysis tasks.

In this paper, we characterize numerical issues into many types. At one end of the spectrum, we have issues that arise from floating-point errors and approximate answers, since numerical solvers seldom reach a true optimal solution. At the other end, certain problems are not well posed, depending on the nature of the solution technique used. One common reason involves the failure of strict feasibility. Using actual examples from the literature, we show how the answers from popular numerical SDP solvers can be wrong and potentially mislead even a careful user who pays due attention to the various errors reported by the SDP solver.

Finally, we address some of the numerical problems raised. We first present a sound verification procedure that can check the answer from the solver and help us decide whether the answer is *qualitatively* correct. Next, we provide a padding procedure that helps reformulate a given problem into a stricter version so that if an approximate, floating-point solver can find a reliable answer to the stricter version, then we conclude feasibility of the original version. We integrate our framework into a polynomial invariant synthesis/verification task, showing how our ideas can successfully address numerical issues arising from the solver.

2   Motivating Examples

In this section, we illustrate through two examples the scenario where numerical SDPs give seemingly sensible solutions to simple invariant generation problems, and yet the generated invariants are not sound.

```
(x1, x2) ∈ {x1,x2 | x1² + x2² ≤ 1.5²}
while (1) {   // Find Inv. p(x1,x2) ≥ 0
  x1 = x1 * x2;
  x2 = -x1;
}
```

$$p(x_1,x_2): \begin{pmatrix} 1 + 2.46x_1^2 + 2.46x_2^2 - 5 \times 10^{-7}x_1^4 \\ -2.46x_1^2x_2^2 - 5 \times 10^{-7}x_2^4 \end{pmatrix}$$

Fig. 1. (**Left**) An example program, and "loop invariant" $p(x_1, x_2) \geq 0$ synthesized using numerical solvers. (**Right**) The claimed "invariant" and dashed lines showing violations.

Consider the program in Fig. 1. Does there exist an inductive invariant[1] in the form $\{(x_1, x_2) \in \mathbb{R}^2 \mid p(x_1, x_2) \geq 0\}$ for some polynomial p? A *tractable* sufficient condition that guarantees this can be formulated using the SOS optimization approach (see Sect. 3), resulting in an SDP instance that can be solved by numerical solvers. The widely used SDPT3 [59] solver reports a solution. Although all the DIMACS errors [53] are less than 10^{-8}, not raising any suspicion, we found traces of the program that violate this purported invariant (see Fig. 1).

```
(x1, x2) ∈ [0.9, 1.1] × [0, 0.2]
while (1) {
  pre_x1 = x1; pre_x2 = x2;
  if (x1^2 + x2^2 <= 1) {
    x1 = pre_x1^2 + pre_x2^3;
    x2 = pre_x1^3 + pre_x2^2;
  } else {
    x1 = 0.5 * pre_x1^3
         + 0.4 * pre_x2^2;
    x2 = -0.6 * pre_x1^2
         + 0.3 * pre_x2^2;
  }
}
```

$$2.510902467 + 0.0050x_1 + 0.0148x_2 - 3.0998x_1^2$$
$$+ 0.8037x_2^3 + 3.0297x_1^3 - 2.5924x_2^2$$
$$- 1.5266x_1x_2 + 1.9133x_1^2x_2 + 1.8122x_1x_2^2 - 1.6042x_1^4$$
$$- 0.0512x_1^3x_2 + 4.4430x_1^2x_2^2 + 1.8926x_1x_2^3 - 0.5464x_2^4$$
$$+ 0.2084x_1^5 - 0.5866x_1^4x_2 - 2.2410x_1^3x_2^2 - 1.5714x_1^2x_2^3$$
$$+ 0.0890x_1x_2^4 + 0.9656x_2^5 - 0.0098x_1^6 + 0.0320x_1^5x_2$$
$$+ 0.0232x_1^4x_2^2 - 0.2660x_1^3x_2^3 - 0.7746x_1^2x_2^4$$
$$- 0.9200x_1x_2^5 - 0.6411x_2^6 \geq 0$$

Fig. 2. (**Left**) An example program taken from from ADJÉ et al. [1] (Example 4). (**Right**) Purported invariant at loop head synthesized using SDP solvers [1].

As another example, we consider a program from ADJÉ et al. [1] and the "invariant" they offer, generated with numerical solvers (Fig. 2). Note that the purported invariant is indeed not inductive: one can find points in it whose image after one iteration of the loop body exits the invariant (Fig. 3). Figure 3 also depicts an actual invariant, proved using the method in this paper.

---

[1] In the remainder of this paper, the word "invariant" is used for inductive invariant.

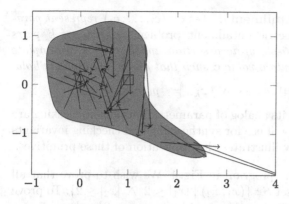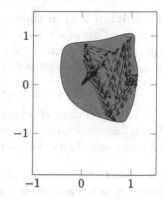

Fig. 3. (Left) The candidate invariant from Fig. 2 with arrows showing concrete transitions. The arrows leaving it are counterexamples to its inductiveness. **(Right)** The invariant of degree 8 whose soundness is proved using the approach in this paper.

3 Sum of Squares (SOS) and Semidefinite Programs (SDP)

In this section, we provide the background for sum of squares (SOS) optimization from the perspective of proving entailments for program analysis (invariant synthesis/verification) tasks. We then trace the steps along which SOS optimization problems are relaxed to semidefinite programs (SDP).

Let $\mathbb{R}$ denote the set of real numbers and $\mathbf{x} : (x_1, \ldots, x_n)$ denote a vector of real-valued variables. The ring of multivariate real polynomials over $\mathbf{x}$ is denoted by $\mathbb{R}[\mathbf{x}]$. The degree of any polynomial $p(\mathbf{x}) \in \mathbb{R}[\mathbf{x}]$ is denoted by $\deg(p)$. A *template polynomial* is of the form $p(\mathbf{c}, \mathbf{x}) : \sum_{j=1}^{s} c_j\, p_j(\mathbf{x})$, where $p_1, \ldots, p_s$ are *basis polynomials* and $\mathbf{c} : (c_1, \ldots, c_s)$ is a placeholder for parameters serving as scalar multiples of the basis polynomials. A *generic template polynomial* of degree $d > 0$ is formed by choosing all monomials of degree up to d as the basis polynomials, and has $s = \binom{n+d}{d}$ parameters.

3.1 Semi-algebraic Assertions and Entailment Problems

A *semi-algebraic* assertion φ is a finite conjunction of polynomial inequalities:

$$\varphi : p_1(\mathbf{x}) \geq 0 \,\wedge\, \cdots \,\wedge\, p_m(\mathbf{x}) \geq 0.$$

It denotes a corresponding semi-algebraic set $[\![\varphi]\!] : \{\mathbf{x} \in \mathbb{R}^n \mid \mathbf{x} \models \varphi\}$. As such, semi-algebraic assertions subsume useful abstract domains such as polyhedra and ellipsoids. They also represent a rich class of constraints with a decidable entailment checking problem [7]. We define two classes of problems involving semi-algebraic sets that are commonly used as primitives.

Definition 1 (Entailment Checking). *Given two semi-algebraic assertions φ and ψ over $\mathbf{x}$, check if $\varphi \models \psi$, i.e., for all $\mathbf{x} \in \mathbb{R}^n$, if $\mathbf{x} \models \varphi$, then $\mathbf{x} \models \psi$.*

Definition 2 (Parametric Entailment). *Let* $\mathbf{c} : (c_1, \ldots, c_s)$ *represent parameters. The input to a* parametric entailment problem *consists of* k *pairs* $(\varphi_i, p_i)_{i=1}^k$, *wherein* φ_i *is a semi-algebraic assertion and* $p_i(\mathbf{c}, \mathbf{x})$ *is a template polynomial. The goal is to compute a value* $\mathbf{c}$ *such that all the entailments hold:*

$$(\varphi_1 \ \models \ p_1(\mathbf{c}, \mathbf{x}) \geq 0) \ \wedge \ \cdots \ \wedge \ (\varphi_k \ \models \ p_k(\mathbf{c}, \mathbf{x}) \geq 0).$$

The entailment checking and its analog of parametric entailment checking are fundamental primitives that we will use for synthesizing and checking invariants of programs. The example below illustrates the application of these primitives.

Invariant checking: Consider the program in Fig. 4. We wish to prove that all executions remain inside a safe set $S : \{(x_1, x_2) \mid |x_1| \leq 2 \ \wedge \ |x_2| \leq 2\}$. To prove this, we consider an inductive invariant $\{(x_1, x_2) \mid p(x_1, x_2) \geq 0\}$, where

$$p(x_1, x_2) : 37 - x_2^2 + x_1^3 - 2x_1^2 x_2 + 2x_2^3 - 12x_1^4 - 10x_1^2 x_2^2 - 6x_1 x_2^3 - 6x_2^4. \tag{1}$$

```
(x1, x2) ∈ I : {(x₁,x₂) | x₁² ≤ 1 ∧ x₂² ≤ 1}
while (1) {
  pre_x1 = x1; pre_x2 = x2;
  if (x1 >= x2) {
    x1 = 0.687 * pre_x1 + 0.558 * pre_x2
       - 0.0001 * pre_x1 * pre_x2;
    x2 = -0.292 * pre_x1 + 0.773 * pre_x2;
  } else {
    x1 = 0.369 * pre_x1 + 0.532 * pre_x2
       - 0.0001 * pre_x1^2;
    x2 = -1.27 * pre_x1 + 0.12 * pre_x2
       - 0.0001 * prex_x1 * pre_x2;
  }
}
```

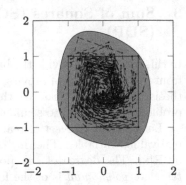

Fig. 4. (Left) An example program. **(Right)** Invariant $[\![p(x_1, x_2) \geq 0]\!]$, along with executions that start inside the initial set I (square).

Fig. 4 shows the invariant region $p(x_1, x_2) \geq 0$. To show that it is indeed an invariant that establishes S as a safe set, we check that the following conditions hold:

(a) *Initial condition:* $1 - x_1^2 \geq 0 \ \wedge \ 1 - x_2^2 \geq 0 \ \models \ p(x_1, x_2) \geq 0$,

(b) *Consecution (loop) conditions:* Let $\tau_1(x_1, x_2) \ : \ (0.687x_1 + 0.558x_2 - 0.0001x_1x_2, \ -0.292x_1 + 0.773x_2)$ denote the transition enabled by the condition $x_1 \geq x_2$, and $\tau_2(x_1, x_2) : (0.369x_1 + 0.532x_2 - 0.0001x_1^2, \ -1.27x_1 + 0.12x_2 - 0.0001x_1x_2)$ denote the transition enabled by the condition $x_1 < x_2$.
  We require two conditions, corresponding to the two transitions in the loop:
  (i) $x_1 - x_2 \geq 0 \ \wedge \ p(x_1, x_2) \geq 0 \ \models \ \hat{p_1} \geq 0$, where $\hat{p_1} = p \circ \tau_1$, and
  (ii) $x_2 - x_1 \geq 0 \ \wedge \ p(x_1, x_2) \geq 0 \ \models \ \hat{p_2} \geq 0$, where $\hat{p_2} = p \circ \tau_2$.

(c) *Safety conditions:* $p(x_1, x_2) \geq 0 \ \models \ -2 \leq x_1 \leq 2 \ \wedge \ -2 \leq x_2 \leq 2$.

The invariant checking problem is then a series of polynomial entailment checking.

Invariant synthesis: The invariant synthesis problem requires us to synthesize polynomials that satisfy some entailment conditions, such as $p(x_1, x_2)$ in (1) satisfying the initial, loop and safety conditions. To do so, we parameterize a *template* polynomial as follows:

$$p(\mathbf{c}, \mathbf{x}) : \begin{pmatrix} c_1 + c_2 x_1 + c_3 x_2 + c_4 x_1^2 + c_5 x_1 x_2 + c_6 x_2^2 + c_7 x_1^3 + c_8 x_1 x_2^2 + \\ c_9 x_1^2 x_2 + c_{10} x_2^3 + c_{11} x_1^4 + c_{12} x_1^3 x_2 + c_{13} x_1^2 x_2^2 + c_{14} x_1 x_2^3 + c_{15} x_2^4 \end{pmatrix} . \quad (2)$$

We then search for values of $\mathbf{c} = (c_1, \dots, c_{15})$ such that the following entailments hold:

(a) *Initial condition:* $1 - x_1^2 \geq 0 \ \wedge \ 1 - x_2^2 \geq 0 \ \models \ p(\mathbf{c}, \mathbf{x}) \geq 0$,
(b) *Loop conditions:* The loop condition for the transition τ_1 is $(x_1 - x_2 \geq 0 \ \wedge \ p(\mathbf{c}, \mathbf{x}) \geq 0 \ \models \ \hat{p}_1(\mathbf{c}, \mathbf{x}) \geq 0)$, where $\hat{p}_1 = p \circ \tau_1$. However, we note that in this condition, a parametric polynomial inequality appears on the antecedent side. This leads to hard *bilinear optimization* problems that are beyond the scope of this paper (see [51] for a discussion of this issue). We impose a stronger condition on p that states that p must be non-decreasing for each loop iteration[2]:
   (i) $x_1 - x_2 \geq 0 \ \models \ \hat{p}_1(\mathbf{c}, \mathbf{x}) \geq p(\mathbf{c}, \mathbf{x})$, and
   (ii) $x_2 - x_1 \geq 0 \ \models \ \hat{p}_2(\mathbf{c}, \mathbf{x}) \geq p(\mathbf{c}, \mathbf{x})$, where $\hat{p}_2 = p \circ \tau_2$.

The invariant synthesis problem is thus reduced to a *parametric* entailment problem.

3.2 Solving Entailment Problems

There are numerous approaches to solving semi-algebraic entailment checking and parametric entailment problems. We classify these into four broad classes: (a) quantifier elimination for the theory of polynomial inequalities, (b) interval arithmetic with branch-and-bound, (c) linear programming relaxations, and (d) sum of squares relaxations that will be the focus of our exposition.

Exact Approaches: It is well-known that the logical theory of polynomial inequalities admits effective decision procedures and a quantifier elimination procedure, originally discovered by TARSKI and further developed by COLLINS, HONG, WEISPFENNING and others [7,13,14,57,61]. These procedures attempt to solve the entailment problem $\varphi \models \psi$ by checking the unsatisfiability of the assertion $\varphi(\mathbf{x}) \wedge (\neg \psi(\mathbf{x}))$. This problem is known to be NP-hard in theory, and hard to solve, in practice. Typical sizes of problems that can be tackled involve polynomials with ~ 5 variables, and degrees ~ 3 [19].

Likewise, an exact approach for the parametric entailment problem requires to perform a quantifier elimination of the form:

$$(\forall \ \mathbf{x}) \ \left(\varphi_1(\mathbf{x}) \ \Rightarrow \ p_1(\mathbf{c}, \mathbf{x}) \geq 0 \ \wedge \ \cdots \wedge \ \varphi_k(\mathbf{x}) \ \Rightarrow \ p_k(\mathbf{c}, \mathbf{x}) \geq 0 \right) .$$

Doing so leads to an assertion that can be expressed purely in terms of $\mathbf{c}$. If this assertion is satisfiable, a solution $\mathbf{c} = \mathbf{c}^*$ can be extracted.

---

[2] Control theorists call (opposite of) such functions *Lyapunov functions* [22].

Branch-and-Bound (BnB) Approaches: They work over states **x** that are a priori restricted to a compact set X. They proceed by subdividing X into finitely many interval (hyper-rectangular) cells. Inside each interval, the entailment is evaluated using interval arithmetic [23,24] or a branch-and-bound scheme using linear programming relaxation of the constraints [8]. BnB approaches can be used to check whether an entailment $\varphi \models \psi$ holds by checking the unsatisfiability of the assertion $\varphi(\mathbf{x}) \wedge (\neg\psi(\mathbf{x}))$. They can conclude soundly that the entailment holds or even find a *witness* **x** such that $\varphi(\mathbf{x}) \wedge (\neg\psi(\mathbf{x}))$ is satisfied. Unfortunately, due to computational limitations, these techniques may also terminate without an answer. Recent work on delta-satisfiability procedures have carefully analyzed this condition to conclude that a "nearby" formula is satisfiable [24]. BnB approaches can extend beyond polynomial programs and invariants. Currently, BnB approaches are restricted to solving entailment problems. Their application to solving parametric entailment problems remains an open challenge. Part of the challenge involves the optimal subdivision of X to search for solutions **c**.

Linear Programming (LP) Relaxations: Linear programming relaxations have been considered for checking polynomial entailment and solving parametric entailment problems (see BEN SASSI et al. for details and further references [8]). LP approaches are primarily based on so-called *Handelman relaxation* and *reformulation linearization*. Given an entailment problem with $p_1, \ldots, p_k$ as antecedents. We generate "valid inequalities" that are consequences of the original antecedents. This is achieved by simply multiplying the antecedents together, enriching the set of possible antecedents. This step is inspired by the Handelman positivstellensatz [29]. Next, we introduce fresh variables corresponding to each monomial term and turn our polynomial entailment problem into a *linear entailment* problem that can be checked using solvers. This step is called *reformulation linearization technique* (RLT) [54]. BEN SASSI et al. show that the generation of linear constraints can be performed in the Bernstein polynomial basis [9,21], rather than the monomial basis to obtain a larger set of valid inequalities. The LP approach has the main advantage that Simplex solvers can be used with exact arithmetic to completely avoid numerical issues. The recent work of MARÉCHAL et al. use this approach and generate machine checkable proofs of polynomial entailments [38]. However, LP relaxations yield a "weak" proof system that requires higher degree terms or a BnB decomposition of the domain, to prove "simple consequences" such as $-1 \leq x \leq 1 \wedge -1 \leq y \leq 1 \models (x^2 + y^2 \geq 0)$ [8]. Interestingly, the Handelman relaxation and RLT are implicit in the polyhedral abstract domain for computing semi-algebraic invariants proposed by BAGNARA et al. [6]. A related approach of *diagonal SOS* (DSOS) has been proposed by ALI AHMADI and MAJUMDAR [3]. Their approach is based on the SOS relaxation wherein instead of reducing to a SDP, they reduce to an LP by imposing the stronger condition of *diagonal dominance* on the associated matrix rather than the semi-definiteness condition that will be described subsequently in this section. A full comparison of DSOS with SOS relaxations for program analysis problems is currently open.

Positivstellensatz/Sum of Squares (SOS) Relaxations: The SOS relaxation [36,43] is an incomplete but efficient way to numerically solve polynomial entailment problems.

Definition 3 (SOS Polynomial). *A polynomial $p \in \mathbb{R}[\mathbf{x}]$ is said to be SOS if there exist polynomials $h_i \in \mathbb{R}[\mathbf{x}]$ such that for all $\mathbf{x}$, $p(\mathbf{x}) = \sum_i h_i^2(\mathbf{x})$.*

Although not all nonnegative polynomials are SOS, being SOS is a sufficient condition to be nonnegative.

Example 1. Consider $p : 2x_1^4 + 2x_1^3x_2 - x_1^2x_2^2 + 5x_2^4$. Since $p = h_1^2 + h_2^2$, where $h_1 : \frac{1}{\sqrt{2}}\left(2x_1^2 + x_1x_2 - 3x_2^2\right)$ and $h_2 : \frac{1}{\sqrt{2}}\left(3x_1x_2 + x_2^2\right)$, the polynomial p is nonnegative, i.e., $p(x_1, x_2) \geq 0$ holds for all $x_1, x_2 \in \mathbb{R}^2$.

Now consider a polynomial entailment problem of the form:

$$\underbrace{p_1(\mathbf{x}) \geq 0 \wedge \cdots \wedge p_k(\mathbf{x}) \geq 0}_{\varphi} \models p(\mathbf{x}) \geq 0. \qquad (3)$$

Our goal is to write p as a *combination* of $p_1, \ldots, p_k$ in the following form:

$$p = \sigma_0 + \sigma_1 p_1 + \cdots + \sigma_k p_k \qquad (4)$$

such that $\sigma_0, \ldots, \sigma_k$ are SOS polynomials over $\mathbf{x}$. Let K denote the semi-algebraic set $[\![\bigwedge_{j=1}^{k} p_j \geq 0]\!]$, let $R(K)$ denote the cone of consequences of K, i.e., $R(K) = \{p(\mathbf{x}) \mid \varphi \models p(\mathbf{x}) \geq 0\}$ and $M(K)$ denote all polynomials expressible in the form (4):

$$M(K) = \left\{p(\mathbf{x}) \;\middle|\; p = \sigma_0 + \sum_{j=1}^{k} \sigma_j p_j, \; \sigma_i \text{ SOS}\right\}.$$

Theorem 1 (Putinar's Positivstellensatz). *For all K, $M(K) \subseteq R(K)$. Conversely, if K is compact and $M(K)$ contains a polynomial of the form $s(\mathbf{x}) = \sum_{i=1}^{n} x_i^2 - L$ for some constant $L > 0$, then $M(K) = R(K)$.*

Proof. We will prove the "easy" direction that $M(K) \subseteq R(K)$. Let $p \in M(K)$. There exist SOS polynomials $\sigma_0, \ldots, \sigma_k$ such that $p = \sigma_0 + \sum_{i=1}^{k} \sigma_i p_i$. Let $\mathbf{x}$ be such that $p_i(\mathbf{x}) \geq 0$ for all $i \in [1, k]$. We have that $\sigma_i(\mathbf{x}) \geq 0$ since each σ_i is a SOS polynomial. Therefore, we conclude that $p(\mathbf{x}) = \sigma_0(\mathbf{x}) + \sum_{i=1}^{k} \sigma_i(\mathbf{x})p_i(\mathbf{x}) \geq 0$. For the converse, we refer the reader to Putinar's work [48]. $\qquad \square$

Thus, a polynomial entailment problem of the form (3) is relaxed to an SOS problem:

$$\begin{aligned}
\text{find}: \; & \text{polynomials } \sigma_0, \ldots, \sigma_k \in \mathbb{R}_d[\mathbf{x}] \\
\text{s.t.} \quad & p = \sigma_0 + \sum_{i=1}^{k} \sigma_i p_i, \\
& \sigma_0, \ldots, \sigma_k \text{ are SOS}.
\end{aligned} \qquad (5)$$

First, we choose a degree limit $d > 0$ (d must be an even number because all positive polynomials have even maximum degree), and select *templates* $\sigma_0(\mathbf{c}^{(0)}, \mathbf{x}), \ldots, \sigma_k(\mathbf{c}^{(k)}, \mathbf{x})$ with unknowns $\mathbf{c}^{(0)}, \ldots, \mathbf{c}^{(k)}$. We then require that p

be equal to a polynomial combination of $p_1, \ldots, p_k$ with "multipliers" $\sigma_0, \ldots, \sigma_k$ as shown above. This yields a set of linear equations involving $\mathbf{c}^{(0)}, \ldots, \mathbf{c}^{(k)}$ and the coefficients of p, obtained by comparing both sides monomial by monomial and setting their coefficients to be the same. Finally, we require $\sigma_0, \ldots, \sigma_k$ to be SOS. This will be tackled through a reduction to a *semidefinite programming* (SDP) problem, as will be explained subsequently.

Example 2. Consider the initial condition check for the program in Fig. 4: $p_1(x_1, x_2) \geq 0 \ \wedge \ p_2(x_1, x_2) \geq 0 \ \models \ p(x_1, x_2) \geq 0$ with $p_i(x_1, x_2) = 1 - x_i^2$ and p given in (1). Our goal here is to find polynomials $\sigma_0, \sigma_1, \sigma_2$ such that $p = \sigma_0 + \sigma_1 p_1 + \sigma_2 p_2$. For simplicity, let us write $\sigma_0 = c_1 + c_2 x_1 + \cdots + c_{15} x_2^4$, $\sigma_1 = d_1 + \cdots + d_{15} x_2^4$ and $\sigma_2 = e_1 + \cdots + e_{15} x_2^4$. We obtain equality constraints by equating terms corresponding to the same monomial on both sides:

$$c_1 + d_1 + e_1 = 37 \ \text{(comparing constant terms)}, \ldots, -e_{15} = 0 \ \text{(comparing } x_2^6 \text{)}.$$

The SOS problem seeks to satisfy these equalities, and additionally make $\sigma_0, \sigma_1, \sigma_2$ SOS. Solving this as an SDP problem (as will be explained below), we obtain: $\sigma_1 \approx 11 - 0.13x_1 + 1.5x_2 + 24x_1^2 - 3x_1x_2 + 8.2x_2^2$ and $\sigma_2 \approx 8.8 + 0.63x_1 - 1.4x_2 + 6.5x_1^2 + 1.6x_1x_2 + 18x_2^2$.

SOS formulation of parametric entailment problems. Consider now a parametric entailment problem of the form $(\varphi_j \models p_j(\mathbf{c}, \mathbf{x}) \geq 0)$ for $j = 1, \ldots, K$ involving parameters $\mathbf{c}$. Let us write $\varphi_j : \ p_{j_1}(\mathbf{x}) \geq 0 \ \wedge \ \cdots \ \wedge \ p_{j_l}(\mathbf{x}) \geq 0$. This is reduced to a *sum of squares* problem:

$$\begin{aligned} \text{find}: \ & \text{polynomials } \sigma_{j,0}, \ldots, \sigma_{j,j_l} \in \mathbb{R}_d[\mathbf{x}], j \in \{1, \ldots, K\} \\ \text{s.t.} \ & p_j = \sigma_{j,0} + \sum_{i=1}^k \sigma_{j,i} p_{j_i}, \ j \in \{1, \ldots, K\}, \\ & \sigma_{j,0}, \ldots, \sigma_{j,j_l} \text{ are SOS}, j \in \{1, \ldots, K\}. \end{aligned} \qquad (6)$$

The unknowns include the coefficients $\mathbf{c}$ involved in each $p_j(\mathbf{c}, \mathbf{x})$ for the original parametric entailment and the coefficients $\mathbf{c}^{(j,i)}$ corresponding to SOS multipliers $\sigma_{j,i}$.

Next, we provide a reduction from SOS problems to a well known class of optimization problems: *semidefinite programs* (SDPs). Any polynomial p of degree $2d$ (a nonnegative polynomial is necessarily of even degree) can be written as a quadratic form in the vector z of all monomials of degree less or equal d:

$$p(\mathbf{x}) = z^T Q z, \qquad (7)$$

where $z = [1, x_1, \ldots, x_n, x_1 x_2, \ldots, x_n^d]^T$ and Q is a constant symmetric matrix.

Example 3. Consider $p(x_1, x_2) : 2x_1^4 + 2x_1^3 x_2 - x_1^2 x_2^2 + 5x_2^4$. To satisfy the equality

$$\begin{aligned} p(x_1, x_2) &= \begin{bmatrix} x_1^2 \\ x_2^2 \\ x_1 x_2 \end{bmatrix}^T \begin{bmatrix} q_{11} & q_{12} & q_{13} \\ q_{12} & q_{22} & q_{23} \\ q_{13} & q_{23} & q_{33} \end{bmatrix} \begin{bmatrix} x_1^2 \\ x_2^2 \\ x_1 x_2 \end{bmatrix} \\ &= q_{11} x_1^4 + 2q_{13} x_1^3 x_2 + (q_{33} + 2q_{12}) x_1^2 x_2^2 + 2q_{23} x_1 x_2^3 + q_{22} x_2^4, \end{aligned}$$

the equalities $q_{11} = 2$, $2q_{13} = 2$, $q_{33} + 2q_{12} = -1$, $2q_{23} = 0$ and $q_{22} = 5$ must hold. Two possible examples for the matrix Q are shown below:

$$Q = \begin{bmatrix} 2 & 1 & 1 \\ 1 & 5 & 0 \\ 1 & 0 & -3 \end{bmatrix}, \qquad Q' = \begin{bmatrix} 2 & -3 & 1 \\ -3 & 5 & 0 \\ 1 & 0 & 5 \end{bmatrix}.$$

The polynomial p is then SOS if and only if there exists a positive semidefinite matrix Q satisfying (7). A matrix Q is said to be *positive semidefinite*, denoted by $Q \succeq 0$, when for all vectors y, $y^T Q y \geq 0$. A matrix Q is said to be *positive definite*, denoted by $Q \succ 0$, when for all nonzero vectors y, $y^T Q y > 0$.

Example 4. In Example 3, the first matrix Q is not positive semidefinite (for $y : [0, 0, 1]^T$, $y^T Q y = -3$). However, the second matrix Q' is positive semidefinite as it can be written $Q' = L^T L$ with

$$L = \frac{1}{\sqrt{2}} \begin{bmatrix} 2 & -3 & 1 \\ 0 & 1 & 3 \end{bmatrix}$$

(then, for all y, $y^T Q y = (Ly)^T (Ly) = \|Ly\|_2^2 \geq 0$). This gives the SOS decomposition of Example 1: $p(x_1, x_2) = \frac{1}{2}(2x_1^2 + x_1 x_2 - 3x_2^2)^2 + \frac{1}{2}(3x_1 x_2 + x_2^2)^2$.

As a result, SOS programming problems can be written as semidefinite optimization problems involving matrices. Let z be a vector of monomials over $\mathbf{x}$ chosen so that we may write each polynomial $\sigma_i(\mathbf{c}^{(i)}, \mathbf{x})$ as a quadratic form $\sigma_i(\mathbf{c}^{(i)}, \mathbf{x}) = z^T C_i z$. Thus, the SOS programming problems (5) and (6) can be written down as an SDP problem:

$$\begin{aligned} &\text{find} : c, C_0, \ldots, C_k \\ &\text{s.t.}\ a_i^T c + \sum_{j=0}^{k} \text{tr}(A_{i,j} C_j) = b_i,\ i = 1, \ldots, m, \\ &\quad C_j \succeq 0,\ j = 0, \ldots, k. \end{aligned} \qquad (8)$$

wherein the vector c encodes the parameters $\mathbf{c}^{(i)}$ of (5) (or $\mathbf{c}$ and $\mathbf{c}^{(j,i)}$ of (6)) and the $A_{i,j}$ and C_j are symmetric matrices. Note that the expression $\text{tr}(XY)$ equals $\sum_{i=1}^{n} \sum_{j=1}^{n} (X)_{i,j} (Y)_{i,j}$ for $n \times n$ matrices X, Y when $X^T = X$.

Example 5. We check whether the entailment $(p_1(x, y) : x - y \geq 0 \models p(x, y) : x - y + 2x^2 - 2y^2 + x^3 + x^2 y - xy^2 - y^3 \geq 0)$ is true using an SOS relaxation: we look for degree 2 SOS polynomials $\sigma_0, \sigma_1 \in \mathbb{R}[x, y]$ such that $p = \sigma_0 + \sigma_1 p_1$. In other words, we seek coefficients $\mathbf{c}^{(0)} : (c_1, \ldots, c_6)$ and $\mathbf{c}^{(1)} : (c_7, \ldots, c_{12})$ such that $\sigma_0(x, y) : c_1 + c_2 x + c_3 y + c_4 x^2 + c_5 xy + c_6 y^2$ and $\sigma_1(x, y) : c_7 + c_8 x + c_9 y + c_{10} x^2 + c_{11} xy + c_{12} y^2$ are SOS and the coefficients of p and $\sigma_0 + \sigma_1 p_1$ coincide, i.e., with $z : [1, x, y]^T$,

$$
\begin{array}{ll}
\text{comparing} \\
\text{coeffs of} \\
\sigma_0 + \sigma_1\, p_1 \\
\text{and } p
\end{array} :
\left\{
\begin{array}{ll}
\text{const. term} & c_1 = 0, \\
\text{coeff. of } x & c_2 + c_7 = 1, \\
\text{coeff. of } y & c_3 - c_7 = -1, \\
\text{coeff. of } x^2 & c_4 + c_8 = 2, \\
\text{coeff. of } xy & c_5 - c_8 + c_9 = 0, \\
\text{coeff. of } y^2 & c_6 - c_9 = -2, \\
\text{coeff. of } x^3 & c_{10} = 1, \\
\text{coeff. of } x^2 y & c_{11} - c_{10} = 1, \\
\text{coeff. of } xy^2 & c_{12} - c_{11} = -1, \\
\text{coeff. of } y^3 & -c_{12} = -1,
\end{array}
\right.
\quad
\begin{array}{l}
\text{comparing} \\
\text{coefficients} \\
\text{of } \sigma_0 \text{ and} \\
z^T C_0\, z
\end{array} :
\left\{
\begin{array}{l}
c_1 = (C_0)_{1,1}, \\
c_2 = (C_0)_{1,2} + (C_0)_{2,1}, \\
c_3 = (C_0)_{1,3} + (C_0)_{3,1}, \\
c_4 = (C_0)_{2,2}, \\
c_5 = (C_0)_{2,3} + (C_0)_{3,2}, \\
c_6 = (C_0)_{3,3},
\end{array}
\right.
$$

$$\text{same for } \sigma_1 \text{ and } z^T C_1\, z. \tag{9}$$

Each of the $m = 22$ equality constraints in (9) is then encoded as in (8). For instance, the second constraint on σ_0 is encoded by the vector $a_{12} = [0, 1, 0, 0, 0, 0, 0, 0, 0, 0, 0, 0]^T$ and the matrices $A_{12,0} = \begin{bmatrix} 0 & -1 & 0 \\ -1 & 0 & 0 \\ 0 & 0 & 0 \end{bmatrix}$ and $A_{12,1} = 0$.

Thus, we have eliminated the formal variables $\mathbf{x}$ from the problem and reduced it to finding matrices that satisfy some linear equality constraints, and are positive semidefinite. In fact, moving one step further, we write a single unknown matrix C in the block diagonal form: $C = \mathrm{Diag}(c_1^+, c_1^-, \ldots, c_s^+, c_s^-, C_0, C_1, \ldots, C_k)$, encoding c_i as $c_i^+ - c_i^-$ with $c_i^+, c_i^- \in \mathbb{R}_+$. This allows us to write (8) as:

$$
\begin{aligned}
\text{find}: C \ \text{ s.t. } \ & \mathrm{tr}(A_i C) = b_i, \ i = 1, \ldots, m, \\
& C \succeq 0.
\end{aligned}
\tag{10}
$$

Problems that follow this form, or equivalently (8), are called *semidefinite programming problems* (SDP). They form a well known class of convex optimization problems that generalize linear programs and can be solved numerically even for large[3] problem matrices C. Numerical solvers also allow to optimize a linear objective function of the coefficients of C. Finally, we define the notion of strict feasibility.

Definition 4 (Strict Feasibility). *The SDP in (10) is said to be strictly feasible when there exists a solution to the problem wherein the matrix C is positive definite.*

If every feasible solution C to the problem (10) is positive semidefinite but not positive definite (in other words, the matrix has zero eigenvalues, or alternatively is rank deficient), the problem is said to *fail strictly feasibility*.

Remark 1. For a strictly feasible problem, there exist solutions C such that any $\widetilde{C}$ in a neighborhood from C and satisfying the equality constraints $\mathrm{tr}(A_i \widetilde{C}) = b_i$ is also a solution. In contrary, problems that are not strictly feasible are also said to have an *empty (relative) interior* because, for any solution C, there exist $\widetilde{C}$ arbitrarily close from C that satisfy the equality constraints but are not solutions. This is illustrated on Fig. 5.

---

[3] Typically, matrices C_j can be of size $n \times n$ for n up to a few hundreds.

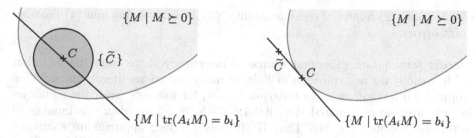

Fig. 5. The line represents the equality constraints $\text{tr}(A_iC) = b_i$ and the shaded area the matrices $C \succeq 0$. The set of solutions is the intersection of the line and the shaded area. (**Left**) A strictly feasible SDP problem. (**Right**) An empty interior problem.

4   Verified SDPs

In Sect. 3, we laid out a procedure for formulating invariant checking and synthesis as a general SOS feasibility problem, which in turn is an SDP feasibility problem. There are SDPs with rational problem data whose solutions are irrational [58]. However, under some regularity conditions, SDP problems can theoretically be solved *efficiently* up to *arbitrarily small* error tolerance (see e.g., [62, Chap. 8–10]). In practice, many numerical solvers are available to solve SDP instances satisfactorily (see [5, Part III]). Currently, the default choice for solving SDPs are specialized second order methods (i.e., using second order derivatives) called *interior point methods* (IPMs)[4].

We discuss in Sect. 4.1 issues leading to inaccuracy or poor solution quality in SDP solving via IPMs. Then in Sect. 4.2, we consider solutions to guarantee soundness.

4.1   Sources of Solution Inaccuracy in Solving SDPs

Before we discuss ways to ensure soundness of solutions to the invariant checking and synthesis problem generated by SDP solvers, we first focus on a few issues that could possibly make an SDP solution inaccurate, leading to potential unsoundness. We will concentrate on SDP solutions obtained from general IPMs.

How do IPMs Work? The convergence of a general IPM *assumes strict feasibility* (Definition 4). Using positive definite matrices as initial points, a general IPM repeatedly solves a perturbed linearization of the Karush-Kuhn-Tucker optimality conditions for a search direction, and moves along that search direction with a fractional step size that maintains the positive definiteness of the iterates. (See e.g. [58, 62].)

In the following, we discuss the four potential issues that can cause solution inaccuracy when a general IPM is used for obtaining SDP solutions: (1) inexact

---

[4] There also exist first order methods handling larger problems but with less accurate solutions.

termination, (2) failure of strict feasibility, (3) ill-conditioning and (4) floating-point errors.

Inexact termination. The first source of inaccuracy stems from the fact that IPMs usually do not converge in finitely many iterations. Iterations are then stopped when some *stopping criterion* is met, for instance when the equalities in (10) are ϵ-approximated (i.e., $|\mathrm{tr}(A_i C) - b_i| \leq \epsilon$) or when the number of iterations becomes too big. Thus IPMs only produce approximate solutions. Nonetheless, under strict feasibility assumption, most common IPMs enjoy a convergence result of the following form: for any $\varepsilon \in (0, 1)$, if an appropriate initial point is chosen, then it takes at most a number of steps polynomial in the problem size and $\log(\frac{1}{\varepsilon})$ to obtain an ε-approximate solution. (See e.g. [62, Chap. 10].)

Failure of Strict Feasibility. Strictly feasibility is a desirable property. For instance, as seen above, it guarantees that a SDP can be solved to arbitrary accuracy by an IPM. "Random" SDP problems are strictly feasible with probability one [20, Theorem 3.2]. However, strict feasibility can fail *systematically* for SDP instances arising from applications due to the inherent problem structure. In particular, strict feasibility can fail for entailment problems (Sect. 3.1), as shown in the following example.

Example 6. The SDP feasibility problem in Example 5 fails the strict feasibility. Indeed, for any solution (c, C_0, C_1), the equality constraints imply $(C_0)_{1,1} = 0$, hence[5] $(C_0)_{1,2} = (C_0)_{2,1} = (C_0)_{1,3} = (C_0)_{3,1} = 0$ which means that C_0 is rank deficient.

While the failure of the strict feasibility in small instances such as Example 6 usually does not cause much numerical issues, significant inaccuracy can often be observed as the number of variables and the degrees of the polynomials increase [60]. Facial reduction techniques proposed by Borwein and Wolkowicz can be used for preprocessing SDP instances that are not strictly feasible [11]. A more efficient version using linear programming reduction, called partial facial reduction, was proposed by Permenter and Parrilo [44].

Ill Conditioning. The coefficients of the polynomials in the entailment problems can influence the condition number of the linear system that is solved in IPMs, and a large condition number can affect the convergence of IPMs. While most SDP solvers use *preconditioning* to enhance the numerical stability, it is important to caution against the possible inaccuracy caused simply by the large input coefficients, which can occur even when preconditioning is used.

---

[5] If a matrix is PSD and one of its diagonal entry (e.g. the $(1, 1)$ entry) equals 0, then the entire row and column that contain that diagonal entry (e.g., the first row and column) equal 0.

Example 7. Consider the entailment checking problem instance:

$$\underbrace{q_1(x,y)}_{x+y} \geq 0 \ \wedge \ \underbrace{q_2(x,y)}_{\gamma \cdot (x^2+y-1)} \geq 0 \ \wedge \ \underbrace{q_3(x,y)}_{x-4y^2} \geq 0 \ \models \ p(x,y) \geq 0, \tag{11}$$

where $p : (x^2 + y^2)(q_1(x,y) + q_2(x,y) + q_3(x,y) + 8)$ and γ is a user-specified constant. For any $\gamma \in \mathbb{R}$, (11) is true, and the corresponding SOS problem has an obvious solution $(\sigma_i : x^2 + y^2$ for $i = 1, \ldots, 3)$ that is independent of γ. Even though theoretically the solution set remains the same for varying γ, we see from Table 1 that a mere change in the value of γ can affect the solution accuracy in some SDP solvers: in this example, SDPT3 appears more robust against ill conditioning than SeDuMi. The large value of γ worsens the conditioning of the linear system solved in each iteration of an IPM and can lead to significant inaccuracy.

Table 1. The relative residual norm of the solutions returned by SDPT3 [59] and SeDuMi [56] for varying values of γ.

	$\gamma = 1$	$\gamma = 10^3$	$\gamma = 10^6$	$\gamma = 10^9$
SDPT3	2.1×10^{-8}	5.4×10^{-10}	5.1×10^{-9}	2.3×10^{-8}
SeDuMi	5.5×10^{-9}	2.6×10^{-9}	3.3×10^{-5}	0.00023

Floating-Point Errors. For the sake of efficiency, IPMs are implemented using floating-point arithmetic. Thus, the precision of the floating-point format used limits the accuracy of the result. The most commonly used floating-point format offers a precision of about 10^{-16} for arithmetic operations and SDP solvers usually offer accuracies ϵ around 10^{-8} [10,63]. Higher accuracies can be reached using more precise (and expensive) floating-point formats such as done by the SDPA-GMP solver (see [5, Chap. 24] and [41]).

4.2 Proving Soundness

Now we describe several different techniques for proving that SDP feasibility problems (10) arising from the SOS formulation of parametric entailment problems admit solutions. These techniques can be separated in two main approaches:

(a) Techniques that attempt to get an actual solution. They are able to solve some empty interior problems but this is often expensive.
(b) Techniques that prove the existence of an actual solution, nearby to an approximate one. They require strict feasibility but are much cheaper.

After a quick review of the first approach, we detail the second one, since numerical tests in Sect. 5 indicate that it is the most useful one for proving polynomial invariants.

Deriving Exact Solutions. As already mentioned in Sect. 3.2, the problem (10) is decidable. Unfortunately, even the most recent algorithms [32] are not meant to be competitive with numerical solvers. Another approach consists in assuming the existence of a rational solution, using a numerical solver and attempting by various means to project its approximate solution to an exact rational solution [30, 35, 39, 45, 46]. These methods are truly impressive as they are able to solve some empty interior problems. It is also worth noting that since they provide an exact SOS decomposition, mechanically checking it with a proof assistant like Isabelle/HOL or Coq is particularly simple [30, 39]. Unfortunately they require heavy computations in rational arithmetic, which incurs the risk of an exponential blow-up of the size of the denominators.

Proving Existence of a Nearby Solution. We now assume that (10) is strictly feasible, call a numerical solver that returns an approximate solution $\widetilde{C}$ and attempt to derive from it a proof that there exists an actual solution C (without actually computing C), based on the following proposition, whose proof is similar to that of [37, Theorem 4].

Proposition 1. *If* (10) *results from the SOS programming problem* (5) *or* (6), *and* $\widetilde{C} \in \mathbb{R}^{s \times s}$ *satisfies the inequality* $\left(s \max_{i \in \{1,\ldots,m\}} |\mathrm{tr}(A_i \widetilde{C}) - b_i| \right) \leq \lambda_{\min}(\widetilde{C})$ *(the smallest eigenvalue of* $\widetilde{C}$*), then* (10) *admits an actual solution* C.

This suggests the following method to prove that a SOS problem is feasible:

Step 1. Obtain an approximate solution $\widetilde{C}$.
Step 2. Compute (an overapproximation of) $\epsilon' := \max_{i \in \{1,\ldots,m\}} |\mathrm{tr}(A_i \widetilde{C}) - b_i|$.
Step 3. Check that $\widetilde{C} - s\,\epsilon'\,I \succeq 0$ (which implies $s\,\epsilon' \leq \lambda_{\min}(\widetilde{C})$).

Step 1 is achieved using a numerical solver and Step 2 is performed using floating-point interval arithmetic. The hard step is to provide a sound and efficient way to check $\widetilde{C} - s\,\epsilon' I \succeq 0$. We rely on a check suggested by the following theorem. Let $\mathbb{F}$ be a floating-point format with unit roundoff eps and underflow unit eta. For any symmetric floating-point matrix $M \in \mathbb{F}^{s \times s}$ with $2(s+2)\mathtt{eps} < 1$, define $\alpha : \frac{(s+1)\mathtt{eps}}{1-(2s+2)\mathtt{eps}}\mathrm{tr}(M) + 4(s+1)(2(s+2) + \max_i M_{i,i})\mathtt{eta}$.

Theorem 2 ([50, **Corollary 2.4**]). $M \succeq 0$ *if there exists* $\widetilde{M} \in \mathbb{F}^{s \times s}$ *such that the following conditions hold:*

- $\widetilde{M}_{ij} = M_{ij}$, *for any* $i \neq j$;
- $\widetilde{M}_{ii} \leq M_{ii} - \alpha$, *for any* i; *and*
- *the Cholesky algorithm implemented in floating-point arithmetic succeeds on* $\widetilde{M}$, *i.e., "concludes" that* $\widetilde{M}$ *is positive semidefinite,*

Theorem 2 is used to prove that $\widetilde{C} - s\,\epsilon'\,I \succeq 0$, as follows:

- compute $M := \widetilde{C} - s\,\epsilon'\,I$ using floating-point arithmetic with rounding toward $-\infty$. It follows that the error $(\widetilde{C} - s\,\epsilon'\,I) - M$ will be a diagonal matrix with nonnegative entries. Hence, if $M \succeq 0$ then $\widetilde{C} - s\,\epsilon'\,I \succeq 0$, as well.
- check that M is symmetric and that $2(s+2)\mathtt{eps} < 1$;
- compute $\widetilde{M} := M - \alpha\,I$ with rounding toward $-\infty$ (the closest $\widetilde{M}$ to $M - \alpha\,I$, the more likely its Cholesky decomposition is to succeed);
- compute the Cholesky decomposition of $\widetilde{M}$.

If the Cholesky decomposition succeeds (which happens when, e.g., $\lambda_{\min}(\widetilde{C}) \geq s\,\epsilon' + 2\alpha$ [18]), then $\widetilde{C} - s\,\epsilon'\,I \succeq 0$.

Remark 2. For the IEEE 754 [33] binary64 format with rounding to nearest[6], $\mathtt{eps} = 2^{-53}$ ($\simeq 10^{-16}$) and $\mathtt{eta} = 2^{-1075}$ ($\simeq 10^{-323}$). Thus, the hypothesis $2(s+2)\mathtt{eps} < 1$ is always satisfied for practical values of s. Moreover, for typical values ($s \leq 1000$ and elements of M of order of magnitude 1), $\alpha \leq 10^{-10}$. This is negligible in front of $s\,\epsilon' \sim 10^{-8}s$ (10^{-8} being the typical default stopping tolerance), which means that the incompleteness of this positive definiteness check is not an issue in practice.

Steps 2 and 3 can be performed in only $O(s^3)$ floating-point operations (cost of the Cholesky decomposition) so the cost of the whole method is dominated by the call to the numerical SDP solver in Step 1.

Remark 3. For ease of exposition, the above technique was presented on the whole matrix C, although it is preferable to apply it on each block C_j of C.

Padding the SDP Problem. Naturally, all this requires that the least eigenvalue of the solution returned by the numerical solver be larger than $s\,\epsilon'$. It could seem that ϵ' is known only after numerically solving the SDP problem, since it is computed from its result in Step 2. In fact, ϵ' will be less than the stopping criterion ϵ of the solver, which is known in advance. Thus instead of solving (10), we solve the slightly modified problem

$$\text{find}: \ C \ \text{ s.t. } \text{tr}(A_i C) = b_i, \ i = 1, \ldots, m,$$
$$C - s\,\epsilon\,I \succeq 0,$$

which is an SDP (up to the change of variable $C \mapsto C + s\,\epsilon\,I$).

The simple criterion in Proposition 1 assumes SDP problems translated from SOS problems. On the other hand, the tool VSDP [31,34] verifies the solutions of general SDP problems using interval arithmetic results.

Remark 4. Mechanically checking proofs generated by the three step method of this section is an ongoing project. To this end, Theorem 2 has been verified [49] in Coq.

---

[6] Type **double** in C.

5 Experiments

This section presents an experimental evaluation of the methods described in Sects. 3 and 4 on the examples of ADJÉ et al. [1]. We first synthesize polynomial invariants for these programs, following [1], then attempt to formally prove their soundness. As seen in Sect. 2, these formal proofs are particularly worthwhile as synthesizing incorrect invariants is quite easy.

$x \in \left\{ x \in \mathbb{R}^n \ \middle| \ \wedge_{j=1}^k i_j(x) \geq 0 \right\}$

```
while (1)
  if (g(x) <= 0)
    x = τ₁(x)
  else
    x = τ₂(x)
```

Fig. 6. Benchmarks form.

Considered programs are of the form in Fig. 6. An invariant $p(\mathbf{c}, \mathbf{x}) \geq 0$ can be provided by any solution[7] of the parametric entailment problem:

$$\begin{cases} i_1(\mathbf{x}) \geq 0 \ \wedge \ \cdots \ \wedge \ i_k(\mathbf{x}) \geq 0 \models p(\mathbf{c}, \mathbf{x}) \geq 0 \\ g(\mathbf{x}) \leq 0 \models (p \circ \tau_1)(\mathbf{c}, \mathbf{x}) \geq p(\mathbf{c}, \mathbf{x}) \\ g(\mathbf{x}) \geq 0 \models (p \circ \tau_2)(\mathbf{c}, \mathbf{x}) \geq p(\mathbf{c}, \mathbf{x}). \end{cases}$$

(See Sect. 3.) Thus, any solution of the following SOS problem gives an invariant:

find : polynomials $\sigma_j \in \mathbb{R}_{d-d_{i_j}}[\mathbf{x}]$ $(j \in \{1, \ldots, k\}), \sigma_{k+1}, \sigma_{k+2} \in \mathbb{R}_{d-d_g}[\mathbf{x}]$

$$\begin{aligned} \text{s.t.} \quad & p - \sum_{j=1}^k \sigma_j i_j \text{ is SOS,} \\ & (p \circ \tau_1) - p + \sigma_{k+1} g \text{ is SOS,} \\ & (p \circ \tau_2) - p - \sigma_{k+2} g \text{ is SOS,} \\ & \sigma_1, \ldots, \sigma_{k+2} \text{ are SOS,} \end{aligned}$$

(12)

where d is the degree of p and $d_{i_1}, \ldots, d_{i_k}$ and d_g are the degrees of $i_1, \ldots, i_k$ and g respectively (all assumed to be less than d).

Table 2 gives the time needed to synthesize candidate invariants of degree d equal to 4, 6, 8 and 10 by solving the above SOS problem. "Example 4" in this table corresponds to the program of Fig. 2. The candidate invariant obtained for degree $d = 6$ is given in Fig. 2 and displayed in Fig. 3. The one obtained for $d = 8$ is also displayed in Fig. 3. "Example 8" corresponds to Fig. 4.

Unfortunately, the problem (12) usually has an empty interior[8]. This means that the candidate invariant obtained from numerical solvers does not precisely satisfy (12). In fact, there often exist values $\mathbf{x}_0$ such that $i_1(\mathbf{x}_0) \geq 0, \ldots, i_k(\mathbf{x}_0) \geq 0$ and $p(\mathbf{x}_0)$ is a tiny negative value. To fix that, we look for a small[9] $c \in \mathbb{R}$ such that $p + c - \sum_{j=1}^k \sigma_j i_j$ is SOS for SOS polynomials σ_j. This is done using the padding technique of Sect. 4. Times in Table 2 include this fixing step.

---

[7] To get a "small" invariant, one minimizes the radius of the ball enclosing it [1].

[8] Assignments τ often admit a fixpoint $\mathbf{x}_0 = \tau(\mathbf{x}_0)$ meaning that the condition $(p \circ \tau) - p + \sigma g \geq 0$ boils down in $\mathbf{x}_0$ to $\sigma(\mathbf{x}_0) g(\mathbf{x}_0) \geq 0$ implying $\sigma(\mathbf{x}_0) = 0$ when $g(\mathbf{x}_0) < 0$.

[9] In practice, $c < 10^{-3}$ when coefficients of p are of order of magnitude 1.

Table 2. Time to synthesize candidate invariants for benchmarks [1]. n is the number of variables and d_τ the degree of the polynomial assignments. All times are in seconds, TO means timeout (900 s) and MO out of memory (4 GB).

	$d = 4$	$d = 6$	$d = 8$	$d = 10$
Example 4 ($n = 2$, $d_\tau = 3$)	0.25	0.95	3.31	8.85
Example 5 ($n = 3$, $d_\tau = 2$)	0.48	2.83	22.75	112.37
Example 6 ($n = 4$, $d_\tau = 2$)	2.12	64.07	TO	MO
Example 7 ($n = 2$, $d_\tau = 3$)	0.25	0.96	3.15	10.45
Example 8 ($n = 2$, $d_\tau = 2$)	0.17	0.34	0.74	1.93

Table 3. Checking the candidate invariants with the implementation of MONNIAUX and CORBINEAU [39]. All times are in seconds, NS means that no proof is found, TO means timeout (900 s) and MO out of memory (4 GB).

	$d = 4$		$d = 6$		$d = 8$		$d = 10$	
	init	ind	init	ind	init	ind	init	ind
Example 4 ($n = 2$, $d_\tau = 3$)	1.43	NS	3.35	TO	19.80	MO	142.33	MO
Example 5 ($n = 3$, $d_\tau = 2$)	3.82	TO	142.49	MO	TO	MO	TO	MO
Example 6 ($n = 4$, $d_\tau = 2$)	32.20	TO	TO	MO	—	—	—	—
Example 7 ($n = 2$, $d_\tau = 3$)	1.48	NS	3.36	TO	18.36	MO	120.40	MO
Example 8 ($n = 2$, $d_\tau = 2$)	1.93	12.81	3.78	NS	26.29	TO	193.79	TO

We now attempt to prove that the fixed candidate invariants p are correct by considering the following entailment checking problem

$$i_1(\mathbf{x}) \geq 0 \wedge \cdots \wedge i_k(\mathbf{x}) \geq 0 \models p(\mathbf{x}) \geq 0$$
$$g(\mathbf{x}) \leq 0 \wedge p(\mathbf{x}) \geq 0 \models (p \circ \tau_1)(\mathbf{x}) \geq 0 \qquad (13)$$
$$g(\mathbf{x}) \geq 0 \wedge p(\mathbf{x}) \geq 0 \models (p \circ \tau_2)(\mathbf{x}) \geq 0.$$

We first evaluated methods looking for exact solutions with the implementation of MONNIAUX and CORBINEAU [39]. Table 3 gives the results. The checking process is split in two parts: init for the initialization property (first entailment of (13)) and ind. for the inductiveness property (remaining entailments). As seen in the table, most of the initialization properties are indeed proved but proofs of the inductiveness property fail for all but the smallest example. This can be explained by the size of the corresponding SDP problems. For the initialization property, the largest block is a matrix of size $\binom{n+\frac{d}{2}}{n} \times \binom{n+\frac{d}{2}}{n}$ whereas for inductiveness it is of size $\binom{n+\frac{d\,d_\tau}{2}}{n} \times \binom{n+\frac{d\,d_\tau}{2}}{n}$. This is too much[10] to perform heavy computations with exact rational arithmetic.

Although (12) usually has an empty interior, it is worth noting that this unfortunate property is due to the relaxation and is not intrinsic to the prob-

---

[10] For $n = 2$, $d_\tau = 3$ and $d = 8$, $\binom{n+\frac{d}{2}}{n} = \binom{6}{2} = 15$ whereas $\binom{n+\frac{d\,d_\tau}{2}}{n} = \binom{14}{2} = 91$.

Table 4. Checking the candidate invariants with the method of Sect. 4 (computing strictly feasible SDP solutions and verifying them). All times are in seconds. As seen in Sect. 2, counter-examples are easily found for Ex. 4, $d = 4$ and 6 and Ex. 7, $d = 4$. No such counter-examples were found for the other unproved cases and it remains unknown whether they are actually inductive or not.

	$d = 4$		$d = 6$		$d = 8$		$d = 10$	
	init	ind	init	ind	init	ind	init	ind
Example 4 ($n = 2$, $d_\tau = 3$)	0.05	NS	0.07	NS	0.19	3.03	0.17	NS
Example 5 ($n = 3$, $d_\tau = 2$)	0.08	0.33	0.23	2.20	0.74	14.55	2.50	92.15
Example 6 ($n = 4$, $d_\tau = 2$)	0.22	1.52	1.26	38.94	—	—	—	—
Example 7 ($n = 2$, $d_\tau = 3$)	0.05	NS	0.07	0.85	0.19	3.32	0.17	NS
Example 8 ($n = 2$, $d_\tau = 2$)	0.05	0.13	0.07	NS	0.09	NS	0.15	NS

lem. Indeed, the loop body τ of the considered programs are usually strictly contractive, i.e., the image of the invariant $\{\mathbf{x} \mid p(\mathbf{x}) \geq 0\}$ by τ is included in its interior. When τ is continuous, this means that any polynomial $\tilde{p}$ close enough from p also defines an invariant $\{\mathbf{x} \mid \tilde{p}(\mathbf{x}) \geq 0\}$. In fact, the entailment checking problem (13) commonly leads to strictly feasible SDP problems. Thus, the method presented in Sect. 4.2 can be used to efficiently prove the soundness of a large part of the candidate invariants, as seen in Table 4. The time needed to compute the proofs (Table 4) is comparable to the time needed to synthesize the invariants (Table 2). Indeed, most of this time is spent running SDP solvers.

These results are confirmed by VSDP [31,34] when we provide it the SDP problems corresponding to (13) and the strictly feasible solutions we computed using SDP solvers. This again indicates that these numerical verification methods only induce a very small overhead compared to the time required to run SDP solvers (Table 5).

Table 5. Rechecking the proofs of Table 4 with VSDP [31,34] (verifying given strictly feasible SDP solutions). All times are in seconds.

	$d = 4$		$d = 6$		$d = 8$		$d = 10$	
	init	ind	init	ind	init	ind	init	ind
Example 4 ($n = 2$, $d_\tau = 3$)	0.04	NS	0.06	NS	0.06	0.30	0.07	NS
Example 5 ($n = 3$, $d_\tau = 2$)	0.06	0.18	0.09	0.26	0.16	0.80	0.27	2.52
Example 6 ($n = 4$, $d_\tau = 2$)	0.10	0.30	0.27	1.11	—	—	—	—
Example 7 ($n = 2$, $d_\tau = 3$)	0.05	NS	0.05	0.15	0.06	0.25	0.07	NS
Example 8 ($n = 2$, $d_\tau = 2$)	0.04	0.07	0.03	NS	0.04	NS	0.05	NS

Implementation. The SOS to SDP translation described in Sect. 3, as well as the validation method described in Sect. 4.2 have been implemented in our OCaml library OSDP. It offers an interface to the SDP solvers Csdp [10], Mosek [40], SDPA [63] and SDPA-GMP [41] and is available at http://cavale. enseeiht.fr/osdp/. Results from Tables 2 and 4 have been obtained thanks to a small static analyzer relying on the library and available, along with all benchmarks, at http://cavale.enseeiht.fr/validatingSDP2016/. All computations were performed with the Mosek solver on a Xeon @ 2.67GHz.

6 Conclusion

Thus far, we have reviewed the use of SOS relaxations and numerical SDP solvers to solve polynomial problems arising in static analysis of programs. We presented some examples and experiments showing that, although erroneous results are often obtained from numerical solvers, rigorous proofs of soundness are possible. Moving forward, we wish to examine the application of our approach inside theorem provers and applications to hybrid systems, as well.

Acknowledgments. The authors would like to thank Didier Henrion, Pierre-Loïc Garoche and Assalé Adjé for interesting discussions on this subject.

References

1. Adjé, A., Garoche, P.-L., Magron, V.: Property-based polynomial invariant generation using sums-of-squares optimization. In: Blazy, S., Jensen, T. (eds.) SAS 2015. LNCS, vol. 9291, pp. 235–251. Springer, Heidelberg (2015)
2. Adjé, A., Gaubert, S., Goubault, E.: Coupling policy iteration with semi-definite relaxation to compute accurate numerical invariants in static analysis. In: Gordon, A.D. (ed.) ESOP 2010. LNCS, vol. 6012, pp. 23–42. Springer, Heidelberg (2010)
3. Ahmadi, A.A., Majumdar, A.: DSOS and SDSOS optimization: LP and SOCP-based alternatives to sum of squares optimization. In: Annual Conference on Information Sciences and Systems (CISS) (2014)
4. Allamigeon, X., Gaubert, S., Goubault, E., Putot, S., Stott, N.: A scalable algebraic method to infer quadratic invariants of switched systems. In: EMSOFT (2015)
5. Anjos, M.F., Lasserre, J.B.: Introduction to semidefinite, conic and polynomial optimization. In: Anjos, M.F., Lasserre, J.B. (eds.) Handbook on semidefinite, conic and polynomial optimization. International Series in Operations Research & Management Science, vol. 166, pp. 1–22. Springer, New York (2012)
6. Bagnara, R., Rodríguez-Carbonell, E., Zaffanella, E.: Generation of basic semialgebraic invariants using convex polyhedra. In: Hankin, C., Siveroni, I. (eds.) SAS 2005. LNCS, vol. 3672, pp. 19–34. Springer, Heidelberg (2005)
7. Basu, S., Pollock, R., Roy, M.-F.: Algorithms in Real Algebraic Geometry, vol. 10. Springer, Heidelberg (2006)
8. Ben Sassi, M.A., Sankaranarayanan, S., Chen, X., Abraham, E.: Linear relaxations of polynomial positivity for polynomial Lyapunov function synthesis. IMA J. Math. Control Inf. (2015)

9. Bernstein, S.N.: Démonstration du théoréme de Weierstrass fondée sur le calcul des probabilités. Communcations de la Société Mathématique de Kharkov **2** (1912)
10. Borchers, B.: CSDP, a C library for semidefinite programming. Optim. Methods Softw. (1999)
11. Borwein, J.M., Wolkowicz, H.: Facial reduction for a cone-convex programming problem. J. Austral. Math. Soc. Ser. A (1980/1981)
12. Chakarov, A., Voronin, Y.-L., Sankaranarayanan, S.: Deductive proofs of almost sure persistence and recurrence properties. In: Chechik, M., Raskin, J.-F. (eds.) TACAS 2016. LNCS, vol. 9636, pp. 260–279. Springer, Heidelberg (2016). doi:10.1007/978-3-662-49674-9_15
13. Collins, G.E.: Quantifier elimination for real closed fields by cylindrical algebraic decomposition. In: Automata Theory and Formal Languages (1975)
14. Collins, G.E., Hong, H.: Partial cylindrical algebraic decomposition for quantifier elimination. J. Symbolic Comput. (1991)
15. Cousot, P.: Proving program invariance and termination by parametric abstraction, lagrangian relaxation and semidefinite programming. In: Cousot, R. (ed.) VMCAI 2005. LNCS, vol. 3385, pp. 1–24. Springer, Heidelberg (2005)
16. Cousot, P., Cousot, R.: Abstract interpretation: a unified lattice model for static analysis of programs by construction or approximation of fixpoints. In: POPL (1977)
17. Dang, T., Gawlitza, T.M.: Template-based unbounded time verification of affine hybrid automata. In: Yang, H. (ed.) APLAS 2011. LNCS, vol. 7078, pp. 34–49. Springer, Heidelberg (2011)
18. Demmel, J.: On floating point errors in Cholesky. Department of Computer Science, University of Tennessee, Knoxville, TN, USA, Lapack working note (1989)
19. Dolzmann, A., Sturm, T.: REDLOG: computer algebra meets computer logic. ACM SIGSAM Bull. (1997)
20. Dür, M., Jargalsaikhan, B., Still, G.: The Slater condition is generic in linear conic programming (2012)
21. Farouki, R.T.: The Bernstein polynomial basis: a centennial retrospective. Comput. Aided Geom. Des. (2012)
22. Féron, É.: From control systems to control software. IEEE Control Syst. (2010)
23. Fränzle, M., Herde, C., Teige, T., Ratschan, S., Schubert, T.: Efficient solving of large non-linear arithmetic constraint systems with complex Boolean structure. J. Satisfiability, Boolean Model. Comput., Special Issue on SAT/CP Integration (2007)
24. Gao, S., Kong, S., Clarke, E.M.: dReal: An SMT solver for nonlinear theories over the reals. In: International Conference on Automated Deduction (CADE) (2013)
25. Gaubert, S., Goubault, É., Taly, A., Zennou, S.: Static analysis by policy iteration on relational domains. In: De Nicola, R. (ed.) ESOP 2007. LNCS, vol. 4421, pp. 237–252. Springer, Heidelberg (2007)
26. Gawlitza, T., Seidl, H.: Precise fixpoint computation through strategy iteration. In: De Nicola, R. (ed.) ESOP 2007. LNCS, vol. 4421, pp. 300–315. Springer, Heidelberg (2007)
27. Gawlitza, T.M., Monniaux, D.: Improving strategies via SMT solving. In: Barthe, G. (ed.) ESOP 2011. LNCS, vol. 6602, pp. 236–255. Springer, Heidelberg (2011)
28. Gawlitza, T.M., Seidl, H.: Computing relaxed abstract semantics w.r.t. quadratic zones precisely. In: Cousot, R., Martel, M. (eds.) SAS 2010. LNCS, vol. 6337, pp. 271–286. Springer, Heidelberg (2010)
29. Handelman, D.: Representing polynomials by positive linear functions on compact convex polyhedra. Pacific J. Math. (1988)

30. Harrison, J.: Verifying nonlinear real formulas via sums of squares. In: Schneider, K., Brandt, J. (eds.) TPHOLs 2007. LNCS, vol. 4732, pp. 102–118. Springer, Heidelberg (2007)
31. Härter, V., Jansson, C., Lange, M.: VSDP: verified semidefinite programming. http://www.ti3.tuhh.de/jansson/vsdp/. Accessed 28 Mar 2016
32. Henrion, D., Naldi, S., Din, M., Safey El Din, M.: Exact algorithms for linear matrix inequalities. arXiv preprint (2015). arXiv:1508.03715
33. IEEE Computer Society. IEEE Standard for Floating-Point Arithmetic. IEEE Standard **754–2008** (2008)
34. Jansson, C., Chaykin, D., Keil, C.: Rigorous error bounds for the optimal value in semidefinite programming. SIAM J. Numer. Anal. (2007)
35. Kaltofen, E., Li, B., Yang, Z., Zhi, L.: Exact certification in global polynomial optimization via sums-of-squares of rational functions with rational coefficients. J. Symb. Comput. (2012)
36. Lasserre, J.B.: Global optimization with polynomials and the problem of moments. SIAM J. Optim. (2001)
37. Löfberg, J.: Pre- and post-processing sum-of-squares programs in practice. IEEE Trans. Autom. Control (2009)
38. Maréchal, A., Fouilhé, A., King, T., Monniaux, D., Périn, M.: Polyhedral approximation of multivariate polynomials using Handelman's theorem. In: Jobstmann, B., Leino, K.R.M. (eds.) VMCAI 2016. LNCS, vol. 9583, pp. 166–184. Springer, Heidelberg (2016). doi:10.1007/978-3-662-49122-5_8
39. Monniaux, D., Corbineau, P.: On the generation of positivstellensatz witnesses in degenerate cases. In: van Eekelen, M., Geuvers, H., Schmaltz, J., Wiedijk, F. (eds.) ITP 2011. LNCS, vol. 6898, pp. 249–264. Springer, Heidelberg (2011)
40. MOSEK ApS. The MOSEK C optimizer API manual Version 7.1 (Revision 40) (2015)
41. Nakata, M.: A numerical evaluation of highly accurate multiple-precision arithmetic version of semidefinite programming solver: SDPA-GMP, -QD and -DD. In: Computer-Aided Control System Design (2010)
42. Oulamara, M., Venet, A.J.: Abstract interpretation with higher-dimensional ellipsoids and conic extrapolation. In: Kroening, D., Păsăreanu, C.S. (eds.) CAV 2015. LNCS, vol. 9206, pp. 415–430. Springer, Heidelberg (2015)
43. Parrilo, P.A.: Semidefinite programming relaxations for semialgebraic problems. Math. Program. (2003)
44. Permenter, F., Parrilo, P.: Partial facial reduction: simplified, equivalent SDPs via approximations of the PSD cone. arXiv preprint (2014). arXiv:1408.4685
45. Peyrl, H., Parrilo, P.A.: Computing sum of squares decompositions with rational coefficients. Theor. Comput. Sci. (2008)
46. Platzer, A., Quesel, J.-D., Rümmer, P.: Real world verification. In: Schmidt, R.A. (ed.) CADE-22. LNCS, vol. 5663, pp. 485–501. Springer, Heidelberg (2009)
47. Prajna, S., Jadbabaie, A.: Safety verification using barrier certificates. In: HSCC (2004)
48. Putinar, M.: Positive polynomials on compact semi-algebraic sets. Indiana Univ. Math. J. (1993)
49. Roux, P.: Formal proofs of rounding error bounds. J. Autom. Reasoning (2015)
50. Rump, S.M.: Verification of positive definiteness. BIT Numer. Math. (2006)
51. Sankaranarayanan, S., Sipma, H., Manna, Z.: Constructing invariants for hybrid systems. Formal Meth. Syst. Des. (2008)

52. Sankaranarayanan, S., Sipma, H.B., Manna, Z.: Scalable analysis of linear systems using mathematical programming. In: Cousot, R. (ed.) VMCAI 2005. LNCS, vol. 3385, pp. 25–41. Springer, Heidelberg (2005)
53. Schmieta, S.H., Pataki, G.: Reporting solution quality for the DIMACS library of mixed semidefinite-quadratic-linear programs. http://dimacs.rutgers. edu/Challenges/Seventh/Instances/error_report.html. Accessed 23 Mar 2016
54. Sherali, H.D., Tuncbilek, Cihan H. C.H. : A global optimization algorithm for polynomial programming using a reformulation-linearization technique. J. Glob. Optim. (1991)
55. Shor, N.Z.: Class of global minimum bounds on polynomial functions. Cybernetics (1987). Originally in Russian: Kibernetika (1987)
56. Sturm, J.F.: Using SeDuMi 1.02, a MATLAB toolbox for optimization over symmetric cones. Optim. Methods Softw. (1999)
57. Tarski, A.: A decision method for elementary algebra and geometry. Univ. of California Press, Berkeley, Technical report (1951)
58. Tuncel, L.: Polyhedral and semidefinite programming methods in combinatorial optimization. Am. Math. Soc. (2010)
59. Tütüncü, R.H., Toh, K.C., Todd, M.J.: Solving semidefinite-quadratic-linear programs using SDPT3. Math. Program. (2003)
60. Waki, H., Nakata, M., Muramatsu, M.: Strange behaviors of interior-point methods for solving semidefinite programming problems in polynomial optimization. Comput. Optim. Appl. (2011)
61. Weispfenning, V.: Quantifier elimination for real algebra–the quadratic case and beyond. In: Applied Algebra and Error-Correcting Codes (AAECC) (1997)
62. Wolkowicz, H., Saigal, R., Vandenberghe, L.: Handbook of Semidefinite Programming. Kluwer Academic Publishers, Boston (2000)
63. Yamashita, M., Fujisawa, K., Nakata, K., Nakata, M., Fukuda, M., Kobayashi, K., Goto, K.: A high-performance software package for semidefinite programs: SDPA 7. Technical report B-460, Tokyo Institute of Technology (2010)

Enforcing Termination of Interprocedural Analysis

Stefan Schulze Frielinghaus(✉), Helmut Seidl, and Ralf Vogler

Fakultät für Informatik, TU München, Munich, Germany
{schulzef,seidl,voglerr}@in.tum.de

Abstract. Interprocedural analysis by means of partial tabulation of summary functions may not terminate when the same procedure is analyzed for infinitely many abstract calling contexts or when the abstract domain has infinite strictly ascending chains. As a remedy, we present a novel local solver for general abstract equation systems, be they monotonic or not, and prove that this solver fails to terminate only when infinitely many variables are encountered. We clarify in which sense the computed results are sound. Moreover, we show that interprocedural analysis performed by this novel local solver, is guaranteed to terminate for all non-recursive programs — irrespective of whether the complete lattice is infinite or has infinite strictly ascending or descending chains.

1 Introduction

It is well known that static analysis of run-time properties of programs by means of abstract interpretation can be compiled into systems of equations over complete lattices [10]. Thereby, various interesting properties require complete lattices which may have infinite strictly ascending or descending chains [6,8,16]. In order to determine a (post-) solution of a system of equations over such lattices, Cousot and Cousot propose to perform a first phase of iteration using a *widening* operator to obtain a post-solution which later may be improved by a second phase of iteration using a *narrowing* operator. This strict arrangement into separate phases, though, has the disadvantage that precision unnecessarily may be given up which later is difficult to recover. It has been observed that widening and narrowing need not be organized into separate phases [2,4,5]. Instead various algorithms are proposed which *intertwine* widening with narrowing in order to compute a (reasonably small) post-fixpoint of the given system of equations. The idea there is to combine widening with narrowing into a single operator and then to iterate according to some fixed ordering over the variables of the system. Still, monotonicity of all right-hand sides is required for the resulting algorithms to be terminating [2,4].

Non-monotonic right-hand sides, however, are introduced by interprocedural analysis in the style of [3] when partial tabulation of summary functions is used. In order to see this, consider an abstract lattice $\mathbb{D}$ of possible program invariants. Then the abstract effect of a procedure call can be formalized as a transformation $f^{\sharp}$ from $\mathbb{D} \to \mathbb{D}$. For rich lattices $\mathbb{D}$ such transformations may be difficult to

© Springer-Verlag GmbH Germany 2016
X. Rival (Ed.): SAS 2016, LNCS 9837, pp. 447–468, 2016.
DOI: 10.1007/978-3-662-53413-7_22

represent and compute with. As a remedy, each single variable function may be decomposed into a set of variables — one for each possible argument — where each such variable now receives values from $\mathbb{D}$ only. As a result, the difficulty of dealing with elements of $\mathbb{D} \to \mathbb{D}$ is replaced with the difficulty of dealing with systems of equations which are infinite when $\mathbb{D}$ is infinite. Moreover, composition of abstract functions is translated into *indirect addressing* of variables (the outcome of the analysis for one function call determines for which argument another function is queried) — implying non-monotonicity [15]. Thus, termination of interprocedural analysis by means of the solvers from [2,4] cannot be guaranteed. Interestingly, the *local* solver SLR_3 [2] terminates in many practical cases. Nontermination, though, may arise in two flavors:

- infinitely many variables may be encountered, i.e., some procedure may be analyzed for an ever growing number of calling contexts;
- the algorithm may for some variable switch infinitely often from a narrowing iteration back to a widening iteration.

From a conceptual view, the situation still is unsatisfactory: any solver used as a fixpoint engine within a static analysis tool should reliably terminate under reasonable assumptions. In this paper, we therefore re-examine interprocedural analysis by means of local solvers. First, we extend an ordinary local solver to a two-phase solver which performs widening and subsequently narrowing. The novel point is that both iterations are performed in a demand-driven way so that also during the narrowing phase fresh variables may be encountered for which no sound over-approximation has yet been computed.

In order to enhance precision of this demand-driven two-phase solver, we then design a new local solver which intertwines the two phases. In contrast to the solvers in [2,4], however, we can no longer rely on a fixed combination of a widening and a narrowing operator, but must enhance the solver with extra logic to decide when to apply which operator. For both solvers, we prove that they terminate — whenever only finitely many variables are encountered: irrespective whether the abstract system is monotonic or not. Both solvers are guaranteed to return (partial) post-solutions of the abstract system of equations only if all right-hand sides are monotonic. Therefore, we make clear in which sense the computed results are nonetheless sound—even in the non-monotonic case. For that, we provide a sufficient condition for an abstract variable assignment to be a sound description of a concrete system — given only a (possibly non-monotonic) abstract system of equations. This sufficient condition is formulated by means of the *lower monotonization* of the abstract system. Also, we elaborate for partial solutions in which sense the domain of the returned variable assignment provides sound information. Here, the formalization of purity of functions based on computation trees and variable dependencies plays a crucial role. Finally, we prove that interprocedural analysis in the style of [3,12] with partial tabulation using our local solvers terminates for all non-recursive programs and every complete lattice with or without infinite strictly ascending or descending chains.

The paper is organized as follows. In Sect. 2 we recall the basics of abstract interpretation and introduce the idea of a lower monotonization of an abstract system of equations. In Sect. 3 we recapitulate widening and narrowing. As a warm-up, a terminating variant of round-robin iteration is presented in Sect. 4. In Sect. 5 we formalize the idea of local solvers based on the notion of purity of functions of right-hand sides of abstract equation systems and provide a theorem indicating in which sense local solvers for non-monotonic abstract systems compute sound results for concrete systems. A first local solver is presented in Sect. 6 where widening and narrowing is done in conceptually separated phases. In Sect. 7, we present a local solver where widening and narrowing is intertwined. Section 8 considers the abstract equations systems encountered by interprocedural analysis. A concept of stratification is introduced which is satisfied if the programs to be analyzed are non-recursive. These notions enable us to prove our main result concerning termination of interprocedural analysis with partial tabulation by means of the solvers from Sects. 6 and 7.

2   Basics on Abstract Interpretation

In the following we recapitulate the basics of abstract interpretation as introduced by Cousot and Cousot [10,13]. Assume that the concrete semantics of a system is described by a system of equations

$$x = f_x, \quad x \in X \tag{1}$$

where X is a set of variables taking values in some power set lattice $(\mathbb{C}, \subseteq, \cup)$ where $\mathbb{C} = 2^Q$ for some set Q of concrete program states, and for each $x \in X$, $f_x : (X \to \mathbb{C}) \to \mathbb{C}$ is the defining right-hand side of x. For the concrete system of equations, we assume that all right-hand sides $f_x, x \in X$, are *monotonic*. Accordingly, this system of equations has a unique least solution σ which can be obtained as the least upper bound of all assignments σ_τ, τ an ordinal. The assignments $\sigma_\tau : X \to \mathbb{C}$ are defined as follows. If $\tau = 0$, then $\sigma_\tau x = \bot$ for all $x \in X$. If $\tau = \tau' + 1$ is a successor ordinal, then $\sigma_\tau x = f_x \sigma_{\tau'}$, and if τ is a limit ordinal, then $\sigma_\tau x = \bigcup \{ f_x \sigma_{\tau'} \mid \tau' < \tau \}$. An *abstract* system of equations

$$y = f_y^\sharp, \quad y \in Y \tag{2}$$

specifies an analysis of the concrete system of equations. Here, Y is a set of *abstract* variables which may not necessarily be in one-to-one correspondence to the concrete variables in the set X. The variables in Y take values in some complete lattice $(\mathbb{D}, \sqsubseteq, \sqcup)$ of abstract values and for every abstract variable $y \in Y$, $f_y^\sharp : (Y \to \mathbb{D}) \to \mathbb{D}$ is the abstract defining right-hand side of y. The elements $d \in \mathbb{D}$ are meant to represent invariants, i.e., properties of states. It is for simplicity that we assume the set $\mathbb{D}$ of all possible invariants to form a complete lattice, as any partial order can be embedded into a complete lattice so that all existing least upper and greatest lower bounds are preserved [22]. In order to relate concrete sets of states with abstract values, we assume that there is a Galois connection between $\mathbb{C}$ and $\mathbb{D}$, i.e., there are monotonic functions $\alpha : \mathbb{C} \to \mathbb{D}$, $\gamma : \mathbb{D} \to \mathbb{C}$ such that for all $c \in \mathbb{C}$ and $d \in \mathbb{D}$, $\alpha(c) \sqsubseteq d$ iff $c \subseteq \gamma(d)$. Between the sets of concrete and abstract variables, we assume that there is a *description relation* $\mathcal{R} \subseteq X \times Y$. Via the Galois connection between $\mathbb{C}$ and $\mathbb{D}$, the description relation $\mathcal{R}$ between variables is lifted to a description relation $\mathcal{R}^*$ between assignments $\sigma : X \to \mathbb{C}$ and $\sigma^\sharp : Y \to \mathbb{D}$ by defining $\sigma \, \mathcal{R}^* \, \sigma^\sharp$ iff for all $x \in X, y \in Y$, $\sigma(x) \subseteq \gamma(\sigma^\sharp(y))$ whenever $x \, \mathcal{R} \, y$ holds. Following [13], we do not assume that the right-hand sides of the abstract equation system are necessarily monotonic. For a sound analysis, we only assume that all right-hand sides respect the description relation, i.e., that for all $x \in X$ and $y \in Y$ with $x \, \mathcal{R} \, y$,

$$f_x \, \sigma \subseteq \gamma(f_y^\sharp \, \sigma^\sharp) \tag{3}$$

whenever $\sigma \, \mathcal{R}^* \, \sigma^\sharp$ holds. Our key concept for proving soundness of abstract variable assignments w.r.t. the concrete system of equations is the notion of the *lower monotonization* of the abstract system. For every function $f^\sharp : (Y \to \mathbb{D}) \to \mathbb{D}$ we consider the function

$$\underline{f}^\sharp \sigma = \bigsqcap \{ f^\sharp \sigma' \mid \sigma \sqsubseteq \sigma' \} \tag{4}$$

which we call *lower monotonization* of $f^\sharp$. By definition, we have:

Lemma 1. *For every function* $f^\sharp : (Y \to \mathbb{D}) \to \mathbb{D}$ *the following holds:*

1. $\underline{f}^\sharp$ *is monotonic;*
2. $\underline{f}^\sharp \sigma^\sharp \sqsubseteq f^\sharp \sigma^\sharp$ *for all* $\sigma^\sharp$;
3. $\underline{f}^\sharp = f^\sharp$ *whenever* $f^\sharp$ *is monotonic.*   □

The lower monotonization of the abstract system (2) then is defined as the system

$$y = \underline{f}_y^\sharp, \qquad y \in Y \tag{5}$$

Since all right-hand sides of (5) are monotonic, this system has a least solution.

Example 1. Consider the single equation

$$y_1 = \text{if } y_1 = 0 \text{ then } 1 \text{ else } 0$$

over the complete lattice of non-negative integers equipped with an infimum element, i.e., let the domain $\mathbb{D} = \mathbb{N} \cup \{\infty\}$. This system is not monotonic. Its lower monotonization is given by $y_1 = 0$.   □

Lemma 2. *Assume that* σ *is the least solution of the concrete system* (1). *Then* $\sigma \, \mathcal{R}^* \, \sigma^\sharp$ *for every post-solution* $\sigma^\sharp$ *of the lower monotonization* (5).

Proof. For every ordinal τ, let σ_τ denote the τth approximation of the least solution of the concrete system and assume that $\sigma^\sharp$ is a post-solution of the lower monotonization of the abstract system, i.e., $\sigma^\sharp y \sqsupseteq \underline{f}_y^\sharp \sigma^\sharp$ holds for all $y \in Y$. By ordinal induction, we prove that $\sigma_\tau \, \mathcal{R}^* \, \sigma^\sharp$. The claim clearly holds for $\tau = 0$. First assume that $\tau = \tau' + 1$ is a successor ordinal, and that the claim holds for τ', i.e., $\sigma_{\tau'} \, \mathcal{R}^* \, \sigma^\sharp$. Accordingly, $\sigma_{\tau'} \, \mathcal{R}^* \, \sigma'$ holds for all $\sigma' \sqsupseteq \sigma^\sharp$. Consider any pair of variables x, y with $x \, \mathcal{R} \, y$. Then $\sigma_\tau \, x = f_x \sigma_{\tau'} \sqsubseteq \gamma(f_y^\sharp \sigma')$ for all $\sigma' \sqsupseteq \sigma^\sharp$. Accordingly, $\alpha(\sigma_\tau \, x) \sqsubseteq f_y^\sharp \sigma'$ for all $\sigma' \sqsupseteq \sigma^\sharp$, and therefore,

$$\alpha(\sigma_\tau \, x) \sqsubseteq \bigsqcap \left\{ f_y^\sharp \sigma' \mid \sigma' \sqsupseteq \sigma^\sharp \right\} = \underline{f}_y^\sharp \, \sigma^\sharp \sqsubseteq \sigma^\sharp \, y$$

since $\sigma^\sharp$ is a post-solution. From that, the claim follows for the ordinal τ. Now assume that τ is a limit ordinal, and that the claim holds for all ordinals $\tau' < \tau$. Again consider any pair of variables x, y with $x \, \mathcal{R} \, y$. Then

$$\sigma_\tau \, x = \bigcup \left\{ \sigma_{\tau'} \, x \mid \tau' < \tau \right\} \sqsubseteq \bigcup \left\{ \gamma(\sigma^\sharp y) \mid \tau' < \tau \right\} = \gamma(\sigma^\sharp y)$$

and the claim also follows for the limit ordinal τ. $\qquad\qquad\square$

From Lemma 2 we conclude that for the abstract system from Example 1 the assignment $\sigma^\sharp = \{y_1 \mapsto 0\}$ is a sound description of every corresponding concrete system, since $\sigma^\sharp$ is a post-solution of the lower monotonization $y_1 = 0$.

In general, Lemma 2 provides us with a sufficient condition guaranteeing that an abstract assignment $\sigma^\sharp$ is sound w.r.t. the concrete system (1) and the description relation $\mathcal{R}$, namely, that $\sigma^\sharp$ is a post-solution of the system (5). This sufficient condition is remarkable as it is an *intrinsic* property of the abstract system since it does not refer to the concrete system. As a corollary we obtain:

Corollary 1. *Every post-solution $\sigma^\sharp$ of the abstract system (2) is sound.*

Proof. For all $y \in Y, \sigma^\sharp y \sqsupseteq f_y^\sharp \sigma^\sharp \sqsupseteq \underline{f}_y^\sharp \, \sigma^\sharp$ holds. Accordingly, $\sigma^\sharp$ is a post-solution of the lower monotonization of the abstract system and therefore sound. $\qquad\square$

3 Widening and Narrowing

It is instructive to recall the basic algorithmic approach to determine non-trivial post-solutions of abstract systems (2) when the set Y of variables is finite, all right-hand sides are monotonic and the complete lattice $\mathbb{D}$ has finite strictly increasing chains only. In this case, *chaotic iteration* may be applied. This kind of iteration starts with the initial assignment $\perp$ which assigns $\perp$ to every variable $y \in Y$ and then repeatedly evaluates right-hand sides to update the values of variables until the values for all variables have stabilized. This method may also be applied if right-hand sides are non-monotonic: the only modification required is to update the value for each variable not just with the new value provided by the left-hand side, but with some upper bound of the old value for a variable with the new value. As a result, a *post-solution* of the system is computed which, according to Corollary 1, is sound.

The situation is more intricate, if the complete lattice in question has strictly ascending chains of infinite length. Here, we follow Cousot and Cousot [9, 10, 13] who suggest to accelerate iteration by means of *widening* and *narrowing*. A widening operator $\nabla : \mathbb{D} \times \mathbb{D} \to \mathbb{D}$ takes the old value $a \in \mathbb{D}$ and a new value $b \in \mathbb{D}$

and combines them to a value $a \sqcup b \sqsubseteq a \nabla b$ with the additional understanding that for any sequence $b_i, i \geq 0$, and any value a_0, the sequence $a_{i+1} = a_i \nabla b_i, i \geq 0$, is ultimately stable. In contrast, a narrowing operator $\Delta : \mathbb{D} \times \mathbb{D} \to \mathbb{D}$ takes the old value $a \in \mathbb{D}$ and a new value $b \in \mathbb{D}$ and combines them to a value $a \Delta b$ satisfying $a \sqcap b \sqsubseteq a \Delta b \sqsubseteq a$ — with the additional understanding that for any sequence $b_i, i \geq 0$, and any value a_0, the sequence $a_{i+1} = a_i \Delta b_i, i \geq 0$, is ultimately stable.

While the widening operator is meant to reach a post-solution after a finite number of updates to each variable of the abstract system, the narrowing operator allows to improve upon a variable assignment once it is known to be sound. In particular, if all right-hand sides are monotonic, the result of a narrowing iteration, if started with a post-solution of the abstract system, again results in a post-solution. Accordingly, the returned variable assignment can easily be verified to be sound. In analyzers which iterate according to the syntactical structure of programs such as ASTREE [14], this strict separation into two phases, though, has been given up. There, when iterating over one loop, narrowing for the current loop is triggered as soon as locally a post-solution has been attained. This kind of intertwining widening and narrowing is systematically explored in [2,4]. There, a widening operator is combined with a narrowing operator into a single derived operator $\boxtimes$ defined by

$$a \boxtimes b = \textbf{if } b \sqsubseteq a \textbf{ then } a \Delta b$$
$$\textbf{else } a \nabla b$$

also called *warrowing*. Solvers which perform chaotic iteration and use warrowing to combine old values with new contributions, necessarily return post-solutions — whenever they terminate. In [4,5], termination could only be guaranteed for systems of equations where all right-hand sides are monotonic. For *non-monotonic* systems as may occur at interprocedural analysis, only practical evidence could be provided for the proposed algorithms to terminate in interesting cases.

Here, our goal is to lift these limitations by providing solvers which terminate for all finite abstract systems of equations and all complete lattices — no matter whether right-hand sides are monotonic or not. For that purpose, we dissolve the operator $\boxtimes$ again into its components. Instead, we equip the solving routines with extra logic to decide when to apply which operator.

4 Terminating Structured Round-Robin Iteration

Let us consider a finite abstract system as given by:

$$y_i = f_i^{\sharp}, \qquad i = 1, \ldots, n \tag{6}$$

In [4], a variation of round-robin iteration is presented which is guaranteed to terminate for monotonic systems, while it may not terminate for non-monotonic systems. In order to remedy this failure, we re-design this algorithm by additionally maintaining a flag which indicates whether the variable presently under consideration has or has not reached a sound value (Fig. 1). Solving starts with a call

```
void solve(b, i) {
    if (i ≤ 0) return;
    solve(b, i − 1);
    tmp := f_i^♯ σ;
    b' := b;
    if (b) tmp := σ[y_i] Δ tmp;
    else if (tmp ⊑ σ[y_i]) {
        tmp := σ[y_i] Δ tmp;
        b' := true;
    } else tmp := σ[y_i] ∇ tmp;
    if (σ[y_i] = tmp) then return;
    σ[y_i] := tmp;
    solve(b', i);
}
```

Fig. 1. Terminating structured round-robin iteration.

solve($\mathbf{false}, n$) where n is the highest priority of a variable. A variable y_i has a higher priority than a variable y_j whenever $i > j$ holds. A call solve(b, i) considers variables up to priority i only. The Boolean argument b indicates whether a sound abstraction (relative to the current values of the higher priority variables) has already been reached. The algorithm first iterates on the lower priority variables (if there are any). Once solving of these is completed, the right-hand side $f_i^♯$ of the current variable y_i is evaluated and stored in the variable tmp. Additionally, b' is initialized with the Boolean argument b. First assume that b has already the value **true**. Then the old value $\sigma\, y_i$ is combined with the new value in tmp by means of the narrowing operator giving the new value of tmp. If that is equal to the old value, we are done and solve returns. Otherwise, $\sigma\, y_i$ is updated to tmp, and solve($\mathbf{true}, i$) is called tail-recursively. Next assume that b has still the value **false**. Then the algorithm distinguishes two cases. If the old value $\sigma\, y_i$ exceeds the new value, the variable tmp receives the combination of both values by means of the narrowing operator. Additionally, b' is set to **true**. Otherwise, the new value for tmp is obtained by means of widening. Again, if the resulting value of tmp is equal to the current value $\sigma\, y_i$ of y_i, the algorithm returns, whereas if they differ, then $\sigma\, y_i$ is updated to tmp and the algorithm recursively calls itself for the actual parameters (b', n). In light of Theorem 1, the resulting algorithm is called *terminating structured round-robin iteration* or TSRR for short.

Theorem 1. *The algorithm in Fig. 1 terminates for all finite abstract systems of the form (6). Upon termination, it returns a variable assignment σ which is sound. If all right-hand sides are monotonic, σ is a post-solution.*

A proof is provided in the long version of this paper [24]. In fact, for monotonic systems, the new variation of round-robin iteration behaves identical to the algorithm SRR from [4].

5   Local Solvers

Local solving may gain efficiency by querying the value only of a hopefully small subset of variables whose values still are sufficient to answer the initial query. Such solvers are at the heart of program analysis frameworks such as the CIAO system [17,18] or GOBLINT. In order to reason about *partial* variable assignments as computed by local solvers, we can no longer consider right-hand sides in equations as black boxes, but require a notion of *variable dependence*.

For the concrete system we assume that right-hand sides are mathematical functions of type $(X \to \mathbb{C}) \to \mathbb{C}$ where for any such function f and variable assignment $\sigma : X \to \mathbb{C}$, we are given a superset $\mathsf{dep}(f, \sigma)$ of variables onto which f possibly depends, i.e.,

$$(\forall x \in \mathsf{dep}(f, \sigma). \, \sigma[x] = \sigma'[x]) \implies f \, \sigma = f \, \sigma' \tag{7}$$

for all $\sigma' : X \to \mathbb{C}$. Let $\sigma : X \to \mathbb{C}$ denote a solution of the concrete system. Then we call a subset $X' \subseteq X$ of variables σ-*closed*, if for all $x \in X'$, $\mathsf{dep}(f_x, \sigma) \subseteq X'$. Then for every x contained in the σ-closed subset X', $\sigma[x]$ can be determined already if the values of σ are known for the variables in X' only.

In [23,25] it is observed that for suitable formulations of interprocedural analysis, the set of all run-time calling contexts of procedures can be extracted from σ-closed sets of variables.

Example 2. The following system may arise from the analysis of a program consisting of a procedure with a loop (signified by the program point u) within which the same procedure is called twice in a row. Likewise, the procedure p iterates on some program point v by repeatedly applying the function g:

$$\langle u, q \rangle = \bigcup \{ \, \langle v, q_1 \rangle \mid q_1 \in \bigcup \{ \, \langle v, q_2 \rangle \mid q_2 \in \langle u, q \rangle \, \} \, \} \cup \{q\}$$
$$\langle v, q \rangle = \bigcup \{ \, g \, q_1 \mid q_1 \in \langle v, q \rangle \, \} \cup \{q\}$$

for $q \in Q$. Here, Q is a superset of all possible system states, and the unary function $g : Q \to 2^Q$ describes the operational behavior of the body of the loop at v. The set of variables of this system is given by $X = \{ \langle u, q \rangle, \langle v, q \rangle \mid q \in Q \}$ where $\langle u, q \rangle, \langle v, q \rangle$ represent the sets of program states possibly occurring at program points u and v, respectively, when the corresponding procedures have been called in context q. For any variable assignment σ, the dependence sets of the right-hand sides are naturally defined by:

$$\mathsf{dep}(f_{\langle u,q \rangle}, \sigma) = \{ \langle u, q \rangle \} \cup \{ \langle v, q_2 \rangle \mid q_2 \in \sigma \langle u, q \rangle \}$$
$$\cup \{ \langle v, q_1 \rangle \mid q_2 \in \sigma \langle u, q \rangle, q_1 \in \sigma \langle v, q_2 \rangle \}$$
$$\mathsf{dep}(f_{\langle v,q \rangle}, \sigma) = \{ \langle v, q \rangle \}$$

where f_x again denotes the right-hand side function for a variable x. Assuming that $g(q_0) = \{q_1\}$ and $g(q_1) = \emptyset$, the least solution σ maps $\langle u, q_0 \rangle, \langle v, q_0 \rangle$ to the set $\{q_0, q_1\}$ and $\langle u, q_1 \rangle, \langle v, q_1 \rangle$ to $\{q_1\}$. Accordingly, the set $\{ \langle u, q_i \rangle, \langle v, q_i \rangle \mid i = 0, 1 \}$ is σ-closed. We conclude, given the program is called with initial context q_0, that the procedure p is called with contexts q_0 and q_1 only. □

In concrete systems of equations, right-hand sides may depend on *infinitely* many variables. Since abstract systems are meant to give rise to effective algorithms, we impose more restrictive assumptions onto their right-hand side functions. For these, we insist that only finitely many variables may be queried. Following the considerations in [19–21], we demand that every right-hand side $f^\sharp$ of the abstract system is *pure* in the sense of [20]. This means that, operationally, the evaluation of $f^\sharp$ for any abstract variable assignment $\sigma^\sharp$ consists of a finite sequence of variable look-ups before eventually, a value is returned. Technically, $f^\sharp$ can be represented by a *computation tree*, i.e., is an element of

$$\text{tree} ::= \text{Answer } \mathbb{D} \quad | \quad \text{Query } Y \times (\mathbb{D} \to \text{tree})$$

Thus, a computation tree either is a leaf immediately containing a value or a query, which consists of a variable together with a continuation which, for every possible value of the variable returns a tree representing the remaining computation. Each computation tree defines a function $[\![t]\!] : (Y \to \mathbb{D}) \to \mathbb{D}$ by:

$$[\![\text{Answer } d]\!]\, \sigma \quad = d$$
$$[\![\text{Query } (y, c)]\!]\, \sigma = [\![c\,(\sigma[y])]\!]\, \sigma$$

Following [20], the tree representation is uniquely determined by (the operational semantics of) $f^\sharp$.

Example 3. Computation trees can be considered as generalizations of binary decision diagrams to arbitrary sets $\mathbb{D}$. For example, let $\mathbb{D} = \mathbb{N} \cup \{\infty\}$, i.e., the natural numbers (equipped with the natural ordering and extended with ∞ as top element), the function $f^\sharp : (Y \to \mathbb{D}) \to \mathbb{D}$ with $\{y_1, y_2\} \subseteq Y$, defined by

$$f^\sharp \sigma = \textbf{if } \sigma[y_1] > 5 \textbf{ then } 1 + \sigma[y_2] \textbf{ else } \sigma[y_1]$$

is represented by the tree

$$\text{Query } (y_1, \textbf{fun } d_1 \to \textbf{ if } d_1 > 5 \textbf{ then } \text{Query } (y_2, \textbf{fun } d_2 \to \text{Answer } (1 + d_2))$$
$$\textbf{else } \text{Query } (y_1, \textbf{fun } d_1 \to \text{Answer } d_1)) \qquad \square$$

A set $\text{dep}(f^\sharp, \sigma^\sharp) \subseteq Y$ with a property analogous to (7) can be explicitly obtained from the tree representation t of $f^\sharp$ by defining $\text{dep}(f^\sharp, \sigma^\sharp) = \text{treedep}(t, \sigma^\sharp)$ where:

$$\text{treedep}(\text{Answer } d, \sigma^\sharp) \quad = \emptyset$$
$$\text{treedep}(\text{Query } (y, c), \sigma^\sharp) = \{y\} \cup \text{treedep}(c\,(\sigma^\sharp[y]), \sigma^\sharp)$$

Technically, this means that the value $f^\sharp \sigma^\sharp = [\![t]\!]\, \sigma^\sharp$ can be computed already for *partial* variable assignments $\sigma' : Y' \to \mathbb{D}$, whenever $\text{dep}(f^\sharp, \top \oplus \sigma') = \text{treedep}(t, \top \oplus \sigma') \subseteq Y'$. Here, $\top : Y \to \mathbb{D}$ maps each variable of Y to $\top$ and $\top \oplus \sigma'$ returns the value $\sigma'[y]$ for every $y \in Y'$ and $\top$ otherwise.

Example 4. Consider the function $f^\sharp$ from Example 3 together with the partial assignment $\sigma' = \{y_1 \mapsto 3\}$. Then $\text{dep}(f^\sharp, \top \oplus \sigma') = \{y_1\}$. $\qquad \square$

We call a partial variable assignment $\sigma' : Y' \to \mathbb{D}$ *closed* (w.r.t. an abstract system (2)), if for all $y \in Y'$, $\mathsf{dep}(f_y^\sharp, \bot \oplus \sigma') \subseteq Y'$.

In the following, we strengthen the description relation $\mathcal{R}$ additionally to take variable dependencies into account. We say that the abstract system (2) *simulates* the concrete system (1) (relative to the description relation $\mathcal{R}$) iff for all pairs x, y of variables with $x \mathrel{\mathcal{R}} y$, such that for the concrete and abstract right-hand sides f_x and $f_y^\sharp$, respectively, property (3) holds and additionally $\mathsf{dep}(f_x, \sigma) \mathrel{\mathcal{R}} \mathsf{dep}(f_y^\sharp, \sigma^\sharp)$ whenever $\sigma \mathrel{\mathcal{R}^*} \sigma^\sharp$. Here, a pair of sets X', Y' of concrete and abstract variables is in relation $\mathcal{R}$ if for all $x \in X'$, $x \mathrel{\mathcal{R}} y$ for some $y \in Y'$. Theorem 2 demonstrates the significance of closed abstract assignments which are sound.

Theorem 2. *Assume that the abstract system (2) simulates the concrete system (1) (relative to $\mathcal{R}$) where σ is the least solution of the concrete system. Assume that $\sigma^\sharp : Y' \to \mathbb{D}$ is a partial assignment with the following properties:*

1. *$\sigma^\sharp$ is closed;*
2. *$\bot \oplus \sigma^\sharp$ is a post-solution of the lower monotonization of the abstract system.*

Then the set $X' = \{ x \in X \mid \exists y \in Y'. x \mathrel{\mathcal{R}} y \}$ is σ-closed.

Proof. By Lemma 2, $\sigma \mathrel{\mathcal{R}^*} (\bot \oplus \sigma^\sharp)$ holds. Now assume that $x \mathrel{\mathcal{R}} y$ for some $y \in Y'$. By definition therefore, $\mathsf{dep}(f_x, \sigma) \mathrel{\mathcal{R}} \mathsf{dep}(f_y^\sharp, \bot \oplus \sigma^\sharp)$. Since the latter is a subset of Y', the former must be a subset of X', and the assertion follows. □

6 Terminating Structured Two-Phase Solving

We first present a local version of a two-phase algorithm to determine a sound variable assignment for an abstract system of equations. As the algorithm is local, no pre-processing of the equation system is possible. Accordingly, variables where widening or narrowing is to be applied must be determined dynamically (in contrast to solvers based on static variable dependencies where widening points can be statically determined [7]). We solve this problem by assigning *priorities* to variables in decreasing order in which they are encountered, and consider a variable as a candidate for widening/narrowing whenever it is queried during the evaluation of a lower priority variable. The second issue is that during the narrowing iteration of the second phase, variables may be encountered which have not yet been seen and for which therefore no sound approximation is available. In order to deal with this situation, the algorithm does not maintain a single variable assignment, but two distinct ones. While assignment σ_0 is used for the widening phase, σ_1 is used for narrowing with the understanding that, once the widening phase is completed, the value of a variable y from σ_0 is copied as the initial value of y into σ_1. This clear distinction allows to continue the widening iteration for every newly encountered variable y' in order to determine an acceptable initial value before continuing with the narrowing iteration. The resulting algorithm can be found in Figs. 2 and 3. Initially, the priority queue Q and the

```
void iterate₀(n) {                          void iterate₁(n) {
    if (Q ≠ ∅ ∧ min_prio(Q) ≤ n) {              if (Q ≠ ∅ ∧ min_prio(Q) ≤ n) {
        y := extract_min(Q);                        y := extract_min(Q);
                                                    solve₁(y, prio[y] − 1);
        do_var₀(y);                                 do_var₁(y);
        iterate₀(n);                                iterate₁(n);
    }                                           }
}                                           }
void solve₀(y) {                            void solve₁(y, n) {
    if (y ∈ dom₀) return;                        if (y ∈ dom₁) return;
    dom₀ := dom₀ ∪ {y};                          solve₀(y);
    prio[y] := next_prio();                      dom₁ := dom₁ ∪ {y};
    σ₀[y] := ⊥;                                  σ₁[y] := σ₀[y];
    infl[y] := ∅;                                forall (z ∈ {y} ∪ infl[y]) insert z Q;
    do_var₀(y);                                  infl[y] := ∅;
    iterate₀(prio[y]);                           iterate₁(n);
}                                           }
```

Fig. 2. The solver TSTP, part 1.

sets dom_0 and dom_1 are empty. Accordingly, the mappings $\sigma_i : dom_i \to \mathbb{D}$ and infl : $dom \to 2^Y$ are also empty. Likewise, the set point is initially empty. Solving for the variable y_0 starts with the call $solve_1(y_0, 0)$.

Let us first consider the functions $solve_0$, $iterate_0$, do_var_0. These are meant to realize a local widening iteration. A call $solve_0(y)$ first checks whether $y \in dom_0$. If this is the case, solving immediately terminates. Otherwise, $\sigma_0[y]$ is initialized with $\perp$, y is added to dom_0, the empty set is added to $infl[y]$, and y receives the next available priority by means of the call $next\_prio$. Subsequently, $do\_var_0(y)$ is called, followed by a call to $iterate_0(prio[y])$ to complete the widening phase for y. Upon termination, a call $iterate_0(n)$ for an integer n has removed all variables of priority at most n from the queue Q. It proceeds as follows. If Q is empty or contains only variables of priority exceeding n, it immediately returns. Otherwise, the variable y with least priority is extracted from Q. Having processed $do\_var_0(y)$, the iteration continues with the tail-recursive call $iterate_0(n)$.

It remains to describe the function do_var_0. When called for a variable y, the algorithm first determines whether or not y is a widening/narrowing point, i.e., contained in the set point. If so, y is removed from point, and the flag isp is set to **true**. Otherwise, isp is set to **false**. Then the right-hand side $f_y^\sharp$ is evaluated and the result stored in the variable tmp. For its evaluation, the function $f_y^\sharp$, however, does not receive the current variable assignment σ_0 but an auxiliary function $eval_0$ which serves as a wrapper to the assignment σ_0. The wrapper function $eval_0$, when queried for a variable z, first calls $solve_0(z)$ to compute a first non-trivial value for z. If the priority of z is greater or equal to the priority of y, a potential widening point is detected. Therefore, z is added to the set point. Subsequently, the fact that z was queried during the evaluation of the right-hand side of y, is recorded by adding y to the set $infl[z]$. Finally, $\sigma_0[z]$ is returned.

```
void do_var_0(y) {                          void do_var_1(y) {
    isp := y ∈ point;                           isp := y ∈ point;
    point := point\{y};                         point := point\{y};
    D eval_0(z) {                               D eval_1(z) {
        solve_0(z);                                 solve_1(z, prio[y] − 1);
        if (prio[z] ≥ prio[y])                      if (prio[z] ≥ prio[y])
            point := point ∪ {z};                       point := point ∪ {z};
        infl[z] := infl[z] ∪ {y};                   infl[z] := infl[z] ∪ {y};
        return σ_0[z]);                             return σ_1[z];
    }                                           }
    tmp := f_y^♯ eval_0;                        tmp := f_y^♯ eval_1;
    if (isp) tmp := σ_0[y] ∇ tmp;              if (isp) tmp := σ[y] Δ tmp;
    if (σ_0[y] = tmp) return;                   if (σ_1[y] = tmp) return;
    σ_0[y] := tmp;                              σ_1[y] := tmp;
    forall (z ∈ infl[y]) insert z Q;           forall (z ∈ infl[y]) insert z Q;
    infl[y] := ∅;                               infl[y] := ∅;
    return;                                     return;
}                                           }
```

Fig. 3. The solver TSTP, part 2.

Having evaluated $f_y^♯$ $eval_0$ and stored the result in tmp, the function do_var_0 then applies widening only if isp equals **true**. In this case, tmp receives the value of $\sigma[y] \nabla tmp$. In the next step, tmp is compared with the current value $\sigma_0[y]$. If both values are equal, the procedure returns. Otherwise, $\sigma_0[y]$ is updated to tmp. The variables in $infl[y]$ are inserted into the queue Q, and the set $infl[y]$ is reset to the empty set. Only then the procedure returns.

The functions $solve_1$, $iterate_1$ and do_var_1, on the other hand, are meant to realize the narrowing phase. They essentially work analogously to the corresponding functions $solve_0$, $iterate_0$ and do_var_0. In particular, they re-use the mapping $infl$ which records the currently encountered variable dependencies as well as the variable priorities and the priority queue Q. Instead of σ_0, dom_0, however, they now refer to σ_1, dom_1, respectively. Moreover, there are the following differences.

First, the function $solve_1$ now receives not only a variable, but a pair of an integer n and a variable y. When called, the function first checks whether $y \in dom_1$. If this is the case, solving immediately terminates. Otherwise, $solve_0(y)$ is called first. After that call, the widening phase for y is assumed to have terminated where the resulting value is $\sigma_0[y]$. Accordingly, $\sigma_1[y]$ is initialized with $\sigma_0[y]$, and y is added to dom_1. As the value of σ_1 for y has been updated, y together with all variables in $infl[y]$ are added to the queue, whereupon $infl[y]$ is set to the empty set, and $iterate_1(n)$ is called to complete the narrowing phase up to the priority n. Upon termination, a call $iterate_1(n)$ for an integer n has removed all variables of priority at most n from the queue Q. In distinction to $iterate_0$, however, it may extract variables y from Q which have not yet been encountered in the present phase of iteration, i.e., are not yet included in dom_1

and thus have not yet received a value in σ_1. To ensure initialization, $\mathsf{solve}_1(y, n)$ is called for $n = \mathsf{prio}[y] - 1$. This choice of the extra parameter n ensures that all lower priority variables have been removed from Q before $\mathsf{do\_var}_1(y)$ is called.

It remains to explain the function $\mathsf{do\_var}_1(y)$. Again, it essentially behaves like $\mathsf{do\_var}_0(y)$ — with the distinction that the narrowing operator is applied instead of the widening operator. Furthermore, the auxiliary local function eval_0 is replaced with eval_1 which now uses a call to solve_1 for the initialization of its argument variable z (instead of solve_0) where the extra integer argument is given by $\mathsf{prio}[y] - 1$, i.e., an iteration is performed to remove all variables from Q with priorities lower than the priority of y (not of z).

In light of Theorem 3, we call the algorithm from Figs. 2 and 3 *terminating structured two-phase solver*.

Theorem 3. *The local solver* TSTP *from Fig. 2 and 3 when started with a call* $\mathsf{solve}_1(y_0, 0)$ *for a variable* y_0, *terminates for every system of equations whenever only finitely many variables are encountered.*

Upon termination, assignments $\sigma_i^\sharp : Y_i \to \mathbb{D}$, $i = 0, 1$ *are obtained for finite sets* $Y_0 \supseteq Y_1$ *of variables so that the following holds:*

1. $y_0 \in Y_1$;
2. $\sigma_0^\sharp$ *is a closed partial post-solution of the abstract system* (2);
3. $\sigma_1^\sharp$ *is a closed partial assignment such that* $\top \oplus \sigma_1^\sharp$ *is a post-solution of the lower monotonization of the abstract system* (2).

A proof is provided in the long version of this paper [24].

7 Terminating Structured Mixed-Phase Solving

The draw-back of the two-phase solver TSTP from the last section is that it may lose precision already in very simple situations.

Example 5. Consider the system:

$$y_1 = \mathsf{max}(y_1, y_2) \qquad y_2 = \mathsf{min}(y_3, 2) \qquad y_3 = y_2 + 1$$

over the complete lattice $\mathbb{N}^\infty$ and the following widening and narrowing operators:

$$a \nabla b = \text{if } a < b \text{ then } \infty \text{ else } a$$
$$a \Delta b = \text{if } a = \infty \text{ then } b \text{ else } a$$

Then $\mathsf{solve}_0(y_1)$ detects y_2 as the only widening point resulting in

$$\sigma_0 = \{y_1 \mapsto \infty, y_2 \mapsto \infty, y_3 \mapsto \infty\}$$

A call to $\mathsf{solve}_1(y_1, 0)$ therefore initializes y_1 with ∞ implying that $\sigma_1[y_1] = \infty$ irrespective of the fact that $\sigma_1[y_2] = 2$. $\qquad\square$

```
void iterate(b, n) {                    void solve(y) {
    if (Q ≠ ∅ ∧ min_prio(Q) ≤ n) {          if (y ∈ dom) return;
        y := extract_min(Q);                 dom := dom ∪ {y};
        b' := do_var(b, y);                  prio[y] := next_prio();
        n' := prio[y];                       σ[y] := ⊥;
        if (b ≠ b' ∧ n > n') {               infl[y] := ∅;
            iterate(b', n');                 b' := do_var(false, y);
            iterate(b, n);                   iterate(b', prio[y]);
        } else iterate(b', n);           }
    }
}
```

Fig. 4. The solver TSMP, part 1.

```
bool do_var(b, y) {                      ...
    isp := y ∈ point;                    if (isp)
    point := point\{y};                      if (b) tmp := σ[y] △ tmp;
    D eval(z) {                              else if (tmp ⊑ σ[y]) {
        solve(z);                                tmp := σ[y] △ tmp;
        if (prio[z] ≥ prio[y])                   b' := true;
            point := point ∪ {z};            } else tmp := σ[y] ▽ tmp;
        infl[z] := infl[z] ∪ {y};        if (σ[y] = tmp) return true;
        return σ[z];                     σ[y] := tmp;
    }                                    forall (z ∈ infl[y]) insert z Q;
    tmp := f_y^♯ eval;                   infl[y] := ∅;
    b' := b;                             return b';
    ...                             }
```

Fig. 5. The solver TSMP, part 2.

We may therefore aim at intertwining the two phases into one — without sacrificing the termination guarantee. The idea is to operate on a single variable assignment only and iterate on each variable first in widening and then in narrowing mode. In order to keep soundness, after every update of a variable y in the widening phase, all possibly influenced lower priority variables are iterated upon until all stabilize with widening and narrowing. Only then the widening iteration on y continues. If on the other hand an update for y occurs during narrowing, the iteration on possibly influenced lower priority variables is with narrowing only. The distinction between the two modes of the iteration is maintained by a flag where **false** and **true** correspond to the widening and narrowing phases, respectively. The algorithm is provided in Figs. 4 and 5.

Initially, the priority queue Q and the set dom are empty. Accordingly, the mappings $\sigma : \text{dom} \to \mathbb{D}$ and infl : dom $\to Y$ are also empty. Likewise, the set point is initially empty. Solving for the variable y_0 starts with the call solve(y_0). Solving for some variable y first checks whether $y \in$ dom. If this is the case, solving immediately terminates. Otherwise, y is added to dom and receives the next available priority by means of a call to next_prio. That call should provide a value which is less than any priority of a variable in dom. Subsequently, the entries $\sigma[y]$ and $\mathsf{infl}[y]$ are initialized to $\perp$ and the empty set, respectively, and do_var is called for the pair $(\mathbf{false}, y)$. The return value of this call is stored in the Boolean variable b'. During its execution, this call may have inserted further variables into the queue Q. These are dealt with by the call $\mathsf{iterate}(b', \mathsf{prio}[y])$.

Upon termination, a call $\mathsf{iterate}(b, n)$ has removed all variables of priority at most n from the queue Q. It proceeds as follows. If Q is empty or contains only variables of priority exceeding n, it immediately returns. Otherwise, the variable y with least priority n' is extracted from Q. For (b, y), do_var is called and the return value of this call is stored in b'.

Now we distinguish several cases. If $b = \mathbf{true}$, then the value b' returned by do_var will necessarily be $\mathbf{true}$ as well. In that case, iteration proceeds by tail-recursively calling again $\mathsf{iterate}(\mathbf{true}, n)$. If on the other hand $b = \mathbf{false}$, then the value b' returned by do_var can be either $\mathbf{true}$ or $\mathbf{false}$. If $b' = \mathbf{false}$ or $b' = \mathbf{true}$ and $n' = n$, then $\mathsf{iterate}(b', n)$ is tail-recursively called. If, however, $b' = \mathbf{true}$ and $n > n'$, then first a sub-iteration is triggered for $(\mathbf{true}, n')$ before the main loop proceeds with the call $\mathsf{iterate}(\mathbf{false}, n)$.

It remains to describe the function do_var. When called for a pair (b, y) consisting of a Boolean value b and variable y, the algorithm first determines whether or not y is a widening/narrowing point, i.e., contained in the set point. If so, y is removed from point, and the flag isp is set to $\mathbf{true}$. Otherwise, isp is just set to $\mathbf{false}$. Then the right-hand side $f_y^\sharp$ is evaluated and the result stored in the variable tmp. For its evaluation, the function $f_y^\sharp$, however, does not receive the current variable assignment σ, but an auxiliary function eval which serves as a wrapper to σ. The wrapper function eval, when queried for a variable z, first calls solve z to compute a first non-trivial value for z. If the priority of z exceeds or is equal to the priority of y, a potential widening/narrowing point is detected. Therefore, z is added to the set point. Subsequently, the fact that the value of z was queried during the evaluation of the right-hand side of y, is recorded by adding y to the set $\mathsf{infl}[z]$. Finally, the value $\sigma[z]$ is returned.

Having evaluated $f_y^\sharp$ eval and stored the result in tmp, the function do_var then decides whether to apply widening or narrowing or none of them according to the following scheme. If isp has not been set to $\mathbf{true}$, no widening or narrowing is applied. In this case, the flag b' receives the value b. Therefore now consider the case $isp = \mathbf{true}$. Again, the algorithm distinguishes three cases. If $b = \mathbf{true}$, then necessarily narrowing is applied, i.e., tmp is updated to the value of $\sigma[y] \Delta tmp$, and b' still equals b, i.e., $\mathbf{true}$. If $b = \mathbf{false}$ then narrowing is applied whenever $tmp \sqsubseteq \sigma[y]$ holds. In that case, tmp is set to $\sigma[y] \Delta tmp$, and b' to $\mathbf{true}$. Otherwise, i.e., if $b = \mathbf{false}$ and $tmp \not\sqsubseteq \sigma y$, then widening is applied by setting tmp to $\sigma[y] \nabla tmp$, and b' obtains the value $\mathbf{false}$.

In the next step, tmp is compared with the current value $\sigma[y]$. If both values are equal, the value of b' is returned. Otherwise, $\sigma[y]$ is updated to tmp. The variables in $\mathsf{infl}[y]$ are inserted into the queue Q, and the set $\mathsf{infl}[y]$ is reset to the empty set. Only then the value of b' is returned.

Example 6. Consider the system of equations from Example 5. Calling solve for variable y_1 will assign the priorities $0, -1, -2$ to the variables y_1, y_2 and y_3, respectively. Evaluation of the right-hand side of y_1 proceeds only after solve(y_2) has terminated. During the first update of y_2, y_2 is inserted into the set point, implying that at the subsequent evaluation the widening operator is applied resulting in the value ∞ for y_2 and y_3. The subsequent narrowing iteration on y_2 and y_3 improves these values to 2 and 3, respectively. Only then the value for y_1 is determined which is 2. During that evaluation, y_1 has also been added to the set point. The repeated evaluation of its right-hand side, will however, again produce the value 2 implying that the iteration terminates with the assignment

$$\sigma = \{y_1 \mapsto 2, y_2 \mapsto 2, y_3 \mapsto 3\} \qquad \square$$

In light of Theorem 4, we call the algorithm from Figs. 4 and 5, *terminating structured mixed-phase solver* or TSMP for short.

Theorem 4. *The local solver* TSMP *from Figs. 4 and 5 when started for a variable y_0, terminates for every system of equations whenever only finitely many variables are encountered.*

Upon termination, an assignment $\sigma^\sharp : Y_0 \to \mathbb{D}$ is returned where Y_0 is the set of variables encountered during solve(**false**, y_0) *such that the following holds:*

- *$y_0 \in Y_0$,*
- *$\sigma^\sharp$ is a closed partial assignment such that $\top \oplus \sigma^\sharp$ is a post-solution of the lower monotonization of the abstract system (2).*

A proof is provided in the long version of this paper [24].

8 Interprocedural Analysis

As seen in Example 2, the concrete semantics of programs with procedures can be formalized by a system of equations over a set of variables $X = \{\langle u, q \rangle \mid u \in U, q \in Q\}$ where U is a finite set of program points and Q is the set of possible system states. A corresponding abstract system of equations for interprocedural analysis can be formalized using abstract variables from the set $Y = \{\langle u, a \rangle \mid u \in U, a \in \mathbb{D}\}$ where the complete lattice $\mathbb{D}$ of abstract values may also serve as the set of abstract calling contexts for which each program point u may be analyzed. The description relation $\mathcal{R}$ between concrete and abstract variables is then given by $\langle u, q \rangle \; \mathcal{R} \; \langle u, a \rangle :\Longleftrightarrow q \in \gamma(a)$ for all $\langle u, q \rangle \in X$ and $\langle u, a \rangle \in Y$ and program points $u \in U$. Moreover, we require that for all right-hand sides f_x of the concrete system and $f_y^\sharp$ of the abstract system that $f_x \, q \subseteq \gamma(f_y^\sharp \, a)$ holds, whenever $x \, \mathcal{R} \, y$ and $q \in \gamma(a)$. Right-hand sides for abstract variables are given by expressions e according to the following grammar:

$$e \quad ::= \quad d \mid \alpha \mid g^\sharp \, e_1 \cdots e_k \mid \langle u, e \rangle \tag{8}$$

where $d \in \mathbb{D}$ denotes arbitrary constants, α is a dedicated variable representing the current calling context, $g^\sharp : \mathbb{D} \to \cdots \to \mathbb{D}$ is a k-ary function, and $\langle u, e \rangle$ with

$u \in U$ refers to a variable of the equation system. Each expression e describes a function $[\![e]\!]^\sharp : \mathbb{D} \rightarrow (Y \rightarrow \mathbb{D}) \rightarrow \mathbb{D}$ which is defined by:

$$[\![d]\!]^\sharp a\,\sigma = d \qquad\qquad [\![g^\sharp\, e_1 \cdots e_k]\!]^\sharp a\,\sigma = g^\sharp\,([\![e_1]\!]^\sharp a\,\sigma)\cdots([\![e_k]\!]^\sharp a\,\sigma)$$
$$[\![\alpha]\!]^\sharp a\,\sigma = a \qquad\qquad [\![\langle u, e\rangle]\!]^\sharp a\,\sigma \quad = \sigma\,\langle u, [\![e]\!]^\sharp a\,\sigma\rangle$$

A finite representation of the abstract system of equations then is given by the finite set of schematic equations

$$\langle u, \alpha\rangle = e_u, \qquad u \in U \tag{9}$$

for expressions e_u. Each schematic equation $\langle u, \alpha\rangle = e_u$ denotes the (possibly infinite) family of equations for the variables $\langle u, a\rangle, a \in \mathbb{D}$. For each $a \in \mathbb{D}$, the right-hand side function of $\langle u, a\rangle$ is given by the function $[\![e_u]\!]^\sharp a$. This function is indeed pure for every expression e_u and every $a \in \mathbb{D}$. Such systems of equations have been used, e.g., in [3,11] to specify interprocedural analyses.

Example 7. Consider the schematic system:

$$\langle u, \alpha\rangle = \langle v, \langle v, \langle u, \alpha\rangle\rangle\rangle \sqcup \alpha \qquad \langle v, \alpha\rangle = g^\sharp\,\langle v, \alpha\rangle \sqcup \alpha$$

for some unary function $g^\sharp : \mathbb{D} \rightarrow \mathbb{D}$. The resulting abstract system simulates the concrete system from Example 2, if $g(q) \subseteq \gamma(g^\sharp(a))$ holds whenever $q \in \gamma(a)$. $\square$

As we have seen in the example, function calls result in indirect addressing via nesting of variables. In case that the program does not have recursive procedures, there is a mapping $\lambda : U \rightarrow \mathbb{N}$ so that for every u with current calling context α, right-hand side e_u and every subexpression $\langle u', e'\rangle$ of e_u the following holds:

– If $\lambda(u') = \lambda(u)$, then $e' = \alpha$;
– If $\lambda(u') \neq \lambda(u)$, then $\lambda(u') < \lambda(u)$.

If this property is satisfied, we call the equation scheme *stratified* where $\lambda(u)$ is the *level* of u. Intuitively, stratification means that a new context is created only for some point u' of a strictly lower level. For the interprocedural analysis as formalized, e.g., in [3], all program points of a given procedure may receive the same level while the level decreases whenever another procedure is called. The system from Example 7 is stratified: we may, e.g., define $\lambda(u) = 2$ and $\lambda(v) = 1$.

Theorem 5. *The solver* TSTP *as well as the solver* TSMP *terminate for stratified equation schemes.*

Proof. We only consider the statement of the theorem for solver TSMP. Assume we run the solver TSMP on an abstract system specified by a stratified equation scheme. In light of Theorem 4, it suffices to prove that for every $u \in U$, only finitely many contexts $a \in \mathbb{D}$ are encountered during fixpoint computation. First, we note that variables $\langle v, a\rangle$ may not be influenced by variables $\langle u, a'\rangle$ with $\lambda(u) > \lambda(v)$. Second, let $D_{v,a}$ denote the set of variables $\langle u, a'\rangle$ with $\lambda(u) = \lambda(v)$

onto which $\langle v, a' \rangle$ may depend. Then all these variables share the same context. We conclude that new contexts for a point v at some level k are created only by the evaluation of right-hand sides of variables of smaller levels. For each level k, let $U_k \subseteq U$ denote the set of all u with $\lambda(u) \leq k$. We proceed by induction on k. Assume that we have proven termination for all calls solve $\langle u, a' \rangle$, $\lambda(u) < k$ for any subset of variables $\langle u', a'' \rangle$ which have already been solved. Then evaluating a call solve $\langle v, a \rangle$ with $\lambda(v) = k$ will either query the values of other variables $\langle v', a' \rangle$ where $\lambda(v') = k$. In this case, $a' = a$. Therefore, only finitely many of these are encountered. Or variables $\langle v', a' \rangle$ are queried with $\lambda(v') < k$. For those which have not yet been encountered solve $\langle v', a' \rangle$ is called. By induction hypothesis, all these calls terminate and therefore query only finitely many variables. As the evaluation of call $\langle v, a \rangle$ encounters only finitely many variables, it terminates. □

A similar argument explains why interprocedural analyzers based on the functional approach of Sharir/Pnueli [1, 26] terminate not only for finite domains but also for full constant propagation — if only the programs are non-recursive.

9   Conclusion

We have presented local solvers which are guaranteed to terminate for all abstract systems of equations given that only finitely many variables are encountered — irrespective of whether right-hand sides of the equations are monotonic or not or whether the complete lattice has infinite strictly ascending/descending chains or not. Furthermore, we showed that interprocedural analysis with partial tabulation of procedure summaries based on these solvers is guaranteed to terminate with the only assumption that the program has no recursive procedures. Clearly, theoretical termination proofs may only give an indication that the proposed algorithms are well-suited as fixpoint engines within a practical analysis tool. Termination within reasonable time and space bounds is another issue. The numbers provided by our preliminary practical experiments within the analysis framework GOBLINT seem encouraging (see Appendix A). Interestingly, a direct comparison of the two-phase versus mixed-phase solver for full context-sensitive interprocedural analysis, indicated that TSMP was virtually always faster, while the picture w.r.t. precision is not so clear. Also, the new solvers always returned post-solutions of the abstract systems — although they are not bound to do so.

There are several ways how this work can be extended. Our techniques crucially require a Galois connection to relate the concrete with the abstract domain. It is not clear how this restriction can be lifted. Also one may think of extending two phased approaches to a many-phase iteration as suggested in [9].

A   Experimental Evaluation

We implemented the solvers TSTP and TSMP presented in Sects. 6 and 7 within the analysis framework GOBLINT[1]. For that, these solvers have been extended

---

[1] http://goblint.in.tum.de/.

to deal with *side-effects* (see [3] for a detailed discussion of this mechanism) to jointly deal with flow- and context-sensitive and flow-insensitive analyses. In order to perform a fair comparison of the new solvers with *warrowing*-based local solving as proposed in [2,4], we provided a simplified version of TSMP. This simplified solver performs priority based iteration in the same way as TSMP but uses the warrowing operator instead of selecting operators according to extra flags. These three solvers were evaluated on the SPECint benchmark suite[2] consisting of not too small real-world C programs (1,600 to 34,000 LOC). Furthermore, the following C programs where analyzed: ent[3], figlet[4], maradns[5], wget[6], and some programs from the coreutils[7] package. The analyzed program wget is the largest one with around 77,000 LOC.

The analyses which we performed are put on top of a basic analysis of pointers, strings and enums. For enum variables, *sets* of possibles values are maintained. The benchmark programs were analyzed with full context-sensitivity of local data while globals were treated flow-insensitively.

The experimental setting is a fully context-sensitive interval analysis of int variables. Therefore, program 482.sphinx had to be excluded from the benchmark suite since it uses procedures which recurse on int arguments. Interestingly, the *warrowing* solver behaves exactly the same as TSMP on all of our benchmark programs. We interpret this by the fact that for the given analysis the right-hand sides are effectively monotonic. Accordingly, Fig. 7 only reports the relative precision of TSTP compared to TSMP.

Figure 6 compares the solvers TSMP and TSTP in terms of space and time. For a reasonable metric for space we choose the total number of variables (i.e., occurring pairs of program points and contexts) and for time the total number of evaluations of right-hand sides of a corresponding variable. The table indicates that the solver TSMP requires only around half of the variables of the solver TSTP. Interestingly, the percentage of evaluations of right-hand sides in a run of TSMP is still around 60 to 70 % of the solver TSTP.

In the second experiment, as depicted by Fig. 7, we compare the precision of the two solvers. For a reasonable metric we only compare the values of variables which occur in both solver runs. As a result, between 80 and 95 % of the variables receive the same value. It is remarkable that the mixed phase solver is not necessarily more precise. In many cases, an increase in precision is observed, yes — there are, however, also input programs where the two-phase solver excels.

---

[2] https://www.spec.org/cpu2006/CINT2006/.

[3] http://www.fourmilab.ch/random/(version 28.01.2008).

[4] http://www.figlet.org/.

[5] http://www.maradns.org/.

[6] https://www.gnu.org/s/wget/.

[7] https://www.gnu.org/s/coreutils/.

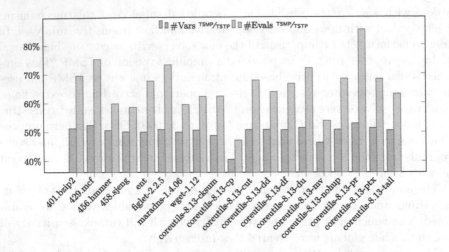

The blue bars (resp. red bars) depict the percentage of required variables (resp. evaluations of right-hand sides) of the solver TSMP compared to the solver TSTP.

Fig. 6. Efficiency of TSMP vs. TSTP. (Color figure online)

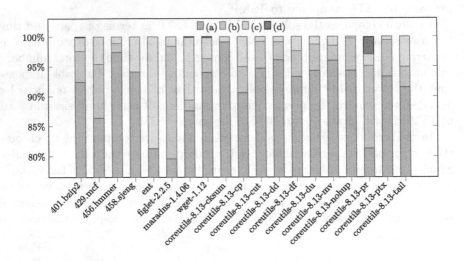

Percentage of variables occurring during a a run of both solvers

(a) for which TSMP and TSTP compute the same value;
(b) for which TSMP computes more precise results then TSTP;
(c) for which TSTP computes more precise results then TSMP;
(d) for which the results computed by TSMP and TSTP are incomparable.

Fig. 7. Precision of TSMP vs. TSTP.

References

1. Alt, M., Martin, F.: Generation of efficient interprocedural analyzers with PAG. In: Mycroft, A. (ed.) SAS 1995. LNCS, vol. 983, pp. 33–50. Springer, Heidelberg (1995)
2. Amato, G., Scozzari, F., Seidl, H., Apinis, K., Vojdani, V.: Efficiently intertwining widening and narrowing. Sci. Comput. Program. **120**, 1–24 (2016)
3. Apinis, K., Seidl, H., Vojdani, V.: Side-effecting constraint systems: a swiss army knife for program analysis. In: Igarashi, A., Jhala, R. (eds.) APLAS 2012. LNCS, vol. 7705, pp. 157–172. Springer, Heidelberg (2012)
4. Apinis, K., Seidl, H., Vojdani, V.: How to combine widening and narrowing for non-monotonic systems of equations. In: 34th ACM SIGPLAN Conference on Programming Language Design and Implementation (PLDI), pp. 377–386. ACM (2013)
5. Apinis, K., Seidl, H., Vojdani, V.: Enhancing top-down solving with widening and narrowing. In: Probst, C.W., Hankin, C., Hansen, R.R. (eds.) Nielsons' Festschrift. LNCS, vol. 9560, pp. 272–288. Springer, Heidelberg (2016). doi:10.1007/978-3-319-27810-0_14
6. Bagnara, R., Hill, P.M., Ricci, E., Zaffanella, E.: Precise widening operators for convex polyhedra. Sci. Comput. Program. **58**(1–2), 28–56 (2005)
7. Bourdoncle, F.: Efficient chaotic iteration strategies with widenings. In: Bjørner, D., Broy, M., Pottosin, I.V. (eds.) Formal Methods in Programming and Their Applications. LNCS, vol. 735, pp. 128–141. Springer, Heidelberg (1993)
8. Chen, L., Miné, A., Wang, J., Cousot, P.: An abstract domain to discover interval linear equalities. In: Barthe, G., Hermenegildo, M. (eds.) VMCAI 2010. LNCS, vol. 5944, pp. 112–128. Springer, Heidelberg (2010)
9. Cousot, P.: Abstracting induction by extrapolation and interpolation. In: D'Souza, D., Lal, A., Larsen, K.G. (eds.) VMCAI 2015. LNCS, vol. 8931, pp. 19–42. Springer, Heidelberg (2015)
10. Cousot, P., Cousot, R.: Abstract interpretation: a unified lattice model for static analysisof programs by construction or approximation of fixpoints. In: Fourth ACM Symposium on Principles of Programming Languages (POPL), pp. 238–252. ACM (1977)
11. Cousot, P., Cousot, R.: Static determination of dynamic properties of generalized type unions. In: ACM Conference on Language Design for Reliable Software (LDRS), pp. 77–94. ACM (1977)
12. Cousot, P., Cousot, R.: Static determination of dynamic properties of recursive procedures. In: IFIP Conference on Formal Description of Programming Concepts, pp. 237–277, North-Holland (1977)
13. Cousot, P., Cousot, R.: Abstract interpretation frameworks. J. Log. Comput. **2**(4), 511–547 (1992)
14. Cousot, P., Cousot, R., Feret, J., Mauborgne, L., Miné, A., Rival, X.: Why does Astrée scale up? Formal Methods Syst. Design **35**(3), 229–264 (2009)
15. Fecht, C., Seidl, H.: An even faster solver for general systems of equations. In: Cousot, R., Schmidt, D.A. (eds.) SAS 1996. LNCS, vol. 1145. Springer, Heidelberg (1996)
16. Gonnord, L., Halbwachs, N.: Combining widening and acceleration in linear relation analysis. In: Yi, K. (ed.) SAS 2006. LNCS, vol. 4134, pp. 144–160. Springer, Heidelberg (2006)
17. Hermenegildo, M.V., Bueno, F., Carro, M., López-García, P., Mera, E., Morales, J.F., Puebla, G.: An overview of Ciao and its design philosophy. Theor. Pract. Log. Program. **12**(1–2), 219–252 (2012)

18. Hermenegildo, M.V., Puebla, G., Bueno, F., López-García, P.: Integrated program debugging, verification, and optimization using abstract interpretation (and the Ciao system preprocessor). Sci. Comput. Program. **58**(1–2), 115–140 (2005)
19. Hofmann, M., Karbyshev, A., Seidl, H.: Verifying a local generic solver in Coq. In: Cousot, R., Martel, M. (eds.) SAS 2010. LNCS, vol. 6337, pp. 340–355. Springer, Heidelberg (2010)
20. Hofmann, M., Karbyshev, A., Seidl, H.: What is a pure functional? In: Gavoille, C., Kirchner, C., Meyer auf der Heide, F., Spirakis, P.G., Abramsky, S. (eds.) ICALP 2010. LNCS, vol. 6199, pp. 199–210. Springer, Heidelberg (2010)
21. Karbyshev, A.: Monadic Parametricity of Second-Order Functionals. Ph.D. thesis, Institut für Informatik, Technische Universität München, September 2013
22. MacNeille, H.M.: Partially ordered sets. Trans. Amer. Math. Soc. **42**(3), 416–460 (1937)
23. Muthukumar, K., Hermenegildo, M.V.: Deriving a fixpoint computation algorithm for top-down abstract interpretation of logic programs. Technical report ACT-DC-153-90, Microelectronics and Computer Technology Corporation (MCC), Austin, TX 78759, April 1990
24. Schulze Frielinghaus, S., Seidl, H., Vogler, R.: Enforcing termination of interprocedural analysis. arXiv e-prints (2016). http://arxiv.org/abs/1606.07687
25. Seidl, H., Fecht, C.: Interprocedural analyses: a comparison. J. Logic Program. **43**(2), 123–156 (2000)
26. Sharir, M., Pnueli, A.: Two approaches to interprocedural data flow analysis.In: Muchnick, S., Jones, N. (eds.) Program Flow Analysis: Theory and Application, pp. 189–233. Prentice-Hall (1981)

From Array Domains to Abstract Interpretation Under Store-Buffer-Based Memory Models

Thibault Suzanne[1](✉) and Antoine Miné[2]

[1] École Normale Supérieure, PSL Research University, CNRS, Inria, Paris, France
thibault.suzanne@ens.fr
[2] Laboratoire d'informatique de Paris 6 (LIP6), Sorbonne Universités,
UPMC Univ Paris 6, Paris, France
Antoine.Mine@lip6.fr

Abstract. We address the problem of verifying concurrent programs under store-buffer-based weakly consistent memory models, such as TSO or PSO. Using the abstract interpretation framework, we adapt existing domains for arrays to model store buffers and obtain a sound abstraction of program states (including the case of programs with infinite state space) parameterised by a numerical domain. Whereas the usual method for this kind of programs implements a program transformation to come back to an analysis under a sequentially consistent model, the novelty of our work consists in applying abstract interpretation directly on the source program, setting a clean foundation for special dedicated domains keeping information difficult to express with program transformations. We demonstrate the precision of this method on a few examples, targetting the TSO model and incidentally being also sound for PSO due to some specific abstraction choice. We discuss an application to fence removal and show that our implementation is usually able to remove as many or more fences, with respect to the state of the art, on concurrent algorithms designed for sequential consistency while still remaining precise enough to verify them.

1 Introduction

Multicore architectures have become increasingly important in the performance race of computers, hence concurrent programming is nowadays a wide-spread technique. Its most abundant paradigm is shared memory: all threads run simultaneously on different cores, and they communicate by accessing the same locations in the common memory.

The intuitive execution model of these concurrent programs is the *sequential consistency*[1] [16]. It states that the possible executions of a concurrent program correspond to sequential executions of the interleavings of its threads. However, for optimisation reasons, modern processors or language implementations do

---

This work is partially supported by the project ANR-11-INSE-014 from the French Agence nationale de la recherche.

[1] We will use the acronym SC, as it is usually done.

© Springer-Verlag GmbH Germany 2016
X. Rival (Ed.): SAS 2016, LNCS 9837, pp. 469–488, 2016.
DOI: 10.1007/978-3-662-53413-7_23

```
                    initial x = 0 && y = 0;

        /* Thread 1 */          |        /* Thread 2 */
        x = 1;                  |        y = 1;
        r1 = y;                 |        r2 = x;
```

Fig. 1. A simple program with counter-intuitive possible results on x86

```
/* Property to check: At labels (bp0; bp1), tail < h1 */
                    int head;

        /* ENQUEUE */           |        /* DEQUEUE */
        int h1;                 |        int tail, h2;

        while true {            |        tail = head;
            h1 = head;          |        while true {
        bp0:                    |            h2 = head;
            h1 = h1 + 1;        |            while (tail >= h2) {
            head = h1;          |                h2 = head;
        }                       |            }
                                |        bp1:
                                |            tail = tail + 1;
                                |        }
```

Fig. 2. A program with unbounded buffers and variable value space

not stick to this description, but add some additional possible behaviours. For instance, after the execution on a x86 CPU of the program described in Fig. 1, it is possible that both registers r1 and r2 are equal to 0, because memory writes are buffered and Thread 1 can read y to 0 even after Thread 2 has executed the assignment y=1.[2]

The example program of Fig. 1 is actually quite simple: the value space of the variables is small (four variables, each one can be equal to 0 or 1), and the size of the write buffers is bounded by a known and computable limit (that is 1). However, the program described in Fig. 2 is much more complicated: none of these properties holds anymore. There are infinitely many reachable states, and unbounded and nested loops. Furthermore, the actual execution model adds again some possible behaviours, with unbounded write buffers. This makes it even harder to reason on its correctness.

Weakly consistent memory models [1] aim to formally describe these additional behaviours in addition to the sequentially consistent ones. However, as this complexity adds to the inherent difficulties of writing correct concurrent programs, automatic verification becomes more and more useful.

---

[2] The result set of this program is $x = 1, y = 1, r1 \in \{0, 1\}, r2 \in \{0, 1\}$. Most static analyses are able to infer it exactly, and ours will too.

Several works [2–5, 10, 14, 15, 17] have been done in this area, using various static analysis techniques and targetting different memory models (see Sect. 6). Our work focuses on abstract interpretation [8], by giving an abstract semantic of concurrent programs which takes into account the relaxed memory effects of the TSO model. Amongst works that use this abstract interpretation framework, the usual method consists in applying a transformation on the source program to obtain another program which exhibits the same behaviour when run under sequential consistency. This resulting program is then verified with existing SC analysers.

This paper describes a general method to adapt existing array abstractions in order to represent the buffer part of the state of a concurrent program. Contrary to existing work, this method applies abstract interpretation directly on the source program. By doing so, we set a clean foundation for special dedicated domains keeping information difficult to express with program transformations. In particular, our analysis is able to prove the program in Fig. 2 correct, which is impossible with the state of the art since existing analyses are limited to bounded write buffers or programs which are finite-state when they run under SC.

After describing in Sect. 2 a concrete operational semantics of programs running under the chosen memory model, Sect. 3 presents the formalisation of an instance of our abstract domain using the summarisation approach from Gopan et al. [11] Sect. 4 then describes how to formalise more precise and complex abstractions. In Sect. 5, we give some experimental results obtained with an implementation of the first instance. We finally discuss a comparison with related works in Sect. 6. Section 7 concludes.

1.1 Weak Memory Models

We focus on two similar weak memory models, TSO and PSO, for *total* (resp. *partial*) *store ordering*. TSO is especially known to be the base memory model of the x86 CPU family [19]. In general, weak memory models can be described in several ways, e.g. by giving axiomatic (based for instance on event reordering) or operational semantics. We will work with the latter.

The operational model of TSO adds to the usual registers (or local variables) and shared memory of the sequentially consistent concurrent programs a *buffer* for each thread of the program. These buffers act as unbounded FIFO queues for the writes issued by the corresponding thread: when some thread executes an instruction such as x := n for some shared variable x, the value n does not reach the memory immediately, but instead the binding x= $\mapsto$ =n is pushed into the buffer. Conversely, when a thread attempts to read the value of some shared variable x, it effectively reads the value corresponding to the most recent binding of x in its own buffer. If this buffer contains no entry for x, then its value is read from the memory: a thread cannot directly access the buffer of another thread.

At any time between the execution of two instructions (which we consider as being atomic), the oldest binding of a buffer can be *flushed*: it disappears from the buffer and its value is used to update the memory at the corresponding variable location. The `mfence` specific instruction also flushes every entry of the buffer, enforcing consistency with memory updates.

This model therefore ensures that two consecutive writes issued by a thread cannot be seen in the opposite order by another one. It also ensures that when a write issued by a thread is visible to another one, then it is visible to every other thread with no corresponding entry in its buffer.

PSO works almost the same way, except that there is not a single buffer per thread, but a buffer per thread per shared variable — or equivalently, entries concerning different variables in the buffer can be reordered before they reach the memory. The `mfence` instruction will flush every buffer of the thread which executes it.

We now illustrate the behaviour of buffers by describing a concrete example of an execution of the program in Fig. 2. We first note that as it involves only one shared variable `head`, TSO and PSO are equivalent for this program: there is only one buffer used (for thread ENQUEUE, as thread DEQUEUE does not write anything to `head`), which we will denote as the list of the values written in it (most recent first). Let us set the initial value of `head` for this particular execution to 0.

- After one iteration of the loop of the ENQUEUE thread, h1 is equal to 1, `head` is still equal to 0 in the shared memory, but the buffer of the ENQUEUE thread contains one entry for `head`: {1}.
- Then thread DEQUEUE executes `tail = head`: it has no entry for `head` in its buffer, thus it reads from the memory, and `tail` is now equal to 0.
- Thread ENQUEUE starts a new iteration. It executes h1 = head and reads the most recent entry in its buffer: h1 is equal to 1.
- Thread ENQUEUE finishes its iteration: its buffer now contains {2, 1} and h1 is equal to 2.
- Thread ENQUEUE starts a new iteration and executes h1 = head: h1 reads from the buffer and is now equal to 2.
- Thread ENQUEUE flushes one entry from its buffer: it now contains {2} and `head` is equal to 1. It reaches label bp0.
- Thread DEQUEUE enters its outer loop. It executes h2 = head, which still reads from the memory. It can now read the write from thread ENQUEUE which has been flushed: h2 is equal to 1.
- `tail` is equal to 0 and h2 is equal to 1: thread DEQUEUE does not enter the inner loop and reaches label bp1.
- `tail` is equal to 0, h1 is equal to 2: the property holds, but we only tested it for a particular reachable state. Our analysis will be able to prove it for every possible execution path.

For three main reasons, our main target is TSO:

- It is a "real-life" model, corresponding to x86 processor architecture, whereas PSO is mainly of theoretical interest.
- It fills a sweet spot in the relaxation scale: most algorithms designed with sequential consistency in mind become incorrect, yet one can usually get back the desired behaviour with only a few modifications, such as fence insertion at selected points.

- It is a conceptually simpler and less permissive model than some other more relaxed ones like POWER, C11 or Java, which is a sensible property to lay the ground for works on the latter.

However, the abstraction choices made in our implementation happens to lose enough information to make our analysis also sound for PSO. For this reason, we mention and use this model in our formalisation. Yet we do not seek a precise abstraction of the special `sfence` instruction of PSO (which ensures that all stores preceding it will be flushed before the following ones), as it does not exist on our target model (if needed, it can soundly be abstracted by the identity). Section 4 will present abstractions able to exploit the additional precision of TSO (though we did not implement them).

1.2 Use of Array Abstractions

Presentation of the Technique. When using these operational models, buffers constitute the main difficulty for abstracting weakly consistent states: they behave as an unbounded FIFO queue whose size can change in a dynamic and non-deterministic way on virtually every execution step. We chose to use array abstractions to build computable abstract representations of these buffers.

On top of usual operations over fixed-size arrays, these abstractions must support (or be extended to support) an operation adding an element, and an operation removing one. Then we adapt them to go from arrays, which are fixed-size structures with immediate access to each element, to buffers, which behave mostly like FIFO queues whose size can change a lot during program execution, but are only accessed either at the beginning or the end, not at arbitrary positions.

A first and direct encoding consists in representing a buffer[3] B of size N with N different variables $B_1, ..., B_N$. Adding an entry E at the top of the buffer amounts to adding B_{N+1}, shifting all the variables $(B_{N+1} := B_N; ...; B_2 := B_1)$, and assigning E to B_1. We also consider, for each shared symbol x, an abstract variable x^{mem} which holds the memory value of x. This model is very concrete and results in unbounded buffers. To ensure termination, existing work enforce a fixed or pre-computed bound on the buffers, and the analysis fails if this bound is exceeded. As we will see shortly, our method does not have this limitation.

Dan et al. [10] propose another encoding of the buffers which does not need the shifting operation. The obtained analysis is usually more precise and efficient, but it suffers from the same limitation: buffer sizes must be statically bounded or the analysis may not terminate.

Summarisation of Unbounded Buffers. To get a computable abstraction which allows unbounded buffers, we use the summarisation technique described by Gopan et al. [11]

---

[3] In TSO, these buffers contain a tuple (variable name, variable value). In PSO, as there is one buffer for each variable, they simply contain integers. The abstract variables B_i share the same type.

This technique consists in regrouping several variables under the same symbol. For instance, if we have a state $(x, y, z) \in \{(1, 2, 3); (4, 5, 6)\}$, we can group x and y in a summarised variable v_{xy} and get the possible states as follows:

$$(v_{xy}, z) \in \{(1, 3); (2, 3); (4, 6); (5, 6)\}$$

This is indeed an abstraction, which loses some precision (since we cannot distinguish anymore between x and y): the summarised set also represents the concrete state $(x, y, z) = (1, 1, 3)$, which is absent of the original concrete set. The advantages are a more compact representation and, more importantly for us, the ability to represent a potentially infinite number of variables within the usual numerical domains.

We consider the PSO memory model, therefore we have a buffer for each variable for each thread, containing numerical values. For each buffer x^T of the variable x and the thread T where they are defined (that is when $N \geq 2$), we group the variables $x_2^T...x_N^T$ into a single summarised variable x_{bot}^T, whose possible values will therefore be all the values of these buffer entries. We distinguish all these older entries from x_1^T because it plays a special role as being the source of all reads of x by the thread T (if it is defined). Hence we need to keep it as a non-summarised variable to prevent a major loss of precision on read events.

Numerical Abstraction of Infinite States. This abstraction only allows to analyse programs with a finite number of reachable states after summarisation (finite state programs when run under SC). To be able to verify more complex programs, we use abstractions such as numerical domains (e.g. Polyhedra) to represent elements with an unbounded (and potentially infinite) number of states (each one still having an unbounded finite buffer). We will develop this abstraction in the next part, but the key idea is to partition the states with respect to the variables they define, so that the states that define the same variables can be merged into a numerical abstract domain. Using widening, we can then verify the program in Fig. 2.

2   Concrete Semantics

We consider our program to run under the PSO memory model (therefore our analysis will *a fortiori* be sound for TSO). We specify in Fig. 3 the direct encoding domain used to define the corresponding concrete semantics.

Notations. *Var* is the set of shared variable symbols, and *VarReg* is the set of registers (or local variables). Unless specified, we use the letters x, y, z for *Var* and r, s for *VarReg*, and e denotes an arithmetic expression over integers and registers only. *Thread* is the set of thread identifiers, typically some $\{1, 2, ..., K\}, K \in \mathbb{N}$. $\mathbb{V}$ is the numerical set in which the variables are valued, for instance $\mathbb{Z}$ or $\mathbb{Q}$ (respectively the set of integers and rational numbers). $\mathbb{N}^{>0}$ is the set of strictly

$$VarMem \triangleq \{x^{mem} \mid x \in Var\} \tag{1}$$

$$Mem \triangleq VarMem \to \mathbb{V} \quad Reg \triangleq VarReg \to \mathbb{V} \tag{2}$$

$$\forall x \in Var, T \in Thread, N \in \mathbb{N}, VarBuf(x, T, N) \triangleq \{x_i^T \mid 1 \leq i \leq N\} \tag{3}$$

$$Buf(x, T, N) \triangleq VarBuf(x, T, N) \to \mathbb{V} \tag{4}$$

$$BufSizes \triangleq (Var \times Thread) \to \mathbb{N} \tag{5}$$

$$\mathscr{S} \triangleq \bigcup_{N \in BufSizes} \left(Mem \times Reg \times \prod_{\substack{x \in Var \\ T \in Thread}} Buf(x, T, N(x, T)) \right) \tag{6}$$

$$\mathscr{D} \triangleq \mathcal{P}(\mathscr{S}) \tag{7}$$

Fig. 3. A concrete domain for PSO programs

positive integers. $\circ$ is the function composition operator.[4] $\prod$ denotes cartesian product: $\prod_{m \leq i \leq n} X_i = X_m \times X_{m+1} \times \ldots \times X_n$.

Bindings of variables in *Var* exist both in the memory and in the buffers, therefore we duplicate the symbols using *VarMem* and *VarBuf*. In the definition of the states set $\mathscr{S}$, for each $x \in Var, T \in Thread$, $N(x, T)$ is the size of the buffer for the variable x in the thread T. For a given state S, such a N is unique. We will note it N_S thereafter. A concrete element $X \in \mathscr{D}$ is a set of concrete states: $\mathscr{D} = \mathcal{P}(\mathscr{S})$.

Remark 1. $\mathscr{D}$ is isomorphic to a usual numerical points concrete domain. As such, it supports the usual concrete operations for variable assignment $(x := e)$, condition evaluation and so on. We will also use the *add* and *drop* operations, which respectively add an unconstrained variable to the environment of the domain, and delete it along with its constraints.

We define in Fig. 4 the concrete semantics of the instructions of a thread. Formally, for each instruction **ins** and thread T of the program, we define the concrete operator $[ins]_T$ that returns the set of concrete states obtained when the thread T performs this instruction from an input set of states. We build $[.]_T$ using basic operations on numerical domains as defined in Remark 1. These operations are noted with $[.]$ and operate from sets of states to sets of states. For convenience, we first define $[.]_T$ on state singletons, and then lift it pointwise on general state sets.

The control graph of a program being the product of the control graphs of each thread, the concrete semantics of a program is then the least fixpoint of the equation system described by this graph where edges are labelled by the corresponding operators of Fig. 4. The non-determinism of flushes is encoded by a self-loop edge of label $[\textbf{flush } x]_T$ for each $x \in Var, T \in Thread$ on each vertex in the graph.

---

[4] $(f \circ g)(x)$ is $f(g(x))$. That means operators are listed in the equations in reverse application order.

$$\forall T \in Thread, [\![.]\!]_T : \mathcal{D} \to \mathcal{D} \tag{8}$$

$$[\![x := e]\!]_T\{S\} \triangleq [\![x_1^T := e]\!] \circ [\![x_2^T := x_1^T]\!] \circ \dots$$
$$\dots \circ [\![x_{N_S(x,T)+1}^T := x_{N_S(x,T)}^T]\!] \circ [\![add \; x_{N_S(x,T)+1}^T]\!]\{S\} \tag{9}$$

$$[\![r := x]\!]_T\{S\} \triangleq \begin{cases} [\![r := x^{mem}]\!]S & \text{if } N_S(x,T) = 0 \\ [\![r := x_1^T]\!]S & \text{if } N_S(x,T) \geq 1 \end{cases} \tag{10}$$

$$[\![\texttt{mfence}]\!]_T\{S\} \triangleq \begin{cases} S & \text{if } \forall x \in Var, N_S(x,T) = 0 \\ \emptyset & \text{otherwise} \end{cases} \tag{11}$$

$$[\![\texttt{flush } x]\!]_T\{S\} \triangleq \begin{cases} \emptyset & \text{if } N_S(x,T) = 0 \\ [\![drop \; x_{N_S(x,T)}^T]\!] \circ [\![x^{mem} := x_{N_S(x,T)}^T]\!]\{S\} & \text{if } N_S(x,T) \geq 1 \end{cases} \tag{12}$$

$$\forall X \in \mathcal{D}, [\![ins]\!]_T X \triangleq \bigcup_{S \in X} [\![ins]\!]_T\{S\} \tag{13}$$

Fig. 4. Concrete semantics in PSO

Remark 2. An equivalent point of view is to consider the asynchronous execution of two parallel virtual processes for each thread: the first one is actually executing the source code instructions of the program and does not perform any flush, and the second one is simply performing an infinite loop of flushes. The non-determinism of this asynchronous parallel execution matches the non-determinism of the flushes.

This equivalent simulation of the execution of the program explains why the concrete operators of each actual instruction do not perform any flush, and especially why $[\![\texttt{mfence}]\!]$ does not actually write anything to the memory: the mfence instruction simply prevents the execution of the actual thread to continue until the associated flushing thread has completely emptied the buffer of every variable. Therefore, its semantics are the same of a instruction like while (some variable can be flushed) {}, that is a filter on states with no possible flush.

Properties of this concrete semantics are usually undecidable: not only because of the classic reasons (presence of loops, infinite value space, infinitely many possible memory states), but also because buffers have an unbounded possible size. Thus we use the abstract interpretation framework [8] to describe abstract operators whose fixpoint can be computed by iteration on the graph.

3 Abstract Semantics

3.1 Partitioning

Our first step towards abstraction consists in partitioning the concrete states of some concret element. We do this partition with respect to a partial information, for each thread, on the presence of each variable in its buffer: either it is absent, or it is present once, or it is present more than once. We respectively use the

$$\mathcal{B}^b \triangleq Var \times Thread \rightarrow \{0; 1; 1+\} \tag{14}$$

$$\delta : \mathcal{S} \rightarrow \mathcal{B}^b \tag{15}$$

$$\delta(S) \triangleq \lambda(x, T). \begin{cases} 0 & \text{if } N_S(x, T) = 0 \\ 1 & \text{if } N_S(x, T) = 1 \\ 1+ & \text{if } N_S(x, T) > 1 \end{cases} \tag{16}$$

Fig. 5. A partial information on states buffers to partition them

$$\mathcal{D} \xrightleftharpoons[\alpha_1]{\gamma_1} (\mathcal{B}^b \rightarrow \mathcal{D}) \tag{17}$$

$$\alpha_1(X) \triangleq \lambda b^b. \left\{ S \in X \mid \delta(S) = b^b \right\} \tag{18}$$

$$\gamma_1(X_{part}) \triangleq \{S \in \mathcal{S} \mid S \in X_{part}(\delta(S))\} \tag{19}$$

Fig. 6. The state partitioning abstract domain

notations 0, 1 and 1+ for these three cases. We define this partitioning criterion δ in Fig. 5.

We then formalise in Fig. 6 the resulting domain. We use the usual state partitioning domain, given as a Galois connection $\mathcal{D} \xrightleftharpoons[\alpha_1]{\gamma_1} (\mathcal{B}^b \rightarrow \mathcal{D})$. We emphasise that this abstraction does not lose any information yet.

3.2 Summarising

In order to be able to represent and compute potentially unbounded buffer states, we then use summarisation [11]. In each concrete partition where they are defined, we group the variables $x_2^T...x_N^T$ into a single summarised variable x_{bot}^T.

We denote by $\mathcal{D}^\natural$ the abstract domain resulting from the summarisation of these variables from $\mathcal{D}$, and suppose we have a concretisation function which matches the *representation* notion of Gopan et al. [11]:

$$\gamma_{sum} : \mathcal{D}^\natural \rightarrow \mathcal{D}$$

$\mathcal{D}^\natural$ should also implement the fold and expand operation described by Gopan et al. [11] We recall that $[\![fold \ x, y]\!]X$ is the summarisation operation: y is removed from the environment of X and, for each state, its value is added as a possible value of x (where the remaining part of the state remains the same); and $[\![expand \ x, y]\!]$ is the dual operation that creates a new variable y whose possible values are the same as x (put in another way, it inherits all the constraints of x, but the value of y is not necessarily equal to that of x).

We give in Fig. 7 an equivalent formulation of fold and expand as described by Siegel and Simon [20], which can also be used for implementing them on domains where they are not natively defined. $[\![swap \ x, y]\!]X$ swaps the value of x and y in each state of X.

$$[\![fold\ x,y]\!]X = [\![drop\ y]\!](X \cup [\![x := y]\!]X) \qquad (20)$$

$$[\![expand\ x,y]\!]X = [\![add\ y]\!]X \cap ([\![swap\ x,y]\!] \circ [\![add\ y]\!]X) \qquad (21)$$

Fig. 7. Summarisation operations fold and expand

$$\gamma_2 : (\mathscr{B}^b \to \mathscr{D}^\natural) \to (\mathscr{B}^b \to \mathscr{D}) \qquad (22)$$

$$\gamma_2(X^\sharp) \triangleq \lambda b^b.\gamma_{sum}(X^\sharp(b^b)) \qquad (23)$$

$$\gamma : (\mathscr{B}^b \to \mathscr{D}^\natural) \to \mathscr{D} \qquad (24)$$

$$\gamma \triangleq \gamma_1 \circ \gamma_2 = \lambda X^\sharp. \{ S \in \mathscr{S} \mid S \in \gamma_{sum}(X^\sharp(\delta(S))) \} \qquad (25)$$

Fig. 8. Summarising the buffers to regain a bounded representation

We formalise in Fig. 8 the resulting abstract domain. As Gopan et al. [11] doe not give an abstraction function (not least since it does not necessarily exist after numerical abstraction, see next Sect. 3.3), we only provide a concretisation function γ_2 from the summarised domain to the partitioned domain. We also define a global concretisation function γ from the summarised domain to the original concrete domain $\mathscr{D}$.

We give the corresponding semantics of our resulting abstract domain in Fig. 9. We first define partial abstract operators $\{\!\!|.|\!\!\}_T^\sharp$ that give, for one abstract input partition $(b^b, X^\natural)$, a partition index b_{result}^b and a summarised element $X_{result}^\natural$. Then the full operator $[\![.]\!]_T^\sharp$ is computed partitionwise, joining the summarised elements sent in the same partition index.

Theorem 1. *The abstract operators defined in Fig. 9 are sound:*

$$\forall X^\sharp \in \mathscr{B}^b \to \mathscr{D}^\natural, [\![ins]\!]_T \circ \gamma(X^\sharp) \subseteq \gamma \circ [\![ins]\!]_T^\sharp(X^\sharp)$$

Proof. Our abstract domain is built as the composition of two abstractions: the state partitioning and the summarisation. Therefore the soundness ensues from the soundness results on these two domains, provided we compute the right numerical elements and send them in the right partitions.

Therefore we will not detail the state partitioning arguments, as it is a fairly common abstraction. We will simply check that $\{\!\!|.|\!\!\}_T^\sharp$ sends its images into the right partition. However, summarising is less usual, thus we provide more explanations about the construction of the numerical content of the partitions.

The read operation involves no summarised variable, therefore its semantics is direct and corresponds almost exactly to the concrete one. The buffers are left unmodified in the concrete, hence the partition does not change. The fence operation is also an immediate translation of the concrete one.

The write operation distinguishes two cases: if the variable has a count of 0 in the abstract buffer, no summarisation is involved. If it has a count of 1, it involves the variable x_{bot}^T, but here summarisation still does not appear, since this variable actually only represents x_2 from the concrete state. In both these

$$\forall T \in Thread, \{\![.]\!\} : (\mathscr{B}^b \times \mathscr{D}^\natural) \to \mathcal{P}(\mathscr{B}^b \times \mathscr{D}^\natural) \tag{26}$$

$$\{\![r := x]\!\}_T^\sharp(b^b, X^\natural) = \begin{cases} \{b^b, [\![r := x^{mem}]\!]X^\natural\} & \text{if } b^b(x^T) = 0 \\ \{b^b, [\![r := x_1^T]\!]X^\natural\} & \text{otherwise} \end{cases} \tag{27}$$

$$\{\![x := e]\!\}_T^\sharp(b^b, X^\natural) = \begin{cases} \{b^b[x^T := 1], [\![x_1^T := e]\!] \circ [\![add\ x_1^T]\!]X^\natural\} & \text{if } b^b(x^T) = 0 \\ b^b[x^T := 1+], \\ [\![x_1^T := e]\!] \circ [\![x_{bot}^T := x_1^T]\!] \circ [\![add\ x_{bot}^T]\!]X^\natural\} & \text{if } b^b(x^T) = 1 \\ \{b^b, [\![x_1^T := e]\!] \circ [\![fold\ x_{bot}^T, x_2^{temp}]\!] \\ \circ [\![x_2^{temp} := x_1^T]\!] \circ [\![add\ x_2^{temp}]\!]X^\natural\} & \text{if } b^b(x^T) = 1+ \end{cases} \tag{28}$$

$$\{\![mfence]\!\}_T^\sharp(b^b, X^\natural) = \begin{cases} \{b^b, X^\natural\} & \text{if } \forall x \in Var, b^b(x_T) = 0 \\ \emptyset & \text{otherwise} \end{cases} \tag{29}$$

$$\{\![flush\ x]\!\}_T^\sharp(b^b, X^\natural) = \begin{cases} \emptyset & \text{if } b^b(x^T) = 0 \\ \{b^b[x^T := 0], [\![drop\ x_1^T]\!] \circ [\![x^{mem} := x_1^T]\!]X^\natural\} & \text{if } b^b(x^T) = 1 \\ \begin{cases} b^b, [\![drop\ x^{temp}]\!] \circ [\![x^{mem} := x^{temp}]\!] \\ \circ [\![expand\ x_{bot}^T, x^{temp}]\!]X^\natural; \\ b^b[x^T := 1], [\![drop\ x_{bot}^T]\!] \circ [\![x^{mem} := x_{bot}^T]\!]X^\natural \end{cases} & \text{if } b^b(x^T) = 1+ \end{cases} \tag{30}$$

$$\forall T \in Thread, [\![.]\!]_T^\sharp : (\mathscr{B}^b \to \mathscr{D}^\natural) \to (\mathscr{B}^b \to \mathscr{D}^\natural) \tag{31}$$

$$[\![ins]\!]_T^\sharp X^\sharp = \lambda b^b. \bigcup_{\substack{\exists b_1^b \in \mathscr{B}^b, \\ (b^b, X^\natural) \in \{\![ins]\!\}_T^\sharp(b_1^b, X^\sharp(b_1^b))}}^\natural X^\natural \tag{32}$$

Fig. 9. Abstract semantics with summarisation

cases, the abstract operator is almost the same as the concrete one, and there is only one partition in the destination, obtained by adding 1 to the presence of x_T.

In the third case, when the variable is present more than once, summarisation does apply. The numerical part is obtained by translating each step of Eq. (9) into $\mathscr{D}^\natural$, following the results of Gopan et al. [11] The steps $[\![x_1^T := e]\!]$, $[\![x_2^T := x_1^T]\!]$ and $[\![add\ x_{N_S(x,T)+1}^T]\!]$ are directly translated into the corresponding parts in Eq. (28). $[\![addx_{N_S(x,T)+1}^T]\!]$ is translated as the identity, since x_{bot}^T already exists. We now consider the operations of the form $[\![x_{i+1}^T := x_i^T]\!]$, for $i \geq 2$. They all translate into:

$$[\![drop\ x']\!] \circ [\![fold\ x_{bot}^T, x'']\!] \circ [\![x'' := x']\!] \circ [\![add\ x'']\!] \circ [\![expand\ x_{bot}^T, x']\!]$$

After applying $[\![x'' := x']\!]$, x'' and x' become interchangeable: they share the exact same constraints. Therefore, we can rewrite this formula as:

$$[\![drop\ x'']\!] \circ [\![fold\ x_{bot}^T, x']\!] \circ [\![x'' := x']\!] \circ [\![add\ x'']\!] \circ [\![expand\ x_{bot}^T, x']\!]$$

Then, $[\![drop\ x'']\!]$ and $[\![fold\ x_{bot}^T, x']\!]$ being independent, we can make them commute:

$$[\![fold\ x_{bot}^T, x']\!] \circ [\![drop\ x'']\!] \circ [\![x'' := x']\!] \circ [\![add\ x'']\!] \circ [\![expand\ x_{bot}^T, x']\!]$$

However, $[\![drop\ x'']\!] \circ [\![x'' := x']\!] \circ [\![add\ x'']\!]$ trivially reduces to the identity. Therefore we obtain $[\![fold\ x_{bot}^T, x']\!] \circ [\![expand\ x_{bot}^T, x']\!]$, which Siegel and Simon also demonstrates to be the identity [20]. All the $[\![x_{i+1}^T := x_i^T]\!]$ for $i \geq 2$ being reduced to the identity in the abstract semantics, we indeed get the formula of Eq. (28).

As for the partition, it does not change, since adding one element to a buffer containing more than one element still makes it contain more than one element.

The flush operation is the most complex. When the partition only has the variable once in the buffer, it is direct (with no summarisation) as in the other operations.

However, when a flush is done from a partition which has more than one variable in its buffer, the abstract element represents concrete states where this variable is present twice — the concrete image states having it once, and more than twice — the image states having it more than once.

Hence, in the 1+ case, the abstract flush operator performs two computations, respectively considering both possibilities, and sends these results into two different partitions. The contents of these partitions follow directly from the results of Gopan et al. [11].   □

Example 1. Let us consider the result of the execution (from a zeroed memory) by the thread 1 of the instructions $x = 1; x = 2$, with no flush yet. The resulting concrete state is $x^{mem} \mapsto 0, x_1^1 \mapsto 2, x_2^1 \mapsto 1$. We now consider the abstraction of this resulting concrete state. In the abstract buffer part, x^1 will be bound to 1+, and the numerical part will be $x^{mem} \mapsto 0, x_1^1 \mapsto 2, x_{bot}^1 \mapsto 1$. This abstract state does not only describe the actual concrete state, but also other concrete states where the buffer could have other entries with the value 1, such as $x^{mem} \mapsto 0$, $x_1^1 \mapsto 2, x_2^1 \mapsto 1, x_3^1 \mapsto 1$. Therefore, for soundness, the abstract flush of the last entry of the buffer should not only yield the abstract state $(x^1 \mapsto 1), (x^{mem} \mapsto 1, x_1^1 \mapsto 2)$, but also the abstract state $(x^1 \mapsto 1+), (x^{mem} \mapsto 1, x_1^1 \mapsto 2, x_{bot}^1 \mapsto 1)$.

3.3 Numerical Abstraction

Eventually, we abstract the $\mathscr{D}^\natural$ part of our elements using numerical domains. We can do this in a direct way because, after partitioning and summarisation, each partition is a set of summarised states which all have the same dimensions (the same variables are defined in each state of one partition).

We obtain the same kind of formulas for our abstract operators as in Fig. 9, as long as we use domains which can provide the fold and expand operations as described by Gopan et al. [11] For instance, the authors define them for Polyhedra and Octagons, and Fig. 7 provides a way to compute them with very common operations of abstract domains, so we can use a wide variety of abstractions at this step. We hence obtain a resulting abstraction which is parameterised by the choice of a numerical abstract domain, which can be fine-tuned to obtain some desirable invariant building capabilities.

The abstract domain built this way allows us to approximate efficiently computations on concrete sets containing an unbounded number of states, each of them presenting buffers of unbounded length. The soundness proof remains the same after using numerical domains to abstract sets of summarised states.

4   Towards a Better Precision

We now describe additional abstractions we designed to gain more precision on the analysis. Unlike the basic abstractions described in the previous section, we did not implement these domains for lack of time, but they use the same idea of adapting some array abstraction and show that our framework is generic enough to add some additional information if needed.

4.1   Non-uniform Abstraction of Shape Information

We can first improve the precision by using non-uniform abstractions, e.g. the ones described by Cousot et al. [9] As example, let us consider the program in Fig. 10.

During the concrete execution of this program, the value of x in the memory can only increase, because of the FIFO property of buffers. However, the previous abstraction does not keep this information: due to summarisation, after widening, the abstract variable x_{bot}^0 will have every possible natural integer value. Therefore the instructions r1 = x and r2 = x in Thread 1 will respectively assign all these possible values to r1 and r2, with no relation between them: the property cannot be verified.

To solve this problem, we can use, together with the summarisation, an abstraction able to keep the information "the buffer is sorted". This information will indeed be valid (say in decreasing order) for the buffer of the first thread, and the analyser can know it because of the relation $x_1^0 > x_{bot}^0$ which ensures it stays true after writes into x. Therefore the flush operator will be able to

```
                         initial x = 0;

        /* Thread 0 */              /* Thread 1 */
        counter = 0;                while(true) {
        while(true) {                   r1 = x;
            counter++;                   r2 = x;
            x = counter;                 assert (r1 <= r2);
        }                            }
```

Fig. 10. A program with writes in ascending order

keep the relation $x_{bot}^0 > x^{mem}$, the last element of the buffer being the smallest one. Then, between r1 = x and r2 = x, the analysis will compute that either nothing happens, and r1 and r2 have the same value, or some combination of writes (not modifying x^{mem}) and flushes (increasing x^{mem}) happens, and r1 is smaller than r2 (or equal if there is no flush). The property holds.

4.2 Handling TSO with Order-Preserving Abstractions

Although all these abstractions were designed to target TSO programs, they are also sound for PSO (and defined using this model, as a consequence). They remain sound for TSO, since PSO is strictly weaker; but may lack precision for some programs to be verified, if these programs rely on the specific guarantee of TSO which is write order preservation even between different variables. Let us consider for instance the program in Fig. 11.

```
/* Property to check: mutual exclusion at (crit1, crit2) */
        initial not flag_0 && not flag_1 && not turn;


        /* Thread 0 */          /* Thread 1 */
        flag_0 = true;          flag_1 = true;
        // mfence;              // mfence;
        turn = true;            turn = false;
        mfence;                 mfence;

        f = flag_1;             f = flag_0;
        t = turn;               t = turn;
        while (f && t) {        while (f && not t) {
            f = flag_1;             f = flag_0;
            t = turn;               t = turn;
        }                       }
        crit1:                  crit2:
        flag_0 = false;         flag_1 = false;
```

Fig. 11. A program where the order between variables is important

This program implements Peterson's lock algorithm for threads synchronisation [18]. In TSO, it is indeed correct as written in Fig. 11. In PSO, the following sequence of events could happen:

- Thread 0 writes true into flag_0 and turn, these are not flushed yet.
- Thread 1 writes true into flag_1 and false into turn. turn is flushed, but not flag_1 (which is possible under PSO).
- Thread 0 flushes its buffers. It immediately overwrites the previous false value of turn, which simulates the absence of this write instruction from the program.

- Thread 0 reads false from flag_1 and true from turn in the memory. It skips the loop and enters the critical section.
- Thread 1 flushes flag_1. It reads true from flag_0 and turn in the memory, skips the loop and also enters the critical section.

In TSO, this kind of execution cannot happen, since Thread 0 cannot flush turn before flag_1 in the memory. However, since our previous abstractions are sound in PSO, they cannot verify that this program is indeed correct in TSO without uncommenting the two additional mfence (which prevent the problematic reordering from happening). To be able to do it, we need to add to the abstraction some information on the write order of different variables. With the summarisation abstraction, the difficulty lies in the non-distinction between the older entries for each variable. If a buffer contains $[y \mapsto 1; y \mapsto 2; x \mapsto 0; y \mapsto 3]$, the summarisation loses the distinction between $y \mapsto 2$ and $y \mapsto 3$, so we cannot express that $x \mapsto 0$ is between them.

We propose to alleviate this problem by extending the summarisation idea to the order between entries: we keep the information that a given abstract variable $x_{\{0,bot\}}$ is more recent than an abstract variable $y_{\{0,bot\}}$ if and only if all the concrete buffer entries represented by this x are more recent that all the concrete entries represented by that y. On the buffer $[y \mapsto 1; y \mapsto 2; x \mapsto 0; y \mapsto 3]$, that gives us the only information "y_0 is more recent than x_0". This can be used to ensure that the flush of the $y \mapsto 1$ entry does not happen before the flush of the $x \mapsto 0$ one, but will allow the flush of $y \mapsto 2$ before $x \mapsto 0$.

Peterson's algorithm could then be proved: turn being more recent than flag_1 in the buffer of Thread 1, it cannot be flushed earlier, hence the problematic behaviour is forbidden.

In these two cases (non-uniform and order-preserving abstractions), the formalisation will be sensibly the same as the one simply using summarisation. The additional precision will be expressed as a finer paritioning: some partitions will have extra information such as "the buffer is sorted", and this information can be used for restricting the possible output values of some abstract operators on these partitions. For instance, the $[\![\text{flush } x]\!]_T$ operator will return $\bot$ on a partition where y_{bot} is known as being older than x_{bot}.

5   Experimentations

We implemented our approach and tested it against several concurrent algorithms (for PSO). Our implementation is written in OCaml. It runs with the library ocamlgraph [7], using a contributed module which iteratively computes the fixpoint of the abstract semantics over the product graph of the interleavings of the threads, with the general method described by Bourdoncle [6]. We used the (logico-)numerical relational domains provided by the libraries Apron [13] and Bddapron [12]. Our experiments run on a Intel(R) Core(TM) i7-3612QM CPU @ 2.10 GHz computer with 4 GB RAM. We used the formulas of Siegel and Simon [20] to implement for the Bddapron domains the expand and fold operations.

Our objective was to be able to verify the correctness of these algorithms after removing the maximal number of fences (with respect to the sequentially consistent behaviour where a fence is inserted after each write). For each algorithm, this correctness was encoded by a safety property, usually some boolean condition expressing a relation between variables that must be true at some given point of the execution.[5]

A secondary goal was to obtain an analysis as fast as possible by adjusting the settings concerning the parametric numerical domain. We tried four relational or weakly relational logico-numerical domains: Octagons, Polyhedra, Octagons with BDD and Polyhedra with BDD.[6] For each of these domains, we give in Fig. 12 the number of fences needed to verify the correctness property of the algorithm, the time needed to compute this verification and the memory used (line `Average resident set size` of $ time -v).

We also give, for comparison, the results obtained for PSO by Dan et al. (domain AGT[7]) [10]. It should be emphasised that we focus on a different problem: while they provide a fence removal algorithm which uses an existing analyser and a program transformation, we design an analysis which works directly on the source program with fences. We discuss fence removal as a case study, removing them with a systematic method not automated for lack of time and measuring the analysis performances on the program with a minimal fence set. The raw Time and Memory numbers comparison is therefore not accurately relevant, but still a reference order of magnitude to evaluate our performances (our test machine being almost as powerful as theirs). However, the number of fences needed is an objective measurement of the precision reachable by the analysis.

When no result is shown for a particular domain, it means that this domain does not allow the verification of the property. It is in particular the case for programs involving some boolean computations with numerical-only domains, because they do not provide abstractions for such operations (we first tried to implement it by encoding booleans into integers, but it usually led to a big loss of precision, making the extra-complexity to implement it non-naively not worthwile against logico-numerical domains.) Some programs verified by Dan et al. [10] are not shown here, because they require operations that our implementation does not provide yet (such as atomic Compare-And-Swap, or more generally patterns requiring cooperative scheduling[8]).

---

[5] On lock algorithms, the correctness being mutual exclusion, this condition was simply `false`, meaning the program state at the given point (the conjunction of the critical sections of each thread) should be $\perp$.

[6] These domains, provided by Bddapron, are essentially numerical domains for the integer variables linked to the leaves of a Binary Decision Diagram which abstracts the boolean variables.

[7] Abstraction Guided Translation.

[8] We did not implement cooperative scheduling nor atomic Compare-And-Swap, but it would make no difference for our abstraction: the only changes would be in the generation of the control graph.

Algorithm	Domain	Fences	Time	Mem	Domain	Fences	Time	Mem
Abp	Oct	-	-	-	Bdd+Oct	0	0.3	32
	Poly	-	-	-	Bdd+Poly	0	0.3	32
	AGT	0	6	167				
Bakery	Oct	-	-	-	Bdd+Oct	-	-	-
	Poly	-	-	-	Bdd+Poly	-	-	-
	AGT	4	3429	10951				
Concloop	Oct	2	0.19	38	Bdd+Oct	2	0.29	34
	Poly	2	0.24	37	Bdd+Poly	2	0.29	34
	AGT	2	6	504				
Dekker	Oct	4	23	52	Bdd+Oct	4	62	42
	Poly	4	22	50	Bdd+Poly	4	66	43
	AGT	4	121	1580				
Kessel	Oct	-	-	-	Bdd+Oct	4	4	33
	Poly	-	-	-	Bdd+Poly	4	4	34
	AGT	4	6	198				
Loop2 TLM	Oct	-	-	-	Bdd+Oct	0	4.3	34
	Poly	-	-	-	Bdd+Poly	0	4.2	34
	AGT	2	36	1650				
Peterson	Oct	4	1.53	39	Bdd+Oct	4	2.77	32
	Poly	4	1.53	39	Bdd+Poly	4	2.94	33
	AGT	4	20	901				
Queue	Oct	0	0.15	36.9	Bdd+Oct	0	0.70	34.3
	Poly	1	0.2	34.7	Bdd+Poly	0	0.31	33.3
	AGT	1	1	108				

Fig. 12. Experimental results. Times in sec, Mem in MB.

Interpretation. These results show that our method is competitive against the state of the art: in most cases, we are able to verify the property of the algorithm with the same number of fences, and in a space and time efficient way if we compare to the characteristic numbers of the abstraction-guided translation.

In two cases (Loop2 TLM and Queue), we strictly improve the result obtained by Dan et al. [10] by being able to verify the algorithm with no inserted fence, compared to respectively 2 and 1. Queue is the program of Fig. 2: on top of an unbounded state space in SC (which their method is able to deal with), it exhibits unbounded buffers. Our method allows performing this verification by being able to precisely represent these buffers, whereas they need a finite computable maximal size, hence they have to insert supplementary fences to prevent an unbounded number of writes to be waiting for a flush.

However, the additional abstraction of summarising the buffer even when its size is actually bounded sometimes comes at a precision cost, and our method is not able with this implementation to verify the Bakery algorithm (yet it is able to verify it when the while true infinite loop of lock/unlock operations is replaced with some for loop of fixed size).

Regarding the numerical domain parameter of our abstraction, the results show that Octagons and Polyhedra almost yield the same precisions and efficiency results. In Queue however, Octagons allow verifying the program with no fence, where Polyhedra fail at it. We did not observe the opposite behaviour, and as Octagons are also usually faster due to complexity results, they seem the best go-to choice for abstracting this kind of programs with our method.

When analysing programs which make some consistent use of logical expressions, the boolean-aware domains of Bddapron offer good properties of precision of efficiency. The overhead over purely numerical domains is however not negligible on programs which do not need this additional expressivity (up to 100% and more time consumed), so these results tend to suggest that they should not be used by default if not necessary on this kind of program.

Another experimental result that does not appear in this table is the number of partitions actually present in the abstract domain. While the maximum theoretical number is $3^{nb\_threads \times nb\_var}$, in practice a lot of them are actually empty. We did not measure it precisely for each test, but for instance, in the Peterson case (3 variables, 2 threads), only one state exhibits 9 non-empty partitions. Most of them have 4 or less, often 2. Our analysis is sparse in that empty partitions are not represented at all; hence, we greatly benefit from the small number of non-empty partitions. Partitioning therefore seems to be a good choice since it yields a significantly better precision while not having too much impact on time and space performances. However we do not know to which level a more precise partitioning, as we describe in Sect. 4, would still verify this statement.

6   Related Work

Ensuring correctness of concurrent programs under weakly memory models has been an increasingly important topic in the last few years.

A lot of work has been focused on finite state programs, usually using model-checking related techniques [2,4,5,15].

Kuperstein et al. [14] propose to use abstract interpretation to model programs with potentially unbounded buffers. However, their method uses abstract domains on a statewise basis: for each state, if the buffer grows above a fixed arbitrary size, it is abstracted; but they do not use abstract domains to represent the possibly still unbounded sets of resulting states. As such, their work is only able to analyse programs which have a finite state space when run under sequential consistency (although they can have an infinite state space in TSO, due to unbounded buffers).

The work of Dan et al. [10], which we compared with in Sect. 5, can manage programs with infinite sequential consistency state space, but they are limited to bounded buffers.

By contrast to these two methods [10,14], our work uses array abstractions and numerical domains to efficiently represent potentially infinite sets of states with unbounded buffers: our analysis has no limitation on the state space of our program, whether it is on state size or on state number.

A common approach for verifying the correctness of weakly consistent executions is to rely on already existing analyses sound under sequential consistency, by performing source-to-source program transformations to bring back the problem to a SC-analysis [3,10,17]. This especially appears to be a useful technique when coupled with automatic fence generation to get back properties verified under sequential consistency. However, some properties can be difficult to express with a program transformation (for instance "the values in the buffer are increasingly sorted"), and the final SC analyser has no way to retrieve information lost by the transformation. Furthermore, these transformations may not be sufficient to efficiently analyse the program, and one may have to modify the SC tool to take into account the original memory model (for instance, by considering that some variables actually come from one buffer, which would make no sense for the original SC analyser).

We believe that, by applying abstract interpretation directly on the original source program, our method can serve as a good baseline for future work on special dedicated abstractions using advanced information related to the model that leverages these two issues.

7   Conclusion

We designed a new method for analysing concurrent programs under store-buffer-based relaxed memory models like TSO or PSO. By adapting array abstractions, we showed how to build precise and robust abstractions, parameterised by a numerical domain, which can deal with unbouded buffer sizes.

We gave a formalisation of a particular abstraction which uses summarisation. We implemented this approach and our experimental results demonstrate that this method gives good precision and performance results compared to the state-of-the-art, and sometimes is able to verify programs with strictly fewer fences thanks to its ability to represent unbounded buffers.

As a future work, we shall focus on scalability. While we obtained good performances on our test cases, our method will suffer from the same problem as the previous ones, that is it does not scale well with the number of threads. By using modular analysis techniques (analysing each thread separately instead of considering the exploding product control graph), we should be able to analyse programs with more than two threads in acceptable times. We believe we can do it while reusing the abstractions defined here. However, it is significantly more complex and raises additional problems that need to be solved.

References

1. Adve, S.V., Gharachorloo, K.: Shared memory consistency models: a tutorial. Computer **29**(12), 66–76 (1996)
2. Alglave, J., Kroening, D., Lugton, J., Nimal, V., Tautschnig, M.: Soundness of data flow analyses for weak memory models. In: Yang, H. (ed.) APLAS 2011. LNCS, vol. 7078, pp. 272–288. Springer, Heidelberg (2011)

3. Alglave, J., Kroening, D., Nimal, V., Tautschnig, M.: Software verification for weak memory via program transformation. In: Felleisen, M., Gardner, P. (eds.) ESOP 2013. LNCS, vol. 7792, pp. 512–532. Springer, Heidelberg (2013)
4. Atig, M.F., Bouajjani, A., Burckhardt, S., Musuvathi, M.: On the verification problem for weak memory models. In: ACM Sigplan Notices, vol. 45, pp. 7–18. ACM (2010)
5. Bouajjani, A., Derevenetc, E., Meyer, R.: Checking and enforcing robustness against TSO. In: Felleisen, M., Gardner, P. (eds.) ESOP 2013. LNCS, vol. 7792, pp. 533–553. Springer, Heidelberg (2013)
6. Bourdoncle, F.: Efficient chaotic iteration strategies with widenings. In: Bjørner, D., Broy, M., Pottosin, I.V. (eds.) Formal Methods in Programming and their Applications. LNCS, vol. 735, pp. 128–141. Springer, Heidelberg (1993)
7. Conchon, S., Filliâtre, J.-C., Signoles, J.: Designing a generic graph library using ML functors. Trends Func. Program. 8, 124–140 (2007)
8. Cousot, P., Cousot, R.: Abstract interpretation: a unified lattice model for static analysis of programs by construction or approximation of fixpoints. In: Proceedings of the 4th ACM SIGACT-SIGPLAN Symposium on Principles of Programming Languages, pp. 238–252. ACM (1977)
9. Cousot, P., Cousot, R., Logozzo, F.: A parametric segmentation functor for fully automatic and scalable array content analysis. In: ACM SIGPLAN Notices, vol. 46, pp. 105–118. ACM (2011)
10. Dan, A., Meshman, Y., Vechev, M., Yahav, E.: Effective abstractions for verification under relaxed memory models. In: D'Souza, D., Lal, A., Larsen, K.G. (eds.) VMCAI 2015. LNCS, vol. 8931, pp. 449–466. Springer, Heidelberg (2015)
11. Gopan, D., DiMaio, F., Dor, N., Reps, T., Sagiv, M.: Numeric domains with summarized dimensions. In: Jensen, K., Podelski, A. (eds.) TACAS 2004. LNCS, vol. 2988, pp. 512–529. Springer, Heidelberg (2004)
12. Jeannet, B.: The BDDAPRON logico-numerical abstract domains library (2009)
13. Jeannet, B., Miné, A.: APRON: a library of numerical abstract domains for static analysis. In: Bouajjani, A., Maler, O. (eds.) CAV 2009. LNCS, vol. 5643, pp. 661–667. Springer, Heidelberg (2009)
14. Kuperstein, M., Vechev, M., Yahav, E.: Partial-coherence abstractions for relaxed memory models. In: ACM SIGPLAN Notices, vol. 46, pp. 187–198. ACM (2011)
15. Kuperstein, M., Vechev, M., Yahav, E.: Automatic inference of memory fences. ACM SIGACT News 43(2), 108–123 (2012)
16. Lamport, L.: How to make a multiprocessor computer that correctly executes multiprocess programs. IEEE Trans. Comput. 100(9), 690–691 (1979)
17. Meshman, Y., Dan, A., Vechev, M., Yahav, E.: Synthesis of memory fences via refinement propagation. In: Müller-Olm, M., Seidl, H. (eds.) Static Analysis. LNCS, vol. 8723, pp. 237–252. Springer, Heidelberg (2014)
18. Gary, L.: Myths about the mutual exclusion problem. Inf. Process. Lett. 12(3), 115–116 (1981)
19. Sewell, P., Sarkar, S., Owens, S., Nardelli, F.Z., Myreen, M.: x86-tso: a rigorous and usable programmer's model for x86 multiprocessors. Commun. ACM 53(7), 89–97 (2010)
20. Siegel, H., Simon, A.: Summarized dimensions revisited. Electronic Notes Theor. Comput. Sci. 288, 75–86 (2012)

Making k-Object-Sensitive Pointer Analysis More Precise with Still k-Limiting

Tian Tan[1(✉)], Yue Li[1], and Jingling Xue[1,2]

[1] School of Computer Science and Engineering,
UNSW Australia, Sydney, Australia
tiantan@cse.unsw.edu.au
[2] Advanced Innovation Center for Imaging Technology, CNU, Beijing, China

Abstract. Object-sensitivity is regarded as arguably the best context abstraction for pointer analysis in object-oriented languages. However, a k-object-sensitive pointer analysis, which uses a sequence of k allocation sites (as k context elements) to represent a calling context of a method call, may end up using some context elements redundantly without inducing a finer partition of the space of (concrete) calling contexts for the method call. In this paper, we introduce BEAN, a general approach for improving the precision of any k-object-sensitive analysis, denoted k-*obj*, by still using a k-limiting context abstraction. The novelty is to identify allocation sites that are redundant context elements in k-*obj* from an Object Allocation Graph (OAG), which is built based on a pre-analysis (e.g., a context-insensitive Andersen's analysis) performed initially on a program and then avoid them in the subsequent k-object-sensitive analysis for the program. BEAN is generally more precise than k-*obj*, with a precision that is guaranteed to be as good as k-*obj* in the worst case. We have implemented BEAN as an open-source tool and applied it to refine two state-of-the-art whole-program pointer analyses in DOOP. For two representative clients (*may-alias* and *may-fail-cast*) evaluated on a set of nine large Java programs from the DaCapo benchmark suite, BEAN has succeeded in making both analyses more precise for all these benchmarks under each client at only small increases in analysis cost.

1 Introduction

Pointer analysis, as an enabling technology, plays a key role in a wide range of client applications, including bug detection [3,25,34,35], security analysis [1,13], compiler optimisation [6,33], and program understanding [12]. Two major dimensions of pointer analysis precision are flow-sensitivity and context-sensitivity. For C/C++ programs, flow-sensitivity is needed by many clients [11,16,32,37]. For object-oriented programs, e.g., Java programs, however, context-sensitivity is known to deliver trackable and useful precision [17,19–21,28–30], in general.

There are two general approaches to achieving context-sensitivity for object-oriented programs, call-site-sensitivity (k-CFA) [27] and object-sensitivity [23,24,29] (among others). A k-CFA analysis represents a calling context of a

© Springer-Verlag GmbH Germany 2016
X. Rival (Ed.): SAS 2016, LNCS 9837, pp. 489–510, 2016.
DOI: 10.1007/978-3-662-53413-7_24

method call by using a sequence of k call sites (i.e., k labels with each denoting a call site). In contrast, a k-object-sensitive analysis uses k object allocation sites (i.e., k labels with each denoting a new statement) as context elements.

Among all the context abstractions (including k-CFA) proposed, object-sensitivity is regarded as arguably the best for pointer analysis in object-oriented languages [14,17,29]. This can be seen from its widespread adoption in a number of pointer analysis frameworks for Java, such as DOOP [4,7], CHORD [5] and WALA [36]. In addition, object-sensitivity has also been embraced by many other program analysis tasks, including typestate verification [9,38], data race detection [25], information flow analysis [1,10,22], and program slicing [21].

Despite its success, a k-object-sensitive pointer analysis, which uses a sequence of k allocation sites (as k context elements) to represent a calling context of a method call, may end up using some context elements redundantly in the sense that these redundant context elements fail to induce a finer partition of the space of (concrete) calling contexts for the method call. As a result, many opportunities for making further precision improvements are missed.

In this paper, we introduce BEAN, a general approach for improving the precision of a k-object-sensitive pointer analysis, denoted k-obj, for Java, by avoiding redundant context elements in k-obj while still maintaining a k-limiting context abstraction. The novelty lies in identifying redundant context elements by solving a graph problem on an OAG (Object Allocation Graph), which is built based on a pre-analysis (e.g., a context-insensitive Andersen's analysis) performed initially on a program, and then avoid them in the subsequent k-object-sensitive analysis. By construction, BEAN is generally more precise than k-obj, with a precision that is guaranteed to be as good as k-obj in the worst case.

We have implemented BEAN and applied it to refine two state-of-the-art (whole-program) pointer analyses, $2obj+h$ and S-$2obj+h$ [14], provided in DOOP [7], resulting in two BEAN-directed pointer analyses, B-$2obj+h$ and B-S-$2obj+h$, respectively. We have considered may-$alias$ and may-$fail$-$cast$, two representative clients used elsewhere [8,29,30] for measuring the precision of a pointer analysis on a set of nine large Java programs from the DaCapo benchmark suite. Our results show that B-$2obj+h$ (B-S-$2obj+h$) is more precise than $2obj+h$ (S-$2obj+h$) for every evaluated benchmark under each client, at some small increases in analysis cost.

This paper presents and validates a new idea on improving the precision of object-sensitive pointer analysis by exploiting an object allocation graph. Considering the broad applications of object-sensitivity in analysing Java programs, we expect more clients to benefit from the BEAN approach, in practice. Specifically, this paper makes the following contributions:

- We introduce a new approach, BEAN, for improving the precision of any k-object-sensitive pointer analysis, k-obj, for Java, by avoiding its redundant context elements while maintaining still a k-limiting context abstraction.
- We introduce a new kind of graph, called an OAG (object allocation graph), constructed from a pre-analysis for the program, as a general mechanism to identify redundant context elements used in k-obj.

- We have implemented BEAN as a soon-to-be released open-source tool, which is expected to work well with various object-sensitive analyses for Java.
- We have applied BEAN to refine two state-of-the-art object-sensitive pointer analyses for Java. BEAN improves their precision for two representative clients on a set of nine Java programs in DaCapo at small time increases.

2   Motivation

When analysing Java programs, there are two types of context, a *method context* for local variables and a *heap context* for object fields. In *k-obj*, a k-object-sensitive analysis [24,29], a method context is a sequence of k allocation sites and a heap context is typically a sequence of $k-1$ allocation sites. Given an allocation site at label ℓ, ℓ is also referred to as an abstract object for the site.

Currently, *k-obj*, where $k = 2$, represents a 2-object-sensitive analysis with a 1-context-sensitive heap (with respect to allocation sites), denoted *2obj+h* [14], which usually achieves the best tradeoff between precision and scalability and has thus been widely adopted in pointer analysis for Java [8,21,29]. In *2obj+h*, a heap context for an abstract object ℓ is a receiver object of the method that made the allocation of ℓ (known as an *allocator object*). A method context for a method call is a receiver object of the method plus its allocator object.

Below we examine the presence of redundant context elements in *2obj+h*, with two examples, one for method contexts and one for heap contexts. This serves to motivate the BEAN approach proposed for avoiding such redundancy.

2.1   Redundant Elements in Method Contexts

We use an example in Fig. 1 to illustrate how *2obj+h* analyses it imprecisely due to its use of a redundant context element in method contexts and how BEAN avoids the imprecision by avoiding this redundancy. We consider a *may-alias* client that queries for the alias relation between variables v1 and v2.

In Fig. 1(a), we identify the six allocation sites by their labels given in their end-of-line comments (in green), i.e., A/1, A/2, O/1, O/2, B/1, and C/1.

In Fig. 1(b), we give the context-sensitive call graph computed by *2obj+h*, where each method is analysed separately for each different calling context, denoted by [...] (in red). C.identify() has two concrete calling contexts but analysed only once under [B/1,C/1]. We can see that B/1 is redundant (relative to C/1) since adding B/1 to [C/1] fails to separate the two concrete calling contexts. As a result, variables v1 and v2 are made to point to both O/1 and O/2 at the same time, causing *may-alias* to report a spurious alias. During any program execution, v1 and v2 can only point to O/1 and O/2, respectively.

In Fig. 1(c), we give the context-sensitive call graph computed by BEAN, where C.identify() is now analysed separately under two different contexts, [A/1, C/1] and [A/2, C/1]. Due to the improved precision, v1 (v2) now points to O/1 (O/2) only, causing *may-alias* to conclude that both are no longer aliases.

```
1 void main(Object[] args) {
2     A a1 = new A(); // A/1
3     Object v1 = a1.foo(new Object()); // O/1
4
5     A a2 = new A(); // A/2
6     Object v2 = a2.foo(new Object()); // O/2
7 }
8 class A {
9     Object foo(Object v) {
10        B b = new B(); // B/1
11        return b.bar(v);
12    }
13 }
14 class B {
15    Object bar(Object v) {
16        C c = new C(); // C/1
17        return c.identity(v);
18    }
19 }
20 class C {
21    Object identity(Object v) { return v; }
22 }
```

(a) Program

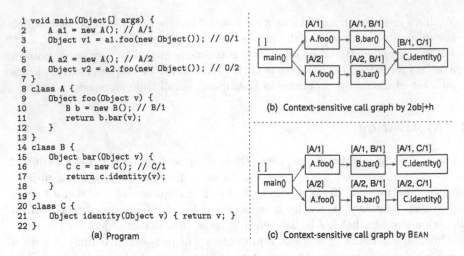

(b) Context-sensitive call graph by 2obj+h

(c) Context-sensitive call graph by BEAN

Fig. 1. Method contexts for *2obj+h* and BEAN. (Color figure online)

2.2   Redundant Elements in Heap Contexts

We now use an example in Fig. 2 to illustrate how *2obj+h* analyses it imprecisely due to its use of a redundant element in heap contexts and how BEAN avoids the imprecision by avoiding this redundancy. Our *may-alias* client now issues an alias query for variables emp1 and emp2. In Fig. 2(a), we identify again its six allocation sites by their labels given at their end-of-line comments (in green).

Figure 2(b) shows the context-sensitive field points-to graph computed by *2obj+h*, where each node represents an abstract heap object created under the corresponding context, denoted [. . .], (in red), and each edge represents a field points-to relation with the corresponding field name being labeled on the edge. An array object is analysed with its elements collapsed to one pseudo-field, denoted arr. Hence, x[i] = y (y = x[i]) is handled as x.arr = y (y = x.arr).

In this example, two companies, Co/1 and Co/2, maintain their employee information by using two different ArrayLists, with each implemented internally by a distinct array of type Object[] at line 22. However, *2obj+h* has modelled the two array objects imprecisely by using one abstract object Obj[]/1 under [AL/1]. Note that AL/1 is redundant since adding it to [ ] makes no difference to the handling of Obj[]/1. As a result, emp1 and emp2 will both point to Emp/1 and Emp/2, causing *may-alias* to regard both as aliases conservatively.

Figure 2(c) shows the context-sensitive field points-to graph computed by BEAN. This time, the Object[] arrays used by two companies Co/1 and Co/2 are distinguished under two distinct heap contexts [Co/1] and [Co/2]. As a result, our *may-alias* client will no longer report emp1 and emp2 to be aliases.

```
 1 void main(String[] args) {
 2     Company comp1 = new Company(); // Co/1
 3     comp1.addEmployee(new Employee()); // Emp/1
 4     Employee emp1 = comp1.getEmployee(0);
 5
 6     Company comp2 = new Company(); // Co/2
 7     comp2.addEmployee(new Employee()); // Emp/2
 8     Employee emp2 = comp2.getEmployee(0);
 9 }
10 class Employee {...}
11 class Company {
12     private ArrayList emps;
13     Company() { emps = new ArrayList(); } // AL/1
14     void addEmployee(Employee emp) { emps.add(emp); }
15     Employee getEmployee(int i) {
16         return (Employee) emps.get(i);
17     }
18 }
19 class ArrayList {
20     private Object[] elems;
21     private int size = 0;
22     ArrayList() { elems = new Object[10]; } // Obj[]/1
23     void add(Object e) { elems[size++] = e; }
24     Object get(int i) { return elems[i]; }
25 }
```

(a) Program

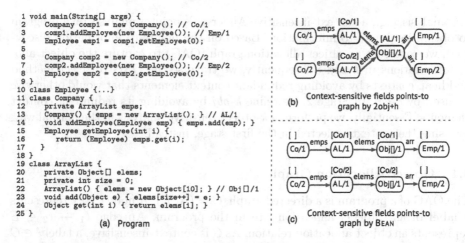

(b) Context-sensitive fields points-to graph by 2obj+h

(c) Context-sensitive fields points-to graph by BEAN

Fig. 2. Heap contexts for *2obj+h* and BEAN. (Color figure online)

2.3 Discussion

As illustrated above, *k-obj* selects blindly a sequence of *k*-most-recent allocation sites as a context. To analyse large-scale software scalably, *k* is small, which is 2 for a method context and 1 for a heap context in *2obj+h*. Therefore, redundant context elements, such as B/1 in [B/1,C/1] in Fig. 1(b) and AL/1 in [AL/1] in Fig. 2(b), should be avoided since they waste precious space in a context yet contribute nothing in separating the concrete calling contexts for a call site.

This paper aims to address this problem in *k-obj* by excluding redundant elements from its contexts so that their limited context positions can be more profitably exploited to achieve better precision, as shown in Figs. 1(c) and 2(c).

3 Methodology

We introduce a new approach, BEAN, as illustrated in Fig. 3, to improving the precision of a *k*-object-sensitive pointer analysis, *k-obj*. The basic idea is to refine *k-obj* by avoiding its redundant context elements while maintaining still a *k*-limiting context abstraction. An element *e* in a context *c* for a call or allocation site is *redundant* if *c* with *e* removed does not change the context represented by *c*. For example, B/1 in [B/1,C/1] in Fig. 1(b) and AL/1 in [AL/1] in Fig. 2(b) are redundant.

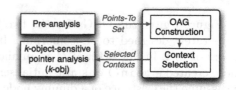

Fig. 3. Overview of BEAN.

BEAN proceeds in two stages. In Stage 1, we aim to identify redundant context elements used in *k-obj*. To do so, we first perform usually a fast but imprecise pre-analysis, e.g., a context-insensitive Andersen's pointer analysis on a program to obtain its points-to information. Based on the points-to information discovered, we construct an object allocation graph (OAG) to capture the object allocation relations in *k-obj*. Subsequently, we traverse the OAG to select method and heap contexts by avoiding redundant context elements that would otherwise be used by *k-obj*. In Stage 2, we refine *k-obj* by avoiding its redundant context elements. Essentially, we perform a *k*-object-sensitive analysis in the normal way, by using the contexts selected in the first stage, instead.

3.1 Object Allocation Graph

The OAG of a program is a directed graph, $G = (N, E)$. A node $\ell \in N$ represents a label of an (object) allocation site in the program. An edge $\ell_1 \to \ell_2 \in E$ represents an object allocation relation. As G is context-insensitive, a label $\ell \in G$ is also interchangeably referred to (in the literature) as the (unique) abstract heap object that models all the concrete objects created at the allocation site ℓ. Given this, $\ell_1 \to \ell_2$ signifies that ℓ_1 is the receiver object of the method that made the allocation of ℓ_2. Therefore, ℓ_1 is called an *allocator object* of ℓ_2 [29].

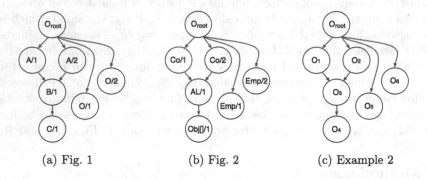

(a) Fig. 1   (b) Fig. 2   (c) Example 2

Fig. 4. The OAGs for the two motivating programs in Figs. 1 and 2.

Figure 4 gives the OAGs for the two programs in Figs. 1 and 2, which are deliberately designed to be isomorphic. In Fig. 4(a), A/1 and A/2 are two allocators of B/1. In Fig. 4(b), AL/1 is an allocator of Obj[]/1. Some objects, e.g., those created in main() or static initialisers, have no allocators. For convenience, we assume the existence of a dummy node, O_{root}, so that every object has at least one allocator. The isomorphic OAG in Fig. 4(c) will be referred to in Example 2.

The concept of allocator object captures the essence of object sensitivity. By definition [24, 29], a context for an allocation site ℓ, i.e., an abstract object ℓ consists of its allocator object (ℓ'), the allocator object of ℓ', and so on. The OAG provides a new perspective for object sensitivity, since a context for an object ℓ is simply a path from O_{root} to ℓ. As a result, the problem of selecting contexts for ℓ can be recast as one of solving a problem of distinguishing different paths from O_{root} to ℓ. Traditionally, a k-object-sensitive analysis selects blindly a suffix of a path from O_{root} to ℓ with length k.

3.2   Context Selection

Given an object ℓ in G, BEAN selects its contexts in G as sequences of its direct or indirect allocators that are useful to distinguish different paths from O_{root} to ℓ while avoiding redundant ones that would otherwise be used in k-obj. The key insight is that in many cases, it is unnecessary to use all nodes of a path to distinguish the path from the other paths leading to the same node. In contrast, k-obj is not equipped with G and thus has to select blindly a suffix of each such path as a context, resulting in many redundant context elements being used.

Method Contexts. Figure 1 compares the method contexts used by $2obj+h$ and BEAN for the first example given. As shown in Fig. 1(b), $2obj+h$ analyses C.identity() under one context [B/1,C/1], where B/1 is redundant, without being able to separate its two concrete calling contexts. In contrast, BEAN avoids using B/1 by examining the OAG of this example in Fig. 4(a). There are two paths from O_{root} to C/1: $O_{root} \rightarrow$ A/1 $\rightarrow$ B/1 $\rightarrow$ C/1 and $O_{root} \rightarrow$ A/2 $\rightarrow$ B/1 $\rightarrow$ C/1. Note that $2obj+h$ has selected a suffix of the two paths, B/1 $\rightarrow$ C/1, which happens to represent the same context [B/1,C/1] for C.identity(). BEAN distinguishes these two paths by ignoring the redundant node B/1, thereby settling with the method contexts shown in Fig. 1(c). As a result, C.identity() is now analysed under two different contexts [A/1,C/1] and [A/2,C/1] more precisely.

Heap Contexts. Figure 2 compares the heap contexts used by $2obj+h$ and BEAN for the second example given. As shown in Fig. 2(b), $2obj+h$ fails to separate the two array objects created at the allocation site Obj[]/1 for two companies Co/1 and Co/2 by using one context [AL/1], where AL/1 is redundant. In contrast, BEAN avoids using AL/1 by examining the OAG of this example in Fig. 4(b). There are two paths from O_{root} to Obj[]/1: $O_{root} \rightarrow$ Co/1 $\rightarrow$ AL/1 $\rightarrow$ Obj[]/1 and $O_{root} \rightarrow$ Co/2 $\rightarrow$ AL/1 $\rightarrow$ Obj[]/1. Note that $2obj+h$ has selected a suffix of the two paths, AL/1 $\rightarrow$ Obj[]/1, which happens to represent the same heap context [AL/1] for Obj[]/1. BEAN distinguishes these two paths by ignoring the redundant node AL/1, thereby settling with the heap contexts shown in Fig. 2(c). As a result, the two array objects created at Obj[]/1 are distinguished under two different contexts [Co/1] and [Co/2] more precisely.

3.3   Discussion

BEAN, as shown in Fig. 3, is designed to be a general-purpose technique for refining k-obj with three design goals, under the condition that its pre-analysis is sound. First, as the pre-analysis is usually less precise than k-obj, the OAG constructed for the program may contain some object allocation relations that are not visible in k-obj. Therefore, BEAN is not expected to be optimal in the sense that it can avoid all redundant context elements in k-obj. Second, if the pre-analysis is more precise than k-obj(e.g., in some parts of the program), then the OAG may miss some object allocation relations that are visible in k-*obj*. This allows BEAN to avoid using context elements that are redundant with respect to the pre-analysis but not k-*obj*, making the resulting analysis even more precise. Finally, BEAN is expected to be more precise than k-*obj* in general, with a precision that is guaranteed to be as good as k-*obj* in the worst case.

4   Formalism

Without loss of generality, we formalise BEAN as a k-object-sensitive pointer analysis with a $(k-1)$-context-sensitive heap (with respect to allocation sites), as in [14]. Thus, the depth of its method (heap) contexts is k ($k-1$).

4.1   Notations

We will use the notations in Fig. 5. The top section lists the domains used. As we focus on object-sensitive analysis, a context is a sequence of objects. The middle section gives the five key relations used. pt and fpt store the analysis results: $pt(c, x)$ represents the points-to set of variable x under context c and $fpt(c, o_i, f)$ represents the points-to set of the field f of an abstract object o_i under context c. $mtdCtxSelector$ and $heapCtxSelector$ choose the method contexts for method calls and heap contexts for allocation sites, respectively. $contextsOf$ maps a method to its contexts. The last section defines the OAG used for a program: $o_i \rightarrow o_j$ means that o_i is an allocator object of o_j, i.e., the receiver object of the method that made the allocation of o_j.

$$
\begin{aligned}
\text{variable} \quad & x, y \in \mathbb{V} \\
\text{heap object} \quad & o_i, o_j \in \mathbb{H} \\
\text{method} \quad & m \in \mathbb{M} \\
\text{field} \quad & f \in \mathbb{F} \\
\text{context} \quad & c \in \mathbb{C} = \mathbb{H}^0 \cup \mathbb{H}^1 \cup \mathbb{H}^2 \ldots
\end{aligned}
$$

$$
\begin{aligned}
pt &: \mathbb{C} \times \mathbb{V} \rightarrow \mathcal{P}(\mathbb{C} \times \mathbb{H}) \\
fpt &: \mathbb{C} \times \mathbb{H} \times \mathbb{F} \rightarrow \mathcal{P}(\mathbb{C} \times \mathbb{H}) \\
mtdCtxSelector &: \mathbb{C} \times \mathbb{H} \rightarrow \mathbb{C} \\
heapCtxSelector &: \mathbb{C} \times \mathbb{H} \rightarrow \mathbb{C} \\
contextsOf &: \mathbb{M} \rightarrow \mathcal{P}(\mathbb{C})
\end{aligned}
$$

$$
\begin{aligned}
\text{OAG} \quad & G = (N, E) \\
\text{node} \quad & o_i, o_j \in N \subseteq \mathbb{H} \\
\text{edge} \quad & o_i \rightarrow o_j \in E \subseteq N \times N
\end{aligned}
$$

Fig. 5. Notations.

4.2   Object Allocation Graph

Figure 6 gives the rules for building the OAG, $G = (N, E)$, for a program, based on the points-to sets computed by a pre-analysis, which may or may not be context-sensitive. As G is (currently) context-insensitive, the context information that appears in a points-to set (if any) is simply ignored. [OAG-NODE] and [OAG-DUMMYNODE] build N. [OAG-EDGE] and [OAG-DUMMYEDGE] build E.

By [OAG-NODE], we add to N all the pointed-to target objects found during the pre-analysis. By [OAG-DUMMYNODE], we add a dummy node o_{root} to N.

By [OAG-EDGE], we add to E an edge $o_i \rightarrow o_j$ if o_i is an allocator object of o_j. Here, m_{this}, where m is the name of a method, represents the this variable of method m, which points to the receiver object of method m. By [OAG-DUMMYEDGE], we add an edge from o_{root} to every object o_i without any incoming edge yet, to

$$\frac{\langle \_, o_i \rangle \in pt(\_, \_)}{o_i \in N} \text{ [OAG-Node]} \qquad \frac{}{o_{root} \in N} \text{ [OAG-DummyNode]}$$

$$\frac{\langle \_, o_i \rangle \in pt(\_, m_{this}) \quad m \in \mathbb{M} \quad o_j \text{ is allocated in } m}{o_i \rightarrow o_j \in E} \text{ [OAG-Edge]}$$

$$\frac{o_i \in N \quad o_i \neq o_{root} \quad o_i \text{ does not have any incoming edge}}{o_{root} \rightarrow o_i \in E} \text{ [OAG-DummyEdge]}$$

Fig. 6. Rules for building the OAG, $G = (N, E)$, for a program based on a pre-analysis.

indicate that o_{root} is now a pseudo allocator object of o_i. Note that an object allocated in `main()` or a static initialiser does not have an allocator object. Due to o_{root}, every object has at least one allocator object.

Example 1. Figure 4 gives the OAGs for the two programs in Figs. 1 and 2. For reasons of symmetry, let us apply the rules in Fig. 6 to build the OAG in Fig. 4(a) only. Suppose we perform a context-insensitive Andersen's pointer analysis as the pre-analysis on the program in Fig. 1. The points-to sets are: $pt(\text{v1}) = pt(\text{v2}) = \{\text{O/1}, \text{O/2}\}$, $pt(\text{a1}) = \{\text{A/1}\}$, $pt(\text{a2}) = \{\text{A/2}\}$, $pt(\text{b}) = \{\text{B/1}\}$, and $pt(\text{c}) = \{\text{C/1}\}$. By [OAG-Node] and [OAG-DummyNode], $N = \{o_{root}, \text{A/1}, \text{A/2}, \text{B/1}, \text{C/1}, \text{O/1}, \text{O/2}\}$. By [OAG-Edge], we add $\text{A/1} \rightarrow \text{B/1}$, $\text{A/2} \rightarrow \text{B/1}$ and $\text{B/1} \rightarrow \text{C/1}$, since B/1 is allocated in `foo()` with the receiver objects being A/1 and A/2 and C/1 is allocated in `bar()` on the receiver object B/1. By [OAG-DummyEdge], we add $o_{root} \rightarrow \text{A/1}$, $o_{root} \rightarrow \text{A/2}$, $o_{root} \rightarrow \text{O/1}$ and $o_{root} \rightarrow \text{O/2}$. □

Due to recursion, an OAG may have cycles including self-loops. This means that an abstract heap object may be a direct or indirect allocator object of another heap object, and conversely (with both being possibly the same).

4.3 Context Selection

Figure 7 establishes some basic relations in an OAG, $G = (N, E)$, with possibly cycles. By [Reach-Reflexive] and [Reach-Transitive], we speak of graph reachability in the standard manner. In [Confluence], $\curlyvee o_i$ identifies a conventional confluence

$$\frac{o_i \in N}{o_i \rightsquigarrow o_i} \text{ [Reach-Reflexive]} \qquad \frac{o_i \rightarrow o_j \in E \quad o_j \rightsquigarrow o_k}{o_i \rightsquigarrow o_k} \text{ [Reach-Transitive]}$$

$$\frac{o_j \rightarrow o_i \in E \quad o_k \rightarrow o_i \in E \quad o_j \neq o_k}{\curlyvee o_i} \text{ [Confluence]}$$

$$\frac{o_i \rightarrow o_j \in E \quad o_i \rightarrow o_k \in E \quad o_j \neq o_k \quad o_j \rightsquigarrow o_t \quad o_k \rightsquigarrow o_t}{o_i \prec o_t} \text{ [Divergence]}$$

Fig. 7. Rules for basic relations in an OAG, $G = (N, E)$.

point. In [DIVERGENCE], $o_i \prec o_t$ states that o_i is a divergence point, with at least two outgoing paths reaching o_t, implying that either o_t is a confluence point or at least one confluence point exists earlier on the two paths.

$$\frac{o_t \in N \quad o_{root} \to o_i \in E \quad o_i \rightsquigarrow o_t}{o_i^t : \langle o_{root} \prec o_t, [] \rangle \quad \textbf{if } o_i = o_t \textbf{ then } heapCtxSelector([], o_i) = []} \ [\text{Hctx-Init}]$$

$$\frac{o_j^t : \langle rep, c \rangle \quad o_j \to o_i \in E \quad o_i \rightsquigarrow o_t \quad o_j \neq o_t}{o_i^t : \langle rep', c' \rangle \quad \begin{cases} rep' = \textbf{true}, & c' = c & \textbf{if } \neg rep \wedge o_j \prec o_t \ ① \\ rep' = o_j \prec o_t, & c' = c \mathbin{+\!\!+} o_j & \textbf{if } rep \wedge \curlyvee o_i & ② \\ rep' = rep, & c' = c & \textbf{otherwise} \end{cases}}{\quad \textbf{if } o_i = o_t \textbf{ then } heapCtxSelector(c \mathbin{+\!\!+} o_j, o_i) = c'} \ [\text{Hctx-Div}]$$

$$\frac{o_j^t : \langle rep, c \rangle \quad o_j \to o_i \in E \quad o_i \rightsquigarrow o_t \quad o_j = o_t}{o_i^t : \langle rep', c' \rangle \quad \begin{cases} rep' = \textbf{true}, & c' = c \mathbin{+\!\!+} o_j, & \textbf{if } rep \wedge \curlyvee o_i & ③ \\ rep' = \textbf{true}, & c' = c, & \textbf{otherwise} \end{cases}}{\quad \textbf{if } o_i = o_t \textbf{ then } heapCtxSelector(c \mathbin{+\!\!+} o_j, o_i) = c'} \ [\text{Hctx-Cyc}]$$

$$\frac{heapCtxSelector(\_, o_i) = c \quad c' = c \mathbin{+\!\!+} o_i}{mtdCtxSelector(c, o_i) = c'} \ [\text{Mctx}]$$

Fig. 8. Rules for context selection in an OAG, $G = (N, E)$. $\mathbin{+\!\!+}$ is a concatenation operator.

Figure 8 gives the rules for computing two context selectors, *heapCtxSelector* and *mtdCtxSelector*, used in refining an object-sensitive pointer analysis in Fig. 11. In *heapCtxSelector*$(c, o_i) = c'$, c denotes an (abstract calling) context of the method that made the allocation of object o_i and c' is the heap context selected for o_i when o_i is allocated in the method with context c. In *mtdCtxSelector*$(c, o_i) = c'$, c denotes a heap context of object o_i, and c' is the method context selected for the method whose receiver object is o_i under its heap context c.

For *k-obj* [24,29], both context selectors are simple. In the case of full-object-sensitivity, we have *heapCtxSelector*$([o_1, ..., o_{n-1}], o_n) = [o_1, ..., o_{n-1}]$ and *mtdCtxSelector*$([o_1, ..., o_{n-1}], o_n) = [o_1, ..., o_n]$ for every path from o_{root} to a node o_n in the OAG, $o_{root} \to o_1 \to ... \to o_{n-1} \to o_n$. For a *k*-object-sensitive analysis with a $(k-1)$-context-sensitive heap, *heapCtxSelector*$([o_{n-k}, ..., o_{n-1}], o_n) = [o_{n-k+1}, ..., o_{n-1}]$ and *mtdCtxSelector* $([o_{n-k+1}, ..., o_{n-1}], o_n) = [o_{n-k+1}, ..., o_n]$. Essentially, a suffix of length of k is selected from $o_{root} \to o_1 \to ... \to o_{n-1} \to o_n$, resulting in potentially many redundant context elements to be used blindly.

Let us first use an OAG in Fig. 9 to explain how we avoid redundant context elements selected by k-obj. The set of contexts for a given node, denoted o_t, can be seen as the set of paths reaching o_t from o_{root}. Instead of using all the nodes on a path to distinguish it from the other four, we use only the five *representative nodes*, labeled by 1–5, and identify the five paths uniquely as ① → ③, ① → ④, ② → ③, ② → ④, and ⑤. The other six nodes are redundant with respect to o_t. The rules in Fig. 8 are used to identify such representative nodes (on the paths from a divergence node to a confluence node) and compute the set of contexts for o_t.

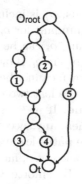

Fig. 9. An OAG.

In Fig. 8, the first three rules select heap contexts and the last rule selects method contexts based on the heap contexts selected. The first three rules traverse the OAG from o_{root} and select heap contexts for a node o_t. Meanwhile, each rule also records at o_i, which reaches o_t, a set of pairs of the form $o_i^t : \langle rep, c \rangle$. For a pair $o_i^t : \langle rep, c \rangle$, c is a heap context of o_i that uniquely represents a particular path from o_{root} to o_i. In addition, *rep* is a boolean flag considered for determining the suitability of o_i as a representative node, i.e., context element for o_t *under c* (i.e., for the path c leading to o_i). There are two cases. If $rep = \mathbf{false}$, then o_i is redundant for o_t. If $rep = \mathbf{true}$, then o_i is potentially a representative node (i.e., context element) for o_t. $c + o$ returns the concatenation of c and o.

Specifically, for the first three rules on heap contexts, [HCTX-INIT] bootstraps heap context selection, [HCTX-CYC] handles the special case when o_t is in a cycle such that $o_j = o_t$, and [HCTX-DIV] handles the remaining cases. In [MCTX], the contexts for a method are selected based on its receiver objects and the heap contexts of these receiver objects computed by the first three rules. Thus, removing redundant elements from heap contexts benefits method contexts directly.

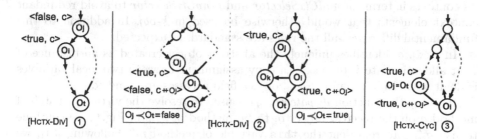

Fig. 10. Three Cases marked for [HCTX-DIV] and [HCTX-CYC] in Fig. 8.

Figure 10 illustrates the four non-trivial cases marked in Fig. 8, i.e., ①, ② (split into two sub-cases), and ③. In ①, o_i appears on a divergent path from o_j leading to o_t, o_i^t's rep' is set to **true** to mark o_i as a potential context element for o_t. In ②, there are two sub-cases: $\neg o_j \prec o_t$ and $o_j \prec o_t$. In both cases, o_j is in a branch (since o_j^t's rep is **true**) and o_i is a confluence node (since $\curlyvee o_i$ holds).

Thus, o_j is included as a context element for o_t. In the case of $\neg o_j \prec o_t$, o_i is redundant for o_t under c. In the case of $o_j \prec o_t$, the paths to o_t diverge at o_j. Thus, o_i can be potentially a context element to distinguish the paths from o_j to o_t via o_i. If o_i is ignored, the two paths $o_j \rightarrow o_k \rightarrow o_t$ and $o_j \rightarrow o_i \rightarrow o_k \rightarrow o_t$ as shown cannot be distinguished. In [HCTX-CYC], its two cases are identically handled as the last two cases in [HCTX-CYC], except that [HCTX-CYC] always sets o_i^t's rep' to **true**. If [HCTX-CYC] is applicable, o_t must appear in a cycle such that $o_j = o_t$. Then, any successor of o_t may be a representative node to be used to distinguish the paths leading to o_t via the cycle. Thus, o_i^t's rep' is set to **true**. The first case in [HCTX-CYC], marked as ③ in Fig. 8, is illustrated in Fig. 10.

To enforce k-limiting in the rules given in Fig. 8, we simply make every method context $c + \!\!\!+ \, o_i$ k-bounded and every heap context $c + \!\!\!+ \, o_j$ $(k-1)$-bounded.

Example 2. For the two programs illustrated in Figs. 1 and 2, BEAN is more precise than *2obj+h* (with $k = 2$) in handling the method and heap contexts of o_4, shown in their isomorphic OAG in Fig. 4(c). We give some relevant derivations for o_i^t, with $t = 4$, only. By [HCTX-INIT], we obtain $o_1^4 : (\textbf{true}, [\,])$ and $o_2^4 : (\textbf{true}, [\,])$. By [HCTX-DIV], we obtain $o_3^4 : (\textbf{false}, [o1])$, $o_3^4 : (\textbf{false}, [o2])$, $o_4^4 : (\textbf{false}, [o1])$ and $o_4^4 : (\textbf{false}, [o2])$. Thus, $heapCtxSelector([o1, o3], o4) = [o1]$ and $heapCtxSelector([o2, o3], o4) = [o2]$. By [MCTX], $mtdCtxSelector([o1], o4) = [o1, o4]$, and $mtdCtxSelector([o2], o4) = [o2, o4]$. For *2obj+h*, the contexts selected for o_4 are $heapCtxSelector([o1, o3], o4) = [o3]$, $heapCtxSelector([o2, o3], o4) = [o3]$ and $mtdCtxSelector([o3], o4) = [o3, o4]$. As result, BEAN can successfully separate the two concrete calling contexts for o_4 and the two o_4 objects created in the two contexts but *2obj+h* fails to do this.   □

4.4   Object-Sensitive Pointer Analysis

Figure 11 gives a formulation of a k-object-sensitive pointer analysis that selects its contexts in terms of $mtdCtxSelector$ and $heapCtxSelector$ to avoid redundant context elements that would otherwise be used in *k-obj*. In addition to this fundamental difference, all the rules are standard, as expected.

In [NEW], o_i identifies uniquely the abstract object created as an instance of T at allocation site i. In [ASSIGN], a copy assignment between two local variables is dealt with. In [LOAD] and [STORE], object field accesses are handled.

In [CALL], the function $dispatch(o_i, g)$ is used to resolve the virtual dispatch of method g on the receiver object o_i to be method m'. As in Fig. 6, we continue to use m'_{this} to represent the **this** variable of method m'. Following [31], we assume that m' has the k formal parameters $m'_{p1}, ..., m'_{pk}$ other than m'_{this} and that a pseudo-variable m'_{ret} is used to hold the return value of m'.

Compared to *k-obj*, BEAN avoids its redundant context elements in [NEW] and [CALL]. In [NEW], $heapCtxSelector$ (by [HCTX-INIT], [HCTX-DIV] and [HCTX-CYC]) is used to select the contexts for object allocation. In [CALL], $mtdCtxSelector$ (by [MCTX]) is used to select the contexts for method invocation.

$$\boxed{m\text{: the containing method for each statement being analysed}}$$

$$\frac{i:\; x = new\; T()\quad c \in contextsOf(m)\quad c' = heapCtxSelector(c, o_i)}{\langle c', o_i \rangle \in pt(c, x)}\; \text{[New]}$$

$$\frac{x = y\quad c \in contextsOf(m)}{pt(c, y) \subseteq pt(c, x)}\; \text{[Assign]}$$

$$\frac{x = y.f\quad c \in contextsOf(m)\quad \langle c', o_i \rangle \in pt(c, y)}{fpt(c', o_i, f) \subseteq pt(c, x)}\; \text{[Load]}$$

$$\frac{x.f = y\quad c \in contextsOf(m)\quad \langle c', o_i \rangle \in pt(c, x)}{pt(c, y) \subseteq fpt(c', o_i, f)}\; \text{[Store]}$$

$$\frac{\begin{array}{c} x = y.g(arg_1, ..., arg_n)\quad c \in contextsOf(m)\quad \langle c', o_i \rangle \in pt(c, y) \\ m' = dispatch(o_i, g)\quad c'' = mtdCtxSelector(c', o_i) \end{array}}{c'' \in contextsOf(m')\quad \langle c', o_i \rangle \in pt(c'', m'_{this})}\; \text{[Call]}$$
$$\forall\, 1 \le k \le n : pt(c, arg_k) \subseteq pt(c'', m'_{pk})\quad pt(c'', m'_{ret}) \subseteq pt(c, x)$$

Fig. 11. Rules for pointer analysis.

4.5 Properties

Theorem 1. *Under full-context-sensitivity (i.e., when $k = \infty$),* BEAN *is as precise as the traditional k-object-sensitive pointer analysis (k-obj).*

Proof Sketch. The set of contexts for any given abstract object, say o_t, is the set P_t of its paths reaching o_t from o_{root} in the OAG of the program. Let R_t be the set of representative nodes, i.e., context elements identified by BEAN for o_t. We argue that R_t is sufficient to distinguish all the paths in P_t (as shown in Fig. 9).

For the four rules given in Fig. 8, we only need to consider the first three for selecting heap contexts as the last one for method contexts depends on the first three. [HCTX-INIT] performs the initialisation for the successor nodes of o_{root}.

[HCTX-DIV] handles all the situations except the special one when o_t is in a cycle such that $o_t = o_j$. [HCTX-DIV] has three cases. In the first case, marked ① (Fig. 10), our graph reachability analysis concludes conservatively whether it has processed a divergence node or not during the graph traversal. In the second case, marked ② (Fig. 10), o_i is a confluence node. By adding o_j to c in $c \mathbin{+\!\!+} o_j$, we ensure that for each path p from o_i's corresponding divergence node to o_i traversed earlier, at least one representative node that is able to represent p, i.e., o_j, is always selected, i.e., to R_t. In cases ① and ②, as all the paths from o_{root} to o_t are traversed, all divergence and confluence nodes are handled. The third case simply propagates the recorded information across the edge $o_j \rightarrow o_i$.

[HCTX-CYC] applies only when o_t is in a cycle such that $o_t = o_j$. Its two cases are identical to the last two cases in [HCTX-DIV] except o_i^t's rep' is always set to **true**. This ensures all the paths via the cycle can be distinguished correctly. In the case, marked ③ and illustrated in Fig. 10, o_j is selected, i.e., added to R_t.

Thus, R_t is sufficient to distinguish the paths in P_t. Hence, the theorem. □

Theorem 2. *For any fixed context depth k,* BEAN *is as precise as the traditional k-object-sensitive pointer analysis (k-obj) in the worst case.*

Proof Sketch. This follows from the fact that, for a fixed k, based on Theorem 1, BEAN will eliminate some redundant context elements in a sequence of k-most-recent allocation sites in general or nothing at all in the worst case. Thus, BEAN may be more precise than (by distinguishing more contexts for a call or allocation site) or has the same precision as *k-obj* (by using the same contexts).   □

5   Evaluation

We have implemented BEAN as a standalone tool for performing OAG construction (Fig. 6) and context selection (Fig. 8), as shown in Fig. 3, in Java. To demonstrate the relevance of BEAN to pointer analysis, we have integrated BEAN with DOOP [7], a state-of-the-art context-sensitive pointer analysis framework for Java. In our experiments, the pre-analysis for a program is performed by using a context-insensitive Andersen's pointer analysis provided in DOOP. To apply BEAN to refine an existing object-sensitive analysis written in Datalog from DOOP, it is only necessary to modify some Datalog rules in DOOP to adopt the contexts selected by *heapCtxSelector* and *mtdCtxSelector* in BEAN (Fig. 8).

Our entire BEAN framework will be released as open-source software at http://www.cse.unsw.edu.au/~corg/bean.

In our evaluation, we attempt to answer the following two research questions:

RQ1. Can BEAN improve the precision of an object-sensitive pointer analysis at slightly increased cost to enable a client to answer its queries more precisely?
RQ2. Does BEAN make any difference for a real-world application?

To address RQ1, we apply BEAN to refine two state-of-the-art whole-program object-sensitive pointer analyses, *2obj+h* and *S-2obj+h*, the top two most precise yet scalable solutions provided in DOOP [7,14], resulting in two BEAN-directed analyses, *B-2obj+h* and *B-S-2obj+h*, respectively. Altogether, we will compare the following five context-sensitive pointer analyses:

– *2cs+h*: 2-call-site-sensitive analysis [7]
– *2obj+h*: 2-object-sensitive analysis with 1-context-sensitive heap [7]
– *B-2obj+h*: the BEAN-directed version of *2obj+h*
– *S-2obj+h*: selective hybrids of 2 object-sensitive analysis proposed in [7,14]
– *B-S-2obj+h*: the BEAN-directed version of *S-2obj+h*

Note that *2obj+h* is discussed in Sect. 2. *S-2obj+h* is a selective 2-object-sensitive with 1-context-sensitive heap hybrid analysis [14], which applies call-site-sensitivity to static call sites and *2obj+h* to virtual call sites. For *S-2obj+h*, BEAN proceeds by refining its object-sensitive part of the analysis, demonstrating its generality in improving the precision of both pure and hybrid object-sensitive analyses. For comparison purposes, we have included *2cs+h* to demonstrate the superiority of object-sensitivity over call-site-sensitivity.

We have considered *may-alias* and *may-fail-cast*, two representative clients used elsewhere [8,29,30] for measuring the precision of pointer analysis. The *may-alias* client queries whether two variables may point to the same object or not. The *may-fail-cast* client identifies the type casts that may fail at run time.

To address RQ2, we show how BEAN can enable *may-alias* and *may-fail-cast* to answer alias queries more precisely for `java.util.HashSet`. This container from the Java library is extensively used in real-world Java applications.

5.1 Experimental Setting

All the five pointer analyses evaluated are written in terms of Datalog rules in the DOOP framework [4]. Our evaluation setting uses the LogicBlox Datalog engine (v3.9.0), on an Xeon E5-2650 2 GHz machine with 64 GB of RAM.

We use all the Java programs in the DaCapo benchmark suite (2006-10-MR2) [2] except `hsqldb` and `jython`, because all the four object-sensitive analyses, cannot finish analysing each of the two in a time budget of 5 hours. All these benchmarks are analysed together with a large Java library, JDK 1.6.0_45.

DOOP handles native code (in terms of summaries) and (explicit and implicit) exceptions [4]. As for reflection, we leverage SOLAR [20] by adopting its string inference to resolve reflective calls but turning off its other inference mechanisms that may require manual annotations. We have also enabled DOOP to merge some objects, e.g., reflection-irrelevant string constants, in order to speed up each analysis without affecting its precision noticeably, as in [7,14].

When analysing a program, by either a pre-analysis or any of the five pointer analyses evaluated, its native code, exceptions and reflective code are all handled in exactly the same way. Even if some parts of the program are unanalysed, we can still speak of the soundness of all these analyses with respect to the part of the program visible to the pre-analysis. Thus, Theorems 1 and 2 still hold.

5.2 RQ1: Precision and Performance Measurements

Table 1 compare the precision and performance results for the five analyses.

Precision. We measure the precision of a pointer analysis in term of the number of may-alias variable pairs reported by *may-alias* and the number of may-fail-casts reported by *may-fail-cast*. For the *may-alias* client, the obvious aliases (e.g., due to a direct assignment) have been filtered out, following [8]. The more precise a pointer analysis is, the smaller these two numbers will be.

Let us consider *may-alias* first. $B\text{-}2obj+h$ improves the precision of $2obj+h$ for all the nine benchmarks, ranging from 6.2 % for `antlr` to 16.9 % for `xalan`, with an average of 10.0 %. In addition, $B\text{-}S\text{-}2obj+h$ is also more precise than $S\text{-}2obj+h$ for all the nine benchmarks, ranging from 3.7 % for `antlr` to 30.0 % for `xalan`, with an average of 8.8 %. Note that the set of non-aliased variable pairs reported under $2obj+h$ ($S\text{-}2obj+h$) is a strict subset of the set of non-aliased variable pairs reported under $B\text{-}2obj+h$ ($B\text{-}S\text{-}2obj+h$), validating practically the validity of Theorem 2, i.e., the fact that BEAN is always no less precise than the

Table 1. Precision and performance results for all the five analyses. The two precision metrics shown are the number of variable pairs that may be aliases generated by *may-alias* ("may-alias pairs") and the number of casts that cannot be statically proved to be safe by *may-fail-cast* ("may-fail casts"). In both cases, *smaller is better*. One performance metric used is the analysis time for a program.

		2cs+h	*2obj+h*	*B-2obj+h*	*S-2obj+h*	*B-S-2obj+h*
xalan	may-alias pairs	25,245,307	6,196,945	**5,146,694**	5,652,610	**3,958,998**
	may-fail casts	1154	711	**653**	608	**550**
	analysis time (secs)	1400	8653	11450	1150	1376
chart	may-alias pairs	43,124,320	4,189,805	**3,593,584**	3,485,082	**3,117,825**
	may-fail casts	2026	1064	**979**	923	**844**
	analysis time (secs)	3682	630	1322	1145	1814
eclipse	may-alias pairs	20,979,544	5,029,492	**4,617,883**	4,636,675	**4,346,306**
	may-fail casts	1096	722	**655**	615	**551**
	analysis time (secs)	1076	119	175	119	188
fop	may-alias pairs	38,496,078	10,548,491	**9,870,507**	9,613,363	**9,173,539**
	may-fail casts	1618	1198	**1133**	1038	**973**
	analysis time (secs)	3054	796	1478	961	1566
luindex	may-alias pairs	10,486,363	2,190,854	**1,949,134**	1,820,992	**1,705,415**
	may-fail casts	794	493	**438**	408	**353**
	analysis time (secs)	650	90	140	88	145
pmd	may-alias pairs	13,134,083	2,868,130	**2,598,100**	2,457,457	**2,328,304**
	may-fail casts	1216	845	**787**	756	**698**
	analysis time (secs)	816	131	191	132	193
antlr	may-alias pairs	16,445,862	5,082,371	**4,768,233**	4,586,707	**4,419,166**
	may-fail casts	995	610	**551**	525	**466**
	analysis time (secs)	808	109	162	105	163
lusearch	may-alias pairs	11,788,332	2,251,064	**2,010,780**	1,886,967	**1,771,280**
	may-fail casts	874	504	**450**	412	**358**
	analysis time (secs)	668	94	153	91	155
bloat	may-alias pairs	43,408,294	12,532,334	**11,608,822**	12,155,175	**11,374,583**
	may-fail casts	1944	1401	**1311**	1316	**1226**
	analysis time (secs)	10679	4508	4770	4460	4724

object-sensitive analysis improved upon. Finally, *2obj+h*, *S-2obj+h*, *B-2obj+h* and *B-S-2obj+h* are all substantially more precise than *2cs+h*, indicating the superiority of object-sensitivity over call-site-sensitivity.

Let us now move to *may-fail-cast*. Again, *B-2obj+h* improves the precision of *2obj+h* for all the nine benchmarks, ranging from 5.4 % for fop to 11.2 % for luindex, with an average of 8.4 %. In addition, *B-S-2obj+h* is also more precise than *S-2obj+h* for all the nine benchmarks, ranging from 6.7 % for fop to 15.6 % for luindex, with an average of 10.8 %. Note that the casts that are shown to be safe under *2obj+h* (*S-2obj+h*) are also shown to be safe by *B-2obj+h* (*B-S-2obj+h*), verifying Theorem 2 again. For this second client, *2obj+h*, *S-2obj+h*, *B-2obj+h* and *B-S-2obj+h* are also substantially more precise than *2cs+h*.

Performance. BEAN improves the precision of an object-sensitive analysis at some small increase in cost, as shown in Table 1. As can be seen in Figs. 1 and 2, BEAN may spend more time on processing more contexts introduced. *B-2obj+h* increases the analysis cost of *2obj+h* for all the nine benchmarks, ranging from 5.8 % for bloat to 109.8 % for chart, with an average of 54.8 %. In addition, *B-S-2obj+h* also increases the analysis cost of *S-2obj+h* for all the nine benchmarks, ranging from 5.9 % for bloat to 70.3 % for lusearch, with an average of 49.1 %.

Table 2 shows the pre-analysis times of BEAN for the nine benchmarks. The pre-analysis is fast, finishing within 2 min for the most of the benchmarks and in under 6 min in the worst case. In Table 1, the analysis times for *B-2obj+h* and *B-S-2obj+h* do not include their corresponding pre-analysis times. There are three reasons: (1) the points-to information produced by "CI" in Table 2 (for some other purposes) can be reused, (2) and the combined overhead for "OAG" and "CTX-COMP" is small, and (3) the same pre-analysis is often used to guide BEAN to refine many object-sensitive analyses (e.g., *2obj+h* and *S-2obj+h*).

Table 2. Pre-analysis times of BEAN (secs). For a program, its pre-analysis time comes from three components: (1) a context-insensitive points-to analysis ("CI"), (2) OAG construction per Fig. 6 (OAG), and (3) object-sensitive context computation per Fig. 8 ("CTX-COMP").

Benchmark	xalan	chart	eclipse	fop	luindex	pmd	antlr	lusearch	bloat
CI	82.6	112.2	49.6	105.5	39.0	65.3	56.9	39.1	52.5
OAG	0.2	0.2	0.1	0.2	0.2	0.1	0.2	0.1	0.1
CTX-COMP	83.0	168.0	32.1	236.5	11.7	13.9	13.9	18.3	13.3
Total	165.8	280.4	81.8	342.2	50.9	79.3	71.0	57.5	65.9

2obj+h and *S-2obj+h* are the top two most precise yet scalable object-sensitive analyses ever designed for Java programs [14]. BEAN is significant as it improves their precision further at only small increases in analysis cost.

5.3   RQ2: A Real-World Case Study

Let us use java.util.HashSet, a commonly used container from the Java library to illustrate how *B-2obj+h* improves the precision of *2obj+h* by enabling *may-alias* and *may-fail-cast* to answer their queries more precisely. In Fig. 12, the code in main() provides an abstraction of a real-world usage scenario for HashSet, with some code in HashSet and its related classes being extracted directly from JDK 1.6.0_45. In main(), X and Y do not have any subtype relation.

We consider two queries: (Q1) are v1 and v2 at lines 5 and 11 aliases (from *may-alias*)? and (Q2) may the casts at lines 6 and 12 fail (from *may-fail-cast*)?

Let us examine main(). In lines 2–6, we create a HashSet object, HS/1, insert an X object into it, retrieve the object from HS/1 through its iterator into v1,

```
 1  void main(String[] args) {              23  class HashMap ... {
 2      HashSet xSet = new HashSet(); // HS/1  24      Entry[] table = new Entry[16]; // Entry[]/1
 3      xSet.add(new X()); // X/1            25      public Object put(Object key, ...) { ...
 4      Iterator xIter = xSet.iterator();    26          table[bucketIndex] =
 5      Object v1 = xIter.next();            27              new Entry(key, ...); // Entry/1
 6      X x = (X) v1;                        28      ... }
 7                                           29      static class Entry {
 8      HashSet ySet = new HashSet(); // HS/2  30          final Object key;
 9      ySet.add(new Y()); // Y/1            31          Entry(Object k, ...) {
10      Iterator yIter = ySet.iterator();    32              key = k;
11      Object v2 = yIter.next();            33          }
12      Y y = (Y) v2;                        34      }
13  }                                        35      private final class KeyIterator ... {
14  class HashSet ... {                      36          public Object next() { ...
15      HashMap map = new HashMap(); // HM/1  37              Entry e = table[index];
16      public boolean add(Object e) {       38              return e.key;
17          return map.put(e, ...) == null;  39          }
18      }                                    40      }
19      public Iterator iterator() {         41      Iterator newKeyIterator() {
20          return map.newKeyIterator();     42          return new KeyIterator(); // KeyIter/1
21      }                                    43      }
22      ...                                  44      ...
23  }                                        45  }
```

Fig. 12. A real-world application for using java.util.HaseSet.

and finally, copy v1 to x via a type cast operation (X). In lines 7–12, we proceed as in lines 1–6 except that another HashSet object, HS/2, is created, and the object inserted into HS/2 is a Y object and thus cast back to Y.

Let us examine HashSet, which is implemented in terms of HashMap. Each HashSet object holds a backing HashMap object, with the elements in a HashSet being used as the keys in its backing HashMap object. In HashMap, each key and its value are stored in an Entry object pointed to its field table.

In main(), the elements in a HashSet object are accessed via its iterator, which is an instance of KeyIterator, an inner class of HashMap.

As before, we have labeled all the allocation sites in their end-of-line comments. Figure 13 gives the part of the OAG related to the two HashSet objects, HS/1 and HS/2, which are known to own their distinct HM/1, Entry/1, Entry[]/1 and KeyIter/1 objects during program execution.

2obj+h. To answer queries Q1 and Q2, we need to know the points-to sets of v1 and v2 found at lines 5 and 11, respectively. As revealed in Fig. 13, *2obj+h* is able to distinguish the HashMap objects in HS/1 and HS/2 by using two different heap contexts, [HS/1] and [HS/2], respectively. However, the two iterator objects associated with HS/1 and HS/2 are still modeled under one context [HM/1] as one abstract object KeyIter/1, which is pointed to by xIter at line 5 and yIter at line 11. By pointing to X/1 and Y/1 at the same time, v1 and v2 are reported as aliases and the casts at lines 6 and 12 are also warned to be unsafe.

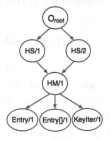

Fig. 13. Part of OAG related to HS/1 and HS/2.

B-2obj+h. By examining the part of the OAG given in Fig. 13, *B-2obj+h* recognises that HM/1 is redundant in the single heap context [HM/1] used by *2obj+h* for representing Entry/1, Entry[]/1 and KeyIter/1. Thus, it will create two distinct sets of these three objects, one under [HS/1] and one under [HS/2], causing v1 (v2) to point to X/1 (Y/1) only. For query Q1, v1 and v2 are no longer aliases. For query Q2, the casts at lines 6 and 12 are declared to be safe.

6 Related Work

Object-sensitivity, introduced by Milanova et al. [23,24], has now been widely used as an excellent context abstraction for pointer analysis in object-oriented languages [14,18,29]. By distinguishing the calling contexts of a method call in terms of its receiver object's k-most-recent allocation sites (rather than k-most-recent call sites) leading to the method call, object-sensitivity enables object-oriented features and idioms to be better exploited. This design philosophy enables a k-object-sensitive analysis to yield usually significantly higher precision at usually much less cost than a k-CFA analysis [8,14,17]. The results from our evaluation have also validated this argument further. In Table 1, *2obj+h* is significantly more precise than *2cs+h* in all the configurations considered and also significantly faster than *2cs+h* for all the benchmarks except xalan.

There once existed some confusion in the literature regarding which allocation sites should be used for context elements in a k-object-sensitive analysis [9,15,17, 24,30]. This has recently been clarified by Smaragdakis et al. [29], in which the authors demonstrate that the original statement of object-sensitivity given by Milanova et al. [24], i.e., full-object-sensitivity in [29], represents a right approach in designing a k-object-sensitive analysis while the other approaches (e.g., [15]) may result in substantial loss of precision. In this paper, we have formalised and evaluated BEAN based on this original design [24,29].

For Java programs, hybrid object-sensitivity [14] enables k-CFA (call-site-sensitivity) to be applied to static call sites and object-sensitivity to virtual call sites. The resulting hybrid analysis is often more precise than their corresponding non-hybrid analyses at sometimes less and sometimes more analysis cost (depending on the program). As a general approach, BEAN can also improve the precision of such a hybrid pointer analysis, as demonstrated in our evaluation.

Type-sensitivity [29], which is directly analogous to object-sensitivity, provides a new sweet spot in the precision-efficiency tradeoff for analysing Java programs. This context abstraction approximates the allocation sites in a context by the dynamic types (or their upper bounds) of their allocated objects, making itself more scalable but less precise than object-sensitivity [14,29]. In practice, type-sensitivity usually yields an acceptable precision efficiently [20,21]. How to generalise BEAN to refine type-sensitive analysis is a future work.

Oh et al. [26] introduce a selective context-sensitive program analysis for C. The basic idea is to leverage a pre-impact analysis to guide a subsequent main analysis in applying context-sensitivity to where the precision improvement is likely with respect to a given query. In contrast, BEAN is designed to improve the precision of a whole-program pointer analysis for Java, so that many clients may benefit directly from the improved points-to information obtained.

7   Conclusion

In the past decade, object-sensitivity has been recognised as an excellent context abstraction for designing precise context-sensitive pointer analysis for Java and thus adopted widely in practice. However, how to make a k-object-sensitive analysis even more precise while still using a k-limiting context abstraction becomes rather challenging. In this paper, we provide a general approach, BEAN, to addressing this problem. By reasoning about an object allocation graph (OAG) built based on a pre-analysis on the program, we can identify and thus avoid redundant context elements that are otherwise used in a traditional k-object-sensitive analysis, thereby improving its precision at a small increase in cost.

In our future work, we plan to generalise BEAN to improve the precision of other forms of context-sensitive pointer analysis for Java that are formulated in terms of k-CFA and type-sensitivity (among others). Their redundant context elements can be identified and avoided in an OAG-like graph in a similar way.

Acknowledgement. The authors wish to thank the anonymous reviewers for their valuable comments. This work is supported by Australian Research Grants, DP130101970 and DP150102109.

References

1. Arzt, S., Rasthofer, S., Fritz, C., Bodden, E., Bartel, A., Klein, J., Le Traon, Y., Octeau, D., McDaniel, P.: Flowdroid: precise context, flow, field, object-sensitive and lifecycle-aware taint analysis for android apps. In: PLDI 2014 (2014)
2. Blackburn, S.M., Garner, R., Hoffmann, C., Khang, A.M., McKinley, K.S., Bentzur, R., Diwan, A., Feinberg, D., Frampton, D., Guyer, S.Z., Hirzel, M., Hosking, A., Jump, M., Lee, H., Moss, J.E.B., Phansalkar, A., Stefanović, D., VanDrunen, T., von Dincklage, D., Wiedermann, B.: The DaCapo benchmarks: Java benchmarking development and analysis. In: OOPSLA 2006 (2006)
3. Blackshear, S., Chang, B.Y.E., Sridharan, M.: Selective control-flow abstraction via jumping. In: OOPSLA 2015 (2015)
4. Bravenboer, M., Smaragdakis, Y.: Strictly declarative specification of sophisticated points-toanalyses. In: OOPSLA 2009 (2009)
5. Chord. A program analysis platform for Java. http://www.cc.gatech.edu/~naik/chord.html
6. Das, M., Liblit, B., Fähndrich, M., Rehof, J.: Estimating the impact of scalable pointer analysis on optimization. In: Cousot, P. (ed.) SAS 2001. LNCS, vol. 2126, pp. 260–278. Springer, Heidelberg (2001)
7. DOOP. A sophisticated framework for Java pointer analysis. http://doop.program-analysis.org

8. Feng, Y., Wang, X., Dillig, I., Dillig, T.: Bottom-up context-sensitive pointer analysis for java. In: Feng, X., Park, S. (eds.) APLAS 2015. LNCS, vol. 9458, pp. 465–484. Springer, Heidelberg (2015). doi:10.1007/978-3-319-26529-2_25
9. Fink, S.J., Yahav, E., Dor, N., Ramalingam, G., Geay, E.: Effective typestate verification in the presence of aliasing. ACM Trans. Softw. Eng. Methodol. **17**(2), 1–34 (2008)
10. Gordon, M.I., Kim, D., Perkins, J.H., Gilham, L., Nguyen, N., Rinard, M.C.: Information flow analysis of android applications in droidsafe. In: NDSS 2015 (2015)
11. Hardekopf, B., Lin, C.: Flow-sensitive pointer analysis for millions of lines of code. In: CGO 2011 (2011)
12. Hind, M.: Pointer analysis: Haven't we solved this problem yet? In: PASTE 2001 (2001)
13. Huang, W., Dong, Y., Milanova, A., Dolby, J.: Scalable and precise taint analysis for android. In: ISSTA 2015 (2015)
14. Kastrinis, G., Smaragdakis, Y.: Hybrid context-sensitivity for points-to analysis. In: PLDI 2013 (2013)
15. Lhoták, O.: Program Analysis using Binary Decision Diagrams. Ph.D. thesis (2006)
16. Lhoták, O., Chung, K.C.A.: Points-to analysis with efficient strong updates. In: POPL 2011 (2011)
17. Lhoták, O., Hendren, L.: Context-sensitive points-to analysis: is it worth it? In: Mycroft, A., Zeller, A. (eds.) CC 2006. LNCS, vol. 3923, pp. 47–64. Springer, Heidelberg (2006)
18. Lhoták, O., Hendren, L.: Evaluating the benefits of context-sensitive points-to analysis using a BDD-based implementation. ACM Trans. Softw. Eng. Methodol. **18**(1), 1–53 (2008)
19. Li, Y., Tan, T., Sui, Y., Xue, J.: Self-inferencing reflection resolution for java. In: Jones, R. (ed.) ECOOP 2014. LNCS, vol. 8586, pp. 27–53. Springer, Heidelberg (2014)
20. Li, Y., Tan, T., Xue, J.: Effective soundness-guided reflection analysis. In: Blazy, S., Jensen, T. (eds.) SAS 2015. LNCS, vol. 9291, pp. 162–180. Springer, Heidelberg (2015)
21. Li, Y., Tan, T., Zhang, Y., Xue, J.: Program tailoring: Slicing by sequential criteria. In: ECOOP 2016 (2016)
22. Mangal, R., Zhang, X., Nori, A.V., Naik, M.: A user-guided approach to program analysis. In: FSE 2015 (2015)
23. Milanova, A., Rountev, A., Ryder, B.G.: Parameterized object sensitivity for points-to and side-effect analyses for java. In: ISSTA 2002 (2002)
24. Milanova, A., Rountev, A., Ryder, B.G.: Parameterized object sensitivity for points-to analysis for Java. ACM Trans. Softw. Eng. Methodol. **14**(1), 1–41 (2005)
25. Naik, M., Aiken, A., Whaley, J.: Effective static race detection for java. In: PLDI 2006 (2006)
26. Oh, H., Lee, W., Heo, K., Yang, H., Yi, K.: Selective context-sensitivity guided by impact pre-analysis. In: PLDI 2014 (2014)
27. Shivers, O.G.: Control-flow Analysis of Higher-order Languages of Taming Lambda. Ph.D. thesis (1991)
28. Smaragdakis, Y., Balatsouras, G.: Pointer analysis. Found. Trends Program. Lang. **2**, 1–69 (2015)
29. Smaragdakis, Y., Bravenboer, M., Lhoták, O.: Pick your contexts well: understanding object-sensitivity. In: POPL 2011 (2011)
30. Sridharan, M., Bodík, R.: Refinement-based context-sensitive points-to analysis for Java. In: PLDI 2006 (2006)

31. Sridharan, M., Chandra, S., Dolby, J., Fink, S.J., Yahav, E.: Alias analysis for object-oriented programs. In: Noble, J., Wrigstad, T., Clarke, D. (eds.) Aliasing in Object-Oriented Programming. LNCS, vol. 7850, pp. 196–232. Springer, Heidelberg (2013)
32. Sui, Y., Di, P., Xue, J.: Sparse flow-sensitive pointer analysis for multithreaded programs. In: CGO 2016 (2016)
33. Sui, Y., Li, Y., Xue, Y.: Query-directed adaptive heap cloning for optimizing compilers. In: CGO 2013 (2013)
34. Sui, Y., Ye, D., Xue, J.: Static memory leak detection using full-sparse value-flow analysis. In: ISSTA 2012 (2012)
35. Sui, Y., Ye, D., Xue, J.: Detecting memory leaks statically with full-sparse value-flow analysis. IEEE Trans. Softw. Eng. **40**(2), 107–122 (2014)
36. Wala, T.J.: Watson libraries for analysis. http://wala.sf.net
37. Yu, H., Xue, J., Huo, W., Feng, X., Zhang, Z.: Level by level: making flow- and context-sensitive pointer analysisscalable for millions of lines of code. In: CGO 2010 (2010)
38. Zhang, X., Mangal, R., Grigore, R., Naik, M., Yang, H.: On abstraction refinement for program analyses in datalog. In: PLDI 2014 (2014)

Author Index

Abdulla, Parosh Aziz   61
Alglave, Jade   3

Balatsouras, George   84

Chatterjee, Krishnendu   23
Christakis, Maria   105

Dalla Preda, Mila   126
De Angelis, Emanuele   147
Deng, Chaoqiang   170

Fioravanti, Fabio   147

Gange, Graeme   189
Gharat, Pritam M.   212
Giacobazzi, Roberto   126
Gonnord, Laure   361
Gupta, Aarti   317

Henzinger, Thomas A.   23
Heo, Kihong   237

Jonsson, Bengt   61
Journault, Matthieu   257

Khedker, Uday P.   212
Kinoshita, Minoru   278
Kojima, Kensuke   278

Li, Yue   489

Mastroeni, Isabella   126
Maurica, Fonenantsoa   300
Menendez, David   317
Mesnard, Frédéric   300
Midtgaard, Jan   338
Miné, Antoine   257, 469
Monniaux, David   361
Mycroft, Alan   212

Nagarakatte, Santosh   317
Namjoshi, Kedar S.   170, 383
Navas, Jorge A.   189
Nielson, Flemming   338
Nielson, Hanne Riis   338

Oh, Hakjoo   237
Otop, Jan   23

Payet, Étienne   300
Pettorossi, Alberto   147
Proietti, Maurizio   147

Ranzato, Francesco   403
Roux, Pierre   424

Sankaranarayanan, Sriram   424
Schachte, Peter   189
Schulze Frielinghaus, Stefan   447
Seidl, Helmut   447
Singhania, Nimit   383
Smaragdakis, Yannis   84
Søndergaard, Harald   189
Spoto, Fausto   39
Stuckey, Peter J.   189
Suenaga, Kohei   278
Suzanne, Thibault   469

Tan, Tian   489
Trinh, Cong Quy   61

Vogler, Ralf   447
Voronin, Yuen-Lam   424

Wüstholz, Valentin   105

Xue, Jingling   489

Yang, Hongseok   237